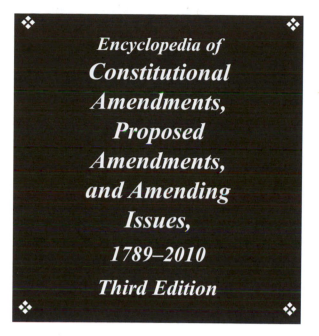

Encyclopedia of
Constitutional
Amendments,
Proposed
Amendments,
and Amending
Issues,

1789–2010
Third Edition

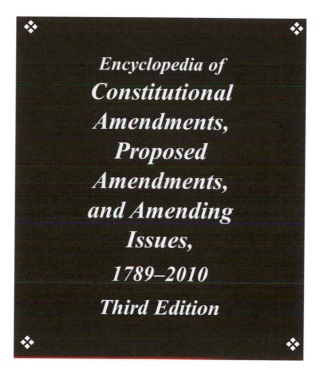

Encyclopedia of
Constitutional Amendments, Proposed Amendments, and Amending Issues, 1789–2010
Third Edition

VOLUME TWO
N–W

John R. Vile

ABC-CLIO

Santa Barbara, California • Denver, Colorado • Oxford, England

Copyright 2010 by ABC-CLIO, LLC

Library of Congress Cataloging-in-Publication Data

Vile, John R.
  Encyclopedia of constitutional amendments, proposed amendments, and amending issues, 1789-2010 / John R. Vile. — 3rd ed.
     p. cm.
  Includes bibliographical references and index.
  ISBN 978-1-59884-316-3 (alk. paper) — ISBN 978-1-59884-317-0 (ebook)
  1. Constitutional amendments—United States. I. Title.
  KF4557.V555 2010
  342.7303--dc22   2010002113

ISBN: 978-1-59884-316-3
EISBN: 978-1-59884-317-0

14 13 12 11 10   1 2 3 4 5

This book is also available on the World Wide Web as an eBook.
Visit www.abc-clio.com for details.

ABC-CLIO, LLC
130 Cremona Drive, P.O. Box 1911
Santa Barbara, California 93116-1911

This book is printed on acid-free paper ∞
Manufactured in the United States of America

This book is dedicated to three great teachers, scholars, and gentlemen: Henry J. Abraham, Alpheus T. Mason, and Walter F. Murphy

❖ CONTENTS ❖

❖ A TO Z LIST OF ENTRIES ❖

N

❖

NASHVILLE CONVENTION

The June 1850 convention of nine Southern states that met in Nashville, Tennessee, was an extralegal (albeit far from secret) affair, rather than one called under provisions of Article V of the U.S. Constitution. In this it resembled the earlier Hartford Convention of Northern States and the later Peace Convention of 1861. Attended by more than 175 delegates, the majority from Tennessee, the Nashville Convention was concerned about many of the issues that led to the Compromise of 1850. Altogether, the convention made 28 proposals, one of which would have extended the Missouri Compromise line dividing slave and free states all the way to the Pacific Coast. It also adopted Robert Barnwell Rhett's radical "Address to the People of the South" before more moderate voices prevailed. A follow-up meeting attended by far fewer delegates in November 1850 affirmed the right of secession, but the two conventions are collectively better known for averting this contingency, at least in the short term, than for their contributions to eventual disunion.

See also Hartford Convention; Peace Convention.

For Further Reading:

Jennings, Thelma. 1998. "Nashville Convention." In *The Tennessee Encyclopedia of History & Culture,* ed. Carroll Van West. Nashville, TN: Rutledge Hill Press, pp. 674–675.

———. 1980. *The Nashville Convention: Southern Movement for Unity, 1848–1851.* Memphis, TN: Memphis State University Press.

NATIONAL ASSOCIATION FOR THE ADVANCEMENT OF COLORED PEOPLE (NAACP)

Few issues have had more impact on the United States than has the issue of race, and few organizations have been as important in addressing this issue as the National Association for the Advancement of Colored People (NAACP). The NAACP was founded in New York City in 1909–1910, at a time when the rights guaranteed to all Americans under the Fourteenth and Fifteenth Amendments (respectively providing for equal rights for all Americans and prohibiting voting discrimination on the basis of race) had been eroded by narrow constructions of these amendments and by practices like Jim Crow segregation laws that the U.S. Supreme Court had approved in *Plessy v. Ferguson* (1896). The NAACP utilized a variety of mechanisms to fight for the rights of African Americans. These included lobbying; the publication of *The Crisis* (a magazine long edited by W. E. B. DuBois); successful legal challenges to grandfather clauses and the all-white primaries, both of which had been designed to deprive blacks of the right to vote; and efforts to adopt anti-lynching legislation.

The NAACP's most important legal efforts came with the establishment of the Legal Defense Fund, long directed by Charles Houston and Thurgood Marshall, who would later serve as the first African American U.S. Supreme Court justice. Initially bringing cases involving law and graduate schools that required states to adhere to the "equal" provision of the "separate but equal" doctrine announced in

Plessy v. Ferguson, the NAACP eventually challenged the doctrine head on, representing individuals in a number of states and the District of Columbia. It achieved success in *Brown v. Board of Education* (1954), when, in a unanimous decision authored by Chief Justice Earl Warren, the U.S. Supreme Court declared that separate educational facilities were inherently unequal. Uncertain whether the Fourteenth Amendment had been specifically adopted with the intention of outlawing racial discrimination, Warren argued that education was so important in the modern context and the effects of segregation were so inimical to the self-image of minority students and so negatively impacted their ability to learn, that segregation could no longer be tolerated.

This decision was the first of many Court decisions on the subject and was, along with actions led by the NAACP and other civil rights organizations, the catalyst for congressional legislation like the Civil Rights Act of 1964 (outlawing discrimination in places of public accommodation) and the Voting Rights Act of 1965, which has been subsequently extended a number of times. Although the Supreme Court has continued consistently to rule against de jure segregation, it has had greater difficulty in addressing de facto racial segregation and in settling issues like affirmative action and school busing, both of which have been the subject of proposed constitutional amendments and continuing court actions.

Pressures exerted by NAACP-sponsored boycotts and marches undoubtedly influenced the adoption of the Twenty-fourth Amendment outlawing poll taxes, as well as the less successful attempt to provide voting representation in Congress for the District of Columbia. However, the NAACP is not so much known for contributing to the adoption of new amendments as it is for insisting that the nation recognize, and its courts enforce, amendments already on the books. The NAACP strategy of utilizing courts to ensure the enforcement of constitutional norms has subsequently been utilized by a variety of other interest groups from those favoring and opposing abortion rights, to those concerned about religious freedoms, to those favoring and disfavoring the death penalty, and so forth.

See also *Brown v. Board of Education;* Fourteenth Amendment; Fifteenth Amendment; Twenty-fourth Amendment; Warren Court.

For Further Reading:

Jonas, Gilbert. 2007. *Freedom's Sword: The NAACP and the Struggle Against Racism, 1909–1969.* New York: Routledge.

NATIONAL INITIATIVE FOR DEMOCRACY

The National Initiative for Democracy is a plan, sponsored in part by former Alaskan senator (and unsuccessful candidate for the 2008 Democratic presidential nomination) Mike Gravel to adopt a constitutional amendment and accompanying legislation through initiative and referendum mechanisms. The initiative is associated with a nonprofit corporation designated "Philadelphia II" and has an extensive website. The Initiative sponsored a conference in February 2002 in Williamsburg, Virginia, that included presentations by numerous scholars, including Akhil Reed Amar of Yale, who believe that "We the People" can exercise sovereignty by amending the U.S. Constitution outside the formal constitutional amending mechanism.

The proposed Democracy Amendment contains seven sections (an earlier version had 11). Section 1 prohibits either state or national governments from denying or abridging "the sovereign authority and the legislative power of citizens of the United States to enact, repeal and amend public policy, laws, charters, and constitutions by local, state and national initiatives." Section 2 sanctions "the national election conducted by the nonprofit corporation Philadelphia II, permitting the enactment of this Article and the Democracy Act." This section is intended to trigger "the self-enacting process of the National Initiative." Section 3 creates a United States Electoral Trust of 53 members. Section 4 specifies that initiatives created under the amendment will assume "the force of law" when "approved by more than half the registered voters of the relevant jurisdiction in each of two successive elections conducted by the Electoral

Trust." In such cases, the second election must occur within six months to a year of the first. Section 5 limits initiative sponsorship to citizens, and Section 6 limits expenditures for or against such initiatives to "natural persons." Section 7 grants "the people" power "to enforce the provisions of this Article by appropriate legislation" and prevents judicial Injunctions against such initiatives "except on grounds of fraud" ("the Democracy Amendment").

The National Initiative for Democracy has also proposed the Democracy Act, which is designed to formalize the initiative process at the national level. Citizens would be able to introduce initiatives of 5,000 words or less through petition, through public opinion poll, or through legislative resolution. The National Initiative for Democracy provides that both the law and the amendment will be ratified when "Philadelphia II has received a number of affirmative votes greater than half the total number of government-validated votes cast in the presidential election occurring immediately prior to the election's certification" provided this exceeds the number of negative votes on the subject.

See also Amar, Akhil Reed; Initiative and Referendum.

For Further Reading:

"The Democracy Act," http://ni4d.us/act.htm. Accessed June 19, 2008.

"The Democracy Amendment," http://ni4d.us/amendment.htm. Accessed June 19, 2008.

Gravel, Mike. 1995. "Philadelphia II: National Initiatives." Campaigns and Elections 16 (December): 25.

"The National Initiative for Democracy," http://ni4d.us/nationalinitiative.htm. Accessed June 19, 2008.

"The Parrish Report." http://ni4d.us/parrishreport.htm. Accessed June 19, 2008.

NATIONAL PROHIBITION CASES (1920)

Seven cases challenging the constitutionality of the Eighteenth Amendment and the Volstead Act, the lead being *Rhode Island v. Palmer,* were grouped together and brought before the Supreme Court in 1920. Justice Willis Van Devanter delivered the Court's opinion. The challengers' primary hope had been to convince the Court that the Eighteenth Amendment exceeded certain limits on the constitutional amending process as well as fell short of a number of procedural qualifications.

Rather than grapple directly with these arguments, Van Devanter basically stated conclusions. He asserted that the power to regulate alcohol "is within the power to amend reserved by Article V of the Constitution" (*National Prohibition Cases* 1920, 386). This prompted Justice Joseph McKenna to note in dissent that such a policy, if established, "will undoubtedly decrease the literature of the court if it does not increase lucidity" (*Id.,* 393). However, in their dissenting opinions, McKenna and John Clarke likewise focused primarily on the meaning of "concurrent powers" in Section 2 of the Eighteenth Amendment rather than providing any in-depth discussion of possible limits on the amending process.

Van Devanter decided that Congress's vote, rather than an explicit statement, was enough to show that it considered the Eighteenth Amendment to be necessary. He also noted that the two-thirds majority required by Article V was two-thirds of a quorum rather than of the entire membership. Van Devanter cited *Hawke v. Smith* (1920) as authority for excluding any state requirements that amendments also be confirmed or rejected by referendum.

On the matter of concurrent powers, which so distressed the dissenters, Van Devanter argued that the clause granting such powers to the nation and the states was intended to allow neither government "to defeat or thwart the prohibition, but only to enforce it by appropriate legislation" (*National Prohibition Cases* 1920, 387). Moreover, he decided that the Eighteenth Amendment, and the accompanying Volstead Act (which applied to all beverages with 0.5 percent or more alcohol content), could be applied both to preexisting alcohol and to that manufactured or imported after its passage.

Opposition to the Eighteenth Amendment was intense, but its opponents ultimately succeeded in the court of public opinion rather than at the bar of the Supreme Court, which rejected another legal challenge in *United States v. Sprague* (1931). Eventually, the Twenty-first Amendment, ratified shortly after the first election of President Franklin D. Roosevelt, repealed the Eighteenth.

See also Constitutional Amendments, Limits on; Eighteenth Amendment; *Hawke v. Smith;* Twenty-first Amendment.

For Further Reading:
National Prohibition Cases, 253 U.S. 350 (1920).

NATIVE AMERICANS

The U.S. Constitution mentions Native Americans in few places, yet their treatment and status have been a perpetual source of shame and controversy throughout American history. Both Article I, Section 2 of the Constitution and Section 2 of the Fourteenth Amendment exclude "Indians not taxed" from the numbers used to calculate representation in the House. Article I, Section 8 further extended congressional power over commerce "with the Indian tribes."

The earliest proposed amendment related to Native Americans was introduced in 1832 when the state of Georgia petitioned Congress for a convention to clarify the rights of Indians. The state had been stung by John Marshall's Supreme Court opinion in *Worcester v. Georgia* (1832), which had invalidated a Georgia statute requiring a minister to obtain a license to live in Cherokee country and enlarged the right of Indian sovereignty. With President Andrew Jackson (who upheld strong national powers in the Nullification Controversy) unwilling to enforce this judgment holding Georgia to treaties it had made, the state proceeded to remove the Cherokees in the historic evacuation known as the "Trail of Tears."

There appears to have been at least one attempt to include Indians within the citizenship guarantee of the Fourteenth Amendment, but in cases such as *Elk v. Wilkins* (1884), the Supreme Court did not interpret the amendment to confer citizenship on Indians. Congress finally took

this action in 1924 (Wunder 1994, 50; Maltz 2002, 572).

In 1937 a South Dakota representative proposed including Indians in apportioning the House of Representatives, and in 1940 a North Dakota representative voted to deprive Congress of the power to regulate intrastate commerce with them. When they were charged with one of a number of major crimes defined by Congress or when they were off reservations, Native Americans were governed by federal constitutional guarantees, but on the reservations, tribal courts were not bound by the Bill of Rights (Wunder 1994, 132–133). Members of Congress introduced at least four proposals from 1939 through 1953—three by Democratic senator Patrick McCarran of Nevada—to restore the same rights to American Indians as were enjoyed by other American citizens. In 1968 Congress adopted legislation known as the Indian Bill of Rights. It applied most, but not all, provisions of the Bill of Rights to proceedings on Indian reservations (Wunder 1994, 135–144).

See also Bill of Rights: Fourteenth Amendment.

For Further Reading:
Maltz, Earl M. 2002. "The Fourteenth Amendment and Native American Citizenship." *Constitutional Commentary* 17 (Winter): 555–573.
Wunder, John R. 1994. *"Retained by the People": A History of American Indians and the Bill of Rights.* New York: Oxford University Press.

NATURAL-BORN CITIZEN

See Presidency, Qualifications for.

NATURAL LAW

Many of the American founders believed strongly in the idea of natural law. This idea, traceable back to ancient Greek and Roman as well as to medieval Christian philosophers, posits the existence of an unwritten set of unchanging moral principles that human reason can ascertain (Sigmund 1971). In the 18th century, such ideas were transfigured into the idea of natural rights.

Thomas Jefferson premised the Declaration of Independence on this latter doctrine, which he linked to the "unalienable rights" of "life, liberty, and the pursuit of happiness." Pointing out that the Declaration is included at the beginning of the U.S. Code, some have argued that it is part of the organic law of the land (Jaffa 1994, 4–5) and that judges should enforce this part of the nation's "unwritten constitution" (Grey 1975). Others prefer to maintain the distinction between natural law and positive law (O'Neil 1995) and think that judges should enforce only those natural-law principles that are embodied in such parts of the Constitution as the Bill of Rights, the Fourteenth Amendment, and other specific provisions.

Prior to 1787 American courts frequently resorted to natural-law concepts in justifying their decisions, but they later devoted greater attention to specific phrases and more general principles of the written Constitution (L. Goldstein 1991, 15). In *Calder v. Bull* (1798), a decision about the scope of the ex post facto provision, Justice Samuel Chase argued for judicial enforcement of such natural-law principles, whereas Justice James Iredell thought that courts should base their judgments only on specific constitutional provisions. From the late 19th century through 1937, the Supreme Court's focus on substantive due process embodied a type of natural-law reasoning that some scholars believe served to usurp the people's role in amending the Constitution. Arguably, modern opinions on the right to privacy, sometimes traced to the Ninth Amendment, have a similar natural-law foundation—as do some of the opposition arguments against abortion. Some advocates of limits on the amending process have based their argument on natural-law principles said to be implicit in the Constitution (Rosen 1991, 1086).

Principles of natural law are generally thought to be unalterable. To the extent that the Constitution is regarded as embodying such natural-law principles, judicial interpretations are likely to be considered largely unalterable. This idea is in tension with some versions of "the living Constitution," whereby judges are expected to adapt constitutional provisions not simply to new developments in technology but also to contemporary changes in thinking.

See also Declaration of Independence; Jefferson, Thomas; Living Constitution; Ninth Amendment.

For Further Reading:

Corwin, Edward S. 1955. *The "Higher Law" Background of American Constitutional Law.* Ithaca, NY: Cornell University Press.

DeHart, Paul R. 2007. *Uncovering the Constitution's Moral Design.* University of Missouri Press.

Goldstein, Leslie F. 1991. *In Defense of the Text: Democracy and Constitutional Theory.* Savage, MD: Rowman and Littlefield.

Grey, Thomas C. 1975. "Do We Have an Unwritten Constitution?" *Stanford Law Review* 27 (February): 703–718.

Hamburger, Philip A. 1993. "Natural Rights, Natural Law, and American Constitutionalism." *Yale Law Journal* 102 (January): 907–960.

Jaffa, Harry V. 1994. *Original Intent and the Framers of the Constitution: A Disputed Question.* Washington, DC: Regnery Gateway.

O'Neil, Patrick M. 1995. "The Declaration as Un-Constitution: The Bizarre Jurisprudential Philosophy of Professor Harry V. Jaffa." *Akron Law Review* 28 (Fall/Winter): 237–252.

Rosen, Jeff. 1991. "Was the Flag Burning Amendment Unconstitutional?" *Yale Law Review* 100: 1073–1092.

Sigmund, Paul E. 1971. *Natural Law in Political Thought.* Cambridge, MA: Winthrop Publishers.

NAYLOR, THOMAS H. (1936–), AND WILLIAM H. WILLIMON (1946–)

Since the end of the U.S. Civil War, there have been relatively few advocates of secession, but the fear that James Madison battled in arguing in *Federalist No. 10* for an extended republic continues to be raised by those who fear bigness in all its forms. Thomas Naylor, a professor emeritus of economics from Duke University, and William H. Willimon, then dean of the chapel and professor of Christian Ministry at the same institution, combine both themes in a book, *Downsizing the U.S.A.*, which they published in 1997.

The authors believe that "small is beautiful," and their primary example is the state of Vermont. Surveying the ills of modern America, they attribute almost all of them to bigness. Corporations are too large; cities are too large; schools and universities are too large; the United States is too large; and many of the 50 states are too large.

For each large institution, there is a set of strategies. Corporations can be brought down to size by "abolishing the U.S. Departments of Commerce and Labor"; encouraging "corporate downsizing"; buying locally; avoiding large chain stores; and spending money at home (Naylor and Willimon 1997, 77). Cities can be downsized by abolishing the U.S. Department of Housing and Urban Development; eliminating "most federal subsidies"; allowing cities to limit their growth; and permitting "cities to secede from the state in which they are located and form independent city-states" (*Id.,* 75). Rural America can be revitalized by abolishing the U.S. Department of Agriculture; subsidizing "family farms, not large corporate farms"; revoking federal aid for interstate highways; and patronizing local merchants (*Id.,* 93). Education can be downsized by abolishing the U.S. Department of Education; using educational vouchers; limiting schools to 300 students (*Id.,* 121); dividing universities with more than 10,000 students into colleges of 3,000, with residential colleges of about 300 students; reducing federal aid to colleges and universities; and replacing tenure with long-term contracts (*Id.,* 135). Religious organizations should "decentralize decision-making power" to "the local congregation," reduce denominational central offices, and cultivate small groups within congregations (*Id.,* 154). Cures for the welfare state include the abolition of Medicare and Medicaid; closing the U.S. Department of Health and Human Services; practicing holistic medicine;

and using more resources to teach people "how to live healthy, meaningful lives and how to die happy" (*Id.,* 171). Superpowers like the United States can be brought to heel by substituting "constructive engagement, tension reduction, and power sharing for military confrontation"; reducing troop commitments abroad; resigning from the United Nations and the World Bank; and substituting voluntary for compulsory alliances (*Id.,* 202). States may be empowered and downsized by reducing federal regulations; allowing large states to split; and allowing large cities to "become separate states" (*Id.,* 236).

Naylor and Willimon proceed to make four arguments for the legitimacy of secession. They believe that states should be permitted to call conventions at which secession is the only issue on the agenda (Naylor and Willimon 1997, 250). Naylor and Willimon believe the central issues that would emerge would be economic, namely:

> (1) compensation for U.S. government-owned property within the state, (2) payment of relocation costs for citizens who want to leave the state but remain in the United States, (3) disposition of the state's share of the federal debt, and (4) settlement of the state's pro rata claim on the total net worth of the United States taken as a whole. (Naylor and Willimon 1997, 256)

Naylor and Willimon believe that the states' share of national wealth will more than compensate for their share of the national debt.

Naylor and Willimon describe their view as "a form of anarchism" (Naylor and Willimon 1997, 259). Once two-thirds of a state's conventional delegates agree to secede, a state would present its petition to the U.S. secretary of state and follow with "a strategy of constructive engagement with the U.S. government" (*Id.,* 276). Naylor and Willimon further envision a system of "free trade and free travel among states having a single currency and a common economic system. Member states might form a mutual defense alliance" (*Id.,* 278). States would, in turn, "have complete responsibility for and total control for and total control of their own taxes, schools, social welfare, health care, law enforcement, highways, airports, housing, and physical environment" (*Id.,* 278).

Naylor and Willimon suggest various regional state groupings including a black nation in the Mississippi Delta. They note, however, that they have "no grand scheme for downsizing America, for such a plan would be antithetical to what we are trying to accomplish" (Naylor and Willimon 1997, 284).

See also Cummings, Richard.

For Further Reading:

Naylor, Thomas H., and William H. Willimon. 1997. *Downsizing the U.S.A.* Grand Rapids, MI: William B. Eerdmans Publishing Company.

NECESSARY AND PROPER CLAUSE

The last clause in Article I, Section 8 of the Constitution grants Congress power "to make all laws which shall be necessary and proper for carrying into Execution the foregoing Powers." Often called the "elastic" or "sweeping" clause, this provision serves as the textual basis for the notion that Congress can exercise certain implied powers. The clause was one of the central constitutional supports by which John Marshall justified the constitutionality of the national bank in *McCulloch v. Maryland* (1819). Marshall argued that the national bank was not an end in and of itself but, rather, a means for effecting ends, or powers (like raising revenue), that were specified within the Constitution. Contrary to the arguments that Thomas Jefferson had made in opposing the establishment of a national bank, Marshall argued that the word "necessary" did not mean "absolutely necessary" but permitted Congress to exercise some choice of means. Without such a provision, many more amendments would undoubtedly have been necessary in order to expand congressional powers.

If not tied specifically to constitutional ends, however, the clause could undermine the whole idea of a constitution of enumerated powers (Engdahl 1994, 13). In 1806 John Clopton, a Democra-

tic representative from Virginia, introduced an amendment to construe the clause so as "to comprehend only such laws as shall have a natural connection with and immediate relation to the powers enumerated in the said section, or such other powers as are expressly vested by the Constitution in the Government of the United States" (Ames 1896, 168). Democratic-Republicans like James Madison were quite concerned that Marshall's decision in *McCulloch v. Maryland* was so broad that it undermined the idea of a government of limited powers, and early Republican presidents often denied that the clause provided justification for federal funding of internal improvements. More recently, a participant in a law review symposium cited the ambiguity of the necessary and proper clause as a reason for nominating it as the most "stupid" provision in the current document (Eskridge and Levinson 1998, 43–50).

See also Internal Improvements; Jefferson, Thomas; Madison, James; Marshall, John; *McCulloch v. Maryland.*

For Further Reading:

Ames, Herman. 1896. *The Proposed Amendments to the Constitution of the United States during the First Century of Its History.* Reprint, New York: Burt Franklin, 1970.

Engdahl, David E. 1994. "The Spending Power." *Duke Law Journal* 44 (October): 1–109.

Eskridge, William N., Jr., and Sanford Levinson. 1998. *Constitutional Stupidities, Constitutional Tragedies.* New York: New York University Press.

NEW DEAL

See Court-packing Plan.

NINETEENTH AMENDMENT

Although they proclaimed human equality, the American founding fathers did little to heed Abigail Adams's plea to "remember the Ladies, and be more generous and favourable to them than your ancestors" (letter to John Adams dated March 31, 1776, quoted in Mason and Baker 1985, 119). New Jersey was the only state that permitted women to vote, and there the doctrine of coverture, by which a married couple constituted a single entity, essentially limited this right to unmarried women (Bernstein with Agel 1993, 129). Moreover, throughout most of the 18th and 19th centuries, laws subjected women to a number of legal disabilities that affected their title to land, custody of their children in the case of divorce, and access to occupations (Van Burkleo 1990, 10).

Origins of the Suffrage Movement

The movement for women's suffrage is usually dated to the Seneca Falls Convention of 1848, where Elizabeth Cady Stanton drew up the Seneca Falls Declaration of Rights and Sentiments that she patterned after the Declaration of Independence. The convention's support for women's suffrage was considered to be one of its more radical stances and was widely ridiculed in the press of the day. Many of the early leaders of the women's suffrage movement were also active in the abolition movement and in the movement for national alcoholic prohibition. These women were understandably upset when the Fourteenth and Fifteenth Amendments made no specific provisions for women. Indeed, the Fourteenth Amendment was the first to introduce the term "male" into the Constitution. Largely because of disputes arising over the proper stance for women to take toward these amendments, women's suffrage proponents split into two main groups. Elizabeth Cady Stanton and Susan B. Anthony, who opposed adoption of the Fourteenth Amendment, formed the National Woman Suffrage Association; Henry Ward Beecher and Lucy Stone, who favored the amendment, formed the American Woman Suffrage Association (Kraditor 1981, 3–4). This rivalry continued until the two groups joined in 1890 to become the National American Woman Suffrage Association (NAWSA).

Democratic representative James Brooks of New York was the first to offer a women's suffrage amendment in Congress. He introduced his proposal in 1866 as an amendment to Section 2 of the Fourteenth Amendment and again in 1869 as an addition to the Fifteenth Amendment. Although Brooks did not succeed, the Fifteenth Amendment subsequently became the model for the women's suffrage amendment (also called the Susan B. Anthony amendment), which was introduced regularly in Congress from 1880 until it was proposed by the necessary majorities in 1919. Few observers could have been surprised when in *Minor v. Happersett* (1875) the Supreme Court rejected the argument that the Fourteenth Amendment extended the right to vote to women.

Western states provided much of the pressure for women's suffrage. They were motivated partly by their desire to get enough voters to qualify for statehood. The Wyoming Territory granted suffrage to women in 1869, and other states and territories followed. Some allowed women to vote in all elections, and others limited such voting to school board elections or elections for the president (Bernstein with Agel 1993, 132).

Debates over Women's Suffrage

As in other amending controversies, most notably the later disputes over the Equal Rights Amendment, both sides of the women's suffrage debate claimed more radical consequences for the amendment than it would eventually generate. Opponents feared that women would be sullied by their participation in politics and forecast dire changes in family and social structures. Whereas some proponents of suffrage argued that it simply recognized women's equality under the law, others anticipated that women would ennoble political life and would inaugurate major political reforms. Some proponents of the amendment also argued from time to time that the votes of educated women might help counteract the votes of African Americans and immigrants (Kraditor 1981, 14–74).

The tie between women's suffrage and other issues was sometimes a disability. Women (especially those in the Women's Christian Temperance Union) had taken such an active part in the movement for national alcoholic prohibition that those opposed to Prohibition feared that women's suffrage would lead to adoption of the

Prohibition Amendment. Especially in the South, fears were raised that an amendment granting women the right to vote might renew federal efforts to enforce the Fifteenth Amendment, prohibiting discrimination in voting on the basis of race. Southerners were a major source of support for the Shafroth-Palmer Amendment of 1914, which would have allowed each state to have a referendum (if so requested by 8 percent or more of the voters) on the women's suffrage issue rather than setting a single national standard (for Southern views, see Wheeler 1993). Some supporters of women's suffrage wanted it limited to white women (Grimes 1978, 91).

Growing Support for the Amendment

As increasing numbers of states extended the right to vote in whole or in part to women, pressures for a federal amendment increased. In 1914 the Senate voted 35 to 34 for the amendment, with the House falling far shorter in 1915 with a vote of 174 to 204. That same year, under the leadership of Alice Paul, the Congressional Union for Woman Suffrage (CU)—later the Woman's Party (WP)—broke with NAWSA and advocated more militant measures, including campaigns against all Democrats, who were generally less supportive of the amendment than Republicans. The CU also led a series of parades and controversial pickets outside the White House.

The adoption of the Eighteenth Amendment probably aided the Nineteenth Amendment, in that some of those who had opposed women's suffrage for fear that it would lead to Prohibition now had nothing more to lose. World War I also mobilized increasing numbers of women into the workforce and increased support for acknowledging their sacrifices. Initially a tepid supporter of the amendment, President Woodrow Wilson addressed the Senate in 1918 in support of it (Flexnor 1974, 307–309), but it again fell short of the necessary votes, as it would in early 1919 as well. Wilson subsequently called a special session of Congress in May 1919, and the amendment finally succeeded, with the final Senate vote coming on May 28, 1919. Proposals to limit the vote to white women, to ratify the amendment by convention rather than by state legislatures, and to entrust states with primary enforcement powers were all rejected at this time (U.S. Senate Committee on the Judiciary, Subcommittee on the Constitution 1985, 56).

Ratification of the Amendment

The amendment was ratified in just over a year. Most opposition came, as expected, in the South. The 36th state to ratify was Tennessee. Several prominent leaders of the women's movement, including Carrie Chapman Catt, president of the National Woman Suffrage Association, came to Nashville to lobby and were met by almost equally well-organized opponents. The Tennessee Constitution contained a provision that the state legislature could not vote for a proposed amendment until after an intervening election (A. Taylor 1957, 104), but both the U.S. solicitor general and Tennessee's attorney general declared this provision invalid after the Supreme Court's two decisions in *Hawke v. Smith* (1920). The Tennessee Senate subsequently adopted the resolution by a vote of 24 to 4 and sent it to the House, where a motion to table the resolution failed by a vote of 48 to 48. When the measure came up for a vote, a 24-year-old state representative named Harry Burn switched votes because of his mother's request to adopt the amendment, and another member did the same in order to call the vote up for reconsideration. The "Red Rose Brigade," consisting of opponents of the amendment (supporters wore yellow roses), subsequently left the state for Alabama to prevent a quorum on reconsideration, but after a series of complicated maneuvers, they proved unsuccessful. The U.S. secretary of state apparently ignored a later House resolution of nonconcurrence (A. Taylor 1957, 122–124).

Subsequent Developments

The amendment was quickly implemented. In *Leser v. Garnett* (1922), the Supreme Court rejected a challenge to this amendment, and in *Adkins v. Children's Hospital* (1923), the Court cited the amendment in striking down a minimum-wage law for women in the District of

Columbia. Partly on the basis of this precedent and on the basis of the long debates on this amendment, some recent authors have argued that the Nineteenth Amendment might be interpreted, particularly in conjunction with the Fourteenth Amendment, as a broader guarantee of women's rights (J. Brown 1993; Siegel 2002).

Celebrations in Tennessee and throughout the nation marked the 75th anniversary of the Nineteenth Amendment in 1995. Events in Washington, D.C., were held in the basement of the Capitol near a statue of Susan B. Anthony, Elizabeth Cady Stanton, and Lucretia Mott, because the House had failed to vote on an earlier Senate resolution to move the monument—donated by the National Woman's Party in 1921—to the main rotunda. Among the dozens of statues of American forefathers there, none depicted American women ("A Celebration" 1995, 9).

See also Anthony, Susan Brownell; Catt, Carrie Lane Chapman; Eighteenth Amendment; Fifteenth Amendment; Fourteenth Amendment; *Hawke v. Smith; Leser v. Garrett; Minor v. Happersett;* Paul, Alice; Seneca Falls Convention; Shafroth-Palmer Amendment; Stanton, Elizabeth Cady; Willard, Frances.

For Further Reading:

Baker, Jean H., ed. 2002. *Votes for Women: The Struggle for Suffrage Revisited.* New York: Oxford University Press.

Bernstein, Richard B., with Jerome Agel. 1993. *Amending America: If We Love the Constitution So Much, Why Do We Keep Trying to Change It?* New York: Random House.

Brown, Jennifer K. 1993. "The Nineteenth Amendment and Women's Equality." *Yale Law Journal* 102 (June): 2174–2204.

"A Celebration of Women's Right to Vote." 1995. *New York Times,* 27 August, 9.

Flexnor, Eleanor. 1974. *Century of Struggle: The Woman's Rights Movement in the United States.* New York: Atheneum.

Grimes, Alan P. 1978. *Democracy and the Amendments to the Constitution.* Lexington, MA: Lexington Books.

Kraditor, Aileen S. 1981. *The Idea of the Woman's Suffrage Movement, 1890–1920.* New York: W. W. Norton.

Siegel, Reva B. 2002. "She the People: The Nineteenth Amendment, Sex Equality, Federalism, and the Family." *Harvard Law Review* 115 (February): 947–1046.

Stevens, Doris. 1995. *Jailed for Freedom: American Women Win the Vote.* Troutdale, OR: New Sage.

Taylor, A. Elizabeth. 1957. *The Woman Suffrage Movement in Tennessee.* New York: Bookman Associates.

U.S. Senate Committee on the Judiciary, Subcommittee on the Constitution, *Amendments to the Constitution: A Brief Legislative History.* 1985. Washington, DC: U.S. Government Printing Office.

Van Burkleo, Sandra F. 1990. "No Rights but Human Rights." *Constitution* 2 (Spring–Summer): 4–19.

Wheeler, Marjorie S. 1995b. *Votes for Women! The Woman Suffrage Movement in Tennessee, the South, and the Nation.* Knoxville, TN: University of Tennessee Press.

Wheeler, Marjorie S., ed. 1995. *One Woman, One Vote: Rediscovering the Woman Suffrage Movement.* Troutdale, OR: New Sage.

NINTH AMENDMENT

The Ninth Amendment is one of the most elusive amendments to the Constitution. It was ratified in 1791 as part of the Bill of Rights. This amendment provides that "the enumeration in the Constitution of certain rights, shall not be construed to deny or disparage others retained by the people."

This provision originated in an amendment proposed by the Virginia ratifying convention (Lash 2009, 24–215). The proposal that Madison introduced in the First Congress actually incorporated the ideas that would later appear in both the Ninth and the Tenth Amendments: "The exceptions here or elsewhere in the Constitution, made in favor of particular rights, shall not be so construed as to diminish the just importance of other rights retained by the people, or to enlarge the powers delegated by the Constitution; but either as actual limitations of such powers, or as inserted merely for greater caution" (Kurland and Lerner 1987, 5:25).

One of the Federalists' original objections to the inclusion of a bill of rights was that it would be impossible to make a complete list of human rights. Such a bill might prove dangerous if observers concluded that because a right was not enumerated it had therefore been forfeited. Madison introduced the Ninth Amendment was with this problem in mind. Speaking before the House of Representatives, he thus noted:

It has been objected also against a bill of rights, that, by enumerating particular exceptions to the grant of power, it would disparage those rights which were not placed in that enumeration; and it might follow by implication, that those rights which were not singled out, were intended to be assigned into the hands of the General Government, and were consequently insecure. This is one of the most plausible arguments I have ever heard urged against the admission of a bill of rights into this system; but, I conceive, that it may be guarded against. I have attempted it [in the Ninth Amendment] (Kurland and Lerner 1987, 5:399).

Professor Kurt Lash has observed that a select congressional committee "deleted Madison's original reference to enlarged construction of federal power and kept the language regarding retained rights" (2009, 49), which he believes to have been collective in nature. The only recorded debate on the subject in the First Congress centered on Elbridge Gerry's unsuccessful motion to substitute the word "impair" for "disparage" (Kurland and Lerner 1987, 5:400); other modifications were insignificant (Caplan 1983, 258). In a letter to Hardin Burnley of the Virginia House of Delegates, Madison further attempted during state ratification debates to assure that the amendment guarded state interests (Lash, 2009, 55–59). In debates opposing the constitutionality of the first national bank, Madison further cited the Ninth and Tenth Amendments, noting that the former guarded "against a latitude of interpretation" and the latter "as excluding every source of power not within the constitution itself" (Quoted in Lash 2009, 68). Others later cited both the Ninth and Tenth Amendments in opposing the Alien and Sedition Acts of 1798 (Lash, p. 160).

In its early years, state courts often paired the Ninth and Tenth Amendments to protect perceived interests of the states. In *Houston v. Moore* (1820),

Justice Joseph Story cited the Ninth Amendment (listing it as the eleventh, its original order in the Bill of Rights, rather than the ninth) to support the position that states should have concurrent power to court-martial individuals who refused to perform their duty as federal militia men. The nationalist Marshall Court largely ignored the Ninth Amendment, but subsequent state and federal courts continued the cite the amendment, usually in conjunction with the Tenth, to affirm that states retained important powers of government under the federal constitution.

The post–New Deal Court largely ignored and emasculated both amendments so that when Justice Arthur Goldberg cited the amendment in the Connecticut birth control case in *Griswold v. Connecticut* (1965), he and other justices were largely unaware of earlier precedents. Goldberg interpreted the amendment as a protection of individual natural rights, among which he thought privacy might be included.

This attempt has led to what a leading student of the Ninth Amendment called a "rights-powers" approach to the amendment. Under this approach, courts considered unenumerated rights under the amendment to consist only of those rights that remained because the government was granted no power over them (Barnette 1989, 14). An alternative approach would be to conceive of the protections for unenumerated rights in the Ninth Amendment, like other protections in the first ten amendments, as "power-constraints" on government (Barnette 1989, 14).

The main obstacles to this "power-constraints" approach appear to be twofold. First is the difficulty of deciding precisely what unenumerated rights the Ninth Amendment protects. Second is the related concern that expansive interpretation of such unenumerated rights might upset the scheme of separation of powers or federalism by unduly empowering the judiciary (DeRosa 1996).

Another way of interpreting the Ninth Amendment is to view it as recognizing that rights protected under state constitutions when it was adopted would continue in force "until modified or eliminated by state enactment, by federal preemption, or by a judicial determination of unconstitutionality" (Caplan 1983, 228).

Arguing that "The history of the Ninth Amendment is inextricably bound to the history of federalism under the American Constitution," Lash (2009, 359) has contended that the Amendment was designed to assure that courts would not interpret federal powers so as to undermine individual state government. He believes it might be a way of protecting states' rights to permit the medical use of marijuana, allow for assisted suicide, or make their own marriage regulations (*Id.*, 360).

Lash further associates the Ninth Amendment with the Eleventh Amendment, in that both appear to have been designed to influence the way that other provisions of the Constitution were construed.

See also Bill of Rights; Eleventh Amendment; *Griswold v. Connecticut;* Madison, James; Natural Law; Tenth Amendment.

For Further Reading:

Barnette, Randy E., ed. 1989. *The Rights Retained by the People: The History and Meaning of the Ninth Amendment.* Fairfax, VA: George Mason University Press.

Caplan, Russell L. 1983. "The History and Meaning of the Ninth Amendment." *Virginia Law Review* 69 (March): 223–268.

DeRosa, Marshall L. 1996. *The Ninth Amendment and the Politics of Creative Jurisprudence: Disparaging the Fundamental Right of Popular Control.* New Brunswick, NJ: Transaction Publishers.

Farber, David A. 2007. *Retained by the People: The "Silent" Ninth Amendment and the Constitutional Rights American Don't Know They Have.* New York: Basic Books.

Houston v. Moore, 18 U.S. (4 Wheat.) (1820) 1.

Kurland, Philip B., and Ralph Lerner, eds. 1987. *The Founders' Constitution.* 5 vols. Chicago: University of Chicago Press.

Lash, Kurt T. 2009. *The Lost History of the Ninth Amendment.* New York: Oxford University Press.

Lutz, Donald S. 1992. *A Preface to American Political Theory.* Lawrence: University Press of Kansas.

Massey, Calvin R. 1995. *Silent Rights: The Ninth Amendment and the Constitution's Unenumerated Rights.* Philadelphia: Temple University Press.

Patterson, Bennett B. 1955. *The Forgotten Ninth Amendment.* Indianapolis, IN: BobbsMerrill.

NORDEEN, ROSS

Ross Nordeen, a Floridian who identifies himself as a an engineer and an amateur economist, has joined those who have used the Internet to reprint the Constitution along with changes that he thinks should be added or deleted. His site (*www.amatecon.com*), which the author of this book first visited in June 2000, is still available and does not appear to have changed in significant measure. Nordeen indicates that he became interested in the idea of constitutional reform because of Florida's look at its own constitution, and cites a number of conservative and libertarian individuals and groups that have influenced his thinking.

In revising Article I, Nordeen proposes to eliminate all indirect references to slavery. He would also limit members of the House of Representatives to three terms and members of the U.S. Senate to two. Both houses would be limited to meeting no more than 60 days per year, except by a two-thirds vote permitting an additional 60-day term. Nordeen proposes a number of alterations in the list of congressional powers in Article I, Section 8. He would: require a two-thirds vote for levying any new taxes; delete the provision giving Congress power to establish post offices and post roads; and alter the necessary and proper clause by giving Congress power "to make only those laws which shall be necessary and proper" and by further providing that all congressional laws shall expire after ten years. Additionally, he would prohibit taxes with retroactive effect as well as prohibit deficit spending unless such spending were approved by three-fourths majorities of both houses.

Nordeen would leave Articles II and III relatively untouched, but he would also add a provision to Article IV specifying that "[a] state may secede from the union by a two-thirds vote of its citizens. Congress may levy additional requirements on the secession of a state with a two-thirds vote of both houses." Nordeen adds, by way of explanation that:

Giving the states an explicit method of secession might have prevented the bloodshed of the Civil War. If the southern states were allowed to peacefully secede, the remaining states could have easily passed an amendment barring slavery and acted as a safe haven for runaway slaves.

Nordeen would further provide in Article V "nor shall a state's method of electing Senators be changed without its consent." He apparently does so in the hopes of allowing states who choose to do so to revert to the method of selecting senators prior to the introduction of the Seventeenth Amendment, which, however, remains unchanged in his document.

Nordeen advocates a number of changes in the Bill of Rights. The word "abridging" in the First Amendment would be changed to "infringing." He further adds a provision, which appears largely to codify existing case law, stating that:

The rights of electoral participation and political association are fundamental; any law burdening their exercise is subject to strict judicial scrutiny for legitimacy regarding ends and means, and must be supported by clear and convincing evidence. Political choices and competition are primary interests of the citizenry.

Nordeen would eliminate the preface to the Second Amendment, thus simply providing that "Congress shall make no law infringing on the right of the people to keep and bear arms." He also adds a provision to the Third Amendment requiring that "Congress shall make no law requiring service in the army, navy, the militia or any civil service." The Fourth Amendment is prefaced with a provision stating that "Congress shall make no law infringing on the right of the people to privacy." Nordeen would further strengthen the takings clause of the Fifth Amendment by providing that private property shall not be taken "except for a substantial, explicit public use and with full compensation therefore paid to each owner." Nordeen adds a provision to the Sixth Amendment providing that "[t]he jury shall have the power to judge the law in all instances in which the government or any of its agencies is an opposing party." Nordeen proposes fairly extensive changes to the Eighth Amendment. It would, like the First Amendment, begin with the words, "Congress shall make no law," and include the following provisions designed to strengthen property rights:

Forfeiture of estate, indefinite imprisonment, and unreasonable detention of witnesses are forbidden. There shall be proportionality between magnitude of felony and the severity of forfeiture of property. No person charged with a crime shall be compelled to pay costs before a judgment of conviction has become final. A person not found guilty of a crime shall not be assessed fees or costs to recover property seized as evidence or otherwise held, impounded, or stored by the government.

Nordeen also adds new language to the Tenth Amendment designed to rein in federal powers:

Relative to the people, no branch of government has inherent or reserved powers, implicit or assumed prerogatives, or presupposed attributes of sovereignty. Powers must be expressly granted to government by the people, and the extent and range of such powers shall be strictly, narrowly construed.

Nordeen does not propose any alterations in the other 17 amendments that have been ratified.

Nordeen's plan of indicating how his proposals would fit into the existing Constitution, although not unique, adds to the clarity of his amendments. The concern by an admitted "novice" about constitutional issues is another indication of the importance that private citizens in the United States often place on the written constitution.

See also Bill of Rights, Eighth Amendment; Fifth Amendment; Fourth Amendment; Sixth Amendment, Tenth Amendment.

For Further Reading:

Nordeen, Ross. "Home Page." www.amatecon. com. Accessed June 30, 2000. Reaccessed for updates on May 17, 2002. There are few significant changes in the two documents. Quotations are taken from the first.

NUMBER OF PROPOSED AMENDMENTS

When historian Herman Ames surveyed the amendments that had been proposed during the nation's first 100 years, he counted 1,736 proposals. He noted, however, that "it is scarcely possible that all the proposed amendments presented to Congress have been included" (Ames 1896, 11). The precision of his count is further undercut by the fact that he included some state petitions and proposals for amendments that presidents made in speeches but that were not necessarily introduced as amendments in Congress. Also, Ames sometimes split a single proposal into several components, each of which he numbered separately. Notwithstanding such limitations, his count still remains the best approximation for the nation's first 100 years.

In the next published list of amendments, the Library of Congress counted 1,316 amendments that had members had introduced in Congress from 1890 through 1926 (Tansill 1926).

When Daryl Harris published an update of amendments in 1992, he counted 10,431 proposals. These included the 3,000-plus amendments counted by Ames and Tansill, as well as 2,340 amendments introduced from 1926 to 1962 (*Proposed Amendments* 1963; this study duplicates parts of *Proposed Amendments* 1957), 1,548 from 1963 to 1968 (*Proposed Amendments* 1969), 3,054 from 1969 to 1984 (Davis 1985), and 437 from 1985 to 1990 (D. Harris 1992, CRS8).

The best count available for the Congresses since 1990 are as follows: 152 proposals for the 102nd Congress (1991–1992); 156 for the 103rd Congress; 287 for the 104th Congress; 110 for the 105th Congress; and 69 for the 106th Congress (1999–2000) (Vile 2003). The 107th Congress proposed 81 amendments; the 108th Congress proposed 92; the 109th Congress proposed 80, the 110th Congress proposed 68 amendments, and as of August 17, 2009, the 111th Congress has proposed 47 amendments (Library of Congress Web site). This would bring the total to 11,573. This number does not include all the petitions that have been made to Congress by private groups and by governments for particular amendments. The most complete list of state applications for a constitutional convention, which was published in 1993, lists 399 such proposals, some of which were included in Ames's count of the first 100 years (Paulsen 1993). Some states have rescinded their calls for a convention either for a specific issue, like balanced budgets, or for a convention in general.

Counting the total number of amendments proposed in Congress is somewhat deceptive, because most such proposals are repetitious. Charles Leedham, writing in 1964, noted the "recent trend toward the introduction, all at once, of dozens of identically worded proposals . . . boosts the total far out of any meaningful relation to the number of topics under consideration (1964, 264). He thus noted that of 328 proposals introduced in the 88th Congress, there were only "37 distinct propositions in the House and 13 in the Senate." He further observed that:

> The Senate manages to keep the total number of proposals rather low by listing each resolution only once and noting that it may have more than one sponsor. The House clutters up the record with dozens of individually entered "Joint Resolutions," each one commemorating no more than the fact that an individual representative likes the idea. (Leedham 1964, 264)

There are thus literally hundreds of proposals to introduce an Equal Rights Amendment, to restore public prayer in schools, to provide for a balanced budget amendment, and the like.

Of the thousands of amendments that members of Congress have introduced, only 34 have been proposed by the requisite congressional majorities. Of these, six remain failed amendments, and the states have ratified only 27. The Twenty-first Amendment repealed the Eighteenth, which had provided for national alcoholic prohibition.

See also Failed Amendments.

For Further Reading:

Ames, Herman. 1896. *The Proposed Amendments to the Constitution of the United States during the First Century of Its History.* Reprint, New York: Burt Franklin, 1970.

Davis, Richard. 1985. *Proposed Amendments to the Constitution of the United States of America Introduced in Congress from the 91st Congress, 1st Session, through the 98th Congress, 2d Session, January 1969–December 1984.* Washington, DC: Congressional Research Service Report no. 85–36 GOV.

Harris, Daryl B. 1992. *Proposed Amendments to the U.S. Constitution: 99th–101st Congresses (1985–1990).* Washington, DC: Congressional Research Service, Library of Congress.

Leedham, Charles. 1964. *Our Changing Constitution: The Story behind the Amendments.* New York: Dodd, Mead & Company.

Paulsen, Michael S. 1993. "A General Theory of Article V: The Constitutional Issues of the Twenty-seventh Amendment." *Yale Law Journal* 103: 677–789.

Proposed Amendments to the Constitution of the United States, Introduced in Congress from the 69th Congress, 2d Session through the 84th Congress, 2d Session, December 6, 1926, to January 3, 1957. 1957. Washington, DC: U.S. Government Printing Office.

Proposed Amendments to the Constitution of the United States of America Introduced in Congress from the 69th Congress, 2d Session through the 87th Congress, 2d Session, December 6, 1926, to January 3, 1963. 1963. Washington, DC: U.S. Government Printing Office.

Proposed Amendments to the Constitution of the United States of America Introduced in Congress from the 88th Congress, 1st Session through the 90th Congress, 2d Session, January 9, 1963, to January 3, 1969. 1969. Washington, DC: U.S. Government Printing Office.

Tansill, Charles C. 1926. *Proposed Amendments of the Constitution of the United States Introduced in Congress from December 4, 1889, to July 2, 1926.* Washington, DC: U.S. Government Printing Office.

Vile, John R., ed. 2003. *Proposed Amendments to the U.S. Constitution, 1787–2001.* 3 vols. Union, NJ: Law Book Exchange.

O

❖

OAKLAND STATEMENT

See Ellis, Frederick, and Carl Frederick.

OBJECTIVIST CONSTITUTION

Objectivism is a philosophy of government grounded in laissez-faire economics that has grown out of the philosophy of Ayn Rand, whose best-known works are *The Fountainhead* and *Atlas Shrugged.* In what may be a first, the Wikipedia Internet entry on objectivism includes a proposed revised U.S. Constitution. Although the proposal does not include commentary, it is tied to a Wikipedia entry that identifies objectivism with the idea that "the proper moral purpose of one's life is the pursuit of one's own happiness or 'rational self-interest'; [and] that the only social system consistent with this morality is full respect for individual rights, embodied in pure, consensual *laissez-faire* capitalism."

The objectivist constitution includes the current text of the U.S. Constitution with proposed additions and deletions, some of the latter of which correspond to changes to be initiated by amendment. Proposed changes to the preamble include deleting the general welfare clause, adding a provision to "protect property," and another "acknowledging that the proper function of government is to protect the freedom of individuals from the initiation of force."

Article I (the legislative branch) incorporates the existing Ninth and Tenth Amendments and adds that "No powers delegated to the United States by the Constitution, nor powers retained by the states nor subsidiary governments or municipalities thereof shall be construed in any way inconsistent with clause 2 [the Ninth Amendment]." Clause 6 of the existing article is changed so that the chief justice will preside over the Senate in the case of both presidential and vice-presidential impeachment trials. Objectivists propose major changes in the allocations of congressional powers in Article I, Section 8. In place of the power "to lay and collect" taxes, the first clause would provide that Congress has power to "charge fees for the services of the United States from those who choose to use those services; but such fees shall be uniform throughout the United States and furthermore to raise revenue through other non-coercive means such as a lottery." The proposal would delete current powers to regulate commerce, coin money, establish post offices, and the like. A clause specifically provides that Congress shall make no law abridging the freedom of production and trade."

Article II (the executive branch) would obligate the president to "veto and negate any law which is in violation of this Constitution." It would further require Senate consent to presidential pardons. Such pardons, like nominations, would stand, unless rejected by the Senate within 90 days. The revisions provide that "[n]o official action of the President, Vice-President, or any civil or military Officer of the United States shall be exempt from Constitutional Review under the Judicial Power of the United States."

Article III (the judicial branch) would incorporate changes inaugurated by the Eleventh

Amendment and is worded so as to prevent Congress from withdrawing judicial review over any laws. Article IV (federalism) remains intact.

Article V (the constitutional amending process) adds a seven-year deadline for ratifying amendments and provides that "[n]o Amendment shall authorize the initiation of force by the United States or any State." Article VI further provides that "[e]ach State retains the option of peacefully seceding from the United States by a vote of three fourths of its citizens in a referendum, if the state on becoming a new nation adopts the protections of individual rights laid out in this constitution."

The Constitution specifies several changes in the Bill of Rights. In addition to its other guarantees, the First Amendment would prohibit any Congressional law abridging "any action that does not harm or threaten another person." The Second Amendment would be stripped of language referring to a well-regulated militia. The Fifth Amendment would require that indictments specify "who is alleged to have been harmed or threatened, and how." The Eighth Amendment would add compensation for "any loss from wrongful imprisonment" and would provide for "the cost of defense against any criminal prosecution that does not result in valid conviction of a crime."

Provisions in the Fourteenth Amendment would apply to both the state and national governments and would apportion representation among states according to "citizens registered to vote in each State." The Sixteenth Amendment, authorizing the national income tax, would be deleted as would the Twenty-fourth Amendment relative to poll taxes.

For Further Reading:

http://wiki.objectivismonline.net/wiki/New_constitution. Accessed June 6, 2008.

OBSCENITY AND PORNOGRAPHY

Laws directed toward the regulation of obscenity and pornography arouse intense emotions. Advocates of such laws believe that they help promote morality and protect minors; opponents believe that they infringe on the freedoms of speech and the press, which the First and Fourteenth Amendments protect. Members of Congress introduced at least half a dozen proposals from 1959 to 1970 to grant that body or the states the power to enact legislation regulating obscenity. During this same period, critics often accused U.S. courts of being too tolerant of obscenity.

In the 19th century, U.S. courts gave fairly wide range to state anti-obscenity statutes under the so-called Hicklin test. Under this formula, obscenity was judged according to "whether the tendency of the matter charged as obscenity is to deprave and corrupt those whose minds are open to such immoral influence and into whose hands a publication of this sort may fall" (quoted in Abraham and Perry 1994, 237). As the Supreme Court began to give increasing scrutiny to such legislation in the 1950s, it liberalized its standards in cases such as *Roth v. United States* and *Alberts v. California* (1957) but still denied that the First Amendment protected obscenity.

Since then, the Court's most difficult problem has been that of identifying obscenity. Some justices, such as William Brennan, eventually concluded that it was impossible to regulate obscenity without infringing on other First Amendment rights. But in *Miller v. California* (1973), Chief Justice Warren Burger formulated a three-part test that, with minor modifications, remains in force today. This test provided that a work is obscene if "(a) the average person, applying contemporary community standards, would find that the work, taken as a whole, appeals to the prurient; (b) the work depicts or describes, in a patently offensive way, sexual conduct specifically defined by the applicable state law; and (c) the work, taken as a whole, lacks serious literary, artistic, political, or scientific value" (*Miller* 1973, 25).

Since then, the Supreme Court has permitted governments to tighten the regulation of pornography involving juveniles (see especially *New York v. Ferber,* 1982) or directed to juveniles or nonconsenting adults. It has also allowed local governments to use zoning ordinances to regulate pornography in towns and cities. Regulation of obscenity on the Internet has proven to be more difficult. Thus, in *Reno v. American Civil Liberties Union* (1997), the Court invalidated provisions of the Communications Decency Act of 1996 that it thought, in protecting children, also unduly restricted access by adults to chat rooms with mature content that fell short of being defined as obscene. Similarly, in *Ashcroft v. Free Speech Coalition* (2002), the Court struck down part of the Child Pornography Prevention Act of 1996 regulating computer-generated depictions of minors engaged in sexual activities; here the Court thought that depictions of actual children engaged in sexual behavior generated concrete harms that depictions of computer-generated images of children did not.

See First Amendment.

For Further Reading:

Abraham, Henry J., and Barbara Perry. 1994. *Freedom and the Court: Civil Rights and Liberties in the United States.* 8th ed. Lawrence: University Press of Kansas.

Miller v. California, 413 U.S. 15 (1973).

Vile, John R., David L. Hudson, Jr, and David Schultz, eds. 2009. *The Encyclopedia of the First Amendment.* Washington, DC: CQ Press.

OCEANIA

See Davidson, Jim.

O'CONOR, CHARLES (1804–1888)

Charles O'Conor was a successful New York attorney who introduced proposals for constitutional reforms in the 1870s and 1880s. Like his contemporaries who were concerned with political corruption, O'Conor hoped to eliminate private legislation at both state and national levels (O'Conor 1877, 29). He also hoped to cut off the source of government graft by eliminating duties and tariffs, limiting government revenues to what could be raised by "immediate taxation," and prohibiting governments from borrowing or coining money (*Id.,* 1314–1316). O'Conor also proposed to reduce the number of laws by adopting general statutes that would be suitable for each kind of political subdivision, and he thought that the invention of the telegraph made it possible to eliminate the diplomatic corps (*Id.,* 1316). He favored shortening the ballot and reducing the number of elected offices, but, convinced that voting was a duty rather than a right, he also favored limiting the franchise and eliminating the secret ballot (*Id.,* 6).

As a Catholic, O'Conor wanted to exclude public schools from teaching religion or other sectarian ideals. O'Conor wanted to outlaw polygamy, and he opposed liberal divorce laws. He also suggested that state autonomy could be preserved and greater uniformity could be achieved if a "court of ultimate appeal" was created to hear cases coming from both state and federal courts. It would be composed of judges selected by the states to deal with "conflicting laws" and "jarring jurisprudence" (O'Conor 1881, 1317).

O'Conor favored making both Congress and state legislatures unicameral, but his most radical proposal related to the presidency. O'Conor proposed filling the office each month by lot from the legislature, "thus substantially extinguishing the great office of President" (O'Conor 1877, 35). He predicted that efforts expended on competition for this office could then be diverted to more productive private enterprises.

For Further Reading:

O'Conor, Charles. 1881. "Democracy." In *Johnson's New Universal Cyclopaedia: A Treasury of Scientific and Popular Treasure of Useful Knowledge.* Vol. 1, Part 2. New York: A. J. Johnson.

———. 1877. Address by Charles O'Conor delivered before the New York Historical Society at the Academy of Music. May 8. New York: Anson D. F. Randolph.

Vile, John R. 1991c. *Rewriting the United States Constitution: An Examination of Proposals from Reconstruction to the Present.* New York: Praeger.

OFFICE OF THE FEDERAL REGISTER

Although the national archivist of the United States is currently entrusted with the official duty of certifying and publishing the state ratification of proposed amendments, the archivist has delegated some of these duties to the director of the federal register. This individual examines ratifications for "facial legal sufficiency and an authenticating signature," and, if a sufficient number of states ratify, subsequently "drafts a formal proclamation for the Archivist to certify that the amendment is valid and has become part of the Constitution." If so, the amendment is then "published in the *Federal Register* and U.S. Statutes at Large and serves as official notice to the Congress and to the Nation that the amendment process has been completed" ("The Constitutional Amendment Process" Archives Web site).

See also Archivist of the United States.

For Further Reading:

"The Constitutional Amendment Process." http://www.archives.gov/federal_register/constitution/amendment_process.html. Accessed August 12, 2009.

OFFICES, FORFEITURE OF, OR INELIGIBILITY FOR

The Constitution does not prohibit individuals who are convicted of crimes from serving in office, but it does provide some mechanisms for removing such individuals. Thus, Article I, Section 2 of the Constitution gives the House of Representatives the sole power of impeachment, and the subsequent section provides that the Senate shall try impeachments. Article I, Section 4 extends the prospect of impeachment to the president, vice president, "and all civil Officers of the United States" but limits the grounds of such impeachment to conviction of "Treason, Bribery, or other high Crimes and Misdemeanors." Article I, Section 3 specifies that conviction requires a two-thirds vote. Conviction is to extend no further "than to removal from Office, and disqualification to hold and enjoy any Office of honor, Trust or Profit under the United States." Of the seven impeachment convictions the Senate has rendered (all of federal judges), it has voted for disqualification to future offices in only two cases (Peltason 1994, 53).

According to Article I, Section 5, each house of Congress may "punish its Members for disorderly Behavior, and, with the Concurrence of two thirds, expel a Member."

Congress may further exclude members by a majority vote. According to the Supreme Court's decision in *Powell v. McCormack* (1969), it can do so only when members fail to meet the constitutionally specified age, citizenship, or residence requirements. If Congress wants to expel a member, it must do so by the two-thirds vote cited above.

As the framers undoubtedly intended, neither the procedure for impeaching and convicting governmental officials nor that for expelling members of Congress is simple. Moreover, unless the Senate so specifies when it convicts an individual of an impeachable offense, even a person removed from one office may be eligible for another. Two proposals were offered in the 19th century, one in 1838 and the other in 1876, to prohibit individuals convicted of embezzlement or bribery from holding office. Some of the contemporary proposals to outlaw polygamy also contained provisions designed to exclude polygamists from holding office.

Since 1985 about 20 more proposals have attempted to prohibit convicted felons from serving as federal officials, as members of Congress, or as judges. These proposals may have been stimulated by the conduct of Harry E. Claiborne, a U.S. district court judge in Nevada who continued to draw his salary after being convicted and imprisoned and subsequently became the fifth federal judge in history to be impeached and convicted (Abraham 1998, 45). In 1992 Florida judge Alcee Hastings was elected to Congress after having been successfully removed from office by a Senate vote of impeachment (Peltason 1994, 53). Ironically, as a congressman, he cast one of the votes against the impeachment of President Bill Clinton.

See also Polygamy

For Further Reading:

Abraham, Henry J. 1998. *The Judicial Process: An Introductory Analysis of the Courts of the United States, England, and France.* 7th ed. New York: Oxford University Press.

Peltason, Jack W. 1994. *Corwin and Peltason's Understanding the Constitution.* 13th ed. Fort Worth, TX: Harcourt Brace College Publishers.

OREGON V. MITCHELL (1970)

The decision for the Supreme Court in *Oregon v. Mitchell* (consolidated with two other cases, *Texas v. Mitchell* and *United States v. Arizona*) precipitated the proposal and ratification of the Twenty-sixth Amendment. The cases also serve as classic examples of differences among the justices as to the meaning of the post–Civil War amendments and the degree to which these amendments permit legislative and judicial extensions of constitutional rights.

The Court considered three questions involving congressional authority exercised in the 1970 amendments to the 1965 Voting Rights Act. These questions involved congressional authority to lower the voting age to 18 in state and federal elections, bar the use of literacy tests, and eliminate state residency requirements in presidential elections.

Justice Hugo Black's opinion, which garnered four votes from the two major divisions of the Court, recognized congressional authority under Article I, Section 4; Article II, Section 1; and the necessary and proper clause to lower the voting age for federal elections. Black also stated that Article I, Section 2 limited federal power to lower the voting age in state and local elections. He further denied that the equal protection clause of the Fourteenth Amendment, which was directed primarily to discrimination on the basis of race, provided such authority. Black accepted the literacy test ban on the basis of the enforcement clauses of the Fourteenth and Fifteenth Amendments, and elimination of residency requirements on the basis of congressional authority over federal elections.

Justice William O. Douglas would have relied on the authority of the equal protection and privileges and immunities clauses of the Fourteenth Amendment to lower the voting age in both state and federal elections. He would also have upheld the other provisions of the law.

Justice John Marshall Harlan accepted the congressionally imposed literacy ban on the basis of the Fifteenth Amendment. However, he used exhaustive analysis of the framing of the Fourteenth Amendment to deny that the amendment intended to provide authority for other federal measures at issue. Citing powers reserved to the states by the Tenth Amendment, Harlan suggested that federal authority over these other voting matters would require amendments similar to the Fifteenth, Nineteenth, and Twenty-fourth Amendments. Harlan also rejected Black's analysis of Article I, Sections 2 and 4.

Justices William Brennan, Byron White, and Thurgood Marshall disputed Harlan's narrow reading of the Fourteenth Amendment. They would have upheld all aspects of the law under the equal protection clause and congressional enforcement powers under the Civil War amendments.

Justices Potter Stewart, Warren Burger, and Harry Blackmun accepted Black's distinction between congressional power over federal elections and that over state and local elections. However, they grounded congressional power over residency requirements on the privileges and immunities of American citizens, including the right to travel.

See also Black, Hugo Lafayette; Fifteenth Amendment; Fourteenth Amendment; Supreme Court Decisions Reversed by Constitutional Amendments; Tenth Amendment; Twenty-sixth Amendment.

For Further Reading:

Banks, Christopher P. 2003. "The Constitutional Politics of Interpreting Section 5 of the Fourteenth Amendment." *Akron Law Review* 36: 425–471.

Oregon v. Mitchell, 400 U.S. 112 (1970).

P

❖

PACE, JAMES O. (1954–)

New York attorney James Pace advanced one of the most novel and racist contemporary proposals for constitutional amendment in a book titled *Amendment to the Constitution: Averting the Decline and Fall of America* (Pace 1986). Addressing a variety of concerns related to the decline of the family, permissive sexual relations, crime, disrespect for religion, poverty, and declining educational standards, Pace's primary concern was the nation's increasing racial diversity. He was also troubled by the way that the Fourteenth Amendment had enabled the federal courts to oversee traditional state and local controls in areas such as pornography and crime.

Pace called for the adoption of an amendment that would repeal the Fourteenth and Fifteenth Amendments and alter the Tenth Amendment by adding the word "expressly" before the word "delegated." This would thereby foreclose the possibility of implied congressional powers that Chief Justice Marshall recognized in *McCulloch v. Maryland* (1819). Pace would further limit citizenship to "non-Hispanic white [people] of the European race, in whom there is no ascertainable trace of Negro blood, nor more than one-eighth Mongolian, Asian, Asia Minor, Middle Eastern, Semitic, Near Eastern, American Indian, Malay or other non-European or nonwhite blood" (Pace 1986, 140). Pace would restrict the right to reside permanently in the United States to citizens. He advocated programs for resettling noncitizens in other nations while allowing those who were needed—for example, blacks, who, "because of

their physical abilities," might be employed as police officers to enforce the amendment—to get temporary work permits (Pace 1986, 118). Pace favored calling a constitutional convention to inaugurate his plans.

See also Constitutional Conventions; Fifteenth Amendment; Fourteenth Amendment; *McCulloch v. Maryland;* Tenth Amendment.

For Further Reading:

Pace, James O. 1986. *Amendment to the Constitution: Averting the Decline and Fall of America.* Los Angeles, CA: Johnson, Pace, Simmons and Fennell.

PALKO V. CONNECTICUT (1937)

Palko v. Connecticut remains one of the leading cases dealing with the incorporation controversy (Abraham and Perry 2003, 62–65). At issue was a Connecticut law that permitted the state to retry an individual if there had been errors in that individual's first trial. Here, the state retried a case in which Palka (his name was misspelled in the official case reporter) had been sentenced to life in prison for second-degree murder. On retrial, the state won a conviction of murder in the first degree, carrying the death penalty. If that had occurred in a federal court, it would have been considered to be double jeopardy, in violation of the Fifth Amendment. Palka argued for the view that all the prohibitions in the Bill of Rights that applied to the federal government should also apply to the states through the due process clause of the Fourteenth Amendment.

In an 8-to-1 decision for the Court, Justice Benjamin Cardozo rejected this contention. His task was complicated by the fact that, by 1937, the Court had accepted the idea that some provisions of the Bill of Rights—for example, protections for freedom of speech and the press—did apply to the states through the Fourteenth Amendment, although it had rejected the application of other rights. Cardozo attempted to reconcile these cases by articulating the doctrine of selective incorporation, or fundamental rights. According to this view, the due process clause of the Fourteenth Amendment incorporated only those provisions that are "of the very essence of a scheme of ordered liberty" or that are based on principles of justice "so rooted in the traditions and conscience of our people as to be ranked as fundamental" (*Palko* 1937, 325). Seeing this case as a legitimate state attempt to remedy past errors rather than as an attempt to wear the defendant down, Cardozo decided that no violation of due process had taken place.

The arguments in *Palko* would later be repeated in *Adamson v. California* (1947), where Justice Hugo Black advanced his support for the doctrine of total incorporation and Justice Felix Frankfurter advocated a view akin to Cardozo's. Although continuing to profess adherence to the doctrine of selective incorporation or fundamental fairness, over time, the Court ruled that most provisions in the Bill of Rights were fundamental and should be applied to the states. In *Benton v. Maryland* (1969), the Court finally applied the double-jeopardy provision to the states, thus overruling the specific decision in *Palko*.

See also *Adamson v. California;* Fourteenth Amendment; Incorporation.

For Further Reading:

Abraham, Henry J., and Barbara Perry. 2003. *Freedom and the Court: Civil Rights and Liberties in the United States.* 8th ed. Lawrence: University Press of Kansas.

Palko v. Connecticut, 302 U.S. 319 (1937).

PALM, KIRBY (1955–)

Kirby Palm is a Floridian who graduated from Florida Technological University in 1977 and has since retired from engineering. He has a Web site on which he has proposed adding three kinds of amendments to the U.S. Constitution.

The first concerns "applicability." In this section Palm would clarify and distinguish the rights of natural-born U.S. citizens from naturalized citizens, the latter of which he does not think should have the right to vote: "Immigrants should be very happy to be able to become U.S. citizens even if they don't get full rights; their children born here *will* get full rights, which is a valuable objective for immigrating." He also believes that the Constitution should specifically describe the rights of criminals, of children, and even of the unborn.

Palm proposes another section dealing with "Offense and Recourse." He proposes making the existing constitution much more specific. He thus favors a textual explanation of the Second Amendment right to bear arms specifically denying the government power to require a license, outlaw ammunition, outlaw particular types of arms, or prohibiting the bearing of arms in particular situations. He favors a variation of the U.S. Supreme Court with no "connections to the other branches of the federal government" and with the power "to expel elected officials from office, if necessary." Much as monarchs can call new elections in parliamentary systems, such a body would be able to expel "all the Senators, Congressmen, and the President whose signatures appeared on a piece of legislation that was in clear violation of the Constitution."

Palm proposes a third section specifying how a state can peacefully secede. He doubts that any would choose to do so, but he argues that "having the threat of secession might be just what the federal government needs to keep them from usurping more and more of the states' rights."

On his personal Web site, Palm has also proposed an amendment that would repeal the Twenty-seventh Amendment and provide that "No persons shall hold successive terms in an elected office." He makes it clear that this would apply to all offices within the United States at either state or national levels. His stated goal is that of eliminating "the career politician."

See also Twenty-seventh Amendment.

For Further Reading:
Palm, Kirby. "The U.S. Constitution: Formal Additions." http://www.nettally.com/palmk/Constitution Sections.html. Accessed June 23, 2008.

———. "Proposed Constitutional Amendment." http://www.nettally.com/palmk/terms.html. Accessed June 23, 2008.

PARDON POWER

See Presidency, Pardon Power.

PARENTAL RIGHTS AMENDMENTS

Proponents of parental rights, including Republican Senator Charles Grassley of Iowa and Republican Representative Steve Largent of Oklahoma, have proposed a Parental Rights and Responsibility Act to limit governmental regulation of family life absent a "compelling state interest." The bill focuses on four main areas: education, health care, discipline, and religious training. Similarly, since 1994 "parental rights amendments" have been introduced both in Congress and in a majority of states, where action is more prominent. Such amendments would alter state constitutions to provide that "the rights of parents to direct the upbringing and education of their children shall not be infringed" (Lawton 1996, 57).

The U.S. Supreme Court has recognized related rights in *Meyer v. Nebraska* (1923), in *Pierce v. Society of Sisters* (1925), and in *Wisconsin v. Yoder* (1972). The first struck down a state law prohibiting the teaching of modern foreign languages in school, the second permitted parents to send their children to parochial rather than to public schools, and the third allowed Amish parents to withdraw their children, who were in Amish-directed apprenticeship programs, from school after the eighth grade. In *Troxel v. Granville* (2000), the Court further asserted parental control over visits by third parties (in this case, grandparents) with their children.

Michale Ferris, chancellor of Patrick Henry College and president of the Home School Legal Defense League, has drafted a Parental Rights Amendment with three sections. The first would recognize that "[t]he liberty of parents to direct the upbringing and education of their children is a fundamental right." The second would provide that "[n]either the United States nor any state shall infringe upon this right without demonstrating that its governmental interest as applied to the person is of the highest order and not otherwise served." The third would specify that "[n]o treaty nor any source of international law may be employed to supersede, modify, interpret, or apply to the rights guaranteed by this article" ("The Solution"). The latter provision reflects Ferris's concern, similar to that which once led to calls for the Bricker Amendment, that the proposed U.S. ratification of the UN Convention on the Rights of the Child might supersede existing laws that permit homeschooling and other parental rights. Critics fear that the proposed parental rights amendments might increase parental rights at the expense of those of children, and spawn unnecessary litigation that might give parents too much control of school curricula (Sabourin 1999; Ross 2000).

See also Bricker Amendment.

For Further Reading:
Lawton, Kim A. 1996. "'The Right to Parent': Should It Be Fundamental." *Christianity Today* (April 29): 57.

Ross, William G. 2000. "The Contemporary Significance of *Meyer* and *Pierce* for Parental Rights Issues Involving Education." *Akron Law Review* 34: 1277–1207.

Sabourin, Jennifer L. 1999. "Parental Rights Amendments: Will a Statutory Right to Parent Force Children to 'Shed Their Constitutional Rights' at the Schoolhouse Door?" *Wayne State University Law Review* 44 (Winter): 1899–2926.

"The Solution: A Constitutional Amendment."
ParentalRights.org. http://www.parentalrights.org/
learn/the-solution-a-constitutional-amendment.
Accessed May 26, 2008.

PARLIAMENTARY SOVEREIGNTY

In Great Britain the central struggle for liberty centered on the struggle for power between the Crown and Parliament. Because the Crown was a hereditary office and Parliament was an elected body, the idea of democracy came to be identified with the latter body. Over time, the British embraced the idea that democratic rule required that Parliament be sovereign.

By contrast, in America, the struggle for independence began with the rejection of parliamentary sovereignty, especially as it related to taxation (Reid 1993). Moreover, as American constitutional theory developed, it increasingly emphasized that the written constitution limited all three branches of the new government.

In consequence of these developments, Americans had to formulate a different theory of constitutional amendment than did the British. When the British refer to their constitution, they do not refer to a single document but to a host of documents, practices, and understandings that have developed over a long period. In practice, this system has adopted constitutional change fairly cautiously (Vile 1993c), but in theory, constitutional changes can be effected simply by parliamentary action. By contrast, the U.S. system is based on a written constitution that is not changeable by ordinary acts of legislation but requires extraordinary majorities at both state and national levels. Thus, James Bryce, an English observer, appears to have initiated characterizations of the U.S. Constitution as "rigid" (Bryce 1905, 1906; Vile 1992, 137–138). However, because the United States' written constitution is a brief outline that leaves many matters to legislative majorities, many policy changes can be initiated short of constitutional amendment.

Although the U.S. Constitution does not use the term "sovereignty," the reference in the preamble to "We the People" is often cited as an indication that the people are the ultimate sovereigns in the United States. The constitutionally designated method for exercising this sovereignty to pass laws is through procedures specified within the document. Article V further delineates a method for supermajorities of the people to alter that document. Many contemporary proposals for initiatives and referendums would shift this sovereignty more directly to popular majorities.

See also Rigid Constitution; Sovereignty.

For Further Reading:
Bryce, James. 1905. "Flexible and Rigid Constitutions." In *Constitutions*. Germany: Scientia Verlag Aalen. Reprint of New York and London edition, 1980.

Reid, John P. 1993. *Constitutional History of the American Revolution. The Authority of Law.* Madison, WI: University of Wisconsin Press.

Vile, John R. 1993c. "Three Kinds of Constitutional Founding and Change: The Convention Model and Its Alternatives." *Political Research Quarterly* 46: 881–895.

———. 1992. *The Constitutional Amending Process in American Political Thought.* New York: Praeger.

PARLIAMENTARY SYSTEM

Among those who have proposed major constitutional changes, few alterations have been more popular than those designed to incorporate one or another aspect of parliamentary systems, especially as this system is practiced in Great Britain. This system generally avoids the problem of divided government, wherein the legislative majority and the chief executive are from different parties. It does so by allowing the majority party or majority coalition within the legislative branch, generally designated as the parliament, to choose the chief executive, who is usually called a prime minister.

In contrast to the U.S. system, which forbids members of Congress from holding executive office, members of the British cabinet are chosen from and continue to serve in the Parliament. Fairly strict party discipline is the norm, and if Parliament rejects one of the prime minister's major bills or gives a vote of "no confidence" in the existing administration, the monarch dissolves the Parliament and calls new parliamentary elections, in which all members of the House of Commons are up for election. The parliamentary system also stresses norms of collective decision making and ministerial responsibility, and it requires the prime minister to appear before Parliament on a regular basis to answer questions—the so-called question hour. Professor Sudha Setty of the Western New England College School of Law has recently advocated the adoption of a similar mechanism, which she believes would provide for greater accountability and transparency in the U.S. (1998). She does not believe this would require adoption of a constitutional amendment. In the British system, the lower house, designated as the House of Commons, has substantially greater powers than does the upper house, the House of Lords.

Although some individuals have advocated an entirely new U.S. Constitution along British lines, many members of Congress have introduced amendments to adopt one or more parts of this system. Such proposals have included plans allowing members of Congress to serve in the cabinet or permitting Congress to take a vote of "no confidence" in the president.

Proponents of the parliamentary model defend it as a way of making government more responsive to the people and of overcoming problems of stalemate and inaction attributed in the U.S. system to the separation of powers. One important study, however, suggested that the problems of divided government in the United States may be exaggerated (Mayhew 1991); another study denies that separation of powers is responsible for many of the problems that have been attributed to it (Sargentich 1993). Others suggest that systems that appear from a distance to have advantages may, on closer inspection, demonstrate weaknesses. Moreover, the strengths of some parliamentary systems may result in part from greater social homogeneity and from factors other than constitutional structures (Ceaser 1986).

Yale's Bruce Ackerman has argued that nations considering new constitutional systems might consider adopting a model of what he describes as "constrained parliamentarianism" like governments in Germany, Japan, Canada, and other nations, rather than the pure parliamentary model in Britain. Such constrained parliamentarianism seeks "to check the power of the cabinet and the chamber [parliament] . . . by giving independence to a variety of other checking institutions, including a constitutional court" (Ackerman 2000, 634).

See also Ackerman, Bruce; Divided Government; Presidency, Vote of No Confidence.

For Further Reading:

Ackerman, Bruce. 2000. "The New Separation of Powers." *The Harvard Law Review* 113 (January): 633–728.

Ceaser, James W. 1986. "In Defense of Separation of Powers." In *Separation of Powers—Does It Still Work?* Ed. Robert A. Goldwin and Art Kaufman. Washington, DC: American Enterprise Institute.

Gerring, John and Strom C. Thacker. 2008. *A Centripetal Theory of Democratic Governance.* New York: Cambridge University Press.

Mayhew, David R. 1991. *Divided We Govern: Party Control, Lawmaking, and Investigations, 1946–1990.* New Haven, CT: Yale University Press.

Sargentich, Thomas O. 1993. "The Limits of the Parliamentary Critique of the Separation of Powers." *William and Mary Law Review* 34 (Spring): 679–739.

Setty, Sudha. 2008. "The President's Question Time: Power, Information, and the Executive Credibility Gap." *Cornell Journal of Law and Public Policy* 17 (Spring): 247–294.

PAROCHIAL SCHOOLS, AID TO

Long before courts applied the First Amendment's establishment clause to the states through the due process clause of the Fourteenth Amendment, proponents of the Blaine Amendment sought to restrict state governmental funding of parochial schools. This issue reemerged when members of Congress introduced at least four proposals from 1973 to 1975 to allow tax credits or other types of state financial assistance to parochial schools.

In several cases, most notably *Lemon v. Kurtzman* (1971), the Supreme Court has invalidated most forms of direct aid to parochial schools, claiming that they either favor religion over irreligion or that they lead to excessive entanglement between church and state. The Supreme Court has, however, upheld the constitutionality of state payments to parents for bus fares to parochial schools (*Everson v. Board of Education* [1947]) and the provision of secular textbooks for such schools (*Meek v. Pittenger* [1973]). In *Mueller v. Allen* (1983), the Court upheld a state law that permitted tax deductions for all parents for school expenses, including tuition for parochial schools. After ruling in *Witters v. Washington Department of Services for the Blind* (1986) that a blind student at a Christian college could use a vocational tuition grant and deciding in *Zobrest v. Catalina Foothills School District* (1993) that a deaf student could bring a state-employed sign language teacher to a parochial school, in *Agostini v. Felton* (1997) the Court reversed an earlier ruling that had barred the state from sending public school teachers into parochial schools in order to provide remedial education. Recent debates have shifted attention to the constitutionality of voucher systems that allow parents to use such state-provided vouchers for publicly or privately administered schools of the parents' own choosing (Skillen 1993). A narrowly divided Supreme Court upheld the constitutionality of such a voucher system in Cleveland, Ohio, in the case of *Zelman v. Simmons-Harris* (2002), in which it ruled that the state was pursuing a secular legislative purpose that furthered parental, rather than governmental, choices.

See also Blaine Amendment; First Amendment.

For Further Reading:
Skillen, James W., ed. 1993. *The School Choice Controversy: What Is Constitutional?* Grand Rapids, MI: Baker Books.
Zelman v. Simmons-Harris, 122 S. Ct. 2460 (2002).

PATENTS AND COPYRIGHTS

Article I, Section 8 of the Constitution grants Congress power "to promote the Progress of Science and useful Arts, by securing for limited Times to Authors and Inventors the exclusive Right to their respective Writings and Discoveries." The 1952 Patent Act grants inventors a 17-year monopoly over their inventions (Lieberman 1992, 371). Copyrights now extend 50 years beyond an author's death (*Information Please Almanac* 1993, 594–595).

In 1953, New Jersey Democratic Representative Hugh Addonizio introduced an amendment to grant copyrights and patents "in perpetuity." Although such an amendment might increase rewards for authors and inventors, it might also slow progress by retarding the free flow of ideas.

In early 2003, the U.S. Supreme Court, in *Eldred v. Ashcroft,* 537 U.S. 186, upheld the constitutionality of the Copyright Term Extension Act of 1998. This act extended copyrights for an additional ten years and protected, among other properties, the copyright that the Disney Company owns in Mickey Mouse, which was otherwise scheduled to expire in 2003 (Hudson 2002, 1).

See also Progress and the Amending Process.

For Further Reading:
Hudson, David L, Jr. 2002. "Top Court Docket: Copyright to Cross Burning." *Chicago Daily Law Bulletin* (September 16): 1.
Information Please Almanac: Atlas and Yearbook. 1993. 43d ed. Boston: Houghton Mifflin.
Lieberman, Jethro K. 1992. *The Evolving Constitution: How the Supreme Court Has Ruled on Issues from Abortion to Zoning.* New York: Random House.

PAUL, ALICE (1885–1947)

Scholars often identify Alice Paul as one of the "new suffragists" (Lunardini 1986, 17). Paul, who never married, earned a PhD in political science from the University of Pennsylvania and law degrees from the Washington College of Law and American University. After taking part in suffragist demonstrations in England—where she met fellow American Lucy Burns, with whom she would subsequently work quite closely—Paul was appointed chair of the Congressional Committee of the National American Woman Suffrage Association (NAWSA) in 1912. Paul subsequently founded the Congressional Union for Woman Suffrage, which became independent in 1914 and firmly opposed the Shafroth-Palmer Amendment (which would have left women's suffrage to be determined by individual state referendums), which NAWSA representatives had initially approved.

Paul was a persistent organizer who sponsored a suffragist parade the day before Woodrow Wilson's inaugurations in 1913 and 1917 and founded the National Woman's Party in 1916. This organization, which was regarded as more radical than the NAWSA, worked to oppose candidates who did not support the Anthony Amendment. It also sponsored a series of pickets in front of the Wilson White House for 18 months beginning in January 1917, the same year that the Congressional Union merged with the National Woman's Party (NWP). Picketers, including Paul, were jailed; Paul was force-fed after she declared a hunger strike. Unlike the NAWSA, the NWP refused to support Wilson's war efforts. Still, the combined pressures from the NAWSA and the NWP, along with Wilson's hopes that such a measure would help boost war morale, convinced him to endorse the Anthony Amendment, which became the Nineteenth Amendment in 1920.

Thereafter, the NWP continued its push for women's rights. Initially, it was the only such women's organization to support the Lucretia Mott, or Equal Rights, Amendment. The amendment was written and first proposed by Paul at the 75th anniversary of the Seneca Falls Convention and subsequently was introduced in Congress in December 1923 by Republican Senator Charles Curtis (S.J. 21) and Republican Representative Daniel Anthony, both of Kansas.

Paul crusaded for the League of Nations in the 1920s and 1930s. She was also instrumental in getting recognition of equal gender rights in the preamble to the United Nations Charter (McHenry 1980, 320). Paul opposed the seven-year deadline for ratification of the Equal Rights Amendment, as well as the deletion of concurrent enforcement power in the states (Fry 1986, 21).

See also Equal Rights Amendment; Mott, Lucretia Coffin; Nineteenth Amendment; Seneca Falls Convention; Shafroth-Palmer Amendment.

For Further Reading:

Flexnor, Eleanor. 1974. *Century of Struggle: The Woman's Rights Movement in the United States.* New York: Atheneum.

Fry, Amelia R. 1986. "Alice Paul and the ERA." In *Rights of Passage: The Past and Future of the ERA,* ed. Joan Hoff-Wilson. Bloomington, IN: Indiana University Press.

Lunardini, Christine A. 1986. *From Equal Suffrage to Equal Rights: Alice Paul and the National Woman's Party, 1910–1928.* New York: New York University Press.

PEACE CONVENTION

In February 1861, the same month that the states of the Deep South were meeting in Montgomery, Alabama, to draw up a new Confederate constitution, the governor of Virginia called for a convention of the states to devise a plan of reconciliation. Such a call deviated from the convention procedure specified in Article V of the Constitution but was especially popular in border states that were still undecided as to how to respond to Abraham Lincoln's election and were interested in averting civil war.

Twenty-one of the 34 states responded by sending 132 delegates to the Willard Hotel in Washington D.C. (Dumond 1973, 241). Because Virginia did not specify how states would be represented, states sent anywhere from five to eleven delegates

The convention created a committee of one delegate from each state, which former secretary of the treasury James Guthrie of Kentucky headed. This committee reported seven proposals to the full convention on February 15; these were in turn modified and proposed collectively to Congress as what would have been the Thirteenth Amendment. Many of the provisions resembled those of the Crittenden Compromise, being hammered out in Congress.

Section 1 of the amendment proposed reinstating the 36 degrees 30 minutes line of latitude created under the Missouri Compromise of 1820. Thus proposing to reverse that portion of the *[Dred] Scott* decision (1857) declaring such legislation invalid, this section would have permitted slavery south of the line and prevented it north of the line in all existing territories, with new states in each area permitted to join the Union when they had sufficient populations to do so.

Section 2 would have prohibited the acquisition of new territory except by a majority vote of both free and slave states in the Senate and agreement by the requisite two-thirds majority required to approve a treaty. Section 3 of the amendment would have prohibited Congress from interfering with slavery in those states where it existed or abridging slavery in the nation's capital without the consent of Maryland (from which what remained of the District had been originally carved) without giving compensation to slave owners. This section would also have permitted the continuing transit of slaves between slave states, albeit not through states that disapproved of that institution. This section did prohibit the transit of slaves to the capital for transfer to other states.

Section 4 was designed to enforce the fugitive slave law. Similarly, Section 5 prohibited the "foreign slave trade." Section 6 would have added an entrenchment clause to the Constitution by providing that Sections 1, 3, and 5 of the amendment, as well as other constitutional provisions relating to slavery, "shall not be amended or abolished without the consent of all the States." Section 7 further provided that the national government would compensate owners who lost their slaves as a result of "violence or intimidation from mobs or riotous assemblages," but such compensation would not preclude further attempts to secure such individuals. Finally, the proposal would authorize Congress to "provide by law for securing to the citizens of each State the privileges and immunities of citizens of the several States" (Gunderson 1961, 62, 86, 107–109). Majorities of states at the convention favoring these proposals varied from as low as nine to eight (Section 1) to sixteen to five (Section 5).

Although the Peace Convention had no specific constitutional authorization, the convention arguably kept border states within the Union long enough for Lincoln to be inaugurated as president. Apparently, the convention hoped that Congress would submit its proposed amendments directly to the states for their approval. This would have bypassed the requirement in Article V for a prior congressional sanction by a two-thirds vote of both houses. The convention further proposed ratification, as in the case of the original Constitution, by state conventions (Keogh 1987, 291). Never considered by the full House, which failed to muster the necessary two-thirds majority to consider the proposals, the convention proposals (substituted for the Crittenden Compromise) were defeated on the closing day of the lame-duck Senate by a vote of 7 to 28. The House and Senate did adopt the Corwin Amendment, which would have protected states from amendments interfering with slavery, but like the Peace Convention's proposals, this failed to avert civil war.

See also Corwin Amendment; Crittenden Compromise; Nashville Convention.

For Further Reading:

Crittenden, L. E. 1864. *A Report of the Debates and Proceedings in the Secret Sessions of the Conference Convention for Proposing Amendment to the Constitution of the United States held at Washington D.C., in February A.D. 1861.* New York: D. Appleton & Company.

Gunderson, Robert Gray. 1961. *Old Gentleman's Convention: The Washington Peace Conference of 1861.* Madison, WI: University of Wisconsin Press.

Labunski, Richard. 2000. *The Second Constitutional Convention: How the American People Can Take Back Their Government.* Versailles, KY: Marley and Beck Press.

PEI, MARIO (1901–1978)

Mario Pei, a professor of Romance languages at Columbia University, called for a constitutional convention in the late 1960s (Pei 1967–1968; Vile 1991c, 100–101). He argued that such a convention would be a better way of revising and clarifying ambiguous sections of the current document than would more piecemeal reform.

Pei's proposals included four-year terms for the members of the House of Representatives; clarification of constitutional provisions relative to declarations of war; reform of the electoral college system; and the popular election and/or confirmation of Supreme Court justices, with the possibility of limited terms of office. Other ideas included having the president run on a ticket with members of the cabinet and reconsidering Supreme Court rulings relative to the establishment clause of the First Amendment and the right of peaceable assembly. Pei would also examine existing interpretations of the Second Amendment and the relation between the nation and the states. Among his proposed tax reforms was a plan to repeal the Sixteenth Amendment and to allocate different kinds of taxes among the different levels of government.

Pei envisioned a convention that would meet for a year or two. He thought that the voters of each state should choose delegates on nonpartisan ballots, with elected delegates to resign from any other offices. He also thought that proposed reforms should require the approval of two-thirds of the delegates. Pei argued that the convention mechanism was democratic. He suggested that one of the major parties should propose such a convention as part of its platform.

See also Constitutional Conventions.

For Further Reading:

Pei, Mario. 1967–1968. "The Case for a Constitutional Convention." *Modern Age* 12 (Winter): 8–13.

Vile, John R. 1991c. *Rewriting the United States Constitution: An Examination of Proposals from Reconstruction to the Present.* New York: Praeger.

PENDLETON, EDMUND (1721-1803)

Born in Caroline County, Virginia, Pendleton overcame the early death of his father and a mediocre education to become one of Virginia's finest lawyers. He served as a member of Virginia's Committee of Correspondence, as a delegate to both continental congresses, as Virginia's de facto governor, as a member of the Virginia House of Burgesses and speaker of its House of Delegates, and ended his career as chief justice of Virginia's highest court of chancery, and later of its court of appeals.

Pendleton presided over the Virginia convention that ratified the U.S. Constitution and, despite his friendship with George Washington, gravitated to the Democratic-Republican Party that Thomas Jefferson and James Madison led. On October 5, 1801, not long after Jefferson was elected president, Pendleton proposed a series of eight constitutional amendments in an article titled "The Danger Not Over," which he first published in the *Richmond Examiner.* Lance Banning has observed that these reforms "would eventually flower into an Old Republican opposition to the more moderate course of Jefferson's and Madison's administrations" (2004). Although many had heralded the election of 1800 as a revolution, Pendleton clearly feared that this revolution might not go far enough in restoring what he considered to be lost principles.

In introducing his plan, Pendleton indicated that he did not intend "to damp the public joy occasioned by the late changes of our public agents or disturb the calm which already presages the most beneficial consequences." He thought, however, that it was time "to erect new barriers against folly, fraud, and ambition; and to explain such parts of the Constitution as have been already, or may be, interpreted contrary to the intention of those who adopted it." Many of Pendleton's principles reflected concerns that Anti-Federalists had raised when the Constitution was being ratified.

Pendleton outlined six principles, which he thought the federal government had violated. The first stressed that government was instituted for the common good and should not increase debt or multiply public offices. The second observed that "standing armies, fleets, severe penal laws, way, and a multitude of civil officers" could undermine "civil liberty." The third focused on executive powers to involve the nation in an undeclared war. The fourth warned against "a consolidated general government" and its power of taxation. The fifth focused on Pendleton's support of separation of powers and his fears that violation of this principle could lead to "a dangerous aristocracy." His sixth warned again about multiplying offices and patronage.

Acknowledging that some of these concerns had been raised at the time the Constitution was ratified, he thought that the nation might now learn from subsequent experience. He accordingly offered eight amendments.

The first would have made the president ineligible for reelection and transfer his power to make appointments to Congress. The second would trim the Senate "of all executive power" (possibly its power to ratify treaties) and either shorten its members' terms or subject them to recall (which states had practices under the Articles of Confederation). The third would prevent federal legislators and judges from accepting offices within a specified period after leaving office. In a provision that might have severely eroded judicial review, it also provided for "subjecting the judges to removal by the concurring vote of both houses of Congress." The fourth proposed "some check upon the abuse of *public credit.*" The fifth favored "instituting a fair mode of impaneling juries." The sixth would prevent most treaties from becoming law until ratified by the legislature. The seventh, harkening back to Pendleton's express concern over constitutional construction, and especially its abuse in the adoption of the Sedition Act of 1798, which had threatened First Amendment rights, proposed "to inderdict laws relating to the freedom of speech, of the press, and of religion, to declare that the common law of England or of any other foreign country in criminal cases shall not be considered as a law of the United States, and that treason shall be confined to the cases stated in the Constitution, so as not to be extended further by law or construction or by using other terms such as sedition, etc." The eighth proposed "marking out with more precision the distinct powers of the *general* and *state* governments." Pendleton ended with an appeal to the language of the Virginia Bill of Rights.

The only constitutional amendment adopted during Jefferson's two terms in office, the Twelfth, modified the electoral college. However, a Pendleton biographer observes that

Pendleton's proposals along with Madison's Report [on the Alien and Sedition Acts] of 1799 [actually 1800] soon "became the 'Old and the New Testaments' of the 'political faith' of Thomas Ritchie, for so many years editor of the Richmond *Enquirer*" and that they became prominent again when Andrew Jackson was elected as president (Mays 1984, 2:234).

See also Anti-Federalists: First Amendment; Twelfth Amendment.

For Further Reading:

Mays, David John. 1984. *Edmund Pendleton, 1721–1803: A Biography.* 2 vols. Richmond: Virginia State Library. Reprint of Harvard University Press edition of 1952.

Pendleton, Edmund. 2004. "The Danger Not Over." Found in *Liberty and Order: The First American Party Struggle,* ed. Lance Banning (Indianapolis: Liberty Fund). http:oll.libertyfund .org/title/875/63994. Accessed May 24, 2008.

Vile, John R. "Pendleton, Edmund." *Great American Lawyers: An Encyclopedia,* ed. John R. Vile, 2 vols. Santa Barbara, CA: ABC-CLIO.

PENN, WILLIAM (1644–1718)

William Penn was an English Quaker. Along with parishioner William Mead, Penn had been arrested and tried in 1670 for preaching to his congregation, and he was subjected to a kangaroo judicial proceeding that led to his popular vindication (Peck 1992, 85–87). The king later granted him land in America. Penn's Frame of Government for Pennsylvania (1682–1683) was the first such document to contain an amending mechanism (Beatty 1975, 61).

In the preamble to this document, Penn observed, "I do not find a model in the world that time, place, and some singular emergences have not necessarily altered" (Thorpe 1909, 5:3053–3054). Here and in subsequent charters that he drew up for Delaware and Pennsylvania, Penn allowed for future charter alterations with the consent of the governor and six-sevenths of the assembly. Drawing on his view that freedom of conscience was especially fundamental, however, Penn provided that protections for this right should never be altered (*Id.,* 5:3079–3080). Both the required supermajorities to initiate change and the presence of entrenchment mechanisms find echoes in the amending article of the U.S. Constitution.

See also Entrenchment Clauses.

For Further Reading:

Beatty, Edward C. 1975. *William Penn as Social Philosopher.* New York: Octagon Books.

Calvert, Jane E., *Quaker Constitutionalism and the Political Thought of John Dickinson.* New York: CambridgeUniversity Press, 2009.

Peck, Robert S. 1992. *The Bill of Rights and the Politics of Interpretation.* St. Paul, MN: West.

Penn, William. 2002. *The Political Writings of William Penn,* intro by Andrew R. Murphy. Indianapolis: Liberty Fund.

Thorpe, Francis N. 1909. *The Federal and State Constitutions, Colonial Charters and Other Organic Laws of the States, Territories, and Colonies Now or Heretofore Forming the United States of America.* 7 vols. Washington DC: U.S. Government Printing Office.

PENSIONS

The Constitution makes no explicit mention of pensions. There was no general scheme of government pensions in the nation's early history, but controversy periodically surfaced with respect to military pensions, bonuses, and land grants. These compensated those who had served in the military, provided care to those wounded in the service, or supported the widows and children of such veterans (Glasson and Kinley 1918). In the 1880s and 1890s, members of Congress introduced amending resolutions to prevent the decrease or repeal of promised pensions, to limit pensions to those provided under law at the time an individual enlisted, or to restrict pensions to individuals or to the families of individuals actually wounded in service (Musmanno 1929, 129–131).

Although there are still occasional disputes about veterans' benefits, today primary atten-

tion has shifted from military pensions to old-age and disability pensions provided under the Social Security system established in 1935 (Myles 1989). At least one amendment proposed in 1935 attempted to give Congress power to establish this program. Despite Supreme Court decisions upholding the taxation provisions of the act in *Steward Machine Co. v. Davis* (1937) and *Helvering v. Davis* (1937), several amendments were introduced from 1939 to 1941 to formalize this power. A handful of subsequent proposals have attempted to place limits on the extent to which Social Security and other related taxes can be raised.

There are continuing concerns that the Social Security program might become bankrupt as the number of senior citizens and the ratio of non-working to working individuals increase. In 1964, Massachusetts submitted a petition for a constitutional convention to deal with this issue, but no other state joined in this call. In recent years, some members of Congress have added provisions to calls for a Balanced Budget Amendment that would require that current Social Security surpluses could not be used in such budget calculations.

See also Balanced Budget Amendment; Social Security.

For Further Reading:

Glasson, William H., and David Kinley. 1918. *Federal Military Pensions in the United States.* New York: Oxford University Press.

Musmanno, M. A. 1929. *Proposed Amendments to the Constitution.* Washington DC: U.S. Government Printing Office.

Myles, John. 1989. *Old Age in the Welfare State: The Political Economy of Public Pensions.* Lawrence: University Press of Kansas.

PETITIONS FOR AMENDMENTS

Before they become law, amendments must be proposed by sufficient majorities in Congress (or by a Constitutional convention called at the behest of the states) and ratified by three-fourths of the states. Members of Congress generally introduce amendments as joint resolutions. In addition, the Congress frequently receives petitions from a variety of private groups and state and local governmental entities on behalf of various causes, including adoption of constitutional amendments. These petitions are not nearly as well publicized as are those which individual members of Congress introduce (and are not included in the lists of proposed amendments that have been published from time to time), but they reflect a basic American right to petition the government that has been advocated since the Declaration of Independence, that is incorporated into the First Amendment, and that has been recognized by U.S. Supreme Court Justice Anthony Kennedy in a concurring opinion (see *Cook v. Gralike* 2001, 60). There does not appear to be any systematic study of petitions to Congress specifically on the subject of constitutional amendments.

See also First Amendment; Joint Resolution.

For Further Reading:
Cook v. Gralike, 531 U.S. 510 (2001).

PHILADELPHIA II

See National Initiative for Democracy.

PHILIPPINE INDEPENDENCE

In July 1930, Democratic Senator Royal Copeland of New York introduced an amending resolution to grant independence to the Philippines, an objective that ordinary legislation subsequently accomplished. After defeating the Spanish in the Spanish-American War of 1898, the United States purchased these Pacific islands from Spain and, much to the chagrin of American anti-imperialists, forcefully overwhelmed the independence movement there.

Subsequently, the Jones Act of 1916 promised eventual independence ("Philippines"

1994). After the Filipinos rejected the provisions for independence in the 1933 Hawes-Cutting-Hare bill, Congress adopted the Tydings McDuffie Act of 1934 (Grunder and Livezey 1973, 220–223). It provided for an interim commonwealth to be followed by complete independence in 1946 ("Philippines" 1994).

This timetable was followed despite the disruptions caused by the Japanese seizure of the islands in World War II. The United States, however, continued to view the Philippines as a special area of responsibility and influence (Shalom 1981), and it maintained military bases there until quite recently. After the terrorist attacks on the United States on September 11, 2001, and the capture of a number of Americans by Muslim extremists, the U.S. government again sent troops to the Philippines to help its government combat terrorism.

For Further Reading:
Grunder, Garel A., and William E. Livezey. 1973. *The Philippines and the United States.* Westport, CT: Greenwood Press.

"Philippines, Republic of the." 1994. *Microsoft Encarta Multimedia Encyclopedia.*

Shalom, Stephen R. 1981. *The United States and the Philippines: A Study of Neocolonialism.* Philadelphia: Institute for the Study of Human Issues.

PIBURN, JOHN L. (1872–?)

John Piburn was a medical doctor who authored a book published in 1932 proposing the text of a new U.S. constitution and a revised code suitable for California and other states. Although much of his proposed constitution simply rearranged the provisions in the existing document, it also contained a number of innovative ideas.

Most prominent was the creation of the Educational Department and Educational College, the organization of which led off the document. Consisting of five recent graduates elected by each college and initially governed by the first member to be selected from the University of Missouri (Piburn 1932, 12), the department was to have extensive powers to promote and oversee education, including power to specify how grading would be done (*Id.,* 20–24), designate what size diplomas should be (*Id.,* 24), and set tax rates for education (*Id.,* 14). "Religious," "denominational," and "sectarian" schools were to be prohibited, as would night classes, the use of initials on diplomas (*Id.,* 16), and the issuance of any doctoral degrees other than in medicine (*Id.,* 27). BS and MS degrees were to be designated as outranking BAs or MAs (*Id.,* 27).

In Piburn's scheme, the House of Representatives would be designated as the House of Solons (Piburn 1932, 32). Piburn would prohibit laws from being rewritten; any changes would have to be adopted as new laws and their predecessors repealed (*Id.,* 39). Piburn's prohibition against "sumptuary laws" (*Id.,* 46) was apparently designed to abolish the Eighteenth Amendment, which he described in his introduction as "a crime"—an introduction in which he likewise saw the only good in the Nineteenth Amendment as the fact that "it will help to un-Christianize women." Piburn would replace the congressional power to declare war with the power to call an election for declaring war, which election would require a majority of males under age 40—presumably those most likely to serve—to approve (*Id.,* 41). Piburn applied the restraints in the Bill of Rights directly to Congress, although he extended the establishment clause of the First Amendment to both the nation and the states and specified that "all the promoters of religion, and their followers, are jointly and severally liable for damages, libel, and slander for their utterances and practices" (*Id.,* 49–50). Piburn further proposed explicitly providing for civil and criminal libel (*Id.,* 46–47). On another matter, he would have prohibited miscegenation laws "restricting the amalgamation of the races; or the mating of the sexes" (*Id.,* 50), a move that the U.S. Supreme Court did not make until its 1967 decision in *Loving v. Virginia.*

Piburn would have eliminated the office of vice president and provided that presidential vacancies be filled by the oldest senator from the president's party (Piburn 1932, 55). Piburn also included a provision for presidential disability similar to that now found in the Twenty-fifth Amendment (*Id.,* 55). Piburn would have explicitly provided for the exercise of judicial review (*Id.,* 59) and would have imposed a one-term limit on all offices (*Id.,* 66).

Piburn's constitution was to be ratified by the people in three-fourths of the states, and he would have altered the amending process so that amendments could be ratified in the same fashion. In a scheme somewhat reminiscent of Thomas Jefferson, a nine-member committee appointed by the Educational College, the Senate, and the House of Solons was to consider revising the document in the year 2000 and "once every fifty years thereafter" (Piburn 1932, 71).

See also Education, Right to: Eighteenth Amendment; Jefferson, Thomas; Nineteenth Amendment; Twenty-fifth Amendment.

For Further Reading:
Piburn, John L. 1932. *A Constitution and a Code.* San Diego: Bowman Printing Company.

PLACEMENT OF CONSTITUTIONAL AMENDMENTS

The 27 amendments that have been adopted are found at the end of the constitutional text that was written in 1787, but it was not initially clear that they would be so. Indeed, Virginia's James Madison, the individual most responsible for compilation of what became the first 10 amendments, originally proposed integrating new amendments into the constitutional text, giving the amended document greater coherence than if amendments trailed behind in a postscript. Connecticut's Roger Sherman, who initially opposed the Bill of Rights, argued instead that new amendments should be listed separately, so, among other reasons, it would not appear as though George Washington and other framers had signed on to provisions that they had not contemplated. Congress initially voted to accept Madison's plan but changed its mind a week later and adopted Sherman's. There is some evidence that "Madison compromised on form to secure the substance of the larger project of amendments" (Marshall 1998, 110).

Because Sherman's view was victorious, it is much easier to trace American constitutional history than if amendments were scattered within the text and earlier conflicting provisions had been deleted. Moreover, some scholars have argued that the Bill of Rights has achieved more prominence as a separate section of the Constitution than had these provisions been incorporated into the text. However, one prominent scholar has also argued that "[t]he decision to make amendments supplementary increased the need for an arbiter of disputes over constitutional interpretation," thereby increasing the power of U.S. courts (Kyvig 1996a, 102).

Similarly, Professor Edward Hartnett of Seton Hall University has argued that incorporating new amendments within the text would have made the Constitution more comprehensible and would have forced Congress to give greater consideration as to how new amendments are designed to relate to existing constitutional provisions. In surveying how the current Constitution would be different, Hartnett begins by showing where Madison would have placed the provisions of the Bill of Rights, and then surmises where subsequent amendments would have been placed. He notes that some provisions in the current Bill of Rights would have ended up by Madison's specification in Article I, Section 9, which limits Congress, whereas other provisions (including provisions for a grand jury indictment and jury trials in civil cases, neither of which has been applied as most other provisions in the Bill of Rights to limit the states as well as the national government) would have been moved to Article III, the judicial article. The Tenth Amendment would have become a separate article. Hartnett believes that had Madison's suggestion been heeded, the current Constitution would be shorter and more coherent. Superseded provisions would have been eliminated from the document, and one would not have to depend on notes or italics within the text to identify provisions that have been subsequently altered. Hartnett argues that the purpose of some amendments, for example, the Eleventh, which he believes would have been incorporated into the judicial article (Article III), would have been clearer, whereas the array of amendments that remove barriers to voting rights would be grouped together, probably after the provision in Article IV granting each state a "republican" form of government. Hartnett includes a copy of the Constitution as he believes it would be had Madison's ideas been followed (Hartnett 1998, 284–299).

Some state and foreign constitutions do incorporate constitutional changes into the text much as Madison had recommended, with attendant advantages and disadvantages similar to those discussed above.

See also Madison, James

For Further Reading:

Blocker, Joseph. 2008. "Amending the Exceptions Clause." *Minnesota Law Review* 92 (April): 971–1030.

Hartnett, Edward. 1998. "A 'Uniform and Entire' Constitution: Or, What if Madison Had Won?" *Constitutional Commentary* 15 (Summer): 251–297.

Kyvig, David E. 1996a. *Explicit and Authentic Acts: Amending the Constitution, 1776–1995.* Lawrence: University Press of Kansas.

Marshall, Price. 1998. "'A Careless Written Letter'—Situating Amendments to the Federal Constitution." *Arkansas Law Review* 51: 95–115.

PLEDGE OF ALLEGIANCE

See Flag Salute.

PLESSY V. FERGUSON (1896)

Plessy v. Ferguson was one of the most important 19th-century decisions about the meaning of the Thirteenth and Fourteenth Amendments (Lofgren 1987). In the *Slaughterhouse Cases* (1873), the Supreme Court had given a restrictive reading to the privileges and immunities clause. In the *Civil Rights Cases* (1883), the Supreme Court had further ruled that Congress did not have the power to remedy individual acts of racial discrimination that were not the result of state action. By contrast, in *Plessy v. Ferguson,* the Court upheld a Louisiana Jim Crow law requiring white and black passengers to sit in separate train cars. Homer Plessy, who was seven-eighths white and one-eighth black, challenged the law after he was denied seating on a car reserved for whites.

In rejecting Plessy's Thirteenth Amendment claim, Justice Henry Brown, writing the Court's 7-to-1 majority decision, cited the *Civil Rights Cases* as evidence that the Thirteenth Amendment had the limited purpose of freeing the slaves. In interpreting the Fourteenth Amendment, Brown distinguished between legal and social rights and concluded that "it could not have been intended to abolish distinctions based on color, or to enforce social, as distinguished from political, equality, or a commingling of the two races upon terms unsatisfactory to either" (*Plessy* 1896, 544). In response to John Marshall Harlan's dissenting opinion suggesting that racial discrimination was as arbitrary as requiring members of different races to walk on different sides of the street or to live in houses of different colors, Brown upheld Jim Crow laws as reasonable. He ascertained such reasonableness by deferring to the state's "liberty to act with reference to the established usages, customs, and traditions of the people, and with a view to the promotion of their comfort, and the preservation of the public peace and good order" (*Id.,* 550). Brown further denied that segregation was a badge of inferiority: "If this be so, it is not by reason of anything found in the act, but solely because the colored race choses [*sic*] to put that construction upon it" (*Id.,* 551).

John Marshall Harlan's dissent took a broad view of both the Thirteenth and the Fourteenth Amendments, suggesting that they did much more than simply providing freedom for former slaves. Harlan is best known for articulating his vision of a color-blind Constitution: "But in view of the Constitution, in the eye of the law, there is in this country no superior, dominant, ruling class of citizens. Our Constitution is colorblind, and neither knows nor tolerates classes among citizens. In respect of civil rights, all citizens are equal before the law" (*Plessy* 1896, 559).

Plessy v. Ferguson remained the law of the land until the Supreme Court's decision in *Brown v. Board of Education* (1954) reversed it. Contemporary affirmative action programs, often designed to make up for past inequalities in the areas of race or sex, continue to raise questions as to whether the Fourteenth Amendment was designed to eliminate all considerations of race (and thus provide for a color-blind Constitution) or simply those that invidiously discriminated against minority groups.

See also Affirmative Action; *Brown v. Board of Education;* Fourteenth Amendment; Thirteenth Amendment.

For Further Reading:
Plessy v. Ferguson, 163 U.S. 537 (1896).

POLITICAL QUESTIONS

The political questions doctrine is one of the most elusive doctrines of U.S. constitutional law. The doctrine is designed to allow courts to defer judgments on issues that they think are, for one reason or another, best left to the "political," that is, the elected, branches of government. The Supreme Court has sometimes equivocated as to whether this doctrine is motivated by constitutional or practical concerns. Moreover, the Court no longer classifies some issues as political that it once did (Scharpf 1966).

As early as *Marbury v. Madison* (1803), Chief Justice John Marshall asserted that the Supreme Court dealt with individual rights and that "questions in their nature political . . . can never be made in this Court" (*Marbury* 1803, 168). The major 19th-century case involving the political questions doctrine, however, was *Luther v. Borden* (1849). Asked to determine which of two rival Rhode Island governments was "republican" under the guarantee clause in Article IV, Section 4 of the Constitution (an issue precipitated by the fact that Rhode Island had made no provision for formal constitutional changes), the Court deferred to the decisions already made by the president and Congress.

Although it had previously answered a number of important amending issues, in *Coleman v. Miller* (1939) the Supreme Court applied the political questions doctrine to the amending process. It proclaimed itself "equally divided" on the issue of whether a state's lieutenant governor could break a tie on a state's ratification of an amendment. The Court decided, however, that the decision as to whether a state could ratify an amendment it had previously rejected, and the related question of whether a state could rescind its previous ratification, were political questions for Congress to decide. Similarly, it vested Congress with the responsibility for ascertaining whether amendments were ratified in a timely fashion (Vile 1993b, 24–35).

A number of developments have affected the political questions doctrine since *Coleman.* Most significantly, in *Baker v. Carr* (1962), the Supreme Court reversed course on the justiciability of state legislative apportionment. Whereas in *Colegrove v. Green* (1946) it had decided that such issues fell under the guarantee clause and were nonjusticiable, in *Baker v. Carr* it ruled that such issues could be reached under the equal protection clause of the Fourteenth Amendment. In *Powell v. McCormack* (1969), the Court subsequently ruled that the question of qualifications of a member of Congress was not a political question but was one that the Court could decide. By contrast, in *Nixon v. United States* (1993), the Court decided that the Constitution vested the issue of impeachment proceedings exclusively in Congress.

In *Dyer v. Blair* (1975), a U.S. district court decided that the political questions doctrine did not preclude it from deciding that a state legislature (albeit not a state constitution) had the right to set an extraordinary majority requirement for ratification of an amendment. Similarly, in *Idaho v. Freeman* (1981), another district court sought to settle a number of issues surrounding ratification of the Equal Rights Amendment.

Justice William Brennan offered the most complete catalog of questions that are considered political in *Baker v. Carr,* where he cited six:

[1] a textually demonstrable constitutional commitment of the issue to a coordinate political department; [2] or a lack of judicially discoverable and manageable standards for resolving it; [3] or the impossibility of deciding without an initial policy determination of a kind clearly for nonjudicial discretion; [4] or the impossibility of a court's undertaking independent resolution without expressing lack of the respect due coordinate branches of government; [5] or an unusual need for unquestioning adherence to a political decision already made; [6] or the potentiality of embarrassment from multifarious pronouncements by various departments on one question. (*Baker* 1962, 217)

Applying these principles, especially in light of precedents that have been written since *Coleman v. Miller,* a number of scholars have argued that the Supreme Court has considerable leeway in deciding modern amending controversies (Dellinger 1983; Rees 1986; Vile 1993a). In *Bush v. Gore* (2000), the Supreme Court took jurisdiction of vote counting in a presidential election that many thought should have been left to the political branches.

See also *Baker v. Carr; Coleman v. Miller; Dyer v. Blair;* Guarantee Clause; *Idaho v. Freeman; Luther v. Borden.*

For Further Reading:

Baker v. Carr, 369 U.S. 186 (1962).

Barkow, Rachel E. 2000. "More Supreme Than Court? The Fall of the Political Question Doctrine and the Rise of Judicial Supremacy." *Columbia Law Review* 102 (March): 237–336.

Dellinger, Walter. 1983. "The Legitimacy of Constitutional Change: Rethinking the Amending Process." *Harvard Law Review* 97 (December): 380–432.

Marbury v. Madison, 5 U.S. (1 Cranch.) 137 (1803).

Rees, Grover, III. 1986. "The Amendment Process and Limited Constitutional Conventions." *Benchmark* 2: 67–108.

Scharpf, Fritz W. 1966. "Judicial Review and the Political Question: A Functional Analysis." *Yale Law Journal* 75 (March): 517–597.

Vile, John R. 1993a. *Contemporary Questions Surrounding the Constitutional Amending Process.* Westport, CT: Praeger.

POLL TAXES

See Twenty-fourth Amendment.

POLLOCK V. FARMERS' LOAN & TRUST CO. (1895)

In one of the most controversial rulings in its day, the Supreme Court first invalidated taxes on income from state and municipal bonds and on income from property (*Pollock I* [1895]); on reargument, it invalidated the federal tax on personal and corporate income (*Pollock II* [1895]). Although the decisions conflicted with earlier rulings, including dicta in *Hylton v. United States* (1796) and a decision upholding a Civil War income tax in *Springer v. United States* (1881), in the second *Pollock* decision, Chief Justice Melville Fuller stated that the Court was doing no more than reading the constitutional language about direct taxes in its "obvious sense" (1895, 618). He further noted that if the people desired to change this language, "the ultimate sovereignty may be . . . called into play by a slow and deliberate [constitutional amending] process, which gives time for mere hypothesis and opinion to exhaust themselves, and for the sober second thought of every part of the country to be asserted" (1895, 635).

In one of four dissenting opinions, Justice John Marshall Harlan criticized the majority for departing from precedents. He stated, "If this new theory of the Constitution . . . is justified by the fundamental law, the American people cannot too soon amend their Constitution" (1895, 674).

The nation heeded Harlan's advice and ratified the Sixteenth Amendment in 1913, effectively overturning *Pollock*. This was only the third such amendment in U.S. history to have such an effect.

See also Sixteenth Amendment; Supreme Court Decisions Reversed by Constitutional Amendments.

For Further Reading:

Jensen, Erik M. 2001. "The Taxing Power, the Sixteenth Amendment, and the Meaning of 'Income.'" *Arizona State Law Journal* 33 (Winter): 1057–1158.

Pollock v. Farmers' Loan & Trust Co. (I), 157 U.S. 429 (1895).

Pollock v. Farmers' Loan & Trust Co. (II), 158 U.S. 601 (1895).

POLYGAMY

Legislators have introduced numerous bills and amendments to prohibit polygamy, or the practice of allowing men to have multiple wives. The catalyst for such action was a decision in 1852 by the Mormon Church, which Joseph Smith had founded, to approve of this form of marriage, which its leaders had previously practiced (G. Larson 1971, 37). Contemporaries often argued that polygamy, like chattel slavery, which took a Civil War and the Thirteenth Amendment to end, was a relic of barbarism. President Ulysses S. Grant expressed such a view in his seventh annual message in 1875.

States are responsible for enacting most laws involving domestic relations, including marriage and divorce, under the "police powers" that they retain under the Tenth Amendment. Because Article IV, Section 1 of the Constitution provides for "Full Faith and Credit . . . to the public Acts, Records, and judicial Proceedings of every other State," changes adopted in marriage regulations in one state can affect those of another.

Many states were territories prior to statehood. Article IV, Section 3 of the Constitution entrusts Congress with the power to "make all needful Rules and Regulations respecting the Territory or other Property belonging to the United States." In exercising this power, Congress adopted several laws in the 19th century to regulate polygamy. Such laws included the Morrill Act of 1862 restricting polygamy; a bill sponsored by Vermont

Republican Luke Porter Poland in 1874 strengthening federal judicial power in the Utah Territory where many Mormons had settled; and the Edmunds Bill of 1874 (strengthened by the Tucker Amendment in 1887), which restricted voting rights of polygamists (G. Larson 1971, 58–59; Peterson 1977, 102).

The U.S. Supreme Court unanimously upheld the constitutionality of congressional laws against polygamy beginning in *Reynolds v. United States* (1879), the first case in which it ever ruled on the First Amendment. In upholding Reynolds's conviction for polygamy, the Court said that although the federal government could not legislate belief, it could regulate conduct. It has subsequently applied this distinction to numerous cases involving interpretation of the religious clauses of the First Amendment.

Congress did not admit Utah as a state until January 1896, after Mormon Church leaders had renounced polygamy (Lyman 1986). In 1879, Republican Representative Julius Caesar Burrows of Michigan introduced the first of the 55 proposed amendments that members of Congress introduced from then until 1924. Several such amendments were proposed after Utah elected polygamist Brigham Roberts to Congress in 1899 (Stein 2004, 634). From 1906 to 1913, 16 states applied for a convention to deal with this issue. Most such amendments specifically sought to outlaw polygamy, but some were phrased to allow Congress to make uniform rules on marriage and divorce (see Godkin 1864) or to prohibit polygamists from assuming office.

From time to time, states prosecute members of fundamental Mormon groups that still practice polygamy. In 2008, several hundred children of the Fundamentalist Latter Day Saints were rounded up from the Yearning for Zion ranch in Eldorado, Texas, and distributed to foster homes after allegations of polygamy, underage marriage, and child abuse, most of which proved unsubstantiated.

The modern debates over same-sex marriage and a Federal Marriage Protection Amendment involve some of the same issues as this earlier controversy (Stein 2004).

See also Federal Marriage Protection Amendment; First Amendment; Thirteenth Amendment.

For Further Reading:

Godkin, E. L. 1874. "The Constitution and Its Defects." *North American Review* 99 (July): 117–143.

Gordon, Sarah Barringer. 2002. *The Mormon Question: Polygamy and Constitutional Conflict in Nineteenth-Century America.* Chapel Hill: University of North Carolina Press.

Langum, David J. 1994. *Crossing Over the Line: Legislating Morality and the Mann Act.* Chicago: University of Chicago Press.

Larson, Gustave O. 1971. *The "Americanization" of Utah for Statehood.* San Marino, CA: Huntington Library.

Lyman, Edward L. 1986. *Political Deliverance: The Mormon Quest for Utah Statehood.* Urbana, IL: University of Illinois Press.

Richardson, James E., ed. 1908. *A Compilation of the Messages and Papers of the Presidents, 1789–1908.* 11 vols. Washington DC: Bureau of National Literature and Art.

POPULIS

See Vanguard, Virginia.

PORNOGRAPHY

See Obscenity and Pornography.

POST OFFICE

Throughout much of U.S. history, the post office has been a major source of political patronage. In 1829, President Andrew Jackson made the postmaster general a cabinet official "not so much to honor the Post Office as to control it" (Cullinan 1968, 44). The president subsequently exercised the right both to appoint (subject to Senate confirmation) and fire first-, second-, and third-class postmasters (Cullinan 1968, 221). The Supreme Court affirmed the president's power to fire such officials without Senate approval in *Myers v. United States* (1926).

There have been a number of proposals throughout U.S. history to make the positions of postmasters and other presidential appointees (for example, revenue assessors) elective. Although most such proposals came in the 19th century, Democratic Texas representative Olin Teague offered several such proposals in the 1960s. The Postal Reorganization Act of 1970 removed the postmaster general from the cabinet and converted the U.S. Postal Service into a public corporation with its own civil service system. It thus dried up what has been called the "last great pool of patronage" (M. Nelson 2008, II, 1311). Calls to make postmasters' positions elective appear to have ceased, but some libertarians have proposed constitutions to turn over tasks currently performed by the post office to private enterprise.

In 1973, Democratic Representative Tom Bevill of Alabama proposed an amendment prohibiting the use of U.S. mail for "the transmission, carriage, or delivery of communications hostile to or subversive of this Constitution and the laws and form of government of the U.S. or of any State" (H.J. Res. 131). This proposal, which is similar to regulations adopted during World War I and the cold war period, could modify the free speech provision of the First Amendment.

For Further Reading:

Cullinan, Gerald. 1968. *The Post Office Department.* New York: Praeger.

Nelson, Michael, ed. 2008. *Guide to the Presidency.* 4th ed. 2 vols. Washington DC: Congressional Quarterly.

PRAYER IN PUBLIC SCHOOLS

Since 1962, members of Congress have introduced several hundred amendments to allow spoken prayer in public schools and/or public buildings, making this one of the most frequently offered proposals in U.S. history.

Catalysts for the Prayer Amendment

The proposals began in the aftermath of the Supreme Court's decision in *Engel v. Vitale* (1962), which struck down a nondenominational prayer composed by the New York State Board of Regents for public schools. In an 8-to-1 decision written by Justice Hugo Black, the Court found that the prayer constituted an impermissible establishment of religion in violation of the First Amendment. In *Abington v. Schempp* (1963), in an 8-to-1 decision written by Justice Tom Clark, the Court subsequently extended its ruling to prohibit devotional readings from the Bible and recitation of the Lord's Prayer.

These two cases, especially the first, hit like bombshells and provoked numerous cries of outrage. One congressman noted that "we ought to impeach these men in robes who put themselves up above God," and another commented that "they put the Negroes in the schools and now they've driven God out" (cited in Laubach 1969, 2). Although Congress did not act on one member's proposal to buy a Bible "for the personal use of each justice," the House voted, in September 1962, to put the words "In God We Trust" behind the Speaker's desk (Laubach 1969, 3).

Congressional Amending Efforts

Early efforts to overturn the Supreme Court's decisions centered on a proposal by New York Democratic representative Frank J. Becker. A devout Roman Catholic who was not running for reelection, Becker devoted much effort toward securing a discharge petition to pry the amendment from the House Judiciary Committee, where fellow New York Democrat Emanuel Celler was trying to keep it bottled up.

Becker's proposal, as modified in conjunction with other House sponsors, had four sections, the last of which contained a seven-year ratification deadline. The other three sections were as follows:

Sec. 1: Nothing in this Constitution shall be deemed to prohibit the offering, reading from, or listening to prayers or Biblical scriptures, if participation therein is on a voluntary basis, in any governmental or public school, institution or place.

Sec. 2: Nothing in this Constitution shall be deemed to prohibit making reference to, belief in, reliance upon, or invoking the aid of God or a Supreme Being in any governmental or public document, proceeding, activity, ceremony, school, institution, or place, or upon any coinage, currency, or obligation of the United States.

Sec. 3: Nothing in this article shall constitute an establishment of religion. (Beaney and Beiser 1973, 32)

Celler reluctantly called for hearings, but an increasing number of scholars and religious leaders began to raise questions about the implications of this amendment—for example, which version of the Bible would be used—and others questioned the wisdom of altering the Bill of Rights. Becker's discharge petition failed.

In 1964, the Republican platform called for an amendment to permit prayer and Bible reading in schools. In 1966, Illinois Republican senator Everett Dirksen (who had also been active in trying to repeal the Supreme Court's reapportionment decisions) introduced an amendment, which provided that "nothing contained in this Constitution shall prohibit the authority administering any school, school system, educational institution or other public building supported in whole or in part through the expenditure of public funds from providing for or permitting the voluntary participation by students or others in prayer" (Laubach 1969, 142).

Indiana Democratic senator Birch Bayh subsequently presided over hearings on this amendment. Again, scholars and religious leaders raised questions. Dirksen subsequently brought his amendment to the floor without the support of the Senate Judiciary Committee. The vote of 49 to 37 fell short of the required two-thirds (Laubach 1969, 149).

In 1967, Dirksen revised his amendment to provide that "nothing in this Constitution shall abridge the rights of persons lawfully assembled, in any public building that is supported in whole or in part through the expenditure of public funds, to participate in nondenominational prayer" (Laubach 1969, 149). Again the amendment proved unsuccessful, as did a similar amendment sponsored in 1970 by Tennessee

Republican senator Howard Baker. A 1971 vote in the House of Representatives on a similar measure garnered 240 votes to 163, again falling short of the necessary two-thirds (Keynes with Miller 1989, 194).

In 1979, Ronald Reagan made prayer in school part of his platform for the presidency. The year before, Congress had held hearings on a proposal by North Carolina Republican senator Jesse Helms to curb the jurisdiction of the Supreme Court over such issues. Helms's proposal was eventually stopped by a filibuster (R. Smith 1987, 276).

Congress subsequently considered Reagan's amendment. It provided that "nothing in this Constitution shall be construed to prohibit individual or group prayer in public schools or other public institutions. No person shall be required by the United States or by any state to participate in such prayer" (R. Smith 1987, 276). In March 1984, the amendment received a vote of 56 to 44 in the Senate, again falling short of the required two-thirds majority (R. Smith 1987, 278). However, that same year, Congress adopted the Equal Access Act, designed to allow religious groups to meet on public school property if noncurricular nonreligious groups were also permitted to meet there.

In *Wallace v. Jaffree* (1985), the Supreme Court struck down an Alabama law that specifically allowed students to use a moment of silence for the purpose of prayer. The Court decided that, because the law had been altered specifically to mention prayer, it did not have a "secular legislative purpose," the first of three requirements that the Supreme Court generally applies under the so-called *Lemon* test. This test, named after the case in which it was announced *(Lemon v. Kurtzman* (1971)), also requires that laws neither "advance nor inhibit" religion and that they avoid "excessive entanglement" between church and state. *Wallace v. Jaffree,* however, did not resolve the issue of whether a moment of silence that does not specifically endorse prayer might be valid. Utah Republican senator Orrin Hatch subsequently introduced an amendment providing that "nothing in this Constitution shall be construed to prohibit individual or group silent prayer or reflection in public schools. Neither the United States nor any state shall require any person to participate in such prayer or reflection, nor shall they encourage any particular form of prayer or reflection" (Smith

1987, 188). Again, hearings were held, with the Judiciary Committee favorably reporting out the amendment.

Current Developments

Doubts remain as to both the proper wording of such an amendment and the wisdom of modifying any part of the Bill of Rights. Some proponents of greater religious freedom retain the hope that the Supreme Court will eventually ease the tension by officially sanctioning some existing moment-of-silence laws. In 1995, President Clinton attempted to fend off a prayer amendment by stressing religious rights that schoolchildren already have under the Equal Access Act and other judicial decisions. A majority of the House of Representatives adopted a prayer amendment in 1998, but it did not muster the two-thirds vote required of amendments (Marshall 2001, 5). Although in *Sante Fe Independent School District v. Doe* (2000) the U.S. Supreme Court struck down a provision whereby a student council chaplain offered a prayer broadcast over the public address systems prior to football games, more recently it declined to review a U.S. Fourth Circuit Court of Appeals decision allowing Virginia's moment of silence law (Masters 2001, B01).

The proposed Religious Equality Amendment is chiefly designed to protect the free exercise rights of religious believers in the wake of U.S. Supreme Court decisions in *Employment Division v. Smith* (1990) and *City of Boerne v. Flores* (1997). These decisions did not require states to show a "compelling interest" when applying generally applicable laws that fall more heavily on religious believers than on others. Some versions of this amendment specifically provide for reinstitution of public prayer in schools.

See also *Abington v. Schempp;* Dirksen, Everett; *Engel v. Vitale;* First Amendment; Religious Equality Amendment.

For Further Reading:

Beaney, William M., and Edward N. Beiser. 1973. "Prayer and Politics: The Impact of *Engel* and *Schempp* on the Political Process." In *The Impact of Supreme Court Decisions: Empirical Studies.* 2d ed. Eds. Theodore L. Becker and Malcolm M. Feeley. New York: Oxford University Press.

Keynes, Edward, with Randall K. Miller. 1989. *The Court vs. Congress: Prayer, Busing, and Abortion.* Durham, NC: Duke University Press.

Laubach, John H. 1969. *School Prayers: Congress, the Courts and the Public.* Washington DC: Public Affairs Press.

Marshall, Patrick. 2001. "Religion in Schools." *CQ Researcher* (January 12). http://library.cqpress.com/cqres/1pext.dll/cqpres/print/print20010112. Accessed March 18, 2002.

Masters, Brooke A. 2001. "Va. Minute of Silence Survives Test in High Court: 4th Circuit Ruling Allowed to Stand Without Comment." *The Washington Post* (October 30): B01.

Schotten, Peter, and Dennis Stevens. 1996. *Religion, Politics and the Law: Commentaries and Controversies.* Belmont, CA: Wadsworth.

Smith, Rodney K. 1987. *Public Prayer and the Constitution: A Case Study in Constitutional Interpretation.* Wilmington, DE: Scholarly Resources.

PREAMBLE TO THE BILL OF RIGHTS

When Congress proposed the Bill of Rights in 1789, it recognized that it was creating a pattern for future amendments. While Virginia's James Madison had sought to incorporate amendments at appropriate places within the constitutional text, Connecticut's Roger Sherman succeeded in convincing his fellow congressmen that they should add amendments to the end of the document.

In reporting the Bill of Rights to the states for ratification, Congress adopted a resolution of explanation. Referring to the state ratifying conventions, Congress observed that several had "expressed a desire," in order to prevent misconstructions or abuse of its powers, that further declaratory and restrictive clauses should be added." This division suggests at least two different functions for amendments. The paragraph proceeded to associate both sorts of amendments with "extending the ground of public confidence in the Government" so as to "best answer the beneficent ends of its institution."

Congress then resolved by the constitutionally-prescribed two-thirds majority to propose amendments to the state legislatures (the Constitution itself had been ratified by special conventions within the states). The closing paragraph refers to these proposals as "ARTICLES in addition to, and Amendment of the Constitution of the United States of America, proposed by Congress, and ratified by the Legislatures of the several States, pursuant to the fifth Article of the original Constitution."

In parsing these words, Joseph Blocher observes that the term "articles" suggests that amendments are on an equal basis to other constitutional provisions, which are classified in the same manner (2008, 989). He further suggests that the words "in addition to and amendment of" suggest two functions of amendments (990). Similarly, he concludes that "the Preamble's reference to the 'Original' Constitution indicates that there is a document other than the pre-amendment Constitution—that the Constitution itself changes and becomes a 'new' constitution when amended" (990).

Blocher believes that placing amendments at the end of the Constitution often accentuates difficulties in deciding whether new amendments are mere constitutional "additions" or actual "amendments," and, if the latter, in deciding which prior provisions they amend.

See also Bill of Rights; Madison, James; Placement of Constitutional Amendments; Sherman, Roger.

For Further Reading:

Blocher, Joseph. 2008. "Amending the Exceptions Clause." *Minnesota Law Review* 92 (April): 971–1030.

PREAMBLE TO THE CONSTITUTION

The first paragraph of the Constitution is called the preamble. In elegant language, it delineates the primary purposes of the document. The pre-amble has an "aspirational tone" (S. Barber 1984, 34). However, a scholar of the Constitution has observed that "[t]he Preamble does not confer any power upon any branch or agency of the national government. A person cannot go into a federal court and claim any right under the Preamble" (Cooke 1984, 26).

There have been at least four proposals to alter the preamble, one in 1869 and three in the 1960s. At least one wanted to incorporate the principles of the Declaration of Independence there. Many of those who have proposed texts of new constitutions have also altered the preamble to reflect new or widened purposes for government to achieve. The Confederate constitution altered the preamble to reinforce Southern claims of state sovereignty (a matter that the opening words of the preamble, "We the people of the United States," arguably left ambiguous). In a move later advocated by proponents of the Christian Amendment, the Confederate constitution preamble also mentioned "Almighty God" (DeRosa 1991, 135).

Most proposals for a new constitution include a new preamble, often designating contemporary problems that their authors believe they are needed to solve. In proposing a "Court of Generations," futurist Bruce E. Tonn suggested an amendment that would incorporate some of the language in the existing preamble by specifying that "[t]he power to judge threats to the security of the blessings of liberty to our posterity shall be vested in the Court of Generations" (Tonn 1991, 483). In suggesting that the U.S. Constitution should be rewritten, Joseph Church proposed adding many additional provisions to the existing preamble.

See also Christian Amendment; Church, Joseph; Tonn, Bruce E.

For Further Reading:

Barber, Sotirios A. 1984. *On What the Constitution Means*. Baltimore: Johns Hopkins University Press.

Cooke, Edward F. 1984. *A Detailed Analysis of the Constitution*. 5th ed. Savage, MO: Littlefield Adams Quality Paperbacks.

DeRosa, Marshall L. 1991. *The Confederate Constitution of 1861: An Inquiry into American Constitutionalism*. Columbia, MO: University of Missouri Press.

Tonn, Bruce E. 1991. "A Court of Generations: A Proposed Amendment to the U.S. Constitution." *Futures* 21: 413–431.

PRESIDENCY, AGE LIMITS FOR

The Constitution sets a minimum age of 35 for the president but does not specify a maximum age. When Ronald Reagan was inaugurated for his first term in 1981, he was just shy of his 70th birthday, and the "age issue" had already emerged when he first sought the Republican nomination five years earlier (Ceaser 1988, 183). Republican Bob Dole of Kansas began his third attempt for the Republican nomination for president in 1995 at the age of 72, the same age as Republican John McCain in 2008.

A number of amending proposals introduced in the 1970s would deny eligibility to presidential or vice-presidential candidates who had reached the age of 70. Most would have provided that the president serve for a single six-year term.

The Twenty-fifth Amendment limits a president to two full terms, but the amendment is not specifically tied to age and applies equally to a relatively young individual like Bill Clinton who leaves the presidency after two full terms as well as to an older one like Ronald Reagan.

See also Twenty-fifth Amendment.

For Further Reading:

Ceaser, James W. 1988. "The Reagan Presidency and American Public Opinion." In *The Reagan Legacy: Promise and Performance.* Ed. Charles O. Jones. Chatham, NJ: Chatham House.

PRESIDENCY, APPOINTMENT AND REMOVAL POWERS OF

Article II, Section 2 of the Constitution outlines the power to appoint executive officials and vests this power largely in the president, who must operate with the "Advice and Consent of the Senate." The Constitution does not specify who has the power to remove executive officials. This issue was especially controversial in the 19th century and was a major bone of contention between President Andrew Johnson and the Reconstruction Congress. Johnson's secretary of war, Edwin M. Stanton, refused to accept Johnson's authority to fire him until the impeachment effort against Johnson failed in the Senate.

In *Myers v. United States* (1926), Chief Justice (and ex-president) William Howard Taft upheld President Wilson's authority to fire a first-class postmaster without Senate concurrence. Relying heavily on James Madison, Taft argued that the framers intended to vest this power in the president, who would best be able to ascertain the capabilities and performance of his subordinates. Taft further argued that "the power to remove inferior executive officers, like that to remove superior officers, is an incident of the power to appoint them, and is in its nature an executive power" (*Myers* 1926, 161).

Two subsequent cases have somewhat qualified this power. In *Humphrey's Executor v. United States* (1935), the Supreme Court unanimously ruled that a president could not fire a member of the Federal Trade Commission— considered a quasi-legislative and quasi-judicial body. Similarly, in *Wiener v. United States* (1958), the Court denied that President Eisenhower could remove without cause a member of the War Claims Commission, also described by the Court as a quasi-judicial body.

Most proposals for altering or clarifying presidential appointment and removal powers came in the 19th century. Some would give Congress the power to appoint and remove the secretary of the Treasury Department, members of the Post Office Department, or various other members of the cabinet; some proposed including the House of Representatives in the advice and consent function and in removals; some would have permitted cabinet officers (rather than the president) to select officers under them; others attempted to set specific terms for executive officials; and still others attempted to exclude various individuals— members of Congress, for example—from executive offices (Ames 1896, 134–138). The 19th century also witnessed the development of the civil service system.

Judicial decisions have clarified the appointment and removal power in the 20th century, and the executive's power to remove members of his or her administration is generally accepted. Periodically, members of Congress have introduced proposals to provide a means, in addition to impeachment and conviction, to remove judicial officers. Members of Congress have also periodically called for the people's right to recall elected or appointed officials.

See also Civil Service Reform; Madison, James; Post Office.

For Further Reading:

Ames, Herman. 1896. *The Proposed Amendments to the Constitution of the United States during the First Century of Its History.* Reprint, New York: Burt Franklin, 1970.

Bailey, Jeremy D. 2008. "The New Unitary Executive and Democratic Theory: The Problem of Alexander Hamilton." *American Political Science Review* 102 (November): 453–466.

Greenfield, Kent. 1993. "Original Penumbras: Constitutional Interpretation in the First Year of Congress." *Connecticut Law Review* 26 (Fall): 79–144.

Myers v. United States, 272 U.S. 52 (1926).

PRESIDENCY, COMPENSATION FOR

Article II, Section 1 of the Constitution provides that "the President shall, at stated Times, receive for his Services, a Compensation, which shall neither be increased nor diminished during the period for which he shall be elected, and he shall not receive within that Period any other Emolument from the United States, or any of them."

The first Congress set the president's salary at $25,000 a year (although Washington, and later Kennedy, refused such compensation), a figure that was doubled in 1873. As of 2001, the president's pay was raised from $200,000 to $400,000 annually, but there are other perquisites, such as travel, expense accounts, use of the White House, and the like (Kalb and Bledsoe 2008, II, 1279).

In 1808, Federalist Senator James Hillhouse of Connecticut introduced an amendment to cut the president's salary to $15,000 a year, and in 1822, Democrat Timothy Fuller of Massachusetts proposed that such compensation be fixed—along with that of members of Congress—every 10 years. Amendments introduced in 1882 and 1884 to limit the president to one term also had a provision to grant him a pension (Ames 1896, 129). The United States did not provide such pensions until 1958. Today, ex-presidents receive a salary equal to that of a cabinet secretary (Kalb and Bledsoe 2008, II, 1292), but some have made millions of dollars in writing, speaking, and consulting fees.

For Further Reading:

Kalb, Deborah and Craig W. Bledsoe. 2008. "Executive Pay and Perquisites." In *Guide to the Presidency,* 4th ed., 2 vols. Ed. Michael Nelson. Washington DC: Congressional Quarterly Press.

PRESIDENCY, CREATION OF A SEPARATE CHIEF OF STATE

In Great Britain, the prime minister serves as chief of government, and the monarch serves as ceremonial chief of state. In the United States, by contrast, the president carries out both sets of responsibilities. Although ceremonial tasks can be wearisome, a president can also manipulate them to increase his or her visibility and prestige. President Richard M. Nixon was especially fond of the ceremonial aspects of his office.

In 1975, after the collapse of Nixon's presidency, Democratic Representative Henry Reuss of Wisconsin proposed a constitutional amendment to create a ceremonial chief of state who would be confirmed by a majority vote of both houses of Congress. The chief of state could serve an unlimited number of four-year terms and would receive the same salary as the president. Terms of the chief of state would overlap with those of presidents, the first to be appointed two years into the president's term. Reuss's proposal generated little support (Diller

1989, 594). A number of proposed new constitutions have, however, called for making a similar distinction between the head of the U.S. government and its head of state.

For Further Reading:

Stuckey, Mary, and David C. Diller. 2008. "Chief of State." In *Guide to the Presidency.* 4th ed., 2 vols. Ed. Michael Nelson. Washington DC: Congressional Quarterly.

PRESIDENCY, MEMBERSHIP IN SENATE FOR EX-PRESIDENTS

In a parliamentary system, unsuccessful candidates for prime minister generally continue to lead their party in that body, assuming that they are reelected to the parliament. In contrast, once U.S. presidents leave office, they have no official governmental post, although the visibility and government-provided financial support for such individuals have grown fairly dramatically in recent years. As early as 1875, proposals were introduced to make ex-presidents lifetime at-large or ex officio nonvoting members of the U.S. Senate, a proposal apparently later supported by perpetual presidential candidate William Jennings Bryan (William Howard Taft, who humorously proposed that ex-presidents, like himself, be chloroformed, noted that Bryan seemed to prefer that such individuals "should expire under the anaesthetic effect of the debates of the Senate") (Vile 2002b, 188). A resolution introduced in 1917 would have given ex–vice presidents at-large membership in the House of Representatives. The period from 1960 to 1963 witnessed at least seven proposals to give ex-presidents ex officio status in the Senate. One of these proposals, offered by Democratic Representative Morris Udall of Arizona, would also apply to all unsuccessful candidates for president.

In 1963, the Senate altered its rules to provide that "former presidents of the United States shall be entitled to address the Senate upon appropriate notice to the presiding officer who shall thereupon make the necessary arrangements." The next year, Truman made some remarks to the Senate, but to date, no ex-president has delivered a formal address there (M. Nelson 1989, 1080).

See also Parliamentary Systems.

For Further Reading:

Clark, James C. 1985. *Faded Glory: Presidents out of Power.* New York: Praeger.

Nelson, Michael, ed. 1989. *Guide to the Presidency.* Washington DC: Congressional Quarterly.

Vile, John R. 2002b. *Presidential Winners and Losers: Words of Victory and Concession.* Washington DC: Congressional Quarterly.

PRESIDENCY, OATH OF

The only oath specifically included in the U.S. Constitution is the oath of the president. The president swears or affirms faithfully to "execute the office of President . . . and . . . preserve, protect, and defend the Constitution of the United States."

The Constitution does not specify a number of the practices currently associated with the oath—for example, swearing on a Bible and having the oath administered by the chief justice of the United States (Nelson, Euchner, and Maltese 2008, I, 339). The words "so help me God" are not included in the Constitution either; there is debate about whether George Washington was the first to initiate this practice. Several proposals—the most persistent being that of Democrat John Rarick of Louisiana—have called for adding these words to the text of the Constitution. Some atheists filed a suit in December 2008 to prevent President-elect Barrak Obama from adding these words to the oath and to prevent members of the clergy from delivering prayers at the event (CNN, 2008).

See also Christian Amendment.

For Further Reading:

"Bloomquist, Robert F. 2004. "The Presidential Oath, The American National Interest and a Call for presiprudence." *University of Missouri–Kansas City Law Review* 73 (Fall): 1–52.

CNN, "Lawsuit seeks to take 'so help me god' out of inaugural," cnn.com. http://www.cnn.com/2008/POLITICS/12/31/inauguration.lawsuit/index.html. Accessed December 31, 2008.

Nelson, Michael, Charles C. Euchner, and John Anthony Maltese. "The Electoral Process and Taking Office," In *Guide to the Presidency.* 4th ed., 2 vols. Ed. Michael Nelson. Washington DC: Congressional Quarterly.

PRESIDENCY, PARDON POWER

Since 1974, members of Congress have introduced more than 25 amending proposals to modify the president's pardon power. This power is delineated in Article II, Section 2 of the Constitution, which grants the president "[p]ower to grant Reprieves and Pardons for Offenses against the United States, except in Cases of Impeachment."

In *Federalist No. 74,* Alexander Hamilton defended this provision not simply as a way of mitigating individual injustices but also as a means of restoring domestic peace. Hamilton noted that "in seasons of insurrection or rebellion, there are often critical moments when a well-timed offer of pardon to the insurgents or rebels may restore the tranquillity of the commonwealth: and which if suffered to pass unimproved, it may never be possible afterwards to recall" (Hamilton, Madison, and Jay 1961, 449).

The Supreme Court has interpreted the pardon power broadly. In *Ex parte Garland* (1867), upholding a pardon that President Andrew Johnson issued to a former Confederate, the Court said that the executive pardon "extends to every offense known to the law, and may be exercised at any time after its commission, either before legal proceedings are taken, or during their pendency, or after conviction and judgment" (380). Similarly, in *Schick v. Reed* (1974), which upheld a condition to a pardon that President Eisenhower issued, the Court said that the purpose of the power was "to allow plenary author-ity in the President to 'forgive' the convicted person in part or entirely, to reduce a penalty in terms of a specified number of years, or to alter it with conditions which are themselves constitutionally unobjectionable" (266). The pardon power includes the authority to issue general amnesties, which several presidents have granted. President Carter made such provision for Vietnam-era draft evaders.

President Ford issued the most controversial pardon in U.S. history in 1974 when he extended a "full, free, and absolute pardon" to former President Nixon "for all offenses against the United States which he had committed or may have committed or taken part in" (McDonald 1992, 620). This pardon was the catalyst for most amendment proposals that followed. Most such proposals, including one that Minnesota Democratic senator (later Vice President) Walter Mondale introduced, would have allowed Congress to disapprove such pardons by a two-thirds vote within 180 days (Duker 1977, 537). In 2007, Tennessee Representative Steve Cohen proposed a similar amendment that would require approval of a two-thirds majority of the U.S. Supreme Court. Other proposals would have limited the president to pardoning only those convicted of crimes or, like a proposal offered by California's Democratic Senator Barbara Boxer, would have prohibited the president from pardoning individuals employed in his own administration. As he left office, President George Bush Sr. pardoned a number of former members of his administration including former secretary of defense Caspar Weinberger, who had been implicated in the Iran-Contra Scandal involving the illegal sale of arms to Iran to raise money to fight communism in Nicaragua.

Questions about presidential pardons were renewed at the end of President Bill Clinton's administration. Although he had not previously issued many pardons, at the end of his administration he made a flurry of last-minute pardons that some thought were influenced either by campaign contributions to his party (Clinton was prohibited by the Twenty-second Amendment from running for a third term), by attempts to influence his wife's election to the U.S. Senate seat in the state of New York, or by undue pressure on the part of the president's brother-in-law on behalf of some of his clients. Clinton issued pardons to fugitive Marc Rich for tax fraud, to his brother, Roger Clinton, for conspiring to distribute cocaine, and to Susan McDougal (who had stayed in jail rather than testify in the Whitewater land deal investigation) for bank fraud. This was the impetus for a proposal by Massachusetts Democratic representative Barney Frank in February 2001 that would have prohibited presidential pardons and reprieves between October 1 of an election year and the inauguration of a new president. Although presidents presumably still care about their historical legacies, outgoing presidents have fewer political constraints on issuing pardons during such time periods than they might if they planned to serve another term in office (Sisk 2000).

See also Twenty-second Amendment.

For Further Reading:

Crouch, Jeffrey. 2009. *The Presidential Pardon Power.* Lawrence: University Press of Kansas.

Duker, William F. 1977. "The President's Power to Pardon: A Constitutional History." *William and Mary Law Review* 18 (Spring): 475–538.

Ex parte Garland, 71 U.S. 333 (1867).

Hamilton, Alexander, James Madison, and John Jay. 1787–1788. *The Federalist Papers.* Reprint, New York: New American Library, 1961.

McDonald, Forrest. 2005. "Pardon Power." In *The Oxford Companion to the Supreme Court of the United States.* 2nd ed. Ed. Kermit L. Hall. New York: Oxford University Press.

Schick v. Reed, 419 U.S. 256 (1974).

Sisk, Gregory C. 2002. "Suspending the Pardon Power During the Twilight of a Presidential Term." *Missouri Law Review* 67 (Winter): 13–27.

PRESIDENCY, PLURAL EXECUTIVE

Delegates to the Constitutional Convention decided to fashion the presidency as a singular office rather than to entrust such powers in a dual executive or executive council. Pennsylvania's James Wilson defended a singular executive to those who feared that it would assume monarchical powers. He argued that a single individual would be better able to assume responsibility for executive tasks (M. Nelson 2003, I, 24). In *Federalist No. 70,* Alexander Hamilton further defended a singular executive as a means of achieving "energy" and "unity" in government (Hamilton, Madison, and Jay 1961, 423–434).

As the slavery controversy grew, however, some began to fear that a single president might tilt the resolution of this issue toward the interest of a single section of the nation. Indeed, the election of Abraham Lincoln eventually prompted the Southern secession movement. Picking up on an earlier idea of John C. Calhoun's, Virginia Democratic representative Albert Jenkins introduced a resolution in 1860 to create a dual executive; that same year, Democratic Representative John Noell of Missouri proposed replacing the president with a three-person executive council. In 1878, Ohio Democratic representative Milton Southard, who feared that the presidency was becoming too monarchical, proposed creating a presidency of three men representing the western, eastern and middle, and southern states (Ames 1896, 69–70). In 1975, Democratic Representative Henry Reuss of Wisconsin introduced proposals to create a separate chief of state to perform ceremonial functions now assumed by the president.

From a somewhat different perspective, political scientist Matthew Holden Jr. advocated an amendment to create a plural executive, with the prospect of guaranteeing that at least one of the vice presidents forming the resulting executive would be an African American (Holden 1973b, 252–253). Herman Finer proposed adding 11 vice presidents, who, with the president, would exercise collective responsibility in much the same way as the cabinet in Great Britain (Finer 1960, 304). William Marshall of the University of North Carolina School of Law has argued that the Justice Department should (as in most corresponding state counterparts) be given independence from the executive branch so that it could make judgments about the constitutionality of presidential exercises of power without being beholden to the president (2008).

Some proponents of new constitutions have proposed either eliminating the presidency or making the president, as in parliamentary systems, a spokesperson for Congress.

See also Calhoun, John C.; Presidency, Creation of a Separate Chief of State; Parliamentary Systems.

For Further Reading:

Ames, Herman. 1896. *The Proposed Amendments to the Constitution of the United States during the First Century of Its History.* Reprint, New York: Burt Franklin, 1970.

Finer, Herman. 1960. *The Presidency, Crisis and Regeneration: An Essay in Possibilities.* Chicago: University of Chicago Press.

Hamilton, Alexander, James Madison, and John Jay. 1787–1788. *The Federalist Papers.* Reprint, New York: New American Library, 1961.

Holden, Matthew, Jr. 1973b. *The White Man's Burden.* New York: Chandler.

Marshall, William. 2008. "Recalibrating Checks and Balances: Dividing the Executive." Part of "Imaging a New Constitution for the United States in the 21st Century." University of Alabama School of Law, January 11, 2008.

Nelson, Michael, ed. 2008. *Guide to the Presidency.* 4th ed., 2 vols. Washington DC: Congressional Quarterly.

PRESIDENCY, PROPERTY SEIZURE POWERS OF

The Takings Clause of the Fifth Amendment prohibits "private property" from being taken "for public use, without just compensation." However, in April 1952, President Harry Truman issued Executive Order 10340, which directed the secretary of commerce to seize and operate U.S. steel mills. Truman took this action, which he immediately reported to Congress, to avert a strike that threatened the U.S. war efforts in Korea (Westin 1990). In so acting, Truman decided against simply delaying the strike by calling for a cooling-off period under the Taft-Hartley Act of 1947. Instead, he relied on the

broad grants of executive power within the Constitution itself. As a consequence, at least three members of Congress introduced resolutions that April and May calling for a constitutional amendment to limit executive seizure powers.

Such an amendment proved to be unnecessary. On June 2, 1952, the Supreme Court ruled in *Youngstown Sheet & Tube Co. v. Sawyer* (often known simply as the *Steel Seizure Case*) that the president had exceeded his constitutional powers. Justice Hugo Black authored the 6-to-3 decision, which was especially skeptical of the president's broad claim of inherent executive authority. The equally celebrated concurring opinion of Justice Robert Jackson, however, suggested that the president's actions might have been constitutional if Congress had authorized them.

See also Takings Clause.

For Further Reading:

Westin, Alan. 1990. *The Anatomy of a Constitutional Law Case:* Youngstown Sheet and Tube Co. v. Sawyer; *the Steel Seizure Decision.* New York: Columbia University Press.

PRESIDENCY, QUALIFICATIONS FOR

The Constitution requires that the president be at least 35 years old and have resided in the United States for 14 years or more. Article II, Section 1 of the U.S. Constitution further specifies that the president must be "a natural born Citizen" or citizen when the Constitution was adopted, a provision that appears to have been inserted in part at the insistence of Pennsylvania delegate James Wilson, who had been born in Scotland (Miller 2001, 23). The provision forbidding other immigrants from becoming president was apparently designed to ease fears that the delegates to the Constitutional Convention of 1787 might be planning to invite a European monarch to serve as chief executive. The Twelfth Amendment makes it clear that the qualifications for presidential nominees apply equally to nominees for vice-president.

The term "natural born citizen" has been subject to some dispute and could one day be clarified by an amendment. Meanwhile, it probably already includes individuals—such as George Romney, who ran unsuccessfully for the 1968 Republican nomination—born overseas to parents who were American citizens (Gordon 1968). The U.S. Senate adopted a resolution (co-sponsored by both Barack Obama and Hillary Clinton) on April 30, 2008, declaring that John McCain, who was born to U.S. citizens on a U.S. military base in the Panama Canal Zone in 1936, was "natural born." The Supreme Court subsequently rejected a case alleging that President-elect Barack Obama was not a citizen because his father had dual-citizenship in the U.S. and Kenya when Barack was born.

Members of Congress have proposed a number of amendments to alter presidential qualifications, many in the first 100 years of the nation's history. These included proposals to raise the age of eligibility from 35 to 45, to exclude former secessionists from the office (a qualified version of which appeared in Section 3 of the Fourteenth Amendment), and to bar members of Congress or those who are holding office or have held office within two or four years of a presidential election from the job (Ames 1896, 74–75).

In 1976, House Minority Leader John Rhodes and Senator Barry Goldwater, both Arizona Republicans, sponsored a version of this last proposal that would bar members of Congress from the presidency for two years after they left office. Their primary intention was to avoid excessive absences by members of Congress running for chief executive. As the 1964 Republican presidential candidate, Goldwater could testify from personal experience to the difficulty of pursuing both tasks. Their proposal would not have affected the provisions for appointing vice presidents under the Twenty-fifth Amendment.

The most popular proposal affecting presidential qualifications, first offered in the 1860s and periodically introduced from the 1940s to the present, would alter the requirement that a president be a natural-born citizen. Authors of an article have divided these proposals into three types. Some would eliminate the requirement entirely; others would exempt certain groups from the requirement; and yet others would eliminate the natural-born requirement but add others (Duggin and Collins 2005, 148). Proponents of the second option generally include a specific exemption for individuals who were born abroad while their parents were serving in the U.S. military or in other capacities. Proponents of the third option generally propose ending the disability on natural-born citizens but requiring a length of residence in the United States or number of years of citizenship, often 14 to 20 years, prior to being eligible to be president.

See also Citizenship, Officeholding Rights; Fourteenth Amendment; Twelfth Amendment; Twenty-fifth Amendment.

For Further Reading:

Ames, Herman. 1896. *The Proposed Amendments to the Constitution of the United States during the First Century of Its History.* Reprint, New York: Burt Franklin, 1970.

Duggin, Sarah Helene, and Mary Beth Collins. 2005. "'Natural Born' in the USA: The Striking Unfairness and Dangerous Ambiguity of the Constitution's Presidential Qualifications Clause and Why We Need to Fix It." *Boston University Law Review* 85 (February): 53–154.

Gordon, Charles. 1968. "Who Can Be President of the United States: The Unresolved Enigma." *Maryland Law Review* 28 (Winter): 1–32.

Herlihy, Sarah P. 2006. "Amending the Natural Born Citizen Requirement: Globzlization as the Impetus and the Obstacle." *Chicago-Kent Law Review* 81: 275–300.

Ho, James C. 2000. "Unnatural-Born Citizens and Acting Presidents," *Constitutional Commentary* 17: 575–585.

Nelson, Michael. 1987. "Constitutional Qualifications for President." *Presidential Studies Quarterly* 17 (Spring): 383–399.

PRESIDENCY, ROLE IN THE AMENDING PROCESS

Article V of the Constitution does not designate a role for the president in the amending process.

However, Article I, Section 7 specifies that "every order, resolution, or vote to which the concurrence of the Senate and the House of Representatives may be necessary (except on the question of adjournment) shall be presented to the President of the United States" for approval or veto. Does this clause require the president's signature to be valid?

Historically, the answer has been negative. Delegates to the Constitutional Convention of 1787 discussed the veto in the context of legislation rather than with respect to constitutional amendments (Edel 1981, 33–38). Moreover, in an early decision in *Hollingsworth v. Virginia* (1798), the U.S. Supreme Court declared that the president's signature was not necessary. Even a critic of this decision, who wants it confined as narrowly as possible, does not appear to advocate reversal of the ruling (C. Black 1978).

On two occasions, presidents have signed amendments before Congress sent them to the states for approval. The first such signature occurred in 1861, when outgoing president James Buchanan signed the Corwin Amendment (which was not subsequently ratified), designed to prevent any congressional interference with the institution of slavery; the second occurred in 1865, when President Abraham Lincoln signed the Thirteenth Amendment abolishing slavery (Bernstein with Agel 1993, 91, 100). President Lyndon Johnson also insisted on having a ceremony in which he signed as a witness to ratification of the Twenty-fifth Amendment, which provided for presidential disability and, in cases where the need arose, for the replacement of vice presidents.

Although their signatures are not required, presidents frequently take positions on constitutional amendments. Article II, Section 3 of the Constitution grants the president power to "recommend" to Congress "such Measures as he shall judge necessary and expedient." Presidents from George Washington to the present have recognized that this right encompasses power to recommend constitutional amendments (Sidak 1989, 2085).

See also Constitutional Convention of 1787; Corwin Amendment; *Hollingsworth v. Virginia;* Lincoln, Abraham; Thirteenth Amendment; Twenty-fifth Amendment.

For Further Reading:

Bernstein, Richard B., with Jerome Agel. 1993. *Amending America: If We Love the Constitution So Much, Why Do We Keep Trying to Change It?* New York: Random House.

Black, Charles L., Jr. 1978. "Correspondence: On Article I, Section 7, Clause 3—and the Amendment of the Constitution." *Yale Law Journal* 87: 896–900.

Edel, Wilbur. 1981. *A Constitutional Convention: Threat or Challenge?* New York: Praeger.

Sidak, J. Gregory. 1989. "The Recommendation Clause." *Georgetown Law Journal* 77 (August): 2070–2135.

PRESIDENCY, SUCCESSION

See Twenty-fifth Amendment.

PRESIDENCY, TERM LIMITS

See Twenty-second Amendment.

PRESIDENCY, VETO POWER OF

Of all the domestic powers exercised by the president, few are as formidable as the veto, which Article I, Section 7 of the Constitution outlines. Qualified rather than absolute, a two-thirds vote of both houses of Congress can override the presidential veto. The veto's placement within Article I of the Constitution indicates that the framers understood it to be a legislative power and that it therefore represents a departure from strict separation of powers (Spitzer 1988, 18). The threat of such a veto can give a president considerable influence over the formulation of pending legislation. Although presidents may use the veto to void laws they consider to be unconstitutional, the Constitution did not limit use of the mechanism to such circumstances.

President Andrew Jackson reflected his view that the presidency embodied popular will by exercising the veto 12 times, more than all his predecessors combined (Spitzer 1988, 33). Jackson's administration also marked the introduction of the first of at least 11 proposals that members of Congress introduced in the 19th century to allow it to override such vetoes by a simple majority vote (Spitzer 1988, 38). Former president John Quincy Adams and perpetual presidential candidate Henry Clay both offered such proposals during the administration of John Tyler, who was especially criticized for his use of the veto power. The House of Representatives voted 99 to 90 in favor of one such bill in 1842, thus falling substantially below the two-thirds majority required (Ames 1896, 132). Proposals to override presidential vetoes by majority vote were reintroduced in Congress in 1912 and 1913 and from 1943 to 1945.

There were two proposals in the first half of the 19th century to eliminate the presidential veto. A number of other proposals later in the century would have required two-thirds of the members elected in each house rather than by two-thirds of a quorum to override vetoes. The latter was a long-standing practice that the Supreme Court eventually legitimated in *Missouri Pacific Railway Co. v. Kansas* (1919).

New York Democratic representative Jonathan Bingham introduced an amendment resolution in the House in 1975 to allow Congress to override a veto by a three-fifths vote of both houses, but it applied only in the case of an unelected president (such as Gerald Ford, who was then serving) appointed under the Twenty-fifth Amendment (H.J. Res. 529). After the Supreme Court's opinion in *Immigration and Naturalization Service v. Chadha* (1983), declaring the so-called legislative veto to be unconstitutional, members of Congress introduced at least two resolutions to restore this mechanism, one within a week of the decision. Such a veto, a part of about 200 laws, allowed Congress to delegate to the president certain powers, with the understanding that one or both houses could later veto his or her action. The Court found that such legislative vetoes violated the presentment clause (requiring bills to be presented to the president for a possible veto) and,

in some cases, the requirement that legislation be passed by both houses of Congress.

A president exercises a pocket veto by deciding not to sign a bill presented to him or her within 10 days of a congressional adjournment. In early American history, questions were raised as to whether a president could sign a bill once Congress had adjourned. President Ulysses S. Grant accordingly proposed an amendment that would have forbidden Congress to pass any laws in its final 24 hours (Spitzer 1988, 110).

The most popular proposed reform of the veto power has been the proposal to give the president a so-called line-item veto, similar to that which many state governors wield. Such a power was entrusted to, but never exercised by, the president of the Confederate States of America (Spitzer 1988, 126) and has been advocated by members of Congress from both parties and from both ends of the political spectrum. Georgia's Republican senator Mack Mattingly introduced a bill that received substantial support in the Senate in 1985. It provided that all major spending proposals would be divided into separate bills before being presented to the president (Cronin and Weill 1985, 127).

Most proposed amendments dealing with item vetoes have been limited specifically to appropriations bills. The 1880s witnessed the introduction of at least two such item-veto proposals for rivers and harbors bills. A number of 19th-century presidents, including James Madison, vetoed legislation on the basis that Congress had no constitutional authority to pass legislation for internal improvements.

President Grant asked for an item veto in his annual message of 1873, and the first such proposal was introduced in Congress three years later by West Virginia Congressman James Faulkner. Since then, members have introduced more than 150 item-veto amendments, but on the one occasion in 1884 when the amendment was favorably reported out of committee, the Senate did not act on it (Spitzer 1988, 127). Modern advocates of the item veto have included Presidents Harry S Truman, Dwight D. Eisenhower, Gerald Ford, Ronald Reagan, George Bush, and Bill Clinton. Indeed, all three presidential candidates in the 1992 election endorsed this proposal. The only presidents on record against such an item veto are William Howard Taft (Ross and Schwengel 1982, 72), who later served as chief justice of the United States, and Jimmy Carter, who initially supported the proposal but later changed his mind (Cronin and Weill 1985, 130).

Advocates of the item veto believe that it represents a return to the founders' original intention, which has been subverted by the increased use of "riders," or nongermane amendments, that Congress often adds to appropriations bills (Best 1984a). There have been at least half a dozen proposals in U.S. history to prevent such riders or to limit each bill to a single subject as well as a recent law review article on the subject (Denning and Smith 1999). Proponents also see the item veto as a way of trimming the federal budget, which has itself been the subject of numerous proposed amendments. Critics of the item veto doubt that it would have a significant effect on the budget and fear that it might unduly increase presidential powers. Some critics even suggest that it might ultimately result in greater spending, as members of Congress add items in the expectation of some presidential vetoes and as presidents accept such items in exchange for support of other bills.

The item veto was one of the proposals in the Republicans' Contract with America. In March 1996, Republicans agreed on a "functional equivalent of the line-item veto" by means of legislation rather than amendment (Taylor 1996b, 637). Incorporated into the Line Item Veto Act that went into effect in January 1997, this law allowed presidential rescissions of individual budget items to stand unless Congress disapproved within 30 days. It also contained a "lockbox mechanism" designed to dedicate any savings from the item veto to a reduction of the national debt (Taylor 1996b, 866). The U.S. Supreme Court struck the Line Item Veto Act down in *Clinton v. City of New York* (1998), indicating that if a line-item veto were to be enacted, it would have to be adopted by constitutional amendment.

See also Congress, Legislative Veto; *Clinton v. City of New York;* Contract with America; Internal Improvements.

For Further Reading:

Ames, Herman. 1896. *The Proposed Amendments to the Constitution of the United States during the First Century of Its History.* Reprint, New York: Burt Franklin, 1970.

Best, Judith. 1984a. "The Item Veto: Would the Founders Approve?" *Presidential Studies Quarterly* 14 (Spring): 183–188.

Clinton v. City of New York, 524 U.S. 417 (1998).

Cronin, Thomas E., and Jeffrey J. Weill. 1985. "An Item Veto for the President?" *Congress & the Presidency* 12 (Autumn): 127–151.

Denning, Brannon P., and Brooks R. Smith. 1999. "Uneasy Riders: The Case for a TruthinLegislation Amendment." *Utah Law Review:* 957–1025.

Ross, Russell M., and Fred Schwengel. 1982. "An Item Veto for the President?" *Presidential Studies Quarterly* 12 (Winter): 66–79.

Sidak, J. Gregory. 1995. "The Line-Item Veto Amendment." *Cornell Law Review* 80 (July): 1498–1505.

Spitzer, Robert J. 1988. *The Presidential Veto: Touchstone of the American Presidency.* Albany: State University of New York Press.

Taylor, Andrew. 1996b. "Republicans Break Logjam on Line-Item Veto Bill." *Congressional Quarterly Weekly Report* 54 (16 March): 687.

PRESIDENCY, VOTE OF NO CONFIDENCE

Unless they are impeached and convicted for constitutionally designated offenses, U.S. presidents serve for fixed terms of office. In American history, only President Richard Nixon has resigned under the threat of impeachment. Although the House of Representatives impeached presidents Andrew Johnson and Bill Clinton, the required two-thirds majority in the Senate failed to convict them. By contrast, new elections are called in parliamentary systems when parliament votes "no confidence" in the prime minister. Commended for making government responsive to the people, such a mechanism has been proposed as part of a number of plans to rewrite the Constitution. Although his attorney general eventually convinced him that the idea was not feasible, during debates over the League of Nations, Democratic President Woodrow Wilson proposed that senators opposing the plan resign and put themselves up for reelection, with the understanding that if a majority were reelected, Wilson would resign and allow a Republican to assume office (Link 1963, 70–71).

Congressional amending proposals for a vote of "no confidence" in the president have been clustered in two periods—the early 1950s and the early 1970s. Republican Representatives Frederick R. Coudert Jr. of New York and Charles Kersten of Wisconsin and Republican Senator Robert Hendrickson of New Jersey offered the first set of proposals, perhaps in reaction to the fact that the presidency had been occupied by Democrats from 1933 to 1953. Democrat Edith Green of Oregon introduced a resolution in July 1973 (H.J. Res. 666) tied to concerns over President Nixon's abuse of office. It provided that Congress could, by a two-thirds vote of both houses, adopt a resolution stating that the president had failed to execute the laws, had willfully exceeded his powers, or had violated individual rights. In such a case, Congress could call for a new publicly funded election to be held within 90 days. With a view to the situation at hand, Green further specified that such an election would not preclude use of the impeachment procedure.

Democratic Representative Henry Reuss of Wisconsin, who also advocated creation of a separate chief of state and a number of other reforms (Vile 1991c, 119–121), was another supporter of such a mechanism. In 1974, he proposed that a three-fifths vote of both houses of Congress should be able to declare "no confidence" in the president and institute an election within 90 to 110 days. His initial proposal contemplated that the vice president would serve during the interim period, but a subsequent proposal left the president in office during this time and required that all members of Congress also stand for reelection. Reuss's resolution was the subject of deliberation, both in a special law review symposium ("Symposium on the Reuss Resolution" 1975) and in subsequent congressional hearings (*Political Economy and Constitutional Reform* 1982).

See also: Parliamentary Systems; Wilson, Thomas Woodrow.

For Further Reading:

Link, Arthur S. 1963. *Woodrow Wilson: A Brief Biography.* Cleveland: World.

Political Economy and Constitutional Reform. 1982. Hearings before the Joint Economic Committee of the Congress of the United States. 97th Cong., 2d Sess.

"Symposium on the Reuss Resolution: A Vote of No Confidence in the President." 1975. *George Washington Law Review* 43 (January): 328–500.

Vile, John R. 1991c. *Rewriting the United States Constitution: An Examination of Proposals from Reconstruction to the Present.* New York: Praeger.

PRICE CONTROLS

In 1932 and 1933, members of Congress introduced at least four amendments to allow it to control prices and prevent profiteering during war. Especially during wartime, power to control prices already appears to have been well established when these amendments were introduced. During World War I, over a dozen federal agencies regulated prices, with the Food and Fuel Administrations having primary control over consumer prices (C. May 1989, 95). During World War II, the Supreme Court also upheld the Emergency Price Control Act of 1942 in *Yakus v. United States* (1944). At the state level, the Court had already sanctioned New York's regulation of milk prices in *Nebbia v. New York* (1934).

For Further Reading:

May, Christopher N. 1989. *In the Name of War.* Cambridge, MA: Harvard University Press.

PRIOR STATE REJECTION OF AMENDMENTS

Article V of the Constitution does not specifically address whether a state legislature or convention can ratify an amendment that it has previously rejected. Precedents indicate that this practice is on far firmer ground than a state's power to rescind its ratification of a pending amendment (Edel 1981, 47–48).

One challenge to Kansas's ratification of the proposed child labor amendment in *Coleman v. Miller* (1939) was that the legislature had previously rejected the amendment. Although acknowledging "that Article V says nothing of rejection but speaks only of ratifications," the Supreme Court ultimately grounded its refusal to intervene in the matter on the idea that the issue was a political question for Congress to resolve (*Coleman* 1939, 447–450).

Subsequent cases have called into question the application of the political questions doctrine to some amending issues, but it seems doubtful that the Supreme Court would deny a state the right to ratify an amendment it has previously rejected. Without such authority, the Fourteenth Amendment would probably not have been ratified, and the amending process would be even more difficult than it is now. Although never adopted, most proposed legislation on the subject has recognized such a right.

See also *Coleman v. Miller;* Fourteenth Amendment; Legislation Proposed on Constitutional Conventions; Rescission of Ratification of Pending Amendments.

For Further Reading:

Coleman v. Miller, 307 U.S. 433 (1939).

Edel, Wilbur. 1981. *A Constitutional Convention: Threat or Challenge?* New York: Praeger.

PRIVACY, RIGHT TO

Although the U.S. Constitution does not specifically list a right to privacy, modern Supreme Court decisions have carved out such a right, most notably in *Griswold v. Connecticut* (1965) and in *Roe v. Wade* (1973). Faced in the first decision with a longstanding state law that banned the use or prescription of contraceptives, even for married couples, a court majority led by Justice William O. Douglas decided that the law was an unconstitutional infringement on the right to privacy that, although not directly stated in the Constitution, could be ascertained by the "penumbras," or shadows, cast by provisions of the First Amendment (with its presumption of a right of association), the Third Amendment (limiting the quartering of troops in private residences), the Fourth Amendment (with its protections against "unreasonable searches and seizures"), the Fifth Amendment (with its prohibition against self-incrimination), the Ninth Amendment (with its reference to unspecified rights), and the Fourteenth Amendment (with its reference to due process). Justice Hugo Black registered a strong dissent in this case, acknowledging that, while he enjoyed his own privacy, he did not find a sufficient constitutional basis for the judicial construction of such a right and thought the Court was effectively amending the constitution by relying on such a right.

Roe v. Wade extended *Griswold v. Connecticut* by ruling that the right of privacy was extensive enough to permit a woman and her doctor to choose to terminate her pregnancy, especially during the first two trimesters, or six months. Numerous subsequent decisions have allowed for some state regulations of abortion procedures that do not constitute an "undue burden" on a woman's right to choose this procedure. In *Bowers v. Hardwick* (1986), the Supreme Court narrowly refused to overturn a Georgia sodomy law, but it reversed itself in *Lawrence v. Texas* (2003) when deciding that consensual sexual acts between consenting adults were constitutionally protected.

In related Fourth Amendment developments that were highlighted in the U.S. Supreme Court decision in *Katz v. United States* (1967) outlawing warrantless electronic surveillance, Justice John Marshall Harlan articulated a two-part standard that continues to be applied. The test specified that, when ascertaining whether an individual had a right to privacy, the Court would ask whether such an individual had an expectation of privacy and whether that expectation was reasonable.

In *Cruzan v. Missouri Department of Health* (1990) and companion cases in *Washington v. Glucksberg* and *Vacco v. Quill* (1997), the Supreme Court has refused to recognize a "constitutional right to die," especially when such a "right" would imply an "obligation" on the part of medical personnel to prescribe lethal doses of medication.

A number of state constitutions have specific provisions that acknowledge a right to privacy, and a number of proposed new constitutions for the United States contain similar provisions. These often include specific language regarding abortion, the right to die, or private sexual conduct between consenting adults.

See also Abortion; Black, Hugo Lafayette; *Griswold v. Connecticut;* Right to Life; *Roe v. Wade.*

For Further Reading:

Garrow, David J. 1994. *Liberty & Sexuality: The Right to Privacy and the Making of* Roe v. Wade. New York: Macmillan Publishing.

Johnson, John W. 2005. *Griswold v. Connecticut: Birth Control and the Constitutional Right of Privacy.* Lawrence: University Press of Kansas.

Murdock, Joyce, and Deb Price. 2001. *Courting Justice: Gay Men and Lesbians v. the Supreme Court.* New York: Basic Books.

PROGRESS AND THE AMENDING PROCESS

The constitutional amending process is a means of correcting errors in the existing constitutional structure and of adapting to new and unforeseen circumstances. However, it also presents the possibility of incorporating new ideas and even new rights into the Constitution. Throughout much of human history, the emphasis within law has been on stability rather than progress. A historian has noted that "[d]uring most of history, people were more impressed by the destructive effects of time than by the good things it held in store" (Lasch 1995, 546). Many early notions of history were cyclical. Periods of progress would be followed by periods of decline, and the cycle would repeat itself again.

Although not completely unique, Christianity tends to view time in a more linear fashion.

In particular, Christians believe that God revealed himself more clearly in the New Testament than he had in the Old, and there was a still better world to follow. Although most Christians understand that ultimate progress awaits another world, the idea of such progress has taken on secular (and sometimes even utopian) overtones, especially during the Enlightenment period during which the U.S. Constitution was written. This notion was further secularized when philosophers applied ideas of Darwinian biological evolution to political and social structures. Progress was especially associated with the idea of increased human freedom (Nisbet 1980, 179–236), although it was often balanced with a darker view linking it to increased power to bring about totalitarian visions of new societies (Nisbet 1980, 237–296).

In allowing Congress to provide for copyright and patent protection, Article I, Section 8 of the Constitution refers specifically to "the Progress of Science and useful Arts." Although this is the only specific reference to progress in the document, the constitutional amending process provides a means to incorporate progress into the Constitution. In recognition that majorities in favor of a particular constitutional reform could prove to be mistaken or ephemeral, this process requires supermajorities at both the proposal and ratification stages. Although making such written reforms difficult to initiate, the amending mechanism also assures that, once incorporated into the text, they will also be quite difficult to repeal.

Thomas Jefferson was among those who argued that, with increased knowledge and experience, it was foolish to be permanently bound by ancient constitutions, so much so that his friend James Madison had to temper Jefferson's view that each generation should write its own constitution. Many proposals for new constitutions have similarly been predicated on the idea that new forms of government are needed either to respond to or to initiate greater progress. The idea of progress is often tied to economic growth, and constitutions predicated on releasing new human energies are often based on ideas of removing governmental regulations that are viewed as obstacles to further economic development. Similarly, many proposals for more direct forms of democracy are based either on the assumption that more widespread education, or more modern forms of communication and other forms of technology, have made such direct citizen participation more feasible and less dangerous than in the past.

Writers have often described the history of the constitutional amending process in America in progressive terms. Alan Grimes's *Democracy and the Amendments to the Constitution* (1978) is a good example. Certainly, the amending process has allowed for the wide expansion of suffrage and democracy as well as for increased guarantees of civil liberties, especially in the Bill of Rights (and its subsequent application to state governments) and the adoption of the Thirteenth Amendment eliminating slavery and the Fourteenth Amendment expanding the rights of citizenship. A number of democratizing amendments were specifically associated with the Progressive Era in American history and that other mechanisms from this period like the initiative, referendum, and recall continue to be proposed. To date, the only serious restriction on civil liberties to be added to the U.S. Constitution by amendment, namely national alcoholic prohibition, has been repealed (see the Eighteenth and Twenty-first Amendments).

This rosy view of constitutional progress may mask less savory extraconstitutional developments like increases in wars and other forms of violence, increased overcrowding, environmental degradation, family disintegration, moral degeneration, or even increased feelings of spiritual emptiness. Although many of these problems may not be amenable to constitutional solution, the constitutional amending process remains a viable mechanism for incorporating newly discovered or better appreciated rights and advanced procedural mechanisms into the constitutional text.

See also Amendment, Definition; Democracy and Constitutional Amendments; Jefferson, Thomas; Madison, James; Progressive Era.

For Further Reading:

Grimes, Alan P. 1978. *Democracy and the Amendments to the Constitution.* Lexington, MA: Lexington Books.

Lasch, Christopher. 1995. "Progress." *A Companion to American Thought,* eds. Richard Wightman Fox and James T. Kloppenberg. Malden, MA: Blackwell Publishers.

Nisbet, Robert. 1980. *The Idea of Progress.* New York: Basic Books.

Pollack, Malla. 2001. "What is Congress Supposed to Promote?: Defining 'Progress' in Article I, Section 8, Clause 8 of the United States Constitution, or Introducing the Progress Clause." *Nebraska Law Review* 80: 754–813.

PROGRESSIVE ERA

Amendments have not been proposed and ratified at a uniform pace in U.S. history but have tended to be adopted in clusters. The Bill of Rights was adopted as a unit, three amendments were ratified in the five years that followed the end of the Civil War, and four more were ratified from 1913 to 1920.

This latter period corresponds roughly with the end of the Progressive Era, a time during which reformist sentiments were strong and reformers were optimistic about their ability to solve social problems (Ekirch 1974; Gould 1974; Link and McCormick 1983). Prominent Progressives included Herbert Croly, Theodore Roosevelt, and—to a lesser degree—Woodrow Wilson.

Many Progressives, undoubtedly influenced by the long hiatus of the amending process, started out with fairly critical views of the U.S. Constitution and its possibility for change. Progressives were also especially critical of the political party system—with its bosses, patronage, and vote buying—that had developed in the wake of Jacksonian politics. Progressives wanted to transfer power from the parties to the people, but they combined this desire with that of elevating and reforming individuals as well.

The four amendments ratified from 1913 to 1920 illumine different aspects of Progressive thought. The Sixteenth Amendment, which legalized the income tax, is, in a sense, the foundation of the powers of the modern national government. Without this or an equivalent revenue source, the national government simply could not take on all its modern functions. The fact that this tax can also be made progressive, so that it takes a higher percentage of the income of the rich than of the poor, means that it has the ability to redistribute income, the disparities of which concerned Progressive reformers.

The Seventeenth Amendment, providing for the direct election of senators, struck at the party politics that had dominated senatorial selection in the state legislatures. The Eighteenth Amendment, providing for national alcoholic prohibition, was tied to Progressive strands of Protestant moralism (often directed against Catholic immigrants, who generally had more tolerant attitudes toward alcohol consumption) and to a desire to combat a genuine social evil. Finally, the Nineteenth Amendment capped more than half a century of reform efforts on behalf of women's suffrage, which many believed would not only promote fairness but also bring women's elevated moral sensibilities to bear at the ballot box.

In addition to these amendments, Progressive leaders advocated numerous other reforms, many of which still influence U.S. politics. These include the direct primary; the initiative, referendum, and recall (also closely associated with mid-western Populism, with at least indirect ties to Progressivism); compulsory schooling; and such economic reforms as antitrust measures, protections against child labor, maximum-hours legislation, and minimum wages (Eisenach 1994, 8–9). Although it was adopted later, the Twentieth Amendment, limiting the terms of "lame-duck" representatives and presidents, and introduced by Progressive Senator George Norris, was also a product of sentiments that grew out of the Progressive Era.

See also Child Labor Amendment; Eighteenth Amendment; Initiatives and Referendums; Seventeenth Amendment; Sixteenth Amendment; Twentieth Amendment

For Further Reading:

Eisenach, Eldon J. 1994. *The Lost Promise of Progressivism.* Lawrence: University Press of Kansas.

Ekirch, Arthur A., Jr. 1974. *Progressivism in America: A Study of the Era from Theodore Roosevelt to Woodrow Wilson.* New York: New Viewpoints.

Epstein, Richard A. 2006. *How Progressives Rewrote the Constitution.* Washington, DC: Cato Institute.

Gould, Lewis L., ed. 1974. *The Progressive Era.* Syracuse, NY: Syracuse University Press.

Link, Arthur S., and Richard L. McCormick. 1983. *Progressivism.* Arlington Heights, IL: Harlan Davidson.

PROMULGATION OF AMENDMENTS

In *Coleman v. Miller* (1939) the Supreme Court indicated that most issues surrounding the constitutional amending process were "political questions" for Congress to resolve. In so ruling, the Court appears to have been influenced in large part by the actions of the Reconstruction Congress regarding the dispute as to whether the Fourteenth Amendment had been ratified. The situation was messy, but on that occasion, faced with attempts by Ohio and New Jersey to rescind their ratifications of the amendment, Congress adopted a joint resolution counting those states in the final total and stating that the Fourteenth Amendment was "hereby declared to be a part of the Constitution of the United States, and it shall be duly promulgated by the Secretary of State" (quoted in Dellinger 1983, 397). More recently, Congress adopted a similar resolution declaring that the Twenty-seventh Amendment had been ratified. There was good reason for taking such action as the amendment, which had originally been proposed as part of the Bill of Rights, was not ratified by the requisite number of states until 1992.

Article V of the Constitution does not mention the need for congressional promulgation of amendments. Moreover, the Supreme Court's decision in *Dillon v. Gloss* (1921) indicated that amendments become part of the law of the land when ratified by the necessary number of states rather than when acknowledged, or promulgated, by the secretary of state, or, in later practice, the administrator of the General Services Administration or the archivist of the Library of Congress.

Law professor Walter Dellinger has argued that congressional promulgation can neither add to nor detract from the legitimacy of an amendment. Believing that such a mechanism is likely to be "an unwieldy, uncertain and unpredictable mechanism for resolving amendment disputes" (Dellinger 1983, 392), he thinks that such matters can better be resolved through the exercise of judicial review.

See also Coleman v. Miller: *Dillon v. Gloss;* Fourteenth Amendment; Twenty-seventh Amendment.

For Further Reading:

Dellinger, Walter. 1983. "The Legitimacy of Constitutional Change: Rethinking the Amending Process." *Harvard Law Review* 97 (December): 380–432.

PROPER GOVERNMENT

Proposals for constitutional change often come from unexpected places. Increasingly, the Internet is one source of proposals. In 1998, a site was established under the title of "Proper Government," with four proposals (although recent updates suggest that the project was first constructed in 1981 or 1982), and it has continued to grow into a site of well over 100 pages (see *http://www.ebtx.com*). The author was not identified on the original site and remains anonymous. Self-described as "an intellectual pig," who "will investigate anything no matter how common, bizarre or crude," he (deprecatory remarks about women on the site indicate that the author is a man) lists his "immediate goals" as attempting to "figure out the universe; fix the world, conquer life; and think & do & run & jump & play." The site continues to change and includes e-mail messages, many of which appear to question the sanity of the author of the site.

The four central reform proposals offered by the author of "Proper Government" appear under the title of "The New Proposed Constitution" and are unusual. The first proposal is likely to be the most unpopular. It calls for limiting the right to vote (or at least the right to votes that count; he seems to have no problem with advisory votes) to men and would therefore reverse the Nineteenth Amendment. Perhaps to counter problems with representative government, the author's second main proposal would require that each individual would have to vote for a "personal acquaintance." Votes would be cast by computer and aggregated with individuals getting the highest votes, and in any event no "less than twice the votes of any of his electors," selected as representatives. The third plank of this plan calls for paying representatives on the basis of how many votes they captured. A president winning 100 million votes could thus earn $2 billion, thus presumably shielding him from the possibility of bribery. The fourth plank of the plan would allow votes collectively to decide by what percentage taxes would go up or down each year. Through a point system, voters would also determine how tax dollars would be distributed.

Guided largely by libertarian ideals, the author believes that "[t]he goal of law must be to preserve the autonomy of the individual" and that "no individual can be punished for NOT performing an action." This would exempt individuals from being required to file tax returns, serve in the military, or buy insurance. The author expresses disdain for the income tax and for welfare programs. Although advocating the formation of an online "American Party," he favors nonparticipation and disrespect for existing governmental officials in the meantime. Believing that a second civil war is inevitable, his advice to "[a]rm yourselves as heavily as possible" is qualified: citizens should be armed "with a purpose and a plan."

The plan for "Proper Government" demonstrates both the strength and weakness of the Internet in advancing ideas for constitutional change. The Internet serves as a platform for points of view that might not otherwise be aired, but it can also insulate anonymous authors from scholarly reviews and criticisms that they might receive were their views to be published in more traditional printed forms.

For Further Reading:

"Proper Government." http://www.ebtx.com. Accessed May 17, 2002.

PROPOSAL OF AMENDMENTS

Article V of the Constitution divides the amending process into two steps, proposal and ratification. Although rules in the House of Representatives once provided that committees would introduce both bills and amendments, individual members of both houses may do so. Members who propose amendments generally do so through joint resolutions. Members have introduced more than 11,700 proposals (most redundant) in U.S. history. A contemporary study links this large number to "grand standing," "credit seeking," and "careerism." (Latham 2005, 152).

Whereas ratification requires three-fourths of the states to approve, the Constitution requires that amendments be proposed by two-thirds majorities of both houses of Congress or by a convention called by Congress when it receives petitions from two-thirds of the states. However, perhaps because American parties are relatively decentralized and there is relatively little party discipline by comparison to the legislative bodies in other democratic nations, the mechanisms for proposing amendments have been greater obstacles to the adoption of new amendments than have the proposals for ratification (Ferreres-Comella 2000, 48). Thus, states have ratified 27 of 33 amendments proposed by Congress.

In the *National Prohibition Cases* (1920), the Supreme Court declared that when Congress proposed an amendment by the requisite two-thirds majorities, it did not need to adopt a separate resolution stating its judgment that such an amendment was necessary. In the same decision, the Court decided that the required two-thirds majority vote "is a vote of two-thirds of the members present—assuming the presence of a quorum—and not a vote of two-thirds of the entire membership, present and absent" (1920,

386). On at least some occasions, such majorities have been ascertained by voice vote rather than by roll call.

The most controversial issue involving the proposal of amendments involves the still-untried Article V mechanism for a convention to propose amendments, which Congress is supposed to call after two-thirds of the state legislatures petition it to do so. As is the case with the ratification of amendments, the Constitution does not specify how contemporaneous such applications must be; it also does not specify whether such calls have to center on the same topic.

Some scholars argue that the states can call for only a general convention and that other calls are invalid (C. Black 1979; Dellinger 1979). Others scholars believe that states may call a convention on a single topic or subject area (Rees 1986; Van Alstyne 1978; for discussion of this issue, see Vile 1993a, 54–73). Some scholars argue that, based on the nature of petitions it has received, Congress is already bound to call such a convention (Paulsen 1993, 1995; Van Sickle and Boughey 1990).

See also Constitutional Conventions; Joint Resolution; *National Prohibition Cases;* Number of Proposed Amendments.

For Further Reading:

Black, Charles L., Jr. 1979. "Amendment by a National Constitutional Convention: A Letter to a Senator." *Oklahoma Law Review* 32: 626–644.

Dellinger, Walter. 1979. "The Recurring Question of the 'Limited' Constitutional Convention." *Yale Law Journal* 88: 1623–1640.

Ferreres-Comella, Victor. 2000. "A Defense of Constitutional Rigidity." In *Analysis and Right,* ed. Paul Comanducci and Riccardo Guastine. Turin, Italy: G. Biappichelli Publisher.

Latham, Darren R. 2005. "The Historical Amendability of the American Constitution: Speculations on an Empirical Problematic." *American University Law Review* 55 (October): 145–269.

Paulsen, Michael S. 1995. "The Case for a Constitutional Convention." *Wall Street Journal* 3, May, A15.

———. 1993. "A General Theory of Article V: The Constitutional Issues of the Twenty-seventh Amendment." *Yale Law Journal* 103: 677–789.

National Prohibition Cases, 253 U.S. 350 (1920).

Rees, Grover, III. 1986. "The Amendment Process and Limited Constitutional Conventions." *Benchmark* 2: 67–108.

Van Alstyne, William. 1978. "Does Article V Restrict the States to Calling Unlimited Conventions Only?—A Letter to a Colleague." *Duke Law Journal* 1978 (January): 1295–1306.

Van Sickle, Bruce M., and Lynn M. Boughey. 1990. "Lawful and Peaceful Revolution: Article V and Congress' Present Duty to Call a Convention for Proposing Amendments." *Hamline Law Review* 14 (Fall): 1–115.

Vile, John R. 1993b. *Contemporary Questions Surrounding the Constitutional Amending Process.* Westport, CT: Praeger.

PROPOSED AMENDMENTS THAT FAILED

See Failed Amendments.

PUBLIC CHOICE AND CONSTITUTIONAL AMENDMENTS

Public choice is an approach to economics with implications for politics. Most frequently associated with Nobel-prize winner James M. Buchanan and his collaborator Gordon Tullock, public choice economists anticipate that individuals, interest groups, and elected officials will use political processes for personal gain. They understand constitutions as one mechanism that people may use to reduce such "rent-seeking." Constitutions may do so by making both the processes of legislation and of constitutional amendment difficult.

Lawyers Donald J. Boudreaux and A. C. Pritchard have sought to apply these insights to the U.S. Constitution. In describing constitutions, they associate them with "precommitment," which they describe as "a device that restrains majorities from taking actions that they might later regret" (1993, 114). Constitutions precommit members of a polity to foreclose future choices, much as classical literature described Ulysses as ordering his men to tie himself to a ship mast in order that he could hear the beautiful sounds of sirens without being able to yield to their destructive and deadly charms.

Constitutions further seek to reduce "agency costs" by attempting "to limit the damage willful government actors impose on the public" (*Id.,* 114). Bicameralism and separation of powers are among the constitutional mechanisms used to thwart law-makers from enhancing their purely self-interests.

In seeking to pursue their interests, lobby groups must weigh the comparative costs of laws or amendments. Because they are more difficult to adopt, the latter cost more. It is easier for minorities to block the latter than the former, although once enacted, the latter are more difficult to repeal.

Boudreaux and Pritchard identify two requirements in the Article V amending process that "advantage minority interest groups that oppose amendments," namely splitting decision-making between Congress and the states and requiring supermajorities at both levels (*Id.,* 129). Although these mechanisms do not guarantee that "a majority of the *people* support a constitutional amendment," "[t]he supermajority requirement at least increases the odds that a majority of people favor an amendment" (*Id.,* 130). However, "Amendments that confer a small benefit on a large percentage of the population are unlikely to find much support in Congress, particularly if that amendment impairs the interests of its members" (*Id.,* 131).

Boudreaux and Pritchard believe that the delegates to the Constitutional Convention of 1787 were most concerned with what they saw as rent-seeking at the state level (the enactments of state tariffs, the issuance of paper money, and the like) under the Articles of Confederation whereas their anti-federalist opponents were more concerned about "agency costs of the federal government" (*Id.,* 137) Boudreaux and Pritchard attribute the successful adoption of the Bill of Rights in part to the fact that members of the new national government not only wanted to guard against the possibility of a second convention that might undo the work of the first but also to the fact that members of Congress had not yet developed significantly different interests from the people they represented. Boudreaux and Pritchard point out that successful subsequent amendments have tended to augment national powers, often against the states. They conclude that:

> Congressional control over the agenda of constitutional amendments restricts the ability of the people to control Congress effectively through the Constitution. As a consequence, Article V poorly serves the normative efficiency theories of constitutionalism. By placing the foxes in charge of the chicken coop, the Framers made Article V useless for achieving those efficiency goals of constitutionalism: precommitment and the reduction of agency costs. (*Id.,* 160)

Writing in 1993, they predicted that there were long odds against amendments like balanced-budget requirements or term limits, which would restrict congressional powers.

Boudreaux and Pritchard believe that some vested interests might be bypassed if Article V were amended to permit the people to petition for amendments, but they believe that such amendments "would surely fall prey to the same forces that doom the term-limits and balanced-budget amendments" (*Id.,* 161).

James Buchanan has advocated three amendments. In seeking to impose "fiscal responsibility," he favors a balanced budget amendment that requires Congress to limit spending to anticipated tax revenues absent a waiver of three-fourths of both houses to deal with extraordinary circumstances. A second amendment, which he attributes to the philosopher F. A. Hayek, would provide that "congress shall make no law authorizing government to take any discriminatory measures of coercion" He likens this to an equal protection clause. It would aim at distinguishing permissible legislation that benefits "citizens of the polity generally" from legislation aimed "to benefit members of identified groups." Finally, he favors an amendment interfering with voluntary economic exchanges

both within the domestic sphere and in respect to foreign trade. Buchanan observes that the three proposals are "internally redundant" in that "effective enforcement of any one would do much toward meeting the need for the implementation of the others" (2005).

See also Balanced-Budget Amendment; Bill of Rights: Supermajorities; Term Limits.

For Further Reading:

Boudreaux, Donald J., and A. C. Pritchard. 1993. "Rewriting the Constitution: An Economic Analysis of the Constitutional Amending Process." *Fordham Law Review* 62 (October): 111–162.

Brennan, Geoffrey, and James M. Muchanan. 2000. "Is Constitutional Revolution Possible in Democracy?" The Reason of Rules: Constitutional Political Economy, vol. 10 of *The Collected Works of James M. Buchanan.* Indianapolis: Liberty Fund.

Brennan, Geoffrey, and Alan Hamlin. 1998. "Constitutional Economics." *The New Palgrave Dictionary of Economics and the Law.* 3 vols. Ed. Peter Newman. New York: Stockton Press, 401–410.

Buchanan, James M. and Gordon Tullock. 1962. *The Calculus of Consent: Logical Foundations of Constitutional Democracy.* Ann Arbor: The University of Michigan Press.

Buchanan, James M. 2005. "Three Amendments: Responsibility, Generality, and Natural Liberty." Cato Unbound. http://www.cato-unbound.org/2005/12/05/james-m-buchanan/three-amendments/. Accessed July 26, 2008.

Holmes, Stephen. 1988. "Precommitment and the paradox of democracy." *Constitutionalism and Democracy.* Eds. Elster, Jon, and Rune Slagstad. New York: Cambridge University Press, 195–240.

Zwicki, Todd J. 1994. "Senators and Special Interests: A Public Choice Analysis of the Seventeenth Amendment." *Oregon Law Review* 73 (Winter): 1007–1055.

PUBLIC OPINION AND THE AMENDING PROCESS

The U.S. Constitution begins with the words "We the People," and Americans pride themselves on living in a democracy. However, as

James Madison argued in *Federalist No. 10,* the system created by the Constitution is a system of republican, or representative, rather than direct democracy, and it falls short of true democracy in many respects. Although it is difficult to gauge public opinion at the time with any precision, the U.S. Constitution did not go into effect in any state until it was approved by a popular convention there, and subsequent states cast similar votes before deciding whether to join the Union. Article VII specified that the Constitution would not go into effect until ratified by nine or more of the 13 states, and subsequent amendments have all been adopted by two-thirds majorities in both houses of Congress and three-fourths of the states. Amendments have been ratified as early as 1791 (the Bill of Rights) and as late as 1992 (the Twenty-seventh Amendment).

As in the case of the original Constitution, new amendments call for supermajorities rather than for mere majorities, although because of differential state populations and federalism, it is possible to imagine scenarios both in which amendments that majorities favor are not adopted and scenarios in which amendments are proposed and/or ratified with less than majority support. The fact that the Eighteenth Amendment providing for national alcoholic prohibition is the only one specifically to have been repealed (by the Twenty-first Amendment) is probably testimony not only to the difficulty of the amending process, but also to the fact that, hypotheticals aside, few amendments can pass through the current amending gauntlet without a solid majority of the people supporting them.

Unlike some states, the United States has not adopted a mechanism whereby the people can propose or ratify constitutional amendments directly. Some scholars have proposed altering the Constitution so as to allow for national initiatives and referendums. Akhil Reed Amar (1994) has argued that such a power exists even without direct constitutional language providing for its support. Moreover, Bruce Ackerman (1991) argues that public opinion might be expressed in certain "constitutional moments" (as, for example, during the New Deal period) that are incorporated into constitutional understandings without necessarily being incorporated into the constitutional text. Such understandings would appear to be less stable than those that are incorporated specifically into constitutional language. Moreover, a study of the New Deal period suggests that the people might not have been very well informed about the "Constitutional" changes that were being adopted (Somin 2003).

The Founders designed the current amending process to promote deliberation and stability. At least during certain periods, large majorities of the people have clearly supported proposals— like prayer in schools, electoral college reform, or an amendment to prohibit flag desecration— that were not adopted as national amendments. In some cases, reforms can be carried out within individual states that do not require amendments of the national constitution. Still, most amendments that have been ratified have promoted greater democracy and an expansion of civil rights and liberties, and it would be difficult to identify a constitutional amendment that has been adopted and that remains in effect that would currently be disfavored by a majority of the people.

As fundamental law, most Americans probably understand that the Constitution is not intended to embody the latest public sentiment on every issue. The government takes no official notice of public opinion polls as such, and even elections are imperfect measures of such opinion. The First Amendment guarantees that individuals can express their views on the desirability or undesirability of constitutional amendments, just as they can on other matters. If the system is properly functioning, existing constitutional amending mechanisms should, at least over time, reflect consistent thoughtful majority opinion with nationwide support as to what the Constitution should include and what it should not.

See also Ackerman, Bruce; Amar, Akhil Reed; Deliberation and the Amending Process; Democracy and Constitutional Amendments; Federalism and the Amending Process; First Amendment; Initiative and Referendum; Madison, James; Supermajorities.

For Further Reading:
Ackerman, Bruce. 1991. *We the People: Foundations.* Cambridge, MA: Belknap.

Amar, Akhil Reed. 1994. "The Consent of the Governed: Constitutional Amendment outside Article V." *Columbia Law Review* 94 (March): 457–508.

Cushman, Barry. 2002. "Mr. Dooley and Mr. Gallup: Public Opinion and Constitutional Change in the 1930s." *Buffalo Law Review* 50 (Winter): 7–101.

Somin, Ilya. 2003. "Voter Knowledge and Constitutional Change: Assessing the New Deal Experience." *William and Mary Law Review* 45 (December): 595–674.

PUERTO RICO, REPRESENTATION IN ELECTORAL COLLEGE

In 1961, the states ratified the Twenty-third Amendment granting the District of Columbia representation in the electoral college equivalent to that of the least populous state—presently three votes. In the two years that followed, representatives from New York, Texas, and New Mexico, all states with sizable Hispanic populations, introduced amendments to grant similar representation for Puerto Rico, a U.S. commonwealth acquired from Spain in the Spanish–American War of 1898.

The commonwealth now holds presidential primaries and sends delegates to both major party conventions. It remains unrepresented, however, in the electoral college. Either the adoption of a constitutional amendment like the Twenty-third giving electoral votes to the District of Columbia, or Puerto Rico's admission as a state, a long-discussed option (Melendez 1988) appears to be a prerequisite to such representation. However, the allocation of electoral votes under the Twenty-third Amendment for the District of Columbia (that of the smallest state, or three votes) would arguably be inadequate for a jurisdiction with more than six times its population. With or without such representation in the electoral college for Puerto Rico, American Hispanics are exerting increased influence on American politics. Hispanic support appears to have been one of the reasons for George Bush's ultimate success in the state of Florida, and, consequently, in the electoral college, in the presidential election of 2000.

See Voting Rights, Constitutional Amendments Relating to.

For Further Reading:

Malawet, Pedro, A. 2000. "Puerto Rico: Cultural Nation, American Colony." *Michigan Journal of Race and Law* 6 (Fall): 1–106.

Melendez, Edgardo. 1988. *Puerto Rico's Statehood Movement.* New York: Greenwood Press.

R

❖

RATIFICATION OF AMENDMENTS

Article V of the Constitution specifies how amendments are proposed and ratified. After being proposed either by the necessary congressional majorities or by a special convention, they become part of the Constitution "when ratified by the Legislatures of three fourths of the several States, or by Conventions in three fourths thereof, as the one or the other Mode of Ratification may be proposed by the Congress." Acknowledging the difficulty of amendment, one author noted that "ratification isn't beanbag" (Vose 1979, 113). Yet to date the states have failed to ratify only six of 36 amendments that Congress has submitted to them. State legislatures ratified 26 amendments; special state conventions ratified the Twenty-first Amendment. Congress specified this form of ratification within the Twenty-first Amendment; in the other three times that Congress has specified the mode of ratification within an amendment (the Eighteenth, Twentieth, and Twenty-second Amendments) rather than in accompanying legislation, it provided for state legislative ratification.

Although ratification by state constitutional conventions would appear to be more democratic than ratification by state legislative delegations (whose members are often chosen for their positions on issues other than their approval or disapproval of pending amendments), a scholarly study has pointed to serious flaws in the ratification of the Twenty-first Amendment, which repealed national alcoholic prohibition. This study notes that the off-year elections had low voter turnouts; selection by at-large, rather than single-member, districts greatly exaggerated popular approval of the amendment; and the conventions engaged in little deliberation. Only in Indiana does there appear to have been any real deliberation at the convention, and in New Hampshire, delegates voted for repeal and adjourned within 17 minutes (Schaller 1998)!

The ratification process has raised a number of legal questions. In an early case, *Hollingsworth v. Virginia* (1798), the Supreme Court decided that the president's signature was not required for amendment ratifications. In *Hawke v. Smith* (1920), it subsequently decided that a state could not require such amendments to be approved by referendum. Although the Supreme Court later ruled in *Kimble v. Swackhamer* (1978) that a nonbinding referendum to ascertain state sentiment was acceptable, in *Cook v. Gralike* (2001) it prohibited states from instructing legislators as to how they should vote on amendments or making negative notations on ballots of those who did not follow the state's will. In *Dillon v. Gloss* (1921), the Court declared that ratification must follow soon enough after Congress has proposed an amendment to reflect a contemporary consensus of the states; it also held that such ratification was complete on the date that the last of the necessary number of states approved rather than on the date that the secretary of state declared such ratification complete. In *United States v. Sprague* (1931), the Supreme Court affirmed that Congress had the responsibility of designating which of the two modes specified in the Constitution the states would follow when ratifying an amendment.

Coleman v. Miller (1939) subsequently raised additional issues, including whether prior rejection of an amendment precluded subsequent ratification, whether a state's lieutenant governor could cast a tie-breaking vote in the state legislature in favor of an amendment, and whether a state had ratified an amendment within a reasonable length of time. The Court declared itself "equally divided" on the issue of the lieutenant governor's veto and decided that the other issues were "political questions" for Congress to resolve.

The Equal Rights Amendment brought renewed attention to ratification issues. A lower court case, *Dyer v. Blair* (1975), raised the issue of whether a state could require the ratification of amendments by supermajority—in this case, a three-fifths vote. Future Supreme Court Justice John Paul Stevens ruled that this issue was justiciable and that the state ratifying bodies should ascertain the majority that would be required; he did, however, rule that any requirements found in a state's constitution on the subject were invalid.

Another district court decision, in *Idaho v. Freeman* (1981), also focused on whether a state could rescind the Equal Rights Amendment prior to its adoption by the necessary three-fourths of the states. Also at issue was the right of Congress to extend the ratification deadline. Like the issues that Stevens had examined, these issues were deemed justiciable by the district judge. Working from the principle of contemporary consensus, the judge declared that a state should be able to rescind ratification of a pending amendment. He further argued that Congress had no power to extend the original deadline for the Equal Rights Amendment, and even if it did, such action would require a two-thirds vote of both houses (Vile 1993b, 49–51). This decision became moot when states failed to ratify the Equal Rights Amendment. A seemingly surefire way to avoid future controversies over ratification deadlines is to include them within the text of proposed amendments (as was done in the case of the Eighteenth, Twentieth, Twenty-first, and Twenty-second Amendments), where they will be self-executing (Dellinger 1983, 409).

The proposal that became the Twenty-seventh Amendment did not have such a deadline. Considerable controversy was generated by the decision of the national archivist—subsequently affirmed by Congress—to accept this amendment that was originally proposed in 1789 but not ratified by the necessary majority of states until 1992. The Twenty-seventh Amendment, like the previous ones, had to be ratified by three-fourths of the states in existence at the time of ratification, rather than at the time the amendment was proposed (Silversmith 1999, 595–597).

There is no conclusive decision regarding whether states can rescind ratifications prior to adopt of amendments, but many states have ratified amendments they have previously either failed to adopt or attempt to rescind. Chin and Abraham have observed that "[t]he Thirteenth, Fourteenth, Fifteenth, and Nineteenth Amendments have been ratified by all of the states in the Union at the time each became effective" (2008, 26). They further note that "although challenges to the validity of particular ratifications are a common feature of the post-ratification legal landscape, post-adoption ratifications render them moot" (*Id.,* 27).

Chin and Abraham observe that many such ratifications are fairly contemporaneous. Thus, Oregon, California, Florida, Iowa, New Jersey, and Texas all ratified the Thirteenth Amendment between its formal adoption in 1865 and 1870 (*Id.,* 18). Similarly, Nebraska, Texas, and New Jersey ratified the Fifteenth Amendment not long after its adoption in 1870. Congress required the Southern states to ratify the Fourteenth Amendment as a condition of reentering the union. However, many states ratified the postwar amendments in the 20th century as a sign of "substantive support for civil rights and principles of equality" (*Id.,* 30) Some states specifically ratified one or more of the Reconstruction Amendments as a way to demonstrate support for the Supreme Court decision invaliding racial segregation in *Brown v. Board of Education* (1954). African American legislators led some of these movements. Postratifications sometimes correspond with constitutional commemorations or celebrations.

In observations that could be important to various theories that posit the illegality of one or more of the Reconstruction Amendments, Chin and Abraham observe that "post-amendment ratifications . . . stabilize and legitimize amendments that otherwise might be doubtful because of shenanigans associated with particular ratifications. If forty or forty-two states ratify, it matters not if a parliamentary trick (or worse) was used to get one or two of the bare minimum thirty-eight (three-fourths of fifty)" (*Id.,* 38). Such ratifications raise challenging questions for those who believe in interpreting amendments through the original intent of states that ratified. Chin and Abraham are somewhat shocked that Supreme Court decisions interpreting original intent sometimes consider practices of 20th-century ratifiers along with those whose ratifications actually made a difference (*Id.,* 42–43). They also suggest that postadoption ratifications "offer some support for the idea that rescission [prior to ratification] is valid" (*Id.,* 46).

See also *Cook v. Gralike; Coleman v. Miller; Dillon v. Gloss; Dyer v. Blair;* Equal Rights Amendment; *Hawke v. Smith; Hollingsowrth v. Virginia; Idaho v. Freeman; Kimble v. Swackhamer;* Rescission of Ratification of Pending Amendments; Twenty-first Amendment; Twenty-seventh Amendment; *United States v. Sprague.*

For Further Reading:

Chin, Gabriel J., and Anjali Abraham. 2008. "Beyond the Supermajority: Post-Adoption Ratification of the Equality Amendments." *Arizona Law Review* 50 (Spring): 25–47.

Dellinger, Walter. 1983. "The Legitimacy of Constitutional Change: Rethinking the Amending Process." *Harvard Law Review* 97 (December): 380–432.

Schaller, Thomas F. 1998. "Democracy at Rest: Strategic Ratification of the Twenty-First Amendment." *Publius: The Journal of Federalism* 28 (Spring): 81–97.

Schwartzberg, Melissa. 2008. "Ratification Rules and the New (and Old) Constitutional Convention." Paper presented at the Annual Meeting of the American Political Science Association in Boston.

Silversmith, Jol A. 1999. "The 'Missing Thirteenth Amendment': Constitutional Nonsense and Titles of Nobility." *Southern California Interdisciplinary Law Journal* 8 (Spring): 577–611.

Vile, John R. 1993b. *The Theory and Practice of Constitutional Change in America: A Collection of Original Source Materials.* New York: Peter Lang.

Vose, Clement E. 1979. "When District of Columbia Representation Collides with the Constitutional Amendment Institution." *Publius: The Journal of Federalism* 9 (Winter): 105–125.

RATIFICATION OF THE EXISTING U.S. AND/OR FUTURE U.S. CONSTITUTIONS

The Articles of Confederation provided that Congress would propose amendments and that they would have to be unanimously ratified by the state legislatures. This process was so difficult that no amendments were adopted during the duration of the Articles, and the process would have become even more difficult had other states joined. When the delegates gathered at the U.S. Constitutional Convention in Philadelphia, they decided to pursue a new form of government rather than attempting to build on existing foundations. The result was a Congress with substantially greater powers, as well as a government of three coordinate branches (the Articles only had one) that embodied checks and balances that were missing under the Articles.

The state of Rhode Island never sent delegates to the Constitutional Convention, making the prospect of ratification of the new document through existing means quite unlikely indeed; moreover, there was intense opposition to the new Constitution by Anti-Federalists in many states. Not only did delegates to the convention reasonably fear that existing state legislators might be reluctant to give up powers to the new national government, but they also hoped to put the new Constitution on firmer ground than mere legislative ratification. The delegates addressed both concerns by providing in Article VII of the new document that it would go into effect with "the Ratification of the Conventions of nine States." Such conventions were widely believed to embody popular sovereignty, and the contest between Federalists and Anti-Federalists was quite spirited.

New Hampshire became the critical ninth state to ratify on June 21, 1788. But, because of the size and population of Virginia and New York, the fate of the new Union was still not secure until these states joined shortly thereafter. The first Congress under the new system did not meet until March 4, 1789, and the president was not sworn in until April 30, 1789. In *Owings v. Speed* (1820), Chief Justice John Marshall ruled that the Constitution did not become effective until the first Congress met, but two scholars have suggested that some provisions of the new document were self-executing and should be considered to have gone into effect on June 21, 1788, with others going into effect at various subsequent dates (Lawson and Seidman 2001).

Debates over the U.S. Constitution produced *The Federalist Papers,* which are still considered to be among the best sources for understanding that document; Alexander Hamilton, James Madison, and John Jay wrote the essays under the name Publius. Anti-Federalists also produced notable tracts. One of the results of the intense debate surrounding the document was that key Federalists (most notably James Madison) understood the need to adopt a bill of rights to ease public fears about the power of the new central government. Madison subsequently took the lead in the first Congress to proposed 12 amendments, 10 of which became the Bill of Rights. Had there been no process for introducing such amendments, the fate of the new constitution might have been very much at risk.

Were a new constitution to be formulated today, its authors might also seek to bypass existing requirements in Article V for constitutional amendment. If Article V were followed, amendments proposed through the unused Article V convention mechanism would continue to require ratification of three-fourths of the state legislatures or of specially called state conventions (as happened in the case of the Twenty-first Amendment repealing national alcoholic prohibition), but fears continue to linger about what a "runaway" convention might propose and, perhaps, about how it might seek to have its proposals ratified. Given advances in technology and increased clamor for forms of direct democracy like the initiative and referendum, proponents of a new constitution might well seek to have it affirmed either by a majority, or perhaps a supermajority, of the voters. Despite the failure of the current Constitution to specify any such mechanism, a number of scholars like Akhil Reed Amar and Sanford Levinson believe that popular electoral majorities already have the inherent authority both to initiate and ratify amendments in this manner.

See also Amar, Akhil Reed; Articles of Confederation; Bill of Rights; Constitutional Convention of 1787; Constitutional Conventions; Levinson, Sanford; Ratification of Amendments.

For Further Reading:

Flaherty, Martin S. 2002. "The Legacy of Justice John Marshall: John Marshall, *McCulloch v. Maryland,* and 'We the People': Revisions In Need of Revising." *William and Mary Law Review* 43 (March): 1339–1397.

Fritz, Christian G. 2004. "Fallacies of American Constitutionalism." *Rutgers Law Journal* 32 (Summer): 1327–1369.

Gillespie, Michael L., and Michael Lienesch, eds. 1989. *Ratifying the Constitution.* Lawrence: University Press of Kansas.

Gonzalez, Carlos E. 2005. "Representational Structures Through Which We the People Ratify Constitutions: The Troubling Original Understanding of the Constitution's Ratification Clauses." *University of California, Davis Law Review* 38 (June): 1373–1504.

Lawson, Gary, and Guy Seidman. 2001. "When Did the Constitution Become Law?" *Notre Dame Law Review* 77 (November): 1–37.

Utley, Robert L., Jr., and Patricia B. Gray. 1989. *Principles of the Constitutional Order: The Ratification Debates.* Lanham, MD: University Press of America.

RECALL

See Congress, Recall of Members; Judiciary, Removal of Members; Presidency, Vote of No Confidence.

REFERENDUM

See Initiative and Referendum.

REID V. COVERT (1957)

This case set aside the convictions by courts-martial of Clarice Covert and Dorothy Smith, wives of U.S. military personnel stationed overseas who had killed their husbands. The courts-martial had been held under putative authority of executive agreements that had been reached with the nations involved.

Writing for Chief Justice Earl Warren and for Justices William O. Douglas, William Brennan, and himself, Justice Hugo Black ruled that provisions of the Bill of Rights—including Fifth and Sixth Amendment guarantees of grand jury indictment and trial by a petit jury—applied to U.S. citizens abroad. Black argued that "no agreement with a foreign nation can confer power on Congress, or on any other branch of Government, which is free from the restraints of the Constitution" and that allowing agreements with foreign governments to override the Constitution would be to "permit amendment of that document in a manner not sanctioned by Article V" (*Reid* 1957, 16–17).

Although Black denied that his decision conflicted with *Missouri v. Holland* (1920), his opinion helped ease fears that that case had raised. In easing such fears, the *Reid* decision may well have undercut support for the Bricker Amendment, designed to limit the scope of federal treaties.

More recent attention appears to have shifted to whether the United States has ceded some of its sovereignty to international trade organizations, membership in which is sometimes approved by majority vote in both houses of Congress rather than by the two-thirds majority required in the Senate under the Constitution for approval of treaties.

See also Bricker Amendment; *Missouri v. Holland*.

For Further Reading:
Reid v. Covert, 354 U.S. 1 (1957).

RELEVANCE OF CONSTITUTIONAL AMENDMENTS

Although amendments are the constitutionally prescribed means for adding language to the written Constitution, changes in understanding of that document are also brought about through judicial interpretations, through changes in social customs, through the development of extraconstitutional institutions like presidential nominating conventions and political parties (somewhat recognized by the changes the Twelfth Amendment made in the electoral college), and through presidential and congressional practices. Although this has long been known, if not always celebrated, most scholars of the subject have still understood constitutional amendments to be a dynamic part, if not the driving force, in this mix.

By contrast, Davis A. Strauss, a Chicago law professor, has advanced the provocative thesis that constitutional amendments are essentially irrelevant, at least in what he calls "a mature democratic society," like the United States is today (Strauss 2001, 1460). This reservation may be significant in that it essentially allows Strauss to exclude the effect of the Bill of Rights (the first 10 amendments, which were adopted just as the nation was getting established) from his analysis, as well as any effect that the presence of an amending process may have initially had in leading to acceptance of that document. Still, Strauss's thesis is bold, and it certainly poses a challenge to those who consider the process to be important.

Strauss advances four main arguments:

First . . . sometimes matters addressed by the Constitution change even though the text of the Constitution is unchanged. Second, and more dramatically, some constitutional changes occur even though amendments that would have brought about those very changes are explicitly rejected. Third, when amendments are adopted, they often do no more than ratify changes that have already taken place in society without the help of an amendment. The changes produce the amendment, rather than the other way around. Fourth, when amendments are adopted even though society has not changed, the amendments are systematically evaded. They end up having little effect until society catches up with the ambitions of the amendment. (Strauss 2001, 1459)

Strauss acknowledges that amendments serve "certain ancillary functions," among which he lists the role of "establishing 'rules of the road'" by "settling matters that are not themselves controversial but that must be settled clearly, one way or another" (Strauss 2001, 1461). He also believes that amendments serve "the distinct function of suppressing outliers," often turning "all-but-unanimity into unanimity" (*Id.*, 1461).

Professors Brannon Denning and John R. Vile have acknowledged some of the points that Strauss has made, while arguing that he has dramatically overstated his argument. They believe that Strauss has minimized the "settling function" that amendments perform as well as the role of amendments in suppressing outliers—it is important (especially to the women involved) that all states, and not simply 90 percent, allow women to vote. Denning and Vile argue that some changes that have been brought about in the absence of amendments that were not adopted may nonetheless have been hastened by such proposals, if not directly attributable to them. Moreover, even "premature" amendments (like the Fifteenth Amendment, which sought to deny discrimination against voters on the basis of race) may ultimately succeed in a way that they would not have been able to do in the absence of a specific text.

Denning and Vile further argue that amendments serve several discrete functions that Strauss does not adequately appreciate. These include the "corrective function" in remedying constitutional defects that become apparent over time; a "checking function" allowing for checks on U.S. Supreme Court decisions (at least four amendments have overturned such decisions); the function of providing an alternative to violence and thus "domesticating revolution"; the function of "legitimization" of changes that are incorporated into formal amendments; and the function of giving "publicity" to those changes that are so incorporated (Denning and Vile 2002–2003).

Adrian Vermeule has argued that while Strauss has demonstrated that amendments are not "necessary" or "sufficient" conditions for change, he has not shown that they do not "cause" such change (2006, 233). In another article, Yale law professor Reva B. Siegel has argued that Strauss's argument underestimates the role that the movement for women's rights, and the accompanying Nineteenth Amendment prohibiting discrimination in voting on the basis of gender, has had on American constitutional understandings (Siegel 2001).

See also Bill of Rights; Twelfth Amendment; Fifteenth Amendment; Nineteenth Amendment.

For Further Reading:

Denning, Brannon P., and John R. Vile. 2002. "The Relevance of Constitutional Amendments: A Response to David Strauss." *Tulane Law Review* 77 (November): 247–282.

Siegel, Reva B. 2001. "Gender and the Constitution from a Social Movement Perspective." *University of Pennsylvania Law Review* 150 (November): 297–351.

Strauss, David A. 2001. "Commentary: The Irrelevance of Constitutional Amendments." *Harvard Law Review* 114: (March): 1457–1505.

Vermeule, Adrian. 2006. "Constitutional Amendments and the Constitutional Common Law." *The Least Examined Branch: The Role of Legislatures in the Constitutional State.* Bauman, Richard W. and Tsvi Kahana, eds. New York: Cambridge University Press.

RELIGIOUS EQUALITY AMENDMENT

For decades, members of some religious groups have complained that they have been treated unfairly. They believe that, in attempting to enforce the First Amendment's prohibition against an establishment of religion, courts and other governmental agencies have often denied the legitimate free exercise and free speech rights of those with strong religious beliefs (Reed 1995, 1–12; but see Folton 1996).

In *Employment Division v. Smith* (1990), the Supreme Court denied unemployment compensation to state employees who had been fired from their jobs for ingesting peyote as part of their Native American religious practice. In so doing, the Court apparently abandoned the strict scrutiny it had previously extended to laws impinging on free exercise rights in cases like *Sherbert v. Verner* (unemployment compensation for Sabbatharians) and *Wisconsin v. Yoder* (Amish parents who took their children out of school after the eighth grade). Although this decision was blunted by subsequent adoption of the Religious Freedom Restoration Act (Vile 1994a, 61), concerns were renewed with the federal court of appeals decision in *Rosenberger v. Rector and Visitors of the University of Virginia* (1994). This ruling upheld the University of Virginia's decision to deny expenditure of student activity fee funds to an evangelical Christian publication while funding similar publications that did not have such an evangelical orientation. Although the Supreme Court overturned this ruling in 1995 and decided that the university could not deny funding to a group simply because it was religious, concerns remained that the free exercise clause of the First Amendment was not being fully honored. These concerns led a number of individuals to advocate a Religious Equality Amendment (Casey 1995; Goodstein 1995).

In November 1995, two Republicans introduced separate amending resolutions in Congress. Representative Henry Hyde of Illinois proposed in H.J. Res. 121 that

> neither the United states nor any state shall deny benefits to or otherwise discriminate against any private person or group on account of religious expression, belief, or identity; nor shall the prohibition on laws respecting an establishment of religion be construed to require such discrimination.

In contrast to Hyde's proposal, the proposal introduced by Representative Ernest Istook Jr. of Oklahoma (H.J. Res. 127) specifically mentioned prayer in the public schools:

> To secure the people's right to acknowledge God according to the dictates of conscience: Nothing in this Constitution shall prohibit the acknowledgements of the religious heritage, beliefs, or traditions of the people, or prohibit student-sponsored prayer in public schools. Neither the United States nor any State shall compose any official prayer or compel joining in prayer, or discriminate against religious expression or belief.

Although Istook's proposal specifically permits student-sponsored prayer in schools, advocates of a religious equality amendment generally note that it differs from earlier proposals to permit public prayer in schools or to acknowledge God in the Constitution. One advocate specifically asserts that the proposal "is not a 'school prayer' amendment (as that term is commonly understood) because it does not permit state-sponsored teacher-led prayer." He further notes, however, that "if a school board sets aside a time for a student message at a graduation ceremony, the student speaker would have the right to say a prayer under the proposed amendment." Moreover, although the amendment would not permit "special funding of religious schools and social service providers," under such an amendment, "the Constitution would no longer prohibit religious entities from participating in neutrally available government funding programs" including a school voucher system (Baylor 1995, 4–5).

The Religious Equality Amendment was the first of 10 proposals included in the Christian Coalition's Contract with the American Family—a takeoff of the earlier Republican Contract with America (Reed 1995, 1–12).

In a related vein, in 1995 Republican Senator Thad Cochrane of Mississippi introduced an amendment prohibiting the state or national governments from abridging the free exercise of religion and granting Congress power to enforce this amendment. Cochrane noted on the Senate floor that the First Amendment already contained a free exercise clause, but he feared that the adoption of the Religious Freedom Restoration Act of 1993 (RFRA) might have shifted the protection of religious liberty from the Constitution, where it had been secure, to Congress, where it might be more vulnerable (Cochrane 1994, S6867).

The Court's decision in *City of Boerne v. Flores* (1997), that the Religious Freedom Restoration Act was an unconstitutional attempt by

Congress to interpret (rather than simply to enforce) the provisions of the Fourteenth Amendment, stimulated renewed calls for a constitutional amendment to provide broader protection for religious liberty. In the meantime, Congress adopted the Religious Land Use and Institutionalized Persons Act (RLUIPA) of 2000, providing more partial coverage than the earlier Religious Freedom Restoration Act by limiting its effect to cases that substantially affect interstate commerce or cases arising from federal programs (Farris 1999, 703). The Court has upheld provisions of this act that applied to prisoners in *Cutter v. Wilkinson* (2005). State courts are also free to interpret religious freedoms more broadly under their state constitutions than the U.S. Supreme Court currently does under the First Amendment.

See also *Boerne, City of v. Flores;* Christian Amendment; Prayer in Public Schools.

For Further Reading:

Baylor, Gregory S. 1995. "The Religious Equality Amendment." Christian Legal Society Quarterly 16 (Summer): 4–5.

Casey, Samuel B. 1995. "Religious Freedom Makes Good Neighbors." *Christian Legal Society Quarterly* 16 (Summer): 3.

Cochrane, Thad. 1994. "Constitutional Amendment Restoring the Right to the Free Exercise of Religion." *Congressional Record,* U.S. Senate, 14 June, 103rd Cong., 2d sess., 1994, Vol. 140, pt. 9.

Farris, Michael P. 1999. "Only a Constitutional Amendment Can Guarantee Religious Freedom for All." *Cardozo Law Review* 21 (December): 689–706.

Folton, Richard T. 1996. "Horror Stories." *Liberty* (March–April): 6–8.

Goodstein, Laurie. 1995. "Religious Freedom Amendment Passed." *Washington Post* (June 9): A12.

Greenawalt, Kent. 1998a. "Introduction: Should the Religion Clauses of the Constitution Be Amended?" *Loyola of Los Angeles Law Review* 32 (November): 9–25.

Reed, Ralph. 1995. *Contract with the American Family: A Bold Plan by Christian Coalition to Strengthen the Family and Restore Common-Sense Values.* Nashville, TN: Moorings.

"Symposium: A Religious Equality Amendment?" 1996. *Brigham Young University Law Review* 561–688.

Vile, John R. 1994a. *Constitutional Change in the United States: A Comparative Study of the Role of Constitutional Amendments, Judicial Interpretations, and Legislative and Executive Actions.* Westport, CT: Praeger.

REPRODUCTIVE RIGHTS

Since the Supreme Court's decision in *Roe v. Wade* (1973), American women have had the legal right to obtain abortions, especially during the first two trimesters of pregnancy. Abortion opponents have introduced numerous calls for a right-to-life amendment to overturn this decision. Although such an amendment has not been adopted, in cases such as *Webster v. Reproductive Health Services* (1989) and *Planned Parenthood of Southeastern Pennsylvania v. Casey* (1992), the Supreme Court has permitted states to impose greater restrictions on this procedure.

Perhaps with a view to such restrictions, in April 1993, Democratic Representative Patsy Mink of Hawaii introduced an amendment to protect the rights of individuals "to have full control over reproductive decisions affecting their own bodies" (H.J. Res. 176). If the Supreme Court ever reversed its decision in *Roe v. Wade,* there might be considerable support for such an amendment.

See also Abortion; Right to Life; *Roe v. Wade.*

For Further Reading:

Garrow, David J. 1994. *Liberty and Sexuality: The Right to Privacy and the Making of* Roe v. Wade. New York: Macmillan.

RESCISSION OF RATIFICATION OF PENDING AMENDMENTS

The Constitution is silent as to whether states can rescind the ratification of pending amendments. Congress has yet to adopt legislation to deal with the subject, although legislation proposed by

North Carolina Democratic senator Sam Ervin and Utah Republican senator Orrin Hatch relative to constitutional conventions would have accepted the legitimacy of such rescissions.

In dealing with ratification of the Fourteenth Amendment, Congress refused to accept the legitimacy of two attempted rescissions, but the precedent is a muddy one, and it is not clear whether the congressional judgment was actually essential to the amendment's ratification (Vile 1990, 112). Moreover, when the issue of rescissions reemerged during the controversy over the Equal Rights Amendment, a U.S. district court ruled in *Idaho v. Freeman* (1981) that such rescissions are permissible. This precedent is complicated, however, by the fact that Congress had not only extended the original ratification deadline but had done so by simple majority vote. Also, the decision was eventually mooted when the amendment failed to receive the necessary number of state ratifications.

One argument for permitting states to rescind ratification of pending amendments is an argument from balance, because states have been permitted to ratify amendments that they have previously rejected (Grinnell 1959, 1164). The doctrine of contemporary consensus that the Supreme Court articulated in *Dillon v. Gloss* (1921) also suggests that states should not be included in a consensus they no longer share. The ability to rescind also guards against hasty change.

Arguments against rescission include the value of finality (Orfield 1942, 70). Some also fear that state legislators might treat ratification less seriously if they thought that the decision was not final (Freedman and Naughton 1978, 11). Also, the process of amendment is arguably difficult enough without allowing states additional leeway in rejecting amendments.

In the absence of clear precedents, Congress is likely to resolve this issue on a case-by-case basis. Although this is consistent with the Supreme Court's decision in *Coleman v. Miller* (1939) that amending issues are "political questions," such discretion continues the uncertainty about a matter that might benefit from preordained rules (Dellinger 1983, 395–396).

See also *Dillon v. Gloss;* Equal Rights Amendment; Fourteenth Amendment; *Idaho v. Freeman;* Ratification of Amendments.

For Further Reading:

Baker, A. Diane. 1979. "ERA: The Effect of Extending the Time for Ratification on Attempts to Rescind Prior Ratifications." *Emory Law Journal* 28: 71–110.

Burke, Yvonne B. 1976. "Validity of Attempts to Rescind Ratification of the Equal Rights Amendment." *University of Los Angeles Law Review* 8: 1–22.

Dellinger, Walter. 1983. "The Legitimacy of Constitutional Change: Rethinking the Amending Process." *Harvard Law Review* 97 (December): 380–432.

Freedman, Samuel S., and Pamela J. Naughton. 1978. *ERA: May a State Change Its Vote?* Detroit, MI: Wayne State University Press.

Ginsburg, Ruth B. 1969. "Ratification of the Equal Rights Amendment: A Question of Time." *Texas Law Review* 57: 919–945.

Grinnell, Frank W. 1959. "Petitioning Congress for a Convention: Cannot a State Change Its Mind?" *American Bar Association Journal* 45: 1164–1165.

Kanowitz, Leo, and Marilyn Klinger. 1978. "Can a State Rescind Its Equal Rights Amendment Ratification: Who Decides and How?" *Hastings Law Journal* 28 (March): 969–1009.

Orfield, Lester B. 1942. *The Amending of the Federal Constitution.* Ann Arbor, MI: University of Michigan Press.

Planell, Raymond M. 1974. "The Equal Rights Amendment: Will States Be Allowed to Change Their Minds?" *Notre Dame Lawyer* 49 (February): 657–670.

Vierra, Norman. 1981. "The Equal Rights Amendment: Rescission, Extension and Justiciability." *Southern Illinois Law Journal* 1981: 1–29.

Vile, John R. 1990. "Permitting States to Rescind Ratifications of Pending Amendments to the U.S. Constitution." *Publius: The Journal of Federalism* 20 (Spring): 109–122.

RESPONSIBILITIES

See Bill of Responsibilities.

REVENUE SHARING

In the early 1960s, the national government appeared to have a much stronger and fairer revenue base than did the states. Between 1965 and 1971, 14 states petitioned Congress to call a constitutional convention to amend the Constitution to provide for federal revenue sharing.

In contrast to more traditional categorical grant-in-aid programs and block grants, revenue sharing was designed to give maximum leeway to state funding decisions. Georgia Republican representative Standish Thompson introduced amendments providing for revenue sharing in 1967 and 1969. Under his plan, the national government would eventually have provided 10 percent of the money it collected through income taxes to the states, based on their populations and with no strings other than an antidiscrimination provision.

Although little progress was made on proposed amendments, in 1972 the Nixon administration successfully launched revenue sharing for state and local governments. State governments were dropped from the program in 1980, and the Reagan administration terminated the entire program—under which Congress had funneled some $85 billion to states and localities—in 1986 (Harrigan 1994, 41).

See also Constitutional Conventions.

For Further Reading:

Harrigan, John J. 1994. *Politics and Policy in States and Communities.* 5th ed. New York: Harper-Collins College Publishers.

REVERENCE FOR THE CONSTITUTION

Members of Congress have introduced more than 11,700 proposals (most redundant) to amend the U.S. Constitution, but it has only been successfully amended 27 times. In more than 220 years, neither has it been completely revised nor has a sufficient majority of states called on Congress to call a new convention to do so. Moreover, there have been two fairly long periods in American history—one from 1804 through 1865 and the second from 1870 through 1913—when no amendments were added to the document.

James Madison defended the amending mechanisms as guarding "equally against that extreme facility, which would render the Constitution too mutable; and that extreme difficulty, which might perpetuate its discovered faults" (Hamilton et al. 1961, 278). However, by comparison to mechanisms in other nations and in the states, the processes for formal change of the Constitution that Article V outlines are fairly onerous (Lutz 1994). The difficulty of these procedures lends stability to the document.

An additional obstacle to constitutional amendment is the feeling of reverence, or veneration, that the existing written document often generates. The reputations and achievements of many of its authors (including George Washington and Benjamin Franklin) as well as its relatively early successes in alleviating many of the more obvious problems under the Articles of Confederation have contributed to the document's permanence. These factors have been further enhanced by the age of the document and remain as continuing barriers to major or precipitous changes.

In the United States, the written Constitution arguably plays the role in unifying the nation that monarchs play in other nations, and critics of existing policy, for example, gun control, often take the position that it is not the Constitution, or, in the case of gun control, the Second Amendment, that needs amending so much as current misunderstandings of that document. To the extent that Christians, Jews, Muslims, and other groups who guide their lives by a set of written scriptures associate the Constitution with such sacred scripture, they find it sacrilegious to add to or alter it (see Levinson 1990b). A historian who has examined the role of the U.S. Constitution in U.S. history has observed that it has often been an item of near worship and that early schoolbooks often "stated that the Constitution had been divinely inspired" (Kammen 1987, 3).

The framers' decision to include a formal amending process within the document and to add the Bill of Rights indicate that they did not regard the document as perfect when written. They recognized that it embodied many compromises and that alterations would be required as circumstances changed. They did, however, reject proposals to require periodic review, and

Madison argued in *Federalist No. 49* that veneration for the Constitution would help prevent precipitious change.

Perhaps partly as a result, prior to the Civil War the Constitution often seemed to assume so much of the character of a sacred text and the founders the character of demigods that reformers were reluctant to seek constitutional changes, even when it was clear that they were needed (Vorenberg 2001, 192–193); up until late 1863, many of the individuals advocating constitutional reforms in the United States were "radical, foreign-born reformers who were not burdened by the illusion that amending the Constitution necessarily jeopardized American democracy" (*Id.,* 14). By contrast, some abolitionists, like William Lloyd Garrison, clearly blamed the Constitution, calling it a "Covenant with Death, an agreement with Hell" (Pease and Pease 1965, lx). Although this was clearly a minority view, to some extent the outbreak of the Civil War helped individuals to see that the framers and their solutions to the nation's problems had been imperfect.

Many of today's fears of a possible "runaway" convention stem from concerns that excessive "tinkering" could destroy the existing Constitution. To some extent the Bill of Rights has assumed a quasi-constitutional status of its own, with opponents of amendments prohibiting flag desecration or other alterations in rights guaranteed in the first 10 amendments often citing the fact that no amendments (the Eighteenth Amendment providing for national alcoholic prohibition, which has since been repealed, is a possible exception) have ever restricted existing rights.

Reverence for the existing Constitution has not, of course, prevented many alterations in constitutional understandings initiated through judicial interpretations and through congressional and presidential practices. Although changes in the constitutional text do not always prove to be immediately effective (the Fifteenth Amendment, prohibiting discrimination in voting on the basis of race, was largely moribund for almost a hundred years), changes effected through constitutional interpretation, like broader interpretations of congressional powers that followed Franklin D. Roosevelt's court-packing plan, could prove to be even less permanent. However much the Con-

stitution continues to be venerated, ultimately the amending process continues to lie "at the very center of American constitutionalism" (Kyvig 1996a, xvii).

See also Bill of Rights; Constitutional Conventions; Council of Censors; Fifteenth Amendment; Garrison, William Lloyd; Jefferson, Thomas; Lieber, Francis; Madison, James; Rigid Constitution.

For Further Reading:

Godkin, E. L. 1864. "The Constitution and Its Defects." *North American Review* 99 (July): 117–143.

Greenawalt, Kent. 1998b. "Symposium: Reflections of *City of Boerne v. Flores:* Why Now Is Not the Time for Constitutional Amendment: The Limited Reach of *City of Boerne v. Flores.*" *William & Mary Law Review* 39 (February): 689–698.

Hamilton, Alexander, James Madison, and John Jay. 1787–1788. *The Federalist Papers.* Reprint, New York: New American Library, 1961.

Kammen, Michael. 1987. *A Machine That Would Go of Itself: The Constitution in American Culture.* New York: Alfred A. Knopf.

Kyvig, David E. 1996a. *Explicit and Authentic Acts: Amending the Constitution, 1776–1995.* Lawrence: University Press of Kansas.

Levinson, Sanford. 1990b. "'Veneration' and Constitutional Change: James Madison Confronts the Possibility of Constitutional Amendment." *Texas Tech Law Review* 21: 2443–2461.

Lutz, Donald S. 1994. "Toward a Theory of Constitutional Amendment." *American Political Science Review* 88 (June): 355–370.

Pease, William H., and June H. Pease, eds. 1965. *The Antislavery Argument.* Indianapolis, IN: Bobbs-Merrill.

Vorenberg, Michael. 2001. *Final Freedom: The Civil War, the Abolition of Slavery, and the Thirteenth Amendment.* Cambridge, UK: Cambridge University Press.

REYNOLDS, EUSTACE

In 1915, Eustace Reynolds of New York published a modified constitution for consideration. Aside from the fact that a number of his ideas were similar to those advocated by William Jennings Bryan, who was then secretary of state (Boyd 1992, 129), and that Reynolds promised to use any money from reprints of his constitution for the cause of international peace (Reynolds 1915, 18), no biographical information is available. Most of Reynolds's plan is simply a reprint of the existing Constitution with proposed changes highlighted in bold type. Although most changes involved the conduct of foreign affairs, some other alterations were also proposed.

"Sex qualifications" for voting were to be eliminated (as they soon would be in the Nineteenth Amendment), but the voting age was to be raised to 25 and limited to those who could read and write (Reynolds 1915, 1–2). The vice president, who would serve with the president in a single six-year term, was assigned to represent the United States in a council of other viceroys and vice presidents. With approval of another body consisting of "undersecretaries of state and deputy-ministers for foreign affairs," this council would have power to "make and promulgate decrees in all matters affecting international intercourse, commerce, affairs, or relations"; to "regulate commerce with foreign nations"; and to punish "offenses against the law of nations" (*Id.,* 2–3). Such regulations would be recognized in Article VI as the supreme law of the land (*Id.,* 13). Congress would, in turn, lose its power to "enter into any agreement or contract with another state, or with a foreign power, to engage in war," except in cases of "invasion" or "imminent danger" (*Id.,* 7).

Reynolds favored altering the judicial power to require the chief justice to appoint another Supreme Court justice to sit en banc with members of judiciaries from other nations "and pass upon international questions as they come properly before the court for adjudication" (Reynolds 1915, 10–11). This international court would have appellate jurisdiction in cases involving controversies between American states or their citizens and foreign citizens, and it would have original jurisdiction when the United States and foreign governments were involved. United States courts would be given explicit authority to disregard unconstitutional laws and decrees.

Reynolds would have maintained the guarantees in the Bill of Rights, but he favored allowing a prosecutor to comment, and a jury to weigh this fact, when a defendant chose to exercise the Fifth Amendment right against self-incrimination. He would also have restricted the national government's right to collect income tax on state securities.

See also Nineteenth Amendment.

For Further Reading:

Boyd, Steven R., ed. 1992. *Alternative Constitutions for the United States: A Documentary History.* Westport, CT: Greenwood Press.

Reynolds, Eustace. 1915. *A New Constitution: A Suggested Form of Modified Constitution.* New York: Nation Press.

REYNOLDS V. SIMS (1964)

This case was one of the most important and controversial cases that the Warren Court decided. It established that the equal protection clause of the Fourteenth Amendment required that both houses of a state legislature—in this case, Alabama's—need to be apportioned according to the "one person, one vote" standard.

In so ruling, Chief Justice Earl Warren extended the earlier decision in *Baker v. Carr* (1962), which had established that state legislative apportionment schemes were justiciable under the equal protection clause but had not specified the standard to be utilized. Over the objections of dissenting Justice John Marshall Harlan that the Court was misinterpreting the Fourteenth Amendment, Warren argued that "the right of suffrage can be denied by a debasement or dilution of the weight of a citizen's vote just as effectively as by wholly prohibiting the free exercise of the franchise" (*Reynolds* 1964, 555).

Together, *Baker v. Carr* and *Reynolds v. Sims* provoked numerous calls for an amendment to give states greater leeway. Illinois Republican senator Everett Dirksen led the call for a constitutional convention on the subject. These efforts failed, and both decisions remain in effect. As the Court indicated in the *Reynolds* case, however (1964, 578), it is willing to accept somewhat greater population disparities among state legislative districts than it permits with respect to state-drawn congressional districts.

See also *Baker v. Carr;* Dirksen, Everett; Fourteenth Amendments; States, Legislative Apportionment.

For Further Reading:
Reynolds v. Sims, 377 U.S. 533 (1964).

RHODE ISLAND V. PALMER

See *National Prohibition Cases.*

RICE, ISAAC L. (1850–1915)

Isaac Rice was born in Bavaria and educated at Columbia Law School, where he stayed an additional six years to study and teach before going into the practice of law (Malone 1961, 3:541). In 1884 Rice published an article in which he advocated calling a constitutional convention to address a number of problems, most of which he attributed to the U.S. system of separation of powers and checks and balances. Rice believed that this system was "both weak and irresponsible" (Rice 1884, 534) and that it led to political corruption. In its place, he hoped to establish a parliamentary system (Vile 1991c, 37–38).

Rice proposed three major reforms. The first was to expand the powers of Congress to enable it "to settle all questions of national concern" (Rice 1884, 540). Specifically, he wanted to institute "a uniform code of commerce for the whole country" so that "powerful combinations" would be unable to hide behind artificial state boundaries (Id.). Second, Rice proposed ending the separation of legislative and executive powers. In his words, "the executive must be entitled to propose laws necessary for the preservation of the public welfare, and the legislative must be enabled to control the execution of all laws passed" (Id.). As in a parliamentary system, Rice wanted the heads of executive agencies to serve in Congress; although he did not use the term, he also appears to have contemplated the creation of a prime minister. Third, Rice proposed making the legislature "the sole and responsible judge of the constitutionality of its acts," leaving the judiciary to "interpret" congressional will rather than "to control it" (Id.).

See also Constitutional Conventions: Parliamentary Systems.

For Further Reading:
Malone, Dumas, ed. 1961. *Dictionary of American Biography.* 10 vols. New York: Charles Scribner's Sons.

Rice, Isaac. 1884. "Work for a Constitutional Convention." *Century Magazine* 28 (August): 534–540.

Vile, John R. 1991c. *Rewriting the United States Constitution: An Examination of Proposals from Reconstruction to the Present.* New York: Praeger.

RIGHT TO LIFE

Few issues have proved to be more emotionally wrenching or politically divisive than the issue of abortion. From the time shortly after *Roe v. Wade* was first argued in 1971 to the present, members of Congress have introduced more than 325 proposals to restrict abortions, and at least 19 states have called for a constitutional convention to address this issue. The fact that most such proposals have been made by those opposed to abortion does not indicate that congressional opinion on the subject is uniform but that, throughout this period, those who accept a woman's right to choose an abortion have had the weight of judicial precedents on their side and thus had less need to introduce such amendments.

Background to *Roe v. Wade*
Prior to 1973, the issue of abortion was largely a state matter. Most states had adopted laws

restricting abortions in the second half of the 19th century, at which time abortions were often medically dangerous for women. By 1972, 19 states had liberalized their laws to permit therapeutic abortions, but this meant that, in most states, such procedures were still illegal (Keynes with Miller 1989, 249).

In 1965, the Supreme Court ruled in *Griswold v. Connecticut* that there was a constitutional right to privacy grounded in various penumbras of the Bill of Rights and the Fourteenth Amendment. This decision, in turn, served as the basis for the Court's decision in *Roe v. Wade* (1973), which overturned a Texas abortion law. Written by Justice Harry Blackmun for a 7-to-2 majority of the Court, the opinion stated that the constitutional right to privacy was sufficient to permit a woman to choose to have an abortion without state interference, at least through the first two trimesters (the first six months) of pregnancy. Thereafter, a state could legislate on behalf of the fetus, except in cases in which the life or health of the mother was threatened (Garrow 1994).

Reactions to *Roe v. Wade*

Perhaps because *Roe v. Wade* was thrust so suddenly into the public consciousness (Glendon 1987), it engendered strong responses from both supporters and opponents. Undoubtedly, the decision galvanized public opinion in a way that would not have occurred in the face of state liberalization of abortion laws and the ever-increasing number of legal abortions that were being performed in the years leading up to the decision (Rosenberg 1991, 178–180). Subsequent developments have proceeded on a number of different fronts.

Legislatively, opponents of abortion have followed four distinct strategies: (1) adopting amendments; (2) limiting judicial jurisdiction over the subject of abortion; (3) restricting abortion funding; and (4) passing other laws, including those defining the moment that human life begins as being before birth, requiring informed consent prior to an abortion, establishing waiting periods, regulating clinics, or otherwise restricting abortion access without outlawing it completely (Keynes with Miller 1989, 247).

Such strategies are sometimes pursued independently and sometimes in tandem.

The idea of restricting judicial jurisdiction has also been advocated by opponents of prayer in school and school busing. Republican Representative Philip Crane of Illinois introduced such a proposal relative to abortion in 1979. It provided that:

> [T]he Supreme Court shall not have jurisdiction to review, by appeal, writs of certiorari, or otherwise, any case arising out of any State statute, ordinance, rule, regulation or any part thereof, or arising out of any Act interpreting, applying, or enforcing a State statute, ordinance, rule or regulation, which relates to abortion. The district courts shall not have jurisdiction of any case or question which the Supreme Court does not have jurisdiction to review. (Keynes with Miller 1989, 292)

Much of the controversy over attempts to restrict abortion funding have focused on the Hyde amendment, named after its sponsor, Republican Representative Henry Hyde of Illinois. The Supreme Court upheld this law, which limits federal funding for nontherapeutic abortions, in *Harris v. McRae* (1980). It decided that the right to an abortion did not include the right to government funding for such an abortion. In *Beal v. Doe* (1977), the Court had previously decided that states did not have to provide such funding either.

Judicial Responses to Legislation

The Supreme Court's reactions to other legislative attempts to regulate abortions have arguably zigged and zagged with the mood of the nation, the nature of the specific controversy, and the individuals who have occupied the judiciary. For example, the Court struck down laws that require spousal consent for abortions or that absolutely mandate parental consent for minors to obtain abortions. It has been more sympathetic, however, to laws providing for parental consent when such laws permit some form of judicial bypass. In *Webster v. Reproductive Health Services* (1989) and in

Planned Parenthood of Southeastern Pennsylvania v. Casey (1992), the Court accepted various other state-imposed restrictions on abortion. The latter case is especially significant; the majority, although arguing that such restrictions should not impose an "undue burden" on a woman's right to choose an abortion, appeared largely to scuttle the trimester analysis that was a significant part of the Court's decision in *Roe v. Wade.* In a decision arguably consistent with the trimester analysis, in *Gonzales v. Carhart,* 550 U.S. 124 (2007), the Supreme Court upheld a 2003 congressional law banning partial-birth abortion.

Amendments Designed to Overturn
Roe v. Wade

Amendments on abortion have been divided into four categories:

> Those amendments [that] would (1) restore the states' authority to restore the status quo ante, (2) authorize Congress and the states to protect human life at every stage of biological development, (3) prohibit Congress and the states from interfering with human life at every stage of development, or (4) define the fetus as a person within the meaning of the Fifth and Fourteenth amendments' due process clauses and extend due process rights to the unborn child. (Keynes with Miller 1989, 280)

North Carolina Republican senator Jesse Helms unsuccessfully pushed for legislation in 1982 that would accomplish the last of these four objectives. The law was based on the premise that, since the Court had stated in *Roe v. Wade* that it did not know when human life began, it might defer to congressional judgments and congressional enforcement powers under Section 5 of the Fourteenth Amendment.

At times, abortion opponents have been split between those who want to use the amending process to restrict or prohibit abortion throughout the nation and those who are willing to settle for returning this matter to the states. In 1981, Utah Republican senator Orrin Hatch sponsored legislation to give both Congress and the states con-

current authority to restrict abortions. The Senate subsequently voted 49 to 50 against a substitute amendment offered by Missouri Democratic senator Thomas Eagleton that provided simply that "a right to abortion is not secured by the Constitution." Most recent proposals to restrict abortion have mandated exceptions in cases when a woman's life is at stake. Rather than focusing on a constitutional amendment, the Christian Coalition's Contract with the American Family advocates legislation protecting states that do not choose to fund abortion, limiting late-term abortions, and eliminating federal funding of groups that support abortion (Reed 1995, 63–84).

Other Consequences of *Roe v. Wade*

The abortion controversy has been a major bone of contention in a number of congressional confirmation hearings, including the unsuccessful confirmations of Judge Robert Bork (who was thought to be unsympathetic to a constitutional right to privacy) to the Supreme Court in the Reagan administration, and of Dr. Henry Foster (who had performed abortions) to be surgeon general in the Clinton administration. Presidents have also used executive orders to permit or restrict fetal tissue research and abortion counseling (Vile 1994a, 58). Although more than 30 years have elapsed since the Court's historic attempt to resolve the abortion issue in *Roe v. Wade,* emotional debates continue in Congress and elsewhere (Fraley 1995).

See also Abortion; Privacy, Right to; Reproductive Rights; *Roe v. Wade.*

For Further Reading:

Fraley, Colette. 1995. "House Opponents Savor Gains; Senate Outlook Is Unclear." *Congressional Quarterly Weekly Report* 53 (July 29): 2276–2277.

Garrow, David J. 1994. *Liberty and Sexuality: The Right to Privacy and the Making of* Roe v. Wade. New York: Macmillan.

Glendon, Mary A. 1987. *Abortion and Divorce in Western Law.* Cambridge, MA: Harvard University Press.

Keynes, Edward, with Randall K. Miller. 1989. *The Court vs. Congress: Prayer, Busing, and Abortion.* Durham, NC: Duke University Press.

Lugosi, Charles I. 2005. "Respecting Human Life in 21st Century America: A Moral Perspective to Extend Civil Rights to the Unborn from Creation Until Death." *Issues in Law & Medicine* 20 (Spring): 211–258.

O'Connor, Karen. 1996. *No Neutral Ground? Abortion Politics in an Age of Absolutes.* Boulder, CO: Westview.

Rosenberg, Gerald N. 1991. *The Hollow Hope: Can Courts Bring about Social Change?* Chicago: University of Chicago Press.

RIGHT TO WORK

A major piece of legislation that covers U.S. labor relations is the Taft-Hartley Act of 1947. This law permits states to adopt a closed, or union, shop requiring all workers to belong to unions that a majority has selected (Tomlins 1985, 282–316). It also permits states to adopt open shops, or right-to-work laws, allowing individuals to choose whether to belong to such unions. Union advocates argue that the open shop is unfair because it allows nonmembers to benefit from contract negotiations made by an organization to which they did not contribute. Some civil libertarians respond that a closed shop violates individual First Amendment freedom of association.

In the years immediately prior to the Taft-Hartley Act, members of Congress proposed a number of amendments to guarantee an open shop. The most persistent supporter of such an amendment was Democratic Representative Wilbert O'Daniel of Texas. In July 1955, Indiana Representative William Jenner introduced another resolution to guarantee the rights of workers for hire "to receive their earnings in full"; Jenner probably thereby intended also to prohibit a union shop under which nonunion workers must pay dues to the union.

Representative Jesse Jackson Jr. has recently proposed a "Full-Employment Amendment" to the U.S. Constitution. Although he criticizes the baneful influence of "right to work" laws, his specific proposal, which is also designed to guarantee "equal pay for equal work" and a decent minimum wage, does not appear specifically to abolish such laws. It does, however, provide that "every citizen who works has the right to form and join trade unions for the protection of their interests" (Jackson with Watkins 2001, 252).

See also First Amendment; Jackson, Jesse L., Jr.

For Further Reading:

Jackson, Jesse L., Jr., with Frank E. Watkins. 2001. *A More Perfect Union: Advancing New American Rights.* New York: Welcome Rain Publishers.

Tomlins, Christopher L. 1985. *The State and the Unions: Labor Relations, Law, and the Organized Labor Movement in America, 1880–1960.* Cambridge, UK: Cambridge University Press.

RIGID CONSTITUTION

In his acclaimed book on American politics (1906, 1:370), as well as in an essay (1905), Lord James Bryce of England developed a distinction between flexible and rigid constitutions. This distinction was a frequent point of reference in the early years of the 20th century and a basis for many of the criticisms of the amending process that were made by reformers of the Progressive Era.

Bryce offered his classification as an alternative to early distinctions between written and unwritten constitutions. Like those earlier schemes, however, Bryce's distinguished between constitutions that had developed by customs and usages, like that of Great Britain, and constitutions that were considered to be paramount law unchangeable by ordinary legislative means, like the United States'.

Although Bryce noted that rigid constitutions "mark a comparatively advanced stage in political development, when the idea of separating fundamental laws from other laws has grown familiar, and when considerable experience in the business of government and in political affairs generally has been accumulated" (Bryce 1905, 46), the designation of such a constitution as "rigid" may not have been an altogether impartial designation (Vile 1992, 138). At one point likening a rigid constitution to an iron bridge, Bryce noted that "the fact that it is very strong and all knit tightly into one fabric, while enabling it to stand firm under small oscillations or disturbances, may aggravate small ones" (Bryce 1905, 68), and he cited the U.S. Civil War as an example. Moreover, writing in the time between the post–Civil War amendments and the Progressive Era amendments, Bryce identified the U.S. Constitution as "the most difficult to change" (Bryce 1905, 61).

Today, the older distinction between written and unwritten constitutions is more common than Bryce's distinction between flexible and rigid constitutions. One writer has suggested a classification of constitutions into those formulated by a single lawgiver, those based on immemorial customs and usages, and those formulated by a constitutional convention (Vile 1993c). Another author notes that constitutions vary in rigidity according to "the number of political institutions that are legally required to participate in the amending process," "the size of the majorities that are needed to approve an amendment," and "whether the participation of the people is required" either directly or indirectly (FerreresComella 2000, 46–47). This same author believes that moderate, albeit not absolute, rigidity is an appropriate means of protecting fundamental rights within political systems that utilize judicial review.

See also Parliamentary Systems; Progressive Era.

For Further Reading:

Bryce, James. 1906. *The American Commonwealth.* 3d ed., 2 vols. New York: Macmillan.

———. 1905. "Flexible and Rigid Constitutions." In *Constitutions.* Germany: Scientia Verlag Aalen. Reprint of New York and London edition, 1980.

FerreresComella, Victor. 2000. "A Defense of Constitutional Rigidity." In *Analysis and Right.* Paul Comanducci and Riccardo Guastini, eds. Turin, Italy: G. Giappichelli Publisher.

Vile, John R. 1993c. "Three Kinds of Constitutional Founding and Change: The Convention Model and Its Alternatives." *Political Research Quarterly* 46: 881–895.

———. 1992. *The Constitutional Amending Process in American Political Thought.* New York: Praeger.

ROBINSON, DONALD L. (1936–)

Donald Robinson, a professor of political science at Smith College, has been closely associated with the Committee on the Constitutional System (CCS). Robinson has published two books designed to elicit discussion about reforms considered and proposed by this committee (Robinson 1985, 1989; for discussion, see Vile 1991c, 129–131).

In an article reflecting his own views, Robinson advocated three constitutional reforms: lengthening the terms of members of the House of Representatives to four years and those of senators to eight, allowing members of Congress to head executive agencies, and allowing the president and one-third of both houses of Congress or a majority of either house to call an election (Robinson 1987).

For Further Reading:

Robinson, Donald. 1989. *Government for the Third American Century.* Boulder, CO: Westview Press.

———. 1985. *Reforming American Government: The Bicentennial Papers of the Committee on the Constitutional System.* Boulder, CO: Westview Press.

Vile, John R. 1991c. *Rewriting the United States Constitution: An Examination of Proposals from Reconstruction to the Present.* New York: Praeger.

ROE V. WADE (1973)

Roe v. Wade is one of the most controversial and far-reaching decisions of the 20th century, and it stimulated numerous efforts to adopt a "right to life" amendment. In *Roe,* a 7-to-2 majority of the Supreme Court, led by Justice Harry Blackmun, struck down state abortion laws for the first time. The Court based its decision on the constitutional right of privacy, which it had recognized in *Griswold v. Connecticut* (1965) and other cases.

Blackmun argued that most U.S. abortion laws had been enacted in the second half of the 19th century. He traced the origins of such laws to three causes: the desire to discourage illicit sexual activity, protect women's health, and guard prenatal life. In this case, the state did not assert the first interest. Blackmun further found that the state's interest in prohibiting abortion to protect women's health was not as pressing as it had been before the discovery of antiseptics, when abortion was a far riskier procedure. As to the protection of prenatal life, Blackmun argued that no consensus had emerged as to when human life begins. However, the common law generally did not punish abortions that were performed prior to "quickening," and even then, the offense was not generally regarded as murder.

In an attempt to balance the state's concern with the potential life of the fetus and the health of the mother, Blackmun formulated different rules for each of the three trimesters of pregnancy. During the first, the decision of the woman and her doctor was to be decisive. In the second trimester, the state could establish requirements as to the licensing and qualifications of doctors, types of facilities, and the like, which were designed to ensure that the abortion procedure was safe for the woman. In the third trimester, the outset of which generally marked the period of "viability" where a fetus could survive outside its mother's womb, Blackmun said that the state could pass laws protecting the fetus. He made an exception, however, when abortion might be "necessary to preserve the life or health of the mother" (*Roe* 1973, 164).

In addition to stimulating calls for an amendment, *Roe v. Wade* has stirred considerable controversy. The Supreme Court has subsequently faced numerous issues related to its first decision. Prominent cases have included *Harris v. McRae* (1980), upholding the constitutionality of the Hyde amendment, which prohibits federal funding of nontherapeutic abortions; *Webster v. Reproductive Health Services* (1989), upholding a number of restrictions imposed by the state of Missouri; and *Planned Parenthood of Southeastern Pennsylvania v. Casey* (1992), upholding several state-imposed restrictions on abortion—including a twenty-four-hour waiting period and a requirement for a parent's or judge's consent for a minor to obtain an abortion—that it claimed were not substantial enough to impose an "undue burden." In the *Planned Parenthood* opinion written by Justices Sandra Day O'Connor, Anthony Kennedy, and David Souter, the Court professed to be upholding the central holding of *Roe* even while rejecting much of its rigid trimester analysis.

See also *Griswold v. Connecticut;* Privacy; Right to Life.

For Further Reading:

Garrow, David J. 1994. *Liberty and Sexuality: The Right to Privacy and the Making of* Roe v. Wade. New York: Macmillan.

Roe v. Wade, 410 U.S. 113 (1973).

S

❖

SABATO, LARRY (1952–)

Larry Sabato is a professor of government and director of the Center for Politics at the University of Virginia, where he earned his undergraduate degree before getting a graduate degree from Oxford. The author of numerous books and articles on American politics, Sabato is one of the most quoted political scientists in the nation. More known for his political punditry than for constitutional analysis, Sabato published a book in 2007 in which he made the case for a series of 23 constitutional reforms that he thinks Congress could propose, but that would more likely be the product of a constitutional convention. Notably, a number of reforms involve issues relative to political parties and the nomination of their candidates that the Constitution does not currently address.

Although Sabato's proposals are far-reaching, he does not believe they are radical. Constitutional reform should be consistent with American principles of idealism, pragmatism, fairness, and "the needs of the present and the future" (Sabato 2007, 13). He further says that any proposals should honor the idea of a written constitution, republicanism, separation of powers, federalism, and the rule of law. He thus specifically rejects: the adoption of a parliamentary system; a nationwide initiative and referendum; getting sidetracked by hot-button issues like abortion, capital punishment, and gay rights; or altering the existing Bill of Rights (*Id.,* 13–14). He organizes his proposals under several headings.

In examining Congress, Sabato proposes adding two additional senators for states with the greatest population and one for the next 15. He would also award representation in the Senate to the District of Columbia and to former presidents and vice presidents. He does not initially note that Article V prohibits states from being deprived of their equal representation in the Senate without their consent, but he does recognize later in the book (*Id.,* 149, 219) that this might be a problem. Sabato is quite concerned about the lack of competitive districts in the House of Representatives and proposes changing this by providing for a system of nonpartisan redistricting. He favors expanding House terms from two years to three and aligning Senate terms so that they coincide with presidential elections. He thinks that the House of Representatives should be expanded to 1,000 members, who would, like senators, be subject to unspecified term limits. Sabato also favors a Balanced Budget Amendment, with 55 percent being permitted to override the requirement, and he favors allowing for gubernatorial appointment of members of the House in cases of mass catastrophe.

Sabato favors a modified six-year term for the president, which would allow the president in his 5th year to seek an additional two-year extension to his term. He also favors institutionalizing provisions of the War Powers Act of 1973 by expanding congressional oversight of the president's war powers. He would also grant the president a line-item veto and allow non–natural born citizens to be elected if they have been U.S. citizens for at least 20 years.

In dealing with the judiciary, Sabato seeks mandatory retirement ages and 15-year term limits on all federal judges, although he would allow lower judges to apply for five more years.

He also favors increasing the number of justices (something that the current Constitution does not forbid) from nine to twelve, partly believing that the possibility of a tie might reduce judicial powers and would, in any event, make it less likely that a justice could serve as a "swing" justice. Sabato further thinks that federal judges and justices should receive automatic cost-of-living adjustments without having to depend on Congress to enact them.

Sabato proposes "a new, separate constitutional article specifically for the *politics* of the American system" (*Id.,* 227). He thinks the current presidential nominating system gives undue influence to states like New Hampshire, which conducts the first primary, and Iowa, which conducts the first caucus. He proposes dividing the nation into four regions and determining when sections would vote through a lottery. He would limit the nominating process to the four months immediately preceding national nominating conventions in August. Consistent with his proposed increase in the size of both houses of Congress, Sabato would add electors to the electoral college and eliminate the possibility of faithless electors. He also favors "reasonable limitations on campaign spending by the wealthy from their family fortunes" as well as "partial public financing for general election House and Senate campaigns" (*Id.,* 228). He would encourage voting by having an "automatic registration system for all qualified American citizens" (*Id.,* 228).

Although acknowledging that such a proposal would probably cost about $65.7 billion annually (*Id.,* 174), Sabato favors requiring all Americans to give two years of national service between the ages of 18 and 26. He observes that "[t]his universal civil duty would be, in essence, a Bill of Responsibilities to accompany the Bill of Rights" (*Id.,* 228–29).

Finally, Sabato proposes convening an Article V constitutional convention for the purpose of making such proposals. He takes some comfort from a poll that he conducted that suggest that Americans favor many of his proposals, but he recognizes that the process could take some time. He thinks that delegates to such a convention should be elected by the people according to the "one person, one vote" principle and that

a convention of 436 delegates (the current number of House members plus one for the District of Columbia) would be ideal. He thinks that members of Congress should be excluded from participating and envisions that the chief justice of the United States might preside over the initial meeting. Although he does not include it in his later list of proposals, he suggests that future conventions should be convened at the turn of each century.

In a fairly clever move, the back flyleaf of the book includes "early backing" for "a more perfect constitution" in the form of quotations that begin and end with Thomas Jefferson (who founded the university where Sabato teaches) and includes James Madison, George Washington, and George Mason.

Commentator Fred Barnes observes in a review of Sabato's book that he "makes a more persuasive case for calling a convention than for passing any specific amendment" (2007).

See also Balanced Budget Amendment; Congress, Size of; Term Limits; Presidency, Term Length.

For Further Reading:
Barnes, Fred. "A Meeting to Amend." *Wall Street Journal,* October 18, 2007.
Sabato, Larry J. 2007. *A More Perfect Constitution: 23 Proposals to Revitalize Our Constitution and Make America a Fairer Country.* New York: Walker and Company,

SAFETY-VALVE ANALOGY

Just as early American commentators often likened the Constitution to a machine (Kammen 1987), so too they often compared the amending process to a safety valve. Justice Joseph Story probably coined the term when he wrote that the amending process was "the safety valve to let off all temporary effervescences and excitements; and the real effective instrument to control and adjust the movements of the machinery, when out of order, or in danger of self-destruction" (Story 1987, 680).

In critiquing this analogy, Sidney George Fisher later claimed that Article V had been more like an "iron fetter" than a safety valve; "the efficacy of a safety-valve depends on the promptness with which it can be opened and the width of the throttle. If defective in either of these, when the pressure of steam is too high the boiler will burst" (S. Fisher 1862, 33). Attorney Frederic B. Johnstone later criticized the amending process during the Progressive Era by noting that the difficulty of constitutional amendment made the Constitution like a dangerous boiler that "becomes a source of danger under pressure in the absence of a safety valve" (1912, 282).

However mechanical, the safety-valve analogy highlights the way in which a method for peaceful and legal change helps alleviate pressures that might otherwise be channeled into violence and revolution. In modern discourse that goes at least as far back as Woodrow Wilson, the Constitution is less frequently referred to as a Newtonian "mechanism" than as a Darwinian "organism," and as prominent scholars and judges have adopted the analogy of a "living Constitution" that they can adapt through constitutional interpretation, the safety-valve analogy has accordingly been used less frequently (Gillman 1997, 215). Today the analogy is sometimes used to describe First Amendment rights, which also permits speech rather than leave critics with no recourse other than violence (Vile, Hudson, and Schultz, 2008, 52).

See also Fisher, Sidney George; Living Constitution; Story, Joseph; Wilson, Thomas Woodrow.

For Further Reading:

Fisher, Sidney G. 1862. *The Trial of the Constitution.* Reprint, New York: Da Capo Press, 1972.

Gillman, Howard. 1997. "The Collapse of Constitutional Originalism and the Rise of the Notion of the 'Living Constitution' in the Course of American State-Building." *Studies in American Political Development* 11 (Fall): 191–247.

Story, Joseph. 1987. *Commentaries on the Constitution of the United States.* Durham, NC: Carolina Academic Press.

Vile, John R. David L Hudson, Jr., and David Schultz. 2008. *The Encyclopedia of the First Amendment.* 2 vols. Washington DC: CQ Press.

SCHLAFLY, PHYLLIS (1924–)

Phyllis Schlafly is the individual most frequently associated with the defeat of the Equal Rights Amendment. As the 1972 founder and current president of the conservative Eagle Forum, Schlafly continues to take credit for leading "the pro-family movement to victory over the principal legislative goal of the radical feminists, called the Equal Rights Amendment" (1995 biographical data sheet provided by the Eagle Forum). Her views on the subject are more thoroughly explained in an Eagle Forum video entitled "What's Wrong with ERA?"

Schlafly has a master's degree in political science from Harvard University as well as undergraduate and law degrees from Washington University. She continues to be a prominent conservative spokesperson on college campuses, writes a widely distributed syndicated column, publishes the *Phyllis Schlafly Report,* and has authored or edited sixteen books. These include *A Choice Not an Echo* (1964), which supported Republican Senator Barry Goldwater's bid for the presidency in 1964, and books on U.S. foreign policy, illiteracy, and education.

Schlafly believes strongly in the U.S. Constitution and in Article V, which outlines the amending process. She opposed plans by the Council of States for a conference of the states, fearing that it might develop into an open-ended convention to rewrite the U.S. Constitution (*Phyllis Schlafly Report* April 1995, May 1995). She also opposes an amendment to make the District of Columbia a state. The mother of six children, Schlafly was named 1992 Illinois Mother of the Year.

See also Equal Rights Amendment.

For Further Reading:

Critchlow, Donald T. 2008. *Phillis Schlafly and Graceroots Conservatism.* Princeton, NJ: Princeton University Press.

Critchlow, Donalt T. and Cynthia L. Stachecki. 2008. "The Equal Rights Amendment Reconsidered: Politics, Policy, and Social Mobilization in a Democracy." *Journal of Policy History* 20:1: 157–176.

Phyllis Schlafly Report, April 1995, May 1995.

SCHMITENDORF, JAMES A.
(1933–)

Schmitendorf describes himself as a retired pilot and engineer who "taught engineering at a small mid-west university for 15 years." He appears to be the guiding force behind Abe's Indignation League and a petition that it has posted on the Internet to assert rights under Article V and the First Amendment to request states to call a constitutional amendment.

Schmitendorf directs much of his concern to what he perceives to be dishonesty in government, and especially in the presidency in the aftermath of Richard Nixon and Bill Clinton. Schmitendorf wants the Convention to consider at least 12 proposals that would seek three objectives: "to (1) minimize the future possibility of a dishonest or unsuitable president, (2) consider other important issues and grievances of the people, and (3) consolidate the language for easier citizen reading."

Consistent with his concern over the presidency, the first proposal would require the president to comply with the ethics requirements of the Uniform Code of Military Justice. A second would seek to "reduce the conflict of interest when active lawyers make the nation's laws." The third would address states' rights by restricting the ability of the national government to condition funding on state compliance with federal regulations. The fourth calls for reconsidering "the method of electing federal senators." The fifth would consider removing the Department of Justice from the executive branch. The sixth would limit income tax rates to 15 percent or less except during times of war. The seventh would clarify existing constitutional provisions relative to rights. Schmitendorf is especially concerned about the right to bear arms, but he also favors clarifying phrases like "high crimes," "speedy trial," "post roads," "Armies" and "Navy," and the like consistent with current language usage. The eighth provision calls for validating the use of paper money, providing for a balanced budget, and reducing the current debt. The ninth would limit federal grants and subsidies. The tenth would prohibit ownership of local media by "large, out of state, media corporations." The eleventh would establish congressional term limits, and the twelfth would clarify the amounts of money that Individuals and Political Action Committees can contribute.

Schmitendorf favors excluding federal officials from the constitutional convention and granting states from three to seven delegates, depending on their size. He would further specify that less than 50 of each state delegation should be lawyers and at least one from each state should be "a person of science."

Schmitendorf urges individuals who sign a petition for a constitutional convention to refrain from jury duty, to keep all bills with Lincoln's picture on them, to fly flags at three-quarter mast, and to engage in political action. He suggests that the league might use kitchen brooms as a symbol of the need to sweep dishonest politicians out of office.

See also Constitutional Convention.

Further Reading:

"Abe's Indignation League: Petition for a Constitutional Convention." http://www.abesindignation league.org/. Accessed June 23, 2008.

"Abe's Indignation League: Questions and Answers." http://www.abesindignationleague.org/qanda.html. Accessed June 23, 2008.

"Justifying a Constitutional Convention for the 21st Century (Plain Talk and Common Sense." http://www.abesindignationleague.org/justification.html. Accessed June 23, 2008.

"A Petition for a Constitutional Convention." http://www.abesindignationleague.org/petition1.html. Accessed June 23, 2008.

SCHOOL BUSING

In the wake of the Supreme Court's decision in *Brown v. Board of Education* (1954), which called for an end to school segregation, a number of congressmen from the South proposed amendments to give states exclusive administrative control over public schools. Over time, most proposed amendments focused specifically on the assignment of students to schools on the basis of race and the use of busing to achieve racial balance.

On this issue, individuals who supported the decision in *Brown* were divided. Praise for the effectiveness of busing as a means of promoting desegregation was balanced by concerns about the associated costs, the impact of busing on the quality of education and the idea of community schools, and the resulting creation of private one-race schools and the "white flight" that sometimes resulted from forced busing.

Members of Congress introduced about 25 amending proposals dealing with busing in the 1960s, over 225 in the 1970s, and more than 20 in the 1980s. Congressional sponsors from outside the South increased in the late 1970s and the 1980s. Ten states, including Michigan (1971) and Massachusetts (1974, 1976), also petitioned Congress for a convention on this issue during the 1960s and 1970s.

Contrary to President Richard Nixon's hopes, the Burger Court unanimously upheld the use of busing as a tool to remedy past cases of de jure (legalized) segregation in *Swann v. Charlotte-Mecklenburg Board of Education* (1971). The Court's decision indicated that there were limits to the use of busing, however, and in *Milliken v. Bradley* (1974), in a 5-to-4 decision also written by Chief Justice Burger, the Supreme Court refused to uphold a district court mandate providing for an interdistrict remedy for an intradistrict case of de jure segregation. This and subsequent decisions appeared to limit the scope of busing in cases of de facto segregation that resulted from voluntarily chosen housing patterns rather than from discriminatory governmental actions.

A summary of amending proposals has divided them into five categories:

> [those] that would prohibit: (1) the federal courts from assigning students to public schools on the basis of their race; (2) *any* governmental authority from assigning students to public schools on the basis of their race; (3) governmental authorities from assigning students on the basis of their race to any public school other than the one closest to their residence; (4) governmental authority from assigning stu-

dents to schools other than the one closest to their residence, without exception; and (5) governmental interference with parents' or guardians' rights to choose a public school for their children. (Keynes with Miller 1989, 225)

In the 1970s, both the House and Senate Judiciary Committees held hearings on anti-busing amendments. A proposed amendment by Democratic Representative Ronald M. Mottl of Ohio was discharged from committee, but it was defeated in 1979 by a vote of 209 to 206 in the House of Representatives (Keynes with Miller 1989, 226). There were other attempts to limit busing through restrictions on the Department of Health, Education, and Welfare; through restrictions on the Justice Department; and through controversial and unsuccessful congressional attempts to restrict judicial jurisdiction over this issue (Keynes with Miller 1989, 219).

See also *Brown v. Board of Education.*

For Further Reading:

Keynes, Edward, with Randall K. Miller. 1989. *The Court vs. Congress: Prayer, Busing, and Abortion.* Durham, NC: Duke University Press.

Schwartz, Bernard. 1986. *Swann's Way: The School Busing Case and the Supreme Court.* New York: Oxford University Press.

Wilkinson, J. Harvie, III. 1979. *From* Brown *to* Bakke: *The Supreme Court and School Integration: 1954–1978.* New York: Oxford University Press.

SCHOOLS, PUBLIC

The U.S. Constitution does not say anything directly about education. Many states provided for public education in constitutional reforms made in the 1840s and 1850s (Butts 1978, 81). Others, especially in the South, lagged behind in establishing public school systems. In the decades immediately following the Civil War, several members of Congress introduced amendments calling on states to provide public education for their citizens. In his annual message of

December 1875, President Ulysses S. Grant tied this proposed amendment to a restriction on aid to parochial schools (J. Richardson 1908, 8:334), which resulted in the proposal of the unsuccessful Blaine Amendment.

All states eventually established public schools. The Supreme Court endorsed racial segregation in *Plessy v. Ferguson* (1896), and this policy extended to schools and did not change until the Court's decision in *Brown v. Board of Education* (1954). Modern amending proposals have attempted to limit the use of school busing and to permit prayer and Bible reading in public schools.

See also Blaine Amendment; Education, Right to; Prayer in Public Schools; School Busing.

For Further Reading:

Butts, R. Freeman. 1978. *Public Education in the United States: From Revolution to Reform.* New York: Holt, Rinehart, and Winston.

Richardson, James E., ed. 1908. *A Compilation of the Messages and Papers of the Presidents, 1789–1908.* 11 vols. n.p.: Bureau of National Literature and Art.

SCOTT, RODNEY D. (1949–)

Rodney D. Scott of Fort Wayne, Indiana, has offered one of the most discursive proposals for a new constitution in a book entitled *The Great Debate.* Identified in his book as being from the University of St. Francis, Scott's primary occupation is that of a social worker, and his connection to St. Francis in Fort Wayne is that of an adjunct professor of political science. He has masters' degrees in social work and political science from Indiana University at Indianapolis and from Ball State University. Scott discusses the U.S. Constitution for 276 pages before proposing a constitution consisting of a preamble and 73 articles, and then following with another 200 pages of commentary and various appendices.

Scott's discussion of the Constitution identifies sections of the Constitution that are "not

being followed," sections that are "no longer needed," and sections that "are confusing or contradictory." He views his own proposal as an obligation since "[i]t seems incredibly unjust to criticize a document, especially the image of democracy that the American Constitution represents, without equally putting forth an alternative" (Scott 1999, 274).

Scott makes little attempt in his own preamble to match the rhetoric of the existing document. One of its announced goals is to "verify axioms of law."

Article 1 specifies that his proposal will "be considered a continuation of the rights and responsibilities of the current Constitution" (*Id.*, 277). Article 2 announces Scott's intention to create a parliamentary system, and Article 3 provides for record-keeping.

Articles 4 through 7 deal with Congress. Scott wants to have one representative for every 77,000 citizens, which he estimates would create a house of 3,240 members based on the 1990 census (*Id.*, 330). Members would operate from home districts and do most of their work through teleconferencing, meeting physically together for only two weeks each year. Each state would continue to elect two senators, but elections would coincide with those for governors. The senate would act much like the British House of Lords, voting on, but not originating or amending, acts of the House. It would retain its current power to ratify appointments and treaties.

Article 8 outlines the responsibility of the prime minister, who would be chosen by the House and serve as the head of government. Although Scott says the nation will not have a head of state, he invests the prime minister with power as commander in chief and other powers currently exercised by the president. Scott also proposes that the prime minister engage congress in question and answer periods. Articles 10 and 11 address the cabinet, which would be appointed by the prime minister and confirmed by the Senate.

Articles 12 through 21 address government duties and powers. Article 12 thus declares the supremacy of federal law, and Article 13 vests Congress with the power to declare war. Article 14 provides for balanced budgets, except in time of declared war, and Article 15 vests the power of adjusting congressional districts to the General Accounting Office. Article 16 further makes English the official language of the federal government, Article 17 grants Congress power to tax, and Article 18 provides that the government will release information upon request. Article 19 limits the duration of treaties to 99 years, Article 20 provides for a census every 10 years, and Article 21 grants Congress power over commerce, bankruptcy laws, copyrights and patents, and weights and measures.

Articles 22 through 24 deal with the political process. Article 22 recognizes political parties and gives them the responsibility of formulating platforms. Article 23 guarantees free elections, and Article 24 specifies that "universal suffrage shall exist, with the view of one person, one vote."

Articles 25 through 41 address the judicial system and various rights, many of which elaborate protections currently found within the First Amendment. Scott specifies that "the court system shall consist of a Supreme Court, a Court of Appeals [currently, there are 13 such courts], and district courts" (*Id.,* 291). Judges would continue to serve for life. In listing "the order of authority of laws," Scott puts "international treaties" above the "Federal Constitution" and other laws. Scott places the rights of litigation among those that he would protect and specifically delineates a "right to privacy," "Freedom of movement," and provisions against discrimination based on "race, creed, color, gender, age, national origin, economic status, physical capacity, handicaps, or sexual orientation" (*Id.,* 294). Among the "inherent rights" that he lists are "liberty, life, acquiring possessions, being productive, and seeking happiness and security" (*Id.,* 295).

Articles 41 through 47 list various judicial entitlements including elaborations of various provisions in the Bill of Rights related to the rights of defendants. Article 44 prohibits torture, and Article 45 prohibits capital punishment, although an earlier provision of Article 6 provided that using legislative voting certification codes of members of the House would be "a capital crime" (*Id.,* 280). Article 47 provides for victims' rights.

Article 48 prohibits titles of nobility, Article 49 provides for the right to an education, Article 50 for academic freedom, and Article 51 for the federal reserve system. Articles 52 through 55 deal with the military. Article 53 allows for conscription after a Declaration of War. Article 54 constitutionalizes the system of military justice.

Articles 56 through 62 deal with state directives. Highlights include a provision allowing states to establish "a Rite of Passage" into adulthood.

Articles 63 through 65 deal with the family. The first article provides that "it is the natural right of parents to care for, support, and direct the upbringing of their children" but specifies that "the state has an equal responsibility to supervise this exercise" (*Id.,* 302).

Article 66 provides for labor unions, while Article 67 prohibits child labor. Article 68 further abolishes the District of Columbia, allowing for the land to recede to the states that contributed it.

Article 69 deals with the relation between the national government and the states and territories.

The last four articles deal with modification and termination of the constitution. Amendments will be proposed by a two-thirds vote of the Senate and a majority of the House and ratified by two-thirds of the states within seven years. Three-fourths of the states may further provide for a constitutional convention or conference. The new constitution would go into effect when ratified by two-thirds of the states and would become "null and void" after 200 years (*Id.,* 305).

In his commentary on his proposal, Scott says that the issue "is not whether the United States Constitution will ever be replaced, but more a matter of when" (*Id.,* 515). He thinks a constitutional convention is the best method to adopt his proposal but recognizes that the creation of such a system "would take years to work through" (*Id.,* 510). Citing the examples of Thomas W. Door [Rhode Island] and Vatican II, Scott believes that change is possible, but thinks that without a "Constitutional crisis," it is doubtful that either the people or their leaders will act. He ends on the hope that "great nations do great things" (*Id.,* 521).

Records indicate that Scott lost an appeal based on sex discrimination for reinstatement as a social worker at Parkview Memorial Hospital after the hospital was reorganized, and he was not rehired (*Scott v. Parkview Memorial Hospital* [1999]). In 2001, he announced his bid for the Democratic nomination from Indiana's third congressional district with the slogan, "It is Not a Democracy Unless the People Have a Voice." Focusing on a variety of issues "that never seem to get addressed," he supported eliminating the national debt, addressing Medicare, and allocating money for research on the energy crisis (Herrold 2001).

John W. Whitehead, founder and president of the Rutherford Institute, cited Scott in an article advocating constitutional reform (2005).

See also Parliamentary System.

Further Reading:

Herrold, Lee. 2001. "Fort Wayne man announces House bid." *The Goshen News* (June 9).

Scott, Rodney D. 1999. *The Great Debate: The Need for Constitutional Reform.* Chicago: Rampant Lion Press.

Whitehead, John W. "It's Time for Constitutional Reform." http://www.rutherford.org/articles+db/commentary.asp?record_id=363. Accessed May 19, 2008.

SCOTT V. SANDFORD (1857)

The majority opinion in *Scott v. Sandford* is one of the most controversial in U.S. history. It was written by Chief Justice Roger B. Taney, a Jackson appointee from Maryland who served on the Court from 1836 to 1864 and had succeeded Chief Justice John Marshall. Dred Scott, a slave, had been taken by his master, Dr. Emerson, an army surgeon, to a free state and a free territory and back to Missouri, which was a slave state. Scott and his wife Harriet sued Sanford (incorrectly spelled by the Court reporter as Sandford), the executor of Emerson's estate, for their freedom on the basis of their residence on free soil.

Taney ruled against the Scotts. He declared that however states might choose to define state citizenship, the Constitution limited national citizenship to whites. He interpreted the Declaration of Independence and other founding documents as applying only to whites. Taney cited both the slave importation clause and the fugitive slave clause (omitting the three-fifths clause from his discussion) to indicate that the American framers had regarded African Americans as an inferior class not entitled to the privileges of citizenship. Taney further held it to be the Court's duty to interpret the Constitution with the same words and meaning it had when it was adopted. In a reference to the amending provisions, Taney noted that if parts of the Constitution were thought to be unjust, "there is a mode prescribed in the instrument itself by which it may be amended, but while it remains unaltered, it must be construed now as it was understood at the time of its adoption" (*Scott* 1857, 426). As a noncitizen, Scott therefore had no right to appear in a federal court.

Taney went on, however, to examine the Missouri Compromise of 1820, which had excluded slavery from much of the Louisiana Territory. Again, Taney gave a narrow construction to the Constitution. He claimed that the provision related to the governance of territories referred only to territories in possession of the government in 1789 and not subsequent purchases. People in such territory were guaranteed the same constitutional protections as other citizens, including the Fifth Amendment right not to be deprived of their property (slaves) without their consent. This interpretation served as the basis for the notion of substantive due process that would so affect constitutional interpretation during the next 75 years of Court history.

As to Scott's claim to have become free by reason of his residence in a free state, Taney ruled that such matters were governed by state law. He thus accepted the judgment of the Missouri Supreme Court that such residence in Illinois had not given Scott his freedom.

This case served as a catalyst to civil war rather than, as Taney had hoped, providing a solution to a vexing national problem. *Scott* was subsequently overturned by the Thirteenth and Fourteenth Amendments. The former abolished slavery, and the latter defined citizenship to apply to all persons born in the United States. Ironically, however, in the *Slaughterhouse Cases* (1873), the first Supreme Court decision to interpret the Fourteenth Amendment, the Court continued to rely on the distinction between state and federal citizenship that Taney had developed in *Scott* to give a restrictive reading of the amendment.

See also Fifth Amendment; Fourteenth Amendment; *Slaughterhouse Cases;* Substantive Due Process; Supreme Court Decisions Reversed by Constitutional Amendments; Thirteenth Amendment.

For Further Reading:

Finkelman, Paul. 1997. *Dred Scott v. Sandford: A Brief History with Documents.* Boston: Bedford Books.

Graber, Mark. 2006. *Dred Scott and the Problem of Constitutional Evil.* New York: Cambridge University Press.

Scott v. Sandford, 60 U.S. (19 How.) 393 (1857).

SECESSIONISTS, LIMITING THE RIGHTS OF

The Civil War was followed by numerous attempts to exclude individuals who had been active in or had supported the Confederate States of America from holding office, voting, or participating in certain professions. Some of these attempts took the form of legislation, and some were proposed as amendments.

In *Cummings v. Missouri* (1867), the Supreme Court invalidated a Missouri law requiring individuals in certain professions to swear that they had never supported the Confederacy. Similarly, a companion case, *Ex parte Garland* (1867), struck down a similar oath required of attorneys practicing in federal courts. In both cases, the Court decided that such laws were unconstitutional ex post facto laws (retroactive criminal laws) and bills of attainder (legislative punishments without benefit of a trial), which Article I, Section 9 of the Constitution prohibited.

Congress introduced numerous amendments to exclude former members of the Confederacy from civil office or from voting. Republican Senator Jacob Howard of Michigan eventually introduced the resolution that became Section 3 of the Fourteenth Amendment. This section provided:

No person shall be a Senator or Representative in Congress, or elector of President and Vice President, or hold any office, civil or military, under the United States, or under any State, who, having previously taken an oath, as a member of Congress, or as an officer of the United States, or as a member of any State legislature, or as an executive or judicial officer of any State, shall have engaged in insurrection or rebellion against the same, or given aid or comfort to the enemies thereof.

This section also gave Congress the power to remove this disability by a two-thirds vote, and it did so on behalf of most Southerners in a vote in 1872 (Grimes 1978, 55).

See also Fourteenth Amendment.

For Further Reading:

Grimes, Alan P. 1978. *Democracy and the Amendments to the Constitution.* Lexington, MA: Lexington Books.

SECOND AMENDMENT

The Second Amendment is one of the most controversial amendments to the Constitution. States ratified it in 1791 as part of the Bill of Rights. It provides that "a well regulated Militia, being necessary to the security of a free State, the right of the people to keep and bear Arms, shall not be infringed."

Several states that had ratified the Constitution proposed such an amendment (Vandercoy 1994, 1029–1032), and such an amendment was among those that James Madison proposed in the First Congress in 1789. His original proposal contained a related provision that would have established a right of conscientious objection for religious reasons (see Kurland and Lerner 1987, 5:25), but the Senate deleted it.

In recent years, the Second Amendment has drawn renewed scholarly attention (S. Heller 1995) and has even prompted a full-page advertisement signed by scholars who believe that the amendment has been too narrowly interpreted (Academics for the Second Amendment 1995, A23). Interpretations of the Second Amendment differ radically. The National Rifle Association (NRA) has argued for an absolutist view of this amendment as guaranteeing individual rights, and it has opposed legislation that would ban certain types of guns, including handguns and assault rifles. By contrast, the American Civil Liberties Union has supported gun regulations and has interpreted the amendment to refer to the protection of collective state militia rather than of individual rights (for contrasting positions, see Levinson 1989). This debate has encompassed both historians and political scientists, with great attention being given to a Bancroft Prize–winning book by Michael A. Bellesiles entitled *Arming America: The Origins of a National Gun Culture* (2000). Bellesiles had argued that the modern pervasiveness of guns did not arise from the early republic but from the period after the Civil War. Now generally discredited, the book continues to be the center of academic debate including a forum in the January 2002 issue of *The William and Mary Quarterly.*

The difficulty of interpreting the Second Amendment centers on its statement of purpose. Interpreters have to decide whether the purpose limits the meaning of the entire amendment or whether the right to "keep and bear Arms" that follows has independent meaning.

Even a resolution of this issue does not necessarily solve the interpretive problems, because it can and has been argued that the framers interpreted the idea of the militia quite broadly, believing that an armed citizenry was a guard against tyranny. Thus, during debates in the First Congress, Elbridge Gerry noted that the proposal that became the Second Amendment "is intended to secure the people against the maladministration of the Government." He further connected the militia with the desire "to prevent the establishment of a standing army" (Kurland and Lerner 1987, 5:210). Thus, some proponents of original intent argue that the amendment should be interpreted quite expansively (see Halbrook 1994; Cramer 1994).

By contrast, others argue that the basic thrust of the amendment was simply to ensure "that citizens have a constitutionally protected right to serve in militia in defense of state and country" (Spitzer 1995, 35). Under this interpretation, "the Second Amendment is founded on federalism, balancing powers between the federal government and the states; and military necessity, developing a political compromise between politically popular militias and a politically unpopular but militarily necessary national professional army." Such a view would denigrate arguments on behalf of "hunting, sporting, recreation, or even personal protection" (*Id.,* 35–36). Because state militias have for all practical purposes ceased, those who hold this view also hold that "the Second Amendment has been rendered essentially irrelevant to modern American life" (*Id.,* 38). Moreover, under such an interpretation, both state and federal governments have the power to regulate gun ownership, which is blamed by many for the rising tide of violence in the nation.

Until recently, the Supreme Court has said little on the subject. In *United States v. Miller* (1939), it unanimously upheld a federal law against the use of sawed-off shotguns by ruling that the Second Amendment protected only weapons that could be used as part of a militia. In *Quilici v. Village of Morton Grove* (1983), the Court refused to review a lower court decision upholding a ban on the ownership of handguns. To date, the Second Amendment remains one of the few guarantees in the Bill of Rights that has not been applied to the states via the due process clause of the Fourteenth Amendment and has been described as an "underenforced constitutional norm" (Denning 1998).

In *District of Columbia v. Heller,* 554 U.S. ____ (2008), however, Justice Antonin Scalia authored a 5–4 decision affirming a lower court decision and striking down two provisions of a DC law that had banned all new registrations of handguns and that had required earlier purchasers to keep them in a disabled state. The Court majority came down firmly on the side of the view that the right to bear arms is an individual right that was not restricted to individuals who were members of the state militia. Scalia also observed, however, that the right "is not unlimited." He suggested that individuals who were felons or mentally ill might face restrictions. Similarly, the government might limit "the carrying of firearms in sensitive places such as schools and government buildings" or limit "the commercial sale of arms." He further said that the original right applied to weapons "in common use at the time." Because this decision came out of the District of Columbia, it did not decide whether the Second Amendment also limited the states, but to the extent that the case identified the right as fundamental, it arguably created a rationale for so doing.

Members of Congress introduced two proposed amendments in 1913 to authorize Congress to regulate the carrying of concealed weapons in the District of Columbia and the territories. The next proposal appears to have been the one that New York Democratic representative Major Owens introduced in 1992. He made another appeal for an amendment designed to clarify the Second Amendment in June 1995, calls that have been subsequently repeated.

The paucity of proposed amendments certainly does not stem from disinterest in the Second Amendment. The likely explanation is that most proponents and opponents of gun control have preferred to battle over the meaning of the existing constitutional provision rather than to introduce a new one.

For Further Reading:

Academics for the Second Amendment. 1995. "An Open Letter on the Second Amendment." *Chronicle of Higher Education* 41 (11 August): A23.

Bellesiles, Michael A. 2000. *Arming America: The Origins of a National Gun Culture.* New York: Alfred A. Knopf.

Cottrol, Robert J., ed. 1994. *Gun Control and the Constitution: Sources and Explorations of the Second Amendment.* 3 vols. New York: Garland.

Cramer, Clayton E. 1994. *For the Defense of Themselves and the State: The Original Intent and Judicial Interpretation of the Right to Keep and Bear Arms.* Westport, CT: Praeger.

Denning, Brannon P. 1998. "Gun Shy: The Second Amendment as an 'Underenforced Constitutional Norm.'" *Harvard Journal of Law & Public Policy* 21 (Summer): 719–791.

Doherty, Brian. 2008. *Gun Control on Trial: Inside the Supreme Court Battle Over the Second Amendment.* Washington DC: Cato Institute.

Emerson v. United States, 122 S. Ct. 2362 (2002).

"Forum: Historians and Guns." 2002. *William and Mary Quarterly* 59, 3d Series (January): 203–268.

Halbrook, Stephen P. *The Founders' Second Amendment: Origins of the Right to Bear Arms.* Chicago, IL: Ivan R. Dee, 2008.

Halbrook, Stephen P. 1994. *That Every Man Be Armed: The Evolution of a Constitutional Right.* Oakland, CA: Independent Institute.

Haney v. United States, 122 S. Ct. 2362 (2002).

Heller, Scott. 1995. "The Right to Bear Arms." *Chronicle of Higher Education* 41 (21 July): A8, A12.

Kurland, Philip B., and Ralph Lerner, eds. 1987. *The Founders' Constitution.* 5 vols. Chicago: University of Chicago Press.

Levinson, Sanford. 1989. "The Embarrassing Second Amendment." *Yale Law Journal* 99 (December): 637–660.

McClurg, Andrew J., David B. Kopel, and Brannon P. Denning, eds. 2002. *Gun Control & Gun Rights: A Reader and Guide.* New York: New York University Press.

"Second Amendment Symposium." 1995. *Tennessee Law Review* 62 (Spring): 443–821.

Spitzer, Robert J. 1995. *The Politics of Gun Control.* Chatham, NJ: Chatham House Publishers.

Tushnet, Mark V. 1997. *Out of Range: Why the Constitution Can't End the Battle over Guns.* New York: Oxford University Press.

Vandercoy, David E. 1994. "The History of the Second Amendment." *Valparaiso University Law Review* 28 (Spring): 1007–1039.

Walsh, Edward. 2002. "U.S. Argues for Wider Gun Rights: Supreme Court Filing Reverses Past Policy," *The Washington Post* (8 May): A01.

SECRETARY OF STATE

The secretary of state served until 1818 by custom, and from then until 1951 by statute, as the person responsible for certifying and proclaiming the ratification of constitutional amendments. Congress transferred this function to the administrator of the General Services Administration in 1951 and to the archivist of the Library of Congress in 1984 (Bernstein with Agel 1993, 246).

The action of certifying amendments is generally routine, but Secretary William Seward faced anything but a routine situation when deciding what to do about the Fourteenth Amendment. Although one more than the necessary 28 states had ratified, North and South Carolina had done so in the face of prior rejections of the amendment, and Ohio and New Jersey had subsequently voted rescissions (Dellinger 1983, 389). Seward reported these facts to Congress, directing particular attention to the attempted rescissions. Congress subsequently voted to promulgate the amendment, which Seward then did (James 1984, 289–304). The issue is further confused, however, by the fact that a telegram had been introduced in congressional debates indicating that Georgia had also ratified. This provided the necessary three-fourths majority whether the two rescissions were counted or not (A. Baker 1979, 79–80).

Walter Dellinger has argued that the congressional promulgation of the Fourteenth Amendment was unique, unwarranted, and unnecessary. In his view, an amendment becomes effective the moment it is ratified by the necessary states, whether it is so noted at the time by the official responsible or not (Dellinger 1983, 402).

The controversial ratification of the Twenty-seventh Amendment brought renewed attention to the role of the official responsible for certifying amendments. In that case, the decision by the archivist of the Library of Congress to certify the amendment was confirmed by an overwhelming vote in Congress, whose members were feeling heat from their constituents for being unresponsive to public sentiments. In the minds of critics concerned about the possible absence of a contemporary consensus, however, this did little to justify the ratification of an amendment more than 200 years after it had been proposed.

See also Archivist of the Library of Congress; Fourteenth Amendment; Promulgation of Amendments; Twenty-seventh Amendment.

For Further Reading:

Baker, A. Diane. 1979. "ERA: The Effect of Extending the Time for Ratification on Attempts to Rescind Prior Ratifications." *Emory Law Journal* 28: 71–110.

Bernstein, Richard B., with Jerome Agel. 1993. *Amending America: If We Love the Constitution So Much, Why Do We Keep Trying to Change It?* New York: Random House.

Dellinger, Walter. 1983. "The Legitimacy of Constitutional Change: Rethinking the Amending Process." *Harvard Law Review* 97 (December): 380–432.

SEGREGATION

One of the Supreme Court's most important decisions of the 20th century was its ruling in *Brown v. Board of Education* (1954). In this decision, the Court unanimously declared an end to the system of state-mandated segregation that it had previously sanctioned in *Plessy v. Ferguson* (1896).

In 1948, even before the *Brown* decision, Democratic Representative Oren Harris of Arkansas had introduced an amendment designed to allow individuals to segregate themselves from others voluntarily. He reintroduced this amendment in 1958 and 1961. Three days after the *Brown* decision, Democratic Representative John Bell Williams of Mississippi introduced an amendment to allow states to maintain racial segregation in schools. Other proposals with a similar aim were introduced to limit federal interference with state police powers, protected by the Tenth Amendment. Numerous other proposals have been introduced specifically to limit the use of school busing to achieve racial balance. Supreme Court decisions often distinguish de jure from de facto segregation as well as between state and private action. Racially discriminatory laws are almost always subjected to "strict scrutiny" and declared unconstitutional; discrimination by individuals that does not have state sanction or segregation that results from personal choice is far less likely to be invalidated.

See also *Brown v. Board of Education; Civil Rights Cases; Plessy v. Ferguson;* School Busing; States, Police Powers.

SELF-INCRIMINATION

The Fifth Amendment provides that no person "shall be compelled in any criminal case to be a witness against himself." In *Malloy v. Hogan* (1964), the Supreme Court reversed earlier rulings and decided that this guarantee applied to state as well as federal trials. The Warren Court further expanded this right in *Miranda v. Arizona* (1966) to preclude the use of confessions made in the absence of warnings about self-incrimination and the right to an attorney. Although *Miranda* significantly expanded the right against self-incrimination, this right has deep roots in English common law and has variously been defended as a way of promoting fairness in an accusatorial legal system, as a way to prevent cruel and inhumane treatment of defendants, and as a way of protecting personal privacy (D. O'Brien 2005, 1022–25).

A number of congressmen have proposed modifications of the Fifth Amendment. Among the most prominent advocates of a modification from 1968 to the present has been Democratic Representative Andrew Jacobs Jr. of Indiana, who worked as a police officer while in law school (Barone and Ujifusa 1994, 464). His proposal has three parts: it would stipulate that individuals could not be compelled to incriminate themselves "except in open court"; it would prevent the introduction of prior criminal convictions, "except where they are an element of the crime charged"; and it would alter the Sixth Amendment so that defendants would be informed not only of the nature and cause of the accusations against them but also of the evidence (H.J. Res. 314, 1979). In 1971, Republican Representative Carleton King of New York introduced a proposal (H.J. Res. 903) prohibiting the use of physical or mental torture to extract confessions, but permitting inferences that might be made from failure to testify. King would also have permitted "the reasonable in-custody questioning of suspects by police."

See also Fifth Amendment.

For Further Reading:

Barone, Michael, and Grant Ujifusa. 1994. *The Almanac of American Politics 1994.* Washington DC: National Journal.

O'Brien, David M. 2005. *Civil Rights and Civil Liberties.* Vol. 2 of *Constitutional Law and Politics.* 6th ed. New York: W. W. Norton.

SENECA FALLS CONVENTION (1848)

Although the Nineteenth Amendment prohibiting discrimination against women in voting was not ratified until 1920, scholars often trace the movement for women's suffrage to the Seneca Falls Convention, which met at the Wesleyan Chapel (now a national historic site) in Seneca Falls, New York, on July 19 and 20, 1848. Elizabeth Cady Stanton and Lucretia Mott, who literally called it just days before it was held, largely organized the convention, which about 300 men and women attended.

The convention adopted a "Declaration of Sentiments." Patterned after the U.S. Declaration of Independence, it declared that "all men and women are created equal," and listed numerous deprivations that women faced. These included the denial of the right to vote, the requirement that women submit to laws that they had no part in making, the moribund legal status of married women, the subjection of women to physical punishment by their husbands, the denial of the guardianship of children to women who were divorced, the exclusion of women from key professions, and the like (see Wheeler 1995a, 40–42). In one highly controversial passage, the declaration noted that "He [mankind] has withheld from her [women] rights which are given to the most ignorant and degraded men—both natives and foreigners" (Wheeler 1995a, 40).

Although the convention was the brainchild of Stanton and Mott, Mott's husband, as well as the husband of another participant, presided over the meeting to prevent undue offense to public sensibilities at a time when women did not speak in public unless it was to a group of other women. One hundred delegates, both men and women, subsequently signed a set of resolutions designed to provide for women's equality. Although the Nineteenth Amendment (as well as future calls for an Equal Rights Amendment) can be traced to these resolutions, they did not specifically call for a constitutional amendment or set of amendments. Interestingly, the provision for "the elective franchise" was considered to be the most controversial (so much so, that it was the only provision not to be adopted unanimously, and many who signed the resolutions later renounced them). It probably would not have been included but for the insistence of Elizabeth Cady Stanton and Frederick Douglass that this right was a key to others. Stanton's own husband absented himself from the convention; her father reportedly "rushed to Seneca Falls fearing for his daughter's sanity," and her older sister "wept over . . . her involvement in such a radical cause" (Bernard and Fox-Genovese 1995, 11). Not surprisingly, the resolution for women's suffrage was long subject of journalistic ridicule, and the task of obtaining suffrage proved to be far more extended than many probably would have anticipated. Only one young woman who was present at the Seneca Falls Convention, Charlotte Woodward, survived long enough to cast her vote in a presidential election 72 years later (Palmer 2000, 433).

In the meantime, the Seneca Falls Convention sparked other conventions, including one that was held two weeks later in Rochester, New York, and the first of many subsequent national women's rights conventions, which was held in Worcester, Massachusetts, in 1850. During the next seven decades, Carrie Chapman Catt noted that women participated in a total of

> 56 campaigns of state referenda, 480 campaigns to convince state legislatures to submit suffrage amendments to voters, 47 campaigns attempting to get state constitutional conventions to write woman suffrage into state constitutions, and 19 campaigns with 19 successive Congresses. (Summarized in Palmer 2000, 429)

See also Declaration of Independence; Douglass, Frederick; Equal Rights Amendment; Mott, Lucretia Coffin; Nineteenth Amendment; Stanton, Elizabeth Cady.

For Further Reading:

Bernhard, Virginia, and Elizabeth Fox-Genovese, eds. 1995. *The Birth of American Feminism: The Seneca Falls Woman's Convention of 1848.* St. James, NY: Brandywine Press.

Palmer, Kris E. 2000. *Constitutional Amendments: 1789 to the Present.* Detroit, MI: Gale Group.

Wheeler, Marjorie S., ed. 1995a. *One Woman, One Vote: Rediscovering the Woman Suffrage Movement.* Troutdale, OR: New Sage.

SEPARATION OF POWERS AND THE AMENDING PROCESS

One of the unstated innovations of the U.S. Constitution was its creation of a system of separation of powers. This principle was reflected in the division of its first three articles of the document—the first outlining the legislative, the second the executive, and the third the judicial branches. Although the framers generally understood that the legislative branch would, as an elective body, be the one closest to the people, they did not entrust it, like the British Parliament, with complete sovereignty, which the American framers equated with tyranny. Instead, Congress was to share its powers with an independently elected executive branch and a judicial branch appointed by the executive with the advice and consent of the Senate.

The framers based separation of powers on their belief that men were not "angels" and their fear that individuals with power would seek to abuse it. James Madison explained in *Federalist No. 51* that the presence of three branches, the concurrence of at least two of which would be needed for the adoption of legislation, would result in a system of checks and balances in which each branch would protect liberty by resisting encroachments on their own power by the other two:

> But the great security against a gradual concentration of the several powers in the same

department consists in giving to those who administer each department the necessary constitutional means and personal motives to resist encroachments of the others. The provision for defense must in this, as in all other cases, be made commensurate to the danger of attack. Ambition must be made to counteract ambition. The interest of the man must be connected with the constitutional rights of the place. (Ford 1898, 345)

Although the framers adopted separation of powers to keep the three branches of the national government in check, the division of power between the national government and the states, or federalism, was thought to create additional security for liberty. Provisions for federalism are included in Article IV of the Constitution and reflected in a number of subsequent amendments, most notably the Tenth and Fourteenth, in the latter of which state powers were somewhat reduced in order to provide for greater federal protections of individual rights.

Curiously, in contrast to federalism, separation of powers appears to play relatively little role in the constitutional amending process. The process calls for Congress or a constitutional convention to propose amendments, which state legislatures or state conventions must then ratify.

Of the three branches of the existing national government, Congress has had the central role in the amending process. This role might be curtailed, but not eliminated, if the Article V provision granting two-thirds of the states the power to petition Congress to call a special convention to propose amendments were utilized. Although this provision has not been directly exercised, it has sometimes prompted Congress to take preemptive action by proposing amendments that the states favored.

Article V does not mention a role for the president in the amending process. In *Hollingsworth v. Virginia* (1798), the Supreme Court decided that the president's signature was not required for amendments to become the law of the land. When presidents lobby for, or (as on occasion) sign, amendments, they do so in an extraconstitutional capacity.

The role of the judiciary in the amending process is more complex and debatable. Until its decision in *Coleman v. Miller* (1939), the Supreme Court fairly regularly resolved amending issues—as, for example, in *Hollingsworth v. Virginia* cited above. In *Coleman,* the Court indicated that most amending issues (and particularly the issue of whether states had ratified amendments within an appropriate time period) were "political questions" for Congress to resolve. In the case of extending the deadline for the Equal Rights Amendment and affirming the belated ratification of the Twenty-seventh Amendment related to the timing of congressional pay raises, the Congress has made important decisions in this area. However, the Court has occasionally patrolled the boundaries of the process since *Coleman,* and the status of that decision remains in some doubt after significant changes in the political questions doctrine. Moreover, there is something of a dialectical relationship between courts and constitutional amendments. Amendments can and have reversed decisions of the courts, but courts, in turn, must interpret amendments that are adopted, and their interpretations, particularly of the post–Civil War Amendments, have sometimes been more restrictive than they might have been.

To date, amendments have done far more to address issues of federalism than to adjust mechanisms connected with the doctrine of separation of powers. Although the First Amendment is stated as a limitation on Congress, the Court has applied it, like most of the rest of the Bill of Rights, to all branches of the national government and, since the adoption of the Fourteenth Amendment and the incorporation doctrine, to state governments as well. The Tenth Amendment is a specific recognition of powers reserved to the states, and the Eleventh is designed to provide state immunity against certain lawsuits. The Twelfth Amendment probably undercut congressional power by making it less likely that Congress would have to resolve future presidential elections, but it was chiefly designed to remedy what was regarded as a flaw in the original electoral college mechanism. The post–Civil War amendments, and others with enforcement clauses, increased congressional powers, but chiefly served to limit the states. The Sixteenth Amendment (providing for a national income tax) increased congressional powers but had the same effect on other branches of the national government. In providing for direct election of senators, the Seventeenth Amendment did more to decrease state legislative control of senators than to increase national powers. The Eighteenth Amendment, providing for national alcoholic prohibition, increased powers of both state and national governments, but its repeal limited the powers of the latter.

The Twenty-second Amendment, limiting a president to two full terms in office, arguably decreased the power of second-term presidents (by making them "lame ducks" vis-à-vis the Congress), but this result seems largely to have been an unintended consequence of a more important objective. Amendments (the Fifteenth, Nineteenth, and Twenty-sixth) denying voting discrimination again appear to have largely affected state powers rather than the allocation of national ones. The Twentieth Amendment, relating to lame-duck terms of both Congress and the president, was not aimed at lessening the power of these institutions per se, but only in assuring their accountability. Amendments like the Twenty-fifth, providing for presidential disability and succession, have arguably protected the executive branch against future dangers without significantly altering its relation to the other two branches.

It is curious to see how little connection the amending process has toward what is generally considered to be a major principle of American government, but separation of powers continues to shape judicial interpretations of the Constitution, as in its decisions to reject the so-called "legislative veto" or the "item veto." Similarly, the amending process could still alter the relation among the three branches of the national government either by approving one of these mechanisms that the Court has struck down, by otherwise investing one of the existing branches of government with increased power, or by divesting one of them of powers they now wield. Authors who call for replacing the existing system with a parliamentary form of government often cite existing delays and inefficiencies under separated powers.

See also *Coleman v. Miller;* Equal Rights Amendment; Federalism and the Amending Process; *Hollingsworth v. Virginia;* Parliamentary Sovereignty; Supreme Court Decisions Reversed by Constitutional Amendments; Twenty-seventh Amendment.

For Further Reading:
Campbell, Tom. 2004. *Separation of Powers in Practice.* CA: Stanford Law and Politics.

Ford, Paul L., ed. 1898. *The Federalist.* New York: Henry Holt.

SEVENTEENTH AMENDMENT

The American framers considered bicameralism, the division of Congress into two branches, to be quite important. Anticipating that the legislative body would be the most powerful in a republic, the framers hoped that the Senate would be a somewhat smaller, wiser body capable of tempering "the sudden and violent passions" thought to be more characteristic of larger legislative chambers (Hamilton, Madison, and Jay 1961, 379). This was one reason that the term of senators was set at six years rather than two, as in the case of members of the House of Representatives.

The Framers' Plan
Whereas the Constitution apportioned the House of Representatives according to population, it guaranteed each state two senators. The framers of the Constitution further entrenched the latter guarantee, which they adopted as part of the Great Compromise, to reconcile the interests of the large and small states (Vile 2001, 16–17), by specifying in Article V that no state shall be deprived of its equal Senate representation without its consent. In an attempt to give the Senate a different electoral base than the House, the framers specified in Article I, Section 3 that it would be composed of "two Senators from each State, chosen by the Legislature thereof, for six Years." Although senators were permitted to cast separate votes (thus potentially representing differing political bases within

their states), on key issues, including the proposal of constitutional amendments, state legislatures sometimes attempted to "instruct" their senators. Senators did not always comply and could not, under the Constitution, be recalled when they failed to do so, but a number of senators resigned when they found that their consciences required them to vote differently than their state legislature had mandated (Bybee 1997, 526).

Calls for Change

Beginning in 1826, calls increased to change this method of selection to popular election, a movement notably supported by Tennessee senator (and later president) Andrew Johnson. This movement hit full stride at the end of the 19th century. By the time the amendment was ratified in 1913, members of Congress had introduced close to 200 proposals to this effect, including over 50 petitions (some redundant) from 31 states. The threat of a convention appears to have been a strong motive that finally prompted the Senate to act.

Early in American constitutional history, there had been considerable controversy about how state legislatures were to make their choices. Congress adopted legislation on the subject on July 25, 1866, but the legislation proved singularly ineffective in solving many of the problems (Haynes 1960, 85), and may even have complicated them by requiring that state legislatures had to select senators by majority vote, thus increasing the possibility of deadlocks (Bybee 1997, 536–537). Many thought that the system allowed money and influence to control the political system (Grimes 1978, 79).

A close scholar of the subject identified the following problems: deadlocks, stampeded elections, bribery and corruption, unfilled vacancies depriving states of their constitutionally entitled equal representation, misrepresentation of popular wishes, interference with the states' regular legislative business, and confusion and corruption of state politics (Haynes 1960, 86–95). In one notorious example in Missouri in 1904, representatives attempted to stop the legislative clock to give time for a senatorial election. Tactics included hoisting a ladder, fist-fighting, and throwing books. It was reported that "the glass of the clock front was broken, but the pendulum still persisted in swinging until, in the midst of a yelling mob, one member began throwing ink bottles at the clock, and finally succeeded in breaking the pendulum" (Haynes 1960, 90).

Action by the States

After the Senate repeatedly refused to act, a number of states took matters into their own hands. Most popular was a method, initially adopted in Oregon by popular referendum, and thereby usually referred to as the "Oregon Model," which asked candidates for the state legislature to pledge their votes for the candidate who won the party primary (Haynes 1960, 101–104). Senators so selected naturally felt obligated to support an amendment for popular election. As Idaho senator Borah remarked, "I should not be here if it [election by the legislature under direct instructions of a popular vote] had not been practiced, and I have great affection for the bridge which carried me over" (Haynes 1960, 108).

Proposal and Ratification

The House of Representatives first adopted a proposed amendment providing for the direct election of senators on July 21, 1894, which it did again in 1898, 1900, and 1902. The Senate's first vote in 1911 proved unsuccessful. The so-called race rider, introduced by Republican Representative Horace Young of Michigan and largely supported by Southern Democrats, generated considerable friction. This would have tied direct election of senators to a provision removing such elections from federal supervision, including protections offered to black voters by the Fifteenth Amendment. Eventually, Republican Senator Francis Bristow of Kentucky succeeded in invalidating the race rider by adding an amendment to the resolution that became the Seventeenth Amendment (Grimes 1978, 79–81). On April 11, 1911, Socialist Representative Victor Berger of Wisconsin introduced a resolution to abolish the Senate (H.J. Res. 79), probably as a way to pressure senators. Both houses finally agreed on the Seventeenth Amendment in May 1912.

The necessary number of states ratified the amendment on April 8, 1913. Massachusetts was the first and Connecticut the 36th to ratify (U.S. Senate 1985, 46). As ratified, the amendment calls for the direct election of senators by state voters with the qualifications "requisite for electors of the most numerous branch of the State legislatures." These were the same qualifications that Article I, Section 2 of the Constitution had introduced for voting for members of the House of Representatives. The amendment also provides that state executives may temporarily fill vacancies until the people vote.

Critiques and Implications of the Amendment

The Seventeenth Amendment has been called "the most drastic alteration in the system of federalism since the Civil War Amendments" (Bernstein with Agel 1993, 122). The amendment had the effect of leading to the election of more people on the basis of their governmental experience than on the basis of their wealth or family connections. The Senate has also become more responsive to fluctuations in popular party preferences (Crook and Hibbing 1997, 352). One result, however, is that, since adoption of the Seventeenth Amendment, the senators of a state often represent a different party than the one that dominates the state legislature (Bybee 1997, 553–554).

In June 1939, a Montana representative proposed repealing the amendment. Critics charge that the amendment weakens political parties and reduced the proper influence of the states in the federal system. With the increasingly high costs of political campaigns and the lack of any limits on what an individual can contribute to his or her own efforts, the goal of seeing that the Senate is not a "millionaires club" may also have been thwarted (R. Peters 1990). A recent law graduate has argued that the amendment needs to be repealed to secure state interests; he has proposed that it might be coupled with a more popular amendment like the Federal Marriage Protection Amendment (Ure, 2007).

In her dissenting opinion in *Garcia v. San Antonio Metropolitan Transit Authority,* a case involving congressional authority to set wage regulations for state and local governments, Justice Sandra Day O'Connor, a former Arizona legislator, referred to the direct election of senators as one factor that may have "lessened the weight Congress gives to the legitimate interests of States as States" (1985, 584).

Citing the implications of the Seventeenth Amendment as "unchartered waters," one author criticized a U.S. circuit court opinion in *Trinsey v. Pennsylvania* (1991). This case dealt with the procedures used to select party nominees for the election of a successor to Republican Senator John Heinz of Pennsylvania, who died in a plane crash. The author of the article argued that the amendment should be interpreted to prohibit a state from selecting candidates for senatorial vacancies without following normal primary election procedures (Little 1991).

See also Federal Marriage Protection Amendment; Federalism and the Amending Process; Fifteenth Amendment.

For Further Reading:

Bernstein, Richard B., with Jerome Agel. 1993. *Amending America: If We Love the Constitution So Much, Why Do We Keep Trying to Change It?* New York: Random House.

Bybee, Jay S. 1997. "Ulysses at the Mast: Democracy, Federalism, and the Sirens' Song of the Seventeenth Amendment." *Northwestern University Law Review* 91 (Winter): 500–569.

Crook, Sara Brandes, and John R. Hibbing. 1997. "A Not-So-Distant Mirror: the 17th Amendment and Congressional Change." *American Political Science Review* 91 (December): 845–853.

Garcia v. San Antonio Metropolitan Transit Authority, 469 U.S. 528 (1985).

Grimes, Alan P. 1978. *Democracy and the Amendments to the Constitution.* Lexington, MA: Lexington Books.

Hamilton, Alexander, James Madison, and John Jay. 1787–1788. *The Federalist Papers.* Reprint, New York: New American Library, 1961.

Haynes, George H. 1960. *The Senate of the United States, Its History and Practice.* New York: Russell and Russell.

Hoebeke, C. H. 1995. *The Road to Mass Democracy: Original Intent and the Seventeenth Amendment.* New Brunswick, NJ: Transaction.

Little, Laura E. 1991. "An Excursion into the Uncharted Waters of the Seventeenth Amendment." *Temple Law Review* 674 (Fall): 629–658.

Peters, Ronald M., Jr. 1990. "Repeal the Seventeenth!" *Extensions* 2 (Spring): 16–17.

Rossum, Ralph A. 2001. *Federalism, the Supreme Court, and the Seventeenth Amendment: The Irony of Constitutional Democracy.* Lanham, MD: Lexington Books.

Ure, James Christian. 2007. "You Scratch My Back and I'll Scratch Yours: Why the Federal Marriage Amendment Should Also Repeal the Seventeenth Amendment." *South Texas Law Review* 49 (Fall): 277–305.

U.S. Senate, Subcommittee on the Constitution, Committee on the Judiciary. 1985. *Amendments to the Constitution: A Brief Legislative History.* Washington DC: U.S. Government Printing Office.

Vile, John R. 2001. *A Companion to the United States Constitution and Its Amendments.* Westport, CT: Praeger.

SEVENTH AMENDMENT

The First Congress proposed the Seventh Amendment in 1789, and the states ratified it as part of the Bill of Rights in 1791. The amendment provides that "in suits at common law, when the value in controversy shall exceed twenty dollars, the right of trial by jury shall be preserved, and no fact tried by a jury, shall be otherwise reexamined in any Court of the United States, than according to the rules of common law." The Seventh Amendment thus complements the Sixth, which provides for jury trials in criminal cases.

The absence of a guarantee of juries in civil cases was a prominent Anti-Federalist criticism of the new document, and the ratifying conventions of Massachusetts, Maryland, Virginia, and North Carolina all called for guarantees of juries in civil cases (Lutz 1992, 57). Accordingly, when James Madison introduced his proposal for a bill of rights, he included a provision that "in suits at common law, between man and man, the trial by jury as one of the best securities to the rights of the people, ought to remain inviolate" (Kurland and Lerner 1987, 5:26).

Supreme Court decisions have extended guarantees for jury trials to federal statutory law, as well as to common, or judge-made, law cases.

However, courts have limited civil juries in four types of cases: those in which individuals sue the government; cases involving congressionally created rights; maritime cases; and equity cases that do not involve money (Pendergast, Pendergast, and Sousanis 2001, 1:142). Moreover, as in the case of the Sixth Amendment, the Supreme Court has not required that such juries consist of the traditional 12 members. Whereas courts have applied the Sixth Amendment provision for a jury trial in criminal cases to the states via the due process clause of the Fourteenth Amendment, they have not so applied the provision in the Seventh Amendment. States are therefore free to dispense with such requirements in their civil proceedings.

In the past dozen years, at least two individuals have advocated repeal of the Seventh Amendment (Antieau 1995; Kennedy 1991).

See also Madison, James; Sixth Amendment.

For Further Reading:

Antieau, Chester J. 1995. *A U.S. Constitution for the Year 2000.* Chicago: Loyola University Press.

Kennedy, Devin C. 1991. "We Need a Fresh Start; Repeal the Seventh Amendment." *Detroit College of Law Review* (Winter): 1289–1301.

Kurland, Philip B., and Ralph Lerner, eds. 1987. *The Founders' Constitution.* 5 vols. Chicago: University of Chicago Press.

Lutz, Donald S. 1992. *A Preface to American Political Theory.* Lawrence: University Press of Kansas.

Pendergast, Tom, Sara Pendergast, and John Sousanis, with Elizabeth Shaw Grunow, eds., 2001. *Constitutional Amendments: From Freedom of Speech to Flag Burning.* 3 vols. Detroit, MI: U.X.L. imprint of Gale Group.

SHAFROTH-PALMER AMENDMENT

Sometimes simply referred to as the Shafroth Amendment, Democratic Senator John F. Shafroth of Colorado and Democratic Representative Mitchell Palmer of Pennsylvania introduced this proposal in Congress in March 1914

(Kraditor 1981, 204–209). Initially, Ruth Hanna McCormick of the National American Woman Suffrage Association (NAWSA) also supported the amendment.

The amendment proposed allowing 8 percent of a state's voters to petition to place women's suffrage on the state ballot, the issue subsequently to be decided by a state referendum. This would have left the issue of women's suffrage a matter for state rather than for federal action (Lunardini 1986, 55). NAWSA dropped its endorsement of the proposal in 1915 when it elected Carrie Chapman Catt as its president, and the organization directed renewed attention to the alternative Anthony Amendment, which became the Nineteenth Amendment in 1920 (Lunardini 1986, 182).

See also Initiative and Referendum; Nineteenth Amendment.

For Further Reading:

Kraditor, Aileen S. 1981. *The Idea of the Woman's Suffrage Movement, 1890–1920.* New York: W. W. Norton.

Lunardini, Christine A. 1986. *From Equal Suffrage to Equal Rights: Alice Paul and the National Woman's Party, 1910–1928.* New York: New York University Press.

SHOGAN, ROBERT

Journalist Robert Shogan advanced a series of ideas for constitutional change in a 1982 book entitled *None of the Above*. Shogan was concerned that there was "a gap between politics and government" (Shogan 1982, 5), which he documented in presidential leadership from John F. Kennedy through Ronald Reagan. Throughout his book, he sought to demonstrate, through discussion of individual campaigns, that campaigns had become increasingly personalized and that there was little coordination between candidates and the party organizations that they represented.

His book ends with eight proposed changes in the U.S. Constitution. He first proposed combining presidential and congressional elections. He thought this might involve changing House and Senate terms to four-years and requiring a straight-ticket ballot. He also suggested that it might require a change in the electoral college to ensure that the winner of the popular vote was selected.

Shogan borrowed his second proposal from Charles Hardin. It proposed giving the winning party 100 votes in the House and the losing party 50. He suggested that this might also require "reducing the power of the Senate" (*Id.*, 270).

Shogan's third proposal was to lift the constitutional ban that prohibited members of Congress from serving on the cabinet. His fourth proposal called for allowing a sitting president to call one intraterm election, and his fifth called for eliminating the vice-presidency. Collectively, he argued that "such alterations in the separation of powers, by making the government more cohesive, more accountable, and more responsive, could pave the way for parties to help make politics more relevant."

Shogan's sixth proposal was for a coordinating party council. His seventh would replace the primary system with nomination by party caucus, perhaps allowing the primaries to sort out the top candidate. His eighth proposal called for "institutionalizing the opposition party" (*Id.*, 272).

Recognizing the difficulty of instituting such drastic changes, he suggested forming a national commission. It would be "composed of elected officials, party leaders, scholars, and representatives of interest groups, which would spend an extensive period on research and evaluation, and supplement these activities with public hearings and educational programs" (*Id.*, 277). He concluded by defending his proposals against those who thought it would make government too strong; against those who thought the nation was "too variegated to support a party system which offers distinct choices on policy to the voters" (*Id.*, 278); against those who feared "a massive unraveling of the American system" (*Id.*, 279); and against those who defended the current system on the basis that none was perfect.

See also Hardin, Charles.

For Further Reading:

Shogan, Robert. 1992. *None of the Above: Why Presidents Fail—And What Can Be Done About It.* New York: New American Library.

SIMSON, VIRGINIA

One of the newest proposals for extensive constitutional change is found on the Web site of Virginia Simpson, who describes herself as "a spiritual journalist/activist who runs a visionary planetary tutorial blogspot, www.ladybraodoak. Blogspot.com" and who seeks to education the young about "economics, clean energy, a drug free lifestyle, friendship and concern for the environment." She states her unconditional support for "impeachment and a war crimes tribunal of the current DC administration—including Congress," and many of her proposals are directed to reigning in war powers, which she believed the Bush Administration was abusing. She outlines her proposals in seven articles.

The first deals with "Powers and Rights Reserved To We the People." The article would limit the designation of "human beings" to exclude corporations and entrust humans with the right to "believe anything, including the possible belief that this Constitution must be discarded and replaced with a superior document." Article I would increase public access to public documents and provide for "affordable housing" and freedom of travel. It would prohibit all electronic surveillance except "on probable cause and a warrant before a judicial tribunal."

Article II deals with "Powers and Rights Reserved to States." It would prosecute "failure to enforce the laws of war" as a war crime and allow states to initiate impeachment investigations. Indeed, states would be permitted "to use deadly combat force to enforce this Constitution against US government officials."

Article III outlines an Independent Branch, which would conduct electronic surveillance of the national government, store it, and make it available as public records. Indeed it would impose the death penalty in cases where the doctrine of "state secrets" was used to hide such information.

Article IV would outline a prosecutorial branch with power "to raise independent combat power, support them, and . . . lawfully use that deadly combat force to confront" members of the other branches.

Article V deals with the Judicial Branch, which it describes as "above the Legislative Branch and Executive Branch only in order of precedence.

Article VI provides that members of congress "may be stopped between sessions and held to account for their failure to enforce the laws of war." Its failure to investigate or impeach officials could result in imposition of the death penalty. Simson would add a "Superior Chamber" to the legislature, which would "decide, before any debate, whether the proposed bill is or is not Constitutional," albeit "subject to approval, challenge, and rejection by the People, States, and Judicial Branch."

Article VII provides for three coequal presidencies. The executive is described as "the least responsive to the People, and the greatest threat of tyranny to this Constitution." The article specifically describes a Domestic Affairs President and a Foreign Affairs President. As commander in chief, the executive would "only have the power to lead combat operations during war time." All correspondence between the executive and legislative branches "shall pass through the Prosecutorial Branch." The article further provides that "presidents are denied a presumption of competence until proven." Moreover, the branch "shall have no power to block the Congress, States, Judiciary, Prosecutorial, and Independent Branch from having a co-equal status to oversee, manage, and organize that lesser branch."

For Further Reading:

"We the People: A New Constitution for the United States." http://www.opednews.com/articles/We-the-People-A-New-Cons.by-labybroadoak-08-531-929 .html. Accessed July 3, 2008.

SIXTEENTH AMENDMENT

The Sixteenth Amendment provides that "the Congress shall have power to lay and collect taxes on incomes, from whatever source derived, without apportionment among the several States, or without regard to any census or enumeration." By constitutionalizing the income tax, this amendment has had a profound effect on everyday life (Carson 1973). Coming 43 years after the adoption of the Fifteenth Amendment, the

Sixteenth Amendment also restored faith in the efficacy of the constitutional amending process and initiated a seven-year period in which three additional amendments were proposed and ratified (Kyvig 1988).

Although the U.S. Supreme Court narrowly decided to void the income tax law of 1894 in *Pollock v. Farmers' Loan & Trust Co.* (1895), it had previously accepted a wartime income tax in *Springer v. United States* (1881). Not only had war ceased in the interim, but opponents of the tax, including New York attorneys Joseph H. Choate and William D. Guthrie, had raised their rhetoric by charging that the tax, with its potential for redistributing income by charging higher rates on higher incomes, smacked of populism and socialism (Kyvig 1988, 187).

In addition to Populists, Democrats generally favored the income tax, as did the Progressive wing of the Republican Party. Support was especially strong in the South, Midwest, and West; there was greater opposition in the northeast industrial states, which could be expected to bear a greater percentage of the tax. When Congress debated the Payne-Aldrich Tariff Bill in 1909, a number of individuals, including Tennessee's Democratic representative Cordell Hull, wanted to include an income tax provision in the hope that the Supreme Court would reconsider its decision in *Pollock*. Others, including President (and future chief justice) William Howard Taft, feared that such a judicial turnabout might weaken the prestige of the Supreme Court (Kyvig 1988, 191–192).

The leader of the Senate Republicans, Conservative Rhode Island millionaire Nelson Aldrich, sought to stymie the so-called Bailey-Cummins income tax addition by proposing an income tax amendment in its place. Aldrich's proposal was a tactical maneuver based on the premise, supported by more than 40 years of Article V quiescence, that such an amendment would never be adopted. Voting 77 to 0, however, the Senate approved the amendment in July 1909, and the House followed by a 318 to 14 majority that same month. The necessary number of states ratified the amendment in 1913. Ironically, such ratification closely followed a unanimous Supreme Court decision that upheld a corporate tax adopted in 1909 (*Flint v. Stone Tracy Co.* [1911]).

Relying on arguments from the Tenth Amendment similar to those advanced by Selden Bacon and others that the Court would soon dismiss, at least one commentator argued that the Sixteenth Amendment was the type of amendment that only the people of a state—as opposed to its legislature—could ratify (R. Brown 1920). In more recent years, a number of individuals on the far right, who have received almost no scholarly notice, have attempted to challenge the validity of the ratification of the Sixteenth Amendment largely on the basis of minute differences in wording between various ratifications that were sent to Congress (Benson and Beckman, 1985; Linne, 1985). A U.S. appellate court decision (*United States v. Benson,* 941 F.2d 598 [1991]) has rejected this claim.

In the 1930s, opponents of big government often focused their wrath on the income tax, and the American Taxpayers Association and the Committee for Constitutional Government both proposed to repeal the amendment or provide for a maximum limit of 25 percent. Although this proposal got some support in Congress (see *Hearings* 1954, 1956), where it was introduced by, among others, Democratic Representative Emanuel Celler of New York, its proponents were far more successful in mobilizing calls from the states for a convention. Apparently, 34 states filed such petitions, although 12 of these also appear to have rescinded their calls (Caplan 1988, 69). In recent years, Republican Representative Ron Paul of Texas, who ran unsuccessfully for the Republican nomination for president in 2008, proposed an amendment abolishing the personal income tax as well as estate and gift taxes; his proposal would also prohibit the U.S. government from competing with private businesses.

Political liberals often favor the income tax over other taxes because of its ability to be progressive, taking a higher percentage of income from those who earn more, as opposed to regressive taxes, like sales or property taxes, which are more frequently used at the state level and that sometimes fall more harshly on the poor. Illinois Democrat representative Jesse Jackson Jr. has proposed an amendment to require that Congress "tax all persons progressively in proportion to the income which they respectively enjoy under the protection of the United States" (Jackson with Watkins, 2001, 385). Jackson apparently intends for this proposal to apply to state taxation as well (Jackson with Watkins, 2001, 403). No constitutional provision either provides for or prohibits such redistributive uses of the amendment.

See also Bacon, Seldon; Jackson, Jesse L., Jr.; *Pollock v. Farmers' Loan & Trust Co.;* Tenth Amendment.

For Further Reading:

Benson, Ben, and M. J. "Red" Beckman. 1985. *The Law That Never Was—The Fraud of the 16th Amendment and Personal Income Tax.* South Holland, IL: Constitutional Research Association.

Brown, Raymond G. 1920. "The Sixteenth Amendment to the United States Constitution." *American Law Review* 54: 843–854.

Caplan, Russell L. 1988. *Constitutional Brinkmanship: Amending the Constitution by National Convention.* New York: Oxford University Press.

Carson, Gerald. 1973. "The Income Tax and How It Grew." *American Heritage* 25 (December): 5–9, 79–88.

Graetz, Michael J. 1997. *The Decline (and Fall?) of the Income Tax.* New York: W.W. Norton & Company.

Jackson, Jesse L., Jr., with Frank E. Watkins. 2001. *A More Perfect Union: Advancing New American Rights.* New York: Welcome Rain Publishers.

Kyvig, David E. 1988. "Can the Constitution Be Amended? The Battle over the Income Tax, 1895–1913." *Prologue* 20 (Fall): 181–200.

Linne, Burtoon. *XVI: The Constitution's Income Tax Amendment Was Not Ratified.* Washington DC: American Liberty Information Society.

Schrader, George D. 1970. "Constitutional History of the Income Tax." *Georgia State Bar Journal* 7 (August): 39–55.

SIXTH AMENDMENT

The First Congress proposed the Sixth Amendment in 1789 as part of the Bill of Rights, which the states ratified in 1791. It contains multiple guarantees, all of which relate to the rights of an accused in criminal proceedings:

> In all criminal prosecutions, the accused shall enjoy the right to a speedy and public trial, by an impartial jury of the State and district wherein the crime shall have been committed; which district shall have been previously ascertained by law, and to be informed of the nature and cause of the accusation; to be confronted with the witnesses against him; to have compulsory process for obtaining witnesses in his favor, and to have the assistance of counsel for his defense.

Most of the provisions of the Sixth Amendment were found in the Bill of Rights that James Madison presented to the First Congress (Kurland and Lerner 1987, 5:25). He, in turn, drew from provisions in existing state constitutions and proposals that state conventions that had ratified the Constitution had advanced.

Each of the provisions of the Sixth Amendment has been fleshed out in judicial decisions. Although the guarantees in the Bill of Rights applied initially only to the national government, courts have subsequently applied all the provisions of the Sixth Amendment to the states via the due process clause of the Fourteenth Amendment. The provisions of the Sixth Amendment that have evoked the most attention and controversy in recent years are those related to jury trials and the right to counsel.

The jury specified in the Sixth Amendment is known as a petit jury. Unlike the grand jury required by the Fifth Amendment, which decides whether to indict individuals, a petit jury in a criminal case (the Seventh Amendment deals with juries in civil cases) determines guilt or innocence and, in some instances, decides on an appropriate penalty. In recent years, the issues of jury size and unanimity have dominated discussion of this institution. In *Williams v. Florida* (1970), the Supreme Court ruled that juries of six persons were appropriate in noncapital criminal cases. Similarly, in *Johnson v. Louisiana* (1972) and *Apodaco v. Oregon* (1972), the Court upheld the use of nonunanimous juries, although it decided in *Burch v.*

Louisiana that juries of six did have to be unanimous.

The right to counsel has also undergone substantial reevaluation in recent years. Originally, courts interpreted it merely to guarantee that an individual had the right to employ an attorney. However, in the famous trial of the Scottsboro Boys, a group of black youths arrested in Alabama and charged with the rape of two white girls, the Court decided that certain extraordinary situations called for state-appointed counsel when individuals could not afford to defend themselves (*Powell v. Alabama* [1932]; D. Carter 1964). Then, in *Gideon v. Wainwright* (1963), the Supreme Court extended the right to court-appointed counsel to indigents in all felony cases (see Lewis 1974). *Argersinger v. Hamlin* (1972) extended the guarantee to all cases in which imprisonment was possible. More recently the Court has begun to pay some attention to the quality of representation, especially in death-row cases. In refusing to hear an appeal of a Texas case in 2002, the Court left standing a decision that had invalidated a death penalty conviction in a case where a defendant alleged that his attorney had fallen asleep during the proceedings (Lane 2002). In *Miranda v. Arizona* (1966), the Supreme Court required police officers to inform suspects being interrogated of this right. The Court reaffirmed this right in *Dickerson v. United States* (2000).

As concerns about law enforcement have increased in recent years, some scholars have expressed concern that Supreme Court decisions have eroded some of the guarantees in the Sixth Amendment (Garcia 1992), but this very debate may reflect the continuing relevance of the rights of criminal defendants (Bodenhamer 1992, 138). Although members of Congress have often reacted angrily to Supreme Court decisions expounding the rights of criminal defendants, they have offered no provisions to repeal this amendment.

Some scholars have expressed concern about the effect of the USA PATRIOT Act of 2001, passed in the aftermath of the September 11 terrorist attacks on the United States, on the Sixth Amendment. Not only does the law appear to allow for possible military trials of noncitizens engaged in terrorist activities, but it also allows for detaining "enemy combatants" (even those who are not citizens) without giving them access to their attorneys (Whitehead 2002, 1118–1127).

See also Seventh Amendment; Terrorism.

For Further Reading:

Bodenhamer, David J. 1992. *Fair Trial: Rights of the Accused in American History.* New York: Oxford University Press.

Carter. Dan T. 1964. *Scottsboro: A Tragedy of the American South.* New York: Oxford University Press.

Garcia, Alfredo. 1992. *The Sixth Amendment in Modern American Jurisprudence: A Critical Perspective.* New York: Greenwood Press.

Kurland, Philip B., and Ralph Lerner, eds. 1987. *The Founders' Constitution.* 5 vols. Chicago: University of Chicago Press.

Lane, Charles. 2002. "High Court Denies Texas Death Appeal: Court Declines to Intervene in 'Sleeping Lawyer Case,'" *The Washington Post,* 3 June, at *washingtonpost.com.*

Lewis, Anthony. 1974. *Gideon's Trumpet.* New York: Vintage Books.

Whitehead, John W. 2002. "Forfeiting 'Enduring Freedom' for 'Homeland Security': A Constitutional Analysis of the USA Patriot Act and the Justice Department's AntiTerrorism Initiatives." *American University Law Review* 51 (August): 1081–1133.

SLAUGHTERHOUSE CASES (1873)

A group of Supreme Court decisions known collectively as the *Slaughterhouse Cases* were the first adjudicated under the Thirteenth and Fourteenth Amendments. They had a profound impact on the interpretation of these amendments and their subsequent legal evolution. At issue was a series of regulations that the state of Louisiana had imposed on those who butchered animals in New Orleans and surrounding parishes. Apparently motivated by a combination of noble concerns about health and crass political considerations, the law limited butchering to the facilities of a single privately owned company; these facilities were to be open to all, with both price and safety regulations.

Butchers with their own facilities sued and challenged this law as a violation of the Thirteenth and Fourteenth Amendments, with special emphasis on the privileges and immunities clause of the latter. Writing for a majority of five, Justice Samuel Miller rejected these claims. In looking at the postwar amendments, Miller stated that "the one pervading purpose found in them all" was "the freedom of the slave race." Although acknowledging that the amendments might also forbid "Mexican peonage or the Chinese coolie labor system," he found that their central purpose needed to be kept in view.

Miller interpreted the privileges and immunities clause as requiring states to extend the same rights to citizens of other states within their jurisdiction as they extended to their own citizens. Noting that the Fourteenth Amendment distinguished between state and national citizenship, Miller argued that it intended to leave the protection of most citizen privileges and immunities where it had always been, that is, at the state level. In rejecting the idea of broad nationally based rights, Miller stated that this would make courts "a perpetual censor upon all legislation of the States" and would be inconsistent with American notions of federalism:

The argument, we admit, is not always the most conclusive which is drawn from the consequences urged against the adoption of a particular construction of an instrument. But when, as in the case before us, these consequences are so serious, so far-reaching and pervading, so great a departure from the structure and spirit of our institutions; when the effect is to fetter and degrade the State governments by subjecting them to the control of Congress, in the exercise of powers hitherto-fore universally conceded to them of the most ordinary and fundamental character; when in fact it radically changes the whole theory of the relations of the State and Federal Governments to each other and of both these governments to the people; the argument has a force that is irresistible, in the absence of language which

expresses such a purpose too closely to admit of doubt. (*Slaughterhouse Cases* 1873, 78)

Miller also rejected pleas based on the Thirteenth Amendment and on the due process and equal protection clauses of the Fourteenth Amendment.

In dismissing Miller's narrow reading of the Fourteenth Amendment, Justice Stephen Field said in his dissent that if the privileges and immunities guaranteed by the amendment were so limited, the Fourteenth Amendment "was a vain and idle enactment, which accomplished nothing, and most unnecessarily excited Congress and the people on its passing" (*Slaughterhouse Cases* 1873, 96). Similarly, in his dissent, Justice Noah Swayne said that the post–Civil War amendments had been designed "to rise to the dignity of a new Magna Carta." He further noted that the Fourteenth Amendment was designed to "embrace equally all races, classes and condition of men" and that, however novel such power might seem, "the novelty was known and the measure deliberately adopted" (*Id.,* 125, 129).

Courts have subsequently interpreted the due process and equal protection clauses of the Fourteenth Amendment quite broadly, but the privileges and immunities clause has never rebounded from the narrow reading it received in this case. Scholars are still divided as to whether the decision appropriately recognized necessary state police powers and the continuity with the federal system that the authors of the postwar amendments intended, or whether the decision represented a judicial "amendment" of these additions in the guise of interpretation.

See Also Fourteenth Amendment; Thirteenth Amendment.

For Further Reading:
Agnes, Richard L. 1994. "Constricting the Law of Freedom: Justice Miller, the Fourteenth Amendment, and the *SlaughterHouse Cases.*" *Chicago-Kent Law Review* 70: 627–688.
Labbe, Donald M., and Jonathan Lurie. 2005. *The* Slaughterhouse Cases*: Regulation, Reconstruction,*

and the Fourteenth Amendment. Lawrence: University Press of Kansas.

Slaughterhouse Cases 83 U.S. (16 Wall.) 36 (1873).

SLAVEHOLDERS, COMPENSATION TO

A critical obstacle to slave emancipation was the financial loss that such emancipation represented to the owners. William Lloyd Garrison was among abolitionists who adamantly opposed any compensation for owners, but, in his annual message of 1862, President Abraham Lincoln proposed a scheme of compensation for states that abolished slavery by January 1900 (J. Richardson 1908, 6:136), and the government actually paid such compensation to slaveholders in the District of Columbia who remained loyal to the Union.

Lincoln later issued the Emancipation Proclamation freeing slaves behind enemy lines, and the Thirteenth Amendment abolished the remnants of this institution in 1865. Fearful that slaveholders might later press their claims for compensation, a number of congressmen introduced resolutions to prohibit it. Section 4 of the Fourteenth Amendment subsequently prohibited the United States from assuming any debts incurred by those in rebellion "or any claim for the loss or emancipation of any slave."

See also Emancipation Proclamation; Garrison, William Lloyd; Lincoln, Abraham; Slavery, District of Columbia; Thirteenth Amendment.

For Further Reading:

Richardson, James E., ed. 1908. *A Compilation of the Messages and Papers of the Presidents, 1789–1908*. 11 vols. n.p.: Bureau of National Literature and Art.

SLAVERY AND COLONIZATION

One of the obstacles to slave emancipation was the fear that the white and black races would find it difficult to live together. Thus, in favor-ably reporting a proposed plan in Virginia to alter the laws so as to free slaves born after the act and to colonize them "to such place as the circumstances of the time should render most proper," Thomas Jefferson noted the problem with allowing them to stay:

> Deep-rooted prejudices entertained by whites; ten thousand recollections, by the blacks, of the injuries they have sustained; new provocations; the real distinctions which nature has made; and many other circumstances, will divide us into parties and produce convulsions, which will probably never end but in the extermination of the one or the other race. (Jefferson 1964, 132–133)

An American Colonization Society was founded in December 1816–January 1817, with the hope that the colonization of free blacks in Africa might eventually be followed by complete emancipation (see letter of Robert G. Harper in Pease and Pease 1965, 18–59). In 1832, Whig Representative William Archer of Virginia introduced an amendment calling on Congress to aid the colonization movement from the sale of public lands, a resolution seconded that same congressional session by the Maryland state legislature.

A number of similar plans were introduced in the early 1860s, one of which was part of a series of proposals by Democratic Senator Stephen A. Douglas of Illinois in 1860. In his annual message of 1862, President Abraham Lincoln recommended three amendments, one of which called on Congress to provide money for the recolonization of free blacks who were willing to relocate (J. Richardson 1908, 6:136). With the final emancipation of all African Americans by the Thirteenth Amendment, the financial and other practical obstacles to such a plan became overwhelming, and calls for such an amendment ceased.

See also Jefferson, Thomas.

For Further Reading:

Jefferson, Thomas. 1785. *Notes on the State of Virginia*. New York: Harper and Row, 1964.

Pease, William H., and June H. Pease, eds. 1965. *The Antislavery Argument*. Indianapolis, IN: Bobbs-Merrill.

Richardson, James E., ed. 1908. *A Compilation of the Messages and Papers of the Presidents, 1789–1908.* 11 vols. n.p.: Bureau of National Literature and Art.

SLAVERY, DISTRICT OF COLUMBIA

The existence of slavery in the District of Columbia caused special consternation among representatives of the free states. In 1839, former President John Quincy Adams, then serving as a Whig representative from Massachusetts, proposed the abolition of slavery and the slave trade in the nation's capital after 1845. The Compromise of 1850 subsequently abolished the slave trade in that city.

A number of proposals relating to slavery in the District of Columbia were among the wave of amendments introduced in Congress beginning in 1860. Some sought to guarantee the continuing legality of slavery in the district, and some attempted to abolish it. Others sought to have the question determined by practices in nearby Virginia and Maryland or in the latter state alone, and still others proposed to guarantee the right of federal officers who owned slaves to bring them into the district with them. Congress abolished slavery in the district in April 1862 (prior to the Thirteenth Amendment) and provided for the compensation of owners who were loyal to the Union (Urofsky 1988, 419).

See also Thirteenth Amendment.

For Further Reading:

Urofsky, Melvin I. 1988. *A March of Liberty: A Constitutional History of the United States.* New York: Alfred A. Knopf.

SLAVERY, FOREIGN COMMERCE

Even many slave owners who attended the Constitutional Convention of 1787 expressed antipathy for the slave trade. Largely at the insistence of the South Carolina delegation, however, Article I, Section 9 of the Constitution withheld power over this trade from Congress until 1808.

In the years immediately preceding this date, seven state legislatures, the first of which was North Carolina's, petitioned for amendments to end the slave trade. In 1807, during Thomas Jefferson's administration, Congress adopted legislation outlawing American participation in the slave trade beginning the following January. This legislation was later strengthened in 1818 (Finkelman 1992, 792).

United States law did not, of course, apply internationally. Thus, the Supreme Court had to deal with a number of subsequent cases, most notably *The Antelope* (1825), involving slaves who had come ashore from other nations. It generally took the position that the slave trade, although contrary to natural law, was not contrary to international law but was rather subject to the rules adopted by individual nations. Moreover, the continuing submission of amendments to end the slave trade right up to the Civil War indicated that existing laws on the subject were not always effective.

Although the constitution of the Confederate States of America was in many ways a slave document, it banned the importation of additional slaves, thus effectively reaching beyond the U.S. Constitution on this point. The adoption of the Thirteenth Amendment ended any incentive to bring slave ships to the United States.

See also Confederate Constitution; Thirteenth Amendment.

For Further Reading:

Finkelman, Paul. 1992. "Slavery." In *The Oxford Companion to the Supreme Court of the United States,* ed. Kermit L. Hall. New York: Oxford University Press.

Rawley, James A. 1981. *The Transatlantic Slave Trade: A History.* New York: W. W. Norton.

Reynolds, Edward. 1985. *Stand the Storm: A History of the Atlantic Slave Trade.* London: Allison & Busby.

SLAVERY, INSURRECTIONS

One of the catalysts to the Civil War was the raid that abolitionist John Brown led on Harpers

Ferry in 1859. He hoped that this action would trigger a general slave revolt. Although his hope was not realized, his raid renewed fears among Southern slaveholders.

Three proposals were offered in 1861 to give Congress power to pass penal laws to punish individuals who incited or aided such insurrections or conspiracies, and another was proposed in 1864 as a substitute for the Thirteenth Amendment (Ames 1896, 206). Ironically, federal powers under the Fourteenth Amendment were later evoked in cases such as *United States v. Guest* (1966) and *United States v. Price* (1966) to punish conspiracies against the rights of African Americans.

See also Abolitionists; Brown, John; Fourteenth Amendment; Thirteenth Amendment.

For Further Reading:

Ames, Herman. 1896. *The Proposed Amendments to the Constitution of the United States during the First Century of Its History.* Reprint, New York: Burt Franklin, 1970.

SLAVERY, INTERSTATE COMMERCE

Article I, Section 9 granted Congress power to limit the foreign slave trade after 1808, but it did not directly address congressional control of the interstate slave trade. Although Congress never attempted to restrict slavery through use of this mechanism, Southerners feared that such a use was a real possibility. Several amendments proposed on the eve of the Civil War, including those by Tennessee's Democratic representative (and future president) Andrew Johnson, Kentucky's Unionist representative John Crittenden, and Illinois' Democratic senator Stephen Douglas, attempted expressly to guarantee the right to engage in such interstate trade.

Long before, in 1823, Georgia had proposed an amendment supported by three other states that had been designed to keep any part of the Constitution from being interpreted "to authorize the importation or ingress of any person of color into any one of the United States contrary to the law of such State" (quoted in Ames 1896, 210). This proposal was prompted by the South Carolina Seaman Act of 1822. The original law, later modified, had provided for the jailing and possible enslavement of free blacks who left their ships for shore. In his role as a circuit court judge, Associate Supreme Court Justice William Johnson described the law as conflicting with both federal commerce power and a treaty with Great Britain. William Wirt, President John Quincy Adams's attorney general, subsequently reaffirmed Johnson's opinion. President Andrew Jackson's attorney generals, John Macpherson Berrien and future chief justice Roger B. Taney, later reversed Wirt's opinion, and the issue continued to be contested until the Thirteenth Amendment abolished slavery (Wiecek 1977, 133–139).

See also Slavery, Foreign Commerce; Thirteenth Amendment.

For Further Reading:

Ames, Herman. 1896. *The Proposed Amendments to the Constitution of the United States during the First Century of Its History.* Reprint, New York: Burt Franklin, 1970.

Wiecek, William. 1977. *The Sources of Antislavery Constitutionalism in America, 1760–1848.* Ithaca, NY: Cornell University Press.

SLAVERY, PROTECTION FOR

Slavery was an issue long before the Civil War (Lively 1992, 11–37). The South's greatest fears, which eventually led to secession, was that the more populous Northern states might one day use the law or the constitutional amending process to abolish slavery.

In 1850, Democratic Representative John Daniels of North Carolina introduced an amendment to prevent such abolition. Beginning in 1860, there were a number of similar proposals (one introduced by Mississippi Democratic representative Jefferson Davis, future president of the Confederacy) designed to protect slavery by specifically recognizing the institution or prohibiting any federal interference with it.

The best known of these proposals, designed to be unalterable, was the Corwin Amendment, which President Abraham Lincoln supported, at least for a time. Southern secession marked the failure of this proposal and prepared the way for the very thing that the Southerners had feared. In 1865, the Thirteenth Amendment abolished slavery.

See also Corwin Amendment; Thirteenth Amendment.

For Further Reading:

Lively, Donald E. 1992. *The Constitution and Race.* New York: Praeger.

SLAVERY, RETURN OF FUGITIVES

One of the most persistent problems engendering controversy between Northern and Southern states prior to the Civil War concerned the pursuit and capture of slaves who fled north to obtain their freedom.

Article IV, Section 2 of the Constitution provided that "no Person held to Service or Labour in one State, under the Laws thereof, escaping into another, shall, in Consequence of any Law or Regulation therein, be discharged from such Service or Labour, but shall be delivered upon Claim of the Party to whom such Service or Labour shall be due." This provision did not explicitly designate who had the obligation to return fugitives. High-handed actions by some Southern slave catchers—who tended to presume that all blacks were escaped slaves—led many Northern states to adopt personal liberty laws designed to provide legal protections against false kidnappings.

Congress adopted a fugitive slave law in 1793, which it later strengthened in 1850 as part of the compromise adopted that year, but as abolitionist sentiment grew, Northern states became increasingly uncooperative. Court decisions written by Joseph Story (a Northerner) in *Prigg v. Pennsylvania* (1842) and by Chief Justice Roger Taney (a

Southerner) in *Abelman v. Booth* (1859) attempted to uphold the rights of slaveholders, but sentiment in some Northern states remained hostile, and Southerners were unsatisfied. In his annual message of 1860, President James Buchanan proposed an "explanatory amendment" recognizing "the right of property in slaves." He further proposed "a like recognition of the right of the master to have his slave who has escaped from one State to another restored and 'delivered up' to him, and the validity of the fugitive-slave law enacted for this purpose, together with a declaration that all State laws impairing or defeating this right are violations of the Constitution, and are consequently null and void" (J. Richardson 198, 5:638).

For his part, incoming president Abraham Lincoln was willing to enforce the fugitive slave law against any conflicting state legislation, but he did not think that a constitutional amendment was necessary (T. Morris 1974, 205).

About thirty amending resolutions followed in the year after Buchanan's speech. Most would have affirmed or strengthened the fugitive slave law. Some would have struck down conflicting state legislation. Some, like a proposal by future president Andrew Johnson, would have obligated the government to provide compensation for fugitive slaves who were not returned. A few, reflecting the sentiments that had led to the personal liberty laws, provided that fugitive slaves would be entitled to a jury or to other procedural protections of regular criminal trials.

In June 1864, Congress repealed the fugitive slave law, and subsequent adoption of the Thirteenth Amendment ended this controversy. One writer believes that the Thirteenth and Fourteenth Amendments "carried forward the commitment that had been embodied in the Personal Liberty Laws" (T. Morris 1974, 218).

See also Fourteenth Amendment; Lincoln, Abraham; Thirteenth Amendment.

For Further Reading:

Morris, Thomas D. 1974. *Free Men All: The Personal Liberty Laws of the North, 1780–1861.* Baltimore: Johns Hopkins University Press.

Richardson, James E., ed. 1908. *A Compilation of the Messages and Papers of the Presidents, 1789–1908.* 11 vols. n.p.: Bureau of National Literature and Art.

SLAVERY, RIGHT TO TRAVEL WITH SLAVES

In the early years of the Republic, Northern free states generally made provision for slave owners to travel there with their slaves. By 1860, however, most Northern states explicitly denied this right (Finkelman 1981, 340).

A notorious case was initiated in 1852 when a Virginia slave owner, Jonathan Lemmon, came by ship to New York with his slaves, intending to take a steamboat to New Orleans. When Lemmon brought his slaves ashore, New York courts, including New York's highest tribunal, held that the slaves had become free (*Lemmon* [1860]). Many slavery opponents subsequently feared, however, that *Scott v. Sandford* (1857) signaled an increased willingness on the part of the U.S. Supreme Court to protect slavery, even in the Northern states (Finkelman 1981, 313–338).

In attempts to reduce the friction that this issue was causing, members of Congress introduced four amendments on December 12, 1860, with provisions to protect the rights of slave owners to travel with their slaves. A substitute for the Thirteenth Amendment, which was introduced in 1864, would have limited the right to such travel to other slave states. For its part, the Constitution of the Confederate States of America granted citizens "the right to travel and sojourn in any State of this Confederacy, with their slaves and other property," thus attempting to guarantee the kind of comity that had ended in the North (Finkelman 1981, 21).

See also Confederate Constitution; *Scott v. Sandford.*

For Further Reading:

Finkelman, Paul. 1981. *An Imperfect Union: Slavery, Federalism and Comity.* Chapel Hill, NC: University of North Carolina Press.

SLAVERY, THE TERRITORIES AND

Members of Congress introduced numerous amending proposals just before the outbreak of the Civil War to resolve the issue of slavery in the territories. This issue was important because these territories were the breeding ground for new states and because such states threatened the precarious balance that had been established in the early years of the Republic between free states and slave states, which eventually ended with the admission of California.

The Northwest Ordinance of 1787, adopted under the Articles of Confederation and reauthorized by the new government in 1789, had prohibited slavery in that area. Subsequent congressional legislation regarding the Southwest Territory and the Louisiana and Missouri Territories prohibited the federal government from interfering with the institution there. Slavery was, however, later forbidden in the Illinois, Indiana, and Michigan Territories (Lively 1992, 12).

The divergent policy for northern and southern territories was formalized with the Missouri Compromise of 1820. Under this plan, Congress admitted Missouri as a slave state, Maine as a free state, and forbade slavery in the Louisiana Territory north of a line at 36 degrees 30 minutes of latitude. The failed Wilmot Proviso, which was introduced during the Mexican-American War, subsequently stirred passions by proposing to abolish slavery in any territories acquired from Mexico. Moreover, the Kansas-Nebraska Act of 1854 effectively repealed the Missouri Compromise line between free and slave states by specifying that Kansas and Nebraska, both north of the line, would decide for themselves whether they wanted to be slave or free. This law embodied the principle of popular sovereignty, which Illinois Democratic senator Stephen Douglas had championed. Similarly, in 1857 Chief Justice Roger Taney decided in *Scott v. Sandford* that the provisions of the Missouri Compromise that restricted slavery in the northern territories were unconstitutional.

Members of the newly formed Republican Party were especially concerned about the Kansas-Nebraska Act and the *Scott* decision. Both actions opened the prospect for the expansion of slavery, and Republicans were committed to the principle that slavery could be tolerated only if it were placed on a course of ultimate extinction (Foner 1970). Many Southern Democrats were just as concerned that, as the balance of the Union tipped toward the free states, slavery would be jeopardized.

Proposed constitutional amendments reflected national divisions. In an apparent attempt to reaffirm the much-criticized *Scott* decision, President James Buchanan called for federal protection of slavery in the territories in his 1860 annual message. Other proposals repeated Buchanan's call for federal protection of slavery in the territories, called for resurrection of the 36 degrees 30 minutes line drawn by the Missouri Compromise, proposed to take away any authority of the federal government or the territorial legislatures regarding slavery, or called for states to decide whether they wanted to have slaves at the time they joined the Union.

Ultimately, no compromises proved successful, and the nation plunged into the Civil War. The Thirteenth Amendment subsequently prohibited slavery not only in the northern territories but also in those Southern states where the institution had been so entrenched.

See also *Scott v. Sandford;* Thirteenth Amendment.

For Further Reading:

Foner, Eric. 1970. *Free Soil, Free Labor, Free Men: The Ideology of the Republican Party before the Civil War.* New York: Oxford University Press.

Lively, Donald E. 1992. *The Constitution and Race.* New York: Praeger.

SMITH, GOLDWIN
(1823–1910)

British-born Goldwin Smith, a barrister (lawyer) and professor who eventually settled in Canada, presented his views on the need for American constitutional reform in an article published in 1898. His thoughts appear to have been largely stimulated by the threat of "Bryanism" in the previous presidential contest, and like others of his day, his solution was that of a cabinet, or parliamentary, government (Vile 1991c, 40–42).

Smith favored reducing the power of the Senate; he thought that some states, such as Nevada,

had been introduced prematurely into the Union and that small states had inordinate influence. He also considered the two-year term for members of the House of Representatives to be too short to allow members to gain the requisite knowledge or perform as statesmen. In Smith's judgment, however, the most urgent weakness in U.S. government was "the want of initiative and control in legislation and, still more palpably, in finance, arising from the exclusion of the responsible ministers of state from the assembly which makes the laws, regulates the expenditure, and imposes the taxes" (G. Smith 1898, 262).

Smith also believed that the change of administration every four years needlessly destroyed continuity in the State Department. Because he was especially concerned about the Supreme Court's acceptance of inconvertible paper money, Smith thought that the Court should be limited to interpreting, rather than modifying, the Constitution. Pointing to the sectional strife that disputes over tariff policy had spawned throughout American history, Smith advocated "an equal *ad valorem* duty on all imports, variable in amount with the necessities of the treasury" (G. Smith 1898, 266).

Believing that the Fifteenth Amendment had become a dead letter, Smith favorably cited a petition by Louisiana and two other states for a convention to repeal it. He also favored immigration (and possibly suffrage) restrictions, especially in the case of "the Russian or Hungarian Jew" (G. Smith 1898, 267). Anticipating that Cuba might be annexed to the United States, he also favored an amendment to regulate the governing of such dependencies.

Elsewhere, Smith speculated that "a union of this Northern Continent" might be an appropriate occasion for revising the Constitution (G. Smith 1906, 851). Sharing the common belief of his day that it was extremely difficult to change the U.S. Constitution, Smith did not, however, hold out much prospect for the reforms he advocated.

See also Fifteenth Amendment; Parliamentary Systems.

For Further Reading:

Smith, Goldwin. 1906. "Chief Justice Clark on the Defects of the American Constitution." *North American Review* 183 (1 November): 845–851.

———. 1898. "Is the Constitution Outworn?" *North American Review* 166 (March): 257–267.

Vile, John R. 1991c. *Rewriting the United States Constitution: An Examination of Proposals from Reconstruction to the Present.* New York: Praeger.

SMITH V. UNION BANK (1831)

Smith v. Union Bank involved the disposition of an estate. The specific question was whether debts should be paid according to the laws where the decedent had been domiciled or according to the laws of the state where he held his property. The Supreme Court decided that the latter rule should govern.

In so ruling, Justice William Johnson noted, "Whether it would or would not be politic to establish a different rule by a convention of the States, under constitutional sanction, is not a question for our consideration" (*Smith* 1831, 528). A modern scholar who believes that constitutional conventions may be limited to a single subject has cited this decision as support for his view (Caplan 1988, 45–46).

See also Constitutional Conventions.

For Further Reading:
Caplan, Russell L. 1988. *Constitutional Brinkmanship: Amending the Constitution by National Convention.* New York: Oxford University Press.

Smith v. Union Bank, 30 U.S. (5 Pet.) 518 (1831).

SOCIAL AND ECONOMIC RIGHTS

By contrast to many 20th-century constitutions, the 18th-century authors of the U.S. Constitution, who preceded the birth of the modern welfare state, were more concerned about protecting citizens from government (so-called "negative rights") than they were for guaranteeing that government would provide certain social, economic, and welfare-related rights (so-called "positive rights"). From time to time, individuals, U.S.

Representative Jesse Jackson Jr. among them, have proposed amendments, similar to those in some Western European nations, to guarantee education, housing, vacations, welfare, work, or the like. However, to date no such amendments have been adopted. Even the prohibition against child labor (which was still phrased as a negative rather than as a positive right) was eventually enacted through legislation, and confirmed by judicial acquiescence, rather than through constitutional amendment. Similarly, although the U.S. Supreme Court agreed that the right to an education was an important right in *Brown v. Board of Education* (1954), it subsequently refused in *San Antonio Independent School District v. Rodriguez* (1973) to declare that the right to a particular level of education was a fundamental right or to require that states fund all schools equally.

Harvard Law professor Mary Ann Glendon has observed that those nations that do include social and economic rights within their constitutions usually list them as aspirations rather than as judicially enforceable guarantees, such as those with which Americans accustomed to fairly broad exercises of judicial review are familiar (Glendon 1992, 528). She thinks that adding such rights as amendments to the U.S. Constitution might increase litigation without necessarily resulting in higher levels of welfare-related benefits. Frank E.L. Deale, of the CUNY School of Law, thinks that it might be more productive to lobby for such rights at the state and local level rather than the national level (2000).

See also Child-Labor Amendment; Housing; Jackson, Jesse L., Jr.; Welfare Payments, Right to.

For Further Reading:
Bentley, Curt. 2007. "Constrained by the Liberal Tradition: Shy the Supreme Court Has Not Found Positive Rights in the American Constitution." *Brigham Young University Law Review* 2007: 1721–1765.

Deale, Frank E.L. 2000. "The Unhappy History of Economic Rights in the United States and Prospects for Their Creation and Renewal." *Howard Law Journal* 43 (Spring): 281–342.

Glendon, Mary Ann. 1992. "Rights in Twentieth-Century Constitutions," *University of Chicago Law Review* 59 (Winter): 519–538.

Klein, Alana. 2008. "Judging as Nudging: New Governance Approaches for the Enforcement of Constitutional Social and Economic Rights." *Columbia Human Rights Law Review* 39 (Spring): 351–422.

San Antonio Independent School District v. Rodriguez, 411 U.S. 1 (1973).

———. 2008. *U.S. Social Security: A Reference Handbook.* Santa Barbara: ABC-CLIO.

SOCIAL SECURITY

Introduced during the administration of Franklin D. Roosevelt, Social Security has become one of the largest entitlement programs in America today. It provides both for the children of working individuals who die and retirement pensions for individuals who have paid into the program. Partly because of this program, poverty, once pervasive in this age group, has significantly decreased among retired individuals in the United States. The program, which is financed by mandatory payments from most American workers and their employers, is intended to supplement savings and other retirement pensions rather than as an exclusive means of support for senior citizens. Highly controversial when Roosevelt first proposed it, the program is now supported by leaders of both major political parties.

Some recent projections have indicated that the program could run out of money during the time when the large number of "baby boomers," born in the relatively prosperous years directly following the soldiers' return home from World War II, retire. Largely as a result, there has been increased political concern about the continuing viability of this program.

A number of proposals in recent years that have called for balanced budgets have included provisions that Social Security funds (which are currently in the black) not be used in computing the budget. Republican backers of the Balanced Budget Amendment sometimes charged that Democratic opponents were using the highly emotional Social Security issue as a smokescreen for more deep-seated opposition to the amendment.

See also Balanced Budget Amendment.

For Further Reading:

Livingston, Steven G. 2002. *Student's Guide to Landmark Congressional Legislation on Social Security and Welfare.* Westport, CT: Greenwood Press.

SOCIALIST PARTY OF AMERICA

Although Socialist candidates for president such as Eugene Debs and Norman Thomas have occasionally attracted national attention, unlike many Western European democracies, the United States has never had a strong Socialist Party (Shannon 1967). This may reflect the comparative weakness of organized labor in the United States, but it may also stem from Americans' tendency to associate the agenda of the Socialists with that of the Communists. Although both parties favor governmental ownership of major industries, Socialists favor reform through the ballot box and are committed to other democratic methods. By contrast, Communists are traditionally committed to revolutionary violence and show little respect for democracy.

Of all their platforms, the Socialist platform of 1932 focused the most on constitutional reforms. Many of these reforms showed clear consistency with those of earlier progressivists (Vile 1991c, 67–68) and included provisions for "proportional representation" in Congress, "direct election of the President and Vice President," and adoption of "the initiative and referendum" (Porter and Johnson 1966, 353). The platform also called for the elimination of the Supreme Court's power to declare laws unconstitutional and liberalization of the amending process. In addition, the platform proposed repeal of the Eighteenth Amendment and national alcoholic prohibition.

See also Eighteenth Amendment; Progressive Era.

For Further Reading:

Porter, Kirk H., and Donald B. Johnson. 1966. *National Party Platforms, 1840–1964.* Urbana, IL: University of Illinois Press.

Shannon, David A. 1967. *The Socialist Party of America: A History.* Chicago: Quadrangle Books.

Vile, John R. 1991c. *Rewriting the United States Constitution: An Examination of Proposals from Reconstruction to the Present.* New York: Praeger.

SOUTH CAROLINA V. BAKER (1988)

This case involved a section of the Tax Equity and Fiscal Responsibility Act of 1982, which had removed the federal tax exemption for interest earned on unregistered state bonds. South Carolina argued that this provision violated both the Tenth Amendment and the doctrine of intergovernmental tax immunities.

Writing for a 7-to-1 majority of the Court, Justice William Brennan upheld the law. Working from the precedent in *Garcia v. San Antonio Metropolitan Transit Authority* (1985), Brennan dealt with the Tenth Amendment argument by ruling that states "must find their protection from congressional regulation through the national political process, not through judicially defined spheres of unregulated state activity" (*South Carolina* 1988, 512). On the related matter of the national government's authority to force states to adopt regulations on behalf of federal interests (an issue also raised by the amendment to prohibit unfunded federal mandates), Brennan found that the law in question did not significantly differ from other such laws that the Court had upheld.

The issue of intergovernmental tax immunity dated back to the decision in *Pollock v. Farmers' Loan & Trust Co.* (1895), which immunized interest earned on state bonds from federal taxation. Even after the adoption of the Sixteenth Amendment, the Court had upheld this exemption, prompting numerous amending proposals to permit the taxation of state securities. Noting that the *Pollock* decision regarding state bonds represented but one of a number of intergovernmental tax immunities that were recognized at that time, Brennan pointed out that most such immunities had since been abandoned. He therefore decided that the *Pollock* decision was no longer valid on this point, and he overturned it.

Justices John Paul Stevens, Antonin Scalia, and William Rehnquist each wrote concurring opinions. Justice Sandra Day O'Connor dissented. She believed that the existing tax immunity doctrine, which accepted taxes that were not directly imposed on—or discriminatory with regard to—state governments, was inadequate to protect state sovereignty.

Delaware Republican senator William Roth has since proposed an amendment to limit federal taxation of state and local obligations issued to finance governmental activities or public purposes. Cosponsors included South Carolina Republican senator Strom Thurmond, South Carolina Democratic senator Ernest Hollings, and Kansas Republican senator Bob Dole.

See also *Garcia v. San Antonio Metropolitan Transit Authority; Pollock v. Farmers' Loan & Trust Co;* Tenth Amendment.

For Further Reading:
South Carolina v. Baker, 485 U.S. 505 (1988).

SOVEREIGNTY

Once at the center of much of the discussion of law and politics, the idea of sovereignty is often traced back to the French philosopher Jean Bodin and the English philosophers Thomas Hobbes and John Austin. A modern writer noted that "sovereignty was an attribute of a determinate person or body to whom the generality of the society gave habitual obedience and who or which was not itself habitually obedient to any other person or body. Within that society the sovereign had ultimate power to lay down the law" (Walker 1980, 1163).

It is difficult to identify the sovereign in a system like that of the United States, which divides state and national powers in a federal system and separates national powers into three major branches. There is, however, considerable warrant for suggesting that the ultimate sovereign—what one writer called the "pro-sovereign" (Radin 1930) to distinguish it from the regularly functioning government—is the amending mechanism. Lester B. Orfield noted that "in the last analysis, one is brought to the conclusion that sovereignty in the United States, if it can be said to exist at all, is located in the amending body" (1942, 154). Orfield further noted that "the sovereign is a real sovereign, though one fluctuating in its composition" (1942, 159).

The idea that the amending process is sovereign is sometimes called into question by the entrenchment provision providing for equal state representation in the Senate. However, since this limit can be overridden with the states' consent, it is not absolute, and in any case, it has little "practical significance" (Orfield 1942, 162).

The idea advanced by some writers that there are implicit limits on the amending process suggests that sovereignty rests elsewhere, namely, in whatever body or bodies—perhaps the courts—have responsibility for ascertaining or enforcing such limits. Some such authors may, however, simply be claiming, like Thomas Jefferson, Abraham Lincoln, and others, that popular sovereignty must accord with natural justice in order to be right. The preamble and the Ninth and Tenth Amendments also suggest that "the people" are the sovereign. Akhil Reed Amar has accordingly argued that the people have the power to amend the Constitution outside of the specific procedures designated by Article V. Proposals to amend Article V to provide for greater popular participation are often based on theories of popular sovereignty.

See also Amar, Akhil Reed; Establishment Clause; Federalism and the Amending Process; Initiative and Referendum.

For Further Reading:
Orfield, Lester B. 1942. *The Amending of the Federal Constitution*. Ann Arbor, MI: University of Michigan Press.
Radin, Max. 1930. "The Intermittent Sovereign." *Yale Law Journal* 30: 514–531.
Walker, David M. 1980. *The Oxford Companion to Law*. Oxford: Clarenden Press.

SPECIAL PROSECUTOR

Although the Watergate scandal did not mark the first use of a special prosecutor, this position has assumed increased visibility and been more frequently utilized since this historic event. Great concern was raised over the independence of this office on October 20, 1973, when, in the so-called Saturday Night Massacre, President Richard Nixon fired Watergate special prosecutor Archibald Cox. After the consequent public

uproar, Nixon appointed Leon Jaworski to this post on November 1, 1973.

Shortly thereafter, Missouri Democrat William Randall offered what he called "the Executive Investigation and Prosecution Amendment." Randall wanted to alleviate questions—later largely resolved in favor of the arrangement in *United States v. Nixon* (1974)—about the propriety of one executive official, namely, the president, appointing another officer to investigate other executive officials. Randall therefore proposed giving this authority to Congress.

The Ethics in Government Act of 1978—subsequently revised and reauthorized in 1982, 1987, and 1992—provided that a special court could appoint such prosecutors at the request of the attorney general, who could remove them only for cause. The Supreme Court upheld this arrangement in *Morrison v. Olson* (1988), a decision notable for a strong dissent by Justice Antonin Scalia, who thought the special prosecutor was too independent of executive authority and thus violated separation of powers. After costly investigations of the Iran-Contra Affair in the Reagan Administration (involving the sale of weapons to Iran in exchange for money to fight against communism in Nicaragua) and then first, of President Bill Clinton's Whitewater land deal, and then of his truthfulness about sexual affairs that led to his impeachment by the U.S. House of Representatives, even Special Prosecutor Kenneth Starr joined those who questioned the efficacy of the mechanism. The special prosecutor law has accordingly been allowed to lapse.

For Further Reading:
Harriger, Katy J. 2000. *The Special Prosecutor in American Politics*. 2nd ed. Lawrence: University Press of Kansas.

STABILITY AND THE AMENDING PROCESS

One typically associates the constitutional amending process with change and progress, but the difficulty of the process also indicates that it also helps promote stability. Without any process of constitutional change, progress would be difficult, and individuals might be tempted to follow the example of the American revolutionaries and seek to overthrow the government by force. Once established, however, constitutions are designed to be fundamental law. It is important to protect this law against unnecessary upheavals that could prove to be more disquieting than changes in ordinary legal statutes.

Professor Michael Van Alstine has pointed both to the increased range and velocity of legal change in recent years and to the fact that all changes in law involve costs (Van Alstine 2002). Although he does not specifically focus on changes in constitutional law, such changes would undoubtedly involve similar, if not greater, costs. In early discussions between Thomas Jefferson and James Madison, after Jefferson suggested that the people should rewrite constitutions every generation, Madison pointed out that such continual change could create instability and other unwanted consequences, and he defended the mechanism in Article V as guarding against either too much or too little change. Scholars have classified the U.S. Constitution as a "rigid" constitution in that the framers rejected the idea of parliamentary sovereignty whereby ordinary legislation could alter fundamental law.

Although some constitutional amendments, like the Thirteenth Amendment abolishing slavery or the Nineteenth Amendment guaranteeing that women would not be denied the right to vote on the basis of their sex, have brought about and/or ratified significant changes in American history, the nation continues to operate under the document written in 1787, as amended. To date the only convention that has met to formulate a completely new Constitution was that which by the seceding Confederate States of America held. In most matters not involving slavery, it continued to be patterned on the Constitution for the United States that was already in existence.

Article VII specified that the Constitution of 1787 would not go into effect until nine states ratified. So too, modern amendments do not go into effect until the requisite number of states adopt them. Such amendments sometimes provide for a stated implementation period—the Eighteenth Amendment, for example, specified that it would not go into effect until one year after it was ratified.

The constitutional amending process attempts to provide for stability in the fundamental law through supermajority requirements that promote deliberation and consensus. Article V of the Constitution requires two-thirds majorities to propose amendments and three-fourths majorities to ratify them. To date, only 27 such amendments have been adopted. At least one such amendment, the Eighteenth (imposing national alcoholic prohibition), proved so costly that it was later repealed by the Twenty-first. The Eighteenth Amendment serves as a good example of the unintended consequences that an unwise or unenforceable amendment can impose.

Because amendments are so difficult to adopt, many changes in constitutional understandings are initiated through judicial interpretations and changing customs and practices. These bring their own costs and generate their own instability (especially if they are not stated in clear language), although they may typically be altered more easily than changes incorporated into the constitutional text.

See also Confederate States of America, Constitution of; Implementation Dates of Amendments; Jefferson, Thomas; Madison, James; Progress and the Amending Process; Rigid Constitution; Unintended Consequences of Constitutional Amendments.

For Further Reading:

Scheuerman, William E. 2002. "Constitutionalism in an Age of Speed." *Constitutional Commentary* 19 (Summer): 353–390.

Van Alstine, Michael P. 2002. "The Costs of Legal Change." *UCLA Law Review* 49 (February): 789–870.

STANTON, ELIZABETH CADY (1815–1902)

Elizabeth Cady Stanton was one of the nation's foremost proponents of women's rights and women's suffrage. Her husband, Henry Brewster Stanton, whom she married in 1840, was then an executive of the abolitionist American Anti-Slavery Society. Elizabeth was a proponent of abolition and temperance when she met Lucretia Mott at the London Anti-Slavery Convention in 1840 and became more active in feminist issues.

In 1848, Stanton and Mott helped organize the historic Seneca Falls Women's Rights Convention in New York. In what has been described as "a brilliant propagandistic stroke" (Banner 1980, 41), delegates chose to pattern their plea for women's equality on the language of the Declaration of Independence. At the time, many citizens regarded Stanton's call for women's suffrage as radical. This label often stuck with her, despite the fact that she was married and raised seven children.

Stanton is often associated with Susan B. Anthony. Stanton made Anthony's acquaintance in 1851, and she worked with her (sometimes envying the unmarried Anthony's greater mobility) for much of her remaining life. In 1863, Stanton and Anthony helped gather 300,000 petitions for the emancipation of slaves, an objective accomplished with the Thirteenth Amendment. In 1866, Stanton became the first woman to run for the U.S. House of Representatives. In 1868, Stanton and Anthony founded the Workingwoman's Association, and in 1869, they founded the National Woman Suffrage Association. They did so after having opposed women who had supported the Fourteenth and Fifteenth Amendments despite the failure of these amendments to extend legal protections to women. When Stanton and Anthony's group merged with the rival American Woman Suffrage Association to form the National American Woman Suffrage Association (NAWSA) in 1890 and to push for what was to become the Nineteenth Amendment, Stanton became the first president. She served until Anthony became president in 1892.

In the 1880s, Stanton opposed those who sought an amendment for uniform marriage and divorce laws. She feared that such laws were likely to make divorce more difficult in states that had liberalized laws on the subject (Thomas, 2005).

Stanton generally kept little distance between herself and those espousing radical causes.

Stanton's *Woman's Bible,* which she published in 1895 and which reflected her own religious skepticism, provoked considerable controversy, and NAWSA disavowed any tie with the work the following year. A list of causes Stanton supported in addition to suffrage includes "coeducation, girls' sports, job training, equal wages, labor unions, birth control, cooperative nurseries and kitchens, property rights for wives, child custody rights for mothers, and reform of divorce laws" (Griffith 1984, xiv). The decision to acknowledge Anthony rather than Stanton as the mother of the Nineteenth Amendment was part of a conscious strategy to avoid what was perceived to be Stanton's more radical stigma (Griffith 1984, xv).

See also Abolitionists; Anthony, Susan Brownell; Marriage and Divorce Laws; Nineteenth Amendment; Seneca Falls Convention; Thirteenth Amendment.

For Further Reading:

Banner, Lois W. 1980. *Elizabeth Cady Stanton: A Radical for Women's Rights.* Boston: Little, Brown.

Davis, Sue. *The Political Thought of Elizabeth Cady Stanton.* New York: NYU Press.

Griffith, Elisabeth. 1984. *In Her Own Right: The Life of Elizabeth Cady Stanton.* New York: Oxford University Press.

Thomas, Tracy A. 2005. "Elizabeth Cady Stanton and the Federal Marriage Amendment: A Letter to the President." *Constitutional Commentary* 22 (Spring): 137–159.

STARE DECISIS

One element that contributes to the stability of interpretations of the U.S. Constitution is the legal doctrine of *stare decisis*. Under this generally accepted doctrine, which is nowhere stated in the Constitution, courts usually adhere to the rulings in prior cases and constitutional interpretations without examining the document *de novo,* or "anew," each time they have to make a decision.

If the principle were absolute, unwise or mistaken judicial interpretations like those upholding the doctrine of "separate but equal" in *Plessy v. Ferguson* (1896) or mandating compulsory flag salutes in *Minersville School District v. Gobitis* (1940) could never be reversed other than by the difficult process of constitutional amendment. Although courts thus pay great deference to the principle, it is not absolute. Lower federal courts, which are subservient to the Supreme Court, are generally less likely to depart from established U.S. Supreme Court decisions than is the Supreme Court itself.

The result complicates constitutional changes in the United States. Individuals who might otherwise work for the proposal and ratification of constitutional amendments might simply vote for the election of presidents and senators who they think will appoint and confirm Supreme Court justices who will reverse existing decisions with which they disagree. In *Planned Parenthood of Southeastern Pennsylvania v. Casey* (1992), Justices Sandra Day O'Connor, Anthony Kennedy, and David Souter put particular emphasis on the doctrine in upholding the central ruling in the Supreme Court's decision in *Roe v. Wade* (1973) recognizing the right to obtain legal abortions. These three justices were particularly concerned that if the Supreme Court reversed course, it might look as though it were caving in to popular pressure.

The Child Labor Amendment is an example of a proposal whose need was undercut by judicial decisions that reversed earlier rulings and accepted regulation of this subject. Arguably too, the Equal Rights Amendment may have lost momentum in part due to Supreme Court decisions expanding its interpretations of women's rights under the equal protection clause of the Fourteenth Amendment and to related fears that expansive new constitutional language might give the Court greater leeway in interpreting women's rights than the public actually desired.

One advantage of precisely drawn amendments is that they are unlikely to be altered or reversed through judicial interpretation. Broadly worded provisions like "due process" or "equal protection of the laws" (both found in the Fourteenth Amendment) clearly give greater leeway for judicial decision making than do more narrowly worded provisions.

See also Child Labor Amendment; Equal Rights Amendment; Stability and the Amending Process; Supreme Court Decisions Reversed by Constitutional Amendments.

For Further Reading:
Monaghan, Henry Paul. 1988. "Stare Decisis and Constitutional Adjudication." *Columbia Law Review* 88: 723.

STATE-FEDERAL RELATIONS

Political scientists recognize three basic forms of government: confederal, federal, and unitary. Confederal governments, such as the Articles of Confederation, divide powers between the states and a national government, but because the latter must operate through the former—in raising taxes and armies, for example—the former is more powerful. A unitary government, like that in Great Britain, has no permanent state governments. By contrast, a federal government retains states but allows both state and national governments to operate directly upon individuals. Both confederal and federal governments require written constitutions. Otherwise, there would be no clear way to allocate power between the two levels of government (Vile 2002a, 104).

By its very nature, a federal government is complex. Even with a written constitution, disputes about the appropriate allocation of authority between the nation and the states are likely to arise, and adjustments may be needed. A number of constitutional amendments have addressed federal concerns. These include the Bill of Rights, especially the Tenth Amendment; the Eleventh, Fourteenth, and Seventeenth Amendments; and amendments (for example, the Fifteenth, Nineteenth, and Twenty-sixth) that have set national standards for voting rights.

Of all the conflicts over federalism in the United States, none proved more irreconcilable than that which led to the Civil War. This conflict, in turn, reflected tensions in the original debates between the Federalists and the Anti-Federalists (Mason 1964) and had roots in the conflict from 1828 to 1832 over federal tariff policies. This tariff controversy led to a number of proposals, some for a constitutional convention, to deal with the situation.

The period from 1860 to 1861, just before the outbreak of the Civil War, led to a virtual avalanche of proposals. Many were designed to deal specifically with the issue of slavery and its many ramifications, but others were directed more generally to state-federal relations. Proposals included defining those powers that were reserved to the states or denied to the national government, guaranteeing state equality, providing that states should be permitted to appoint federal officers within their boundaries, creating a plural executive or otherwise guaranteeing that legislation could not be adopted without the concurrence of each section of the nation, providing a legal means for states to secede, prohibiting such secession, or recognizing federal law as supreme.

Within five years of the end of the Civil War, the nation adopted three amendments (the Thirteenth, Fourteenth, and Fifteenth Amendments), and in *Texas v. White* (1869), the Supreme Court declared that the Constitution had created "an indestructible Union of indestructible States" (*Id.*, 725). The vigorous debates reflected in the *Slaughterhouse Cases* (1873), however, indicated that even the postwar amendments had not resolved federalism issues. State-federal conflict was especially prominent in the wake of the Supreme Court's ruling in *Brown v. Board of Education* (1954), which declared de jure segregation to be illegal. This decision subsequently led to calls for protection of state police powers. More recently, the belief that federal regulations have become stifling has led to renewed attention to the Tenth and Eleventh Amendments and to calls for adjusting state-federal relations by amendment ("Conference of the States" 1995).

See also Federalism and the Amending Process; Fourteenth Amendment; Tenth Amendment.

For Further Reading:

"Conference of the States: An Action Plan to Restore Balance in the Federal System." 1995. Concept paper adopted by the Council of State Governments, the National Governors' Association, and the National Conference of State Legislatures. 1 February.

Mason, Alpheus T. 1964. *The States' Rights Debate: Antifederalism and the Constitution.* Englewood Cliffs, NJ: Prentice-Hall.

Vile, John R. 2006. *A Companion to the United States Constitution and Its Amendments.* 4th ed. Westport, CT: Praeger.

STATES, ADMISSION OF NEW

The framers of the Constitution were far-sighted enough to provide in Article IV, Section 3 that "new states may be admitted by Congress into the Union." They subjected this provision to the reservation that new states would be formed neither within existing states nor by joining two or more states or parts of states without their consent. In cases such as *Coyle v. Smith* (1911), involving Oklahoma's authority to move its capital after it became a state, the Supreme Court has established that new states enter on an equal basis with older ones.

The admission of new states was especially controversial in the nation's early history, when both North and South examined each new candidate for statehood with a view to its impact on the respective balance that free and slave states would have in the Senate. Apparently with this issue in mind, in 1815 Senator Joseph Varnum of Massachusetts introduced a resolution to prevent the admission of new states except by a two-thirds vote. In 1839, former President John Quincy Adams, then serving as a Whig in the House of Representatives, sought an amendment to impose a flat ban on the admission of new slave states.

Controversy shifted but continued after the Civil War, when the admission of Utah, where polygamy was then practiced, became especially controversial. In 1871, Democratic Representative Abram Comingo of Missouri introduced an amendment requiring that a new state have at least enough population to entitle it to one member in the House of Representatives under the ratio for representation then in use.

In 1896, Ohio Republican representative Lucien Fenton introduced an amendment to prohibit the admission of states from any territories south of 30 degrees north latitude, thus excluding Hawaii from future statehood. Several other proposed amendments sought either to prevent the acquisition of any noncontiguous territories, several of which the United States acquired as a result of the Spanish-American War, or to require the admission of such territories by approval of two-thirds votes of both houses of Congress and three-fourths of the state legislatures.

Close to 30 amending resolutions were introduced in Congress from 1953 to 1961 regarding the admission of new states. These amendments were apparently aimed at Alaska and Hawaii. Concerns were raised about the nation's ability to defend these areas and, especially in the case of Hawaii, about the Americanization of an area with such a large Asian population (Bell 1984).

Most of the proposals introduced in the 1950s resurrected the idea that new states should be admitted only by the procedures and majorities needed to amend the federal Constitution. Almost as if their sponsors feared that such a policy might be applied retroactively, a number of such resolutions specifically exempted the procedure under which the Republic of Texas (which joined as a republic rather than as a prior territory) had been admitted as a state. Perhaps as a way of highlighting population disparities, especially in the case of Alaska, some resolutions in the 1950s would have allowed Congress to limit the representation of new states in the U.S. Senate.

See also Polygamy.

For Further Reading:

Bell, Roger. 1984. *Last Among Equals: Hawaii Statehood and American Politics.* Honolulu: University of Hawaii Press.

Onuf, Peter. 1984. "Territories and Statehood." In *Encyclopedia of American Political History: Studies of Principal Movements and Ideas,* ed. Jack P. Greene, 3: 1283–1304. New York: Charles Scribner's Sons.

STATES, BOUNDARIES OF

Numerous proponents of a new constitution for the United States have suggested that state boundaries need to be redrawn along more functional lines. Political scientist Rexford Tugwell, for example, wanted to divide existing states into approximately 20 "newstates" (Tugwell 1974); historian Leland Baldwin (1972) called for approximately 15 states, with Alaska being permitted to join Oregon or become a commonwealth. Political scientist Charles Merriam also thought that state boundaries needed to be redrawn, with some large cities being given status as states. He noted that the *Chicago Tribune* received some 3,000 proposed maps when it held a contest for redrawing the boundaries of existing states (Merriam 1931, 58).

More recently, political scientist Matthew Holden Jr. suggested giving statehood to the 19 cities with populations over 500,000, thereby ensuring greater representation to African Americans and urban interests (Holden 1973b, 245–252). In a related vein, radical African Americans such as Detroit's Brother Imari (formerly Richard B. Henry) have argued for setting aside five Gulf Coast states to create a special black nation (Holden 1973a, 69; Imari 1968, 30–31).

The fact that members of Congress are elected from states may account for the paucity of proposals that have been introduced there for redrawing state boundaries. Several proposals introduced before the Civil War attempted to ensure that legislation would require the consent of the nation's major regions, and others called for a plural executive representing the nation's major sections.

Whig Senator Garrett Davis of Kentucky also introduced two proposals in 1864 for a new division of New England. One such proposal would have combined Maine and Massachusetts into East New England and the other states in the region into West New England, leaving the latter state composed of two noncontiguous parts. Apparently, Davis's proposal was designed to express his disdain for Massachusetts, whose leaders' rhetoric he believed had largely precipitated the Civil War (Ames 1896, 215–16).

See also Baldwin, Leland; Merriman, Charles; Tugwell, Rexford.

For Further Reading:

Ames, Herman. 1896. *The Proposed Amendments to the Constitution of the United States during the*

First Century of Its History. Reprint, New York: Burt Franklin, 1970.

Baldwin, Leland. 1972. *Reframing the Constitution: An Imperative for Modern America.* Santa Barbara, CA: ABC-CLIO.

Holden, Matthew, Jr. 1973a. *The Politics of the Black Nation.* New York: Chandler.

———. 1973b. *The White Man's Burden.* New York: Chandler.

Imari, Brother (Richard B. Henry). 1968. *War in America: The Malcolm X Doctrine.* Detroit, MI: Malcolm X Doctrine.

Merriam, Charles E. 1931. *The Written Constitution and the Unwritten Attitude.* New York: Richard R. Smith.

Tugwell, Rexford. 1974. *The Emerging Constitution.* New York: Harper and Row.

STATES, CONSTITUTIONAL REVISION

The federal amending mechanism developed in large part from the experience with such provisions in state constitutions and charters, but the traditions of state and federal reform now differ significantly.

The federal Constitution is a brief document that has been in force since 1789 and has been formally amended only 27 times. By contrast, state constitutions are often codelike documents and are much more frequently amended and revised. The constitutions of the southern states have been revised and replaced particularly frequently. This difference between federal and state constitutions has led one observer to comment on what he calls "the Dual American Constitutional Tradition" (Cornwell 1981, 9). The fact that the guarantee clause in Article IV of the U.S. Constitution provides only that a state have a "republican" form of government gives states considerable leeway in initiating constitutional reforms.

State constitutions may be altered in one of three ways. Like the national Constitution, they may be altered by interpretation, especially by the judicial branch. They may also be altered by piecemeal amendments or through wholesale constitutional reform (Cornwell, Goodman, and Swanson 1975, 8–9). Such reforms are often initiated by either constitutional conventions or constitutional commissions, although the former are becoming less common as fears of "runaway" conventions become more widespread (see Benjamin and Gais 1996).

Piecemeal amendments usually follow two stages—initiation and ratification. Unlike the national government, where this reform has been the subject of amending proposals, a number of states permit amendments to be introduced by popular initiatives (J. May 1987, 158–160). More commonly, however, amendments to state constitutions are introduced by constitutional conventions, by constitutional commissions, or by the state legislatures (Cornwell et al. 1975, 8–9). Most states require that the state legislature propose amendments by extraordinary majorities; some require votes in successive sessions of the legislature. All states except Delaware require ratification of amendments by popular vote. Most states require ratification by a simple majority, but at least two require extraordinary majorities (*Id.*).

Constitutional conventions are the most frequent vehicle for complete state constitutional overhauls, and most state constitutions explicitly provide for them. Although the topic has generated considerable disagreement (compare Jameson 1887 and Dodd 1910), most states subject such conventions to at least some legislative control. Like regular amendments proposed at the state level, most new constitutions must be approved by the voters. In a proposal reminiscent of one that Thomas Jefferson made at the national level, a number of states require the people to vote periodically on constitutional revision (Sturm and May 1982, 122).

See also Initiative and Referendum; Jefferson, Thomas.

For Further Reading:
Benjamin, Gerald, and Thomas Gais. 1996. "Constitutional Conventionphobia." *Hofstra Law and Policy Symposium* 1: 53–77.

Cornwell, Elmer E., Jr. 1981. "The American Constitutional Tradition: Its Impact and Development." In *The Constitutional Convention as an Amending Device,* ed. Kermit L. Hall, Harold M. Hyman, and Leon V. Sigal. Washington DC: American Historical Association.

Cornwell, Elmer E., Jr., Jay S. Goodman, and Wayne R. Swanson. 1975. *State Constitutional Conventions: The Politics of the Revision Process in Seven States.* New York: Praeger.

May, Janice C. 1987. "Constitutional Amendment and Revision Revisited." *Publius: The Journal of Federalism* 17 (Winter): 153–179.

Sturm, Albert L., and Janice May. 1982. "State Constitutions and Constitutional Revision: 1980–81 and the Past 50 Years." In *The Book of the States: 1982–1983.* Lexington, KY: Council of State Governments.

Grad, Frank P. and Robert F. Williams. 2006. *Drafting State Constitutions—Revisions, and Amendments.* Vol. 2 of *State Constitution for the Twenty-first Century.* Albany: State University of New York Press.

Tarr, G. Alan and Robert F. Williams, eds. 2006. *The Politics of State Constitutional Reform.* Vol. 1 of *State Constitutions for the Twenty-first Century.* Albany: State University of New York Press.

———. 2006. *The Agenda of State Constitutional Reform.* Vol. 2 of *State Constitutions for the Twenty-first Century.* Albany: State University of New York Press.

STATES, CONTROL OVER NATURAL RESOURCES

In *United States v. California* (1947) and related cases, the U.S. Supreme Court decided the national government owned offshore oil. In 1953, Congress enacted the Submerged Lands Act to vest ownership of lands within three miles of the coast in the states.

Beginning in the 1950s, the national government has become increasingly active in environmental regulation, an area previously left largely to state control. In March 1956, even before the adoption of much federal legislation on the subject, Democratic Representative Walter Rogers of Texas introduced an amendment to allow states "to conserve and regulate the exploration, production, and distribution of their petroleum products, water, sulfur, and all other minerals and natural resources" (H.J. Res. 588).

See also Environmental Protection.

STATES, LEGISLATIVE APPORTIONMENT

One of the most influential and disputed areas in which the Warren Court intervened was the area of state legislative apportionment; it also issued decisions on the apportionment of congressional districts. The Constitution provides for reapportionment of House seats after each census. From 1842 to 1929, Congress required states to establish "contiguous equal districts," but it omitted the requirement in its 1929 and subsequent apportionment laws (D. O'Brien 2000b, 1:790).

Throughout most of the 19th century, states entering the Union were also required to guarantee representation in their state legislatures based on population. At the turn of the century, however, states began to react to the flood of new immigrants and the rise of large cities by refusing to reapportion their legislatures (D. O'Brien 2005, 823). The result was that thinly populated rural areas often had the same representation within states as did urban areas with many times the population.

In *Colegrove v. Green* (1946), the Supreme Court rejected a challenge brought under the guarantee clause of the Constitution to overturn an Illinois legislative apportionment scheme in which population discrepancies were fairly large. Pointing to *Luther v. Borden* (1849), the Court decided that such matters were political questions, more appropriate for other branches of the government to resolve. In *Gomillion v. Lightfoot* (1960), the Court did strike down a clear scheme of racial gerrymandering in Tuskegee, Alabama, but the case in which the Court truly reversed the course it had proclaimed in *Colegrove* was *Baker v. Carr* (1962). This case challenged the system of representation in Tennessee, which had last reapportioned itself in 1902. Justice William Brennan authored a decision ruling that the Court could examine state legislative apportionment under the equal protection clause of the Fourteenth Amendment.

In *Gray v. Sanders* (1963), the Court invalidated Georgia's system of primary elections, and Justice William O. Douglas articulated the principle of "one person one vote" that the

Court applied in future cases. Most notably, in *Reynolds v. Sims* (1964), the Court applied this standard to both houses of a state legislature, and in *Wesberry v. Sanders* (1964), it applied it to House congressional districts. The Court reiterated the principles of both decisions in a series of related rulings.

Few decisions have led to sharper criticisms than those dealing with the apportionment question. Senate Minority Leader Everett Dirksen led a personal crusade to overturn *Reynolds v. Sims,* and members of Congress introduced more than 200 proposals on the subject from the decision in *Baker v. Carr* through the 1960s. The Council of State Governments pushed for amendments to overturn the reapportionment decisions, make the amending process easier, and clip the power of the Supreme Court. Twice failing to win a Senate vote for an amendment to permit states to apportion at least one house on a basis other than population (Urofsky 1988, 835), proponents of such an amendment pushed for a constitutional convention. By 1969, thirty-three states had applied for such a convention ("33 States Ask Congress" 1969).

As more and more states reapportioned, however, and previously neglected urban and suburban areas received fairer representation, there was increasing support for the Court's rulings. A few more proposals were introduced in the 1970s, but the issue now appears largely to have faded from public consciousness.

Even while equalizing district populations, many states continue to be adept at gerrymandering, that is, at configuring district boundaries to advantage particular parties or candidates. In cases such as *Shaw v. Reno* (1993) and *Miller v. Johnson* (1995), attention has gradually shifted to this issue, with special focus on whether districts can be gerrymandered in ways designed to increase representation for racial minorities. To date the U.S. Supreme Court has overturned extreme examples of racial gerrymandering without making altogether clear the extent to which racial considerations may influence district line-drawing.

See also *Baker v. Carr;* Council of State Governments; Dirksen, Everett McKinley; Political Questions; *Reynolds v. Sims.*

For Further Reading:

Kromkowski, Charles A. 2002. *Recreating the American Republic: Rules of Apportionment, Constitutional Change, and American Political Development, 1700–1870.* New York: Cambridge University Press.

O'Brien, David M. 2005. *Struggles for Power and Governmental Accountability.* 6th ed., Vol. 1 of *Constitutional Law and Politics.* New York: W. W. Norton.

"33 States Ask Congress for Constitutional Convention." 1969. *Congressional Quarterly Weekly Report* 27 (1 August): 1372–1373.

Urofsky, Melvin I. 1988. *A March of Liberty: A Constitutional History of the United States.* New York: Alfred A. Knopf.

STATES, POLICE POWERS

Throughout U.S. history, scholars and politicians have argued about the proper allocation of power between the state and national governments. Powers that the Tenth Amendment reserves to the states are designated as state police powers. Such powers typically involve regulation of morality, of marriage and family matters, of health and safety, and of property, but the term *police powers* is amorphous and clearly resists easy definition (Scheiber 1992, 639).

Although the national government does not have direct constitutional authority over most such matters, it may affect them in the course of exercising its powers over interstate commerce, taxation, and the like (Curry, Riley, and Battistoni 1989, 250–252). Thus, in *Champion v. Ames* (1903), the Supreme Court upheld the federal government's prohibition of the interstate sale of lottery tickets, and other cases upheld congressional regulation of "white slavery," or prostitution.

Beginning with a resolution that Democratic Senator James Eastland introduced on May 24, 1954, and continuing through 1973, members of Congress introduced about 25 proposals to limit interference with state powers over health, morals, education, marriage, and good order; to give states the right to manage their own internal affairs; or to protect the reserved rights of the states. Almost without exception, the sponsors of these amendments were southerners, most from the Deep South, seeking to limit the Supreme Court's decision in *Brown v. Board of Education,* issued on May 17, 1954, and subsequent cases that called for an end to racial segregation. A key rationale for *Plessy v. Ferguson* (1896)—the Supreme Court decision mandating the doctrine of "separate but equal" that *Brown* overturned—had been the states' right to follow local custom and preserve public order.

See also Tenth Amendment.

For Further Reading:

Curry, James A., Richard B. Riley, and Richard M. Battistoni. 1989. *Constitutional Government: The American Experience.* St. Paul, MN: West.

Scheiber, Harry N. 2005. "Police Power." In *The Oxford Companion to the Supreme Court of the United States,* ed. Kermit L. Hall., 2nd ed. New York: Oxford University Press.

STICKNEY, ALBERT (1839–1908)

New York lawyer Albert Stickney published a book in 1879 advocating major constitutional changes (Vile 1991c, 27–29). Stickney's central objective was to create a system to secure in each governmental department the "best men" and see that they gave "their best work" (Stickney 1879, 15). In Stickney's view, the primary obstacle to such objectives was the political party system, which he linked to a system of limited terms in office. He associated both parties and fixed terms with political corruption. In contrast to those who advocated a pure parliamentary system, however, Stickney favored neither the fusion of the legislative and executive branches nor the system of calling for a vote of no confidence by the majority.

Stickney began describing proposed reforms by focusing on the judiciary. In a sense, this branch of government provided a model for the other branches in that its members already serve during good behavior. Believing that such tenure provided security against abuse, Stickney

thought that judges, even at the federal level, could be elected rather than appointed. Stickney believed that voters would take their cues from the legal profession in making their selections.

Stickney advocated lodging executive power in one man with the power to appoint all heads of departments. These heads would, in turn, have authority over their subordinates. The president would serve during good behavior and would be responsible to the legislature, which could remove him only by a two-thirds vote. Stickney proposed to revive the electoral college as a deliberative body, free of partisanship, that would choose the president.

Initially, Stickney indicated that the real work of the legislature should not be making and revising laws—a task for judges—but rather "supervision and control" (Stickney 1879, 214). Specialists within departments would submit spending plans, and then the legislature would look them over, approve, authorize, and supervise them. Stickney favored a legislature (presumably unicameral) of 500 men who would devote their full time to their duties and would not have fixed terms. The legislature would have "absolute control of the money," power of "making *all necessary laws,*" power to remove any governmental official by a two-thirds vote, but no power over appointments (*Id.,* 218). Stickney clearly believed that there were many areas of legislation, including the laws of marriage and divorce, where Congress should have greater authority. Believing that there must be a supreme power within the state, Stickney proposed eliminating the executive veto, but in its place, he proposed that all legislation would have to be adopted by a two-thirds majority.

Stickney favored eliminating the vice presidency. In cases of presidential vacancies, he would allow the senior cabinet officer to serve until the electoral college could choose a new president. Believing that only men with established reputations would be selected to legislative office, Stickney thought that the average member would serve about 12 years. Moreover, freed from party influence, such legislators would be able to serve the public. Legislatures would exercise greater wisdom than the people could exercise on their own behalf.

Stickney acknowledged that his plan would establish an aristocracy, but it would be an aristocracy of talent rather than of heredity. Whereas the American founders had sought the solution to government in institutions, Stickney professed to find the key in selecting men of good character to govern (Stickney 1879, 258). Woodrow Wilson cited Stickney's criticism of political parties in arguing for responsible cabinet government (Wilson 1882, 208–210).

For Further Reading:

Stickney, Albert. 1879. *A True Republic.* New York: Harper and Brothers.

Vile, John R. 1991c. *Rewriting the United States Constitution: An Examination of Proposals from Reconstruction to the Present.* New York: Praeger.

Wilson, (Thomas) Woodrow. 1882. "Government by Debate: Being a Short View of Our National Government as It Is and as It Might Be." In *The Papers of Woodrow Wilson,* Vol. 2, ed. Arthur S. Link. Reprint, Princeton, NJ: Princeton University Press, 1967.

real effective instrument to control and adjust the movements of the machinery, when out of order, or in danger of self-destruction" (Story 1987, 680). Although the analogy of the Constitution to a machine was frequently evoked in the 19th century (Kammen 1987), Story appears to have been the first to use the "safety-valve" analogy in reference to the amending process.

See also Deliberation and the Amending Process; Fisher, Sidney George; Safety-valve Analogy.

For Further Reading:

Kammen, Michael. 1987. *A Machine That Would Go of Itself: The Constitution in American Culture.* New York: Alfred A. Knopf.

Story, Joseph. 1833. *Commentaries on the Constitution of the United States.* Boston: Hilliard, Gray. Reprint New York: Da Capo Press, 1970.

STORY, JOSEPH (1779–1845)

In addition to serving as an associate justice of the U.S. Supreme Court from 1811 to 1845, Joseph Story was one of the most influential legal commentators of the 19th century. His analysis of the amending process reflected the general esteem with which the process was held, at least until the criticisms initiated by Sidney George Fisher at the time of the Civil War and the later criticisms that were raised during the Progressive Era.

Story commended the founders for recognizing the need for an amending process while also recognizing that "a government forever changing and changeable, is, indeed, in a state bordering upon anarchy and confusion" (Story 1987, 678–679). Summarizing his view, Story observed that "the great principle to be sought is to make the changes practicable, but not too easy; to secure due deliberation, and caution; and to follow experience, rather than to open a way for experiments, suggested by mere speculation or theory" (*Id.,* 679).

Story went on to describe the amending process as "the safety valve to let off all temporary effervescences and excitements; and the

STRITTMATTER, BILL

One of the more novel, and far-reaching, attempts to rewrite the U.S. Constitution was composed by Bill Strittmatter, who was identified in the pamphlet only as the pastor of the Church of Jesus Christ in Lakemore, Ohio, a group with possible ties to the Ku Klux Klan. The document is titled "A Christian Constitution and Civil Law for the Kingdom of Heaven on Earth," with the cover picturing an early American flag and identifying America with the words "Ameri meaning heavenly and rica (reich) meaning kingdom."

The pamphlet was not dated but contained a cartoon on p. 12 featuring presidential appointees Dr. [Henry] Kissinger and Dr. [Arthur] Burns, thus probably dating it to the early 1970s. The introduction noted that:

1. The United States was founded as a Christian Nation.
2. Article 1 of the Constitution of The United States of America DOES NOT SAY "separation of Church and State." Read it for yourself.
3. The Supreme Court of the United States has declared that America is a Christian

Nation (Holy Trinity Church vs. United States, 143 U.S.471). (Strittmatter, unnumbered introduction)

This section further indicated that "civil Rulers are God's Ministers," and showed a diagram of an open Bible in which 71 percent of the material there is identified as relating to government and 29 percent as relating to that which is "personal" (Strittmatter 1).

Strittmatter composed his entire constitution around the Ten Commandments, with scripture citations to each section. Most of the passages were from that part of Hebrew Scriptures that Christians refer to as the Old Testament, but some are entwined with passages from the New Testament as well.

Like the Ten Commandments, the first articles of Strittmatter's constitution dealt with individuals' relations with God. Article One thus began with the declaration, "I AM THE LORD THY GOD, THOU SHALT HAVE NO OTHER GODS BEFORE ME" (Strittmatter, 4). This article identified God as Jesus Christ, with the penalty of stoning provided for those who worship others. It further identified Christ as the nation's Commander and Chief, and vested all citizens with the responsibility of receiving military training. Under specified "rules of war," all enemies who did not surrender as tributaries should be slaughtered, and covenants were forbidden with "heathen people" (Strittmatter, 6). This article contained admonitions to cleanliness, and it limited citizenship to "the Christian Race," with persons of "mixed race" being denied citizenship, and "hyphenated citizens such as German-Americans, Mexican-Americans or Italian-Americans" being prohibited (*Id.,* 7). Generally, Strittmatter had little to say about rights, and the "Christian religion" and only that religion was to be accorded "freedom of religion," with only citizen members of the "Christian Race" permitted to hold office in the church; the writings and other productions of "the children of Belial" were to be burned (*Id.,* 7).

Article Two of the Constitution prohibited the worship of "graven images," and Article Three prohibited the taking of God's name in vain. The penalty for blasphemy against Jesus Christ was specified as death (Strittmatter, 9).

Article Four provided for the keeping of the Sabbath, with "those rendering essential services" on the Sabbath taking off Wednesdays. As in other articles, the constitution prescribed death as a punishment for noncompliance. Specific feast days and holidays were also specified, including Pentecost and Thanksgiving. This section also recognized the Passover and the year of Jubile[e] in which every man's land would be returned to him.

The second part of the constitution dealt with individuals' relations with their neighbors, again following the structure of the Ten Commandments. Article Five focused on honoring one's parents, with penalties of death for those who smite or curse their parents. Civil power was to be committed to "a[n] elder . . . whom Jesus Christ your King shall choose" (Strittmatter, 13), and who shall take his judgments from the Bible. "Judges, elders and officers" were also cited, with people further divided into tens, fifties, hundreds, and thousands, and "priests" making final judgments in difficult cases (*Id.,* 16). Punishment by "stripes" was specified. This Article further specified that "Once elected, selected or appointed, elders officers and ministers have absolute authority under and within law, likewise the principle of absolute responsibility" (*Id.,* 17). Church and state would both be supported by tithes.

Article Six dealt with murder. Like the Old Testament, it provided cities of refuge for those who commit involuntary manslaughter. The inclusion of matters of criminal law in this national constitution would tend to indicate that Strittmatter was not (like previous defenders of racial segregation) particularly committed to a division of power between state and federal authorities. Strittmatter also included a section on liability based on Old Testament passages relating to damage done by animals belonging to others.

Article Seven, prohibiting adultery, defined the practice to include "interracial marriage and miscegenation" (Strittmatter, 19). The penalty for such miscegenation was to be stoning to death. Rules were also specified indicating which plants, animals, and foods were to be considered unclean. One prohibition included that of plowing "with an ox and an ass together" (*Id.,* 20).

Article Eight prohibited theft, and dealt with weights and measures, restitution, lost and found articles, confessions of guilt, usury, and wages. Usury (excessive interest) was permitted to strangers but not to fellow citizens. The spoils of war were to be divided between Jesus and those who fought in a war, with "the five hundreth part" going to the "National Cathedral" (Strittmatter, 23).

Article Nine dealt with bearing false witness. It also committed individuals to the keeping of vows.

Article Ten dealt with coveting. This included explicit instructions about the obligations of husbands and wives and sexual relations. It permitted divorce in certain cases but prohibited incest. It also related to inheritance. A welfare provision was included for "the stranger, the fatherless, [and] the widow." It also provided for gleaning, whereby individuals in need are permitted to follow behind harvesters and appropriate any remaining food (Strittmatter, 28).

Article Ten was followed with a specific prohibition against adding amendments to the Constitution: "Ye shall not add unto the word which I command you, neither shall ye diminish ought from it" (Strittmatter, 28). Although officials were permitted to settle controversies under the law, their decisions "shall not become case law to base further decisions thereon" (*Id.,* 28). This section further specified that "[t]he rest of the Bible not mentioned herein is made a part hereof" (*Id.,* 18).

The middle two pages of the pamphlet explained a number of American symbols designed to show that "America has scores of the marks of Israel upon her" (Strittmatter, 14). America was identified as "the 'New Order of the Ages' as prophesied by Daniel" (*Id.,* 15). The last page of the pamphlet, which included a picture of the great seal of America with the all-seeing eye of God shedding a tear, similarly identified America as "the apple" of Christ's eye.

This constitution seems tied to the modern Christian identity movement and other movements motivated by ideals of racial purity and the hope of governing America under a system of divine law.

See also Christian Amendment.

For Further Reading:
Strittmatter, Bill. n.d. "A Christian Constitution and Civil Law for the Kingdom of Heaven on Earth." Lakemore, OH: 28 pp.

STRUBLE, ROBERT, JR.

The Internet has opened up the possibility for individuals to communicate who may not otherwise be able to do so, but it sometimes presents problems for scholars, who would desire more permanent records of proposals that are posted there. One such proposal for constitutional reform that printed out to well over 200 pages was posted by Robert Struble Jr. under the title of "Redeeming U.S. Democracy," and was introduced by former Senator, and onetime presidential contender, Minnesota's Eugene McCarthy. Struble identified himself as a Republican Party official living in Bremerton, Washington, and apparently hoped to solicit comments with the view of publishing a book, which apparently never materialized.

Unfortunately, Struble's Web site, which the author of this book accessed in July 1997, is no longer available. The most important part of the site was the introduction of a Twelve Code, which Struble hoped to propose through constitutional convention. It consisted of a unique blend of proposals, some of which would likely be favored by cultural conservatives chiefly concerned about perceived cultural decay, and others likely favored by liberals concerned about unemployment.

Struble dedicated his work to Mary, the mother of Jesus, and began his preface by asking that God "forgive us the offenses and help us to turn, individually and socially, from license to liberty." In the preamble to his Twelve Code, Struble further noted that "[t]he authority of government is the people's from God," but most of his proposals dealt with quite practical matters.

The first section of Struble's proposal called for limiting members of the U.S. House of Representatives to one term, with the hope of making that body more democratic. Struble thought that the Senate should have more "expertise and institutional memory," and he therefore did not favor imposing limits on this body, although he was willing to allow states to set such limits on their own.

The second section of Struble's Twelve Code clarified the first by indicating that members of the House would begin their first two years of service as tribunates, during which time they would perform functions as ombudsmen, investigators, and assistants to the vice president. The vice president, in turn, would be granted power to veto existing regulations subject to veto by either the U.S. president, both houses of Congress, or the Committee of Cuts. After the Representatives served as tribunates for two years, and were given two months to make a transition, they would in turn become regular House members for their single term. Their income would be set at "twice the median income of the American household." Representatives would be subject to recall. Ex-representatives would serve as a local advisory body to the president and could "propose nominees for the office of Tenth Justice," described later in Struble's proposals.

The third section of the Twelve Code was directed to "Checks against Judicial Usurpation." Concerned chiefly with Congress's power to strip the Supreme Court of its appellate jurisdiction, Struble proposed that whenever jurisdiction was so clipped, "the court of last resort for cases of that class becomes the respective state supreme court." He also suggested that Congress might specify a date, for example 10 years after the decision in *Brown v. Board of Education* (1954) declaring racial segregation in schools to be unconstitutional, as a time before which precedents would remain in force. Struble further provided for automatic "sunset provisions" for limitations of judicial jurisdiction. When jurisdiction is stripped from the Supreme Court, Struble specified that lower courts should abide by six considerations "in order of priority." They are:

First, the written Constitution; second, the intent of the Framers, as best verifiable; third, the federal precedent deriving from decisions rendered since the jurisdiction's restoration; fourth, federal precedent prior to the congressionally specified date . . . ; fifth, federal precedent antedating Appomattox; and sixth, statute law which is not inconsistent with the U.S. Constitution.

Struble devoted sections four and five of the Twelve Code to congressional procedures. His proposals would limit the influence of congressional committees by subordinating their deliberations to the will of the majority and by permitting majority rule on the floor. Committees would be divided into fortnight committees (in which members could serve for a maximum of two weeks), half tribute committees (where tributes or volunteers would make up at least half of the membership), and joint Senate-House Committees. Members would have greater choice over the selection and removal of committee chairs.

Before dealing in sections six through eight of the Twelve Code with problems of unemployment and underemployment, Struble included a preface in which he specified that "we the people require of the American economy that it afford able-bodied citizens the opportunity to make a living by working. We enforce this earning opportunity not by legislating job security or guaranteeing anyone a place, but by making jobs plentiful enough to match the will to work."

Section six would allow Congress to equalize work by "reducing the duration of the workweek, workmonth, or workyear." He also favored "expanding the labor market structurally." To this end, Struble would grant Congress power in section seven to generate jobs by working with private businesses to create Private Enterprise Projects (PEP). Section eight would further use taxation of from 0 percent of those businesses that were most labor intensive to 10 percent for those that used the least.

Sections nine through twelve of Struble's proposals dealt with cultural and religious issues and also came with a preamble in which he noted that "Civil rights and liberties necessitate a sense of community, duty and responsibility." Section nine was designed "to counter the commerce in lewdness which undermines human dignity and degrades the culture in which we must live." To this end, Struble would create a Tenth Justice of the U.S. Supreme

Court, elected by the voters from among five women, and with power to issue injunctions against the importation, exportation, dissemination, or broadcast of "sexually licentious or pornographic phenomena," abbreviated as SLOPP. Struble would provide for "subsequent punishment" of enjoined materials rather than for "prior restraint." Work consisting of "only the written word shall never qualify as SLOPP."

Section ten would provide for a place for scripture in schools. Teachers could read such passages in public schools for up to 12 minutes a day. Similarly, contrary to existing judicial precedents, teachers would be permitted to post the Ten Commandments and up to 10 other scripture verses.

Section eleven provided that pupils who dissented from such readings should "practice silent [and inconspicuous] nonparticipation." States would also be permitted to give money to religious schools or to parents paying tuition to the same, but never in a way so as to "undermine or modify a school's moral and religious character, or to change its religious exercises."

Section twelve explicitly provided for prayers, including the Lord's Prayer, in public schools, as long as they were "initiated in the classroom by the respective teacher." Struble ended with a benediction that included a number of scriptures. Further commenting in an appendix on his Twelve Code, Struble indicated that his amendments were only 20 percent shorter than the Constitution they were amending, but noted that "A few brief sentences will not suffice to streamline today's Capitol City apparatus."

For Further Reading:

Struble, Robert, Jr., "Redeeming U.S. Democracy," http://tcmnet.com/~rusd/. Accessed July 11, 1997. No longer appears to be available.

SUBSTANTIVE DUE PROCESS

Both the Fifth Amendment and the Fourteenth Amendment contain clauses prohibiting deprivation of "life, liberty, or property, without due process of law." The guarantee in the Fifth Amendment applies to the national government, and the guarantee in the Fourteenth Amendment applies to the states. Through the latter clause, the courts have applied most of the guarantees in the Bill of Rights to state governments.

Although the language of the clauses in both the Fifth and the Fourteenth Amendments focuses on *process,* at various times the Court has also given them a substantive meaning (Abraham and Perry 2003, 109–175). Indeed, the courts have interpreted these clauses so flexibly that their decisions have approached the kinds of changes usually reserved for constitutional amendments.

The Supreme Court's first use of substantive due process appears to have been in *Scott v. Sandford* (1857) and the *Slaughterhouse Cases* (1873). Especially from the end of the 19th century until the shift in judicial emphasis and philosophy in 1937, the Supreme Court used the idea of substantive due process to strike down state and federal regulations believed to interfere unreasonably with liberty of contract. *Lochner v. New York* (1905), striking down hours regulations for bakers, and *Adkins v. Children's Hospital* (1923), voiding federal minimum-wage laws for women in the District of Columbia, epitomized this judicial philosophy. More recently, critics have alleged that the Court's decisions in *Griswold v. Connecticut* (1965), striking down Connecticut's prohibition of birth-control devices, and in *Roe v. Wade* (1973), legalizing abortion, were based primarily on substantive ideas of justice not found within the constitutional text.

Numerous amendments, including those attempting to regulate child labor, provide minimum wages, limit workers' hours, and the like, were proposed to overturn decisions by the Court when it was using the due process clause to strike at such economic regulations. More recently, the Right-to-Life Amendment has been intended to strike down the Court's decisions on abortion.

See also Fifth Amendment; Fourteenth Amendment; *Griswold v. Connecticut*; *Lochner v. New York;* Right to Life; *Scott v. Sandford.*

For Further Reading:

Abraham, Henry J., and Barbara Perry. 2003. *Freedom and the Court: Civil Rights and Liberties in the United States.* 8th ed. Lawrence: University Press of Kansas.

Gillman, Howard. 1993. *The Constitution Besieged: The Rise and Demise of Lochner Era Police Power Jurisdiction.* Durham, NC: Duke University Press.

SUBVERSION

The fear of subversion dates at least as far back as the Alien and Sedition Laws of 1798. Such fear was heightened by suspicions directed at the Communist Party during the Cold War, which followed World War II.

Initially, federal courts proved fairly deferential to legislation designed to register and control communists. Focusing specifically on decisions in *Dennis v. United States* (1951) and *Communist Party v. Subversive Activities Control Board* (1961), one observer said that such decisions demonstrated "deference to legislative judgments about the existence of a subversive conspiracy, minimal rationality standards for review of the means chosen to suppress subversion, and a balancing of the rights of individuals to freedom of political expression versus the state's interest in maintaining its power" (Wiecek 1992, 847).

As it began to give greater attention to individual rights, however, the Warren Court began to examine such legislation more closely for possible conflicts with the First Amendment and other constitutional protections. Thus, in *United States v. Robel* (1967), the Supreme Court struck down a provision of the Subversive Activities Control Act of 1950 that prohibited members of the Communist Party from working at defense facilities.

This decision prompted a bevy of amending proposals, most from southern representatives, to allow Congress to exclude from employment at defense facilities individuals who knowingly became or remained a member of any organization committed to overthrowing the government by force. Even before *Robel,* an Alabama representative had introduced an amendment designed to allow public schools to exclude subversives from the classroom. Subsequent proposals also sought to extend federal power to control the transmission of subversive materials through the U.S. mails.

See also First Amendment.

For Further Reading:

Wiecek, William. 2005. "Subversion." In *The Oxford Companion to the Supreme Court of the United States,* ed. Kermit L. Hall. 2nd ed. New York: Oxford University Press.

SUNDQUIST, JAMES (1915–)

Political scientist James Sundquist has authored one of the most historically informed surveys of constitutional reforms in the United States (1986). Although he understood why the American founders settled on a system of checks and balances, he thought they may have solved the problem of tyranny by creating a system that results in excessive deadlock and stalemate (Vile 1991c, 131–133).

As a scholar, Sundquist devoted considerable attention to past reform proposals, but he concluded by advocating consideration of nine constitutional amendments. Many overlap with proposals offered by the Committee on the Constitutional System, for which one edition of his book was published.

Sundquist's recommendations were as follows: combine the president and the president's running mate on a team ticket with members of the House and Senate, so voters would be unable to split their votes; raise terms of members of the House of Representatives to four years and terms of senators to eight; allow either the president or a majority of either house of Congress to call special elections in which all members of the legislative and executive branches would be up for election; remove the constitutional prohibition that prevents members of Congress from serving in the executive branch; create a limited presidential item veto, subject to an override by a majority of both houses of Congress; restore the legislative veto, albeit only when both houses of Congress concur; add an amendment effectively incorporating the provisions of the War Powers Resolution of 1973 into the Constitution; allow majorities of both houses of Congress (rather than two-thirds of the Senate) to approve treaties; and provide for a national referendum to break legislative-executive deadlocks (Sundquist 1986, 241–242).

See also Committee on the Constitutional System; Parliamentary Systems.

For Further Reading:

Sundquist, James L. 1986. *Constitutional Reform and Effective Government.* Washington DC: Brookings Institution.

Vile, John R. 1991c. *Rewriting the United States Constitution: An Examination of Proposals from Reconstruction to the Present.* New York: Praeger.

SUPERMAJORITIES

Although the United States government is often described as a democracy or criticized for not fully embodying democratic ideals (see Dahl 2001), James Madison, writing in *Federalist No. 10,* as well as other framers of the Constitution, specifically distinguished the "republican" form of government that they favored from other forms of "direct democracy" that they thought led to faction and injustice. Law professors John O. McGinnis and Michael B. Rappaport have accordingly argued that "the central principle underlying the Constitution is governance through supermajority rules" (McGinnis and Rappaport 2002, 705). There are seven direct constitutional provisions in the original constitution requiring supermajority approval—for example, it takes two-thirds of the Senate to ratify a treaty and two-thirds of both houses of Congress to override a presidential veto. McGinnis and Rappaport believe that other requirements, like bicameralism and the requirement that all laws be presented to the president for a signature, have a similar impact.

Among the provisions for supermajorities are those in Article V providing that two-thirds of both houses of Congress may propose constitutional amendments or must call a convention for this purpose when petitioned by two-thirds of the states, and that three-fourths of the states must subsequently ratify them. Such requirements clearly pose obstacles to many constitutional changes that temporary majorities, or majorities that are concentrated unduly in one or another region of the nation, may favor. Although McGinnis and Rappaport believe that the idea of supermajorities was a unique contribution of the New World to political theory, the U.S. Constitution is not unique in this respect. Thus, the supermajority requirements in the Articles of Confederation, including a provision for unanimous state consent to amendments, were even more onerous than those in the current Constitution (McGinnis and Rappaport 2002, 717).

McGinnis and Rappaport identify the rules "that govern the adoption and amendment of the Constitution" as "the most important supermajority rules in the Constitution" (McGinnis and Rappaport 2002, 780). They believe that the supermajority requirement in Article V helps answer the question that Jefferson once posed as to why people of today should be bound by decisions made by previous generations (sometimes referred to as "the dead hand of the past") and embodied within the constitutional text (*Id.,* 796). Considering that the initial Constitution was written by delegates from 12 of the existing states, was approved by Congress, and subsequently required ratification of nine or more of the 13 states, McGinnis and Rappaport point out that (with the possible exception of the entrenchment clause forbidding states from being deprived of their equal suffrage in the U.S. Senate without their consent) existing generations face no greater barrier to changing the Constitution than did the original framers (*Id.,* 796–800).

The Fourteenth Amendment contained a provision stipulating that individuals who had served in the Confederacy could not accept public offices without approval by a two-thirds vote of Congress; the Twenty-fifth Amendment further provides for a two-thirds supermajority to certify that a president who says otherwise is not capable of serving (McGinnis and Rappaport 2002, 724). Some proposed amendments have sought to enact supermajority requirements for governmental spending and related matters (McGinnis and Rappaport 1999). Other proposals have called for eliminating existing supermajority requirements, thus, for example, allowing the Senate to approve of treaties by majority vote.

Although Article V is silent on the subject, at least seven states currently specify that their ratifications of constitutional amendments require a supermajority in one or both state legislative chambers (Huckabee, CRS-2).

See also Article V of the U.S. Constitution; Articles of Confederation; Entrenchment Clauses; Fourteenth Amendment; Jefferson, Thomas; Ratification of the Existing U.S. and/or Future U.S. Constitutions.

For Further Reading:

Dahl, Robert. 2001. *How Democratic Is the American Constitution?* New Haven, CT: Yale University Press.

Huckabee, David C. September 30, 1997. "Ratification of Amendments to the U.S. Constitution." Congressional Research Service, Library of Congress.

McGinnis, John O. and Michael B. Rappaport. 2002. "Our Supermajoritarian Constitution." *Texas Law Review* 80 (March): 703–805.

———. 1999. "Supermajority Rules as a Constitutional Solution." *William and Mary Law Review* 40 (February): 365–470.

SUPER-STATUTES

Although it is common to distinguish law established by the Constitution and its amendments from ordinary statutory law, professors William N. Eskridge, Jr. and John Ferejohn have coined the term "super-statutes" (which is sometimes used differently in other contexts) to suggest that there might be a middle category of laws, which while not actually part of the Constitution, serve a similar structuring function.

Eskridge and Ferejohn describe a super-statute as "a law or series of laws that (1) seeks to establish a new normative or institutional framework for state policy and (2) over time does 'stick' in the public culture such that (3) the super-statute and its institutional or normative principles have a broad effect on the law—including an effect beyond the four corners of the statute" (2001, 1216).

Eskridge and Ferejohn cite the Sherman Antitrust Act of 1890, the Civil Rights Act of 1964 (which, of course, rests in large part on the principles established by the Fourteenth Amendment), and the Endangered Species Act of 1973 as examples of such laws, which often derive in part from a dialogue between the judiciary and Congress. The early decision to accept the constitutionality of a national bank, although repudiated for a time, may be another example.

Eskridge and Ferejohn believe that such statutes allow for constitutional "updating" short of the amending process. They distinguish their view from Bruce Ackerman's idea of "constitutional moments" by describing their statutes as "acquiring "their normative force through a series of public confrontations and debates over time and not through a single stylized dramatic confrontation" (1270). They believe that super-statutes reflect a mutual role for both legislators and judges. While requiring adoption by Congress, they do not grant a veto to minorities that the super-majorities required by the constitutional amending process provide. Eskridge and Ferejohn argue that "Prescriptively, super-statutes mediate the tension between democracy or popular accountability and the evolution of higher law at the hands of unelected judges" (1276).

See also Ackerman, Bruce.

Further Reading:

Eskridge, William N., Jr. and John Ferejohn. 2001. "Super-statutes." *Duke Law Journal* 50 (March): 1215-76.

Michelman, Frank I. 2006. "What Do Constitutions Do That Statutes Don't (Legally Speaking)?" in Bauman, Richard W. and Tsvi Kahana, *The Least Examined Branch: The Role of Legislatures in the Constitutional State*. New York: Cambridge University Press, 273-93.

SUPREME COURT DECISIONS REVERSED BY CONSTITUTIONAL AMENDMENTS

At least since John Marshall's decision in *Marbury v. Madison* (1803), the U.S. Supreme Court has asserted its power to interpret both state and federal laws and the Constitution and to interpret laws and strike down those that it believes are in contravention of this document. When the Supreme Court exercises its power (known as statutory interpretation) to interpret a law in a way that Congress thinks is unjustified, Congress can adopt another law, making its intentions clearer, and the Court will generally accept this new interpretation. When the Supreme Court exercises its power to strike down a law that it believes to be unconstitutional (known as judicial review), however, the effects are more profound. In debates with Stephen Douglas, Abraham Lincoln pointed out that the people would no longer be sovereign if all such decisions by unelected judges were considered to be the final word on the subject. Over the course of time, the constitutional amending process has been recognized as one such check on judicial excess or misinterpretation of the document. One of the ironies of this process, which can sometimes look like a dog chasing its tail, is that courts, in turn, interpret new amendments.

The people exercised their power to overturn a Supreme Court interpretation of the U.S. Constitution even before *Marbury*. Thus, in 1795 the Eleventh Amendment reversed a Court decision in *Chisholm v. Georgia* (1793) by limiting suits that individuals could bring against individual states without their consent. When the Supreme Court decided in *[Dred] Scott v. Sandford* (1857) that blacks were not and could not be citizens, this decision was in turn overturned by the Fourteenth Amendment (1868) that declared that all persons born or naturalized within the United States were citizens thereof and were entitled to certain basic rights like due process and equal protection of the laws. The Thirteenth Amendment had already eliminated slavery, and the Fifteenth prohibited discrimination against

voting on the basis of race. Supreme Court decisions in the years immediately after the adoption of the Fourteenth Amendment may have shown some of the limits of the amending process (as well as ambiguity about the amendment's meaning), by interpreting the amendment fairly restrictively. Eventually, however, the Fourteenth Amendment became the vehicle by which the Court reversed the course it had set in *Barron v Baltimore* (1833), where it had declared that the Bill of Rights only limited the national government; subsequent decisions, especially during the Warren Court, would also extend almost all of these limitations to the states.

The Sixteenth Amendment (1913) overturned the Supreme Court's controversial decision in *Pollock v. Farmers' Loan & Trust Co.* (1895) by establishing the constitutionality of the income tax. Similarly, the Twenty-sixth Amendment (1971) responded to the Supreme Court's decision of the previous year in *Oregon v. Mitchell* in which the Court had held that Congress could lower the age of voting in federal, but not in state, elections, by lowering this age in both types of electoral contests.

Some scholars (for example, Kyvig 1996b, 112) would also include the Nineteenth Amendment, which guaranteed women's suffrage, as an example of an amendment that overturned a Court decision because it effectively overturned the Court's ruling in *Minor v. Happersett* (1875) that had declared that the federal constitution did not prevent discrimination against women voters on the basis of their gender. Others believe instead that *Minor* was, and remains, a proper interpretation of the Fourteenth Amendment that has been subsequently and positively modified by the Nineteenth.

Scores of amendments have been proposed to overturn Supreme Court decisions throughout American history. In some cases—for example, child labor—the Court has reversed itself before an amendment was ratified. Recent years have witnessed proposals to reverse Court decisions relative to prayer and Bible reading in schools, state legislative apportionment, abortion, the rights of criminal defendants, the legitimacy of campaign financing laws, the standard of review to be applied in cases related to the free exercise of religion, flag desecration, and so forth. Other amendments have proposed limiting the exercise of judicial review or requiring supermajorities before the Court can overturn legislation. It is not uncommon for members of Congress to propose such amendments within days of controversial decisions.

The line between constitutional amendment and constitutional interpretation is often a fine one—justices not uncommonly accuse one another of attempting to "amend" the Constitution under the guise of interpretation (Vile 1980). Still the amending process vests ultimate power over the Constitution with the people, or at least a people who can muster the supermajorities necessary for an amendment. Because of the difficulty of this process, the Court has reversed far more of its own decisions than have been reversed by amendments. To cite but a few examples, the Supreme Court's decision outlawing racial segregation in *Brown v. Board of Education* (1954) overturned a previous ruling in *Plessy v. Ferguson* (1896); similarly, in *West Virginia Board of Education v. Barnette* (1943), the Court overturned *Minersville School District v. Gobitis* (1940), which had declared that public school students had to salute the American flag. Although the story is often told simplistically, the Supreme Court's historic "switch in time that saved nine," reversing course on some key New Deal programs in 1937, is often attributed to Roosevelt's court-packing plan and has been cited by Bruce Ackerman as one of three important "constitutional moments" in American history.

The Supreme Court's ability to reverse its own decisions, combined with the difficulty of the constitutional amending process, often leads reformers to argue that the problem with a given ruling is not a problem with the constitution itself but simply with its interpretation. This, in turn, often diverts attention away from amendments and toward the election of presidents that reformers believe will introduce new personnel on the Supreme Court who might be willing to reconsider earlier opinions. One of the reasons that Senate confirmation hearings for Supreme Court justices, and indeed for judges in general, have become intense is the belief that new appointees might very well change existing constitutional interpretations.

One reason for declaring issues involving the amending process to be "political questions" for the political branches to resolve is the fact that such issues sometimes arise in cases involving amendments designed to overturn Supreme Court decisions. Although it is difficult to point to provisions since those in the Bill of Rights that have specifically curtailed congressional powers (the Twenty-seventh Amendment made a minor alteration in the timing of congressional pay raises), numerous amendments, including amendments for balanced budgets and term limits, have also been directed at Congress, hardly leaving it as a neutral observer. Questions therefore continue about the validity of the Supreme Court decision in *Coleman v. Miller* (1939) declaring that most amending issues are political questions.

See also Ackerman, Bruce; *Barron v. Baltimore; Child Labor Amendment: Chisholm v. Georgia; Coleman v. Miller;* Court-Packing Plan; Eleventh Amendment; Fourteenth Amendment; *Marbury v. Madison; Oregon v. Mitchell;* Political Questions; *Pollack v. Farmers' Loan & Trust Co.; Scott v. Sandford;* Sixteenth Amendment; Twenty-seventh Amendment; Twenty-sixth Amendment.

For Further Reading:

Kyvig, David E. 1996b. "Appealing Supreme Court Decisions: Constitutional Amendments as Checks on Judicial Review." *Journal of Supreme Court History* 2: 111–119.

Vile, John R. 1980. "The Supreme Court and the Amending Process." *Georgia Political Science Association Journal* 8 (Fall): 33–66.

T

❖

TAKINGS CLAUSE

Immediately after specifying in the due process clause that persons shall not be deprived of their life, liberty, or property without their consent, the Fifth Amendment concludes with the takings clause. It provides: "nor shall private property be taken for public use, without just compensation." Although it does not use the term, the clause permits use of the government's power of eminent domain to take property for public use, with the provision that it must compensate owners for their losses.

This clause has been increasingly litigated in recent years. The U.S. Supreme Court stirred particular controversy with its decision in *Kelo v. City of New London,* 545 U.S. 469 (2005), when it decided that a city could condemn a well-maintained house and then turn it over to a private business for economic development, which the city thought would expand its tax base. Numerous states have subsequently either prohibited or limited such takings, some by constitutional amendment. Professor William N. Eskridge Jr. of Yale University proposed reinvigorating this provision, but he noted that he did not have specific language in mind (2008, 460). Emily Madueno, then a law student, proposed amending the clause to say: "this is not the 'Public Purpose Clause,' and it is definitely not the 'Diverse and Always Evolving Needs of Society Clause'" (2007, 845). Representative Phil Gingrey of Georgia introduced a resolution in Congress on the third anniversary of the *Kelo* decision expressing support for Fifth Amendment property rights protections.

See also Fifth Amendment.

For Further Reading:

Cohen, Charles E. 2006. "Eminent Domain After *Kelo v. City of New London*: An Argument for Banning Economic Development Takings." *Harvard Journal of Law and Public Policy* 29 (Spring): 491–565.

Eskridge, William N., Jr. 2008. "No Easy Constitutional Solution for Big Government." *Northwestern University Law Review* 102 (Winter): 457–460.

Madueno, Emily L. 2007. "The Fifth Amendment's Taking Clause: Public Use and Private Use; Unfortunately, There is no Difference." *Loyola of Los Angeles Law Review* 40 (Winter): 809–852.

Schultz, David. 2006. "Economic Development and Eminent Domain After *Kelo*: Property Rights and 'Public Use' Under State Constitutions." *Albany Law Environmental Outlook Journal* 11:41–88.

TARIFFS

In a book first published in 1903, a scholar identified the tariff as "the most persistent issue in American politics" (Stanwood 1903, 1:1). Yet during the first hundred years of the nation's history, only three amending proposals dealt with it. After the Nullification Crisis of 1828–1832, which largely centered on Southern objections to the sectional character of existing tariff policies that tended—as John C. Calhoun and other Southern statesmen argued—to benefit Northern industrial states at the expense of the more agrarian South, Georgia and Alabama petitioned for a constitutional convention to resolve the issue. An 1864 substitute for the Thirteenth Amendment would have permitted the use of tariffs for raising revenue as long as they were not excessive. A third proposal, offered in 1871, would have substituted direct taxes for tariffs (Ames 1896, 252).

The Payne-Aldrich Tariff Bill of 1907 gave Congress the power to establish a tariff board to give advice on tariff rates, but by the language of Article I, Section 8 of the Constitution, Congress continues to have the duty to set tariff rates. From 1916 to 1922, three proposals were introduced to transfer the power of setting tariff rates to a nonpartisan board or tariff commission. Recent debates over the North American Free Trade Agreement (NAFTA) and whether to extend so-called favorite nation trade status to nations like the People's Republic of China indicate that trade and tariff issues can still stir considerable political controversy.

See also Calhoun, John C.

For Further Reading:

Ames, Herman. 1896. *The Proposed Amendments to the Constitution of the United States during the First Century of Its History.* Reprint, New York: Burt Franklin, 1970.

Stanwood, Edward. 1903. *American Tariff Controversies in the Nineteenth Century.* 2 vols. Reprint, New York: Russell and Russell, 1967.

Taylor, George R., ed. 1993. *The Great Tariff Debate, 1820–1830.* Boston: D. C. Heath.

TAXATION, DIRECT

In an attempt to protect the least populous states, Article I, Section 9 of the Constitution specifies that "no Capitation, or other direct, Tax shall be laid, unless in Proportion to the Census." However, the document does not define what direct taxes are.

In 1793, an amending resolution was introduced to define direct taxes, and three years later, in upholding a federal tax on carriages as an indirect tax, the Supreme Court indicated in *Hylton v. United States* that only taxes on per-

sons and land fell into the direct tax category. *Pollock v. Farmers' Loan & Trust Co.* (1895) subsequently included income taxes in this category, but the Sixteenth Amendment overturned it.

Eighteen provisions were introduced in the nation's first century relative to the apportionment of direct taxes. Some would have overturned the three-fifths clause (as the Fourteenth Amendment eventually did) to require that only free individuals be counted in such apportionment. Others would have apportioned direct taxes according to property values (Ames 1896, 143–144).

Today the issue is moot because the national government relies on the income tax that was sanctioned by the Sixteenth Amendment and on various other excise taxes that are considered to be indirect.

See also *Pollock v. Farmers' Loan & Trust Co;* Sixteenth Amendment; Three-fifths Clause.

For Further Reading:

Ames, Herman. 1896. *The Proposed Amendments to the Constitution of the United States during the First Century of Its History.* Reprint, New York: Burt Franklin, 1970.

TAXATION, EXPORT

In a provision meant to protect the agricultural states, Article I, Section 9 of the Constitution prohibits Congress from levying a tax "on Articles exported from any State." In addition, Article I, Section 10 specifies that "no State shall, without the Consent of Congress, lay any Imposts or Duties on Imports or Exports, except what may be absolutely necessary for executing its inspection Laws."

From 1812 to 1914, 12 attempts were made to repeal the ban on congressional export levies. Most grouped around three periods—the War of 1812, the Civil War, and World War I—when governmental resources were down (Musmanno 1929, 112). Two proposals introduced in 1866 and one in 1884 would have applied specifically to exports of cotton, suggesting a possible intent to retaliate against the South.

In 1974, Michigan Republican representative Robert Huber renewed the call to grant Congress power to levy export fees.

For Further Reading:

Musmanno, M. A. 1929. *Proposed Amendments to the Constitution.* Washington DC: U.S. Government Printing Office.

TAXATION, INCOME

See Sixteenth Amendment.

TAXATION, INHERITANCE

The Supreme Court upheld the constitutionality of a federal inheritance tax in *New York Trust Co. v. Eisner* (1916). Still, at least 10 amendment proposals have contained provisions designed explicitly to recognize such a power in the Constitution, with at least two such proposals declaring that such taxes could be levied only on estates valued at $50,000 or $100,000 or more (Musmanno 1929, 164). Some of the proposals to repeal the Sixteenth Amendment have also called for limits on, or abolition of, inheritance taxes.

In 2001, Congress adopted and President George W. Bush signed the Economic Growth and Tax Relief Reconciliation Act (EGTRRA) of 2001. Under this legislation, the tax rate on estate taxes will be lowered from the 60 percent in effect in 2001 to 45 percent by 2009; during this same time, exclusions from this tax would be raised from $675,000 to $3.5 million. Under the current law, estate taxes would be ended altogether in 2010, but the following year, it would go back to the 60 percent rate with a $1 million exclusion (O'Connell 2001, 588).

For Further Reading:

O'Connell, Frank J., Jr. 2001. "Estate Tax Repeal: What Now?" *The Tax Adviser* 32 (September): 588.

TAXATION, LAND

In 1942, Democratic Representative Horace Voorhis of California proposed an amendment to allow Congress to tax land values; Democratic Representative Herman Eberharter of Pennsylvania did so again in 1944. From a somewhat different perspective, Democratic Senator Morris Sheppard of Texas introduced three resolutions from 1937 to 1941 to provide for a homestead exemption of up to $5,000 for a head of a household. Since Sheppard's proposal, an increasing number of states have exempted such property from taxes (Roemer 1983, 110); it is unclear whether Sheppard intended to universalize such exceptions against state taxation or whether he intended to guard against a future federal tax on land.

For Further Reading:

Roemer, Arthur C. 1983. "Classification of Property." In *The Property Tax and Local Finance,* ed. C. Lowell Harris. New York: Proceedings of the Academy of Political Science.

TAXATION, MAJORITIES NEEDED TO INCREASE

Some proponents of a balanced budget amendment foresee reaching a balanced budget by cuts in spending, but others anticipate that federal taxes will also need to be raised to accomplish this. Opponents of such taxes believe that they simply encourage the government to increase spending.

The Constitution does not set any special majorities for the passage of tax legislation. In the last two decades, several members of Congress have proposed a constitutional amendment that would require a two-thirds vote of both Houses to raise taxes, the same vote now required to override a presidential veto. In January 1995, by a vote of 279 to 152, the House adopted a controversial measure known as Rule XXI, Section 5 (b), requiring a three-fifths vote of the House to enact tax increases. Courts have rejected a challenge to the act (see Leach 1997).

See also Balanced Budget Amendment; Supermajorities.

For Further Reading:

Ackerman, Bruce, et al. 1995. "An Open Letter to Congressman Gingrich." *Yale Law Journal* 104 (April): 1539–1544.

Leach, Robert S. 1997. "House Rule XXI and an Argument against a Constitutional Requirement for Majority Rule in Congress." *UCLA Law Review* 44 (April): 1253–1288.

McGinnis, John O., and Michael B. Rappaport. 1995. "The Constitutionality of Legislative Supermajority Requirements: A Defense." *Yale Law Journal* 105 (November): 483–511.

Soller, Christopher J. 1995. "Newtonian Government: Is the Contract with America Unconstitutional?" *Duquesne Law Review* 33 (Summer): 959–984.

TAXATION, RETROACTIVE

As part of the Revenue Reconciliation Act of 1993, Congress retroactively raised taxes on high incomes and estates. The Supreme Court has subsequently upheld the constitutionality of such provisions ("Retroactive Tax Increases" 1994, 1588). Since the adoption of the 1993 law, however, numerous members of Congress—mostly Republicans—have sponsored what they call a "Citizens Tax Protection Amendment," designed to make such retroactive taxes illegal. Since *Calder v. Bull* (1798), courts have interpreted the current sections of Article I, Sections 9 and 10, which prohibit ex post facto laws, to apply only to criminal laws. Martin J. Bailey is among those who have included provisions against retroactive taxes in his *Constitution for a Future Country* (2001). Under House Rule XXI 5 (c), which could be altered more easily than could a direct constitutional prohibition, the U.S. House of Representatives currently has a prohibition against considering retroactive income tax increases.

See also Bailey, Martin J.

For Further Reading:

Bailey, Martin J. 2001. *Constitution for a Future Country.* New York: Palgrave.

"Retroactive Tax Increases: No Problem, Say Justices." 1994. *Congressional Quarterly Weekly Report* 52 (18 June): 1588.

TAXATION, STATE AND FEDERAL EMPLOYEES

The Constitution does not specifically prohibit the national government from taxing the states or the states from taxing the federal government, but limitations can easily be surmised based on considerations of federalism. As early as *McCulloch v. Maryland* (1819), Chief Justice John Marshall ruled that the states could not tax a branch of the national bank.

In *Dobbins v. Commissioners of Erie County* (1842), the Court extended this rather sensible prohibition to the more problematic cases of states taxing the salaries of federal officials. In *Collector v. Day* (1871), the prohibition was made reciprocal, and it stayed so until *Graves v. New York ex rel. O'Keefe* (1939). There, the Supreme Court repudiated its earlier prohibitions on the taxation of the salaries of governmental officials, now insisting only that such salaries not be singled out for special taxation.

From 1932 to two weeks prior to the *Graves* decision, at least four proposals were introduced in Congress to permit state and federal taxation of governmental officials' incomes. *Graves* made such an amendment unnecessary, and Congress subsequently amended its tax laws in accord with this new precedent.

TAXATION, STATE INCOME TAX OF NONRESIDENTS

From 1953 to 1965, members of Congress introduced about 50 proposals to prohibit states or localities from taxing the income of nonresidents or from discriminating against nonresidents. In 1958, Connecticut also submitted a request to Congress for a convention to deal with this issue.

Representatives of states surrounding New York introduced most of the resolutions. New

York is one of those states that taxes all income earned within the state as well as income that its residents earn in other states (Penniman 1980, 13). Thirteen states permit local governments to levy income or payroll taxes on all who work there, and Philadelphia even applies this law to visiting athletes (Christensen 1995, 273).

For Further Reading:

Christensen, Terry. 1995. *Local Politics: Governing at the Grassroots.* Belmont, CA: Wadsworth.

Penniman, Clara. 1980. *State Income Taxation.* Baltimore: Johns Hopkins University Press.

TAXATION, STATE SECURITIES

Throughout most of American history, the U.S. Supreme Court has upheld a doctrine of intergovernmental tax immunity that prevented both state and national governments from taxing the interest on bonds issued by one another. This prohibition was articulated, among other places, in *Pollock v. Farmers' Loan & Trust Co.* (1895).

From 1920 to 1943, members of Congress introduced more than 100 amendments either to allow Congress to tax the interest on state securities or allow both state and national governments to tax interest on bonds issued by one another. Some such proposals were linked to proposals for the taxation of state and federal employees' income. Others would apply only when such income exceeded a set amount, such as $12,500.

Although Congress still does not tax revenues from registered state securities, its decision in *South Carolina v. Baker* (1988) indicated that the Supreme Court did not see any constitutional barriers preventing it from doing so.

See also Taxation, State and Federal Employees.

TENTH AMENDMENT

The Tenth Amendment was ratified in 1792 as the last provision of the Bill of Rights. The amendment provides that "the powers not delegated to the United States by the Constitution, nor prohibited by it to the states, are reserved to the States respectively or to the people." Throughout early American history, judges often interpreted it along with the preceding Ninth Amendment, which provides that "[t]he enumeration in the Constitution of certain rights shall not be construed to deny or disparage others retained by the people."

Anti-Federalist opponents of the new Constitution expressed concern over the scope of powers of the new central government. Five of the seven states that proposed amendments in the process of ratifying the Constitution suggested an amendment to protect the rights of the states under the new system. James Madison made such a provision part of the Bill of Rights that he offered in the First Congress. His first version of this provision mixed guarantees that are now found in the Ninth and Tenth Amendments.

The primary debate over the Tenth Amendment in the First Congress centered on whether to include the word "expressly" before the word "delegated" (Kurland and Lerner 1987, 5:403–404). Had Congress done so, the provision would have closely resembled Article 2 of the Articles of Confederation, which had provided that "every state retains its sovereignty, freedom, and independence, and every Power, Jurisdiction and right, which is not by this confederation expressly delegated to the United States, in Congress assembled" (5:400). James Madison opposed this emendation, believing that "there must necessarily be admitted powers by implication, unless the Constitution descended to recount every minutia" (5:403). His view was eventually validated by a vote of 32 to 17.

Even before the Tenth Amendment was ratified, Thomas Jefferson, who would soon be allied with James Madison in the Democratic-Republican Party, used it as part of his "strict construction" argument against the constitutionality of the national bank. Similarly, James Madison cited the amendment in his Report of 1800, which questioned the constitutionality of the Alien and Sedition Acts of 1798. In regard to the bank, the Supreme Court vindicated the rival view of Alexander Hamilton in *McCulloch v. Maryland* (1819), in which Chief Justice John

Marshall cited the omission of the word "expressly" as a justification for the doctrine of implied powers.

The great difficulty in interpreting the Tenth Amendment stems from the fact that it does not specify precisely what powers are delegated to the national government. Moreover, those parts of the Constitution that do enumerate such powers—most notably, Article I, Section 10—allow for implied powers.

Early Supreme Court decisions referred to state "police powers" over such matters as education, health, welfare, land management, and the policing of its citizens' activities. However, after the Civil War, the national government asserted full control over most such functions in the states of the former Confederacy, and the Fourteenth Amendment subsequently raised the possibility that the old relationship between the states and the national government had been drastically altered (McDonald 1992, 863).

Initially reluctant to interpret the Fourteenth Amendment so expansively, the Supreme Court adopted somewhat contradictory lines of opinion on the matter from roughly the turn of the century until 1937. In some notable cases involving the regulation of activities such as gambling, prostitution, and the consumption of alcoholic beverages, which the Court regarded as moral evils, it generally recognized broad federal authority under the commerce clause and other federal powers. On other occasions, the Court invalidated legislation. Most notably, in *Hammer v. Dagenhart* (1918), the Court invalidated a federal child labor law adopted under putative authority of the commerce clause; it thought that the law invaded state police powers or interfered with free market forces. In a classic error that showed seeming ignorance of the decision at the Constitutional Convention of 1787 to omit the word "expressly" from the amendment, Justice William Day declared that "to them [the states] and to the people the powers not expressly delegated to the national government are reserved" (*Hammer* 1918, 275).

In 1937, shortly after Franklin D. Roosevelt's court-packing plan, the Supreme Court reversed course in this second area of cases and began interpreting the commerce clause and other grants of federal powers more liberally. In *United States v. Darby* (1941), Justice Harlan Fiske Stone pronounced that the Tenth Amendment "states but a truism that all is retained which has not been surrendered" (124). Until recent years, the amendment lay relatively dormant, but this now appears to be changing.

In *National League of Cities v. Usery* (1976), the Supreme Court relied on the Tenth Amendment to overturn the application of federal minimum-wage laws to certain state employees, but it subsequently overturned this decision in *Garcia v. San Antonio Metropolitan Transit Authority* (1985), in which the Court indicated that the states should look to their representatives in Congress rather than to the courts for protection. The Supreme Court's decision in *United States v. Lopez* (1995), declaring that the federal law prohibiting the carrying of guns within 1,000 feet of a school zone exceeded federal authority under the commerce clause, suggests, however, that the idea of states' rights which the Tenth Amendment articulates continues to be a concern. In a similar decision in *United States v. Morrison* (2000), the U.S. Supreme Court struck down a section of the Violence Against Women Act of 1994 as exceeding congressional authority by infringing on state criminal laws. And in *Jones v. United States* (2000), it limited the reach of the interstate commerce clause in a case involving prosecution for throwing a Molotov cocktail at a private residence. Recent decisions relative to the Eleventh Amendment have further reinforced judicial concerns for the rights traditionally exercised by the states.

Concern for such rights was reflected in reactions to the Supreme Court's reapportionment decisions in the 1960s, in recent proposals for an amendment to forbid unfunded federal mandates, and in increased references to the Tenth Amendment, especially among Republican officeholders. Worldwide, there appears to be increased attention to principles of "devolution" to state and local entities.

See also Articles of Confederation; Eleventh Amendment; Fourteenth Amendment; *Garcia v. San Antonio Metropolitan Transit Authority;* Madison, James; *McCulloch v. Maryland;* Ninth Amendment; States, Police Powers; *United States v. Morrison.*

For Further Reading:

Jones v. United States, 529 U.S. 848 (2000).

Killenback, Mark R. ed. 2002. *The Tenth Amendment and State Sovereignty: Constitutional History and Contemporary Issues.* Lanham, MD: Rowman & Littlefield.

Kurland, Philip B., and Ralph Lerner, eds. 1987. *The Founders' Constitution.* 5 vols. Chicago: University of Chicago Press.

United States v. Morrison, 529 U.S. 528 (2000).

Vile, John R. 1996–1997. "Truism, Tautology or Vital Principle? The Tenth Amendment Since *United States v. Darby.*" *Cumberland Law Review* 27:445–532.

TERM LIMITS

See Congress, Term Limits; Judiciary, Terms of Office; Twenty-second Amendment.

TERRITORIES

Article IV, Section 3 grants Congress power to "make all needful Rules and Regulations respecting the Territory or other Property belonging to the United States." Surprisingly, it makes no specific provision for the acquisition of new territories.

This omission presented a dilemma for President Thomas Jefferson in 1803. Although he favored a strict construction of the Constitution, and therefore wanted a constitutional amendment to legitimize his purchase of Louisiana, he eventually acquiesced with congressional leaders of his party who thought that such an amendment was unnecessary and feared that it might complicate the diplomatic situation (Vile 1992, 70–71).

In the early years of the Republic, most issues relating to the territories centered on the issue of slavery. Ironically, at least one amendment introduced in 1866 sought to reduce the states that had participated in the rebellion to territories. Although this did not happen, Congress did divide the Southern states into military districts during the period of Reconstruction (1865–1877). Congress required that the states ratify the Fourteenth Amendment before their representatives were fully accepted into Congress.

Issues involving territories often centered on the admission of new states, requiring a certain population before this occurred, or seeking to prevent certain territories (especially those that were not contiguous with existing states or those that permitted polygamy) from being admitted into statehood. A resolution introduced by a California representative in 1872 sought to limit grants of public lands in the territories to those who actually settled there. At least three resolutions introduced from 1875 to 1880 proposed that territories should have at least one member in the House of Representatives and one vote in the electoral college. In an idea more fully implemented with the adoption of the Twenty-third Amendment in 1961, at least one such proposal would also have given one electoral vote to the District of Columbia. Since 1975 there have been a number of proposals to provide representation in the electoral college for U.S. territories. Puerto Rico is currently among the territories whose residents are U.S. citizens but who have no right to vote in presidential elections.

See also Fourteenth Amendment; Louisiana Purchase; Puerto Rico, Representation in Electoral College; Slavery, the Territories, Twenty-third Amendment.

For Further Reading:

Onuf, Peter. 1984. "Territories and Statehood." In *Encyclopedia of American Political History: Studies of Principal Movements and Ideas,* ed. Jack P. Greene. Vol. 3: 1283–1304. New York: Charles Scribner's Sons.

Vile, John R. 1992. *The Constitutional Amending Process in American Political Thought.* New York: Praeger.

TERRORISM

To date, the United States has not, like Israel and other nations, faced widespread weekly acts of terrorism, but Timothy McVeigh's bombing of the Murrah Federal Building in Oklahoma City on April 19, 1995, as well as the more recent and even deadlier airplane attacks on the World Trade Center in New York and the Pentagon outside Washington DC on September 11, 2001, have led not only to American intervention in Afghanistan and Iraq in an attempt to destroy the Taliban, but also to renewed questions about whether civil liberties might need to be curtailed in order to combat terrorism.

In what appears to have been designed simply as a teaching exercise to help students think through the implications of this problem, the Constitutional Rights Foundation has designed and posted a "Safe America" Amendment that would begin by providing that U.S. citizens "shall enjoy the right of safety from terrorist attack," and that proceeds to authorize Congress to establish special military courts that could ignore key provisions for individual rights in the Bill of Rights and to ban "the manufacture, sale and possession of all handguns and concealable weapons within the territorial boundaries of the United States" (Constitutional Rights Foundation, 2002), the second issue being one currently addressed by the Second Amendment. A U.S. Supreme Court decision in *Ex parte Milligan* (1866) currently appears to limit military trials of U.S. civilians when regular courts are open, but this decision might or might not be considered to apply to foreign nationals, especially those who have never actually landed in American territory. In *Ex parte Quirin* (1942), the U.S. Supreme Court upheld military trials of German saboteurs who had landed in the United States.

In 2004, the Supreme Court decided three important cases relative to terrorism. In *Hamdi v. Rumsfeld*, it decided that the government did not have a "blank check when it comes to the rights of the Nation's citizens" and that Hamdi, an American citizen arrested in Afghanistan for fighting for the Taliban, was entitled to a showing as to why the government was continuing to hold him. Similarly, it decided in *Rasul et al. v. Bush* that the Court could hear appeals from aliens being held at the Guantanamo navy base and in *Rumsfeld v. Padilla* that an American citizen arrested in America and being held as an "enemy combatant" had brought his case to the

wrong court. In December 2008, the Supreme Court agreed to decide whether the United States could indefinitely confine a Qatari national, Ali al-Marri, without charging him with a crime.

In *Hamdan v. Rumsfeld* (2006), the Court further ruled that a military commission that President Bush had created to try detainees at Guantanamo Bay violated the Code of Military Justice and the Geneva Convention. *Boumediene v. Bush* (2008) further ruled that a military commission that Congress had subsequently established had unconstitutionally denied the right of habeas corpus to Boumediene, a citizen of Bosnia and Herzegovenia whom the United States was holding at Guantanamo.

Most American responses to the threat of terror involving constitutional alterations have focused on how the nation might better prepare to meet the emergency that could be caused by widespread losses of members of the House of Representatives (the Constitution currently provides that such members must be replaced by elections, which take time, whereas state governors are now free to make temporary replacements of members of the U.S. Senate).

See also Congress, Emergency Functioning.

For Further Reading:

Constitutional Rights Foundation. "America Responds to Terrorism." http://www.crfusa/terror/America. Accessed May 18, 2002.

Kay, Julie. 2002. "War of, for Words: South Florida Lawyers on ABA Task Force Lead Fight For Right of Enemy Combatants to Counsel." *Broward Daily Business Review* 43 (October 21): A10.

TEXAS V. JOHNSON (1989)

Texas v. Johnson was one of the Supreme Court's most controversial decisions in recent years. It prompted numerous calls for a constitutional amendment to prohibit flag desecration.

The case involved the actions of Gregory Johnson, who took part in a "Political War Chest Tour" at the Republican National Convention of

1984. At one point in this demonstration, he publicly burned an American flag and was subsequently arrested and convicted under a Texas statute prohibiting desecration of a venerated object. Prior to being appealed to the U.S. Supreme Court, one Texas court of appeals upheld his conviction and another struck it down.

In this case, Justice William Brennan led a 5-to-4 majority affirming that Johnson's conduct was a form of symbolic speech protected by the First and Fourteenth Amendments. The Court ruled that the value of such speech outweighed the two interests advanced by Texas.

The majority rejected Texas's argument that prosecution was needed to prevent a breach of the peace, since no such breach occurred or appeared imminent. Along these lines, the majority further rejected the idea that Johnson's words fell into the small class of "fighting words" that it had recognized in prior cases could be restricted, most notably in *Chaplinsky v. New Hampshire* (1942).

As to Texas's desire to preserve the flag as a symbol of national unity, Brennan noted that the law in question did not prohibit all types of destruction of the flag but only those that would be offensive to others. As such, the restriction on speech was "content based" and subject to special scrutiny (*Texas* 1989, 412). Brennan argued that "government may not prohibit the expression of an idea simply because society finds the idea itself offensive or disagreeable" (*Texas* 1989, 414). Government could adopt precatory, or recommendatory, regulations, but it must use persuasion rather than force when attempting to curb symbolic speech.

Chief Justice William Rehnquist and Justice John Paul Stevens wrote dissenting opinions focusing on the uniqueness of the flag as a national symbol. They argued that Johnson was not being prosecuted for what he said but rather for what he did.

Congress responded to the decision by adopting the Flag Protection Act of 1989 rather than by proposing a constitutional amendment. The Court subsequently struck down this new law in *United States v. Eichman* (1990), and debate over the wisdom of a flag desecration amendment continues.

See also Flag Desecration; *United States v. Eichman*.

For Further Reading:

Goldstein, Robert Justin. 2000. *Flag Burning and Free Speech: The Case of Texas v. Johnson.* Lawrence: University Press of Kansas.

THIRD AMENDMENT

The Third Amendment is part of the Bill of Rights and is among the least controversial amendments to the U.S. Constitution. The amendment, which has deep roots in English prohibitions against billeting troops that go back to a charter that Henry I granted to London in 1131 (Bell 1993, 118), grew more immediately out of some of the abuses by Great Britain under its Quartering Acts that led, in part, to the Boston Massacre, and later to the Revolutionary War. The amendment provides that "no Soldier shall, in time of peace be quartered in any house, without the consent of the Owner, nor in time of war but in a manner to be prescribed by law."

A similar provision was contained in the English Petition of Rights of 1628. In addition, at the time the U.S. Constitution was written, four state constitutions had such a provision, and three state ratifying conventions proposed such a guarantee before James Madison incorporated it in the list of rights he presented to the First Congress (Lutz 1992, 52, 56, 64).

The amendment was little debated in the House of Representatives and was unaltered by either it or the Senate. Although the amendment appears to have been violated during both the War of 1812 and the U.S. Civil War (Bell 1993, 136–137), it has neither been the subject of more than a passing reference by the U.S. Supreme Court nor the subject of a proposed constitutional amendment. Although the Third Amendment remains one of the few provisions of the Bill of Rights that the Supreme Court has not applied to the states via the due process clause of the Fourteenth Amendment, the U.S. Second Court of Appeals ruled in *Engblom v.*

Carey (1982)—a case involving whether the state of New York could quarter National Guard troops at a correctional residence it owned whose members were on strike—that the amendment was so incorporated. Moreover, Justice William O. Douglas cited this amendment in *Griswold v. Connecticut* (1965) as one of a number of amendments that serve as a foundation for a right to privacy.

See Also Bill of Rights; *Griswold v. Connecticut;* Privacy, Right to.

For Further Reading:

Bell, Tom W. 1993. "The Third Amendment: Forgotten but Not Gone." *William & Mary Bill of Rights Journal* 2: 117–150.

Lutz, Donald S. 1992. *A Preface to American Political Theory.* Lawrence: University Press of Kansas.

THIRTEENTH AMENDMENT

The Constitution of 1787 circumspectly omitted direct mention of slavery. Still, a number of clauses—most notably the three-fifths clause (Article I, Section 2), the migration and importation clause (Article IV, Section 9), and the fugitive from labor clause (Article IV, Section 2)—gave implicit sanction to the institution in states where it already existed. The predominant attitude about slavery even in the South was that it was at best a necessary evil, and prominent Southerners were among those who supported the idea of freeing slaves and colonizing them in Liberia.

No constitutional amendments were both proposed and ratified from 1804 to 1865. Indeed, prior to 1860, few proposals were introduced in Congress to eliminate slavery by constitutional amendment. Arthur Livermore, a Democratic representative from New Hampshire, introduced one such proposal in 1818; another was introduced by Whig Representative (and former president) John Quincy Adams of Massachusetts in 1839, who had become an increasingly vocal foe of slavery. The latter

amendment would have abolished hereditary slavery after 1842, prohibited the admission of further slave states into the Union, and abolished slavery and the slave trade in the District of Columbia after 1845.

Just prior to the Civil War, most proposals for dealing with slavery—including the Corwin Amendment and the Crittenden Compromise—sought to reassure the Southern states that were about to secede by guaranteeing that slavery would be perpetual. In 1861 and 1862, Congress adopted confiscation laws relating to slaves who had been used in the rebellion or those who had escaped to or been captured by the Union armies. In 1862, Congress provided for compensated emancipation in the District of Columbia and—despite the 1857 decision in *Scott v. Sandford*—outlawed slavery in the federal territories (Maltz 1990, 13). In September 1862, President Abraham Lincoln issued his preliminary Emancipation Proclamation. Officially proclaimed on January 1, 1863, it freed all slaves held in areas of rebellion and was justified as a war measure (*Id.,* 14).

Although there was some sentiment to abolish slavery by statute, there was general agreement that Congress lacked such power. In December 1863, Republican Representatives James M. Ashley of Ohio and James F. Wilson of Iowa introduced emancipation amendments. Senator John B. Henderson, a Missouri Democrat, introduced a similar amendment in the Senate in January 1864, with Republican Charles Sumner of Massachusetts offering a somewhat different version the next month (Maltz 1990, 15). Proponents justified such amendments both on the grounds of morality and as a means of securing future peace by eliminating the situation of the nation being half slave and half free (*Id.,* 15–16).

Although the amendment had broad Republican support, some of the congressional Democrats who were left after the secession of the Southern states argued that Article V could not legally be used to effect such a major change. Although the amendment passed the Senate by a vote of 38 to 6 in August 1864, the 93-to-65 vote it received in the House in June fell 13 votes shy of the required two-thirds majority (Maltz 1990, 19). Republican James Ashley of Ohio then switched his vote—in a maneuver mimicked by Kansas Republican Senator Bob Dole after the 1995 Senate defeat of the Balanced Budget Amendment—to allow him room to reintroduce the amendment in the second session of the Thirty-eighth Congress *(Id.)*.

The Republicans won substantial victories in the election of 1864. This election and Abraham Lincoln's endorsement of the amendment in his annual message, along with fears among Democrats that they might forever be saddled with the onus of slavery, led to another vote in January 1865, when the House adopted the amendment by a vote of 119 to 56 (Maltz 1990, 20).

Significantly, abolitionist William Lloyd Garrison, who had once described the Constitution as "a covenant with death," now proclaimed that it had been replaced by "a covenant with life" (quoted in Vorenberg 2001, 208). The states ratified the amendment this same year, and, Lincoln, whose signature was not needed, signed the amendment, perhaps in response to Buchanan's earlier signature on the Corwin Amendment *(Id.,* 210). John Wilkes Booth assassinated Lincoln before the amendment was ratified.

The Thirteenth Amendment is divided into two parts. The first section prohibits "slavery" and "involuntary servitude, except as a punishment for crime." This language was taken almost directly from the Northwest Ordinance of 1787. By distinguishing slavery and involuntary servitude, the amendment appears to indicate (and courts have so interpreted the provision) that it outlaws practices like peonage as well as the kinds of practices extant before the U.S. Civil War. Section 1 is fairly unique in that it "covers private conduct as well as state action" (Kares 1995, 375; also see Rutherglen, 2008). Section 2 grants Congress power to enforce the amendment, a statement that a number of subsequent amendments have emulated.

Questions would subsequently be raised as to whether Section 1 was intended to grant any rights other than freedom from bondage (see, for example, *The Civil Rights Cases* of 1883) and precisely what powers Congress was intended to have under Section 2. A scholarly treatment of the Thirteenth Amendment has suggested that subsequent interpreters "failed to remember that the amendment was once seen as the pinnacle of freedom instead of a mere precursor to the Fourteenth and Fifteenth Amendments" (Vorenberg 2001, 239). Still, the precise scope of the Thirteenth Amendment is difficult to resolve on the basis of contemporary debates (Maltz 1990, 21–28), and, at least to some extent, such issues have been mooted by the more explicit and expansive language of the Fourteenth Amendment, and by subsequent legislative reliance on provisions in this and the Fifteenth Amendment.

In *Jones v. Alfred H. Mayer Co.* (1968), the Supreme Court upheld a ban on racial discrimination in housing on the basis of a law adopted under authority of the Thirteenth Amendment. Consistent with the amendment's application to "involuntary servitude," one commentator has suggested that the Thirteenth Amendment could serve as the basis of regulating abusive treatment of "mail-order brides," who are brought to the United States from foreign countries (Vergara 2000).

See also *Civil Rights Cases;* Corwin Amendment; Crittenden Compromise; Emancipation Proclamation; Enforcement Clauses in Amendments; Garrison, William Lloyd; Lieber, Francis; Lincoln, Abraham.

For Further Reading:

Kares, Lauren. 1995. "Note: The Unlucky Thirteenth: A Constitutional Amendment in Search of a Doctrine." *Cornell Law Review* 80 (January): 372–412.

Maltz, Earl M. 1990. *Civil Rights, the Constitution, and Congress, 1863–1869.* Lawrence: University Press of Kansas.

Rutherglen, George. 2008. "State Action, Private Action, and the Thirteenth Amendment." *Virginia Law Review* 94 (October, 2008): 1367–1406.

Tsesis, Alexander. 2004. *The Thirteenth Amendment and American Freedom: A Legal History.* New York: NYU Press.

Vergara, Vanessa B. M. 2000. "Comment: Abusive Mail-Order Bride Marriage and the Thirteenth Amendments." *Northwestern University Law Review* 94 (Summer): 1547–1599.

Vorenberg, Michael. 2001. *Final Freedom: The Civil War, the Abolition of Slavery, and the Thirteenth*

Amendment. Cambridge, UK: Cambridge University Press.

THREE-FIFTHS CLAUSE

At the Constitutional Convention of 1787, representatives of Northern and Southern states had different interests with respect to taxation and representation. Northerners wanted to apportion any direct taxes to include the slave population, but they did not want slaves to figure in the formula for apportioning seats in the U.S. House of Representatives. By contrast, southern representatives did not want their slaves to be taxed, but they did want to count them for representation purposes (Vile 2002a, 29–30).

The delegates settled on an expedient compromise. It was based on a formula proposed, albeit never actually applied, under the Articles of Confederation and was incorporated in Article I, Section 2 of the Constitution. This compromise provided that both taxation and representation would be based on the "whole Number of free Persons" and "three fifths of all other Persons."

The three-fifths clause is arguably one of the foulest compromises that the Constitutional Convention adopted, but it cut both ways. Although it allowed for blacks to count as less than full persons, the term "persons" implicitly recognized their humanity. Significantly, Chief Justice Roger Taney ignored the three-fifths clause when arguing in the *[Dred] Scott* decision (1857) that blacks were not, and could not be, American citizens and must therefore be considered as chattel.

Prior to the Civil War, a number of congressmen, including former president John Quincy Adams, proposed modifying the Constitution to base both taxes and representation solely on the number of free persons. The Thirteenth Amendment ended slavery. This meant that Southern states, and the Democratic Party, might actually gain representation in the House of Representatives. Section 2 of the Fourteenth Amendment subsequently specified that representation would now be apportioned "counting the whole number of persons in each State, excluding Indians not taxed." In an ultimately futile attempt to prevent Southern states from disenfranchising the newly freed slaves, this amendment further provided that if states denied such voting rights, "the basis of representation therein shall be reduced in the proportion which the number of such [disenfranchised] male citizens shall bear to the whole number of male citizens twenty-one years of age in such State."

See also Fourteenth Amendment; *Scott v. Sandford;* Thirteenth Amendment.

For Further Reading:

Vile, John R. 2006. *A Companion to the United States Constitution and Its Amendments.* 4th ed. Westport, CT: Praeger.

THREE-FOURTHS MAJORITY TO RATIFY AMENDMENTS

Article V of the U.S. Constitution proposes that amendments must be proposed by a convention called by Congress at the request of two-thirds of the states or (as has been the practice) by two-thirds majorities in both houses of Congress. These amendments must then be approved, at congressional specification, either by three-fourths of the state legislatures or—as in the solitary case of the Twenty-first Amendment repealing national alcoholic prohibition—by special conventions called within the states.

The supermajority requirement for ratification by the states, like the supermajority requirement for proposing amendments, helps assure that the nation will not adopt amendments unless they have widespread geographical support. Curiously, the Constitution does not specify a time limit during which amendments must be adopted. In *Dillon v. Gloss* (1921), the U.S. Supreme Court agreed that ratification should reflect a contemporary consensus of the states, but in *Coleman v. Miller* (1939), the Court subsequently decided that it was up to Congress to decide whether amendments reflected such a consensus. In the case of the Twenty-seventh

Amendment (relating to the timing of congressional pay raises), the requisite number of states did not ratify the amendment until more than 200 years after it was proposed (a time, however, during which no states attempted to rescind their ratifications). Some proposed amendments have contained self-enforcing provisions stating that they will not go into effect unless ratified within a seven-year period. When such a provision was included in the authorizing resolution, rather than in the text, of the proposed Equal Rights Amendment, Congress subsequently extended the deadline, but the amendment still failed.

Especially considering that Rhode Island had not sent delegates to the Constitutional Convention, the three-fourths requirement for ratification is close to the requirement that the Constitution of 1787 would not go into effect unless and until ratified by nine of the states. Two modern authors have suggested that this parallel is purposeful and helps explain why today's generation continues to be bound to a Constitution made before its members were born. If today's generation wants to alter the Constitution, it must muster majorities similar to those of the founding generation (see McGinnis and Rappaport 2002).

See also Consensus and the Amending Process; Deliberation and the Amending Process; Equal Rights Amendment; Ratification of Amendments; Supermajorities; Twenty-seventh Amendment.

For Further Reading:

McGinnis, John O., and Michael B. Rappaport. 2002. "Our Supermajoritarian Constitution." *Texas Law Review* 80 (March): 703–805.

TIEDEMAN, CHRISTOPHER (1857–1904)

It is common to distinguish the written Constitution of the United States from the unwritten constitution of Great Britain. However, law professor Christopher Tiedeman wrote a book in 1890 that pointed to the similarities of the two constitutions and the way that they change. He argued that law necessarily arose from the legal and moral habits of a people and what he called the "prevalent sense of right" (Tiedeman 1890, 7).

Tiedeman argued that regardless of what the written words of a constitution appear to say, courts use interpretation and construction to see that laws comport with popular understandings. Moreover, in the United States, the written Constitution provides only a skeleton, with most governmental operations less determined by what is written than by what is unwritten. Tiedeman argued that the flesh and blood of a constitution is "not to be found in the instrument promulgated by a constitutional convention, but in the decisions of the courts and acts of the legislature, which are published and enacted in the enforcement of the written Constitution" (Tiedeman 1890, 43).

Changes in the operation of the electoral college, the understanding by which presidents served no more than two terms, and changing interpretations of the contracts clause and of the doctrine of natural rights provided some of Tiedeman's illustrations. Whereas some scholars would criticize judges for going against the original intent of those who wrote the Constitution, Tiedeman praised them for interpreting law in accord with the needs and desires of the present generation.

Nowhere was this clearer than in Tiedeman's discussion of the Fourteenth Amendment. Tiedeman agreed that this amendment was intended to have a broad scope. Still, Tiedeman praised the Court for "keeping the operation of this amendment within the limits which they felt assured would have been imposed by the people, if their judgment had not been blinded with passion, and which in their cooler moments they would ratify" (Tiedeman 1890, 108).

Because the unwritten constitution so frequently limits the written words, Tiedeman inquired into the value of a written constitution. He responded that the Constitution enabled judges with power "to serve as a check upon the popular will in the interest of the minority" (Tiedeman 1890, 163).

See also Fourtenth Amendment; Unwritten Constitution.

For Further Reading:

Halper, Louise A. 1990. "Christopher G. Tiedeman, 'Laissez-Faire Constitutionalism' and the Dilemma of Small-Scale Property in the Gilded Age." *Ohio State Law Journal* 51: 1349–1384.

Mayer, David N. 1990. "The Jurisprudence of Christopher G. Tiedeman: A Study in the Failure of Laissez-Faire Constitutionalism." *Missouri Law Review* 55 (Winter): 93–161.

Tiedeman, Christopher G. 1890. *The Unwritten Constitution of the United States.* New York: G. P. Putnam's Sons.

Vile, John R. 1992. *The Constitutional Amending Process in American Political Thought.* New York: Praeger.

TIME LIMITS ON AMENDMENTS

The Constitution does not specify the length of time during which states may ratify a proposed amendment. When the Eighteenth Amendment was being debated in 1917, however, Republican Senator (later president) Warren G. Harding of Ohio proposed that a deadline for ratification be set at January 1, 1923, apparently in the unrealized hope of putting an effective obstacle in the amendment's path (Bernstein with Agel 1993, 173–174). Similar deadlines were included in the Twentieth Amendment, the Twenty-first Amendment, and the Twenty-second Amendment. Deadlines were also included in the amendment that Congress proposed in 1978 to treat the District of Columbia as a state for purposes of representation in Congress, presidential elections, and the amending process.

In *Dillon v. Gloss,* the Supreme Court ruled that the Constitution implied that ratification must "reflect the will of the people in all sections at relatively the same period" (1921, 375). It thus upheld the constitutionality of the seven-year deadline in the Eighteenth Amendment.

The amendment which Congress proposed in 1924 to give it the power to regulate child labor did not contain such a time limit. In *Coleman v. Miller* (1939), the Court examined Kansas's attempt to ratify the amendment 13 years after it was proposed and ruled that the determination of the contemporaneousness of such a ratification was a "political question" for Congress to resolve.

When Congress proposed the Equal Rights Amendment in 1972, it included a seven-year deadline. Largely to keep the Constitution from being cluttered with ratification deadlines, Congress did not include this deadline in the text of the proposed amendment itself, where it would presumably be self-enforcing, but in an accompanying resolution. In 1978, Congress extended the ratification deadline of the Equal Rights Amendment to 1982. This action was successfully challenged in a U.S. district court in *Idaho v. Freeman* (1981), but the issue became moot when the amendment failed to meet even this new deadline.

The event that has done the most to stretch the idea of contemporary consensus expressed in *Dillon v. Gloss* is the putative ratification of the Twenty-seventh Amendment relative to congressional pay raises. Despite concerns raised by scholars (Vile 1991a), both the national archivist and a majority of Congress accepted the legitimacy of this amendment, first proposed as part of the Bill of Rights in 1789, even though the necessary number of states did not ratify until 1992.

The last two controversies make it a virtual certainty that Congress will place ratification deadlines within the texts of future proposals. Still, there is no apparent legal barrier to keep Congress from departing from the seven-year formula. The author of a law review article has argued that time limits on constitutional amendments are an unconstitutional attempt to alter the specific amending guidelines established in Article V (Kalfus 1999). According to this view, once proposed by Congress, amendments always remain subject to state ratification. Yet another author believes that the omission of a ratification deadline within Article V was a serious omission that should be cured by the adoption of a constitutional amendment (Hanlon 2000). That author, who believes that the decision in *Dillon v. Gloss* calling for a contemporary consensus represented wise social policy but lacked specific constitutional support, believes that an amendment providing for a seven-year deadline would be reasonable.

See also *Coleman v. Miller; Dillon v. Gloss;* Equal Rights Amendment; Failed Amendments; Implementation Dates of Amendments; Twenty-seventh Amendment.

For Further Reading:

Bernstein, Richard B., with Jerome Agel. 1993. *Amending America: If We Love the Constitution So Much, Why Do We Keep Trying to Change It?* New York: Random House.

Dillon v. Gloss, 256 U.S. 368 (1921).

Hanlon, Michael C. 2000. "Note: The Need for a General Time Limit on Ratification of Proposed Constitutional Amendments." *Journal of Law & Politics* 16 (Summer): 663–698.

Kalfus, Mason. 1999. "Why Time Limits on the Ratification of Constitutional Amendments Violate Article V." *University of Chicago Law Review* 66 (Spring): 437–467.

Vile, John R. 1991a. "Just Say No to 'Stealth' Amendment." *National Law Journal* 14 (June 22): 15–16.

TITLES OF NOBILITY

Article I, Section 9 currently contains a provision that

> [n]o Title of Nobility shall be granted by the United States: And no Person holding any Office of Profit or Trust under them, shall, without the Consent of the Congress, accept of any present, Emolument, Office, or Title, of any kind whatever, from any King, Prince, or foreign State.

One of the earliest proposed amendments prescribing loss of citizenship would have supplemented these restrictions by further proposing that

> [i]f any citizen of the United States shall accept, claim, receive or retain any title of nobility or honour or shall, without the consent of Congress, accept and retain any present, pension, office or emolument of any kind whatever, from any emperor, king, prince or foreign power, such person shall cease to be a citizen of the United States, and shall be incapable of holding any office of trust or profit under them, or either of them. (Bernstein with Agel 1993, 178)

Republican Senator Philip Reed of Maryland introduced this amendment in January 1810, and Congress ratified it by May 1 by a vote of 87 to 3 in the House and 19 to 5 in the Senate.

Sometimes called the Reed Amendment, or the "Phantom Amendment," this proposal was included in a congressionally authorized printing of the Constitution made in 1815 (known as the "Bioren edition") (Silversmith 1999, 586) and later copied by other publishers, including a number of states. In 1817, following an inquiry from then President James Monroe, Secretary of State John Quincy Adams determined that the Titles of Nobility Amendment had not been ratified. With 17 states in the Union at the time the amendment was submitted, 13 states would have been required for ratification, and 12, and only 12, apparently ratified. However, new states were admitted during the ratification period, thus apparently never putting the amendment any closer than two states away from ratification (Silversmith 1999, 596–599). Moreover, there is nothing in the act of "publishing" an amendment—especially if done mistakenly—that would give it the force of law.

Long a mystery to historians, who found a lack of contemporary debate on the topic, the amendment might have been motivated by what one author has described as "general animosity to foreigners evident in the United States before the War of 1812" (Silversmith 1999, 583). It might also have been prompted by fears that the son of Jerome Bonaparte (brother to Napoleon) and his onetime Baltimore wife, Elizabeth Patterson, might one day try to claim an American throne. Apparently, Republicans—who were closer on foreign policy matters to France than to England—introduced the measure to defuse criticisms raised by Patterson's pretensions and her associations with top party officials. Federalists had little choice but to concur or face charges that they were hoping to get titles from England (Earle 1987, 37). One historian noted that, with Napoleon's defeat in Europe, "by the time of the amendment's bizarre reappearance in the House of Representatives [in the form of the printed Constitution that included it], it was an anachronism" (Id.). However, Congress apparently applied most provisions of this proposed amendment to American diplomats in 1874 (Pendergast, Pendergast, and Sousanis 2001, 511).

In recent years, David Dodge, the publisher of an extremist magazine called *Anti-Shyster*, has raised the claim (largely based on the publication of the amendment in the Bioren and other editions of the Constitution) that the Titles of Nobility Amendment was legitimately ratified and is part of the U.S. Constitution (Silversmith 1999, 580). Dodge and his followers, who have also posted their views on the Internet, believe that the amendment might be a vehicle for excluding lawyers, who are sometimes called "esquire," from holding office. Even had the amendment been ratified, this interpretation of the amendment is fairly fanciful, since such a title is not "conferred" by any foreign government, and the title when used in the United States seems to be "nothing more than a custom" (Silversmith 1999, 602). An unnamed correspondent to an English magazine noted in 1839 that while the U.S. constitution prohibited titles of nobility, Americans were excessively attached to titles such as colonel, major, and judge.

One scholar of the proposed amendment on titles notes that it carries two important messages:

> That concern about divisions in society in the United States is an historic problem, and that the legal community, both in the nineteenth and the twentieth centuries has not invested sufficient effort into accurately communicating the law to the profession, as well as to the public. (Silversmith 1999, 610)

The Phantom Amendment remains one of six amendments that Congress has proposed but the requisite number of states has never ratified.

See also Failed Amendments.

For Further Reading:

Bernstein, Richard B., with Jerome Agel. 1993. *Amending America: If We Love the Constitution So Much, Why Do We Keep Trying to Change It?* New York: Random House.

Conklin, Curt E. 1996. "The Case of the Phantom Thirteenth Amendment: A Historical and Bibliographic Nightmare." *Law Library Journal* 88 (Winter): 121–127.

An [unnamed] correspondent. 1839. "American Titles," *The Penny Magazine* 487. (November 2): 428–429.

Earle, W. H. 1987. "The Phantom Amendment and the Duchess of Baltimore." *American History Illustrated* 22 (November): 32–39.

Pendergast, Tom, Sara Pendergast, and John Sousanis, with Elizabeth Shaw Grunow, ed., 2001. *Constitutional Amendments: From Freedom of Speech to Flag Burning.* 3 vols. Detroit, MI: U.X.L. imprint of Gale Group.

Silversmith, Jol A. 1999. "The 'Missing Thirteenth Amendment': Constitutional Nonsense and Titles of Nobility. *Southern California Interdisciplinary Law Journal* 8 (Spring): 577–611.

TOFFLER, ALVIN AND HEIDI (1928– , 1929–)

Alvin and Heidi Toffler are known as futurists, whose primary influence has been through the publication of the books *Future Shock* and *The Third Wave*. Taking a broad view of history, the Tofflers argue that civilization has been hit by three primary waves. The first was the conversion from nomadic existence to agriculture; the second was industrialization; and the third was the development and distribution of information. Like the first and second waves, the third wave will involve massive reconfigurations of existing institutions. In a book introduced by then Speaker of the House Georgia Republican Newt Gingrich (a friend of the Tofflers), the Tofflers discuss some of these implications.

The Tofflers begin the final chapter of this book with a letter to the founding fathers. While extolling what the framers did, especially in creating the Bill of Rights, they indicated the need for changes:

You would have understood why even the Constitution of the United States needs to be reconsidered and altered—not to cut the federal budget or embody this or that narrow principle, but to expand its Bill of Rights, taking account of threats to freedom unimagined in the past, and to create a whole new structure of government capable of making intelligent, democratic decisions necessary for our survival in a Third Wave, twenty-first century America. (Toffler and Toffler 1995, 90)

Rather than outlining a whole new plan of government, the Tofflers sketch three key principles that they believe should guide such reconfiguration.

The first is that of "minority power" (Toffler and Toffler 1995, 92). Believing that the "massified" society of the second wave is giving way to more tailored forms of production, the Tofflers note that "we have a configurative society—one in which thousands of minorities, many of them temporary, swirl and form highly novel, transient patterns, seldom coalescing into a consensus on major issues" (Id.). The Tofflers express concern that existing mechanisms for measuring opinion do not always measure the depth of such an opinion, signaling "when a minority feels so threatened or attaches such life-and-death significance to a single issue that its views should perhaps receive more than ordinary weight" (*Id., 95*).

In their second principle, the Tofflers advance "the principle of 'semidirect democracy'—a shift from depending on representatives to representing ourselves" (Toffler and Toffler 1995, 96). Acknowledging that the constitutional framers thought that representative democracy would be "less emotional and more deliberative" (*Id., 97*), the Tofflers believe these problems could be handled through mechanisms "requiring a cooling-off period or second vote before implementation of major decisions taken via referendum or other forms of direct democracy" (*Id., 98*). Moreover, they foresee the possibility of developing arrangements that "*combine* direct and indirect democracy" (*Id.,* 98–99). Noting that legislatures have not always been responsive to popular concerns, the Tofflers suggest that voters might petition legislative bodies "to set up committees on topics the public—not the lawmakers—deem appropriate" (*Id.,* 99).

The Tofflers call their third principle "decision division" (Toffler and Toffler 1995, 99), and it is aimed in two directions. The Tofflers believe that some decisions that are now being made by governments need to be made transnationally. By the same token, they believe that modern central governments, like second-wave industries, are often so top-heavy that they fail from information overload. They think it is necessary "to move a vast amount of decision making downward from the center" (*Id.,* 100), and they argue that "there is no possibility of restoring sense, order and management 'efficiency' to many governments without a substantial devolution of central power. We need to divide the decision load and shift a significant part of it downward" (*Id.,* 101). They note that "the need for new political institutions exactly parallels our need for new family, educational and corporate institutions as well" (*Id.,* 103). They further observe that "we should think not of a single massive reorganization or of a single revolutionary, cataclysmic change imposed from the top, but of thousands of conscious, decentralized experiments that permit us to test new models of political decision making at local and regional levels in advance of their application to the national and transnational levels" (*Id.,* 107).

Bruce E. Tonn is among other futurists who have given some attention to the problem of how modern governmental forms might be adopted to emerging changes.

See also Tonn, Bruce E.

For Further Reading:
  Toffler, Alvin, and Heidi Toffler. 1995. *Creating a New Civilization: The Politics of the Third Wave.* Atlanta: Turner Publishing, Inc.

TONN, BRUCE E. (1955–)

Like Alvin and Heidi Toffler, Bruce E. Tonn, a researcher at the Oak Ridge National Laboratory in Oak Ridge, Tennessee, has written two articles suggesting changes that futurists might consider. He noted in a subsequent interview that his ideas appear to have generated little attention outside this community and will require either extraordinary leadership or a possible crisis before they are likely to get such scrutiny (Pollard and Tonn 1998).

Tonn's first article proposed and described a specific constitutional amendment, which he dubbed the "Court of Generations" Amendment. The amendment, which Tonn divided into four sections, appeared to share characteristics of the Council of Revision that was rejected at the Constitutional Convention, of Thomas Jefferson's idea of periodic revision of constitutions, and the Council of Censors mechanism that was once employed in the State of Pennsylvania.

Section I of the proposed amendments created a "Court of Generations, which shall be an adjunct of the judicial department of the national government" (Tonn 1991, 483). This section specifically employed the language of the U.S. Constitution's preamble in securing "the blessings of liberty to our posterity." Sections II and III indicated that the Court of Generations would consist of a grand jury composed of the Supreme Court and one representative from each of the U.S. states and territories. Its function would be to "return a bill of indictment to the members of the Supreme Court if evidence suggests an intolerable threat to the security of the blessings of liberty to our posterity" (Id.). Interestingly, the Court of Generations would have no authority to do anything about the problems it diagnosed, but "[t]he members of the Supreme Court shall decide whether we and/or our ancestors are in contempt of intolerably threatening the security of the blessings of liberty to our posterity" (Id.). Finally, Section IV provided that the first Court of Generations would meet within five years after the adoption of the amendment and "every subsequent term of five years." Congress would be responsible for assuring that the Court had "reasonable resources at its disposal to assist its deliberations (Id.).

Tonn was especially motivated by his concerns over long-term environmental issues like "species extinction, deforestation and desertification, soil erosion, air and water pollution, toxic waste and radioactive waste" but also about issues like "drug abuse, sexually transmitted diseases (e.g., AIDS), abortion, housing, education and local and national transportation" (Tonn 1991, 484). He was quite concerned with creating a mechanism that was outside of existing partisan structures and wanted to associate the new court with the U.S. Supreme Court so that it would have "the same stature and visibility" (Id., 490). As a grand jury, the Court of Generations would have subpoena power and would meet in secret. States and territories would select members through special processes that they would themselves create. Tonn regarded his proposal not as a substitute for but rather as a "complement" to the existing document that he hoped would "create a dialogue between living generations" (Id. 496).

Tonn subsequently elaborated his ideas in an article that, while not, like the first, proposing specific constitutional language, was far more detailed in the kinds of institutions that Tonn thought would be required for "future-oriented government" (Tonn 1996). Tonn began by listing nine criteria by which he thought a future-oriented government could be judged. These included:

(1) Explicit recognition of future generations and future-oriented issues. [Italics and intervening language here and throughout the rest of this paragraph are omitted.]
(2) Explicit implementation of a structured decision-making process.
(3) Bias toward consensual decision making.
(4) Incentives to include people of wisdom.
(5) Effective and broad-based citizen participation.
(6) Prevention of special-interest lobbying.
(7) Ability to balance long-term and short-term interests.
(8) Ability to make stable commitments to long-term plans and actions [and]
(9) Ability to foster learning. (Tonn 1996, 414–416)

Tonn was especially concerned that the qualities that make for good legislators may not make for individuals with long-term vision. He noted that:

People of wisdom are not self-selected or self-centered. That is, they do not normally declare to the world that they are the wisest, because that would violate their values. Wisdom cannot be conveyed via 20-second commercials. It can be recognized by others only through close association in various difficult and trying contests. Current processes tend to drive people of wisdom away from the fray, do not hold wisdom as a central characteristic for political office, and are, in any case, incapable of identifying people of wisdom and nurturing their growth over the years. (Tonn 1996, 415)

Tonn proceeded to supplement his earlier proposal for a Court of Generations with a proposal for a "Futures Congress" and a "Futures Administration" that would "build and administer (1) a Diagnostic and Decision Support System; (2) the Futures Congress Management System; and (3) systems that integrate with other national and global information systems" (Tonn 1996, 424). His proposal for the Futures Congress was his most elaborate and would consist of four chambers composed (from top to bottom) of Elders, Visionaries, Realists, and Decision Makers (*Id.,* 418–419). Citizens, hypothetically specified at 200 million, would choose 2 million Decision Makers, each of whom would have to be 30 years or older, would have to have the support of 100 to 200 individuals, and would use "moral and ethical judgment" to "choose among future-oriented decision alternatives." The Decision Makers would also choose approximately 20,000 Realists (with a minimum age of 40), whose function would be to evaluate "future-oriented decision alternatives." Realists would choose 200 Visionaries (50 years of age or older), who would create "future-oriented decision alternatives." Finally, a group of 20 elders (60 years of age or older) would set "criteria to guide the creation and evaluation of future-oriented decisions" (*Id.,* 420).

Tonn was not completely sure how the structures he was proposing would relate to structures already in existence, but the basic distinction focused on allowing institutions to handle short-term problems and the new institutions to look toward long-term ones. He also recognized that his new proposals could result in some instability, as individuals in the Futures Congress gain and lose support, but he stressed that, in current circumstances, "the best one can hope for is a retrofit to existing institutions, which this design represents" (Tonn 1996, 430).

See also Council of Censors; Environmental Protection; Jefferson, Thomas; Toffler, Alvin and Heidi.

For Further Reading:

Pollard, Vincent Kelly, and Bruce E. Tonn. 1998. "Revisiting the 'Court of Generations' Amendment." *Futures* 30: 345–352.

Tonn, Bruce E. 1991. 1996. "A Design for Future-Oriented Government." *Futures* 28 (June): 413–431.

———. 1991. "The Court of Generations: A Proposed Amendment to the U.S. Constitution." *Futures* 21 (June): 482–498.

TRADEMARKS

Article I, Section 8 of the Constitution grants Congress power "to promote the Progress of Science and useful Arts, by securing for limited Times to Authors and Inventors the exclusive Right to their respective Writings and Discoveries." In the *Trade Mark Cases* (1879), however, the Supreme Court unanimously ruled that this provision did not grant Congress power over trademarks. The Court ruled that the exercise of any such congressional power would have to be restricted to transactions in interstate or foreign commerce.

Almost immediately, Iowa Republican representative Moses McCoid introduced an amendment to grant Congress power to regulate trademarks. Similar proposals were introduced in 1911 and 1913 and in the late 1940s and early 1950s. As early as 1881, however, Congress had adopted new legislation on trademarks under the authority of its commerce powers, and since 1937, the Supreme Court has interpreted such powers broadly.

Congress has exercised such powers over trademarks in the U.S. Trademark Act of 1946, generally known as the Lanham Act, as well as in the Trademark Counterfeiting Act of 1984. Trademarks are registered with the U.S. Trademarks Office.

For Further Reading:

Widmaier, Uli. 2004. "Use, Liability, and the Structure of Trademark Law." *Hofstra Law Review* 33 (Winter): 603–709.

TREASON

Article III, Section 3 of the Constitution specifies that "treason against the United States, shall consist only in levying War against them, or in adhering to their Enemies, giving them Aid and Comfort." It further specifies that conviction of treason requires either a confession in open court or the testimony of two or more witnesses to an overt act. Although entrusting Congress with the power "to declare the punishment of Treason," the Constitution prevents such penalties from being passed from one generation to another.

In addition to the grounds for treason listed in the U.S. Constitution, the British permitted conviction for "compassing or imagining the death of the king (Chapin 1964, 3). Clearly, the framers feared the impact that such a broad definition might have on freedom of expression which they later protected in the First Amendment. With this in mind, the courts have construed the treason clause strictly throughout most of U.S. history (Hurst 1971, 192).

Members of Congress have introduced about 25 proposed amendments relative to treason. Two such proposals, both introduced in 1901 after the assassination of President William McKinley, would have broadened the definition of treason to include such assassination attempts.

In 1924, Missouri Democratic representative Joseph Wolff introduced a measure, later reflected in concerns that the Nye Commission investigating war-profiteering during World War I raised, that would make it treason to defraud the government with respect to war materials and equipment. That same year, Pennsylvania Republican George Washington Edmonds proposed extending the definition of treason to include any efforts to establish a new form of government except by constitutional amendment.

Most proposals that have been introduced since the end of World War II have attempted to expand the definition of treason to include adherence to or support of groups advocating the overthrow of the government by force; some have specifically mentioned the Communist Party. Louisiana Democratic representative John Rarick introduced a proposal in 1968 to define treason against the United States to include "levying war against them or in adhering to their enemies, giving them aid or comfort, or engaging in acts of subversion." Reflecting his distrust of the courts, Rarick further specified "that the judicial power shall not extend to limit, transfer or negate the powers granted herein, exclusively to the Congress or to alter or amend by interpretation or otherwise the commonly accepted meaning of the language imployed [sic] by Congress in laws enacted pursuant to such powers" (H.J. Res. 1213).

See also First Amendment.

For Further Reading:

Chapin, Bradley. 1964. *The American Law of Treason: Revolutionary and Early National Origins.* Seattle: University of Washington Press.

Hurst, James W. 1971. *The Law of Treason in the United States: Collected Essays.* Westport, CT: Greenwood Press.

TREASURY, DEPARTMENT OF

Although the Constitution grants Congress the power of the purse, the president appoints all cabinet members, including the secretary of the treasury. The Constitution does not specify who has the power to remove such officials, but court decisions, most notably that in *Myers v. United States* (1926), have confirmed that this power is vested in the president. The Supreme Court noted that the president was responsible for enforcing the laws and would presumably be best informed about the performance of his subordinates.

Chief Justice (and former president) William Howard Taft, who wrote the decision in *Myers,* relied heavily on debates in the First Congress, where James Madison had been a strong advocate of the president's removal power. During these debates, however, Madison had suggested that because of the secretary's tie to the power of the purse there might be a reason to treat the secretary of the treasury differently from other officials (D. O'Brien 2005, 1:341). In the nation's early years, at least three members of Congress—States' Rights Democratic representative John Barbour of Virginia (1828) and Whig representatives John Underwood (1836, 1838) and Henry Clay (1841) of Kentucky—proposed amendments to vest either the appointment or the appointment and removal of the treasury secretary in Congress.

In *Bowsher v. Synar* (1986), the Supreme Court reaffirmed presidential authority over budget cuts when it struck down a provision of the Balanced Budget and Emergency Deficit Control Act of 1985. That provision had entrusted the specification of such cuts to the comptroller general, who was subject to removal by Congress rather than by the president.

See also Presidency, Appointment and Removal Powers of.

For Further Reading:

O'Brien, David M. 2005. *Struggles for Power and Governmental Accountability.* 6th ed., Vol. 1 of *Constitutional Law and Politics.* New York: W. W. Norton.

TREATIES, RATIFICATION OF

As disputes about the Bricker Amendment demonstrate, the treaty-making power has been a subject of intense debate. Article II, Section 2 of the Constitution provides that the president "shall have Power, by and with the Advice and Consent of the Senate, to make Treaties, provided two-thirds of the Senators present concur."

Early in American history, the House of Representatives threatened to annul this constitutional provision by failing to appropriate funds needed to carry out the Jay Treaty. The Virginia legislature subsequently proposed that the House of Representatives share in approving treaties, a proposal that was not introduced again until 1884. In 1899, there were two proposals, probably stimulated by the Spanish-American War, to vest treaty ratification in a majority vote of the Senate.

The two world wars both provoked proposals to alter the treaty power. President Woodrow Wilson's failure to get the Treaty of Versailles ratified by the necessary two-thirds of the Senate (the vote was 49 to 35) triggered several proposals from 1919 to 1925. Some proposed that such treaties should become effective by a majority vote in the Senate, some wanted to require a majority vote in both the House and the Senate, and at least one representative wanted to ratify treaties by a national referendum.

Such proposals took on a new urgency with U.S. entry into World War II. In May 1945, the House of Representatives voted 288 to 88 (with 56 members abstaining) for an amendment to enable a majority of both houses to ratify treaties, but the Senate was not keen on giving up its prerogative (Ackerman and Golove 1995, 865, 889). In the meantime, the lines between treaties ratified by the Senate, executive agreements entered into by the president, and other international agreements negotiated by the president with the approval of both houses of Congress were being obscured. The Senate appears to have accepted this situation in part as an alternative to formal constitutional change.

By 1954, Congress, by a simple majority of both houses, adopted an agreement between the United States and Canada regarding the St. Lawrence Seaway, which the president had previously sent to the Senate for approval as a treaty (Ackerman and Golove 1995, 893). In 1993, a similar procedure, negotiated under the Trade Act of 1974, was used to ratify the North American Free Trade Agreement (NAFTA). This bill was put on a legislative "fast track" in exchange for constant presidential-legislative collaboration during the negotiating process. Bruce Ackerman, a prominent theorist on the amending process, has cited this development as an example of constitutional innovation outside the Article V amending process and praised it for its "efficacy, democracy [and] legitimacy" (Ackerman and Golove 1995, 916).

Proposals to alter the formal treaty-making process continued throughout the 1950s, 1960s, and 1970s. A number of the later proposals, undoubtedly precipitated by the United States' experience in Vietnam, would have required the involvement of both houses of Congress in any treaty committing U.S. forces abroad.

Although the Constitution specifies that the Senate must approve treaties by a two-thirds vote, it does not specify how treaties are terminated. In *Goldwater v. Carter* (1979), the Court refused to invalidate a challenge by some senators to President Carter's termination of a treaty with Taiwan that conflicted with U.S. recognition of the People's Republic of China. The justices split as to whether the case was "ripe" for adjudication (the senators who challenged the treaty termination did not constitute a majority of that body), whether the issue was "political" and should be left to the elected branches to solve on their own, or whether the president possessed the power the annul treaties.

See also Ackerman, Bruce; Bricker Amendment.

For Further Reading:
Ackerman, Bruce, and David Golove. 1995. "Is NAFTA Constitutional?" *Harvard Law Review* 108 (February): 799–929.
Goldwater v. Carter, 444 U.S. 996 (1979).

TRUTH-IN-LEGISLATION AMENDMENT

Two authors of a law review article have called for a "Truth-in-Legislation Amendment" (Denning and Smith 1999). Such an amendment is based on a provision of the Tennessee Constitution, which is similar to provisions also adopted in other states. The proposed amendment would require that "Congress shall pass no bill, and no bill shall become law, which embraces more than one subject, that subject being clearly expressed in the title" (*Id.,* 962). This amendment is designed to address the problem of legislative "riders" or "earmarks." Members of Congress often insert such provisions (frequently during last-minute, behind-the-scenes committee negotiations over pieces of legislation) bearing little relation to the title or central purpose of bills in so-called omnibus legislation on behalf of special interests within their districts. If the truth-in-legislation amendment proved effective, whether in influencing the legislative and executive branches or through judicial enforcement, the amendment might serve (much like the proposed item veto, balanced budget, or term limit amending proposals) to limit congressional spending. It might also increase the accountability of Congress to constituents and watchdog groups who are attempting to follow and influence the course of legislation in the public interest.

See also Presidency, Veto Power of.

For Further Reading:
Denning, Brannon P., and Brooks R. Smith. 1999. "Uneasy Riders: The Case for a Truth-in-Legislation Amendment." *Utah Law Review* (1999): 957–1025.

TUGWELL, REXFORD (1891–1979)

No modern would-be constitutional reformer has worked longer or more diligently on a new United States constitution than Rexford Tugwell. One of the three members of Franklin Roosevelt's original "brain trust" who once worked with other scholars on a preliminary draft of a World Constitution, Tugwell had an active life as both a college professor and a public servant before joining the Center for the Study of Democratic Institutions (headed by Robert Hutchins) as a senior fellow (Ashmore 1970).

In his first six years there, Tugwell initiated discussions that led him to draft 37 successive versions of a proposed constitution. This draft was published in a special issue of the center's magazine in 1970. Tugwell continued his revisions and offered his 40th version in a book published in 1974 (for analysis, see Vile 1991c, 106–110).

Tugwell's proposals were quite complex, and are not easily summarized. Certainly, Tugwell put great emphasis on governmental planning, adding numerous new boards, commissions, and positions. He also believed that existing state governments were antiquated and needed to be altered radically. Unlike many 20th-century reformers, however, Tugwell would have maintained the system of separated powers and did not advocate a parliamentary system.

Tugwell's 40th constitution differed significantly in organization from his 37th and consisted of 12 articles. Article I dealt with rights and responsibilities. In addition to most guarantees now found in the Bill of Rights and various amendments, this section contained protections for individual privacy; guarantees against discrimination based on "race, creed, color, origin, or sex"; prohibitions against any public support for religion; a guarantee that those unable to "contribute to productivity shall be entitled to a share of the national product"; and a guarantee of education "at public expense" for those establishing eligibility (Tugwell 1974, 595–596). Citizen responsibilities included respecting the rights of others, participating in democratic processes, and avoiding violence. To promote the latter goal, and in contrast to the Second Amendment of the existing Constitution, Tugwell would reserve the bearing of arms to "the police, members of the armed forces, and those licensed under law" (*Id.,* 597).

Tugwell designated the government under his fortieth constitution the "Newstates of America" (the 37th version referred instead to the "United Republic of America"). Article II dealt with these newstates, none of which was to contain less than 5 percent of the existing population. Each would have its own constitution as well as its own "governors, legislatures, and planning, administrative, and judicial systems" (Tugwell 1974, 598). Like present states, they would exer-

cise "police powers"; all rights and responsibilities applied at the national level would also apply to the states.

Article III established an "electoral branch" of government supervised by an "overseer" selected by the Senate. The overseer would "supervise the organization of national and district parties, arrange for discussion among them, and provide for the nomination and election of candidates for public office" (Tugwell 1974, 599). Duties would include assisting in the nomination of candidates and in arranging and supervising elections. All costs would be paid from public funds, and all private personal expenditures would be prohibited.

Article IV delineated a planning branch headed by a national planning board of 15 members. It would be responsible for submitting six- and twelve-year plans.

Article V described the president, who was designated as "the head of government, shaper of its commitments, expositor of its policies, and supreme commander of its protective forces" (Tugwell 1974, 604). The president would serve a nine-year term subject to recall by 60 percent of the voters after three years. The president would be served by two vice presidents, one for internal affairs and the other for general affairs. The latter would supervise "Chancellors of External, Financial, Legal, and Military Affairs" (*Id.,* 604). Treaties negotiated by the president would go into effect unless rejected by a majority of the Senate. The president would appoint a public custodian in charge of governmental property and an intendant to supervise intelligence and investigation offices.

Article VI described a drastically altered Congress. Various groups and individuals would appoint a Senate of 70 to 80 members who would serve for life terms. The Senate's main function would be to consider, and at times delay, but not initiate legislation. It would also select a three-person national security council to consult with the president about the deployment of American troops abroad. The Senate would also select the national watchkeeper, a type of ombudsman. Members of the House of Representatives would be selected from 100 districts, each of which would select three members for three-year terms; to give the body a more national orientation, there would be another 100 at-large members. The House would be "the original lawmaking body of the Newstates of America" (Tugwell 1974, 609). In contrast to the current Constitution, which is silent on such matters, Tugwell's document outlined the selection of committees and their chairs and included a much longer list of congressional powers, including powers over banking, insurance, communications, transportation, space exploration, welfare, education, libraries, the conservation of natural resources, and civil service.

Article VII established a regulatory branch headed by a national regulator to be selected by the Senate and to serve as head of a regulatory board of seventeen members. The regulator would charter corporations, regulate industrial mergers, and supervise the marketplace.

The judicial branch was delineated in Article VIII in considerable more complexity than the current Constitution. Section 1 of this article began as follows: "There shall be a Principal Justice of the Newstates of America; a Judicial Council; and a Judicial Assembly. There shall also be a Supreme Court and a High Court of Appeals; also Courts of Claims, Rights and Duties, Administrative Review, Arbitration Settlements, Tax Appeals, and Appeals from Watchkeeper's Findings" (Tugwell 1974, 614). The principal justice would preside over the system and appoint all members of the national courts; the justice would serve an 11-year term and would share with the president the power to grant reprieves and pardons. Although Tugwell criticized the extent of judicial review as currently exercised, the Supreme Court would continue to exercise such power under his plan.

Article IX dealt with general provisions, Article X with governmental arrangements, and Article XII with transition to the new government. Article XI dealt with the amending process. The judicial council would have the power to formulate amendments to be approved by the Senate and president and submitted to the people and adopted by majority vote. Every 25 years the overseer would conduct a referendum on whether a new constitution was needed. If approval was given, the judicial council would draw up a constitution to go into effect if not disapproved by a majority.

Tugwell's various proposals were the topic of considerable discussion and criticism (Kelly 1981, 650), some of it quite fanatical (Preston 1972), but they generated little in the way of practical results.

See also World Government.

For Further Reading:

Ashmore, Harry S. 1970. "Rexford Guy Tugwell: Man of Thought, Man of Action." *Center Magazine* 3 (September–October): 2–7.

Kelly, Frank K. 1981. *Court of Reason: Robert Hutchins and the Fund for the Republic.* New York: Free Press.

Preston, Robert L. 1972. *The Plot to Replace the Constitution.* Salt Lake City, Utah: Hawkes Publications.

Tugwell, Rexford. 1974. *The Emerging Constitution.* New York: Harper and Row.

Vile, John R. 1991c. *Rewriting the United States Constitution: An Examination of Proposals from Reconstruction to the Present.* New York: Praeger.

TULLER, WALTER (1886–1939)

California attorney Walter Tuller wrote an article in 1911 that advocated the calling of a constitutional convention to propose an amendment for the direct election of U.S. senators. Although he devoted most of the article to showing that Congress was obligated to call such a convention when two-thirds of the states requested it to do so and that the Court could enforce such a responsibility (see Vile 1991c, 53–54), Tuller also advanced two subjects that he wanted a convention to handle.

First, Tuller wanted to reduce the number of states required to call such a convention from two-thirds to one-half. At a time when many regarded the amending process as too rigid, Tuller saw such a reduction as a way of keeping the Constitution from becoming "too far removed from the people." Second, Tuller wanted an amendment granting the national government power "to regulate corporations or monopolies in any form" (Tuller 1911, 385).

Tuller anticipated a convention of "the strongest and ablest men in the nation" (Tuller 1911, 386). He anticipated that each state would be represented equally, but he was willing to let the convention decide whether members would vote individually or by state.

See also Consitutional Conventions; Seventeenth Amendment.

For Further Reading:

Tuller, Walter K. 1911. "A Convention to Amend the Constitution—Why Needed—How It May Be Obtained." *North American Review* 193: 369–387.

Vile, John R. 1991c. *Rewriting the United States Constitution: An Examination of Proposals from Reconstruction to the Present.* New York: Praeger.

TWELFTH AMENDMENT

There have been hundreds of proposals to alter the process of presidential and vice presidential selection, but the Twelfth Amendment is the only substantial change that has been made in this procedure. This amendment grew out of America's early experience that the original manner of selecting the executive as specified in Article II of the Constitution had some unintended consequences. Many of these were hastened and exaggerated by a development of political parties that most of the framers neither anticipated nor easily welcomed (Turner 1973; Bernstein 1993).

Operation of the Electoral College

The electoral college is a system of indirect election whereby state-designated electors choose the president and vice president. The design of this mechanism was a major development at the Constitutional Convention of 1787 because the electoral college provided a way for the executive to act independently of Congress and thus furthered the idea of a system of separated powers.

Alan Grimes identified six defining features of the electoral college system: (1) it allowed states to determine whether electors would be chosen by the people or by the state legislatures; (2) it gave each state a number of electors equal to its total representation in the House and Senate, thus somewhat advantaging both large states (with the greatest number of representatives) and small states (guaranteed at least three votes); (3) electors met within each state and cast two ballots for president; (4) members of Congress were prohibited from serving as electors; (5) other federal officeholders were also excluded from the job; and (6) electors had to cast at least one of their two votes for someone from another state (Grimes 1978, 20).

The framers thought that such a procedure would avoid the tumult and possible uncertainties of popular election at a time when technology was more primitive. The framers also anticipated that electors would have a better knowledge of candidates from other states than would the populace as a whole.

Early Presidential Elections

Although some scholars assert that the framers anticipated that electors would perform a deliberative function, from the very first election in 1788, electors came ready to cast predetermined votes (Kuroda 1994, 31). Some states selected delegates by direct election (now the universal procedure) and others by legislative appointment; similarly, some used an at-large system of election, and others chose electors by district. In the first election, all 69 delegates who participated (New York was unable to settle on the method of selecting electors and did not cast ballots) each cast one of their two votes for George Washington. They split their second votes among 11 other men, with John Adams's 34 votes putting him in second place and earning him the vice presidency. One representative, knowing Adams's penchant for titles, called him "His Superfluous Excellency" (*Id.,* 24).

By the election of 1792, the Federalist and Democratic-Republican Parties had begun to emerge. Once again, however, Washington was selected unanimously, this time with 132 votes. Adams came in second. The fact that Adams had only 77 votes indicated that the party "ticket" had not yet completely emerged.

Washington retired after his second term, so the election of 1796 was the first without his candidacy. This election saw a closer contest between the top two party candidates and greater cohesion in voting combinations. Because some Federalists who voted for Adams did not vote for Thomas Pinckney, however, the person with the second-highest number of votes was Thomas Jefferson, head of the emerging Democratic-Republican Party. This meant that the president and vice president would be from different parties.

The Election of 1800

Although having a president and vice president from different parties was far from a desirable situation, the election of 1800 finally galvanized action by revealing yet another flaw in the original electoral system. In this election, all 73 electors who cast a vote for Jefferson also voted for Aaron Burr, in an attempt to avoid the different-party problem of the previous election. Because the Constitution did not provide for electors separately to designate presidential and vice presidential candidates, this resulted in a tie in the electoral college, which threw the election into the House of Representatives, where each state had one vote and where the outgoing Federalists effectively had the ability to make the choice. In the initial ballot, Jefferson got the votes of eight states and Burr of six, with two states divided. It took about a week of balloting, and 36 ballots, before enough Federalists abstained (in part at the urging of Alexander Hamilton, who distrusted Burr even more than he distrusted Jefferson and would eventually forfeit his life in a duel with Burr, largely over publication of negative assessments of Burr's character) to give Jefferson the majority of states that he needed to win.

Proposal and Ratification of the Twelfth Amendment

The years immediately following produced scores of proposals, including an automatic plan (which Thomas Jefferson supported for a time) eliminating the office of electors and granting all a state's electoral votes to the person receiv-

ing the plurality of its votes. Other plans proposed eliminating the vice presidency and reconsidering the three-fifths compromise under which electors were allocated to Southern states; specifically designating votes for president and vice president; and requiring district elections both for electors and for members of Congress (Kuroda 1994, 107–126).

The election of 1802 brought substantial gains to the Democratic-Republicans in Congress and renewed pressure for a constitutional amendment. In October 1803, the House voted 88 to 39 for an amendment to require electors to designate which ballot they were casting for president and which for vice president and reducing from five to three the number of candidates the House would choose among if no candidate received a majority.

The Senate then began its own debate, which resulted in the current language of the Twelfth Amendment. Like the version that the House accepted, this proposal specified that when no one received a majority, the House of Representatives would choose from among the top three candidates, rather than the top five. It also provided that if the House did not choose a candidate by March 4 (subsequently changed by the Twentieth Amendment to January 20), the vice president would act as president. The amendment stirred highly partisan debate. Federalists, who purported to represent the interests of the small states, fought the reduction from five candidates to three. Others thought that any constitutional changes might dangerously lower the floodgates to reform (Kuroda 1994, 141).

There was also debate whether amendments required a two-thirds vote of all members or only of those members present. On December 2, 1803, the amendment was narrowly carried by a vote of 22 to 10—although this was short of two-thirds of the entire membership of 34 (Kuroda 1994, 142–143).

The new Senate version then went back to the House, where, on December 8, 1803, after an initial count of 83 to 41, Speaker Nathaniel Macon cast his vote with the majority to give it precisely the two-thirds majority needed. New Hampshire attempted to become the necessary 13th state to ratify in June 1804, but the governor created a state of confusion with a veto, and the honor apparently went to Tennessee in late July. The new amendment set the framework for the 1804 presidential election. In this contest, Jefferson was elected on a ticket that included New York's George Clinton.

Consequences and Implications of the Twelfth Amendment

Although it did not specifically mention them, the amendment affirmed the role that political parties had come to play in designating candidates. It also arguably denigrated the vice presidency. The individual in this position was now clearly recognized as second fiddle; subsequently, vice presidents would often be chosen more for regional or ideological balance than for qualifications to be president (Kuroda 1994, 172).

The political parties subsequently acquired a share in the system that was reaffirmed as large and small states both continued their overrepresentation under the new plan. Despite numerous subsequent proposals, including many calls for complete abolition of the electoral system, it has not been substantially altered by constitutional amendment since 1804. The Twenty-third Amendment did extend some representation in the electoral college to the District of Columbia.

See also Electoral College Reform; Hamilton, Alexander; Jefferson, Thomas; Twentieth Amendment; Twenty-third Amendment.

For Further Reading:

Bernstein, Richard B. 1993. "Fixing the Electoral College." *Constitution* 5 (Winter): 42–48.

Grimes, Alan P. 1978. *Democracy and the Amendments to the Constitution.* Lexington, MA: Lexington Books.

Kuroda, Tadahisa. 1994. *The Origins of the Twelfth Amendment: The Electoral College in the Early Republic, 1878–1804.* Westport, CT: Greenwood Press.

Larson, Edward J. 2008. *A Magnificent Catastrophe: The Tumultuous Election of 1800,* America's First Presidential Campaign. New York: Free Press.

Turner, John J., Jr. 1973. "The Twelfth Amendment and the First American Party System." *Historian* 35: 221–237.

TWENTIETH AMENDMENT

Although it is separated by more than a dozen years from its four immediate predecessors, like them the Twentieth Amendment grew from the democratic sentiment spawned by the Progressive Era. Progressive Republican senator George Norris of Nebraska was a key architect of the amendment that altered the dates that members of the national legislative and executive branches took office (Grimes 1978, 104–105). Adoption followed about 30 proposals made prior to 1900 and about 90 more in the early 20th century. The first two proposals were introduced by famous New Yorkers, Aaron Burr (1795) and Millard Fillmore (1840). These and other proposals suggested that the inauguration date be set as early as December and as late as May.

The Congress under the Articles of Confederation set things in motion when it provided that the first Congress under the new Constitution would begin on March 4. Although the new Constitution did not specify this date, it was perpetuated both by custom and by concern that moving it forward would unconstitutionally shorten terms (Bernstein with Agel 1993, 154). Prior to the adoption of the Seventeenth Amendment, the March 4 date also gave time to state legislatures, which typically did not begin sessions until January, to make their selections (Grimes 1978, 105). Article I, Section 4 of the Constitution, however, specified that the annual meeting of Congress should begin on the first Monday in December. This meant that a new Congress would not come into regular session until 13 months after it was elected in November. In the meantime, the outgoing lame-duck legislature (some of whose members had been electorally wounded but not killed—hence the term "lame duck") could adopt legislation without being accountable to the voters. Thus, in a series of events that eventually led to the Supreme Court's historic decision in *Marbury v. Madison* (1803), an outgoing Federalist Congress adopted the Judiciary Act of 1801, adding fellow Federalists to the judiciary, much to the consternation of the newly elected Republican administration. Similarly, President Warren G.

Harding used his influence with outgoing members of Congress to enact a ship subsidy bill in 1922. This action enraged Nebraska senator George W. Norris, who sponsored a constitutional amendment in 1922 to reduce lame-duck terms and persisted in supporting this amendment over the next decade.

Whereas progressives like Norris viewed the situation as undemocratic, many congressional conservatives, including Republican House Speaker Nicholas Longworth, actually "preferred a cooling-off period before the new Congress came into session" (Grimes 1978, 106). Some also liked the short congressional session (from December through March) in alternate years. Thus, although the amendment passed the Senate in 1923, 1924, and 1926, it failed to receive the necessary majority of votes when first voted on in the House in 1928. In 1929, a conference committee failed to resolve differences between the two houses. A 1930 Democratic landslide broke the deadlock and resulted in the elevation of Democrat John N. Garner of Texas, who favored the amendment, as House Speaker. Although the House of Representatives initially adopted a provision that would have required at least one house of the ratifying state legislatures to be elected before ratifying the amendment, this provision was dropped in conference committee (Grimes 1978, 108). The Senate subsequently voted for the amendment by a vote of 63 to 7 (with 25 abstaining) on January 6, 1932; the House followed with a 336 to 56 vote (1 answering present and 38 not voting) on February 16, 1932. Virginia was the first state to ratify on March 4, 1932; Utah put the amendment over the top on January 23, 1933, and the last of the existing 48 states (Florida) ratified on April 26 of that year (U.S. Senate 1985, 62).

The Twentieth Amendment has six sections. The first, and most important, sets the beginning of congressional terms on January 3 and those of the president and vice president on January 20. Section 2 provides that the annual session of Congress begins on January 3. Anticipating some of the problems later addressed in the Twenty-fifth Amendment, Section 3 specifies that if the president-elect dies prior to inauguration, the vice president–elect becomes president. It also allows the vice president–elect to serve if no one has received a majority of the electoral college and the House of Representatives has not yet chosen among the finalists. It further allows Congress to provide by law for an interim in cases in which neither officer has been selected. Section 4 grants the same power in the case of the death of a candidate during congressional deliberations. Section 5 provides that the amendment would become effective on October 15 after its ratification, and Section 6 makes the Twentieth Amendment the second to contain a seven-year ratification deadline.

A number of subsequent proposals have been introduced to modify the Twentieth Amendment, most by moving inauguration dates even further back to November or December (see Levinson 1995, 185). It is uncertain whether the authors of the Twentieth Amendment anticipated that Congress would meet from the period from current November congressional elections to the January installation of new members (Nagle 1997), thus allowing the perpetuation of lame-duck sessions, albeit shorter ones. Some scholars thus questioned whether the impeachment of President Bill Clinton by the outgoing House of Representatives of 1998 should be valid when reported to the incoming Senate of 1999, but, although it did not result in a conviction, the trial proceeded.

Several other amending proposals have proposed ending congressional sessions in July, probably with a view to shortening the period in which Congress can legislate. In a less hurried time (1878), an amendment was even offered to provide for biennial congressional sessions. Five years earlier, in a speech on December 2, 1873, President Ulysses S. Grant had proposed that when the president called special sessions of Congress (as permitted in Article II, Section 3), such sessions should be limited to subjects the president proposed (J. Richardson 1908, 7:242–243). A number of subsequent proposals would have enabled Congress to call itself into special session. Proposals introduced in 1920 and 1923 by House Republican Edward Browne of Wisconsin, precipitated by President Woodrow Wilson's debilitating stroke, would have enabled Congress to provide for cases of such presidential disability, an issue that the Twenty-fifth Amendment later addressed.

See also Progressive Era; Twenty-fifth Amendment.

For Further Reading:

Bernstein, Richard B., with Jerome Agel. 1993. *Amending America: If We Love the Constitution So Much, Why Do We Keep Trying to Change It?* New York: Random House.

Grimes, Alan P. 1978. *Democracy and the Amendments to the Constitution.* Lexington, MA: Lexington Books.

Levinson, Sanford. 1995. "Presidential Elections and Constitutional Stupidities." *Constitutional Commentary* 12 (Summer): 183–186.

Nagle, John Copeland. 1997. "Essay: A Twentieth Amendment Parable." *New York University Law Review* 72 (May): 470–494.

Richardson, James E., ed. 1908. *A Compilation of the Messages and Papers of the Presidents, 1789–1908.* 11 vols. n.p.: Bureau of National Literature and Art.

U.S. Senate, Subcommittee on the Constitution, Committee on the Judiciary. 1985. *Amendments to the Constitution: A Brief Legislative History.* Washington DC: U.S. Government Printing Office.

TWENTY-FIFTH AMENDMENT

Amendments have been introduced throughout American history to deal with presidential disability and with vacancies in the office of vice president.

Although a number of early vice presidents died in office and Vice President John C. Calhoun resigned to become a senator, no president died until 1841, when the elderly William Henry Harrison passed away shortly after his inauguration. His successor, John Tyler, made it clear that he considered himself to be the president and not simply an "acting" president until a reelection could be called. Despite ambiguity about the framers' intentions on this matter, this precedent became standard practice for other vice presidents who replaced chief executives. Tyler's precedent, however, neither addressed the issue of what would happen in cases of presidential disability nor made provision for filling vice-presidential vacancies.

Laws Dealing with Presidential Succession

Congress addressed the issue of vice-presidential vacancies in a number of laws, but their diversity demonstrated the lack of consensus on how to resolve the issue. In 1792, Congress adopted legislation putting the president pro tempore of the Senate and the Speaker of the House of Representatives behind the vice president in the line of succession, but this arrangement made it possible that, in cases of a double vacancy, the presidency might change political parties without an intervening election. After a period during which both the president pro tempore and the Speaker positions were vacant, Congress revised the law in 1886 to provide that the heads of the executive departments, beginning with the secretary of state and the secretary of the treasury, would be in the line of succession. Because it is possible that such officials may never have held elective office (a particular concern of President Harry S. Truman), however, this law was altered in 1947 to place the Speaker and the president pro tempore ahead of cabinet officers in the line of succession (Feerick 1992, 37–47). Scholar Norman Ornstein, writing in light of the terrorist attack on the World Trade Center and the Pentagon on September 11, 2001, suggested that this law of presidential succession needs to be revisited. He pointed specifically to the possibility that, under existing legislation, succession could be passed from one party to another and to the fact that the president pro tempore of the Senate is usually chosen because he or she is the oldest (but not necessarily the fittest) member. He also noted the possibility that some governors, outside the Washington DC area, should be included on the list of presidential successors (Ornstein 2002).

Presidential Disability

In the meantime, the issue of presidential disability remained. In 1881, President James A.

Garfield lingered for eighty days before dying from an assassin's bullet. President William McKinley also lived several days before dying of another assassin's bullet in 1901, and President Woodrow Wilson suffered a debilitating stroke in 1919. The problem of such disabilities became especially acute with the advent of nuclear weapons. President Dwight D. Eisenhower suffered a number of health problems during his tenure, and he eventually drew up a letter of understanding allowing Vice President Richard Nixon to assume his duties during such times as President Eisenhower might be disabled.

Adoption of the Twenty-fifth Amendment

Following President John F. Kennedy's assassination, calls increased to transform informal arrangements into a viable constitutional procedure. Shortly after the assassination, Indiana Democratic senator Birch Bayh, who chaired the Senate Judiciary Committee's Subcommittee on Constitutional Amendments, held hearings on the subject. The Senate subsequently approved a proposed amendment in 1964 by a vote of 64 to 0. In 1965, it again approved an amendment by a 72 to 0 vote, with the House concurring by a vote of 368 to 29. The House subsequently adopted a conference committee version by voice vote and the Senate concurred by a vote of 68 to 5 on July 6, 1965. Ratification by the necessary number of states was completed on February 10, 1967 (Feerick 1992, 95–111). Informed that he had no official role in the ratification of amendments, President Lyndon Johnson insisted on holding a televised ceremony in the White House Rose Garden when he signed a proclamation indicating that he had received official notice of state ratification of the amendment (Kyvig 1996a, 362).

Provisions of the Twenty-fifth Amendment

The Twenty-fifth Amendment has four sections. An observer noted that it "rivals the Fourteenth in length, and surpasses all other amendments in wordage" (Young 1974, 395). The first section officially confirms John Tyler's 1841 precedent by specifying that when the president dies or resigns, "the Vice President shall become president."

Section 2 provides for filling vice-presidential vacancies. It rejected earlier proposals to provide for multiple vice presidents (New York Senator Kenneth Keating wanted to create separate executive and legislative vice presidents) or to provide that vice-presidential vacancies be filled by a vote of the last electoral college (a position that Richard Nixon advocated for a time). Instead, this section provides that the president shall nominate a replacement when the vice presidency is vacant, and that both houses of Congress shall confirm by a majority vote.

Although they do not specifically define it, Sections 3 and 4 of the Twenty-fifth Amendment deal with the problem of presidential disability. Section 3 provides that when the president informs the president pro tempore of the Senate and the Speaker of the House that he or she is unable to perform his or her duties, "such powers and duties" shall be performed by the vice president until such time as the president sends a letter stating that his or her disability is over.

Section 3 handles an ideal case, but what happens if the president fails to recognize or acknowledge that he or she has a disability? Section 4 creates a complicated system of checks and balances. Rejecting earlier proposals to require a special commission to deal with such matters or to entrust such decisions to the Supreme Court, Section 4 outlines another route. Under this provision, the vice president assumes the president's duties if the vice president and a majority "of the principal officers of the executive departments or such other body as Congress may by law provide" transmit a written declaration to the president pro tempore of the Senate and the Speaker of the House that the president is unable to carry out his or her duties. The president may subsequently submit his or her own written declaration that the disability has ended and resume his or her duties, assuming that the vice president and members of the cabinet or other congressionally designated body do not disagree within four days. If there is such a disagreement, the vice president continues to exercise presidential duties. Congress, in turn, assembles within 48 hours. If, within 21 days, two-thirds of both houses of Congress affirm that the president is disabled, the vice president continues in office. If Congress reaches no such agreement, the president resumes his or her duties.

Operation of the Twenty-fifth Amendment

After John Hinckley wounded President Ronald Reagan in an attempted assassination in 1981, Reagan was reluctant to invoke the disability provisions of the Twenty-fifth Amendment for fear that it would cause popular alarm (Feerick 1992, xiii–xiv; also see Abrams 1994). Although he later declared that he was not invoking provisions of this amendment when he underwent cancer surgery, he adhered fairly closely to the amendment's procedures (Feerick 1992, xvi–xvii). Citing the fact that the nation was "at war" [with terrorists], President George Bush Jr. did specifically follow the guideline of the Twenty-fifth Amendment when he was under brief sedation for a colonoscopy (a procedure designed to detect polyps or cancer of the lower intestine) on June 29, 2002 (Bumiller 2002, A1).

The provision of the Twenty-fifth Amendment that has been most frequently exercised is the section dealing with filling vice-presidential vacancies. President Nixon nominated, and Congress subsequently confirmed, Gerald Ford when Vice President Spiro Agnew resigned in 1973 after being charged with accepting bribes while in the Maryland government. When Ford was subsequently elevated to the presidency after Nixon resigned in the wake of the Watergate scandal, he selected, and Congress confirmed, former New York governor Nelson Rockefeller as vice president. The Twenty-fifth Amendment took on new importance during the electoral controversy and first term of George W. Bush when Vice President Dick Cheney, who had a past history of heart attacks, was twice admitted to the hospital for chest pains.

Proposals to Alter the Twenty-fifth Amendment

There have been several proposals to repeal either Section 2 (dealing with filling vice-presidential vacancies) or the entire Twenty-fifth Amendment. Some such proposals stem from concerns that the existing disability provision is too complex and might be abused by an overly ambitious vice president. Other proposals flow from concern that the Twenty-fifth Amendment allows the office of both president and vice president to be filled by individuals who have not been popularly elected.

Focusing in part on the latter concern and in part on the putative failure of the office to attract strong characters from the adoption of the Twelfth Amendment through the Nixon administration, historian Arthur M. Schlesinger Jr. (1974) has advocated eliminating the vice presidency. He proposes allowing the secretary of state or another eligible cabinet officer to serve in cases of a presidential vacancy (assuming there is more than a year until the next regularly scheduled election) until a new election can be held. A Twentieth Century Fund Task Force Report on the Vice Presidency (1988) opposed this recommendation.

Another scholar has suggested that Congress should act under Section 4 of the amendment (with its reference to "such other body as Congress may by law provide") to provide for a medical advisory committee that would, with the president's personal physician, review the results of the president's annual physical and assemble at times when there were serious questions about the president's health. The advocate of this committee, which he believes should include internists, neurologists, a surgeon, and a psychiatrist, believes that it would be more likely to provide objective information than would the president's personal physician, who might have a conflict of interest in the case of his patient being removed because of disability (Abrams 1999).

See also Congress, Emergency Functioning; Vice President.

For Further Reading:

Abrams, Herbert L. 1999. "Can the Twenty-Fifth Amendment Deal with a Disabled President? Preventing Future White House Cover-Ups." *Presidential Studies Quarterly* 29 (March): 115–133.

Bayh, Birch. 1968. *One Heartbeat Away: Presidential Disability and Succession.* Indianapolis: The Bobbs-Merrill Company, Inc.

Bumiller, Elisabeth. 2002. "Bush to Undergo Colon Procedure: President Will Transfer Power to Cheney before Sedation." *The New York Times* (June 29): A1, A11.

Feerick, John D. *From Failing Hands: The Story of Presidential Succession.* New York: Fordham University Press.

———. *The Twenty-fifth Amendment: Its Complete History and Applications.* New York: Fordham University Press.

Kyvig, David E. 1996a. *Explicit and Authentic Acts: Amending the Constitution, 1776–1995.* Lawrence: University Press of Kansas.

Ornstein, Norman J. 2002. "Preparing for the Unthinkable: Bush's 'Shadow Government' Plan Is a Start—But Only a Start." *The Wall Street Journal* (March 11): A18.

Schlesinger, Arthur M., Jr. 1974. "On the Presidential Succession." *Political Science Quarterly* 89 (Fall): 475–505.

Twentieth Century Fund Task Force on the Vice Presidency. 1988. *A Heartbeat Away.* New York: Printing Press Publications.

"The Twenty-fifth Amendment: Preparing for Presidential Disability." 1995. *Wake Forest Law Review* 30 (Fall): 427–648.

Young, Donald. 1974. *American Roulette: The History and Dilemma of the Vice Presidency.* New York: Viking Press.

TWENTY-FIRST AMENDMENT

The Twenty-first Amendment is both the only amendment ever to have repealed another, and the only amendment ever to be ratified by state conventions rather than by state legislatures.

The Eighteenth Amendment, ratified in 1919, represented a great social experiment in its attempt to outlaw the consumption of alcoholic beverages. Although the amendment appears to have cut the consumption of alcohol, it was far from successful in eliminating it. Organized crime and its accompanying violence received a major boost, providing a product that so many wanted and were willing to break the law to get. Speakeasies, where one could drink in social settings, flourished. Many feared that true temperance was less likely to be achieved by the flouting of such complete prohibition than by less invasive governmental regulations.

Moreover, almost from the time that the Eighteenth Amendment was adopted, opponents challenged it as an unconstitutional interference with state police powers. Although the Supreme Court rejected this argument in the *National Prohibition Cases* (1920), critics continued to charge that the amendment represented an unwarranted federal intrusion into an area of personal relations best left to state control.

Supporters of the Eighteenth Amendment included Democratic Senator Morris Sheppard of Texas, who boasted that "there is as much chance of repealing the Eighteenth Amendment as there is for a hummingbird to fly to the planet Mars with the Washington Monument tied to its tail" (Kyvig 1985, 14). Despite such predictions, the year that the Eighteenth Amendment was ratified, Captain William H. Slayton founded the Association Against the Prohibition Amendment (AAPA), which lobbied throughout the next decade for repeal of the Eighteenth Amendment (Kyvig 1979, 39–52). A prominent supporter was New York Republican senator James W. Wadsworth. In the mid-1920s, the organization also received important support from the Du Pont family, especially Pierre. He enlisted the aid of John J. Raskob, who later exerted considerable influence for the repeal amendment after Al Smith—the Democratic candidate for president in 1928—appointed him to chair the Democratic National Committee (Kyvig 1979, 101). Also important was the foundation in 1929 of the Women's Organization for National Prohibition Reform (WONPR). It provided something of a counterweight to the Women's Christian Temperance Union, which had been so influential in mustering support for the Eighteenth Amendment.

Almost from the adoption of the Eighteenth Amendment until its repeal, proposals were periodically introduced to modify it. Proposals included plans to repeal the amendment, hold a referendum on the question of repeal of the amendment, permit beverages with alcohol below a certain percentage (the Volstead Act, which enforced the Eighteenth Amendment, had applied even to beer with 3.2 percent alcohol content), or allow the federal government to tax and license alcoholic beverages.

Two events—the Great Depression, which began in 1929, and the election of 1932—eventually gave impetus to adoption of the Twenty-first Amendment. The first event encouraged the government to look at alcohol as a potential source of revenue as well as a source of employment. The second brought the Democratic Party into power. Whereas the Republican Convention of 1932 merely proposed allowing voters to consider repeal of the Eighteenth Amendment, the Democrats took a clear stand against Prohibition.

The vote for Democrats was so overwhelming that the lame-duck Congress repealed the amendment even before the new one came into office. Initially, the Senate version contained four sections: Section 1 would have repealed the Eighteenth Amendment; Section 2 reserved to the states and territories powers to regulate alcohol; Section 3 granted Congress concurrent power to regulate the consumption of alcohol at places of sale (an anti-saloon provision); and Section 4 set a seven-year ratification deadline. Section 3 was subsequently deleted, and Section 4 was modified to provide for ratification by state conventions rather than state legislatures. This move may have been stimulated in part by discussion that the Supreme Court generated in *Hawke v. Smith* (1920), when it struck down Ohio's attempt to decide on the ratification of the Eighteenth Amendment by a state referendum; the convention mechanism also helped bypass state legislatures that were believed to be dominated by dry forces.

The Senate voted 63 to 23 (10 not voting) for this amendment on February 16, 1933, and the House followed with a vote of 289 to 121 (with 16 not voting) on February 20 (U.S. Senate 1985, 67–68). In the absence of federal guidelines, states set up their own ratifying conventions (see E. Brown 1935, 1938). These bodies served more as referendums on Prohibition than deliberative assemblies, and the amendment was ratified in a record (for then) of 10 months. Of some 21 million Americans who voted on the subject, 72.9 percent expressed support of repeal (Kyvig 1979, 178). Ironically, it was predominantly Mormon Utah that jockeyed its deliberations to provide the 36th ratification needed to put the amendment over the top (Kyvig 1979, 182).

On at least five occasions from 1935 to 1939, Texas Democratic senator Morris Sheppard, author of the Eighteenth Amendment, introduced resolutions to repeal the Twenty-first Amendment and reinstate national alcoholic prohibition. In 1938, Democratic Representative Gomer Smith of Oklahoma introduced an amendment prohibiting drunkenness in the United States and its territories.

The Twenty-first Amendment recognizes that states have explicit power over alcohol. Many states use a local option system that gives individual cities and counties considerable autonomy to decide what regulation of alcohol is appropriate. Thus, in *California v. Larue* (1972), the Court permitted a state Department of Alcoholic Beverage Control to limit the kinds of entertainment in establishment that serve alcohol. In her dissenting opinion in *South Dakota v. Dole* (1987), Justice Sandra Day O'Connor argued that the amendment gave states authority to set their own minimum drinking age free of federal threats to cut state highway budgets. In 1996, the U.S. Supreme Court decided in *44 Liquormart v. Rhode Island* that the Twenty-first Amendment does not negate First Amendment free speech rights; the Court thus voided a state law prohibiting the advertisement of liquor prices in newspapers or on billboards. In *Granholm v. Heald,* 125 S. Ct. 1885 (2005), the Supreme Court ruled that the Twenty-first Amendment did not grant states the power to ban direct shipments from out-of-state wineries to consumers if such shipments were open to in-state wineries.

See also Eighteenth Amendment; *Hawke v. Smith;* National Prohibition Cases; Ratification of Amendments.

For Further Reading:

California v. Larue, 409 U.S. 109 (1972).

Kyvig, David E. 1979. *Repealing National Prohibition*. Chicago: University of Chicago Press.

Kyvig, David E., ed. 1985. *Alcohol and Order: Perspectives on National Prohibition*. Westport, CT: Greenwood Press.

Pasahow, Michael A. 2006. "*Granholm v. Heald*: Shifting the Boundaries of California Reciprocal Win Shipping Laws." *Berkeley Technology Law Journal* 21: 569–584.

TWENTY-FOURTH AMENDMENT

Initially intended to guarantee that voters had a financial stake in the community, states increasingly used the poll tax after the Civil War to hinder African Americans from voting. In *Breedlove v. Suttles* (1937), the Supreme Court unanimously upheld such a state law against a challenge under the equal protection clause of the Fourteenth Amendment.

In 1941, Democratic Representative Lee Geyer of California introduced legislation to repeal state poll taxes; Geyer also founded the short-lived National Committee to Abolish the Poll Tax (Lawson 1976, 61). The next year, the House of Representatives voted favorably on the bill, but it was killed in the Senate by a filibuster. By the late 1950s, the House had voted favorably on such legislation on five occasions, but the Senate had never approved it (Ogden 1958, 243).

In part because of continuing questions about the constitutionality of such legislation, opponents of the poll tax increasingly began to focus on proposals for a constitutional amendment that had first been introduced in 1941. Florida Democratic senator Spessard Holland was a persistent and forceful advocate of this amendment. Ironically, the National Association for the Advancement of Colored People (NAACP) did not support the amendment, fearing that it would send the signal that Congress did not have adequate power to eliminate poll taxes under its enforcement authority in Section 5 of the Fourteenth Amendment. Still by June 1961, Holland's proposal (S.J. Res. 58) had 67 cosponsors, but it was tied up in the Senate Judiciary Committee by the committee chair, Democrat James O. Eastland of Mississippi. In order to break this logjam, the Committee on Interior and Insular Affairs subsequently introduced a resolution (S.J. Res. 29) to make Alexander Hamilton's house a national monument. By prearrangement, this resolution instead became the focus of the poll tax issue. After 10 days, debate was cut off, and thereafter, the Holland amendment was successfully offered as a substitute and approved by a vote of 77 to 16 on March 27, 1961. Leaders of the House suspended the rules to limit debate, and it approved the amendment 294 to 86 (with 54 not

voting and 1 voting present) on August 27, 1961 (U.S. Senate 1985, 75–76). The necessary number of states ratified by February 1964, but by then, only five states still retained such a tax (Bernstein with Agel 1993, 138). In a telling demonstration of the symbolic power of amendments, a group of high school students subsequently organized a successful effort to add North Carolina's ratification during the celebration of the bicentennial of the U.S. Constitution ("North Carolina Ratifies the 24th Amendment" 1989).

The Twenty-fourth Amendment provides that "the right of citizens of the United States to vote in any primary or other election for President or Vice President, or for Senator or Representative in Congress, shall not be denied or abridged by the United States or any State by reason of failure to pay any poll tax or other tax." Section 2 vests enforcement authority in Congress.

The language of the amendment covers only federal elections, but in *Harper v. Virginia State Board of Elections* (1966), the Supreme Court overturned *Breedlove v. Suttles* (1937) and held that such a tax violated the equal protection clause of the Fourteenth Amendment. This decision suggests that the Supreme Court might have accepted a legislative rather than a constitutional solution to the poll tax problem.

Bruce Ackerman and Jennifer Nou (2009) observe that the major action taken on behalf of voting rights during the 20th-century civil rights revolution occurred not with the adoption of the Twenty-fourth Amendment, but with the passage of the Voting Rights Act of 1965.

See also Fourteenth Amendment.

For Further Reading:

Ackerman, Bruce, and Jennifer Nou. 2009. "Canonizing the Civil Rights Revolution: The People and the Poll Tax," *Northwestern University Law Review* 103 (Winter): 63–148.

Bernstein, Richard B., with Jerome Agel. 1993. *Amending America: If We Love the Constitution So Much, Why Do We Keep Trying to Change It?* New York: Random House.

Lawson, Steven F. 1976. *Black Ballots: Voting Rights in the South, 1944–1969.* New York: Columbia University Press.

"North Carolina Ratifies the 24th Amendment." 1989. *We the People: A Newsletter of the Commission on the Bicentennial of the United States Constitution* 5 (July): 10.

Ogden, Frederic D. 1958. *The Poll Tax in the South.* University: University of Alabama Press.

U.S. Senate, Subcommittee on the Constitution, Committee on the Judiciary. 1985. *Amendments to the Constitution: A Brief Legislative History.* Washington DC: U.S. Government Printing Office.

TWENTY-SECOND AMENDMENT

One of the most persistent proposals for reform in U.S. history was the one that ultimately resulted in the Twenty-second Amendment. Exempting the then-sitting presidential office-holder, President Harry S. Truman, from its provisions, this amendment limited all subsequent persons from being elected as president more than twice or, in the case of a vice president who succeeded to the presidency, from serving a total of more than ten years.

Proposals for Reform

Members of Congress introduced at least 270 proposals for term limits from 1789 to 1947, with the average frequency increasing from just over one per session in the first 100 years, to two from 1890 to 1928, and to three thereafter (Willis and Willis 1952, 469). Although it is probably true that the American people "show little sign of wanting to abandon the Twenty-second Amendment" (M. Nelson 2008, 56), members of Congress have introduced numerous proposals both to lift the two-term limit and to substitute a single six-year presidential term.

The Constitutional Convention and Early Practices

At the Constitutional Convention of 1787, the original Virginia plan, which contemplated that Congress would select the president, proposed a single term of unspecified length (Padover 1962, 53). Delegates apparently feared that separation of powers might be undermined if a president attempted to bargain with legislators to gain reelection. With the invention of the electoral college mechanism—in which members would meet only once within individual states and then dissolve—this fear largely evaporated, and the delegates decided not to impose any term limits.

President George Washington decided to retire after two terms, and President John Adams was defeated in his bid for a second term. In responding to a request from the Vermont state legislature encouraging him to run for a third term, President Thomas Jefferson, who appears to have left open the possibility of running for a third term if it were necessary to exclude a "monarchist" from gaining the presidency (Peabody and Gant 1999, 579), elevated Washington's prudent decision not to run for a third term into a political principle (M. Nelson 1989, 46–47). The two-term tradition seemed so well fixed by 1925 that Herbert Horwill cited it as part of the United States' customs and usages that rose to the level of constitutional principles.

Adoption of the Twenty-second Amendment

Faced with the outbreak of World War II in Europe, President Franklin D. Roosevelt consented to renomination in 1940 (he sent signals that he would accept a party draft without actively "running" for the renomination) and was eventually elected to four terms, his last being cut short by his death. The fact that he had broken with the two-term tradition was hotly discussed in the 1940 election. Republican frustrations with his multiple terms largely accounted for adoption of the Twenty-second Amendment (Stathis 1990). The Twenty-second Amendment passed the House by a vote of 285 to 121 in February 1947 and the Senate by a vote of 59 to 23 the following month. By a vote of 82 to 1, the Senate rejected a substitute amendment that would have fixed the terms of all federal officeholders at six years (Willis and Willis 1952, 478). The partisan aspects of support for the amendment were demonstrated by the fact that Republicans supported the amendment unanimously in both the House (238 to 0) and the Senate (46 to 0), whereas Democrats opposed it by respective votes of 121 to 47 and 23 to 13. President Harry S. Truman, who criticized the amendment after it had been adopted, basically stayed on the sidelines, and the amendment took almost four full years to be ratified, a record prior to the putative ratification of the Twenty-seventh Amendment in 1993 (M. Nelson 2008, 55). Of thousands of Republican state legislators whose votes were recorded, only 83 voted against the amendment (Stathis 1990, 70).

Issues and Consequences

Some of the debates over presidential term limits were surprisingly similar to more modern debates over congressional term limits, with which such proposals were often conjoined. Proponents argued that long terms threaten a system of separated powers and checks and balances. Opponents said that the people decided whether to impose term limits when they voted (Willis and Willis 1952, 476–478).

Prior to the adoption of the Twenty-second Amendment, there were actually more proposals for a single presidential term—ranging from four to eight years, with four- and six-year proposals being most common—than there were for a two-term limit. A two-term limit appears to have tilted some power away from the president and toward Congress, but a one-term limit would arguably have had a much greater impact, effectively making every elected president a lame duck and thereby increasing congressional control over lawmaking (Willis and Willis 1952, 480). The one-term proposal continues to be introduced, sometimes along with proposals for direct popular election or proposals for limiting other officeholders. Supporters of a single six-year presidential term have included Republican Senator Jesse Helms of North Carolina (1977), Democratic Representative John Conyers of Michigan (1980), Democratic Senator Lloyd Bentsen of Texas (1981), and Republican Senator Strom Thurmond of South Carolina (1981).

Despite the Republican role in ratification of the amendment, to date, its effects have been felt primarily by two Republican presidents, Dwight D. Eisenhower and Ronald Reagan (although there had been some indication prior to the Watergate controversy that Richard Nixon might also be interested in running for a third term, and, despite his impeachment, Bill Clinton continued to be popular enough that a run for a third term could have been a possibility). Interestingly, 24 of 29 scholars who responded to a survey in 1957 indicated their belief that the amendment ought to be repealed (Stathis 1990, 73). As president, Reagan lobbied for repeal of the amendment, and members of Congress continue to introduce resolutions to this effect. In the lead essay in a book published after he left office, Reagan described the Twenty-second Amendment as "a perversion of the Constitution's sound design for a limited but energetic government" (Reagan et al. 1990, 1). He was particularly concerned about the effect the amendment had on a president's effectiveness during his second term.

Parsing the language and examining the history of the Twenty-second Amendment, two scholars have argued that there are at least six circumstances under which it might be possible for an individual who has already served two terms to serve for a period as president or acting president, as long as such service did not involve another *election* to the *presidential* office. Their examples include the case of an individual who had served for two terms as president, was then elected as *vice president,* and either succeeded a president who had died, stepped aside in the ex-president's favor, or served as "acting president" during the newly elected president's illness. These authors succeed in demonstrating that the language of the amendment, the result of apparent compromise between those in Congress who wanted an absolute two-term limit and those who were willing to allow individuals who had succeeded another president in the second half of that president's term to serve two addition terms, is not as clear as it could be. They ultimately conclude, however, that office-holding in the circumstances that they outline, if not absolutely unconstitutional, "would seemingly amount to 'constitutional improprieties'" (Peabody and Gant 1999, 632 citing a term apparently coined by Stephen L. Carter).

See also Congress, Term Limits; Electoral College Reform.

For Further Reading:

Hamilton, Alexander, James Madison, and John Jay. 1787–1788. *The Federalist Papers.* Reprint, New York: New American Library, 1961.

Nelson, Michael, ed. 2008. *Guide to the Presidency*. 2 vols., 4th ed. Washington DC: Congressional Quarterly.

Padover, Saul K. 1962. *To Secure These Blessings*. New York: Washington Square Press/Ridge Press.

Peabody, Bruce G., and Scott E. Gant. 1999. "The Twice and Future President: Constitutional Interstices and the Twenty-second Amendment." *Minnesota Law Review* 83 (February): 565–635.

Reagan, Ronald, et al. 1990. *Restoring the Presidency: Reconsidering the Twenty-second Amendment*. Washington DC: National Legal Center for Public Interest.

Richardson, James E., ed. 1908. *A Compilation of the Messages and Papers of the Presidents, 1789–1908*. 11 vols. n.p.: Bureau of National Literature and Art.

Stathis, Stephen. 1990. "The Twenty-second Amendment: A Practical Remedy or Partisan Maneuver?" *Constitutional Commentary 7* (Winter): 61–88.

Sundquist, James L. 1986. *Constitutional Reform and Effective Government*. Washington DC: Brookings Institution.

Willis, Paul G., and George L. Willis. 1952. "The Politics of the Twenty-second Amendment." *Western Political Quarterly* 5 (September): 469–482.

TWENTY-SEVENTH AMENDMENT

Article I, Section 6 of the U.S. Constitution provides that "the Senators and Representatives shall receive a Compensation for their Services, to be ascertained by Law, and paid out of the Treasury of the United States." The latter part of this clause is especially important because it enabled legislators to gain an independence that they might not have had if their salaries depended on the states (Bernstein 1992, 502).

The prospect that voters might penalize them somewhat limits congressional aggrandizement, but when the Constitution was being debated, three states sensed enough danger that they proposed amendments to limit congressional pay raises. In compiling a bill of rights in the First Congress in 1789, James Madison proposed an amendment specifying that "no law, varying the compensation for the services of the Senators and Representatives, shall take effect, until an election of Representatives shall have intervened." This was originally the second of 12 amendments submitted to the states, but as only six states ratified it, it did not become part of the Bill of Rights.

In the 19th century, congressional pay increases twice provoked renewed pleas for ratification of the congressional pay-raise amendment. In 1817, Congress passed a compensation bill switching its salary from $6 a day to $1,500 a year and provoking such controversy that the bill was repealed—albeit not retroactively. Voters dismissed many members, including Daniel Webster (then representing New Hampshire), out of office (Miller and Dewey 1991, 98). Similarly, in 1873 Congress adopted what became known as the Salary Grab Act, retroactively increasing salaries by $2,500 a year and provoking such outrage that it was repealed (Bernstein 1992, 534). The original second amendment was reintroduced in Congress, and Ohio ratified it 82 years after the last ratification (Strickland 1993, 716).

Congress twice voted to cut its salary during the Great Depression, but the 20th century otherwise witnessed a steady progression of congressional salary increases. Salaries went from $10,000 a year in 1935 to $125,100 in August 1991 (Bernstein 1992, 535). Moreover, Congress invented a number of mechanisms by which pay raises could be recommended by special commissions and go into effect without a direct vote. In 1978, 105 years after Ohio's ratification, Wyoming became the eighth state to ratify the pay-raise amendment. During this same period, faith in Congress appeared to decline, as members were caught in check-kiting controversies involving the congressional credit union and in questions of undue influence in the failure of prominent savings and loan institutions (Vile 1992, 15–16).

In 1982, Gregory Watson, a student at the University of Texas at Austin, wrote a term paper for a government course in which he examined the congressional pay-raise amendment and concluded that it could still be ratified. Although he received a "C" from his skeptical instructor (Bernstein 1992, 537), Watson launched a one-man effort and spent over $5,000 of his own money to persuade additional state legislatures to ratify. The effort was not very public, but from 1983 to 1992, an additional 32 states ratified. On May 14, 1992, Don Wilson, the national archivist, certified the amendment as part of the Constitution, a decision that was approved shortly thereafter by votes of 99 to 0 in the Senate and 414 to 3 in the House (Bernstein 1992, 542).

Wilson's certification and the congressional votes have not necessarily settled the legitimacy issue. In *Dillon v. Gloss* (1921), the Supreme Court indicated that, to be valid, ratifications of amendments should be contemporaneous with their proposal. In *Coleman v. Miller* (1939), the Court later ruled that the issue of contemporaneousness was a political question for Congress to ascertain, but subsequent cases have eroded this precedent. Not surprisingly, the putative ratification of the Twenty-seventh Amendment has stirred considerable rethinking of the amending process (Dalzell and Beste 1994; Paulsen 1993; Levinson 1994; Spotts 1994; Van Alstyne 1993).

A U.S. district court decision in *Boehner v. Anderson* (1992) ruled that automatic cost-of-living adjustments for members of Congress that were provided in the Ethics Reform Act of 1989 were not prohibited by the Twenty-seventh Amendment, and the U.S. Court of Appeals for the District of Columbia subsequently affirmed this decision. This and other developments have led at least some observers to believe that the late ratification of the Twenty-seventh Amendment may have made courts more reticent to enforce its provisions than had the amendment been ratified in a more regularized fashion.

See also *Coleman v. Miller; Dillon v. Gloss;* Madison, James; Ratification of Amendments; Watson, Gregory.

For Further Reading:

Bernstein, Richard B. 1992. "The Sleeper Wakes: The History and Legacy of the Twenty-seventh Amendment." *Fordham Law Review* 56 (December): 497–557.

Boehner v. Anderson, 1809 F. Supp. 138 (1992), *aff'd* 30 F.3d 156 (1994).

Dalzell, Stewart, and Eric J. Beste. 1994. "Is the Twenty-seventh Amendment 200 Years Too Late?" *George Washington Law Review* 62 (April): 501–545.

Levinson, Sanford. 1994. "Authorizing Constitutional Text: On the Purported Twenty-seventh Amendment." *Constitutional Commentary* 11 (Winter): 101–113.

Paulsen, Michael S. 1993. "A General Theory of Article V: The Constitutional Issues of the Twenty-seventh Amendment." *Yale Law Journal* 103: 677–789.

Spotts, JoAnne D. 1994. "The Twenty-seventh Amendment: A Late Bloomer or a Dead Horse?" *Georgia State University Law Review* 10 (January): 337–365.

Strickland, Ruth A. 1993. "The Twenty-seventh Amendment and Constitutional Change by Stealth." *P.S. Political Science and Politics* 26 (December): 716–722.

Van Alstine, William. 1993. "What Do You Think about the Twenty-seventh Amendment?" *Constitutional Commentary* 10 (Winter): 9–18.

Vile, John R. 1992. *The Constitutional Amending Process in American Political Thought.* New York: Praeger.

TWENTY-SIXTH AMENDMENT

Under the Constitution, states set voting qualifications, subject to any restrictions incorporated in constitutional amendments. Prior to 1971 there were no constitutional age restrictions for voting, although Section 2 of the Fourteenth Amendment had implicitly sanctioned the widespread 21-year minimum (as well as all-male suffrage, which was not eliminated until adoption of the Nineteenth Amendment in 1920) by specifying that state representation in Congress could be reduced only when states denied the vote to men 21 years of age or older.

World War II marks the beginning of interest in reducing the voting age to 18. At the time the government was drafting many men for military service at that age, and it seemed unfair to call on individuals who could not vote to defend the nation. In 1942, at least four members of Congress introduced resolutions to reduce the voting age to 18. They were Republican Senator Arthur Vanderberg of Michigan and Democratic

Representatives Jennings Randolph of West Virginia and Jed Johnson and Victor Wickersham of Oklahoma. Members introduced more than 150 proposals between 1942 and 1971, with an occasional proposal to set the age at 19 rather than 18, and with New York Democratic representative Emanuel Celler introducing at least one proposal in 1954 to freeze the age at 21. In 1953, the Senate debated a resolution to lower the voting age to 18, but it failed by a vote of 34 to 24 (U.S. Senate 1985, 89).

Support for the amendment increased during the Vietnam War, and Congress held hearings on the subject in 1968 and 1970. The public and some members of Congress—a number of whom had proposed extending the vote to active-duty military personnel regardless of age—may have been focusing on the link between military service and voting. Perhaps recognizing that the draft only applied to men, however, the hearings emphasized the increased educational levels of modern youth. The hearings also cited other responsibilities and privileges that 18-to-21-year-olds were exercising—including driving automobiles, drinking alcohol (an age that most states have subsequently raised), holding jobs, having families, being tried as adults in court, and attending college. Although some witnesses pointed to antiwar demonstrations as evidence that 18-to-21-year-olds were immature, others, including future Republican senator Samuel I. Hayakawa, joined those who attributed such demonstrations to a small group of radicals rather than to the age group as a whole (*Hearings* 1970, 36–43).

After the hearings, Massachusetts Democratic senator Edward Kennedy focused on the Supreme Court's decision in *Katzenbach v. Morgan* (1966) upholding federal suspension of state literacy tests. He suggested bypassing the amending process and lowering the voting age by statute, and Congress subsequently added such a provision to the Voting Rights Act of 1970. The testimony of Assistant Attorney General (later chief justice) William Rehnquist that this could be accomplished only through amendment (Hearings 1970, 233–249) proved prescient. In *Oregon v. Mitchell* (1970), a narrow Court majority, with Justice Hugo Black holding the balance, decided that Congress could lower the voting age in federal but not in state elections.

Only three states had voting ages of 18 (Georgia was the first to lower the age to 18, in 1943), with three others setting the age at 19, three at 20, and the rest at 21 (Grimes 1978, 142–143). This meant that absent repeal of the Voting Rights provision or adoption of an amendment, most states would have to create a dual voting system. This created the impetus for Jennings Randolph, then a West Virginia senator, to reintroduce the 18-year-old vote as an amendment. Accepted on March 10, 1971, by a vote of 94 to 7 in the Senate and on March 23 by a vote of 401 to 19 (with 12 not voting) in the House (U.S. Senate 1985, 90), states ratified the amendment within three months, the fastest ratification in U.S. history. Altogether, 42 states ratified.

In 1992, Minnesota Democratic Farm-Labor representative Timothy Penny introduced a proposal to repeal the Twenty-sixth Amendment and lower the voting age to 16, but this proposal did not garner significant support.

See also *Oregon v. Mitchell.*

For Further Reading:

Grimes, Alan P. 1978. *Democracy and the Amendments to the Constitution.* Lexington, MA: Lexington Books.

Hearings before the Subcommittee on Constitutional Amendments of the Committee on the Judiciary: *Lowering the Voting Age to 18.* 1968. U.S. Senate, 90th Cong., 2d Sess., 14, 15, 16 May.

U.S. Senate, Subcommittee on the Constitution, Committee on the Judiciary. 1985. *Amendments to the Constitution: A Brief Legislative History.* Washington DC: U.S. Government Printing Office.

Uradnik, Kathleen. 2002. *Student's Guide to Landmark Congressional Laws on Youth.* Westport, CT: Greenwood Press.

TWENTY-THIRD AMENDMENT

Because Article II, Section 1 of the Constitution limited the selection of presidential electors to states, Washington DC had no input in presidential elections up to 1961. Although the district population is now smaller than that of any state except Wyoming (Crockett, 2003, 424), in 1961, its population exceeded that of the 13 least populous states (U.S. Senate 1985, 75). As early as 1883, Republican Representative Henry Blair of New Hampshire introduced an amendment to remedy this situation by granting the district representation in the electoral college. Members introduced more than a dozen such proposals between 1915 and 1923, with others following from 1945 and thereafter.

In 1959, Tennessee Democratic senator Estes Kefauver introduced S.J. Res. 39 to provide for the emergency functioning of Congress by granting state governors the right to fill mass vacancies. When the Senate Committee on the Judiciary reported this amendment favorably to the Senate floor, Florida Democrat Spessard Holland proposed an amendment to abolish the poll tax (a proposal that later became the Twenty-fourth Amendment), and New York Republican Kenneth B. Keating introduced an amendment to grant the District of Columbia both the right to select presidential electors and the right to representation in the House of Representatives (Grimes 1978, 127; U.S. Senate 1985, 76–77). The Senate voted favorably on all three proposals and sent them to the House.

The House decided to concentrate on H.J. Res. 757, a proposal that Democrat Emanuel Celler of New York introduced containing the current language of the Twenty-third Amendment. It grants the district "a number of electors of President and Vice President equal to the whole number of Senators and Representatives in Congress to which the District would be entitled if it were a State, but in no event more than the least populous state [which is entitled to three]." Although opponents criticized this proposal for being too narrow, Celler argued that his proposal was more likely to be ratified and indicated that he had agreed to support Holland's poll tax amendment separately (Grimes 1978, 129).

The House approved the Celler amendment by voice vote on June 14, 1960, and the Senate concurred, also by voice, on June 16, 1960. The amendment was ratified in nine months, with New Hampshire rescinding its March 29 ratifi-

cation and readopting it the next day to become the 38th state to approve, providing the necessary three-fourths (U.S. Senate 1985, 77).

The Twenty-third Amendment did not completely equalize the District of Columbia's weight in the electoral college, because the district still has no role in the event that the House or Senate has to decide an electoral deadlock. Rhode Island Democrat Claiborne Pell introduced amendments in 1963 and 1967 to remedy this situation. The unratified amendment that Congress proposed in 1978 to treat the District of Columbia as a state for purposes of representation in Congress, presidential and vice presidential electors, and the amending process contained an explicit repeal of the Twenty-third Amendment, and at least one scholar has argued that the adoption of the Twenty-third Amendment "had the effect of thwarting a full, not to mention more equitable, resolution of the District of Columbia problem, which, as a result, is ongoing" (Kyvig 2000, 244). In 1990, Virginia Republican representative Stanford Parris introduced an amendment to remove electors for the District of Columbia from the electoral college.

Professor David Crockett has expressed concern that the Twenty-third Amendment makes it more likely to have a tie in the electoral college that could send a presidential election to the House of Representatives for resolution. This is because Congress has set the number of representatives in the House at 435, the number of Senators is even, and when the District of Columbia's three votes are added under the Twenty-third Amendment, the total vote is now even, leading to the possibility of a 269 to 269 tie. He thinks Congress should raise House membership to 436 so that there would be 539 electoral votes (2003).

For Further Reading:

Crockett, David A. 2003. "Dodging the Bullet: Election Mechanics and the Problem of the Twenty-third Amendment." *PS: Political Science and Politics* 36 (July): 423–426.

Grimes, Alan P. 1978. *Democracy and the Amendments to the Constitution.* Lexington, MA: Lexington Books.

Kyvig, David E. 2000. *Unintended Consequences of Constitutional Amendments.* Athens: The University of Georgia Press.

U.S. Senate, Subcommittee on the Constitution, Committee on the Judiciary. 1985. *Amendments to the Constitution: A Brief Legislative History.* Washington DC: U.S. Government Printing Office.

TWO-THIRDS MAJORITY TO PROPOSE AMENDMENTS

Article V of the Constitution specifies that two-thirds majorities are required in both houses of Congress to propose constitutional amendments. Alternatively, in a still unused provision, Article V provides that two-thirds of the states may petition Congress for a constitutional convention. In the *National Prohibition Cases* (1920), the Supreme Court ruled that the two-thirds majority of Congress that Article V specifies "is a vote of two-thirds of the members present—assuming the presence of a quorum—and not a vote of two-thirds of the entire membership, present and absent" (386). Fear that future amendments might be proposed without adequate deliberation, the Citizens for the Constitution authoring the Constitutional Amendment Initiative have recently suggested that the two-thirds requirement should be of the entire house. Gregory Watson, the individual primarily responsible for ratification of the Twenty-seventh Amendment (related to the timing of congressional pay raises), has taken a similar position (Watson 2000, 16). The Citizens for the Constitution have also suggested that amendments should not be reported to the floor of Congress unless they have two-thirds support from the committee from which they originated.

In 1798, the U.S. Supreme Court decided in *Hollingsworth v. Virginia* (1798) that constitutional amendments did not require a president's signature. This decision may have been predicated in part on the fact that amendments are already proposed by the same majority required to overrule a presidential veto.

The two-thirds requirement for proposing amendments, like the three-fourths requirement for ratifying them, indicates that the amending process was not designed to incorporate all changes that the majority favor but only those with an unusually strong consensus behind them. In effect, the requirement for such majorities gives a veto to strong minority interests. The requirement for proposal has been a greater obstacle than the requirement for ratification by three-fourths of the states. To date states have ratified 27 of the 33 amendments that Congress has proposed.

See also Citizens for the Constitution, the Constitutional Amendment Initiative; *Hollingsworth v. Virginia; National Prohibition Cases;* Watson, Gregory.

For Further Reading:
National Prohibition Cases, 253 U.S. 350 (1920).
Watson, Gregory. 2000. "I Have a Better Way." *Insights on Law & Society* 1 (Fall): 16.

U

❖

UNAMENDMENTS

Jason Mazzonne, an assistant professor of law at Brooklyn Law School, coined this term to describe what he calls "proposals to use the procedures of Article V to change the Constitution in ways that are beyond Article V's substantive scope" (2005, 1752). Like others who believe that there are implicit substantive limits on the constitutional amending process, Mazzone thinks that amendments are limited "to fine-tuning what is already in place" (1751). Using language that Bruce Ackerman developd, Mazzone believes other changes can be brought about through "higher lawmaking," which articulates new constitutional principles. He believes this is what happened in the case of the adoption of the U.S. Constitution and the post–Civil War amendments, neither of which completely followed the letter or the spirit of amending mechanisms previously in place.

See also Ackerman, Bruce; Constitutional Amendments, Limits on: Entrenchment Clauses.

For Further Reading:

Mazzone, Jason. 2005. "Unamendments." *Iowa Law Review* 90 (May): 1747–1855.

UNFUNDED FEDERAL MANDATES

The relation between the nation and the states was a concern even before the adoption of the U.S. Constitution, and it has continued to be so ever since. As the Supreme Court has recognized increasingly broad congressional powers under the provisions in Article I, Section 8 related to federal taxation and regulation of commerce between the states (see, for example, the analysis under Child Labor Amendment), some advocates of states' rights have argued that state powers have been unduly eroded in violation of the language and spirit of the Tenth Amendment.

The Supreme Court registered this concern when, in *National League of Cities v. Usery* (1976), it decided by a 5-to-4 vote that the wage and hour provisions of the Fair Labor Standards Act that applied to private industries should not apply to traditional state functions. In 1985, however, in another 5-to-4 decision, the Court reversed course in *Garcia v. San Antonio Metropolitan Transit Authority* and decided that the line between traditional and nontraditional state functions was too difficult for the Court to draw. It further decided that the Constitution gave states adequate representation within Congress and other parts of the national government to protect their own interests.

States have subsequently complained not only about such wage and hour regulations (indeed, states have actually succeeded in having some such regulations repealed) but also about unfunded congressional mandates that pass costs on to states and localities without providing federal funding for such requirements. The U.S. Conference of Mayors even sponsored a National Unfunded Mandate Day to protest what the mayors regarded as the unfair burden and the displacement of local choices that such mandates were imposing on states and localities (Gillmor and Eames 1994, 397).

Ohio Republican congressman Paul Gillmor has proposed an amendment to prohibit Congress from enacting unfunded mandates but would not prohibit states from voluntarily spending their own funds as a condition to receiving federal funds. Gillmor is especially concerned that the adoption of a balanced budget amendment "could increase the pressure for Congress to impose unfunded mandates" (Gillmor and Eames 1994, 410). Estimates of the cost of such mandates run up to $11 billion a year (Pear 1994, 20).

In March 1995, President Bill Clinton signed the Unfunded Mandate Reform Act, which received a boost from the Republican congressional elections of 1994 (Hosanky 1995, 40). This act, which appears to undercut the need for a constitutional amendment, makes it more difficult for Congress to adopt unfunded mandates, requires more information about the projected costs of federal regulations, and restricts unfunded or underfunded federal mandates (Conlan, Riggle, and Schwartz 1995, 23). Members of Congress have continued, however, to propose an amendment that would give greater security to the provisions of this legislation.

See also Balanced Budget Amendment; Child Labor Amendment; Tenth Amendment.

For Further Reading:

Conlan, Timothy J., James D. Riggle, and Donna E. Schwartz. 1995. "Deregulating Federalism? The Politics of Mandate Reform in the 104th Congress." *Publius: The Journal of Federalism* 25 (Summer): 23–40.

Gillmor, Paul, and Fred Eames. 1994. "Reconstruction of Federalism: A Constitutional Amendment to Prohibit Unfunded Mandates." *Harvard Journal on Legislation* 31 (Summer): 395–413.

Hosanky, David. 1995. "Mandate Bill Is More Moderate Than Proposed in 'Contract.'" *Congressional Quarterly Weekly Report* 53 (January 7): 40.

Pear, Robert. 1994. "State Officials Worry That a Federal Budget Will Be Balanced on Their Books." *New York Times* (December 11): 34.

UNINTENDED CONSEQUENCES OF CONSTITUTIONAL AMENDMENTS

Once incorporated into the U.S. Constitution, constitutional amendments become the supreme law of the law. Scholars have long known that laws, court decisions, and constitutional amendments may all have unintended consequences. Although such consequences are therefore not unique to amendments, they can be more substantial in the case of amendments precisely because amendments are so difficult both to enact and repeal. The Twenty-first Amendment (repealing national alcoholic prohibition as established in the Eighteenth Amendment) remains the only example of an amendment that has specifically repealed another.

The consideration of unintended consequences thus becomes important when proposing amendments, especially amendments that appear to be politically popular, such as attempting to mandate balanced budgets or term limits, but whose full consequences may not be perceived until they are enacted. Thus, the individuals who proposed the Eighteenth Amendment did not favor the rise in organized crime that spawned, as gangsters supplied the alcohol that individuals could not legally obtain. Similarly, critics believe that the Twenty-second Amendment, limiting American presidents to two full terms (or a total of 10 years) in office, effectively made presidents "lame ducks" during their second terms and thus enhanced congressional powers, while the Twenty-third Amendment providing representation in the electoral college to the District of Columbia might have dissuaded Congress from proposing a more comprehensive solution to this problem. Many scholars believe that expansive interpretations of the equal protection clause of the Fourteenth Amendment to include rights for women led many individuals to conclude that ratification of the Equal Rights Amendment was unnecessary. Critics charged that the language of the proposed Equal Rights Amendment for women was so general that it left too much leeway to judicial interpretations, and, perhaps again, to unintended consequences (Manifreedi and Lustig 1998, 396–397).

See also Eighteenth Amendment; Fourteenth Amendment; Twenty-third Amendment; Twenty-second Amendment.

For Further Reading:

Ayres, Richard L. 2006. "Unintended Consequences of the Fourteenth Amendment and What

They Tell Us About Its Interpretation." *Akron Law Review* 39: 289–321.

Kyvig, David E., ed. 2000. *Unintended Consequences of Constitutional Amendments.* Athens: The University of Georgia Press.

Manfeedi, Christopher and Michael Lusztig. 1998. "Why Do Formal Amendments Fail? An Institutional Design Analysis." *World Politics* 50:377–400.

UNITED NATIONS

Countries created the United Nations at the end of World War II to promote international cooperation. Some individuals feared that such an organization might undermine the sovereignty of individual nations. This appears to have been the concern of Republican Representative Stephen Day of Illinois, who introduced an amending resolution in May 1944 to preserve "the independence and sovereignty of the United States" (H.J. Res 277). Similarly, North Dakota Democratic representative Quentin Burdick's proposal in 1957 to prohibit the service of United States citizens under any banner other than the stars and stripes (H.J. Res 20) may have been aimed at U.S. participation in U.N. peace-keeping missions.

A key component of the organization is the Security Council. Originally composed of 11 members, five of which (including the United States) were permanent, the council has subsequently expanded to 15 members. The five permanent members each have a veto, which was frequently wielded by both the United States and the Soviet Union during the Cold War period. Had Russia not been boycotting at the time of the Korean conflict, it is unlikely that the body could have taken action to repel North Korea's invasion of the South.

The U.S. president appoints the U.S. ambassador to the United Nations with the advice and consent of the Senate. The year after the United Nations was established, Connecticut Republican congresswoman Clare Boothe Luce introduced a resolution relative to the election of U.S. representatives to the Security Council. The proposal is otherwise obscure and does not appear to have elicited further congressional debate or support.

See also World Government.

For Further Reading:

Claude, Inis L., Jr. 1971. *Swords into Plowshares: The Problems and Progress of International Organization.* 4th ed. New York: Random House.

UNITED STATES OF AMERICA, PROPOSED NAME CHANGES

Simon Willard Jr. authored a proposed new Constitution for the United States in 1816 that gave great attention to the idea of renaming the United States Columbia, in honor of Christopher Columbus. Others at the time also believed the nation should be named after Columbus. Radical Republican Representative George Washington Anderson of Missouri proposed an amendment shortening the nation's name to America in 1866 (H.R. 61). Similarly, Wisconsin Democratic representative Lucas Miller introduced an amendment in 1893 to rename the nation the United States of the World (H.J. Res. 208). This latter name corresponded with that proposed by Victoria Claflin Woodhull in 1870 (Stern 1974). After first suggesting that it be called "the United Republic of America," Rexford Tugwell wrote a proposed constitution for what he designated the "Newstates of America."

See also Tugwell, Rexford; Willard, Simon, Jr.; Woodhull, Victoria Claflin.

For Further Reading:

Stern, Madeline B., ed. 1974. *The Victoria Woodhull Reader.* Weston, MA: M & S Press.

UNITED STATES V. CHAMBERS (1934)

This U.S. Supreme Court ruling upheld a district court decision in North Carolina dismissing an indictment against Claude Chambers and Byrum Gibson for possessing and transporting intoxicating liquors in violation of the National Prohibition Act. They had been indicted on June 5, 1933. Chambers had pled guilty, but his judgment had been deferred until December; Gibson's trial had not yet been held. As the Court had recognized in *Dillon v. Gloss* (1921), the ratification of the Twenty-first Amendment repealing national alcoholic prohibition had been consummated on December 5, at which time Chambers filed to abate his guilty plea, and Gibson filed a demurrer to the indictment based on the contention that the Twenty-first Amendment's repeal of the Eighteenth had deprived the court of jurisdiction.

Chief Justice Charles Evans Hughes wrote the Court's unanimous decision. He observed that "upon the ratification of the Eighteenth Amendment, the Eighteenth Amendment at once became inoperative." Continued prosecution depended on "the continued life of the statute," which was no longer in force. Hughes cited a variety of precedents to establish that "after the expiration or repeal of a law, no penalty can be enforced, nor punishment inflicted, for violations of the law committed while it was in force, unless some special provision be made for that purpose by statute." In this case, the Twenty-first Amendment included no such "saving clause." Hughes thought that a general saving provision that Congress had enacted in regard to the repeal of statutes applied only to statutes, and not to the Constitution itself: "The Congress . . . is powerless to expand or extend its constitutional authority. The Congress, while it could propose, could not adopt the constitutional Amendment or vary the terms or effect of the Amendment when adopted." Hughes rejected an analogy drawn from changes from territorial to state governments, since the Constitution specifically vested Congress with power to admit new states. He also rejected the argument that the Court was enforcing a common-law rule that was at odds with public policy. In his words, "The question is not one of public policy which the courts may be considered free to declare, but of the continued efficacy of legislation in the face of controlling action of the people, the source of the power to enact and maintain it. It is not a question of the developing common law. It is a familiar maxim of the common law that when the reason of a rule ceases the rule also ceases." Once the people repealed a power they had vested in Congress, neither Congress nor the courts could continue to enforce it.

See also *Dillon v. Gloss*; Eighteenth Amendment; Twenty-first Amendment.

For Further Reading:

Murchison, Kenneth M. 1982. "Prohibition and the Fourth Amendment: A New Look at Some Old Cases." *Journal of Criminal Law and Criminology* 73 (Summer): 471–532.

United States v. Chambers, 291 U.S. 217 (1934)

UNITED STATES V. EICHMAN (1990)

After the U.S. Supreme Court invalidated a Texas statute preventing flag desecration in *Texas v. Johnson* (1989), congressional opponents of the decision had to decide whether to respond with an anti-flag-burning amendment or with legislation. A majority adopted the latter course, passing the Flag Protection Act of 1989. Protesters in Seattle and Washington DC immediately challenged this law.

The Flag Protection Act asserted an interest in preserving the nation's flag without making reference to explicit content-based limitations on speech. The Supreme Court found that "it is nevertheless clear that the Government's asserted *interest* is 'related "to the suppression of free expression"' . . . and concerned with the content of such expression" (*Eichman* 1990, 315). As in *Texas v. Johnson,* the Court found that the law "suppresses expression out of concern for its likely communicative impact" (317) and must be subject to strict scrutiny under the First Amendment. In exercising such scrutiny, a majority of five justices led by Justice William Brennan refused to overrule its earlier decision and thus invalidated the new law. Justice John Paul Stevens authored the dissenting opinion, restating his stance in the earlier case.

See also First Amendment; Flag Desecration; *Texas v. Johnson.*

For Further Reading:
United States v. Eichman, 496 U.S. 310 (1990).

UNITED STATES V. MORRISON (2000)

This Supreme Court decision is helpful in understanding the current Court's posture in interpreting congressional powers under its enforcement powers in Section 5 of the Fourteenth Amendment; toward federalism; and, by implication, toward the Tenth Amendment, which reserves certain unspecified powers to the states. *Morrison* dealt with a provision of the Violence Against Women Act of 1994 that allowed citizens to bring federal civil suits against perpetrators of crimes motivated by a victim's gender (prior to this time, an individual would have to bring any such claims under state law). In this case, a former student of Virginia Tech had brought a civil suit against two football players for rape after the university ultimately failed to discipline them.

Chief Justice William Rehnquist issued a narrow 5–4 majority joined by Justices O'Connor, Scalia, Kennedy, and Thomas, that built on an earlier opinion in *United States v. Lopez* (1995)—a case that had invalidated a federal gun law punishing individuals who brought a gun within a specified distance from a school. In *Morrison,* as in *Lopez,* the Court decided that Congress had exceeded its authority both under Article I, Section 8, which supplements specific grants of powers to Congress with the power to make all laws "necessary and proper" to carrying out those listed, and under Section 5 of the Fourteenth Amendment, which provides power to enforce other provisions of that amendment. As in *Lopez,* the Court decided that Congress had not tied the law in question either to the channels or instrumentalities of interstate commerce or of a matter that had a "substantial relation" to such commerce (*Morrison,* 609). Although Congress had demonstrated the pervasiveness and widespread impact of violence against women, the Court thought that the tie to economic damages, and hence to interstate *commerce,* was weak.

The Court majority further expressed concern that, if it accepted the presence of such an impact in a matter previously understood to be governed by criminal law or state tort law (both traditional areas for the exercise of state police powers), there would be literally little or nothing left for state control. In interpreting federal authority under Section 5 of the Fourteenth Amendment, the Court noted that previous interpretations of this amendment had limited congressional remedies to violations of individual rights that were the result of state action rather than to control over the actions of private individuals.

Justices Souter, Stevens, Ginsburg, and Breyer all dissented, believing that Congress had demonstrated adequate connection between the Violence Against Women Act and its power to regulate commerce. This narrow division has long characterized Supreme Court decision making relative to federalism.

See also Fourteenth Amendment; Tenth Amendment.

For Further Reading:
Martin, Jil L. 2000. "United States v. Morrison: Federalism Against the Will of the States." *Loyola University of Chicago Law Review* 32 (Fall): 243–333.
United States v. Lopez, 514 U.S. 549 (1995).
United States v. Morrison, 529 U.S. 528 (2000).

UNITED STATES V. SPRAGUE (1931)

This case, like the *National Prohibition Cases* (1920), arose from a challenge to the Eighteenth Amendment. Although citing its own rationale, the U.S. district court accepted the conclusion of Seldon Bacon and other opponents of the Prohibition Amendment, who argued that, no matter what Congress specified, state legislatures could not appropriately ratify such an amendment restricting the rights of the people. Instead, it required ratification by state conventions.

In writing the unanimous opinion for the Court, in which Chief Justice Charles Evans

Hughes did not participate, Justice Owen Roberts argued that the "plain language of Article V" should take priority over any hypothesized "intent of its framers" (*Sprague* 1931, 729). Citing the language of Article V, Roberts argued that the choice between the two means of ratification "rests solely in the discretion of Congress" (*Id.,* 732). Because Congress in making this selection acts "as the delegated agent of the people in the choice of the method of ratification," it is not limited (as Bacon had argued) by the Tenth Amendment, which refers to powers "not delegated to the United States" rather than to powers specifically delegated to Congress (*Id.,* 733).

Roberts further argued that, contrary to Bacon's argument, a number of prior amendments—most notably "the Thirteenth, Fourteenth, Sixteenth, and Nineteenth," all of which the Court had accepted—also touched on the rights of individual citizens (*Sprague* 1931, 734). The Court's acceptance of the lawfulness of their ratifications was an additional argument for accepting the lawfulness of the Eighteenth Amendment.

Ironically, the Twenty-first Amendment repealed the Eighteenth Amendment within two years of the decision in *United States v. Sprague* by the kind of state conventions by which its opponents said that it should have been ratified.

See also Bacon, Selden; Eighteenth Amendment; National Prohibition Cases; Twenty-first Amendment.

For Further Reading:
United States v. Sprague, 282 U.S. 716 (1931).

UNRATIFIED AMENDMENTS

See Failed Amendments.

UNWRITTEN CONSTITUTION

See Customs and Usages; Relevance of Constitutional Amendments.

UPHAM, THOMAS CARLTON (1894–?)

About the only biographical information that is known about Thomas C. Upham is the proposal for a new constitution that he apparently composed in large part in 1937 and 1938 and offered in a book published in 1941 (Boyd 1992, 176). In this proposal, Upham provided a bit of biographical insight when he noted that part of his antipathy to charity derived from the fact that "I have had to take charity myself a few times" (Upham 1941, 56).

Upham aimed to "retain much of the framework, some of the contents, and all of the spirit—plus—of the old constitution" (Upham 1941, 32). While building on the existing document, Upham proposed a number of utopian and socialistic features, and he was particularly concerned about promoting greater equality. His preamble lists, among other objectives, that of forming a society "of mutual cooperation, human brotherhood, general kindliness, common welfare, equal rights, economic security, material prosperity, and universal peace" (*Id.,* 67).

Upham's constitution begins with the executive branch, consisting of a president nominated by petition and elected by a plurality of voters for a single six-year term. A senator would succeed the president in case of vacancy or incapacity. A three-fourths vote of Congress would be able to override the president's power as commander in chief. The president would have the right to submit legislation directly to Congress or to the people for approval and would be subject to recall by petition and a vote of two-thirds of the population.

The Senate would consist of 17 nonpartisan citizens elected for a maximum of two six-year terms. Each would also head one of 17 departments, including one dealing with "cultural security" and another with "private relations" (Upham 1941, 77). Members of the House would be chosen from 24 newly created districts that would take the place of the existing state and local governments, which Upham would eliminate. Upham would subject congressional laws to an item veto and grant the people the right of petition, referendum, and recall.

Upham would maintain the Supreme Court but require justices to retire at age 75. There would also be district courts and criminal boards. Petit juries would consist of six local citizens and six citizens from another part of the country, with a guarantee that at least one juror would be "of the same race, color, sex, and religious persuasion as the accused" (Upham 1941, 91). Government attorneys would serve both as defense counsel and as prosecutors.

At age 18 every citizen would be obligated to register for citizenship. Citizens would be required to work from age 21 to 70. They could not be required to work more than five days and 35 hours a week and would be guaranteed a two-week vacation. All would be paid on a standard wage scale ranging (for those aged 24 to 60) from $1,000 a year to $10,000 a year so that the maximum wage would be no more than 10 times the minimum. Although individuals would be permitted to own small businesses, the government would own major industries, and individuals would be limited to owning $100,000 of private property. Upham would outlaw strikes and guarantee medical care and education to all. He would forbid charity and require all citizens to learn English. A "work and wages" standard would replace the gold standard (Upham 1941, 113). Rights would be protected against both governmental and private action, with existing rights preserved and occasionally expanded.

Upham would outlaw wars but provided some exceptions for defense and for actions within the Western Hemisphere (Upham 1941, 61). The United States would seek to form an international union that would work for "the attainment of Christian or other good ideals in the world" (*Id.,* 115).

Upham favored calling a convention of 84 individuals to write the constitution, its work to become effective when ratified by the people. Future amendments would be instituted by two-thirds of both houses of Congress and ratified by two-thirds of those voting. The president would also have the right to take proposed changes to the people.

For Further Reading:

Upham, Thomas C. 1941. *Total Democracy: A New Constitution for the United States. A Democratic Ideal for the World.* New York: Carlyle House.

U.S. TERM LIMITS, INC. V. THORNTON (1995)

In this case, the U.S. Supreme Court struck down a term-limit provision in the Arkansas state constitution. By implication, the Court also voided laws and constitutional provisions limiting the terms of national legislators that 22 other states had adopted.

Thornton centered on the provisions of Article I, Sections 2 and 3 of the U.S. Constitution setting forth age, citizenship, and residency requirements for members of the U.S. House and Senate. Arkansas had attempted to keep candidates off the ballot when they had served three terms in the House or two terms in the Senate.

Relying in large part on the decision in *Powell v. McCormack* (1969), the Court majority of five, led by Justice John Paul Stevens, held that the qualifications established in Article I were designed to be exclusive and that the Arkansas constitution added another qualification. Stevens argued that such additional state-imposed qualifications were "inconsistent with the Framers' vision of a uniform national legislature, representing the people of the United States" (*U.S. Term Limits* 1995, 783). He further opined that if states wanted to add to constitutionally specified qualifications, they would need to do so "through the amendment procedures set forth in Article V" (*Id.,* 837).

By contrast, Justice Clarence Thomas, who wrote the dissenting opinion, said that although the Constitution established minimum qualifications for legislators, it was silent about additional qualifications. In Thomas's view, the Tenth Amendment thus reserved such restrictions to the people of the states. Noting that "the Constitution simply does not recognize the mechanism for action by the undifferentiated people of the Nation," Thomas observed that the amending process "calls for amendments to be ratified not by a convention of the national people, but by conventions in each state or by the state legislatures elected by these people" (*U.S. Term Limits* 1995, 928).

Republican Senator Hank Brown of Colorado announced a plan to evade this decision by passing legislation defining the term "inhabitant" to exclude members of Congress who had been gone from their districts for more than half a year for 12 consecutive years (Seelye 1995, A11). Other supporters of term limits renewed calls for a constitutional amendment on the subject. Some versions of this plan would impose a single nationwide standard while others would specifically reverse *U.S. Term Limits v. Thornton* (1995) by allowing states to set their own limits.

The state of Missouri attempted to evade the decision in *U.S. Term Limits* by including a ballot notation indicating whether representatives had supported term limits or not. The U.S. Supreme Court struck down this provision in *Cook v. Gralike* (2001).

See also Congress, Term Limits; *Cook v. Gralike.*

For Further Reading:

U.S. Term Limits, Inc. v. Thornton, 514 U.S. 779 (1995).

V

❖

VANGUARD, VIRGINIA

Virginia Vanguard is the pseudonym under which a book entitled *The Populis: A Draft Constitution for a New Political Age* was published in 1995. The author, who was influenced by futuristic plans for greater voter participation in politics, says that he/she was using the pseudonym not to conceal identity but "rather to focus attention on arguments versus personalities." The author began with a preface describing a voter calling in to a National Decision Center, entering a voting code, and registering her opinion on a matter of public importance. The author then proceeded to describe how the concept of democracy could be enhanced by such forms of direct democracy. The book consisted of the draft of a proposed constitution of a preamble and 12 articles followed by a brief description of how the new constitution would work. The preamble is almost identical to that of the current Constitution except that it omits the words "of the United States"; the proposal was relatively vague as to what role such states, if they remain at all, will play in the new system.

Article I described five elements of the new national government. They were the Populis, responsible for determining basic policies and selecting office holders; the Caucis, which would select and present policy issues and candidates to the voters; the Legis, which would translate public decisions into law; the Executis, which would implement and enforce such laws; and the Judicis, which would interpret the laws and attempt to assure fair treatment for all.

Article II defined citizenship, which was to be limited to individuals born to a citizen parent or naturalized. Citizenship could be forfeited upon "accepting the citizenship of another nation, upon conviction of a serious criminal act, or upon death" (Vanguard 1995, 19). Citizens were charged with gaining adequate education and training and would be required to "possess sufficient financial insurance against personal calamity" (*Id.*, 19). Citizenship carried with it, as a birthright, "all freedoms," and these may only be abridged "with the explicit consent of the Populis" (*Id.*, 20). The constitution describes the right of the Populis "to directly and collectively determine all national policy" as "indelible" (*Id.*, 20).

Citizens 18 years and older "may choose to join the Populis" (*Id.*, 20). Only such individuals could hold office or participate in national elections and referenda. Such citizens would be required to perform at least four years of military and civilian service. Individuals who failed to join the Populis within four years would permanently lose this opportunity, although if they continued on the nation's soil, they would be bound by its laws.

The provision for the Caucis was fairly unique. Patterned after a grand jury, this caucis consisted of "seven willing persons selected randomly and secretly from the rolls of the Populis" (*Id.*, 22). Chosen every two month, members "will be sequestered at a central location, along with their immediate families, to allow full concentration on their tasks" (*Id.*, 22). The Caucis would be responsible for identifying issues of national importance, framing issues for the National Policy Referendum, and presenting candidates, for high offices. It would also oversee the Civis, or National Service Board.

Article V described the unicameral Legis, which might be less democratically accountable than the current Congress, although this arguably matters far less because the new body would be responsible for for incorporating the will of the Populis. The next lower governmental entities, whether "state, province, or territory" (*Id.*, 24), would select two representatives to the Legis who would each serve one three-year term. The Legis would "formulate national laws that faithfully implement the policies of the Populis, as reflected in the results of National Policy Referenda" (*Id.*, 25). These would be known as "the National Code of Justice" (*Id.*, 25). The Legis would have some additional powers in times of national emergency. Each year the Legis would select a chief legislator.

Article VI outlines the duties of the Executis, who had the duty "to faithfully and efficiently implement, administer, and enforce the laws as codified by the Legis" (*Id.*, 27). It would consist of a chief executive, a deputy executive, and administrators of civilian and military programs. Much like the current president, the chief executive would sign treaties, appoint ambassadors, and be commander in chief of the armed forces. The chief and deputy would serve for a single five-year term, with the chief legislator designated as following next in succession. The veto power is not mentioned.

Article VII outlines the Judicis. It would "rule on the correctness of conflicting interpretations of the law, develop consistent guidelines for punishments and awards, and render timely judgments" (*Id.*, 29). However, the Populis could overrule it. The Populis would elect a High Court, consisting of seven judges, serving seven-year single terms, and defining its own jurisdiction. The High Court would also set standards for criminal penalties. The chief justice would be elected annually, with no individual serving for more than a single year.

Article VIII outlines the Civis. It consisted of "all persons employed by the Legis, the Judicicis, the various civilian and military agencies or the Executis and the National Service Board." All would be compensated on a consistent scale, with the chief executive being paid the most, albeit no more than "twenty times that of the lowest full-time employee of the national gov-

ernment" (*Id.*, 32). All new members of the Populis would serve in the Civis for at least four years. Boards of Inquiry would hear charges against members of the Civis accused of not doing their duties.

Article IX dealt with making, amending, and repealing laws. The Causis presented such laws after each meeting, initiating a two-month referendum, during which each member of the Populis was expected to vote. Each action selected by a majority would become law and would have to be implemented by the Legis within 120 days. Laws and policies would be guided by 10 principles. These included the requirement that such laws shall "perpetually strive for Justice, by ensuring equal protection under the law and equal application of the law"; "be applied universally"; be national in scope; not address "infrequent events"; not be ex post facto; not include unrelated clauses; have benefits that outweigh their costs; only regulate personal behavior "where significant harm or risk to self or a fellow Citizen is inevitable"; and expire within 25 years (*Id.*, 36–37). The Legis would review existing laws and would assure that "the nation's Code of Justice will be subjected to a general revalidation at least once per century" (*Id.*, 37).

Article X provided for the election of national representatives. The Caucis was charged with screening all such candidates and was responsible for presenting from two to five candidates to the Populis for each. To obtain office, an individual must receive "at least 3 percent more of the vote than the next most popular candidate" (*Id.*, 39). Otherwise, the Caucis would make the choice.

Article XI provided for governmental financing. All revenues would be raised by a personal income tax. It would not include any "deduction, allowance, or exemption" (*Id.*, 40). The government would be forbidden from "incurring any long-term indebtedness or credits." Likewise, it "may neither borrow money from nor lend money to another government, organization, financial institution, or person without the consent of the Populis" (*Id.*, 40–41). The Executis, with Legis approval, would determine the amount of money in circulation but could not artificially manipulate its value without the consent of the Populis.

Article XII described other governmental entities. The national government was to be carefully circumscribed: "It shall provide no service that can reasonably and more efficiently be made available through a non-governmental entity or a lower government entity" (*Id.*, 42). The Populis might create "the permanent or temporary formation of such states, regions, provinces, territories, etc., as may be necessary" (*Id.*, 42). The structure of subgovernments would complement those of the national government and could be dissolved. All policies of subgovernments would have to conform to those of the national government. Governments would practice reciprocity. Although the nation was encouraged to join "benevolent international organizations," Virginia Vanguard specified that "any surrender of national prerogatives to such an organization must be explicitly approved by the Populis" (*Id.*, 43).

Designed both to enshrine popular sovereignty and to end the "paternal relationship" between the government and the people (*Id.*, 45), the Populis contained a number of unique features. "In the POPULIS, Citizens will conditionally relinquish to government only those powers they deem absolutely necessary and retain the right to reclaim even those" (*Id.*, 56). Accordingly, the document listed very few rights.

For Further Reading:

Vanguard, Virginia. 1995. *The Populis: A Draft Constitution for a Political New Age.* Brentsville, VA: The Wingspread Enterprise.

VANSICKLE, JOHN (1965–)

John VanSickle identifies himself as an individual who has spent 14 years in military service. As of 2002, he was working on a bachelor's degree in computer and information science (personal e-mail correspondence with author, June 10, 2002). His Web site, which includes information on his family, science fiction pages, political pages, and raytracing pages (these have to do with computer simulations), includes proposals for twenty-eighth, twenty-ninth, thirtieth, thirty-first, and thirty-second amendments, each

followed by brief commentary. Most of the amendments are quite complex, and many are fairly novel. Most of VanSickle's ideas are conservative; he says that his "political leanings are the result of reading most of Ayn Rand's works that are presently in print (although I do not agree with everything she says and with even less of what is said in her name by her followers)" (personal e-mail correspondence, June 10, 2002). VanSickle further indicates that he believes he began posting his proposals in 1998 (*Id.*, 11 June 2002).

VanSickle's proposed twenty-eighth amendment, the language of which he models after the First Amendment, would prohibit Congress or the states from making laws "respecting an establishment of production, trade, employment, education, medicine, culture, or charity, or restricting the free exercise thereof." The amendment would further repeal the Sixteenth Amendment (which legitimized the national income tax), and congressional power "to borrow or lend money" or "consider any bill to reverse any part of this amendment."

VanSickle's twenty-ninth amendment is composed of 18 sections, which deal chiefly with the criminal justice system. It would prohibit fines or forfeitures except for a crime of which an individual has been convicted (Section 1); compensate individuals for property damaged during governmental seizures (Section 2); require unanimous jury verdicts and limit their application to crimes involving an "identifiable harm to a specific person or party of persons" (Section 3): eliminate "peculiar courts" (Section 4); provide for the selection of jurors for lottery with exclusions for individuals in law enforcement or with personal interests in the case (Section 5); allow jurors to judge matters of both law and fact "independent of the instructions of the court" (Section 6); prohibit convictions based simply on the testimony of governmental officials or from individuals engaged in plea-bargaining (Section 7); prohibit the use of testimony "obtained by coercion or fraud" (Section 8); separate individuals whose crimes involved bodily harm to others from being incarcerated with those who committed such violent offenses (Section 9); reserve the death penalty for specified crimes (Section 10); limit the definition of cruel and unusual punishment of prisoners to the infliction of "injury or illness" (Section 11); make it an abuse for governmental official to abridge the "rights, privileges, or immunities" of persons under guise of their authority and make them liable for the same (Sections 12 and 13); prohibit punitive damages (Section 14); specify the presumption of innocence and sanity and provide that the "beyond a reasonable doubt" standard be applied in both criminal and civil cases (Section 15); distribute fines to individuals harmed or, if no such individuals can be identified, to taxpayers (Section 16): make it a crime for governmental officials to cover up evidence tending to exonerate a defendant (Section 17); and make "entrapment" by law enforcement officials a crime (Section 18).

VanSickle's proposed thirtieth amendment deals with perceived governmental abuses. Section 1 would apply all laws that Congress passed to itself. Section 2 would require all regulations to be "expressly worded." Section 3 would require all governmental representatives and appointees to divest themselves of "commercial interests" and prohibit pensions to the same. Section 4 would require elected officials to take an oath to tell the truth and make them impeachable for violating this oath. Section 5 would enable each individual to place bills before Congress. Sections 6 and 7 would permit the nomination of presidents and vice presidents by petitions of 1 percent or more of the voters. Section 8 would prohibit monies from the treasury from being spent on petitions, and Section 9 would prohibit felons or ex-felons from serving in office. Section 10 would specify that any crime for which an individual could be incarcerated would be considered to be an impeachable offense. Section 11 would prohibit the use of federal expenditures to induce state behavior. Section 12 would limit congressional powers to regulate trade only when such trade "transacts state borders," and Section 13 would provide an automatic sunset for any law on its tenth anniversary, with the understanding that could adopt new laws to replace them.

VanSickle's proposed thirty-first amendment relates to the military. Section 1 would eliminate the draft. Section 2 would limit the stationing of troops abroad "except in prosecution of a war declared by Congress." Sections 3 and 4, much like some earlier versions of the Bricker Amendment, would prohibit the United States from entering into treaties abridging citizens "rights, privileges, or immunities."

VanSickle's proposed thirty-second amendment largely limits both state and federal powers. Section 1 limits the power of licensing and limits such fess to a minimum. Section 2 affirms the Second Amendment right to "keep and bear arms" without being "subject to any system of governmental consent or license" except for limiting ownership of individuals who used weapons to cause or threaten harm. Section 3 limits legislation designed to preserve endangered species. Section 4 provides that child welfare shall be the basis of "all custody decisions." Section 5 allows states to prohibit governments within their jurisdiction from exercising jurisdiction over matters the sates have reserved to themselves. Section 6 limits restrictions on individual rights "only to those restrictions that are enumerated in this constitution." Section 7 limits the information that governments may collect on private individuals. Section 8 provides for a referendum initiated by 1 percent or more of the voters of any state and enacted into law when favored by "a majority of votes." The amendment further provides that "[a] referendum may repeal any law passed by the legislature of that state, remove from office any appointed official of that State, amend the Constitution of that State, ratify a pending amendment to the Constitution of the United States, or withdraw the State's ratification of a pending amendment to the Constitution of the United States." The final section limits U.S. governmental ownership to "only those lands used in the exercise of the powers reserved to it in this constitution."

Van Sickle's site includes other reflections on government, most notably a copy of "the No Bill of Rights," borrowed from another web-site, which basically lets individuals know, in a structure similar to the original bill of rights, that individuals are entitled to opportunities but not to government largesse in such areas as food, housing, health care, or the like.

For Further Reading:

http://enphilistor.users4.50megs.com/index.htm. Accessed June 8, 2002.

VENERATION FOR THE CONSTITUTION

See Reverence for the Constitution.

VETO

See *Clinton v. City of New York:* Presidency, Veto Power of.

VICE PRESIDENT

No other U.S. constitutional office has been subjected to greater scorn than that of the vice presidency (Twentieth Century Fund Task Force 1988, 21; also see Young 1974). Especially in recent years, however, this office has increased in power and visibility and has become a major springboard to the presidency, much as the position of secretary of state did in early American history. Vice president who have run for president since 1960 have included Richard Nixon, Hubert Humphrey, Gerald Ford (who became president after Nixon's resignation), Walter Mondale, George Bush, Sr. and Al Gore Jr.

The Constitution of 1787 assigns only two functions to the vice president. One is to be available in case the president dies. The second is to preside over and break tie votes in the U.S. Senate.

In large part, the Founders created the vice presidency as a concomitant of the electoral college (Schlesinger 1974, 490). Under the original electoral plan, each elector was to cast two votes. The person with the greatest number would become president, and the runner-up would become vice president. With the emergence of political parties, this scheme hit two major snags. First, it permitted electors to choose a president and vice president from different parties; Federalist John Adams thus had a Democratic-Republican vice president, Thomas Jefferson. Second, it created the possibility of a tie in the electoral college. Such a tie occurred in the election of 1800, when all the Democratic-Republican electors for Thomas Jefferson also cast their votes for fellow party member Aaron Burr, and the Houses of Representatives had to resolve the context. The Twelfth Amendment subsequently required electors to cast separate votes for the two offices.

After adoption of this amendment, the vice presidency declined in stature, and some members of Congress began to introduce resolutions to abolish the office. Alternatively, some congressmen proposed creating multiple vice presidencies or allowing Congress to fill vice-presidential vacancies.

Although the institution was generally weak, in 1841 John Tyler established an important precedent. In succeeding William Henry Harrison, who died in office, Tyler insisted that he was the real and not simply an "acting" president. Subsequent vice president who assumed the presidency have taken similar positions, without which their hands would undoubtedly have been weakened.

The Twentieth Amendment settled one issue surrounding the vice presidency when it specified that if a president is not chosen in time for his or her term, the vice president-elect should be president. The amendment simply allowed Congress to legislate in cases in which neither the president nor the vice president had been so selected, but to date, Congress has yet to adopt such legislation.

The two greatest problems with the vice presidency were that the Constitution did not establish a procedure whereby a vice president could take over in cases of presidential disability, and it made no provision for filling vice presidential vacancies. The Twenty-fifth Amendment addressed both problems; it permitted the president temporarily to transfer power to the vice president (during medical operations, times of ill health, and the like) and established a complex procedure whereby the vice president and cabinet could declare a president disabled. It also allowed a president to nominate, and a majority of Congress to confirm, vice presidential replacements. This second procedure for nominating vice presidents essentially confirmed a practice, first established when Franklin D. Roosevelt was president, of allowing the candidate to pick his running mate, in a choice almost always subsequently confirmed by the party nominating convention; prior to that time, conventions typically made this selection on their own.

Adoption of the Twenty-fifth Amendment has not ended calls to abolish the vice presidency or to clarify procedures to be followed in cases of presidential disability. Some critics are also concerned that presidential candidates too often choose their running mates more for electoral advantage than for their fitness to assume the presidency. Perhaps with such problems in mind, members of Congress introduced proposals in 1956 and 1957 to elect the vice president separately from the president. Since adoption of the Twenty-fifth Amendment, members of congress have also occasionally called to fill vice presidential vacancies by special elections rather than by presidential appointment and congressional confirmation. Health problems of George W. Bush's vice president, Dick Cheney (who had a long history of heart ailments), some of which emerged in the thirty-six-day period during which the presidential election of 2000 was being resolved, further highlighted concerns about the current method of vice presidential selection.

See also Twelfth Amendment; Twentieth Amendment; Twenty-fifth Amendment.

For Further Reading:

Albert, Richard, 2005. "The Evolving Vice Presidency," *Temple Law Review* 78 (Winter): 811–896.

Schlesinger, Arthur M., Jr. 1974. "On the Presidential Succession." *Political Science Quarterly* 89 (Fall): 475–505.

Twentieth Century Fund Fask Force on the Vice Presidency. 1988. *A Heartbeat Away.* New York: Printing Press Publications.

Young, Donald. 1974. *American Roulette: The History and Dilemma of the Vice Presidency.* New York: Viking Press.

VICTIMS' RIGHTS

As courts have widened their understanding of the provisions of the Bill of Rights and the Fourteenth Amendment to extend broader protection to the rights of criminal defendants (the Warren Court applied most of the provisions related to the rights of criminal defendants in the Bill of Rights to the states), attention has begun to focus on the rights of victims. In 1982, a Task Force on Victims of Crime that President Reagan appointed recommended adding a provision to the Sixth Amendment to provide that "Likewise, the victim, in every criminal prosecution shall have the right to be present and to be heard at all critical stages of judicial proceedings" (See Schwartz 2005, 626).

In *Payne v. Tennessee* (1991), the Supreme Court overturned two earlier decisions and upheld the use of victim-impact statements, allowing victims to testify as to the effect of crimes on their lives, in the penalty phase of capital trials. Despite this decision, some observers still believe that prosecutors often ignore the interests of victims at other stages of the trial, denying them the psychological sense of closure that they might feel if they were otherwise consulted during judicial proceedings.

Florida Republican Representative Illena Ros-Lehtinen, the first Cuban-born American to serve in such a capacity, introduced amending resolutions in 1990 and 1991 to guarantee victims' rights, and many proposals have been introduced since. California Senator Diane Feinstein and Arizona Republican Senator Jon Kyle, introduced a proposal on 15 April 2002, which President George W. Bush supported, revising earlier proposals, according to Feinstein, so as not "to abridge the rights of defendants or offenders, or otherwise disrupt the delicate balance of our Constitution." It has four sections. The first applies to both state and national governments and provides that:

> The rights of victims of violent crime, being capable of protection without denying the constitutional rights of those accused of victimizing them, are hereby established and shall not be denied by any State or the United States and may be restricted only as provided in this article.

Section 2 of the proposed Victims' Rights Amendment attempts to flesh out such rights by making them more specific:

A victim of violent crime shall have the right to reasonable and timely notice of any public proceeding involving the crime and of any release or escape of the accused; the rights not to be excluded from such public proceeding and reasonably to be heard at public release, plea, sentencing, reprieve, and pardon proceedings; and the right to adjudicative decisions that duly consider the victim's safety, interest in avoiding unreasonable delay, and just and timely claims to restitution from the offender. These rights shall not be restricted except when and to the degree dictated by a substantial interest in public safety or the administration of criminal justice, or by compelling necessity.

Section 3 is designed to thwart the use of the amendment to "provide [for defendants] grounds for a new trial or to authorize any claim for damages." Similarly, it declares that "[o]nly the victim or the victim's lawful representative may asset the rights established by this article, and no person accused of the crime may obtain any form of relief hereunder." Section 4 provides Congress with appropriate enforcement authority and further specifies that "[n]othing in this article shall affect the President's authority to grant reprieves or pardons" (quoted in "New Proposal for Constitutionalizing Victims' Rights" 2002, 2679).

Congress has in part responded to concerns for victims' rights by adopting the Victims' Bill of Rights in 1994 and the Victims' Rights Clarification Act of 1997 (Cassell 1999, 520). All fifty states have adopted some victims' rights legislation, and twenty-two have adopted constitutional amendments on the subject (Schwartz 2005, 526-27), but laws vary widely from one jurisdiction to another and are not always effective.

This legislation demonstrates that at least some of the goals that proponents of the victims' rights amendment favor can currently be enacted through state and/or federal legislation. However, state legislation currently varies widely from one jurisdiction to another, and does not always appear to be effective (515-22).

For Further Reading:
Browne, Michael K. 2004. "International Victims' Rights Law: What Can Be Gleaned from the Victims' Empowerment Provisions in Germany as the United States Prepares to Consider the Adoption of a Victims Rights Amendment to its Constitution?" *Hamline Law Review* 27 (Winter): 15–44.

Cassell, Paul G. 1999. "Barbarians at the Gates? A Reply to the Critics of the Victims' Rights Amendments, " *Utah Law Review* 1999: 479–537.

Cassell, Paul G. and Steven J. Twist. 1996. "A Bill of Rights for Crime Victims." 127 *Wall Street Journal* (24 April): A15.

Kyl, John. 1996. "Why Victims Need a Bill of Rights." *Washington Times* (22 April): A21.

"New Proposal for Constitutionalizing Victims' Rights Introduced in Congress." 2002. U.S. Law Week 70 (30 April): 2679.

Schwartz, Victoria. 2005. "The Victims' Rights amendment." *Harvard Journal on Legislation* 42 (Summer): 525–555.

Taylor Stuart, Jr. 2000. "Victim's Rights: Leave the Constitution Alone." *National Journal* 32 (April 22): 1254.

VIRGINIA AND KENTUCKY RESOLUTIONS

Although commentators often refer collectively to the American framers and their intent when interpreting the U.S. Constitution, the Virginia and Kentucky Resolutions illustrate that even the framers had different understandings of the document they created. The Resolutions also provide a glimpse of the early limitations of the Bill of Rights.

During John Adams' presidency the nation came close to going to war with France. Federalists were increasingly concerned about the growing opposition of the Democratic-Republican Party that Thomas Jefferson and James Madison were leading. Federalists accordingly adopted the Alien and Sedition Acts. The first made it more difficult for immigrants, many of whom favored the Democratic-Republicans, to become citizens, while the second made it a federal crime to criticize the government or the president of the United States.

Modern-day courts would almost certainly invalidate the Sedition Act under the First

Amendment, but in Adam's administration Federalists nominees who were unsympathetic to such pleas dominated the courts. For their part, Democratic-Republicans, who had opposed the establishment of the national bank, continued to express concern that Federalists were interpreting the Constitution, not as a limited compact among the states that had ratified it, but as a document giving the national government virtually unlimited powers.

Democratic-Republicans accordingly chose to respond to the Alien and Sedition Acts by adopting the Virginia and Kentucky Resolutions, the first largely authored by James Madison and the second by Thomas Jefferson (secretly, because he was vice president at the time). The Virginia and Kentucky legislatures adopted the resolutions to encourage other states to "Interpose" themselves against the laws on the basis that they exceeded federal delegated powers, violated various guarantees of due process, and violated the Tenth Amendment, reserving power to the states. In the Kentucky Resolution, Jefferson observed that "free government is founded in jealousy and not in confidence" and that "[i]n questions of power, then, let no more be heard of confidence by man, but bind him down from mischief, by the chains of the Constitution" (Ford 1898, 683). Although others undoubtedly shared Jefferson's sentiments, others states did not at the time respond positively to these resolutions.

In 1801 Thomas Jefferson was elected to the presidency and members of his party gained control of congress. The Alien and Seditions Acts all either lapsed or were repealed (Willis 2002, 9). Jefferson pardoned Individuals who had been convicted under the sedition law. States' rights sentiment subsequently shifted from the South to the North with the Hartford Convention of 1815, and then back to the South with controversies over tariffs and slavery that ultimately produced the now discredited doctrines of nullification and secession.

See also First Amendment; Hartford Convention; Jefferson, Thomas; Madison, James; Tenth Amendment.

For Further Reading:

Ford, Paul L. ed. 1898. *The Federalist.* New York: Henry Holt.

Watkins, William. 2004. *Reclaiming the American Revolution: The Kentucky and Virginia Resolutions and Their Legacy.* New York: Palgrave Macmillan.

VIRGINIA DECLARATION OF RIGHTS

Largely drafted by George Mason and adopted by state convention in June 1776, prior to the when the rest of the colonies declared their Independence, the Virginia Declaration of Rights influenced both the Declaration of Independence and the wording of the Bill of Rights to the U.S. Constitution. The Virginia Declaration started from the premise that "all men are by nature equally free and Independent, and have certain inherent rights, of which, when they enter into a state of society, they cannot, by any compact, deprive or divest their posterity." The document went on to proclaim that "whenever any Government shall be found Inadequate or contrary to these purposes, a majority of the community hath an Indubitable, unalienable, and Indefeasible right, to reform, alter, or abolish it, in such manner as shall be judged most conducive to the publick weal" (Kurland and Lerner 1987, 5:3).

In addition to announcing the doctrine of separation of powers, the Virginia Declaration enumerated a number of important rights, some of which were later repeated in other state declarations and, eventually, by the U.S. Bill of Rights. Mason, who had served as a representative to the U.S. Constitution Convention of 1787, had vigorously opposed the adoption of the U.S. Constitution in part because it originally lacked such a Bill.

The rights which the Virginia Declaration listed included the right to confrontation in capital cases; the right "to a speedy trial"; a provision against self-incrimination and against deprivation of liberty "except by the laws of the land" (a phrase similar to that later incorporated into the due process clauses of the Fifth and Fourteenth Amendments); a prohibition against "excessive bail" and "cruel and unusual punishments"; a prohibition against general warrants or seizures of persons "whose offense is not particularly described and supported by evidence" (this has a parallel in the Fourth Amendment of the U.S. Constitution); a provision for trial by jury; a provision for freedom of the press, and a provision, largely added at James Madison's insistence, for "the free exercise of religion." The Virginia Declaration's proclamation, similar to language later used in the Second Amendment to the U.S. Constitution, "that a well-regulated Militia, composed of the body of the people, trained to arms, is the proper, natural, and safe defense of a free State" was specifically tied to the principles that "Standing Armies, in time of peace, should be avoided as dangerous to liberty" and that "the military should be under strict subordination to, and governed by, the civil power." The Declaration also refers to the necessity of "frequent recurrence to fundamental principles" (Kurland and Lerner 1987, 5:3-4).

See also Bill of Rights: Declaration of Independence; Madison, James; Mason, George.

For Further Reading:

Conley, Patrick T. and John P. Kaminski. 1992. *The Bill of Rights and the States: The Colonial and Revolutionary Origins of American Liberties.* Madison, WI: Madison House.

Kurland, Philip B., and Ralph Lerner, eds. 1987. *The Founders' Constitution.* 5 vols. Chicago: University of Chicago Press.

VOTING RIGHTS, CONSTITUTIONAL AMENDMENTS RELATING TO

By comparison to other areas of the world, voting in the American colonies was fairly widespread, but many of the colonies essentially limited the franchise to white male property owners, sometimes also requiring that they be church members or that they affirm basic tenets of Protestant Christianity. Delegates to the U.S. Constitutional Convention debated whether to extend voting rights to all males or to limit them to those who owned a specified amount of property. Many framers believed that a modicum of property was necessary both to secure a degree of independence—at a time when many elections were public—and to prevent the poor from using their votes to despoil the rich. Others expressed greater faith in the "common man" and believed that individuals without large amounts of property had demonstrated their commitment to the nation during the Revolutionary War.

Ultimately, the delegates to the Constitutional Convention of 1787 did not provide a universal standard for voting in the United States. Instead, Article I, Section 2 specified that electors for the U.S. House of Representatives "in each State shall have the Qualifications requisite for electors of the most numerous Branch of the State Legislature," thus allowing qualifications to vary from one state to another. The Constitution also specified that individuals who were held in slavery—the specific term was not used—would be counted as three-fifths of a person for purposes of taxation and representation.

Although voting rights have waxed and waned within various time periods in American history (Keyssar 2000), constitutional amendments have gradually eliminated barriers to voting so that the right now applies fairly universally to adults eighteen years of age and older who have met minimal residency requirements. Many states do limit the right to vote of incarcerated felons, or ex-felons (a particularly questionable practice that has fallen especially on some African American and lower-income communities and that arguably continues to depress political participation), or to individuals with mental illnesses. In addition, partly through the development of more democratic selection processes and partly through formal amendments, the electoral college, while not always guaranteeing that the winner of the electoral vote will also win the popular vote (witness the presidential election of 2000), has also become more democratic. Citizens generally cast their votes for presidential electors not in the belief that such individuals will exercise independent judgment but because these electors are pledged to vote for candidates whom the majority favors.

The Twelfth Amendment accommodated the development of political parties by specifying that presidential electors should cast separate votes for president and vice president, generally assuring that the two candidates would be from the same political party and would not tie as Thomas Jefferson and Aaron Burr had done in the presidential election of 1800. Similarly, the Twenty-third Amendment provided for representation in the electoral college for citizens of the District of Columbia. On a related matter, the Seventeenth Amendment, ratified in 1913, provides for direct popular election of U.S. Senators, who had previously been selected by state legislatures. According to the operative language of this amendment, however, state voters continued to be designated as those with "the qualifications requisite for electors of the most numerous branch of the State legislatures."

Qualifications based on property and religious affiliation had largely faded at the state level by the time Andrew Jackson was elected president in 1828. In addition, more offices, including many state judgeships, were made elective during this time. Still, many states continued to restrict the rights of African Americans, and none yet extended the right to vote to women. The Fourteenth Amendment eliminated the three-fifths clause and provided, in Section 2, that Congress could reduce state representation for states that abridged the rights of males over the age of twenty-one, but this provision was never enforced, actually leading to increased representation of some of the Southern states in the U.S. House of Representatives after slave emancipation. The corresponding provision in Section 3 limiting the right of individuals who had engaged in rebellion against the United States to serve as presidential electors or hold office (the only limitation of voting rights ever adopted by constitutional amendment) allowed Congress to remove this "disability" by a two-thirds vote.

At least on paper, the Fifteenth Amendment (1870) remedied the states' exclusion of blacks from their electorates, but states widely evaded this amendment during the first 100 years of its history through mechanisms as diverse as all-white primaries, grandfather clauses, poll taxes, unequal application of literacy tests, and voter intimidation, and not until 1965 did Congress adopt effective legislation on its behalf. Three years earlier, the states had ratified the Twenty-

Fourth Amendment, outlawing use of the poll tax in federal elections, a prohibition that the Supreme Court extended to the states in *Harper v. Virginia State Board of Elections* in 1966.

Women, many of whom had hoped to get the right to vote along with African-American men, when the Fifteen Amendment was adopted in 1870, waged a long campaign for suffrage that won some early successes in the territories and the western states (Wyoming was the first to extend the vote to women). This movement did not finally succeed at the national level until states adopted the Nineteenth Amendment in 1920. In contrast to the Fifteenth Amendment, once this amendment was adopted, it was quickly implemented. Similarly, the Australian, or secret, ballot (named after its nation of origin), which is regarded as a mainstay of modern democracy, was first introduced in the United States in 1888 and quickly spread throughout the nation without a constitutional amendment (Keyssar 2000, 143).

The Supreme Court has often announced that it considers voting to be a "fundamental right" that is subject to "strict scrutiny," but it stated in *Bush v. Gore* (2000) that there was "no federal constitutional right to vote." Accordingly, although individuals born in Puerto Rico have been citizens since 1917, they do not have the right to vote in presidential elections as long as they reside in Puerto Rico, which is not represented in the electoral college.

The fact that there remains no federal constitutional right to vote was demonstrated when the U.S. Supreme Court partially rebuffed Congress in *Oregon v. Mitchell* (1970) when it decided that Congress had power to lower voting ages to eighteen (they had generally been set at twenty-one) in federal, but not state, elections. Congress subsequently proposed and the states ratified the Twenty-sixth Amendment in 1971, which equalized the lower qualifications for both jurisdictions.

Most battles for national amendments relating to voting rights have been preceded by victories in individual states. The roles of amendments as both instruments of effecting policies relative to voting as symbols of national aspirations to equality are difficult to separate; thus the Fifteenth and Nineteenth

Amendments both serve as benchmarks in the progress of African Americans and American women.

Although the Constitution has successfully extended to vote to most citizens, many remain apathetic, and low American electoral turnouts, especially among the young, the poor, and the uneducated, remain a frequent subject of popular and scholarly commentary. Particularly during the populist and progressive eras, many states, especially in the West, developed mechanisms for voter initiatives and referendums on items of legislation and amendment and recalls of elected officials. Similarly, in a move referred to, but not specifically endorsed by the Twenty-fourth Amendment, many states adopted direct primaries as the chief mechanism by which to select electoral candidates. Although the initiative and referendum have been frequent subjects of amendment at the national level, they have not been embodied into amendments. Similarly, despite long-time calls for greater national control (Burns 1963, 327-28), parties continue to select their nominees for national offices largely on the basis of a patchwork of state legislation.

Despite all the constitutional amendments that have been adopted preventing various forms of discrimination related to voting, the Constitution still does not provide an affirmative guarantee of the "right to vote." Professor Jamin B. Raskin, of the Washington College of Law at American University, has pointed out that 135 national constitutions do guarantee such an affirmative right. Raskin advocates a twentieth-eighth, or right-to-vote, amendment consisting of four sections. The first would affirmatively specify the right of citizens to vote in local, state, and national elections. The second would prevent such voting from being denied on the basis of "political party affiliation or prior condition of incarceration." Section three would resurrect an amendment that was proposed by Congress but failed to receive the necessary number of state ratifications by providing that residents of the District of Columbia would have the same congressional representation to which the District would be entitled "if it were a State," and section four would provide enforcement power to Congress. Although Raskin also favors

abolishing the electoral college, he omitted that suggestion from his proposal for fear that opposition to that particular measure would jeopardize the entire amendment (Raskin 2001).

Other reformers, especially those who have actually proposed new constitutional systems, have suggested that voting reforms are needed to enable voters to indicate their second and third choices in elections and/or to change the method whereby members of the U.S. House of Representatives are currently chosen from single-member, winner-take-all districts to a system in which they are selected through proportional representation. Political scientists generally believe that the current system of single-member districts (in combination with a presidential rather than a parliamentary system) supports the existing two-party system by making it unlikely that a party with some support throughout the entire nation, but no majority within a single district or set of districts, will be at all represented in Congress or the presidency. By contrast to the United States, many European democracies use systems of proportional representation.

See also Democracy and Constitutional Amendments; Fifteenth Amendment; Initiative and Referendum; Nineteenth Amendment; Seventeenth Amendment; Twelfth Amendment; Twenty-fourth Amendment; Twenty-sixth Amendment; Twenty-third Amendment; other Voting Rights entries.

For Further Reading:

Burns, James MacGregor. 1963. *The Deadlock of Democracy: Four-Party Politics in America.* Englewood Cliffs, NJ: Prentice-Hall, Inc.

Keyssar, Alexander. 2000. *The Right to Vote: The Constitutional History of Democracy in the United States.* New York: Basic Books.

Pitts, Michael J. 2003. "Section 5 of the Voting Rights Act: A Once and Future Remedy." *Denver University Law Review* 81:225–288.

Raskin, Jamin B. 2001. "A Right to Vote." *The American Prospect* 12 (27 August): 10–12.

Roman, Jose D. 2002. "Trying to Fit an Oval Shaped Island into a Square Constitution: Arguments for Puerto Rican Statehood." *Fordham Urban Law Journal* 29 (April): 1681–1713.

VOTING RIGHTS, LITERACY TESTS

Literacy tests were among the tools that white southerners used to discriminate against African Americans. Although the idea that voters should be able to read and write can be justified under democratic theory, literacy and "understanding" tests were frequently administered so as to permit illiterate whites to vote but exclude highly-educated blacks (Lawson 1976, 86-88).

In *Lassiter v. North Hampton County Board of Elections* (1959), the Supreme Court ruled that state power over suffrage included the right to set literacy requirements. That same year members of Congress introduced amendments to limit state voting restrictions to those concerned with age, residence, or imprisonment. From 1961 through 1963, members of Congress introduced several amendments either to establish free and universal suffrage throughout the United States or specifically to abolish literacy tests in federal elections.

In the Voting Rights Act of 1965, Congress decided to address this issue through legislation instead. In *South Carolina v. Katzenbach* (1966), the Court held that congressional power under Section 2 of the Fifteenth Amendment was sufficient to uphold a literacy test ban in states that congress identified as having low registration and voting rates. Similarly, In *Katzenbach v. Morgan* (1966), the Court upheld a provision of the law granting the right to vote to anyone who had completed a sixth-grade education in an accredited Puerto Rican school. In 1970, in the first of a number of extensions of the 1965 Act that are still in effect, Congress banned literacy tests completely. Relying on the enforcement provisions of the Fourteenth and Fifteenth Amendments, the Court upheld this ban in *Oregon v. Mitchell* (1970).

See also Enforcement Clauses in Amendments; Fifteenth Amendment.

VOTING RIGHTS, RESIDENCY REQUIREMENTS

Members of Congress introduced more than thirty proposals from 1959 to 1971 seeking to address state residency requirements for voting.

Although none were adopted, in *Oregon v. Mitchell* (1970), the Supreme Court upheld a provision in the 1970 revision of the Voting Rights Act of 1965 that standardized such requirements for federal elections at thirty days. Similarly, in *Dunn. v. Blumstein* (1972), the Court struck down a Tennessee residency requirement of one year in the state and three months in the county as violating the equal protection clause of the Fourteenth Amendment and impairing the right to travel. The Court did not oppose the state's desire to avoid fraud but thought there were less intrusive measures to combat it. It also noted that extended periods of residency did not guarantees voter competence or familiarity with the issues. In *Marston v. Lewis* (1973), the Supreme Court upheld a fifty-day requirement designed to allow states to prepare accurate voting lists.

For Further Reading:
Dunn v. Blumstein, 405 U.S. 330 (1972).

W

WADE, EDWIN LEE (1932–)

Described on the flyleaf of his book *Constitution 2000: A Federalist Proposal for the Next Century* (published in 1995) as "a businessman, lawyer, writer, lecturer, and former public official" who worked as a foreign service officer and who holds a number of degrees including a law degree from Georgetown University, Edwin Wade used his book to call for ten new amendments, most of which he designed to strengthen the national government. His first amendment, the 28th, called for reforming Congress by cutting the size of the House to 225 members, apportioned as now according to population. Wade further hoped to cut the total number of House committees to 12 and to limit the number of subcommittees on any committee to five. Wade would restrict the total House employees to no more than 20 times its membership, and curtail expenditures for "partisan or religious" activities (Wade 1995, 292). This, like the rest of the proposed amendments, was to be inoperative unless ratified by conventions in three-fourths of the states by December 31, 2001.

Wade's next proposal applied a similar remedy to the U.S. Senate. Cutting the number of senators in half, Wade proposed limiting its total number of committees to eight and the number of employees to 2,500. A provision subjecting Senate debate to "reasonable limitations" was apparently designed to limit filibusters.

Wade's third proposal specified that House members would serve four-year terms and be selected in presidential election years, with senators also serving four-year terms but being elected in off-year elections, beginning in 2006.

Wade's directed his next three proposals to the executive branch, which he believed has been severely weakened. Wade proposed allowing presidential and vice-presidential tickets to be placed on the ballot if they got petitions "equal to or greater than two percent of the total popular vote cast in the immediately preceding [presidential] election" (Wade 1995, 294). These officeholders would be selected directly by "either a plurality or a majority of the national popular vote" (*Id.,* 295). The president would select a cabinet officer to serve as a personal chief of staff, thus helping to assure their direct access to the president. Wade would have further limited the presidential staff to no more than twice the size of Congress. A separate amendment would repeal the Twenty-second Amendment, so that presidents would no longer be limited to serving two full terms. Wade did not favor a presidential item veto, fearing that with such power the president "will have become the 536th member of Congress" (*Id.,* 145).

In examining justice in the courts, Wade was particularly concerned about pretrial discovery procedures, which be believed were more often used to embarrass litigants than to get to the truth. He accordingly provided in his next amendment that no persons in civil cases should be compelled to give testimony "except before or under the supervision of a judge or other officer or officers of the United States as provided by law" (Wade 1995, 296–297). Wade further proposed establishing and maintaining "a system of pretrial court-annexed mandatory arbitration" to most civil cases (*Id.,* 297). Fearing that judges were leaving the judiciary to take jobs with some of the interests in whose behalf they had previously ruled, Wade further proposed limiting such employment.

Believing that the Federal Reserve System was exercising inordinate power that belonged only to Congress, Wade's next proposal provided that:

Congress shall make no law which delegates any power it possesses pursuant to Article I, Section 8 for the purpose of regulating banks and the banking system or credit and money in its several forms to any department or agency of the government of the United States unless such delegation is based on a clear statement of legislative policy and contains a system of precise, objective standards for application to specific cases, and in no case shall such delegation be made to any private persons, firms, partnerships, corporations, or to any other private enterprises or privately owned organizations. (Wade 1995, 299)

Although citing Supreme Court decisions restricting the regulation of vulgar words and flag burning (*Id.,* 232), Wade focuses his last proposed amendment on campaign financing. Specifically, he proposed allowing Congress to limit expenditures for elections and forbid "federal general revenue of any nature or description" from being "used to finance or otherwise assist any political campaign for any elective office anywhere in the United States of America" (Wade 1995, 300).

Although he proposed ten amendments, Wade also opposed some others. He believed that the existing Second Amendment was directly tied to the maintenance of a militia and not an individual personal right to own guns. He accordingly proposed maintaining the Second Amendment as he believed it already was meant to be. Believing that the U.S. Supreme Court had usurped power when it upheld the right to abortion in *Roe v. Wade* (1973), Wade argued that this issue should be left to the states. Wade was as adamant against a human life amendment as against Supreme Court action, believing that "neither the decision nor the Amendment belong in the Constitution. Our Constitution

again is about the way our federal government is *constituted.* It is not about social policy" (Wade 1995, 259). Finding a number of flaws in proposed balanced budget amendments, Wade also argued that the solution to annual budget deficits lies "in Congress, not in the Constitution" (*Id.,* 267).

In an appendix to his book, Wade included a "Proposed Uniform Application From the Several States to Congress Requesting and Requiring That a Constitutional Convention Be Called" (Wade 1995, 287). Scheduled to meet in Philadelphia no later than January 6, 1999, the convention was to consist of "no more than two hundred twenty-five delegates, to be apportioned among the several states in proportion to the total number of Representatives and Senators possessed by each state" (*Id.,* 287). Wade proposed limiting the convention to the matters addressed in his book, with the results to be ratified by conventions within the states. Wade would forbid federal officeholders from serving as delegates. He would further mandate the convention to establish a nine-member Committee on Consolidation and Restatement, which would "prepare a Consolidation and Restatement of the Constitution as then in effect" (*Id.,* 290).

See also Constitutional Conventions.

For Further Reading:
Wade, Edwin L. 1995. *Constitution 2000: A Federalist Proposal for the Next Century.* Chicago: Let's Talk Sense.

WALLACE, WILLIAM KAY (1886–?)

American diplomat William Kay Wallace offered his critique of the U.S. Constitution and proposals for reform during the Great Depression (see Vile 1991c, 68–70). Wallace believed that the framers had built the Constitution on such ideas as individualism, natural rights, the social contract, and a geographically based state that were now seriously outdated. He further believed that economic reorganization was as important as political change.

Wallace advocated what he identified as "scientific capitalism" and declared it to be "the one best way, or the method of efficiency" (Wallace 1932, 104). His initial description of the state as "the directive agency of social control, a clearinghouse that will expedite and adjust public affairs" (*Id.,* 137), was vague, although he did articulate his belief that a new government should outlaw war. Initially, he indicated that the form, but not the substance, of the existing three branches of government could be maintained.

Wallace presented his specific proposals, which he hoped to initiate through a constitutional convention, in a chapter near the end of his book. There he outlined five broad guarantees that the new government should assume. The first was a guarantee of economic liberty. He included specific rights "to the full fruits of one's labor," "to economic security," "to education," and "to leisure" (Wallace 1932, 182).

The second was a guarantee of social security designed to cover "all of the contingencies and possible caprices of fortune in the life of the individual." More specific guarantees included "social insurance" covering old age and unemployment, "child welfare and training," adjusted work schedules, and "adult education" (Wallace 1932, 183).

Wallace's third guarantee was that of a "more effective government." To this end, he proposed replacing the current states with nine regional states, each with four to six representatives. These representatives would form a national board of directors (presumably unicameral) who would select from its members a president, appoint all governmental officials from the civil service, and exercise legislative functions.

To implement his fourth guarantee of "personal liberty and property," Wallace advocated transferring all corporate enterprises from private to public ownership and paying current holders of such property in governmental bonds. The new industries would be "scientifically regulated," with the profit motive being replaced; individuals would, however, still be able to own other forms of private property "in order to stimulate the creative ingenuity of all the citizens" (Wallace 1932, 188).

Wallace's fifth guarantee was for a "planned national economy" (Wallace 1932, 189). He favored making the state the "supreme economic arbiter," with power to conscript citizens in war and peace. The state would further coordinate economic activities and organize credit "as a public not a private function" (*Id.,* 191).

See also Constitutional Conventions; Social and Economic Rights.

For Further Reading:

Vile, John R. 1991c. *Rewriting the United States Constitution: An Examination of Proposals from Reconstruction to the Present.* New York: Praeger.

Wallace, William Kay. 1932. *Our Obsolete Constitution.* New York: John Day.

WAR, DECLARATION OF

When New York and Rhode Island ratified the U.S. Constitution, they proposed that Congress should not be able to declare war except by a two-thirds vote. This proposal was reintroduced at the Hartford Convention of 1815. Beginning about the time of World War I, members of Congress introduced a number of proposals either to require supermajorities of two-thirds or three-fourths or to prohibit Congress from declaring war except in cases of invasion. Some proposals for a national initiative and referendum would also have required voter initiation or approval of such declarations.

World War II marks the last occasion that the United States officially declared war, yet the nation has subsequently been involved in costly conflicts in Korea and Vietnam as well as in a host of other minor engagements for which congressional approval was either tepid or lacking. Congress attempted to rein in presidential powers in the War Powers Resolution of 1973, but the law has not proved altogether successful (J. H. Ely 1993). Perhaps in part because of this resolution, President George H. W. Bush did get prior congressional consent for what proved to be a successful repulsion of Iraq in 1991 after its invasion of Kuwait, and George W. Bush got subsequent congressional authorization for the invasion of Iraq.

Beginning in 1986, Democratic Representative Andy Jacobs Jr. of Indiana, a veteran of the Korean War, introduced several proposals to repeal the provision in Article I, Section 8 that grants Congress the power to declare war. According to one of his legislative aides, Jacobs intended to call attention to the manner in which presidential foreign policy decisions have encroached on congressional powers (Tom Runge, telephone conversation with author, June 15, 1995).

An author concerned with distortions of the U.S. Constitution by members of the press has proposed an amendment to "clarify the war powers of both Congress and the president" (Bonsell 1995, 345). He would require a three-fourths majority of Congress to declare war, a declaration that would result in the automatic suspension of "the privilege of the Writ of Habeas Corpus and the Thirteenth Amendment [presumably to allow for a draft]." Congress would be permitted to declare war, without the accompanying power to suspend the writ of habeas corpus or the Thirteenth Amendment, by a two-thirds vote. His proposal also called for a provision, relating to the First Amendment, specifying that "[t]he right of the people to peacefully protest or legally resist any military action under this article shall be protected by all governments within the United States" (*Id.,* 345).

See also Hartford Convention; Initiative and Referendum.

For Further Reading:

Bonsell, Thomas. 1995. *The Un-Americans: Trashing of the United States Constitution in the American Press.* Wauna, WA: Country Cottage Publishing.

Ely, John Hart. 1993. *War and Responsibility: Constitutional Lessons of Vietnam and Its Aftermath.* Princeton, NJ: Princeton University Press.

WAR, OPPOSITION TO GOVERNMENT DURING

The U.S. Constitution protects dissent even in times of war. The Supreme Court has ruled,

however, that speech that is normally permissible might be suppressed during wartime when such speech creates a "clear and present danger" that Congress has a right to prevent (*Schenck v. United States* 1919, 52).

Public opposition to U.S. participation in the Vietnam War was particularly intense. Although the Supreme Court upheld a federal law prohibiting the destruction of draft cards (*United States v. O'Brien* (1968)), it was otherwise fairly protective of political protesters during this period.

Between 1966 and 1969, Democratic Representative Olin (Tiger) Teague of Texas, a World War II veteran who chaired the Veterans' Affairs Committee, introduced at least three resolutions to make it unlawful to aid or encourage the United States' enemies during a war. His proposal, in obvious tension with the free speech and press guarantees of the First Amendment, would have included restrictions on "public demonstrations, public writings, [and] public speeches" (H.J. Res. 102, 1967).

See also First Amendment.

For Further Reading:

Schenck v. United States, 249 U.S. 47 (1919).

Vile, John R., David L. Hudson Jr., and David Schultz, eds. 2009. *The Encyclopedia of the First Amendment.* Washington DC: CQ Press.

WAR, POWER DURING

Constitutional provisions have afforded legal authority for extensive expansion of federal war powers, especially in this century. During World War I, the government used such powers to seize the nation's railroads and telephone and telegraph systems. Concern with winning the war also fueled the drive for national alcoholic prohibition (C. May 1989, 26, 60–93) that eventually resulted in adoption of the Eighteenth Amendment.

From 1922 to 1939, at least 25 amendments sought to grant the government power not only to conscript soldiers but also to conscript property during times of war (sponsors included Indiana

Democratic Representative Louis Ludlow and North Dakota Republican Senator Gerald Nye). At least some of these proposals were motivated by a desire to take profits out of war. Some proposals specifically sought to exempt governmental takings in wartime from the Fifth Amendment requirement that the government provide just compensation.

In *Youngstown Sheet & Tube Co. v. Sawyer* (1952), the Supreme Court invalidated President Harry S. Truman's seizure of the steel mills during the Korean War, but the justices focused on the lack of congressional authority for such a seizure (Congress had decided against such authority when it adopted the Taft-Hartley Act of 1947) rather than on any inherent constitutional limitations on the subject.

The "war" on terrorism poses special problems because part of it takes place on American soil. In the aftermath of the terrorist attacks against the United States of September 11, 2001, many questions remain about the appropriateness of military trials, of the detention of suspects, and related issues.

See also Eighteenth Amendment; Fifth Amendment; War, Declaration of.

For Further Reading:
May, Christopher N. 1989. *In the Name of War.* Cambridge: Harvard University Press.

WAR, PROHIBITION OF

Republican Senator Lynn Frazier of North Dakota consistently introduced amending proposals from 1926 to 1939 to prohibit war by declaring it to be illegal. New York Republican (and later American Laborite) representative Vito Marcantonio also submitted such a proposal in 1936. Other proposals called for requiring a popular referendum before the nation could go to war.

The 1920s and 1930s saw substantial growth in antiwar sentiment and an American Committee for the Outlawry of War was established in December 1921. In August 1928, representa-

tives of the United States and 14 other nations signed the Kellogg-Briand Pact renouncing the use of war, but the Senate predicated its 85-to-1 ratification of this treaty in January 1929 on reserving the nation's right to self-defense (Ellis 1961, 212), and the treaty was unable to avert World War II.

See also Initiative and Referendum.

For Further Reading:
Ellis, L. Ethan. 1961. *Frank B. Kellogg and American Foreign Relations, 1925–1929.* New Brunswick, NJ: Rutgers University Press.

Morrison, Charles C. 1972. *The Outlawry of War: A Constructive Policy for World Peace.* New York: Garland Publishing.

WARREN COURT

Earl Warren served as chief justice of the United States Supreme Court from 1953 to 1969, and scholars generally refer to the Court during this period as the Warren Court. A former district attorney, attorney general, three-term California governor, and Republican vice-presidential candidate, Warren proved to be a far more liberal and activist justice than President Eisenhower, who appointed him to the position, had anticipated. Moreover, although not nearly as intellectual as his strong-minded colleagues Hugo Black, William O. Douglas, Felix Frankfurter, John Marshall Harlan, and William Brennan (another liberal appointment that Eisenhower grew to regret), Warren proved to be an effective leader who could often achieve a greater degree of consensus than might otherwise have been expected.

Shortly after Warren assumed the reins of the Court, it issued its unanimous decision in *Brown v. Board of Education* (1954), overturning *Plessy v. Ferguson* (1896) and ending longstanding de jure racial segregation in the United States. In numerous subsequent decisions, the Court showed some flexibility in the implementation of desegregation decisions but never deviated from the central principle articulated in

Brown. Significantly, in *Bolling v. Sharpe* (1954), the Court used the due process clause of the Fifth Amendment to strike down egregious forms of discrimination at the federal level, just as it used the equal protection clause of the Fourteenth Amendment to strike down state segregation laws.

The Warren Court took a relatively strict view of separation of church and state, outlawing vocal prayer in public schools in *Engel v. Vitale* (1962) and devotional Bible reading in *Abington v. Schempp* (1963). These decisions prompted numerous proposals for constitutional amendments.

In *Baker v. Carr* (1962), the Court issued its decision declaring that state legislative apportionment was not a political question but was justiciable under the equal protection clause of the Fourteenth Amendment. In a follow-up case, *Reynolds v. Sims* (1964), the Court applied the "one person one vote" standard to both houses of state legislatures. These decisions stirred considerable sentiment for a constitutional amendment to give states greater leeway. Focusing on the apportionment decisions and other liberal rulings, the conservative John Birch Society launched an effort to impeach Earl Warren.

The Warren Court's rulings on the Fourteenth Amendment contained some of its most influential constitutional interpretations. Before Warren came to the Court, it had already begun the process of selectively incorporating some of the important limitations on the national government that were found in the Bill of Rights and applying them to the states—see *Palko v. Connecticut* (1937) and *Adamson v. California* (1947). The Warren Court rapidly accelerated this process, especially with respect to the rights of criminal defendants. Thus, in *Mapp v. Ohio* (1961), it applied the exclusionary rule to the states; in *Gideon v. Wainwright* (1963), it extended the right to appointed counsel for indigents; and in *Miranda v. Arizona* (1966), it extended a panoply of rights previously required only at the federal level. In *Griswold v. Connecticut* (1965), the Court struck down a Connecticut law proscribing birth control by holding that the provisions in the Bill of Rights had penumbras that encompassed the right to privacy, thus laying a foundation for the Burger Court's liberal abortion decision in *Roe v. Wade* (1973) in the following decade. The Court also broadened protection under the Fourth Amendment, specifically outlawing warrantless eavesdropping in *Katz v. United States* (1967). In his last major decision from the bench, *Powell v. McCormack* (1969), Warren further narrowed the political questions doctrine (overturning an attempt by the House of Representatives by majority vote to refuse to seat of a member who met the age, residency, and citizenship requirements spelled out in the Constitution), with possible implications for future amending cases.

Many of the Warren Court's decisions led to proposed amendments, but none proved successful. The Court did, however, encounter considerable political opposition. When Warren first expressed his desire to resign, many of the criticisms of the Court as being too liberal and too activist fell on President Lyndon Johnson's choice of Justice Abe Fortas, who withdrew from consideration for chief justice and later resigned from the Court. President Richard Nixon subsequently appointed Warren Burger to this position. Both Burger and his successor, William Rehnquist, have issued more conservative decisions, in many cases not so much reversing as slowing earlier trends (Funston 1977). The Courts headed by Warren Burger, William Rehnquist, and John Roberts have been considerably more sympathetic to states' interests than was the Warren Court. The Warren Court stands as one of the clearest examples of the way the Supreme Court can inaugurate a constitutional revolution without the adoption of new amendments.

See also *Abington v. Schempp; Baker v. Carr; Engel v. Vitale;* Fourteenth Amendment; Prayer in Schools; Privacy.

For Further Reading:

Funston, Richard Y. 1977. *Constitution Counterrevolution? The Warren Court and the Burger Court: Judicial Policy Making in Modern America.* New York: Schenkman.

Schwartz, Bernard. 1988. *Super Chief: Earl Warren and His Supreme Court—A Judicial Biography.* New York: New York University Press.

WASHINGTON, GEORGE (1732–1799)

George Washington fought for the colonists and British in the French and Indian War, led American forces during the Revolutionary War, presided over the Constitutional Convention of 1787, and served as the nation's first president. Washington set a noble example for the nation, later incorporated into the presidency, in submitting to civilian authority as commander in chief during the Revolutionary War and in renouncing the use of force against Congress to gain legitimate demands of members of the military. Although he was not as intellectually gifted as John Adams, Thomas Jefferson, or James Madison, he articulated a vision of America's destiny that was remarkably prescient (Bradley 1945). At the Constitutional Convention, over which he presided, Washington did not speak frequently. However, he likely contributed to the Virginia Plan: his regal bearing lent a solemnity to the occasion, and the delegates' conviction that he would serve as the nation's first president led them to create a stronger executive than they probably otherwise would have done. Washington's subsequent wholehearted support of the new Constitution and his service as first president were critical to the forging of the Union. He was supremely conscious that his actions as president would set important precedents, and he acted accordingly. His farewell address, in which he warned about the dangers of encroachments by one governmental branch over others; about what he considered to be the baneful role of political parties (although often identified as a Federalist, Washington had both Federalists and Democratic-Republicans in his cabinet and tried to project the image that he was above parties); and of the danger of entangling foreign alliances, is an important state paper. Washington's precedent of stepping down from the presidency after two terms was not broken until the 20th-century administration of President Franklin D. Roosevelt, after which it was formally reestablished by adoption of the Twenty-second Amendment.

The first ten amendments, known as the Bill of Rights, was proposed and ratified during Washington's first term, as was the Eleventh Amendment, limiting judicial jurisdiction over suits against the states. Like James Madison, Washington believed that although not all the amendments in the Bill of Rights were absolutely necessary, they could do no harm and would help quiet the fears that opponents of the new Constitution had stirred (Vile 1992, 50). As president, Washington agreed to the plan by Alexander Hamilton, his secretary of the treasury, to establish a national bank, even though the creation of such a bank rested on implied, rather than specifically enumerated, constitutional powers and was opposed by Secretary of State Thomas Jefferson, who thought that the bank interfered with powers reserved to the states under the Tenth Amendment. Without Washington and Hamilton's broad interpretation of the Constitution, later ratified by the U.S. Supreme Court in *McCullock v. Maryland* (1819), the Constitution would have required considerably more amendments.

In his farewell address, Washington drew the obligation to obedience to government from the presence of a means of peaceful change:

> The Government . . . containing within itself a provision for its own amendment, has a just claim to your confidence and support. Respect for its authority, compliance with its laws, acquiescence in its measures, are duties enjoined by the fundamental maximums of true liberty. The basis of our political system is the right of the people to make and to alter their constitution of government. But the constitution which at any time exists till changed by an explicit and authentic act of the whole people is sacredly obligatory upon all. (quoted in Kaufman 1969, 21)

The author of one of the most comprehensive books on the history of the amending process has used Washington's reference to "explicit and authentic acts" in the above quotation for the title of his volume (Kyvig 1996a). On many other occasions, Washington referred to the amending process as a "constitutional door" (Norham 1988). Thus, in arguing that the new Constitution was not perfect but was a distinct improvement over the Articles of Confederation, Washington noted that it was one in which "a Constitutional door is left open for its amelioration" (Fitzpatrick 1931–1944, 29:411).

See also Banking; Bill of Rights; Constitutional Convention of 1787; Eleventh Amendment; Hamilton, Alexander; Jefferson, Thomas; Twenty-second Amendment.

For Further Reading:

Bradley, Harold W. 1945. "The Political Thinking of George Washington." *Journal of Southern History* 11 (November): 469–486.

Fitzpatrick, John C. 1931–1944. *The Writings of George Washington.* 39 vols. Washington DC: U.S. Government Printing Office.

Kaufman, Burton I. 1969. *Washington's Farewell Address: The View from the 20th Century.* Chicago: Quadrangle Books.

Kyvig, David E. 1996a. *Explicit and Authentic Acts: Amending the Constitution, 1776–1995.* Lawrence: University Press of Kansas.

Norham, George W. 1988. "A Constitutional Door Is Opened for Amendment." *Texas Bar Journal* 51 (September): 804–806.

Rhodehamel, John. 1998. *The Great Experiment: George Washington and the American Republic.* New Haven, CT: Yale University Press.

Vile, John R. 1992. *The Constitutional Amending Process in American Political Thought.* New York: Praeger.

WATSON, GREGORY (1960–)

Gregory Watson served as an aide to Texas senator Ric Williamson. As a sophomore economics major at the University of Texas at Austin, Watson wrote a paper for a government class in which he examined the amendment to delay congressional pay raises until an election intervened, which had been introduced in 1789 as part of the original Bill of Rights. He concluded that this proposal was still a viable subject for state ratification.

Despite receiving a "C" on this paper, Watson launched a one-man campaign, which he personally financed, to ratify this amendment (Bernstein 1992, 537). Watson's efforts were rewarded in 1992 (Watson was then 30 years old) with the putative ratification of the Twenty-seventh Amendment.

Watson continues to advocate "updating" the constitutional amending process, presumably by constitutional amendment. Watson favors requiring that amendments be proposed by a two-thirds vote of the entire congressional membership (rather than, as at present, by those in attendance), and eliminating state legislative ratification. He advocates ratification by national referendum in an election year, with amendments requiring ratification by "a simple majority of all votes cast in not less than two-thirds of the geographical districts that comprise the U.S. House of Representatives" (G. Watson 2000, 16). Watson would permit only one such amendment to be offered in any given election, and it would have to be proposed "no later than a full calendar year prior to the election date so that there can be public discussion and debate on the matter" (*Id.,* 16).

See also Twenty-seventh Amendment.

For Further Reading:

"The Man Who Would Not Quit." 1992. *People* 37 (April 1): 72.

Watson, Gregory. 2000. "I Have a Better Way." *Insights on Law & Society* 1: (Fall) 16.

WEDGWOOD, WILLIAM B. (?–1888)

William B. Wedgwood was a Maine native who moved to New York, where he joined the bar in 1841. He favored numerous reforms during his life, including civil service reform and the emancipation and recolonization of the slaves and the compensation of their owners (Boyd 1992, 22). An author and educator as well as a lawyer, Wedgwood wrote books on New York law and the U.S. Constitution and helped found the City University of New York School of Law (Boyd 1992, 29). Wedgwood's most novel contribution to thinking about constitutional change was a new constitution included in his 1861 book entitled *The Reconstruction of the Government of the United States of America.*

Wedgwood's immediate aim was to halt the progression of the Civil War, and his solution was to allow North and South to form two republics, joined together as the "Democratic

Empire." Believing that the United States was heir to the blessings that had once been bestowed on ancient Israel, Wedgwood described his proposed plan as a "theocratic Democracy" (Wedgwood 1861, 15). Wedgwood contained an acknowledgment of God in the preamble. He also stated that the primary purpose of government was to "develop and arrange" natural law principles into "a written code, under the sanction of legislative enactment" (Wedgwood 1861, 17). Early articles of Wedgwood's constitution elaborately described the flag and seal of the Democratic Empire, the former to contain seven colors and 13 stripes in a double rainbow containing, among other things, the otherwise unexplained symbolical letters W.C.P.P.

Wedgwood's constitution contained a number of novel features. In several places it went into detail about the relationship between natural rights and political rights. It guaranteed a good education to all and required that all citizens labor (Wedgwood 1861, 16). Although protecting the right to worship, it prohibited "the worship of idols and the sacrifice of human beings" (*Id.,* 17). Several times it sanctioned the government's right to exercise eminent domain.

Wedgwood would have set up three degrees, or levels, of government—state, national, and imperial. Each would comprise officeholders "of high moral and religious character" (Wedgwood 1861, 18). States would fall naturally into "Labor States" and "Capital States," with Wedgwood advocating extension of the Missouri Compromise line "west until it reaches the Atlantic *[sic]* Ocean" (*Id.,* 19). Wedgwood would divide each of the three levels of government into legislative, executive, and judicial branches, with terms in the respective Houses of Representatives being one, two, and four years and those in the respective Senates being two, four, and six years. Similarly, state governors would serve for two years, the president for four years, and the emperor for six years.

Wedgwood described the powers of state government in great detail. State powers would include regulation of property, education, and highways; providing employment for the needy; and enacting laws for domestic relations. National powers seemed to be designed to handle problems between and among the states. The

imperial government (headquartered in New York) would deal with matters of defense and diplomacy, with the emperor serving as commander in chief of the army and navy.

Wedgwood believed that the impending Civil War had been largely precipitated by those who had spoken contemptuously, sometimes from the pulpit, of the old Constitution and of those who owned slaves. Wedgwood accordingly proposed that "slanderous words, coming from whatever source they may come, must be suppressed and punished. All unkind language, by which the feelings of a fellow citizen may be injured, should be carefully avoided" (Wedgwood 1861, 26).

Wedgwood hoped that Canada, Mexico, and other Central and South American republics would eventually join the new empire, "triumphantly" vindicating the Monroe Doctrine (Wedgwood 1861, 27). Wedgwood ended his discourse with reference to the four horses of the biblical book of Revelation.

See also Christian Amendment.

For Further Reading:

Boyd, Steven R., ed. 1992. *Alternative Constitutions for the United States: A Documentary History.* Westport, CT: Greenwood Press.

Wedgwood, William B. 1861. *The Reconstruction of the Government of the United States of America: A Democratic Empire Advocated and an Imperial Constitution Proposed.* New York: John H. Tingley.

WELFARE PAYMENTS, RIGHT TO

Although it is generally accurate to say that "welfare benefits are legislative choices, not constitutional commands" (Lieberman 1992, 574), courts have surrounded welfare recipients with certain constitutional protections. Thus, in *Shapiro v. Thompson* (1969), the Supreme Court ruled that a Connecticut one-year residency requirement for welfare recipients violated the right to travel, and in *Saenz v. Roe* (1999) the Court struck down differential welfare benefits for new state residents. Similarly, in *Goldberg v.*

Kelly (1970), the Court ruled that a New York law that did not provide welfare recipients with a hearing before terminating benefits was unconstitutional.

In 1971, Republican Representative Edwin Eshleman of Pennsylvania introduced an amendment declaring that welfare was "not a right, but is to be determined in accordance with the specific provisions of . . . laws, duly enacted by the Congress of the United States or by the State or political subdivision involved" (H.J. Res. 206). On a related topic, a proposal by Rhode Island's ratifying convention in 1790 would have specified "that Congress should have power to establish a uniform rule of inhabitancy and settlement of the poor of the different States throughout the United States" (Ames 1896, 189).

Congress has largely attempted to deal with the issue of welfare through legislative action. This legislation has allowed states to require that those on welfare seek employment. It has also limited the number of years that recipients can remain on welfare.

See also Social and Economic Rights.

For Further Reading:

Ames, Herman. 1896. *The Proposed Amendments to the Constitution of the United States during the First Century of Its History.* Reprint, New York: Burt Franklin, 1970.

Lieberman, Jethro K. 1992. *The Evolving Constitution: How the Supreme Court Has Ruled on Issues from Abortion to Zoning.* New York: Random House.

WEST, JAMES C. (?–1946)

One of the least accessible proposals for a new constitution was contained in a book published by James C. West in Springfield, Missouri, in 1890. The only known copy is now a fragile document in the Library of Congress, but fortunately, the proposal has been reprinted (Boyd 1992).

West served as a clerk, a newspaper editor, and a prosecuting attorney, and although he was a Democrat, his ideology was close to that of the

Populists (Boyd 1992, 68–69). The historian who reprinted West's constitution noted that it reflected "the limited horizon of a mid-western small town political observer" (*Id.,* 70). Although most of West's proposals followed the outline of the Constitution of 1787, he added several features that made his proposal unique.

Congress remained fairly similar, but West added a requirement that members be natural born and sought to guarantee one representative for every 175,000 persons. He would have excluded individuals from the House who were worth more than $25,000 and senators who were worth more than $50,000. He would reduce the terms of senators to four years, and make an individual ineligible to either house who had "not labored five years, after he had attained the age of ten years, at either agricultural or some mechanical arts" (Boyd 1992, 74). Members would have to attend all congressional sessions except in cases of sickness. Their oath would obligate them to seek "the greatest good of the greatest number," and they would swear not to "approve of anything contrary to the spirit of the Constitution, either express or implied" or risk "the vengeance of God . . . and the universal detestation of mankind" (*Id.,* 74). Wedgwood would limit the wages of members of Congress to no more than 15 times the wage of laboring farmhands. West attempted to guard against committee changes in a bill contrary to its sponsor's intentions and appeared to make provision for the House of Representatives to act alone to override a presidential veto of a finance bill.

In listing the powers of Congress, West attempted to prevent the government from collecting surplus revenue. However, he favored "a tax on the sumptuousness of the people" as well as taxes on land and income. He also sought to limit borrowing except in cases of war and not until "the circulating medium" reached at least $60 per person (Boyd 1992, 78). Generally, he wanted to maintain the circulating capital at $40 per person. West favored making it a crime for persons or corporations to "engage in any pool, combine, trust or rebate system," and he hoped to prevent the immigration of persons who "Congress thinks are detrimental" (*Id.,* 78, 81).

West wanted to limit the president's salary to no more than 125 times the average wage for a laboring farmhand. The president's powers, like those of the judiciary, remained unchanged.

After repeating the core of the current amending process, West suggested that amendments "which will render null and void any provision of this Constitution" would require consent by three-fourths of the House and a majority of voters, whereas amendments adding to the Constitution would require only the former. West proposed that his constitution would go into effect when ratified by two-thirds of the states. His document included all 15 amendments that were then part of the Constitution, except for the Twelfth, which he omitted in favor of choosing the president by popular vote.

For Further Reading:

Boyd, Steven R., ed. 1992. *Alternative Constitutions for the United States: A Documentary History.* Westport, CT: Greenwood Press.

WILLARD, FRANCES
(1839–1898)

Descended from a prominent New England family, Frances Willard was one of the driving forces both for national alcoholic prohibition and for women's suffrage. Both movements began as state-based movements, the first being embodied for a time after her death in the Eighteenth Amendment before being repealed by the Twenty-first, and the second coming to fruition with the ratification of the Nineteenth Amendment in 1920.

Born in new Rochester, New York, but largely raised on a farm in the Wisconsin Territory, Frances Willard, who preferred to be called "Frank," attended college in Milwaukee and at the Northwestern Female College in Evanston, Illinois. In college, Willard had a conversion experience, later joining the Methodist Church. Subsequently serving in a number of teaching and educational administration positions, which included the presidency of the Evanston College of Ladies and, when it was made part of Northwestern University, as dean of women, Willard became actively involved in the temperance movement in Chicago. She rapidly rose from serving as president of the Chicago Woman's Christian Temperance Union to the corresponding secretaryship of the National Women's Temperance Convention, to the presidency of the Woman's Christian Temperance Union, where she served from 1879 until her death, and of the World's Woman's Christian Temperance Union ("Francis Willard," 1928–1936).

Although she would have preferred to be self-supporting, Willard, who remained single, accepted a salary with the organization so that she could devote all her efforts to the cause. At least initially, the organization flourished under her leadership. Rather than focusing on economic arguments, she emphasized protecting the values of home and hearth, and advocated women's suffrage and other reforms. Her later conversion to the ideas of Fabian socialism did not prove particularly popular in America. She traveled and lectured widely for the WCTU and spent considerable time in England in her later years.

See also Eighteenth Amendment; Nineteenth Amendment; Women's Christian Temperance Union.

For Further Reading:

Dubois, Ellen Carol. 1991. "Frances Willard. *The Reader's Companion to American History.* P. 1151. Accessed through *www.galenet.com.*

"Francis Elizabeth Caroline Willard." 1928–1936. *Dictionary of American Biography* Base Set. American Council of Learned Societies. Accessed through *www.galenet.com.*

WILLARD, SIMON, JR.
(1795–1874)

One of the most elaborate plans to rewrite the U.S. Constitution was also one of the earliest, but it slipped quickly into obscurity. Written by Simon Willard Jr., the 195 page proposal was printed in New York in 1815. It has the prolix title *The Columbian Union, Containing General and Particular Explanations of Government,* and the Columbian Constitution, Being an Amendment to the Constitution of the United States: Providing a Yearly Revenue to Government of About Forty Millions of Dollars, and the Inevitable Union of the People by a Rule of Voting, and Exemption from Unnecessary Taxation, Consequently Their Permanent and Perpetual Freedom (Willard 1815).

The author was the descendant of a well-known Indian fighter and colonist also named Simon Willard, the son of a notable Massachusetts clockmaker (to whom the "banjo clock" is attributed) and the father of another. Born in Roxbury, Massachusetts, in 1795, Willard was apprenticed to another watchmaker, and then entered the West Point Military Academy in 1813 at the age of 18. He graduated in 1815, and resigned from the military a year later (Willard 1968, 68). Failing at a crockery-making business, Simon went into clock making with his father, later specializing in chronometers and other nautical devices. He was the oldest living graduate of West Point when he died in 1874 (Robinson and Burt 1996, 13). Biographical information about Willard is sketchy and omits his proposal for a new Union, which, given its date of publication, was probably written while he was at West Point. By contrast, Willard Sr.'s correspondence with Thomas Jefferson about a clock purchased for the Rotunda at the University of Virginia is well known.

As the title of his proposal suggests, Willard was especially interested in renaming the nation. Willard used lots of religious language, with a fairly strong emphasis on the doctrine of original sin, which he associated in politics largely with the baneful influence of political parties, monarchy, and aristocratic privilege. Apart from his religious language, Willard's sentiments were strongly republican, resembling ideas current not only during the French Revolution in France of 1789 but also ideas that American writers such as Joel Barlow and Thomas Jefferson has espoused. Thus, reflecting a Jeffersonian emphasis on farmers, early in his book Willard noted that:

The tiller's soul, forms the patriot of nature, but the civil minds of commodities invites the foreigner of wrong; the move-

ables of traffic, foreign to the fixidity of the soil.

The fixed agriculturalists, are manufacturers most humble servants, and only guardian parent of all commerce. (Willard 1815, 12)

Unlike Jefferson and other contemporary American Republicans (as well as New England Federalists of the day), however, Willard had little interest in federalism, believing that rival governments disrupt civic unity. By contrast:

A general constitution is an agreement, by which not a part, but all the people can understand each other, so as not only to keep out of war, but to direct each other in that kind of pursuit, the most common in society for the general happiness of all. (Willard 1815, 15)

Willard further observed that:

The Columbian Constitution, amendatory to that of the United States, only takes from it partial power, but adds to me more general energy, more liberty, and more unity of general government. (Willard 1815, 23)

In the preamble to his proposed Columbian Constitution, Willard noted "the overthrow of the world's maritime equilibrium" (Willard 1815, 25), an apparent reference to the War of 1812. He also cites the need "for our reformation and the preservation of all that country, that unity of government, and that liberty for which our fathers fought" (Id., 26). The text of the proposed printed Constitution was followed by long explanations that took up almost the last half of the Willard's book. Willard divided his proposed constitution into 27 articles.

Article I of the Columbian Constitution proposed renaming the nation the "Columbian Union" after Christopher Columbus and dividing it into geometrical units. Initially, Columbia would have 34 such districts, populated roughly equally. Many would have been named after existing states, but Willard also hoped to include Canada in the new Union. Willard proposed dividing districts into counties, each with its own capitol, its own towns and town houses, called "Temples" (Willard 1815, 30). Each county with 3,125 or more voters would select a representative to the Columbian Congress, with one representative in the upper house for each five in the lower.

Article II provided for nine annual meetings of states, designated as the May Election, the July Election, the September Election, the Vernal Council, the Summer Council, the Autumnal Council, the August Assembly, the New Year Assembly, and the Columbian Congress, the latter to meet from November through March (Willard 1815, 32–33).

Article III proposed annual elections for the legislative and executive divisions. Six classes of legislators were designated—"actors, directors, commissioners, representers, legislators, and mediators," with the executive being divided into minor presidents, major presidents, special presidents, and the general president (Willard 1815, 34). The Columbian Congress would be bicameral with mediators serving in the higher branch and general legislators in the lower. Suffrage would extent "to every free male person of the Columbian Union, having attained to the age of twenty-one years" (*Id.,* 36). Stockholders, members of a "partial body politic" (presumably, political parties), and, as of the end of the 19th century, slaveholders, would be prevented from holding office (*Id.,* 37).

Article IV provided for other governmental offices. One fascinating proposal would limit the kinds of information in campaign materials (Willard 1815, 43).

Article V contained 11 sections and specified how and when various representatives would be elected. Similarly, Article VI dealt with the elections of presidents, who Willard portrayed—much as in contemporary parliamentary systems—as heads of the respective legislative bodies.

Article VII specified the pay scale for public officials, which was to be paid in "talents," each worth thirteen and one-third cents. The general president would receive 150,000 talents. The Columbian Congress would allocate monies from general revenues to the states to pay for the salaries of county officials.

Article VIII limited the authorization of public monies except through sovereign officials.

Article IX extended the privilege against arrest to such officials. Article X gave equivalences of officers under the old and new constitutions, with, for example, the U.S. Senate to be called the Mediation, the House of Representatives designated as the Grand Council, governors now being called special presidents, and so on. Willard did specify that "[f]or the unity of general government all inferior legislative bodies shall be subservient to those of higher legislative powers" (Willard 1815, 59–60). Similarly, Section 3 voided all conflicting provisions of the current Constitution. Section 4 of this article allowed slavery to continue in states where it then existed while discouraging the slave trade and further growth of slavery. Willard also proposed a slave line, similar to that later enacted in the Missouri Compromise, north of which slavery would have been prohibited.

Article XI allowed Congress to "make all laws necessary for carrying into effect the powers contained in this constitution" (Willard 1815, 52), but Willard does not say whether he intentionally omitted the word "proper." Willard would vest Congress with power to encourage internal improvements.

Article XII authorized the production of Columbian maps with "an accurate projection of uniform points, relatively denoting the places of all capitols, and degree lines describing of Columbia the parallels of latitude, and meridians of longitude, representing oblong squares, in imitation of and equal to all the degrees of Columbia" (Willard 1815, 63). Article XIII further provided for subservient "military, judiciary and other necessary officers" (*Id.,* 64).

Article XIII dealt with Columbian courts, dividing them into four parts. In part tracking and in part elaborating on the language of the Second Amendment, Article XV specified that "[a] well-regulated militia under the general subordination and enfranchisement of all the people being required for their common freedom, the Columbian Congress . . . shall establish . . . a uniform military system of general order throughout the Columbian Union, for training, equipping, instructing, directing and governing the militia" (Willard 1815, 65–66). This article was extensive, specifying military organization, and introducing the general president's executive council, perhaps similar to the modern cabinet.

Article XVI extensively outlined plans for a general currency, protecting against counterfeiting and specifying the denominations of bills (to include bills of $3, $30, $200, and $300). This Article also set interest rates at 6 percent per year (Willard 1815, 78). Article XVII further specified the coins that would be used in the improved union.

Revenue and taxation are the subject of Article XVIII. This article distinguished between "ratemen," who are taxable, and "freeman," who would not be (Willard 1815, 84). To be considered a freeman, an individual:

> shall not be a member privileged, or stockholder of any incorporated company, or partial body politic, or of any pursuit pernicious to the general obedience and welfare of the Columbian Union, who shall be the owner of and not exceeding the quantity of land of either of the following description, viz: an improved farm of one hundred acres of good feasible land. (Willard 1815, 85)

Different standards were set for those pursuing "a necessary mechanical pursuit" (Willard 1815, 85). Taxation would be extended to those who owned or hired slaves, and taxes would be levied on imported luxuries and gambling.

Article XIX provided for clarity in the conveyance of land titles and mortgages. All freemen "shall have an equal right to the common forest of Columbia," with protections provided for "obedient" Indian tribes (Willard 1815, 91). Article XX further provided for uniform weights and measures, while Article XXI provided for copyrights and patents.

Whereas the U.S. Constitution does not specifically mention schools, Willard provided in Article XXII that:

> The Columbian Congress shall establish and make all needful rules and regulations expedient for free schools throughout the Columbian Union under the direction of a general school office, to be kept in the vicinity of the Columbian Capitol: and

which shall provide that the attention of orphans, and minors of poor parents (slaves excepted) shall be as constant and faithful at school, in acquiring a knowledge of government, and other essential advantages of society as those of the rich. (Willard 1815, 93)

Article XXIII further provided for "a general benevolent office" to provide for "the support of the needy" (Willard 1815, 93). Article XXIV would grant Congress full power to regulate marriages and divorces, estates, criminal procedures, bankruptcies, and so forth.

Article XXV provided for the continuing validity of acts of the prior Constitution. Article XXVI permitted inducements to be given to English and Canadian officers who shall cease war against the United States. This novel provision further stated that:

> The Columbian Union shall never assume the superior power and dominion of the seas, but the Columbian Congress shall cause to be kept dismantled, the guns of their vectored ships, so that Columbia shall never excel any combination of naval power. (Willard 1815, 96)

Article XXVII, the final article, provided that the Columbian constitution shall go into effect when ratified in conventions "of three fourths of the compacts of the United States called towns in this constitution, or of two thirds of the legislatures of the several states" (Willard 1815, 96).

After completing the outline of his proposed Columbian Constitution, Willard provided for the adoption of either of two additional provisions (both designated as Article I). The first appeared designed to repeal the three-fifths clause in 1830. The second would have prohibited individuals with direct financial interests in foreign trade from passing laws dealing with the same. Willard further printed the existing U.S. Constitution and specified that the existing Constitution "will remain in full force, and so far constitute a part of the Columbian Constitution" (Willard 1815, 97).

Willard's proposed constitution remains one of the most detailed and enigmatic on record.

Reflecting a mixture of ideas from a variety of sources, as well as an excessive attention to precision and detail that one might expect of a clockmaker, the proposal is not known to have served as a model for others.

See also Jefferson, Thomas; United States of America, Proposed Name Changes.

For Further Reading:

Robinson, Roger W., and Herschel B. Burt, ed. by Robert Edwards. 1996. *The Willard House and Clock Museum and the Willard Family Clockmakers.* Columbia, PA: National Association of Watch and Clock Collectors, Inc.

Willard, John Ware. 1911. *Simon Willard and His Clocks.* Reprint, New York: Dover Publications, 1968. Unabridged and corrected version of 1911, *A History of Simon Willard, Inventor and Clockmaker.*

Willard, Simon, Jr. 1815. *The Columbian Union, Containing General and Particular Explanations of Government, and the Columbian Constitution, Being an Amendment to the Constitution of the United States: Providing a Yearly Revenue to Government of About Forty Millions of Dollars, and the Inevitable Union of the People by a Rule of Voting, and Exemption from Unnecessary Taxation, Consequently Their Permanent and Perpetual Freedom.* Albany, NY: printed for the author.

WILSON, THOMAS WOODROW (1856–1924)

In addition to serving as the 28th president of the United States, Thomas Woodrow Wilson was a college professor and president (of Princeton) who was an influential critic of the constitutional amending process and the U.S. system of checks and balances. He was also a strong advocate of the British parliamentary system and was more influential than many merely academic critics of the U.S. system.

In an early work, *Congressional Government,* Wilson noted that "it would seem that no impulse short of the impulse of self-preservation, no force less than the force of revolution, can nowadays be expected to move the cumbrous machinery of formal amendment erected in Article V" (Wilson 1885, 242). Similarly, in a later work, Wilson contrasted the Newtonian system outlined in the U.S. Constitution with the Darwinian system of the natural world: "The trouble with the [Newtonian] theory is that government is not a machine, but a living thing. It falls, not under the theory of the universe, but under the theory of organic life. It is accountable to Darwin, not to Newton" (Wilson 1908, 56).

Wilson was a strong admirer of the English governmental system and of responsible cabinet government. He believed that parliamentary debates refined and enlarged public views and attracted gifted and principled men to involvement in politics. In a work that was not published in his lifetime, Wilson advocated two constitutional changes to advance the nation closer to such a system. One would allow the president to choose members of Congress for his cabinet. They would, in turn, be permitted to initiate legislation and lead debate (Wilson 1882, 202). Elsewhere, Wilson indicated that such a system would also require "ministerial responsibility," under which the cabinet would resign if Congress rejected "any important part of their plans" (Wilson 1879, 498). Wilson's second proposal called for lengthening the terms of both the president and members of Congress (Wilson 1882, 202). When he feared loss of the presidency in his 1916 contest with Charles Evans Hughes, Wilson apparently considered appointing Hughes as secretary of state and then having him and his vice president resign so that Hughes could assume office early.

Although Wilson's early work focused on congressional government, he increasingly advocated presidential leadership. Competently leading the nation through World War I, Wilson was unable to get the nation to join the League of Nations after the war, and he ruined his health in the process of trying.

The Progressive Era, during which Wilson served as president, witnessed the addition of four constitutional amendments. The Sixteenth and Seventeenth Amendments were ratified almost simultaneously with Wilson's inauguration. Wilson opposed the Eighteenth Amendment but, faced with constant demonstrations in front of the White House, eventually supported the Nineteenth Amendment in part to unify the nation during a time of war. Both amendments were ratified toward the end of his second term.

See also Eighteenth Amendment; Nineteenth Amendment; Parliamentary System; Progressive Era; Seventeenth Amendment; Sixteenth Amendment.

For Further Reading:

Wilson, (Thomas) Woodrow. 1908. *Constitutional Government in the United States.* Reprint, New York: Columbia University Press, 1961.

————. 1885. *Congressional Government: A Study in American Politics.* Boston: Houghton Mifflin.

————. 1882. "Government by Debate: Being a Short View of Our National Government as It Is and as It Might Be." In *The Papers of Woodrow Wilson,* vol. 2, ed. Arthur S. Link. Reprint, Princeton, NJ: Princeton University Press, 1967.

————. 1879. *Cabinet Government in the United States.* In *The Papers of Woodrow Wilson,* vol. 1, ed. Arthur S. Link. Reprint, Princeton, NJ: Princeton University Press, 1966.

WOMEN'S CHRISTIAN TEMPERANCE UNION

Like the struggle for women's suffrage that culminated in the adoption of the Nineteenth Amendment, the movement that led to national alcoholic prohibition and the ratification of the Eighteenth Amendment was decades in the making. The Women's Christian Temperance Union (WCTU) was among the most important groups in the early struggle for Prohibition. The WCTU was founded in Lake Chautauqua, New York, in August, 1874, the year after lectures in Ohio by Dr. Diocletion Lewis sparked the women's crusade to force the closure of saloons.

By the 1880s, the WCTU was "the largest organization of women the United States had yet known" (Bordin 1981, xvi). Indeed, the WCTU has been described as "unquestionably the first mass movement of American women" (*Id.,* 156). At its first national convention held in Cleveland, Ohio, in 1874, the WCTU elected Annie Wittmyer, founder of the Methodist Home Missionary Society and editor of the *Christian Woman,* as its first president. The WCTU selected Frances Willard of Illinois, a college educator, as corresponding secretary. Willard would head the WCTU in its glory days from 1879 until her death in 1898. She was succeeded by Lillian M. Stevens, who served as president from 1898 to 1914.

The WCTU succeeded in mobilizing large numbers of women—mostly, but not exclusively, middle- and upper-class white evangelical Protestants—under the banner of "home protection." Such women engaged in political action in defense of what had traditionally been regarded as women's chief sphere—a sphere often threatened when the male breadwinner became an alcoholic. Moreover, following Willard's "do everything" philosophy, the organization sponsored a variety of political programs, granting state and local chapters considerable discretion in choosing where they would focus their energies. Concerns of the WCTU included women's suffrage, prison reform, the establishment of kindergartens and Sunday schools, Sabbath observance, temperance education, proposals for moral purity and the elevation of prostitutes, labor reforms, eugenics, and antismoking. For a time during the 1880s, the WCTU was closely allied with the National Prohibition Party. Some, but by no means all, members embraced contemporary anti-nativist and anti-Roman Catholic sentiments. The *Union Signal* was the main WCTU newspaper.

Most WCTU members did not join in Willard's espousal of Christian socialism in the 1890s. By the time of her death, the organization had begun a slow decline as women increasingly joined the National Federation of Women's Clubs, the National American Woman Suffrage Association, and other such organizations (Bordin 1981, 149–159). During Lillian Stevens's presidency, the WCTU's earlier broad agenda gradually narrowed. An analyst noted that the WCTU's image changed from that of containing "the best, most respected, most forward-looking women in town to narrow-minded antilibertarians riding a hobbyhorse" (*Id.,* 155).

See also Eighteenth Amendment; Nineteenth Amendment; Willard, Francis.

For Further Reading:

Bordin, Ruth. 1981. *Women and Temperance: The Quest for Power and Liberty, 1873–1900.* Philadelphia: Temple University Press.

Epstein, Barbara L. 1981. *The Politics of Domesticity: Women, Evangelism, and Temperance in NineteenthCentury America.* Middletown, CT: Wesleyan University Press.

WOODHULL, VICTORIA CLAFLIN (1838–1927)

Victoria Claflin Woodhull was a stockbroker and onetime protégé of Cornelius Vanderbilt; a reformer, lecturer, spiritualist, and sometime advocate of free love; a proponent of woman's suffrage who split with Susan B. Anthony's National Woman Suffrage Association; and an editor of *Woodhull and Claflin's Weekly* and later the *Humanitarian.* Woodhull was also a thrice-married member of an eccentric family; her sister was the vivacious Tennessee Celeste Claflin. Victoria Woodhull was the primary catalyst for charges of adultery against popular preacher Henry Ward Beecher (McHenry 1980, 451–52; Marberry 1967; Arling 1972). Woodhull proposed a Constitution of the United States of the World in a speech in 1870, two years before her first of five bids for the presidency.

Her proposed constitution was a unique blend of old and new provisions. Congress would continue to be bicameral, with senators serving terms of 10 years and members of the House serving for five years; all bills would originate in the House (Stern 1974, 6), with the possibility of abolishing the Senate if three-fifths of the House and the American people concurred (*Id.,* 22). Moreover, the House could override presidential vetoes by a simple majority vote (*Id.,* 6). Congress would prescribe a common form of constitution for each state (*Id.,* 7); exercise expanded powers to guarantee equal rights; establish a uniform criminal code, a common law, a system of welfare-workfare, prison discipline, inheritance and other progressive taxes, and a system of national railroads; and propose a world tribunal (*Id.,* 8–11).

An electoral college would select the president and the president's ministerial cabinet of 16 designated officers who would serve 10-year nonrenewable terms (Stern 1974, 12–16). The electoral college would also select judges, with a judicial system consisting of district courts, a three-judge Supreme Court of the States, and a five-person Supreme Court of the United States (*Id.,* 18).

Woodhull would extend the franchise to all 18-year-old citizens other than "idiots and the insane" (Stern 1974, 19), thus anticipating both the Nineteenth and the Twenty-sixth Amendments. Woodhull's constitution further provided for the recall, the initiative, and the referendum, with amendments to be adopted by three-fifths of the voters either on their own or in response to proposals made by a three-fifths vote of the House of Representatives (*Id.,* 22–23). Although Woodhull included a number of provisions for equality, she did not include a bill of rights. Woodhull's proposal received little publicity and "had little discernible impact on the American political process or the condition of women in American life" (Boyd 1992, 43).

In 1893, Congressman Lucas Miller of Wisconsin offered a resolution to change the name of the United States to the United States of the World (H.J. Res. 208). This proposal, which he presented by request, contained a number of whimsical features (Musmanno 1929, 185–186), some of which resembled features of the Woodhull plan.

See also Anthony, Susan Brownell; Nineteenth Amendment.; United States of America, Proposed Name Changes.

For Further Reading:

Arling, Emanie. 1972. *The Terrible Siren: Victoria Woodhull.* New York: Arno Press.

Boyd, Steven R., ed. 1992. *Alternative Constitutions for the United States: A Documentary History.* Westport, CT: Greenwood Press.

Gabriel, Mary. 1998. *Notorious Victoria: The Life of Victoria Woodhull,* uncensored. Chapel Hill: Algonquin Books.

Goldsmith, Barbara. 1998. *Other Powers: The Age of Suffrage, Spiritualism, and the Scandalous Victoria Woodhull.* New York: Alfred A. Knopf.

Marberry, M. M. 1967. *Vicky: A Biography of Victoria C. Woodhull.* New York: Funk and Wagnalls.

McHenry, Robert, ed. 1980. *Liberty's Women.* Springfield, MA: G. and C. Merriam.

Musmanno, M. A. 1929. *Proposed Amendments to the Constitution.* Washington DC: U.S. Government Printing Office.

Stern, Madeline B., ed. 1974. *The Victoria Woodhull Reader.* Weston, MA: M & S Press.

WOODWARD, AUGUSTUS B. (1775?–1827)

Augustus Woodward provided one of the earliest comprehensive analyses of the U.S. Constitution and its operation in an 1825 publication called *The Presidency of the United States.* Woodward concentrated attention on the emerging cabinet system, whose history he described before he enumerated twenty "evils" that needed solutions.

The problems Woodward identified were as follows (Woodward 1825, 43–67):

1. The exclusion of the vice president from cabinet councils that would better familiarize him with the job to which he might succeed;
2. The conflict among cabinet members for the presidential post;
3. The difficulty that noncabinet officers had in becoming presidential candidates;
4. The misuse of patronage;
5. The problems caused by party opposition that was often fueled by sectional jealousies;
6. Variations in the methods of selecting presidential electors;
7. Problems arising when the House of Representatives had to choose among the top candidates for the presidency;
8. Problems arising when presidential electors were not chosen on the same day as the general election;
9. The need for a presidential secretary;
10. The failure of Washington, D.C. to have representatives either in the electoral college [a problem not addressed until 1961 by adoption of the Twenty-third Amendment] or in Congress;
11. Corruption of Congress brought about by inadequate attention to the doctrine of separation of powers;
12. Providing the president with a furnished residence without explicit constitutional sanction and despite the constitutional provision preventing additional emoluments for that office;
13. The need for a mechanism whereby the president could establish a committee of investigators;
14. The failure to standardize rules of presidential etiquette;
15. The need for a method whereby various regions of the country would be granted an opportunity to fill the presidency;
16. The need to acquaint the vice president with presidential duties and relieve him of responsibility for presiding over the Senate;
17. The lack of a cabinet office relating to domestic affairs;
18. Concern that cabinet meetings might detract from cabinet officers' attention to their respective departments;
19. Concern that cabinet officers, fearful of losing their jobs, might fail to provide the president with independent counsel; and
20. Concern that the cabinet system lacked adequate constitutional sanction.

Woodward did not elaborate on how to solve all these problems or provide specific language for constitutional amendments. He did provide an outline for a Department of Domestic Affairs that would include branches for advancing sciences and the arts; for agriculture, commerce, and internal improvements; for preservation of public documents; and so forth. Woodward also proposed dividing the Department of Foreign Affairs into eight bureaus, each to deal with a different area of the world.

For Further Reading:

Woodward, Augustus B. 1825. *The Presidency of the United States.* New York: J. & J. Harper.

WORKERS' COMPENSATION LAWS

In the 19th century, several common-law principles limited employer liability for on-the-job accidents. The fellow-servant rule allowed employers to evade responsibility when other employees were negligent; contributory negligence exempted employers when the injured person shared in the fault; and the assumption-of-risk doctrine presumed that employees who knew of workplace dangers assumed the risks (Urofsky 1988, 558).

At the turn of the century, states began creating insurance pools and requiring employees either to participate or to secure private insurance coverage for on-the-job injuries. Beginning in 1906, the national government adopted legislation to cover industries engaged in interstate commerce. In 1908, the Supreme Court struck down the federal law as overly broad, and in *Ives v. South Buffalo Railway Co.* (1911), the New York Court of Appeals invalidated a state law granting compensation for injured workers (Urofsky 1988, 560–561).

That year, Illinois Democratic representative Frank Buchanan introduced an amendment giving Congress the power to pass laws granting compensation to injured workers. Within months of the *Ives* decision, however, state courts began ruling favorably on other state laws (Hall 1989, 244), and the Supreme Court upheld a revised Federal Employers' Liability Act of 1908 in the *Second Employers' Liability Case* of 1912. Amending proposals on the topic subsequently ceased.

For Further Reading:

Hall, Kermit L. 1989. *The Magic Mirror: Law in American History.* New York: Oxford University Press.

Urofsky, Melvin I. 1988. *A March of Liberty: A Constitutional History of the United States.* New York: Alfred A. Knopf.

WORLD GOVERNMENT

One proposed solution to the problem of international conflict is the establishment of international organizations or a world government. Colorado Democratic senator John Safroth offered an amendment in 1916 to authorize the creation of an international peace tribunal. Despite the intense efforts of Woodrow Wilson, the United States never joined the League of Nations, which was established at the end of World War I. The United States was, however, a founding member of the United Nations, which emerged at the end of World War II.

Allowing each nation-state to preserve its sovereignty and independence, the United Nations fell far short of the world government that many thought was necessary to preserve peace and halt the spread of nuclear weapons. World government appears to have had special support in the 1940s and early 1950s (see Johnsen 1947; Mangone 1951), with prominent advocates including President Harry Truman, General Douglas MacArthur, and Supreme Court Justice Owen Roberts (Johnsen 1948, 65).

In 1949, Democratic Representative Charles Bennett of Florida introduced an amendment to permit U.S. participation in a limited world government. That same year, five states (California, Connecticut, Maine, New Jersey, and North Carolina) petitioned for a convention to propose amendments authorizing U.S. participation in such a body.

Just prior to this, 11 scholars including Robert M. Hutchins and Mortimer Adler of the University of Chicago and Rexford Tugwell issued a *Preliminary Draft of a World Constitution* (1948). The proposal grew out of 13 meetings they had held between 1945 and 1947.

The document began with a "Declaration of Rights and Duties," based on "the law of Nature" and the rights of man. The most controversial proposal in this section, which attempted to work in both socialistic and capitalistic economic systems, provided that:

> The four elements of life—earth, water, air, energy—are the common property of the human race. The management and use of such portions thereof as are vested in or assigned to particular ownership, private or corporate or national or regional, of definite or indefinite tenure, of individualistic or collective economy, shall be sub-

ordinated in each and all cases to the interest of the common good. (Committee 1948, 6)

The first section of the proposed constitution focused on "grants of power." It sought to solve the problem of war by creating a "Federal World Republic," which would be "indivisible and one" (Committee 1948, 7). The Federal Republic would be responsible for maintaining peace, settling conflicts, settling boundary disputes, sending troops, and the like. A provision, similar to the Tenth Amendment of the U.S. Constitution, would have reserved nondelegated rights to composite nations and states.

The Federal Republic would vest primary powers in five bodies: the Federal Convention; the President; the Council and Special Bodies; the Grand Tribunal, the Supreme Court, and the Tribune of the People; and the Chamber of Guardians. The Federal Convention, in which states would have one delegate for each one million people, would meet every three years, and would divide into nine electoral colleges from Europa, Atlantis (including the United States and Britain), Eurasia, Afrasia, Africa, India (and maybe Pakistan), Asia Major, Austrasia, and Columbia (South America). This convention would select a president who would serve for six years.

The World Council of 27 members, drawn from these nine electoral colleges and serving for three-year terms, would "initiate and enact legislation" (Committee 1948, 13). In conjunction with the president, the Council would select a House of Nationalities and States to safeguard "local institutions and autonomies and the protection of minorities *(Id.).* A "Syndical or functional Senate" *(Id.)* would protect both union and corporate interests. The Council would also create an Institute of Science, Education and Culture *(Id.,* 14). An additional planning agency would prepare budgets and plan for "improvement of the world's physical facilities" *(Id.,* 14).

The president would appoint a chancellor who would form a cabinet. The president would have veto power over council legislation and would be subject to impeachment (Committee 1948, 17). The president would also serve as chief justice of the Supreme Court. Sixty justices, a Grand Tribunal, would serve on five branches dealing with different subjects and subject to review by the

seven-member Supreme Court. Other lower courts would also be established.

A Tribune of the People, serving for a three-year term, would protect minority rights. The Constitution would outlaw discrimination on the basis of "race or nation or sex or caste or creed or doctrine" (Committee 1948, 25). It would also establish protections for "the freedom of communication and information, of speech, of the press, and of expression by whatever means, of peaceful assembly, [and] of travel" *(Id.,* 26), and ban federal (albeit not state) capital punishment statutes. Balancing political rights with economic and social rights, the Constitution also provided for "old age pensions, unemployment relief, insurance against sickness and accident, just terms of leisure, and protection to maternity and infancy," as well as a right to publicly funded education *(Id.,* 27).

A Chamber of Guardians would provide for the "control and use" of armed forces, as well as for regulating the size of domestic militias.

The Constitution would further provide for a Federal Capital and for designating a single official language "which shall be standard for the formulation and interpretation of the federal law" (Committee 1948, 33). Amendments would be recommended by concurrent two-thirds majorities of the Council and the Grand Tribunal and by approval by a two-thirds majority of the Federal Convention *(Id.,* 34).

An accompanying "Summary Report" indicated that the authors of the constitution believed that world government was "the only alternative to world destruction" (Committee 1948, 41). The report described the proposed constitution being the "maximal" feasible one that could be made but as not being "utopian." The report presented world federalism as a plan for working within existing national boundaries, which most countries would be reluctant to abrogate. A subsequent section of the report notes that this plan was not necessarily a substitute for the United Nations and might even be adopted as "an all-round amendment to the U.N. Charter" *(Id.,* 82).

Although international organizations have been strengthened in recent years and regions like Europe and the Americas have increased economic and trade ties, the idea of a world government is still a distant dream, unlikely to be adopted absent some kind of worldwide calamity.

In recent years, Herbert C. Kirstein, the author of the *U.S. Constitution for the 21st Century and Beyond,* has also published a book, *Ideology of Freedom and Democracy,* which was subtitled, "Master Plan for FREE-DOM, DEMOCRACY, HUMAN RIGHTS, PROGRESS, SECURITY, and PEACE on Planet EARTH." It proposed a world forum of nation-states to take the place of the current United Nations.

See also Kirstein, Herbert C.; Tugwell, Rexford; United Nations.

For Further Reading:

The Committee to Frame a World Constitution. 1948. *Preliminary Draft of a World Constitution.* Chicago: The University of Chicago Press.

Johnsen, Julia E., ed. 1948. *Federal World Government.* Vol. 19, no. 5 of the Reference Shelf. New York: H. W. Wilson.

Kirstein, Herbert C. 1994. *U.S. Constitution for 21st Century and Beyond.* Alexandria, Virginia: Realistic IDEALIST Enterprise.

Mangone, Gerald J. 1951. *The Idea and Practice of World Government.* New York: Columbia University Press.

❖ APPENDIX A ❖

The Constitution of the United States

Preamble

We the People of the United States, in Order to form a more perfect Union, establish Justice, insure domestic Tranquility, provide for the common defence, promote the general Welfare, and secure the Blessings of Liberty to ourselves and our Posterity, do ordain and establish this Constitution for the United States of America.

Article I

Section 1. All legislative Powers herein granted shall be vested in a Congress of the United States, which shall consist of a Senate and House of Representatives.

Section 2. The House of Representatives shall be composed of Members chosen every second Year by the People of the several States, and the Electors in each State shall have the Qualifications requisite for Electors of the most numerous Branch of the State Legislature.

No Person shall be a Representative who shall not have attained to the age of twenty five Years, and been seven Years a Citizen of the United States, and who shall not, when elected, be an Inhabitant of that State in which he shall be chosen.

Representatives and direct Taxes shall be apportioned among the several States which may be included within this Union, according to their respective Numbers, which shall be determined by adding to the whole Number of free Persons, including those bound to Service for a Term of Years, and excluding Indians not taxed, three fifths of all other Persons [changed by Section 2 of the Fourteenth Amendment]. The actual Enumeration shall be made within three Years after the first Meeting of the Congress of the United States, and within every subsequent Term of ten Years, in such Manner as they shall by Law direct. The Number of Representatives shall not exceed one for every thirty Thousand, but each State shall have at Least one Representative; and until such enumeration shall be made, the State of New Hampshire shall be entitled to choose three, Massachusetts eight, Rhode Island and Providence Plantations one, Connecticut five, New York six, New Jersey four, Pennsylvania eight, Delaware one, Maryland six, Virginia ten, North Carolina five, South Carolina five, and Georgia three.

When vacancies happen in the Representation from any State, the Executive Authority thereof shall issue Writs of Election to fill such Vacancies.

The House of Representatives shall choose their Speaker and other Officers; and shall have the sole Power of Impeachment.

Section 3. The Senate of the United States shall be composed of two Senators from each State, *chosen by the Legislature thereof* [changed by the Seventeenth Amendment], for six Years; and each Senator shall have one Vote.

Immediately after they shall be assembled in Consequence of the first Election, they shall be divided as equally as may be into three Classes. The seats of the Senators of the first Class shall be vacated at the Expiration of the second Year, of the second Class at the Expiration of the fourth Year, and of the third Class at the Expiration of the sixth Year, so that one third may be chosen every second Year; *and if Vacancies happen by Resignation, or otherwise, during the Recess of the Legislature of any State, the Executive thereof may make temporary Appointments until the next Meeting of the Legislature, which shall then fill such Vacancies* [changed by Section 2 of the Twentieth Amendment].

No Person shall be a Senator who shall not have attained to the Age of thirty Years, and been nine Years a Citizen of the United States, and who shall not, when elected, be an Inhabitant of that State for which he shall be chosen.

The Vice President of the United States shall be President of the Senate, but shall have no Vote, unless they be equally divided.

The Senate shall choose their other Officers, and also a President pro tempore, in the Absence of the Vice President, or when he shall exercise the Office of President of the United States.

The Senate shall have the sole Power to try all Impeachments. When sitting for that Purpose, they shall be on Oath or Affirmation. When the President of the United States is tried the Chief Justice shall preside: And no Person shall be convicted without the Concurrence of two thirds of the Members present.

Judgment in Cases of Impeachment shall not extend further than to removal from Office, and disqualification to hold and enjoy any Office of honor, Trust or Profit under the United States: but the Party convicted shall nevertheless be liable and subject to Indictment, Trial, Judgment and Punishment, according to Law.

Section 4. The Times, Places and Manner of holding Elections for Senators and Representatives, shall be prescribed in each State by the Legislature thereof; but the Congress may at any time by Law make or alter such Regulations, except as to the Places of choosing Senators.

The Congress shall assemble at least once in every Year, and such Meeting shall be *on the first Monday in December* [changed by Section 2 of the Twentieth Amendment], unless they shall by Law appoint a different Day.

Section 5. Each House shall be the Judge of the Elections, Returns and Qualifications of its own Members, and a Majority of each shall constitute a Quorum to do Business; but a smaller Number may adjourn from day to day, and may be authorized to compel the Attendance of absent Members, in such Manner, and under such Penalties as each House may provide.

Each House may determine the Rules of its Proceedings, punish its Members for disorderly Behaviour, and, with the Concurrence of two thirds, expel a Member.

Each House shall keep a Journal of its Proceedings, and from time to time publish the same, excepting such Parts as may in their Judgment require Secrecy; and the Yeas and Nays of the Members of either House on any question shall, at the Desire of one fifth of those Present, be entered on the Journal.

Neither House, during the Session of Congress, shall, without the Consent of the other, adjourn for more than three days, nor to any other Place than that in which the two Houses shall be sitting.

Section 6. The Senators and Representatives shall receive a Compensation for their Services, to be ascertained by Law, and paid out of the Treasury of the United States. They shall in all Cases, except Treason, Felony and Breach of the Peace, be privileged from Arrest during their Attendance at the Session of their respective Houses, and in going to and returning from the same; and for any Speech or Debate in either House, they shall not be questioned in any other Place.

No Senator or Representative shall, during the Time for which he was elected, be appointed to any civil Office under the Authority of the United States, which shall have been created, or the Emoluments whereof shall have been increased during such time; and no Person holding any Office under the United States, shall be a Member of either House during his Continuance in Office.

Section 7. All Bills for raising Revenue shall originate in the House of Representatives; but the Senate may propose or concur with amendments as on other Bills.

Every Bill which shall have passed the House of Representatives and the Senate, shall, before it become a Law, be presented to the President of the United States; If he approve he shall sign it, but if not he shall return it, with his Objections to that House in which it shall have originated, who shall enter the Objections at large on their Journal, and proceed to reconsider it. If after such Reconsideration two thirds of that House shall agree to pass the Bill, it shall be sent, together with the Objections, to the other House, by which it shall likewise be reconsidered, and if approved by two thirds of that House, it shall become a Law. But in all such Cases the Votes of both Houses shall be determined by Yeas and Nays, and the Names of the Persons voting for and against the Bill shall be entered on the Journal of each House respectively. If any Bill shall not be returned by the President within ten Days (Sunday excepted) after it shall have been presented to him, the Same shall be a Law, in like Manner as if he had signed it, unless the Congress by their Adjournment prevent its Return, in which Case it shall not be a Law.

Every Order, Resolution, or Vote to which the Concurrence of the Senate and House of Representatives may be necessary (except on a question of Adjournment) shall be presented to the President of the United States; and before the Same shall take Effect, shall be approved by him, or being disapproved by him, shall be repassed by two thirds of the Senate and House of Representatives, according to the Rules and Limitations prescribed in the Case of a Bill.

Section 8. The Congress shall have Power To lay and collect Taxes, Duties, Imposts and Excises, to pay the Debts and provide for the common Defence and general Welfare of the United States; but all Duties, Imposts and Excises shall be uniform throughout the United States;

To borrow Money on the credit of the United States;

To regulate Commerce with foreign Nations, and among the several States, and with the Indian Tribes;

To establish a uniform Rule of Naturalization, and uniform Laws on the subject of Bankruptcies throughout the United States;

To coin Money, regulate the Value thereof, and of foreign Coin, and fix the Standard of Weights and Measures;

To provide for the Punishment of counterfeiting the Securities and current Coin of the United States;

To establish Post Offices and post Roads;

To promote the Progress of Science and useful Arts, by securing for limited Times to Authors and Inventors the exclusive Right to their respective Writings and Discoveries;

To constitute Tribunals inferior to the Supreme Court;

To define and punish Piracies and Felonies committed on the high Seas, and Offences against the Law of Nations;

To declare War, grant Letters of Marque and Reprisal, and make Rules concerning Captures on Land and Water;

To raise and support Armies, but no Appropriation of Money to that Use shall be for a longer Term than two Years;

To provide and maintain a Navy;

To make Rules for the Government and Regulation of the land and naval Forces;

To provide for calling forth the Militia to execute the Laws of the Union, suppress Insurrections and repel Invasions;

To provide for organizing, arming, and disciplining the Militia, and for governing such Part of them as may be employed in the Service of the United States, reserving to the States respectively, the Appointment of the Officers, and the Authority of training the Militia according to the discipline prescribed by Congress;

To exercise exclusive Legislation in all Cases whatsoever, over such District (not exceeding ten Miles square) as may, by Cession of Particular States, and the Acceptance of Congress, become the Seat of the Government of the United States, and to exercise like Authority over all Places purchased by the Consent of the Legislature of the State in which the Same shall be, for the Erection of Forts, Magazines, Arsenals, dock-Yards, and other needful Buildings; And

To make all Laws which shall be necessary and proper for carrying into Execution the foregoing Powers, and all other Powers vested by this Constitution in the Government of the United States, or in any Department or Officer thereof.

Section 9. The Migration or Importation of such Persons as any of the States now existing shall think proper to admit, shall not be prohibited by the Congress prior to the Year one thousand eight hundred and eight, but a Tax or duty may be imposed on such Importation, not exceeding ten dollars for each Person.

The Privilege of the Writ of Habeas Corpus shall not be suspended, unless when in Cases of Rebellion or Invasion the public Safety may require it.

No Bill of Attainder or ex post facto Law shall be passed.

No capitation, or other direct, Tax shall be laid, unless in Proportion to the Census of Enumeration herein before directed to be taken [changed by the Sixteenth Amendment].

No Tax or Duty shall be laid on Articles exported from any State.

No Preference shall be given by any Regulation of Commerce or Revenue to the Ports of one State over those of another; nor shall Vessels bound to, or from, one State, be obliged to enter, clear or pay Duties in another.

No Money shall be drawn from the Treasury, but in Consequence of Appropriations made by Law; and a regular Statement and Account of the Receipts and Expenditures of all public Money shall be published from time to time.

No Title of Nobility shall be granted by the United States: And no Person holding any Office of Profit or Trust under them, shall, without the Consent of the Congress, accept of any present, Emolument, Office, or Title, of any kind whatever, from any King, Prince or foreign State.

Section 10. No State shall enter into any Treaty, Alliance, or Confederation; grant Letters of Marque and Reprisal; coin Money; emit Bills of Credit; make any Thing but gold and silver Coin a Tender in Payment of Debts; pass any Bill of Attainder, ex post facto Law, or Law impairing the Obligation of Contracts, or grant any Title of Nobility.

No State shall, without the Consent of the Congress, lay any Imposts or Duties on Imports or Exports, except what may be absolutely necessary for executing it's inspection Laws: and the net Produce of all Duties and Imposts, laid by any State on Imports or Exports, shall be for the Use of the Treasury of the United States; and all such Laws shall be subject to the Revision and Control of the Congress.

No State shall, without the Consent of Congress, lay any Duty of Tonnage, keep Troops, or Ships of War in time of Peace, enter into any Agreement or Compact with another State, or with a foreign Power, or engage in War, unless actually invaded, or in such imminent Danger as will not admit of delay.

Article II

Section 1. The executive Power shall be vested in a President of the United States of America. He shall hold his Office during the Term of four Years, and, together with the Vice President, chosen for the same Term, be elected, as follows.

Each State shall appoint, in such Manner as the Legislature thereof may direct, a Number of Electors, equal to the whole Number of Senators and Representatives to which the State may be entitled in the Congress: but no Senator or Representative,

or Person holding an Office of Trust or Profit under the United States, shall be appointed an Elector.

The Electors shall meet in their respective States, and vote by Ballot for two Persons, of whom one at least shall not be an Inhabitant of the same State with themselves. And they shall make a List of all the Persons voted for, and of the Number of Votes for each; which List they shall sign and certify, and transmit sealed to the Seat of the Government of the United States, directed to the President of the Senate. The President of the Senate shall, in the Presence of the Senate and House of Representatives, open all the Certificates, and the Votes shall then be counted. The Person having the greatest Number of Votes shall be the President, if such Number be a Majority of the whole Number of Electors appointed; and if there be more than one who have such Majority, and have an equal Number of Votes, then the House of Representatives shall immediately choose by Ballot one of them for President; and if no Person have a Majority, then from the five highest on the list the said House shall in like Manner choose the President. But in choosing the President, the Votes shall be taken by States, the Representation from each State having one Vote; a quorum for this Purpose shall consist of a Member or Members from two thirds of the States, and a Majority of all the States shall be necessary to a Choice. In every Case, after the Choice of the President, the Person having the greatest Number of Votes of the Electors shall be the Vice President. But if there should remain two or more who have equal Votes, the Senate shall choose from them by Ballot the Vice President [changed by the Twelfth Amendment].

The Congress may determine the Time of choosing the Electors, and the Day on which they shall give their Votes; which Day shall be the same throughout the United States.

No Person except a natural born Citizen, or a Citizen of the United States, at the time of the Adoption of this Constitution, shall be eligible to the Office of President; neither shall any Person be eligible to that Office who shall not have attained to the Age of thirty five Years, and been fourteen Years a Resident within the United States.

In Case of the Removal of the President from Office, or of his Death, Resignation, or Inabili-

ty to discharge the Powers and Duties of the said Office, the Same shall devolve on the Vice President, and the Congress may by Law provide for the Case of Removal, Death, Resignation or Inability, both of the President and Vice President, declaring what Officer shall then act as President, and such Officer shall act accordingly, until the Disability be removed, or a President shall be elected [changed by the Twenty-fifth Amendment].

The President shall, at stated Times, receive for his Services, a Compensation, which shall neither be increased nor diminished during the Period for which he shall have been elected, and he shall not receive within that Period any other Emolument from the United States, or any of them.

Before he enter on the Execution of his Office, he shall take the following Oath or Affirmation: "I do solemnly swear (or affirm) that I will faithfully execute the Office of President of the United States, and will to the best of my Ability, preserve, protect and defend the Constitution of the United States."

Section 2. The President shall be Commander in Chief of the Army and Navy of the United States, and of the Militia of the several States, when called into the actual Service of the United States; he may require the Opinion, in writing, of the principal Officer in each of the executive Departments, upon any Subject relating to the Duties of their respective Offices, and he shall have Power to grant Reprieves and Pardons for Offenses against the United States, except in Cases of Impeachment.

He shall have Power, by and with the Advice and Consent of the Senate, to make Treaties, provided two thirds of the Senators present concur; and he shall nominate, and by and with the Advice and Consent of the Senate, shall appoint Ambassadors, other public Ministers and Consuls, Judges of the Supreme Court, and all other Officers of the United States, whose Appointments are not herein otherwise provided for, and which shall be established by Law: but the Congress may by Law vest the Appointment of such inferior Officers, as they think proper, in the President alone, in the Courts of Law, or in the Heads of Departments.

The President shall have Power to fill up all Vacancies that may happen during the Recess of the Senate, by granting Commissions which shall expire at the End of their next Session.

Section 3. He shall from time to time give to the Congress Information of the State of the Union, and recommend to their Consideration such Measures as he shall judge necessary and expedient; he may, on extraordinary Occasions, convene both Houses, or either of them, and in Case of Disagreement between them, with Respect to the Time of Adjournment, he may adjourn them to such Time as he shall think proper; he shall receive Ambassadors and other public Ministers; he shall take Care that the Laws be faithfully executed, and shall Commission all the Officers of the United States.

Section 4. The President, Vice President and all Civil Officers of the United States, shall be removed from office on Impeachment for, and Conviction of, Treason, Bribery, or other high Crimes and Misdemeanors.

Article III
Section 1. The judicial Power of the United States shall be vested in one Supreme Court, and in such inferior Courts as the Congress may from time to time ordain and establish. The Judges, both of the supreme and inferior Courts, shall hold their Offices during good Behaviour, and shall, at stated Times, receive for their Services, a Compensation, which shall not be diminished during their Continuance in Office.

Section 2. The judicial Power shall extend to all Cases, in Law and Equity, arising under this Constitution, the Laws of the United States, and Treaties made, or which shall be made, under their Authority; to all Cases affecting Ambassadors, other public Ministers and Consuls; to all Cases of admiralty and maritime Jurisdiction; to Controversies to which the United States shall be a Party; to Controversies between two or more States; *between a State and Citizens of another State* [changed by the Eleventh Amendment]; between Citizens of different States; between Citizens of the same State claiming Lands under Grants of different States, *and between a State, or the Citi-*

zens thereof, and foreign States, Citizens or Subjects [changed by the Eleventh Amendment].

In all Cases affecting Ambassadors, other public Ministers and Consuls, and those in which a State shall be Party, the Supreme Court shall have original Jurisdiction. In all the other Cases before mentioned, the Supreme Court shall have appellate Jurisdiction, both as to Law and Fact, with such Exceptions, and under such Regulations as the Congress shall make.

The Trial of all Crimes, except in cases of Impeachment, shall be by Jury; and such Trial shall be held in the State where the said Crimes shall have been committed; but when not committed within any State, the Trial shall be at such Place or Places as the Congress may by Law have directed.

Section 3. Treason against the United States shall consist only in levying War against them, or in adhering to their Enemies, giving them Aid and Comfort. No Person shall be convicted of Treason unless on the Testimony of two Witnesses to the same overt Act, or on Confession in open Court.

The Congress shall have Power to declare the Punishment of Treason, but no Attainder of Treason shall work Corruption of Blood, or Forfeiture except during the Life of the Person attainted.

Article IV
Section 1. Full Faith and Credit shall be given in each State to the public Acts, Records, and judicial Proceedings of all other States. And the Congress may by general Laws prescribe the Manner in which such Acts, Records and Proceedings shall be proved, and the Effect thereof.

Section 2. The Citizens of each State shall be entitled to all Privileges and Immunities of Citizens in the several States.

A Person charged in any State with Treason, Felony, or other Crime, who shall flee from Justice, and be found in another State, shall on Demand of the executive Authority of the State from which he fled, be delivered up, to be removed to the State having Jurisdiction of the Crime.

No Person held to Service or Labour in one State, under the Laws thereof, escaping into another, shall, in Consequence of any Law or Regulation therein, be discharged from such Service or Labour, but shall be delivered up on Claim of the Party to whom such Service or Labour may be due [changed by the Thirteenth Amendment].

Section 3. New States may be admitted by the Congress into this Union; but no new State shall be formed or erected within the Jurisdiction of any other State; nor any State be formed by the Junction of two or more States, or Parts of States, without the Consent of the Legislatures of the States concerned as well as of the Congress.

The Congress shall have Power to dispose of and make all needful Rules and Regulations respecting the Territory or other Property belonging to the United States; and nothing in this Constitution shall be so construed as to Prejudice any Claims of the United States, or of any particular State.

Section 4. The United States shall guarantee to every State in this Union a Republican Form of Government, and shall protect each of them against Invasion; and on Application of the Legislature, or of the Executive (when the Legislature cannot be convened) against domestic Violence.

Article V
The Congress, whenever two thirds of both Houses shall deem it necessary, shall propose Amendments to this Constitution, or, on the Application of the Legislatures of two thirds of the several States, shall call a Convention for proposing Amendments, which, in either Case, shall be valid to all Intents and Purposes, as Part of this Constitution, when ratified by the Legislatures of three fourths of the several States, or by Conventions in three fourths thereof, as the one or the other Mode of Ratification may be proposed by the Congress; Provided that no Amendment which may be made prior to the Year One thousand eight hundred and eight shall in any Manner affect the first and fourth Clauses in the Ninth Section of the first Article; and that no State, without its Consent, shall be deprived of its equal Suffrage in the Senate.

Article VI
All Debts contracted and Engagements entered into, before the Adoption of this Constitution, shall be as valid against the United States under this Constitution, as under the Confederation.

This Constitution, and the Laws of the United States which shall be made in Pursuance thereof; and all Treaties made, or which shall be made, under the Authority of the United States, shall be the supreme Law of the Land; and the Judges in every State shall be bound thereby, any Thing in the Constitution or Laws or any State to the Contrary notwithstanding.

The Senators and Representatives before mentioned, and the Members of the several State Legislatures, and all executive and judicial Officers, both of the United States and of the several States, shall be bound by Oath or Affirmation, to support this Constitution; but no religious Test shall ever be required as a Qualification to any Office or public Trust under the United States.

Article VII

The Ratification of the Conventions of nine States, shall be sufficient for the Establishment of this Constitution between the States so ratifying the Same.

Amendment I

[First ten amendments ratified 15 December 1791] Congress shall make no law respecting an establishment of religion, or prohibiting the free exercise thereof; or abridging the freedom of speech, or of the press; or the right of the people peaceably to assemble, and to petition the Government for a redress of grievances.

Amendment II

A well regulated Militia, being necessary to the security of a free State, the right of the people to keep and bear Arms, shall not be infringed.

Amendment III

No Soldier shall, in time of peace be quartered in any house, without the consent of the Owner, nor in time of war, but in a manner to be prescribed by law.

Amendment IV

The right of the people to be secure in their persons, houses, papers, and effects, against unreasonable searches and seizures, shall not be violated, and no Warrants shall issue, but upon probable cause, supported by Oath or affirmation, and particularly describing the place to be searched, and the persons or things to be seized.

Amendment V

No person shall be held to answer for a capital, or otherwise infamous crime, unless on a presentment or indictment of a Grand Jury, except in cases arising in the land or naval forces, or in the Militia, when in actual service in time of War or public danger; nor shall any person be subject for the same offence to be twice put in jeopardy of life or limb; nor shall be compelled in any criminal case to be a witness against himself, nor be deprived of life, liberty, or property, without due process of law; nor shall private property be taken for public use, without just compensation.

Amendment VI

In all criminal prosecutions, the accused shall enjoy the right to a speedy and public trial, by an impartial jury of the State and district wherein the crime shall have been committed, which district shall have been previously ascertained by law, and to be informed of the nature and cause of the accusation; to be confronted with the witnesses against him; to have compulsory process for obtaining witnesses in his favor, and to have the Assistance of Counsel for his defence.

Amendment VII

In Suits at common law, where the value in controversy shall exceed twenty dollars, the right of trial by jury shall be preserved, and no fact tried by a jury, shall be otherwise reexamined in any Court of the United States, than according to the rules of the common law.

Amendment VIII

Excessive bail shall not be required, nor excessive fines imposed, nor cruel and unusual punishments inflicted.

Amendment IX

The enumeration in the Constitution, of certain rights, shall not be construed to deny or disparage others retained by the people.

Amendment X

The powers not delegated to the United States by the Constitution, nor prohibited by it to the States, are reserved to the States respectively, or to the people.

Amendment XI
[Ratified 7 February 1795]
The Judicial power of the United States shall not be construed to extend to any suit in law or equity, commenced or prosecuted against one of the United States by Citizens of another State, or by Citizens or Subjects of any Foreign State.

Amendment XII
[Ratified 15 June 1804]
The Electors shall meet in their respective states and vote by ballot for President and Vice-President, one of whom, at least, shall not be an inhabitant of the same state with themselves; they shall name in their ballots the person voted for as President, and in distinct ballots the person voted for as Vice-President, and they shall make distinct lists of all persons voted for as President, and of all persons voted for as Vice-President, and of the number of votes for each, which lists they shall sign and certify, and transmit sealed to the seat of the government of the United States, directed to the President of the Senate; The President of the Senate shall, in the presence of the Senate and House of Representatives, open all the certificates and the votes shall then be counted; The person having the greatest number of votes for President, shall be the President, if such number be a majority of the whole number of Electors appointed; and if no person have such majority, then from the persons having the highest numbers not exceeding three on the list of those voted for as President, the House of Representatives shall choose immediately, by ballot, the President. But in choosing the President, the votes shall be taken by states, the representation from each state having one vote; a quorum for this purpose shall consist of a member or members from two-thirds of the states, and a majority of all the states shall be necessary to a choice. *And if the House of Representatives shall not choose a President whenever the right of choice shall devolve upon them, before the fourth day of March next following, then the Vice-President shall act as President, as in the case of the death or other constitutional disability of the President* [superseded by Section 3 of the Twentieth Amendment]. The person having the greatest number of votes as Vice-President, shall be the Vice-President, if such number be a majority of the whole number of Electors appointed, and if no person have a majority, then from the two highest numbers on the list, the Senate shall choose the Vice-President; a quorum for the purpose shall consist of two-thirds of the whole number of Senators, and a majority of the whole number shall be necessary to a choice. But no person constitutionally ineligible to the office of President shall be eligible to that of Vice-President of the United States.

Amendment XIII
[Ratified 6 December 1865]
Section 1. Neither slavery nor involuntary servitude, except as a punishment for crime whereof the party shall have been duly convicted, shall exist within the United States, or any place subject to their jurisdiction.

Section 2. Congress shall have power to enforce this article by appropriate legislation.

Amendment XIV
[Ratified 9 July 1868]
Section 1. All persons born or naturalized in the United States and subject to the jurisdiction thereof, are citizens of the United States and of the State wherein they reside. No State shall make or enforce any law which shall abridge the privileges or immunities of citizens of the United States; nor shall any State deprive any person of life, liberty, or property, without due process of law; nor deny to any person within its jurisdiction the equal protection of the laws.

Section 2. Representatives shall be apportioned among the several States according to their respective numbers, counting the whole number of persons in each State, excluding Indians not taxed. But when the right to vote at any election for the choice of electors for President and Vice President of the United States, Representatives in Congress, the Executive and Judicial officers of a State, or the members of the Legislature thereof, is denied to any of the male inhabitants of such State, being twenty-one years of age, and citizens of the United States, or in any way abridged, except for participation in rebellion, or other crime, the basis of representation therein shall be reduced in the proportion which the number of such male citizens shall bear to the whole number of male citizens twenty-one years of age in such State.

Section 3. No person shall be a Senator or Representative in Congress, or elector of President and

Vice President, or hold any office, civil or military, under the United States, or under any State, who, having previously taken an oath, as a member of Congress, or as an officer of the United States, or as a member of any State legislature, or as an executive or judicial officer of any State, to support the Constitution of the United States, shall have engaged in insurrection or rebellion against the same, or given aid or comfort to the enemies thereof. But Congress may by a vote of two-thirds of each House, remove such disability.

Section 4. The validity of the public debt of the United States, authorized by law, including debts incurred for payment of pensions and bounties for services in suppressing insurrection or rebellion, shall not be questioned. But neither the United States nor any State shall assume or pay any debt or obligation incurred in aid of insurrection or rebellion against the United States, or any claim for the loss or emancipation of any slave; but all such debts, obligations and claims shall be held illegal and void.

Section 5. The Congress shall have power to enforce, by appropriate legislation, the provisions of this article.

Amendment XV
[Ratified 3 February 1870]
Section 1. The right of citizens of the United States to vote shall not be denied or abridged by the United States or by any State on account of race, color, or previous condition of servitude.

Section 2. The Congress shall have power to enforce this article by appropriate legislation.

Amendment XVI
[Ratified 3 February 1913]
The Congress shall have power to lay and collect taxes on incomes, from whatever source derived, without apportionment among the several States, and without regard to any census or enumeration.

Amendment XVII
[Ratified 8 April 1913]
The Senate of the United States shall be composed of two Senators from each State, elected by the people thereof, for six years; and each Senator shall have one vote. The electors in each State shall have the qualifications requisite for electors of the most numerous branch of the State legislatures.

When vacancies happen in the representation of any State in the Senate, the executive authority of such State shall issue writs of election to fill such vacancies: Provided, That the legislature of any State may empower the executive thereof to make temporary appointments until the people fill the vacancies by election as the legislature may direct.

This amendment shall not be so construed as to affect the election or term of any Senator chosen before it becomes valid as part of the Constitution.

Amendment XVIII
[Ratified 16 January 1919; repealed by the Twenty-first Amendment]
Section 1. After one year from the ratification of this article the manufacture, sale, or transportation of intoxicating liquors within, the importation thereof into, or the exportation thereof from the United States and all territory subject to the jurisdiction thereof for beverage purposes is hereby prohibited.

Section 2. The Congress and the several States shall have concurrent power to enforce this article by appropriate legislation.

Section 3. This article shall be inoperative unless it shall have been ratified as an amendment to the Constitution by the legislatures of the several States, as provided in the Constitution, within seven years from the date of the submission hereof to the States by the Congress.

Amendment XIX
[Ratified 18 August 1920]
The right of citizens of the United States to vote shall not be denied or abridged by the United States or by any State on account of sex.

Congress shall have power to enforce this article by appropriate legislation.

Amendment XX
[Ratified 23 January 1933]
Section 1. The terms of the President and Vice President shall end at noon on the 20th day of January, and the terms of Senators and Repre-

sentatives at noon on the 3rd day of January, of the years in which such terms would have ended if this article had not been ratified; and the terms of their successors shall then begin.

Section 2. The Congress shall assemble at least once in every year, and such meeting shall begin at noon on the 3d day of January, unless they shall by law appoint a different day.

Section 3. If, at the time fixed for the beginning of the term of the President, the President elect shall have died, the Vice President elect shall become President. If a President shall not have been chosen before the time fixed for the beginning of his term, or if the President elect shall have failed to qualify, then the Vice President elect shall act as President until a President shall have qualified; and the Congress may by law provide for the case wherein neither a President elect nor a Vice President elect shall have qualified, declaring who shall then act as President, or the manner in which one who is to act shall be selected, and such person shall act accordingly until a President or Vice President shall have qualified.

Section 4. The Congress may by law provide for the case of the death of any of the persons from whom the House of Representatives may choose a President whenever the right of choice shall have devolved upon them, and for the case of the death of any of the persons from whom the Senate may choose a Vice President whenever the right of choice shall have devolved upon them.

Section 5. Sections 1 and 2 shall take effect on the 15th day of October following the ratification of this article.

Section 6. This article shall be inoperative unless it shall have been ratified as an amendment to the Constitution by the legislatures of three-fourths of the several States within seven years from the date of its submission.

Amendment XXI
[Ratified 5 December 1933]
Section 1. The eighteenth article of amendment to the Constitution of the United States is hereby repealed.

Section 2. The transportation or importation into any State, Territory or possession of the United States for delivery or use therein of intoxicating liquors, in violation of the laws thereof, is hereby prohibited.

Section 3. This article shall be inoperative unless it shall have been ratified as an amendment to the Constitution by conventions in the several States, as provided in the Constitution, within seven years from the date of the submission hereof to the States by the Congress.

Amendment XXII
[Ratified 27 February 1951]
Section 1. No person shall be elected to the office of the President more than twice, and no person who has held the office of President, or acted as President, for more than two years of a term to which some other person was elected President shall be elected to the office of the President more than once. But this Article shall not apply to any person holding the office of President when this Article was proposed by the Congress, and shall not prevent any person who may be holding the office of President, or acting as President, during the term within which this Article becomes operative from holding the office of President or acting as President during the remainder of such term.

Section 2. This Article shall be inoperative unless it shall have been ratified as an amendment to the Constitution by the legislatures of three-fourths of the several States within seven years from the date of its submission to the States by the Congress.

Amendment XXIII
[Ratified 29 March 1961]
Section 1. The District constituting the seat of Government of the United States shall appoint in such manner as the Congress may direct:

Section 2. The Congress shall have power to enforce this article by appropriate legislation.

Amendment XXIV
[Ratified 23 January 1964]
Section 1. The right of citizens of the United

States to vote in any primary or other election for President or Vice President, for electors for President or Vice President, or for Senator or Representative in Congress, shall not be denied or abridged by the United States or any State by reason of failure to pay any poll tax or other tax.

Section 2. The Congress shall have power to enforce this article by appropriate legislation.

Amendment XXV
[Ratified 10 February 1967]
Section 1. In case of the removal of the President from office or of his death or resignation, the Vice President shall become President.

Section 2. Whenever there is a vacancy in the office of the Vice President, the President shall nominate a Vice President who shall take office upon confirmation by a majority vote of both Houses of Congress.

Section 3. Whenever the President transmits to the President pro tempore of the Senate and the Speaker of the House of Representatives his written declaration that he is unable to discharge the powers and duties of his office, and until he transmits to them a written declaration to the contrary, such powers and duties shall be discharged by the Vice President as Acting President.

Section 4. Whenever the Vice President and a majority of either the principal officers of the executive departments or of such other body as Congress may by law provide, transmit to the President pro tempore of the Senate and the Speaker of the House of Representatives their written declaration that the President is unable to discharge the powers and duties of his office, the Vice President shall immediately assume the powers and duties of the office as Acting President.

Thereafter, when the President transmits to the President pro tempore of the Senate and the Speaker of the House of Representatives his written declaration that no inability exists, he shall resume the powers and duties of his office unless the Vice President and a majority of either the principal officers of the executive department or of such other body as Congress may by law provide, transmit within four days to the President pro tempore of the Senate and the Speaker of the House of Representatives their written declaration that the President is unable to discharge the powers and duties of his office. Thereupon Congress shall decide the issue, assembling within forty-eight hours for that purpose if not in session. If the Congress, within twenty-one days after receipt of the latter written declaration, or, if Congress is not in session, within twenty-one days after Congress is required to assemble, determines by two-thirds vote of both houses that the President is unable to discharge the powers and duties of his office, the Vice President shall continue to discharge the same as Acting President; otherwise, the President shall resume the powers and duties of his office.

Amendment XXVI
[Ratified 1 July 1971]
Section 1. The right of citizens of the United States, who are eighteen years of age or older, to vote shall not be denied or abridged by the United States or by any State on account of age.

Section 2. The Congress shall have power to enforce this article by appropriate legislation.

Amendment XXVII
[Ratified 8 May 1992]
No law, varying the compensation for the services of the Senators and Representatives, shall take effect, until an election of Representatives shall have intervened

❖ APPENDIX B ❖

Date Amendments Were Proposed and Ratified

Amendment Number	Date Congress Proposed	Date Ratified
1–10	26 September 1789	15 December 1791
11	Senate: 4 March 1794 House: 4 March 1794	7 February 1795
12	Senate: 3 December 1803 House: 9 December 1803	15 June 1804
13	Senate: 8 April 1864 House: 31 January 1865	6 December 1865
14	Senate: 8 June 1866 House: 13 June 1866	9 July 1868
15	Senate: 26 February 1869 House: 25 February 1869	3 February 1870
16	Senate: 5 July 1909 House: 12 July 1909	3 February 1913
17	Senate: 9 June 1911 House: 13 April 1911	8 April 1913
18	Senate: 18 December 1917 House: 17 December 1917	16 January 1919
19	Senate: 4 June 1919 House: 21 May 1919	18 August 1920
20	Senate: 6 January 1932 House: 16 February 1932	23 January 1933
21	Senate: 16 February 1933 House: 20 February 1933	5 December 1933
22	Senate: 12 March 1947 House: 6 February 1947	27 February 1951
23	Senate: 2 February 1960 House: 14 June 1960	29 March 1961
24	Senate: 27 March 1962 House: 27 August 1962	23 January 1964
25	Senate: 19 February 1965 House: 13 April 1965	10 February 1967
26	Senate: 10 March 1971 House: 23 March 1971	1 July 1971
27	26 September 1787	8 May 1992

Most of this information was adapted from information found in an appendix entitled "Congressional Votes on Amendments" in U.S. Senate, Subcommittee on the Constitution, Committee on the Judiciary. *Amendments to the Constitution: A Brief Legislative History* (Washington DC: U.S. Government Printing Office, 1985), pp. 99–133.

❖ APPENDIX C ❖

Number of Amendments by Decade

Decade	Amendments Proposed (Approximate)	Amendments Adopted
1780s	196	0
1790s	42	1
1800s	65	1
1810s	93	0
1820s	111	0
1830s	102	0
1840s	59	0
1850s	22	0
1860s	518	3
1870s	177	0
1880s	264	0
1890s	265	0
1900s	269	0
1910s	467	3
1920s	393	1
1930s	646	2
1940s	404	0
1950s	793	1
1960s	2,598	3
1970s	2,019	1
1980s	827	0
1990s	774	1
2000s	368	0

Most Popular Amending Proposals by Year and Key Events, and Publications Related to Constitutional Amendments

Year	Number of Proposals[1]	Key Events[2]	Most Frequent Proposals Introduced in Congress[3]
1683		William Penn includes amending provision in charter	
1775		American Revolution begins	
1776		Declaration of Independence written defending Revolution States begin writing constitutions	
1777		Continental Congress proposes Articles of Confederation	
1781		Articles of Confederation ratified Battle of Yorktown marks defeat of British forces	
1786		Annapolis Convention meets to discuss commercial problems Shays's Rebellion stirs fear of governmental collapse	
1787		Continental Congress adopts Northwest Ordinance regulating settlement in the territories Constitutional Convention meets in Philadelphia	
1788	124	Federalists and Anti-Federalists debate merits of new Constitution	Bill of Rights
1789	173	George Washington assumes presidency Congress decides to add new amendments to the end of the Constitution rather than incorporating them in the text After an effort led by James Madison, Congress proposes 12 amendments, 10 of which will become the Bill of Rights and 1 of which will be putatively ratified in 1992	Bill of Rights
1791	15	States ratify Bill of Rights Washington accepts Hamilton's proposal for national bank	The judiciary
1793	8	*Chisholm v. Georgia* allows states to be sued by out-of-state citizens	Judiciary (suits against the states)
1794	6	Congress proposes Eleventh Amendment limiting suits against states	Judicial jurisdiction
1795	4	States ratify Eleventh Amendment	Legislative terms
1797	1		Selection of executive
1798	5	*Hollingsworth v. Virginia* decides that president's signature not needed for amendment Federalist-dominated Congress passes Alien and Sedition Acts Madison and Jefferson write Virginia and Kentucky Resolutions	Officeholding restricted to native-born

Year	Number of Proposals[1]	Key Events[2]	Most Frequent Proposals Introduced in Congress[3]
1799	2		Electors to designate choice of president
1800	7	Realigning presidential election passes control from Federalists to Democratic-Republicans and results in Jefferson-Burr tie	Selection of president
1801	1	John Marshall becomes chief justice of United States	Uniform method of selecting president
1802	12		Choice of executive
1803	7	John Marshall issues decision in *Marbury v. Madison* establishing judicial review Congress proposes Twelfth Amendment altering electoral college Louisiana is purchased without adoption of constitutional amendment	Choice of executive
1804	4	States ratify the Twelfth Amendment	Slave importation
1805	4	Samuel Chase brought to trial before Senate on impeachment charges but not convicted	Judicial jurisdiction and removal of judges
1806	10		Slave importation
1807	2	Jefferson imposes embargo in attempt to avert war with European powers	Judicial jurisdiction and compensation
1808	16	American participation in slave trade ended	Judicial, legislative, executive reforms
1809	2		Duration of embargoes
1810	3	Congress proposes amendment limiting titles of nobility; never ratified	Titles of nobility Exclusion of congress-men from executive offices
1811	2		Removal of judges Executive appointments
1812	2	U.S. and Britain engage in War of 1812	Export duties Removal of judges Legislative terms
1813	9		Choice of executive and legislators by districts
1814	9		Internal improvements National bank Legislative terms
1815	8	Hartford Convention meets Americans hear of end of war of 1812 after Jackson routs British troops at New Orleans Simon Willard Jr. publishes *The Columbian Union*	Slavery War-power issues

Year	Number of Proposals[1]	Key Events[2]	Most Frequent Proposals Introduced in Congress[3]
1816	30	American Colonization Society founded with intention of settling African Americans abroad	War and embargo powers Choice of executive and legislators by districts
1817	8		Choice of executive and legislators by districts
1818	19		Choice of executive and legislators by districts
1819	3	*McCulloch v. Maryland* upholds constitutionality of U.S. bank	Choice of executive and legislators by districts
1820	10	Congress adopts Missouri Compromise, limiting slavery in the territories	National bank prohibited
1821	8		Choice of executive and legislators by districts
1822	9		Choice of executive Compensation of Congress Internal improvements
1823	18	President James Monroe announces the Monroe Doctrine to deter European expansion in Western Hemisphere	Choice of executive and legislators
1824	5	Election of 1824 results in no winner; contest goes to U.S. House of Representatives, where John Quincy Adams is selected	Choice of executive by districts No third term
1825	9	Augustus B. Woodward publishes *The Presidency of the United States*	Choice of executive by districts
1826	30	Thomas Jefferson and John Adams both die on the fiftieth anniversary of the Declaration of Independence	Choice of executive
1827	5		Choice of executive
1828	6	Andrew Jackson elected president Next four years mark controversy over national tariffs	Choice of executive
1829	11		Choice of executive
1830	5		Choice of executive
1831		Anti-Mason Party holds first national nominating convention; other parties follow, replacing "King Caucus" in Congress	Choice of executive
1832	19		Choice of executive Division of state and federal powers
1833	4	*Barron v. Baltimore* says that Bill of Rights limits only the national government	Choice of executive

Year	Number of Proposals[1]	Key Events[2]	Most Frequent Proposals Introduced in Congress[3]
1834	6		Choice of executive
1835	12	Roger B. Taney is appointed chief justice of United States	Choice of executive Terms and removal of judges
1836	18		Choice of executive
1837	7		Choice of executive
1838	16		Choice of executive
1839	12		Executive powers
1840	5		One term for executive
1841	12	William Henry Harrison dies in office and is succeeded by Vice President John Tyler	One term for executive
1842	14		Executive powers
1843	3		Executive choice and term
1844	8		Choice of executive
1845	1		Choice of executive
1846	6	U.S. enters two-year war with Mexico	Executive selection and term
1847	1		Limit judicial review of state legislation
1848	4	Seneca Falls Convention calls for women's suffrage	Executive powers
1849	5	*Luther v. Borden* clarifies political questions doctrine	Executive offices
1850	9	Congress adopts Compromise of 1850 in unsuccessful attempt to heal growing sectional divisions	Executive powers and offices
1851	4		Assorted
1852	4		Direct election of senators
1853	1		Choice of executive by districts
1854	3	Kansas-Nebraska Act opens decision about slavery in the territories to "popular sovereignty" Republican Party is founded in Ripon, Wisconsin	Executive and legislative branches
1857	0	*Scott v. Sandford* invalidates Missouri Compromise and declares that African Americans cannot become citizens	
1858	1	John Brown and his followers adopt a new provisional constitution	Qualification to vote for Congress

Year	Number of Proposals[1]	Key Events[2]	Most Frequent Proposals Introduced in Congress[3]
1859	0	John Brown and his followers launch unsuccessful raid at Harper's Ferry	
1860	74	Abraham Lincoln becomes first Republican elected president	Slavery-related issues
1861	121	Congress proposes Corwin Amendment, which is never ratified by the states Unsuccessful "Peace Convention" is convened The Civil War starts The Southern states draw up their own constitution William B. Wedgwood publishes *The Reconstruction of the Government of the United States of America*	Slavery-related issues
1862	8	Sidney George Fisher publishes *Trial of the Constitution*, commending British model of constitutional change Congress abolishes slavery in District of Columbia	Slavery and chief executive
1863	2	Emancipation Proclamation goes into effect but applies only behind enemy lines	Slavery prohibited
1864	57	Senate proposes Thirteenth Amendment abolishing slavery Robert Beasley publishes *A Plan to Stop the Present and Prevent Future Wars*, proposing new constitution	Slavery prohibited
1865	26	House proposes and states ratify Thirteenth Amendment Civil War ends Lincoln is assassinated	Slavery Representation Suffrage
1866	129	Congress proposes Fourteenth Amendment extending rights of citizenship Southern Reconstruction begins John A. Jameson publishes first edition of *Treatise on Constitutional Conventions* denying that such conventions are sovereign	Apportionment of representatives Suffrage Equal rights
1867	29		Citizenship Executive term and selection
1868	25	U.S. Senate impeaches President Andrew Johnson; House falls a single vote short of majority needed to convict him	Executive choice and qualifications Suffrage
1869	76	Congress proposes Fifteenth Amendment extending suffrage to blacks Susan B. Anthony and Elizabeth Cady Stanton found the National Woman Suffrage Association; their rivals found the American Woman Suffrage Association The Anti-Prohibition Party is founded Congress establishes number of Supreme Court justices at nine	Suffrage
1870	6	States ratify Fifteenth Amendment Victoria C. Woodhull proposes a Constitution of the United States of the World	Suffrage

Year	Number of Proposals[1]	Key Events[2]	Most Frequent Proposals Introduced in Congress[3]
1871	13		Executive eligibility and terms
1872	16		Executive choice, eligibility, term
1873	19	*Slaughterhouse Cases* restrict privileges and immunities clause of the Fourteenth Amendment	Executive choice and term Legislative compensation
1874	10	Women's Christian Temperance Union is founded	Direct election of senators
1875	11	Decision in *Minor v. Happersett* declares that women are not entitled to vote under the Fourteenth Amendment	Single sixyear executive term
1876	34	Disputed election of 1876 goes to U.S. House of Representatives Centennial of the Declaration of Independence	No establishment of religion Executive choice and terms
1877	22	End of congressional Reconstruction; federal troops leave the South	Choice of executive
1878	20		War claims prohibited
1879	26	Centennial of George Washington's inauguration Albert Stickney publishes *A True Republic*	War claims Item veto
1880	13		Choice of executive
1881		Supreme Court upholds constitutionality of income tax in *Springer v. United States*	Alcoholic prohibition
1882	35		Item veto
1883	29	*Civil Rights Cases* of 1883 restrict Fourteenth Amendment by focusing on distinction between state and federal action Pendleton Act establishes civil service system	Item veto
1884	33	Henry C. Lockwood publishes *The Abolition of the Presidency*	Congressional powers
1885	14		Direct election of senators
1886	35		Prohibition of polygamy
1887	12	Centennial of U.S. Constitution	Dates of congressional sessions
1888	42		Regulation of polygamy
1889	30		Uniform laws on marriage and divorce Beginning of sessions of Congress and president

Year	Number of Proposals[1]	Key Events[2]	Most Frequent Proposals Introduced in Congress[3]
1890	19	Christopher Tiedeman publishes *The Unwritten Constitution of the United States* Rival women's suffrage associations merge into the National American Woman Suffrage Association (NAWSA) *Hans v. Louisiana* effectively interprets the Eleventh Amendment as a restatement rather than an amendment of the Constitution	Popular election of senators
1891	7		Popular election of senators
1892	57	Columbian Exposition in Chicago marks 400th anniversary of Columbus's discovery of the New World	Popular election of senators
1893	27		Popular election of senators
1894	18		Limit president to one term
1895	23	*Pollock v. Farmers' Loan & Trust* outlaws income tax	Direct election of senators
1896	26	*Plessy v. Ferguson* endorses "separate but equal" Herman Ames publishes first list and analysis of constitutional amendments in nation's first century Frederick Upham Adams publishes *President John Smith* with proposed text of new constitution Utah is admitted to the Union after extensive debates about the need for an amendment outlawing polygamy William McKinley defeats William Jennings Bryan in critical presidential election	Direct election of senators Women's suffrage
1897	31	Henry O. Morris publishes *Waiting for the Signal: A Novel*	Income tax
1898	14	U.S. fights Spain in a war that leads to acquisition of overseas territories	Income tax
1899	43		Uniform marriage and divorce laws; prohibit polygamy
1900	27		Uniform marriage and divorce laws Income tax
1901	42		Direct election of senators
1902	20		Income tax Regulation of trusts
1903	25		Direct election of senators Income tax

Year	Number of Proposals[1]	Key Events[2]	Most Frequent Proposals Introduced in Congress[3]
1904	9		Assorted proposals
1905	25	*Lochner v. New York* invalidates New York's limits on the hours of bakers and highlights growth of substantive due process .	Direct election of senators
1906	18		Direct election of senators Six-year presidential term
1907	45		Direct election of senators Election of federal judges
1908	20	Woodrow Wilson publishes *Constitutional Government in the United States*	Direct election of senators
1909	38	Congress proposes Sixteenth Amendment legitimizing income tax	Direct election of senators
1910	25	Walter Dodd publishes *The Revision and Amendment of State Constitutions*	Change date that Congress convenes
1911	47	Congress proposes Seventeenth Amendment providing for direct election of senators The size of the U.S. House of Representatives is capped at 435	Direct election of senators
1912	42		Change presidential term length and limit terms Election and terms for judges
1913	74	States ratify Sixteenth Amendment States ratify Seventeenth Amendment	Change presidential term length and limit terms Popular election of president Prohibition of alcohol
1914	38	World War I begins in Europe Alice Paul forms the Congressional Union for Woman Suffrage	Prohibition of alcohol
1915	39	Eustace Reynolds publishes *A New Constitution: A Suggested Form of Modified Government*	Women's suffrage
1916	48	Jones Act promises eventual independence to Philippines	Election of president by popular vote
1917	75	U.S. enters World War I Congress proposes Eighteenth Amendment providing for national alcoholic prohibition	Women's suffrage
1918	23	*Hammer v. Dagenhart* invalidates use of federal commerce power to regulate child labor	Restricting voting to citizens

Year	Number of Proposals[1]	Key Events[2]	Most Frequent Proposals Introduced in Congress[3]
1919	56	States ratify Eighteenth Amendment Congress proposes Nineteenth Amendment extending suffrage to women President Wilson suffers stroke during unsuccessful attempt to secure U.S. participation in League of Nations "Red scare" reflects fear of communism in aftermath of the Russian Revolution of 1917 Roger Hoar publishes *Constitutional Conventions: Their Nature, Powers and Limitations*	Women's suffrage
1920	20	States ratify Nineteenth Amendment *National Prohibition Cases* declare that "two-thirds" means two-thirds of a quorum *Hawke v. Smith* overturns state requirement that amendments be ratified by state referendum *Missouri v. Holland* raises fears that treaties might take away individual rights	Treaty ratification Presidential disability Amendment ratification
1921	61	*Dillon v. Gloss* expresses need for amendments to reflect contemporary consensus U.S. House of Representatives adopts anti-lynching law that is subsequently defeated in the Senate	Changes in amending procedure
1922	39	*Bailey v. Drexel Furniture Company* invalidates use of federal taxing power to regulate child labor William MacDonald publishes *A New Constitution for a New America*	Child labor amendment
1923	86		Child labor
1924	30	Congress proposes child labor amendment; never ratified	Child labor Income tax
1925	31	Herbert Horwill publishes *The Usages of the American Constitution*, stressing role of customs and usages	Dates of terms for president and Congress
1926	20	*Myers v. United States* upholds broad presidential removal powers	Dates of terms for president and Congress Repeal Eighteenth Amendment
1927	42	Charles Lindbergh crosses the Atlantic in *Spirit of St. Louis*	Repeal or modify Eighteenth Amendment
1928	30		Amending procedures
1929	34	Stock market crash leads to Great Depression M. A. Musmanno publishes second analysis of amendments	Modify Eighteenth Amendment
1930	31		Modify or repeal Eighteenth Amendment

Year	Number of Proposals[1]	Key Events[2]	Most Frequent Proposals Introduced in Congress[3]
1931	61	*United States v. Sprague* says Congress has choice of how amendments are ratified and refuses to accept implicit limits on the amending process	Modify or repeal Eighteenth Amendment
1932	100	Franklin D. Roosevelt is elected president William Kay Wallace publishes *Our Obsolete Constitution*	Repeal Eighteenth Amendment
1933	62	FDR launches his ambitious New Deal programs	Provide for taxation of income from securities
1934	28		Provide for taxation of income from securities
1935	69	William Yandell Elliott publishes *The Need for Constitutional Reform*, advocating parliamentary mechanisms *Schechter Poultry Corp. v. United States* invalidates FDR's National Industrial Recovery Act; other decisions invalidate other New Deal programs U.S. Supreme Court moves into its own building, across from the Capitol	Provide for taxation of income from securities
1936	29		Minimum wage Regulation of agriculture
1937	154	U.S. Constitution has its sesquicentennial FDR introduces "court-packing" plan Court inaugurates historic "switch in time that saves nine" in *West Coast Hotel v. Parrish* and *N.L.R.B. v. Jones & Laughlin Steel Corp.* *Palko v. Connecticut* articulates "selective incorporation" of the Bill of Rights to the states Ralph Cram publishes *The End of Democracy*, advocating an iconoclastic scheme of constitutional reform	Reform of judiciary Taxation of securities War-related issues
1938	24	Justice Stone authors famous footnote in *Carolene Products* case Hugh Hamilton publishes *A Second Constitution for the United States of America*	War-related issues
1939	88	*Coleman v. Miller* declares that most amending issues are "political questions" World War II begins in Europe	War-related issues Old-age assistance
1940	4	FDR runs for unprecedented third term	Two-term presidential limit
1941	45	Japanese attack Pearl Harbor; U.S. enters World War II Thomas Upham publishes *Total Democracy: A New Constitution for the United States, a Democratic Ideal for the World*	Limit terms of president

Year	Number of Proposals[1]	Key Events[2]	Most Frequent Proposals Introduced in Congress[3]
1942	12	Henry Hazlitt advocates a parliamentary system in *A New Constitution Now* Lester Orfield publishes *The Amending of the Federal Constitution*	Suffrage for 18-year-olds
1943	46	Alexander Hehmeyer publishes *Time for Change: A Proposal for a Second Constitutional Convention*	Ratification of amendments 18-year-old vote Presidential term limits
1944	22	FDR successfully runs for unprecedented fourth term	Limit presidential terms
1945	116	Thomas Finletter publishes *Can Representative Government Do the Job?* FDR dies and Harry Truman assumes presidency World War II ends after U.S. drops two atomic bombs on Japan; Cold War follows	Presidential terms Treaty ratification Equal rights amendment
1946	10		Organization of judiciary
1947	78	Congress proposes Twenty-second Amendment, limiting president to two terms *Adamson v. California* reveals diverse judicial views on incorporation controversy	Limit presidential terms
1948	7		Assorted
1949	64		Change or abolish electoral college Equal rights amendment
1950	11	U.S. comes to aid of South Korea under UN flag	Electors for District of Columbia
1951	73	States ratify Twenty-second Amendment	Change or abolish electoral college Equal rights amendment Limit treaties
1952	31	Steel Seizure cases invalidate Truman's takeover of steel industry	Treaties in conflict with Constitution
1953	120	President Eisenhower appoints Earl Warren as chief justice	Limit treaties and executive agreements Reform electoral college Equal rights amendment
1954	43	*Brown v. Board of Education* calls for desegregation and overturns *Plessy v. Ferguson* U.S. Senate narrowly defeats a version of the Bricker amendment designed to limit scope of treaties	Amending procedures
1955	115	Dr. Martin Luther King Jr. leads Montgomery bus boycott after Rosa Parks refuses to give up her seat	Change electoral college Scope of treaties Equal rights amendment

Year	Number of Proposals[1]	Key Events[2]	Most Frequent Proposals Introduced in Congress[3]
1956	27		Electoral college reform
1957	141		Electoral college reform Treaties Equal rights amendment Admission of new states Tax limits
1958	38	President Eisenhower sends troops to Little Rock, Arkansas, to uphold authority of federal law against Southern defiance	Limit state collection of taxes on nonresidents Presidential disability
1959	194	Alaska and Hawaii become 49th and 50th states admitted to the Union	Equal rights amendment
1960	28	Congress proposes Twenty-third Amendment granting electors to District of Columbia	Alter electoral college
1961	291	States ratify Twenty-third Amendment	Equal rights amendment Direct election of president
1962	105	Congress proposes Twenty-fourth Amendment abolishing use of poll tax in federal elections *Engel v. Vitale* outlaws public prayer in public schools *Baker v. Carr* decides that state legislative apportionment is a justiciable issue Council of State Governments calls for liberalization of the amending process Cuban missile crisis stimulates fears about the emergency functioning of the government	Prayer in schools
1963	395	Dr. Martin Luther King Jr. delivers famous "I Have a Dream" speech at March on Washington, D.C. President John F. Kennedy is assassinated	Prayer in schools Equal rights amendment Electoral college reform
1964	130	Civil Rights Act of 1964 outlaws racial discrimination in places of public accommodation States ratify Twenty-fourth Amendment *Reynolds v. Sims* extends one-person, one-vote principle to both houses of state legislatures; *Wesberry v. Sanders* applies standard to House congressional districts	State legislative apportionment
1965	411	Congress proposes Twenty-fifth Amendment on presidential disability Congress adopts Voting Rights Act of 1965 *Griswold v. Connecticut* establishes a constitutional right to privacy and strikes down Connecticut birth-control law	State legislative apportionment Equal rights amendment Presidential disability Prayer in schools
1966	88	*Harper v. Virginia State Board of Elections* strikes down use of poll tax in state elections *Miranda v. Arizona* expands rights of criminal defendants and stirs criticisms of the Supreme Court	Equal rights amendment Prayer in schools

Year	Number of Proposals[1]	Key Events[2]	Most Frequent Proposals Introduced in Congress[3]
1967	403	States ratify Twenty-fifth Amendment Senator Sam Ervin introduces the Federal Constitutional Convention Act, but it is not adopted President Johnson appoints Thurgood Marshall, the first African American to serve on the U.S. Supreme Court	Equal rights amendment Right to vote Prayer in schools Electoral college
1968	122	States appear on verge of calling a constitutional convention on state legislative apportionment Martin Luther King Jr. and Robert Kennedy are assassinated George Wallace makes impressive showing in three-way race for president that Richard Nixon wins	Appointment, tenure, removal of judges Equal rights amendment Electoral college
1969	625	Nixon appoints Warren Burger as chief justice to replace retiring Earl Warren American astronauts take first walk on the moon Number of amendments proposed in Congress is the most in any year since the nation's founding	Equal rights amendment Direct election of president Prayer in public places
1970	149	*Oregon v. Mitchell* rules that Congress can lower voting ages for federal but not for state elections Black Panthers meet in Philadelphia in a "Revolutionary People's Convention"	Equal rights amendment Voting rights School busing
1971	453	Congress proposes Twenty-sixth Amendment extending vote to 18-year-olds; states ratify amendment Supreme Court upholds limited use of school busing in *Swann v. Charlotte-Mecklenburg Board of Education*	Equal rights amendment School busing Prayer in schools Electoral college
1972	73	Congress proposes equal rights amendment; states do not ratify Leland Baldwin publishes *Reframing the Constitution: An Imperative for Modern America* *Furman v. Georgia* outlaws death penalty as then administered	Nomination and election of president School busing
1973	326	Decision in Roe v. Wade extends privacy rights to protect most cases of abortion *Miller v. California* sets standards for regulation of pornography *Frontiero v. Richardson* indicates increasing judicial sensitivity to women's rights Congress adopts war powers resolution to limit future overseas involvements without congressional support Last U.S. troops withdrawn from South Vietnam; it falls to North Vietnamese two years later	School busing Prayer in schools Electoral college Right to life
1974	56	Supreme Court rejects claim of executive privilege in *U.S. v. Nixon* President Nixon resigns from office after Watergate scandal and is pardoned by incoming President Ford Charles Hardin publishes *Presidential Power and Accountability: Toward a New Constitution*	State jurisdiction over abortion Pardon power Balanced budget

Year	Number of Proposals[1]	Key Events[2]	Most Frequent Proposals Introduced in Congress[3]
1974 (cont.)		Rexford Tugwell publishes *The Emerging Constitution*, advancing the most complete scheme of constitutional reform ever offered in the U.S.	
1975	273	Lower court decision in *Dyer v. Blair* upholds Illinois' requirement for amendment ratification by a three-fifths majority	Right to life Balanced budget Electoral college
1976	58	Bicentennial of Declaration of Independence celebrated	Right to life Congressional tenure
1977	300		Right to life Balanced budget Electoral college
1978	70	Congress proposes amendment to treat District of Columbia as state in Congress; states do not ratify Justice Rehnquist upholds a Nevada advisory referendum on the equal rights amendment in *Kimble v. Swackhamer* Supreme Court rules on affirmative action in Bakke case Alan P. Grimes publishes *Democracy and the Amendments to the Constitution*	Balanced budget Right to life
1979	261	Congress extends seven-year deadline on equal rights amendment for an additional three years	Balanced budget Right to life Direct election of president
1980	29		Right to life
1981	186	Lower court decision in *Idaho v. Freeman* calls into question extension of equal rights amendment and raises possibility of state rescissions President Reagan appoints Sandra Day O'Connor as the first woman to serve on the U.S. Supreme Court	Balanced budget Right to life
1982	35		Balanced budget Equal rights amendment
1983	148	*Immigration and Naturalization Service v. Chadha* strikes down the legislative veto Walter Dellinger publishes influential article in *Harvard Law Review* entitled "The Legitimacy of Constitutional Change: Rethinking the Amending Process"	Balanced budget Right to life Prayer in schools
1984	13	Congress designates the administrator of the General Services Administration to certify the ratification of amendments, a task previously entrusted to the secretary of state and the archivist of the United States	Item veto Prayer in public places
1985	113	*Garcia v. San Antonio Metropolitan Transit Authority* appears to withdraw judiciary from most federalism issues	Balanced budget

Year	Number of Proposals[1]	Key Events[2]	Most Frequent Proposals Introduced in Congress[3]
1986	17	James Sundquist publishes *Constitutional Reform and Effective Government* President Reagan appoints William Rehnquist to replace retiring Chief Justice Warren Burger Challenger space shuttle explodes, killing its crew and temporarily halting further shuttle flights	Assorted issues
1987	108	Bicentennial celebrations of U.S. Constitution Committee on the Constitutional System issues proposals for constitutional reform Reagan's nomination of Robert Bork to Supreme Court is rejected but initiates renewed debate about role of the Court	Balanced budget Right to life
1988	10	Russell Caplan publishes *Constitutional Brinkmanship*, a book on the constitutional convention option	Assorted issues
1989	168	*Texas v. Johnson* upholds constitutional right of flag burning Congress adopts the Flag Protection Act	Flag desecration Balanced budget
1990	16	*United States v. Eichman* reaffirms constitutional right of flag burning and overturns Flag Protection Act *Missouri v. Jenkins* stimulates fears that courts might order tax increases	Assorted issues
1991	115	American Operation "Desert Storm" forces Iraqi troops from Kuwait, where they had positioned themselves in a surprise invasion the previous year Bicentennial of the ratification of the Bill of Rights Bruce Ackerman publishes *We the People: Foundations*, stressing unofficial amending mechanisms John Vile publishes *Rewriting the United States Constitution* the first of a number of books on proposed new constitutions and the amending process	Balanced budget Term limits Item veto
1992	55	States ratify putative Twenty-seventh Amendment limiting timing of congressional pay raises Barry Krusch publishes *The 21st Century Constitution* Steven Boyd publishes *Alternative Constitutions for the United States* In *Planned Parenthood v. Casey*, the Supreme Court modifies but does not overturn abortion decision in *Roe v. Wade*	Electoral college Balanced budget
1993	144	Richard Bernstein and Jerome Agel publish *Amending America*, a comprehensive history of the amending process in the U.S.	Congressional term limits
1994	14	House Republicans agree to Contract with America, including a number of proposed amendments Midterm elections end 50-year domination of Congress by Democrats	Congressional tenure
1995	121	*U.S. Term Limits, Inc. v. Thornton* indicates that states cannot limit terms of members of Congress	Congressional term limits

Year	Number of Proposals[1]	Key Events[2]	Most Frequent Proposals Introduced in Congress[3]
1995		*U.S. v. Lopez* recognizes limits on congressional powers under the commerce clause Senate narrowly rejects flag desecration amendment after House approves it Sanford Levinson publishes book of essays on the amending process entitled *Responding to Imperfection* Chester J. Antieau publishes *A U.S. Constitution for the Year 2000*	Budget-related matters
1996	26	Presidential election highlights many of the issues in the Contract with America, especially a balanced federal budget Kenneth Dolbeare and Janette Hubbell publish *USA 2012: After the Middle-Class Revolution* David Kyvig publishes *Explicit and Authentic Acts: Amending the U.S. Constitution, 1776–1995* John R. Vile publishes first edition of *Encyclopedia of Constitutional Amendments, Proposed Amendments, and Amending Issues, 1789–1995*	Victims' rights
1997	93	*Boerne v. Flores* limits congressional enforcement powers under the Fourteenth Amendment	Budget issues Term limits
1998	17	Bruce Ackerman publishes *We the People: Transformations*, second of three volumes U.S. House of Representatives impeaches President Bill Clinton for trying to cover up extramarital affairs U.S. Supreme Court decision in *Clinton v. City of New York* outlaws congressionally enacted item veto	Budget and tax issues
1999	54	U.S. Senate acquits President Clinton on impeachment charges	Budget related issues
2000	15	George Bush gets narrow win in the electoral college after U.S. Supreme Court decision in *Bush v. Gore* brings Florida vote-counting to an end U.S. Supreme Court decision in *Cook v. Gralike* prohibits states from "instructing" members of Congress on how to vote on constitutional amendments Palmer publishes *Constitutional Amendments: 1789 to the Present* Richard Labunski publishes *The Second Constitutional Convention*	Electoral College reform Balanced budget
2001	57	Terrorist attacks against the U.S. raise concern about national security and possible mass losses in Congress *Cook v. Gralike* voids Mo's attempt to note on ballot the candidates who support term limits *Santa Fe Independent School District v. Doe* extends ban on prayer in public schools to high school football games Shaw Grunow, ed., publishes *Constitutional Amendments: From Freedom of Speech to Flag Burning*, 3 vols.	Balanced budget Electoral College

Year	Number of Proposals[1]	Key Events[2]	Most Frequent Proposals Introduced in Congress[3]
2002	16 (list incomplete)	John R. Vile, ed., publishes *Proposed Amendments to the U.S. Constitution, 1787–2001*, 3 vols. U.S. Ninth Circuit Court of Appeals decision prohibiting public school recitations of the words "under God" in the pledge of allegiance stir controversy Republicans recapture U.S. Senate	Victims' rights Balanced budget/ "Under God" in flag salute
2003		U.S. is part of a multinational force that invades Iraq A Massachusetts Supreme Court decision in *Goodridge v. Department of Public Health* extended the rights of civil marriage to gay couples.	
2004		George W. Bush reelected, carrying both popular vote and electoral college. In *Elk Grove v. Newdow*, the Supreme Court declares that a parent who challenged the words "under God" in the Pledge of Allegiance lacked standing.	
2005		*Kelo v. City of New London* raises questions about the scope of the Takings Clause of the Fifth Amendment	
2006		Sanford Levinson publishes *Our Undemocratic Constitution*.	
2007		Melissa Schwartzberg publishes *Democracy and Legal Change*. Larry Sabato publishes *A More Perfect Constitution: 23 Proposals to Revitalize Our Constitution and Make America a Fairer Country*. In *Gonzales v. Carhart*, Supreme Court allows for some restrictions on partial-birth abortions.	
2008		U.S. elects Barack Obama, the first African-American President amid growing concerns about the national economy. *District of Columbia v. Heller* interprets the Second Amendment as a personal right, but does not decide whether the right applies to the states.	
2009		*Citizens United v. Federal Election Commission* expands First Amendment protections for Independent campaign expenditures by unions and corporations on behalf of candidates.	
2010		Health care debate and federal stimulus package stir renewed concern about budget deficits.	

[1]These numbers were compiled from the following lists of amendments:

For the years 1787 through 1889, Herman Ames, The Proposed Amendments to the Constitution of the United States During the First Century of Its History (New York: Burt Franklin, 1970; reprint of 1896 edition). (Numbers in 1788ñ1789 reflect proposals of state ratifying conventions.)

For the years 1889 through 1926, Proposed Amendments of the Constitution of the United States Introduced in Congress from December 4, 1889, to July 2, 1926, arranged by Charles C. Tansil (Washington, DC: U.S. Government Printing Office, 1926).

For the years 1927 through 1962, Proposed Amendments to the Constitution of the United States of America Introduced in Congress from the 69th Congress, 2d Session Through the 87th Congress, 2d Session, December 6, 1926, to January 3, 1963 (Washington, DC: U.S. Government Printing Office, 1963).

For the years 1963 through 1968, Proposed Amendments to the Constitution of the United States of America Introduced in Congress from the 88th Congress, 1st Session Through the 90th Congress, 2d Session, January 9, 1963, to January 3, 1969 (Washington, DC: U.S. Government Printing Office, 1969).

For the years 1969 through 1984, Richard Davis, Proposed Amendments to the Constitution of the United States of America Introduced in Congress from the 91st Congress, 1st Session, Through the 98th Congress, 2d Session, January 1969ñDecember 1984, Congressional Research Service Report No. 8536 GOV (Washington, DC: Congressional Research Service, 1985).

For the years 1985 through 1990, Daryl B. Harris, Proposed Amendments to the U.S. Constitution: 99thñ101st Congresses (1985ñ1990) (Washington, DC: Congressional Research Service, Library of Congress, 1992).

For the years from 1990 to the present, lists taken from the author's compilation as found on pp. 1663ñ1709, vol. 3 of 3 vols. of John R. Vile, ed. Proposed Amendments to the U.S. Constitution, 1787ñ2001 (Union, New Jersey: The Lawbook Exchange, 2002). This set reprints all the sources above providing a "onestop" source for topics of all amendments proposed through 2001.

The list used for the first 100 years includes some proposals that were introduced in state legislatures. Petitions for conventions that occurred in the second 100 years are not included in this survey. Any mistakes made in counting the proposals from each year are mine.

[2]Most events were chosen because of their relation to the amending process, but some are presented merely as markers of contemporaneous events.

[3]I read through each list of amendments and prepared this survey with as much completeness as possible, but with no pretense to absolute accuracy. In a few years marked "assorted," no amendment proposal predominated. In years in which numerous amendments were proposed, the proposals are listed according to their frequency. The number of times that amendments were offered does not necessarily indicate which ones had the most support, since a single amendment might have had multiple cosponsors.

❖ APPENDIX E ❖

Chronological List of Proposals by Individuals
Significantly to Revise or to Rewrite the U.S. Constitution

1789–1865
1801, Edmund Pendleton
1808, James Hillhouse
1815, Simon Willard Jr.
1825, Augustus Woodward
1858, John Brown
1861, Confederate States of America
1861, William B. Wedgwood
1864, Robert Beasley

1866–1900
1870, Victoria Chaflin Woodhull
1879, Albert Stickney
1880, William B. Lawrence
1884, Henry C. Lockwood
1884, Isaac Rice
1885, Caspar Hopkins
1887, Charles O'Connor
1890, James C. West
1896, Frederick Upham Adams
1897, Henry O. Morris
1898, Goldwin Smith

1900–1929
1906, Walter Clark
1911, Walter Tuller
1913, Yendell Henderson
1915, Eustace Reynolds
1922, William McDonald

1930–1945
1931, Charles Merriam
1932, John Piburn
1932, William K. Wallace
1933, Henry S. McKee
1937, Ralph Cram
1937, Malcolm Eiselin
1937, William Yandell Elliott
1938, Charles Coleman
1938, Hugh Hamilton
1941, Thomas Carlyle Upham
1942, Herbert Agar
1942, Henry Hazlett
1943, Alexander Hehmeyer
1945, Thomas Finletter

1946–1969
1967–1968, Mario Pei
1968, Dwight MacDonald
1969, Herman Finer

1970–1979
1970, P. J. Marduke
1972, Leland Baldwin
1973, William Gardiner
1970s, Bill Strittmatter
1974, Conley Dillon
1974, Charles Hardin
1974, Rexford Tugwell
1976, Theodore Becker

1980–1989
1980, Richard Cummings
1980, Lloyd Cutler
1981, Joseph Church
1985, 1989, Donald Robinson
1986, James O. Pace
1986, James Sundquist
1987, Arthur Miller
1987, Jeffrey Miller
1988, Anonymous (Proper Government)
1988, Paul Fisher
1988, Cornelius Murphy

1990–1999
1990, John Mertens
1991, 1996, Bruce E. Tonn
1992, Barry Krusch
1994, Jim Davidson
1994, Herbert C. Kirstein
1995, Chester Antieau
1995, Alvin and Heidi Toffler
1995, Virginia Vanguard
1995, Edwin Lee Wade
1996, A. R. Adams
1996, Kenneth Dolbeare and Janel Hubbell
1996, David Lazare
1997, Thomas H. Naylor and William H. Willimon
1997, Robert Struble Jr.
1999, Michael Marx
1999, Rodney Scott

2000–2009

c2000, Jack Durst

2000, Frederick Ellis and Carl Frederick

2000, David B. Jeffs,

2000,Richard Labunski

2000 Ross Nordeen

2000, John VanSickle

2001, Martin I. Bailey

2001, Jesse L. Jackson Jr.

2006, Sanford Levinson

2007, Larry J. Sabato

2008, Steve Gillman

2008, Kirby Palm

2008, James A. Schmitendorf

❖ APPENDIX F ❖

Major Proposals by Individuals outside Congress Seeking Major Constitutional Changes

Name	Occupation	Title	Year	Did they write a new document?
Adams, Frederick Upham	Labor Editor	*President John Smith* (novel)	1896	Yes
Agar, Herbert (1897–1980)	Historian/Editor	Chapter in *A Time for Greatness*	1942	No
Anonymous	Proper Government (Website)		c1988	Yes
Antieau, Chester (1913–)	Professor Emeritus	*A U.S. Constitution for the Year 2000*	1995	No
Bailey, Martin I. (1927–2000?)	Economist	*Constitution for a Future Country*	2001	Yes
Baldwin, Leland (1897–1981)	Retired Historian	*Reframing the Constitution: An Imperative for Modern America*	1972	Yes
Beasley, Robert	Unknown	*A Plan to Stop the Present and Future Wars*	1864	Yes
Becker, Theodore (1932–)	Law & Pol. Sci. Prof	*American Government— Past—Present—Future*	1976	No
Brown, John (1800–1859)	Abolitionist	Provisional Constitution	1858	Yes
Church, Joseph (1918–)	Psychologist	*America the Possible: Why and How the Constitution Should Be Rewritten*	1982	No
Clark, Walter (1846–1942)	Judge	Speech	1906	No
Coleman, Charles (1900–)	Education	*The Constitution Up to Date*	1938	Yes
Confederate States of America		The Confederate Constitution	1861	Yes
Cram, Ralph (1863–1942)	Architect	*The End of Democracy*	1937	No
Cummings, Richard (1938–)	Attorney, Professor	*Proposition Fourteen: A Secessionist Remedy*	1980	No
Davidson, Jim, et al.		*The Atlantis Papers* & Website	c2000	Yes
Dillon, Conley (1906–1987)	Political Scientist	Public Administration Report	1974	No
Dolbeare, Kenneth (1930–) Hubbell, Janette (1948–)	College Professor Businessperson	*USA 2012: After the Middle Class Revolution*	1996	No
Durst, Jack (1980–)	College student	Constitution of the Republic (Website)	c2000	Yes
Eiselin, Malcolm (1902–1965)	Historian	Journal article	1937	No
Elliott William Yandell (1896–1979)	Political Scientist	*The Need for Constitutional Reform*	1937	No
Ellis, Frederick Frederick Carl	Political Activist	*The Oakland Statement* (novel)	2000	28th and 29th Amendments
Finer, Herman (1898–1969)	Political Scientist	*The Presidency: Crisis and Regeneration*	1969	No
Finletter, Thomas (1893–1980)	Attorney	*Can Representative Government Do the Job?*	1945	No
Gardiner, William (1885–)	Educator	*A Proposed Constitution for the United States of America*	1973	Yes
Hamilton, Hugh	Unknown	*A Second Constitution for the United States of America*	1938	Yes
Hardin, Charles (1908–)	Political Scientist	*Presidential Power and Accountability*	1974	No
Hazlitt, Henry (1894–1993)	Journalist	*A New Constitution Now*	1942	No

Name	Occupation	Title	Year	Did they write a new document?
Hehmeyer, Alexander (1910–1993)	Attorney	*Time for Change: A Proposal for a Second Constitutional Convention*	1943	No
Henderson, Yandell (1873–1974)	Physiologist	Article	1913	No
Hopkins, Caspar (1826–1893)	Businessman	Article	1885	Series of 10 Amendments
Jackson, Jesse L., Jr. (1965–)	Legislator	*A More Perfect Union: Advancing New American Rights*	2001	Series of Amendments
Jeffs, David B.	Police Officer	*America's Crisis* (Website)	2000	Multifaceted Amendment
Kirstein, Herbert C.	Government Employee	*U.S. Constitution for the 21st Century and Beyond*	1994	Yes
Krusch, Barry (1958–)		*The 21st Century Constitution*	1992	Yes
Labunski, Richard	Journalism Professor	*The Second Constitutional Convention*	2000	10 Proposed Amendments
Lawrence, William B.	Diplomat	Article	1880	No
Lazare, David	Journalist	*The Frozen Republic and How the Constitution Is Paralyzing Democracy*	1996	No
Lockwood, Henry C.	Historian	*The Abolition of the Presidency*	1884	Series of Proposals
MacDonald, Dwight (1906–1982)	Journalist	Article	1968	No
MacDonald, William (1863–1938)	Journalist/Professor	*A New Constitution for a New America*	1922	
McKee, Henry S. (1868–1956)	Businessman	*Degenerate Democracy*	1933	No
Marduke, P.J.		*The CASCOT System for Social Control of Technology* (Internet)	1970	No
Merriam, Charles (1874–1953)	Political Scientist	*The Written Constitution and the Unwritten Attitude*	1931	No
Mertens, John	Novelist	*The Second Constitution for the United States of America*	1990	Yes
Miller, Arthur (1917–1988)	Law Professor	*The Secret Constitution and the Need for Constitutional Change*	1987	No
Miller, Jeremy M. (1954)	Law Professor	Article	1987	Yes
Morris, Henry O.	Novelist	*Waiting for the Signal* (novel)	1897	Yes
Murphy, Cornelius F., Jr. (1933–)	Law Professor	Article	1988	No
Naylor, Thomas H. Willimon, William H.	Economics Professor Dean of Chapel	*Downsizing the U.S.A.*	1997	No
Nordeen, Ross	Engineer	Website	c2000	Yes
O'Conor, Charles	Attorney	Articles	1887 1881	No No
Pace, James O.	Attorney	*Amendment to the Constitution: Averting the Decline and Fall of America*	1986	No
Pei, Mario	Linguist	Article	1967–68	No
Piburn, John (1872–)	Medical Doctor	*A Constitution and a Code*	1932	Yes
Reynolds, Eustace	Unknown	*A New Constitution: A Suggested Form of Modified Constitution*	1915	Yes
Rice, Isaac L. (1815–1915)	Attorney	Article	1884	3 major reforms
Robinson, Donald L. (1936–)	Political Scientist	2 books on reform	1985 1989	No No

Name	Occupation	Title	Year	Did they write a new document?
Scott, Rodney D. (1949–)	Social Worker	*The Great Debate: The Need for Constitutional Reform*	1999	Yes
Smith, Goldwin (1823–1920)	Lawyer/Professor	Article	1898	No
Stickney, Albert (1839–1908)	Lawyer	*A True Republic*	1879	No
Strittmatter, Bill	Preacher	*A Christian Constitution and Civil Law for the Kingdom on Earth*	1970s	Yes
Struble, Robert, Jr. (1915–)	Republican Official	*"Redeeming U.S. Democracy"* (Website)	c1997	A Twelve Code
Sundquist, James (1915–)	Political Scientist	*Constitutional Reform and Effective Government*	1986	No
Toffler, Alvin and Heidi (1928– , 1929–)	Journalist/Futurists	*Creating a New Civilization*	1995	No
Tonn, Bruce E.	Researcher	Articles	1991 1996	No No
Tugwell, Rexford (1891–1969)	Professor & Official	*The Emerging Constitution*	1974	Yes, many versions.
Tuller, Walter (1886–1939)	Attorney	Article	1911	No
Upham, Thomas Carlyle		*Total Democracy: A New Constitution for the United States*	1941	Yes
Vanguard, Virginia	Unknown	*The Populis: A Draft Constitution for a New Political Age*	1995	Yes
Vansickle, John	Soldier	Website	c2000	28th–32nd Amendments
Wade, Edwin Lee (1932–)	Businessman/Lawyer	*Constitution 2000: A Federalist Proposal for the Next Century*	1995	10 proposed amendments
Wallace, William K. (1886–)	Diplomat	*Our Obsolete Constitution*	1932	No
Wedgwood, William B. (–1883)	Attorney	*The Reconstruction of the Government of the United States*	1861	Yes
West, James C. (–1946)	Educator/Attorney	*A Proposed New Constitution for the United States*	1890	Yes
Willard, Simon, Jr. (1795–1874)	West Point Cadet	*The Columbian Union*	1815	Yes
Woodhull, Victoria Chaflin (1838–1927)	Activist	Speech	1870	Yes
Woodward, Augustus (1775–1827)		*The Presidency of the United States*	1825	No

❖ BIBLIOGRAPHY ❖

Abraham, Henry J. 1999. *Justices, Presidents, and Senators: A History of the U.S. Supreme Court Appointments from Washington to Clinton.* Lanham, MD: Rowman & Littlefield Publishers, Inc.

———. 1998. *The Judicial Process: An Introductory Analysis of the Courts of the United States, England, and France.* 7th ed. New York: Oxford University Press.

Abraham, Henry J., and Barbara Perry. 2003. *Freedom and the Court: Civil Rights and Liberties in the United States.* 8th ed. New York: Oxford University Press.

Abrams, Herbert L. 1999. "Can the Twenty-Fifth Amendment Deal with a Disabled President? Preventing Future White House Coverups." *Presidential Studies Quarterly* 29 (March): 115–133.

———. 1994. *The President Has Been Shot: Confusion, Disability and the Twenty-fifth Amendment.* Stanford, CA: Stanford University Press.

Abramson, Jeffrey. 1994. *We the Jury: The Jury System and the Ideal of Democracy.* New York: Basic Books.

Academics for the Second Amendment. 1995. "An Open Letter on the Second Amendment." *Chronicle of Higher Education* 41 (11 August): A23.

Ackerman, Bruce. 2007. "The Living Constitution." *Harvard Law Review* 120 (May):1737–1812.

———. 2000. "The New Separation of Powers." *The Harvard Law Review* 113 (January): 633–729.

———. 1996. *We the People: Transformation.* Cambridge, MA: Harvard University Press.

———. 1991. *We the People: Foundations.* Cambridge, MA: Belknap.

———. 1989. "Constitutional Politics/Constitutional Law." *Yale Law Journal* 99 (December): 453–547.

———. 1988. "Transformative Appointments." *Harvard Law Review* 101: 1164–1184.

———. 1984. "The Storrs Lectures: Discovering the Constitution." *Yale Law Journal* 93: 1013–1072.

———. 1979. "Unconstitutional Convention." *New Republic* 180 (3 March): 8–9.

Ackerman, Bruce, et al. 1995. "An Open Letter to Congressman Gingrich." *Yale Law Journal* 104 (April): 1539–1544.

Ackerman, Bruce, and David Golove. 1995. "Is NAFTA Constitutional?" *Harvard Law Review* 108 (February): 801–929.

Ackerman, Bruce, and Ned Katyal. 1991. "Our Unconventional Founding." *University of Chicago Law Review* 62 (Spring): 475–573.

Ackerman, Bruce and Jennifer Nou. 2009. "Canonizing the Civil Rights Revolution: The People and the Poll Tax." *Northwestern University Law Review* 103 (Winter): 63–148.

Adair, Douglas. 1965. "The Federalist Papers." *The William and Mary Quarterly,* 3rd ser. 22 (1965): 131–39.

Adams, Frederick U. 1896. *President John Smith: The Story of a Peaceful Revolution.* Chicago: Charles H. Kerr & Company; reprint, New York: Arno Press, 1970.

Adams, Henry. 1974. *The Formative Years,* ed. Herbert Agar. 2 vols. Westport, CT: Greenwood Press.

Adler, Mortimer J. 1987. *We Hold These Truths: Understanding the Ideas and the Ideals of the Constitution.* New York: Macmillan.

Advisory Commission on Intergovernmental Relations. 1987. *Is Constitutional Reform Necessary to Reinvigorate Federalism? A Roundtable Discussion.* November. Washington, DC: ACIR.

———. 1986. *Reflections on Garcia and Its Implications for Federalism.* February. Washington, DC: ACIR.

Agar, Herbert. 1942. *A Time for Greatness.* Boston: Little, Brown.

Agnes, Richard L. 1994. "Constricting the Law of Freedom: Justice Miller, the Fourteenth Amendment, and the Slaughter-House Cases." *Chicago-Kent Law Review* 70: 627–688.

"Albany Plan of Union." *http://www.constitution. org/bcp/albany.htm.* Accessed 27 April 2002.

Albert, Richard. 2007. "The Constitutional Imbalance." *New Mexico Law Review* 37 (Winter): 1–38.

Alderman, Ellen, and Caroline Kennedy. 1991. *In Our Defense: The Bill of Rights in Action.* New York: William Morrow.

Aldous, Joan. 1997. "The Political Process and the Failure of the Child Labor Amendment." *Journal of Family Issues* 18 (January): 71–92.

Alexander, Herbert E. 1992. *Financing Politics: Money, Elections and Political Reform.* 4th ed. Washington, DC: Congressional Quarterly Press.

Alfange, Dean, Jr. 1994. "*Marbury v. Madison* and Original Understandings of Judicial Review: In Defense of Traditional Wisdom." In *Supreme Court Review, 1993.* Chicago: University of Chicago Press.

Amar, Akhil R. 2005. *America's Constitution: A Biography.* New York: Random House.

———. 1998. *The Bill of Rights: Creation and Reconstruction.* New Haven, CT: Yale University Press.

———. 1997. *The Constitution and Criminal Procedure: First Principles.* New Haven, CT: Yale University Press.

———. 1994. "The Consent of the Governed: Constitutional Amendment outside Article V." *Columbia Law Review* 94 (March): 457–508.

———. 1992. "The Bill of Rights as a Constitution." *Yale Law Journal* 100 (Winter): 1131–1210.

———. 1988. "Philadelphia Revisited: Amending the Constitution outside Article V." *University of Chicago Law Review* 55 (Fall): 1043–1104.

Amar, Vikram David. 2000. "The People Made Me Do It: Can the People of the States Instruct and Coerce Their State Legislatures in the Article V Convention Amendment Process?" *William and Mary Law Review* 41 (March): 1037–1092.

Ambrose, Stephen E. 1966. *Duty, Honor, Country: A History of West Point.* Baltimore: Johns Hopkins University Press.

American Political Science Association, Committee on Political Parties. 1950. *Toward a More Responsible Two-Party System.* New York: Rinehart.

Ames, Herman. 1896. *The Proposed Amendments to the Constitution of the United States during the First Century of Its History.* Reprint, New York: Burt Franklin, 1970.

Anastaplo, George. 1995. *The Amendments to the Constitution: A Commentary.* Baltimore: Johns Hopkins University Press.

———. 1989. *The Constitution of 1787: A Commentary.* Baltimore: Johns Hopkins University Press.

Annenberg Democracy Project. 2007. *A Republic Divided.* New York: Oxford University Press.

Antieau, Chester J. 1995. *A U.S. Constitution for the Year 2000.* Chicago: Loyola University Press.

Arling, Emanie. 1972. *The Terrible Siren: Victoria Woodhull.* New York: Arno Press.

Armey, Cick. 2008. "Whatever Happened to the Contract with America?" *Imprints* 37(May): 4–5.

Aroney, Nicholas. 2006. "Formation, Representation and Amendment in Federal Constitutions." *American Journal of Comparative Law* 54(Spring): 277–336.

Ashmore, Harry S. 1970. "Rexford Guy Tugwell: Man of Thought, Man of Action." *Center Magazine* 3 (September/October): 2–7.

"Assembly Joint Resolution 8." 1952. *Congressional Record,* 82nd Cong., 2d sess. 1952, Vol. 98, pt. 3: 4003–4004.

Atkinson, David N. 1999. *Leaving the Bench: Supreme Court Justices at the End.* Lawrence: University Press of Kansas.

Ayers, Ian, and Bruce A. Ackerman. 2002. *Voting with Dollars: A New Paradigm for Campaign Finance.* New Haven, CT: Yale University Press.

Aynes, Richard L. 2006. "Unintended Consequences of the Fourteenth Amendment and What They Tell Us about Its Interpretation." *Akron Law Review* 39:289–321.

———. 2003. "The Continuing Importance of Congressman John A. Bingham and the Fourteenth Amendment." *Akron Law Review* 36: 589–615.

Babson, Jennifer. 1995. "House Rejects Term Limits: GOP Blames Democrats." *Congressional Quarterly Weekly Reports* 53 (1 April): 918–919.

Bacon, Leonard. 1860. *Sketch of the Life and Public Services of Hon. James Hillhouse of New Haven; with a Notice of His Son Augustus Lucas Hillhouse.* New Haven, CT: n.p.

Bacon, Margaret H. 1980. *Valiant Friend: The Life of Lucretia Mott.* New York: Walker and Company.

Bacon, Selden. 1930. "How the Tenth Amendment Affected the Fifth Article of the Constitution." *Virginia Law Review* 16 (June): 771–791.

Bailey, Martin J. 2001. *Constitution for a Future Country.* New York: Palgrave.

Baker, A. Diane. 1979. "ERA: The Effect of Extending the Time for Ratification on Attempts to Rescind Prior Ratifications." *Emory Law Journal* 28: 71–110.

Baker, Deborah. 1999. "The Fight Ain't Over." *American Bar Association Journal* 85 (August): 52.

Baker, Jean H., ed. 2002. *Votes for Women: The Struggle for Suffrage Revisited.* New York: Oxford University Press.

Baker, Leonard. 1974. *John Marshall: A Life in Law.* New York: Macmillan.

Baker, Lynn A., and Samuel H. Dinkin. 1997. "The Senate: An Institution Whose Time Has Gone?" *Journal of Law & Politics* 13 (Winter): 21–95.

Baker, Richard A. 1992. "Congress, Arrest and Immunity of Members Of." In *The Oxford Companion to the Supreme Court of the United States,* ed. Kermit L. Hall. New York: Oxford University Press.

Bailey, Jeremy D. 2008. "The New Unitary Executive and Democratic Theory: The Problem of Alexander Hamilton." 102 *American Political Science Review* (November): 453–466.

Baker, Thomas E. 2000. "Towards a 'More Perfect Union.'" *Insights on Law & Society* 1 (Fall): 4–7.

———. 1995a. "Can Voters Exclude Homosexuals and Their Interests from the Legislative Process?" *Preview of United States Court Cases* (20 September): 11–18.

———. 1995b. "Exercising the Amendment Power to Disapprove of Supreme Court Decisions: A Proposal for a 'Republican Veto.'" *Hastings Constitutional Law Quarterly* 22 (Winter): 325–357.

"The Balanced Budget Amendment: An Inquiry into Appropriateness." 1983. *Harvard Law Review* 96 (May): 1600–1620.

Baldwin, Leland. 1972. *Reframing the Constitution: An Imperative for Modern America.* Santa Barbara, CA: ABC-CLIO.

Baldez, Lisa, Lee Epstein, and Andrew D. Martin. 2006. "Does the U.S. Constitution Need an Equal Rights Amendment?" *The Journal of Legal Studies* 35 (January):243–83.

Balkin, Jack M. 2005. "How Social Movements Change (or Fail to Change) the Constitution: The Case of the New Departure." *Suffolk University Law Review* 39 (January):27–65.

Ban, Kevin K. 1998. "Does the Internet Warrant a Twenty-Seventh Amendment *[sic]* to the United States Constitution?" *The Journal of Comparative Law* 23 (Spring): 521–540.

Banks, Christopher. 2003. "The Constitutional Politics of Interpreting Section 5 of the Fourteenth Amendment." *Akron Law Review* 36: 425–71

Banner, James M., Jr. 1970. *To the Hartford Convention: The Federalists and the Origins of Party Politics in Massachusetts, 1789–1815.* New York: Alfred A. Knopf.

Banner, Lois W. 1980. *Elizabeth Cady Stanton: A Radical for Women's Rights.* Boston: Little, Brown.

Banning, Lance. 1995. *The Sacred Fire of Liberty: James Madison and the Founding of the Federal Republic.* Ithaca, NY: Cornell University Press.

Barber, Benjamin. 1984. *Strong Democracy.* Berkeley: University of California Press.

Barber, Sotirios A. 1984. *On What the Constitution Means.* Baltimore: Johns Hopkins University Press.

Barkow, Rachel E. 2000. "More Supreme Than Court? The Fall of the Political Question Doctrine and the Rise of Judicial Supremacy." *Columbia Law Review* 102 (March): 237–336.

Barnette, Randy E., ed. 1989. *The Rights Retained by the People: The History and Meaning of the Ninth Amendment.* Fairfax, VA: George Mason University Press.

Barnum, David G. 1993. *The Supreme Court and American Democracy.* New York: St. Martin's Press.

Baron, Dennis. 1990. *The English-Only Question: An Official Language for America?* New Haven, CT: Yale University Press.

Barone, Michael, and Grant Ujifusa. 1994. *The Almanac of American Politics 1994.* Washington, DC: National Journal.

Basch, Norma. 1992. "Reconstructing Female Citizenship: *Minor v. Happersett.*" In *The Constitution, Law, and American Life: Critical Aspects of the Nineteenth-Century Experience,* ed. Donald G. Nieman. Athens: University of Georgia Press.

Basker, James G. 2005. *Early American Abolitionists: A Collection of Anti-slavery Writings, 1760–1820.* New York: Gilder Lehrman Institute of American History.

Bates, Stephen. 1991. "Deconstructing the Flag-Burning Debate." *This World & I* 7 (July): 523–529.

Baumer, Donald C., and Carl E. Van Horn. 1985. *The Politics of Employment.* Washington, DC: Congressional Quarterly Press.

Bayh, Birch. 1968. *One Heartbeat Away: Presidential Disability and Succession.* Indianapolis, IN: Bobbs-Merrill.

———. 1966. *The Making of an Amendment.* Indianapolis, IN: Bobbs-Merrill.

Baylor, Gregory S. 1995. "The Religious Equality Amendment." *Christian Legal Society Quarterly* 16 (Summer): 4–5.

Beaney, William M., and Edward N. Beiser. 1973. "Prayer and Politics: The Impact of *Engel* and *Schempp* on the Political Process." In *The Impact of Supreme Court Decisions: Empirical Studies.* 2d ed. Eds. Theodore L. Becker and Malcolm M. Feeley. New York: Oxford University Press.

Beasley, Robert. 1864. *A Plan to Stop the Present and Prevent Future Wars: Containing a Proposed Constitution for the General Government of the Sovereign States of North and South America.* Rio Vista, CA: Robert Beasley.

Beatty, Edward C. 1975. *William Penn as Social Philosopher.* New York: Octagon Books.

Beauregard, Erving E. 1989. *Bingham of the Hills: Politician and Diplomat Extraordinary.* New York: Peter Lang.

Beck, James M. 1935. "Amending the Constitution." *The Farm Journal* 59: 9, 24.

———. 1922. *The Constitution of the United States.* New York: G. H. Doran Co.

Beck, J. Randy. 2002. "The New Jurisprudence of the Necessary and Proper Clause." *University of Illinois Law Review* 2002: 581–649.

Becker, Carl L. 1970. *The Declaration of Independence: A Study in the History of Political Ideas.* New York: Vintage Books.

Becker, Ryan T. 2007. "The Other Nuclear Option: Adopting a Constitutional Amendment to Furnish a Lasting Solution to the Troubled Judicial Confirmation Process." *Pennsylvania State Law Review* 111 (Spring 2007): 981–1008.

Becker, Theodore L. 1976. *American Government: Past—Present—Future.* Boston: Allyn and Bacon.

Becker, Theodore L., and Crista Daryl Slaton. 2000. *The Future of Teledemocracy.* Westport, CT: Praeger.

Becker, Theodore L., and Malcolm M. Feeley, eds. 1973. *The Impact of Supreme Court Decisions: Empirical Studies.* 2d ed. New York: Oxford University Press.

Beeman, Richard. 2007. *Plain, Honest Men: The Making of the American Constitution.* New York: Random House.

Belknap, Michael R. 1992. "Communism and the Cold War." In *The Oxford Companion to the Supreme Court of the United States,* ed. Kermit L. Hall. New York: Oxford University Press.

Bell, Roger. 1984. *Last Among Equals: Hawaii Statehood and American Politics.* Honolulu: University of Hawaii Press.

Bell, Tom W. 1993. "The Third Amendment: Forgotten but Not Gone." *William & Mary Bill of Rights Journal* 2: 117–150.

Bellamy, Edward. 1888. *Looking Backward.* Reprint, New York: Magnum Books, 1968.

Bellesiles, Michael A. 2000. *Arming America: The Origins of a National Gun Culture.* New York: Alfred A. Knopf.

Benjamin, Gerald, and Thomas Gais. 1996. "Constitutional Conventionphobia." *Hofstra Law and Policy Symposium* 1: 53–77.

Benjamin, Gerald, and Michael J. Malbin, eds. 1992. *Limiting Legislative Terms.* Washington, DC: Congressional Quarterly Press.

Bennett, Robert W. 2001. "Popular Election of the President without a Constitutional Amendment." *Green Bag* 2d 4 (Spring): 241–246.

Benson, Ben, and M. J. "'Red" Beckman. 1985. *The Law That Never Was—The Fraud of the 16th Amendment and Personal Income Tax.* South Holland, IL: Constitutional Research Association.

Benson, Paul R., Jr. 1970. *The Supreme Court and the Commerce Clause, 1937–1970.* New York: Denellen.

Bentley, Curt. 2007. "Constrained by the Liberal Tradition: Why the Supreme Court Has Not Found Positive Rights in the American Constitution." *Brigham Young University Law Review* 2007: 1721–1765.

Berg, Larry L., Harlan Hahn, and John R. Schmidhauser. 1976. *Corruption in the American Political System.* Morristown, NJ: General Learning Press.

Berger, Raoul. 1973. *Impeachment: The Constitutional Problems.* Cambridge, MA: Harvard University Press.

Berke, Richard L. 1995. "Epic Political Realignments Often Aren't." *New York Times,* 1 January, E3.

Bernhard, Virginia, and Elizabeth FoxGenovese, eds. 1995. *The Birth of American Feminism: The Seneca Falls Woman's Convention of 1848.* St. James, NY: Brandywine Press.

Berns, Walter., ed. 1992. *After the People Vote: A Guide to the Electoral College.* Rev. ed. Washington, DC: AEI Press.

Bernstein, Richard B. 1993. "Fixing the Electoral College." *Constitution* 5 (Winter): 42–48.

———. 1992. "The Sleeper Wakes: The History and Legacy of the Twenty-seventh Amendment." *Fordham Law Review* 56 (December): 497–557.

Bernstein, Richard B., with Jerome Agel. 1993. *Amending America: If We Love the Constitution So Much, Why Do We Keep Trying to Change It?* New York: Random House.

Berry, Mary F. 1987. "How Hard It Is to Change." *New York Times Magazine,* 13 September, 93–98.

———. 1986. *Why ERA Failed: Politics, Women's Rights, and the Amending Process of the Constitution.* Bloomington: Indiana University Press.

Best, Judith. 1984a. "The Item Veto: Would the Founders Approve?" *Presidential Studies Quarterly* 14 (Spring): 183–188.

———. 1984b. *National Representation for the District of Columbia.* Frederick, MD: University Publications of America.

———. 1971. *The Case against Direct Election of the President: A Defense of the Electoral College.* Ithaca, NY: Cornell University Press.

Betts, James T. 1967. "The Scope of Immunity for Legislators and Their Employees." *Yale Law Journal* 77 (December): 366–389.

Beveridge, Albert J. 1916. *The Life of John Marshall.* 4 vols. Boston: Houghton Mifflin.

The Bible in the Public Schools. 1870. Cincinnati, OH: Robert Clarke & Co. Reprint, New York: Da Capo Press, introduction by Robert G. McCloskey, 1967.

"A Bicentennial Analysis of the American Political Structure." 1987. Washington, DC: Report and Recommendations of the Committee on the Constitutional System. January.

Bickel, Alexander. 1986. *The Least Dangerous Branch: The Supreme Court at the Bar of Politics.* 2d ed. New Haven, CT: Yale University Press.

"The Bill of Rights." 1991. Bicentennial issue of *Life* (Fall).

Bingham, Jonathan. 1986. "Democracy or Plutocracy? The Case for a Constitutional Amendment to Overturn *Buckley v. Valeo.*" *Annals of the Academy of Political and Social Sciences* 486 (July):103–114.

"Birch Evans Bayh, Jr." 2001. In *Contemporary Authors Online.* The Gale Group. Accessed 7 August 2001.

Birkby, Robert H. 1973. "The Supreme Court and the Bible Belt: Tennessee Reaction to the 'Schempp' Decision." In *The Impact of Supreme Court Decisions: Empirical Studies.* 2d ed. Ed. Theodore L. Becker and Malcolm M. Feeley. New York: Oxford University Press.

"The Birthright Citizenship Amendment: A Threat to Equality." 1994. *Harvard Law Review* 107: 1026–1043.

Biskupic, Joan. 1990. "Critics of Measure Win Fight, but Battle Scars Run Deep." *Congressional Quarterly Weekly Report* 48 (30 June): 2063–2064.

Bittker, Boris I. 1999. *Bittker on the Regulation of Interstate and Foreign Commerce.* Gaithersburg, MD: Aspen Law & Business.

Black, Charles L., Jr. 1979. "Amendment by a National Constitutional Convention: A Letter to a Senator." *Oklahoma Law Review* 32: 626–644.

———. 1978. "Correspondence: On Article I, Section 7, Clause 3—and the Amendment of the Constitution." *Yale Law Journal* 87: 896–900.

———. 1963. "The Proposed Amendment of Article V: A Threatened Disaster." *Yale Law Journal* 72

(April): 957–966. Black, Hugo L. 1969. *A Constitutional Faith.* New York: Alfred A. Knopf.

Black's Law Dictionary. 1969. 5th ed. St. Paul, MN: West.

Bledsoe, Craig W. 1989. "Executive Pay and Perquisites." In *Guide to the Presidency,* ed. Michael Nelson. Washington, DC: Congressional Quarterly Press.

Blocher, Joseph. 2008. "Amending the Exceptions Clause." *Minnesota Law Review* 92 (April): 971–1030.

Blocker, Jack S., Jr. 1976. *Retreat from Reform: The Prohibition Movement in the United States, 1890–1916.* Westport, CT: Greenwood Press.

Bloom, Joshua. 2000. "Black Panther Party." In *Civil Rights in the United States.* 2 vols. Ed. Waldo E. Maqrtin Jr. and Patricia Sullivan. New York: Macmillan Reference USA.

Bloomfield, Maxwell. 2000. *Peaceful Revolution: Constitutional Change and American Culture from Progressivism to the New Deal.* Cambridge, MA: Harvard University Press.

Bloomquist, Robert F. 2004. "The Presidential Oath, the American National Interest and a Call for Presiprudence." [AU: OK?]*University of Missouri-Kansas City Law Review* 73(Fall):1–52.

Bobbitt, Philip. 1992. "Constitutional Interpretation." In *The Oxford Companion to the Supreme Court of the United States,* ed. Kermit L. Hall. New York: Oxford University Press.

Bodenhamer, David J. 1992. *Fair Trial: Rights of the Accused in American History.* New York: Oxford University Press.

Bodenhamer, David J., and James W. Ely Jr., eds. 1993. *The Bill of Rights in Modern America after 200 Years.* Bloomington: Indiana University Press.

Boles, Janet K. 1979. *The Politics of the Equal Rights Amendment: Conflict and the Decision Process.* New York: Longman.

Boller, Paul E., Jr. 1984. *Presidential Campaigns.* New York: Oxford University Press.

Bonfield, Arthur E. 1968. "The Dirksen Amendment and the Article V Convention Process." *Michigan Law Review* 66 (March): 949–1000.

Bonsell, Thomas. 1995. *The UnAmericans: Trashing of the United States Constitution in the American Press.* Wauna, WA: Country Cottage Publishing.

Borden, Morton. 1979. "The Christian Amendment." *Civil War History* 25 (June): 156–167.

Bordin, Ruth. 1981. *Women and Temperance: The Quest for Power and Liberty, 1873–1900.* Philadelphia: Temple University Press.

Borchers, Patrick J. 1998. "Could a Treaty Trump Supreme Court Jurisdictional Doctrine? Judgments Conventions and Minimum Contacts." *Albany Law Review* 62: 1161–1176.

Bork, Robert H. 1997. *Slouching Towards Gomorrah: Modern Liberalism and American Decline.* New York: Harper Perennial.

———. 1990. *The Tempting of America: The Political Seduction of the Law.* New York: Free Press.

Boudreaux, Donald J., and A. C. Pritchard. 1003. "Rewriting the Constitution: An Economic Analysis of the Constitutional Amending Process." *Fordham Law Review* 62(October): 111–162.

Boudreaux, Paul. 2005/2006. "A Case for Recognizing Unenumerated Powers of Congress." *New York University Journal of Legislation and Public Policy* 9: 551–585.

Bowen, Catherine Drinker. 1966. *Miracle at Philadelphia: The Story of the Constitutional Convention May to September 1787.* Boston: Little, Brown.

Bowen, James W. 1994. "Enforcing the Balanced Budget Amendment." *Constitutional Law Journal* 4 (Spring): 565–620.

Bowling, Kenneth R. 1991. *The Creation of Washington, D.C.: The Idea and Location of the American Capital.* Fairfax, VA: George Mason University Press.

Bowman, Scott J. 2004. "Wild Political Dreaming: Constitutional Reformation of the United States Senate." *Fordham Law Review* 72 (March): 1017–1051.

Boyd, Steven R., ed. 1992. *Alternative Constitutions for the United States: A Documentary History.* Westport, CT: Greenwood Press.

Bradford, Gamaliel. 1893. "Congress and the Cabinet—II." *Annals of the American Academy of Political and Social Sciences* 4 (November): 289–299.

———. 1891. "Congress and the Cabinet." *Annals of the American Academy of Political and Social Sciences* 4 (November): 404–424.

Bradford, M. E. 1994. *Founding Fathers: Brief Lives of the Framers of the United States Constitution.* 2d ed. Lawrence: University Press of Kansas.

Bradley, Harold W. 1945. "The Political Thinking of George Washington." *Journal of Southern History* 11 (November): 469–486.

Bradsher, Keith. 1995. "Gap in Wealth in U.S. Called Widest in West." *New York Times,* 17 April, 1, C4.

Brandon, Mark E. 1995. "The 'Original' Thirteenth Amendment and the Limits to Formal Constitutional Change." In *Responding to Imperfection: The Theory and Practice of Constitutional Amendment,* ed. Sanford Levinson. Princeton, NJ: Princeton University Press.

Brasseau, Carl A. 1989. "Four Hundred Years of Acadian Life in North America." *Journal of Popular Culture* 23 (Summer): 3–22.

Brennan, Geoffrey, and James M. Buchanan. 2000. "Is Constitutional Revolution Possible in Democracy?" *The Reason of Rules: Constitutional Political Economy,* vol. 10 of *The Collected Works of James M. Buchanan.* Indianapolis: Liberty Fund.

Bridwell, R. Randall, and William J. Quirk. *Judicial Dictatorship.* New Brunswick, NJ: Transaction Publishers.

Broadwater, Jeff. 2006. *George Mason: Forgotten Father.* Chapel Hill: University of North Carolina Press.

Brown, Everett S. 1938. *Ratification of the Twenty-first Amendment to the Constitution of the United*

States; State Convention Records and Laws. Ann Arbor: University of Michigan Press.

———. 1935. "The Ratification of the Twenty-first Amendment." *American Political Science Review* 29 (December): 1005–1017.

Brown, Jennifer K. 1993. "The Nineteenth Amendment and Women's Equality." *Yale Law Journal* 102 (June): 2174–2204.

Brown, Raymond G. 1920. "The Sixteenth Amendment to the United States Constitution." *American Law Review* 54: 843–854.

Browne, Michael K. 2004. "International Victims' Rights Law: What Can be Gleaned from the Victims' Empowerrment Provisions in Germany as the United States Prepares to Consider the Adoption of a Victims' Rights Amendment to its Constitution?" *Hamline Law Review* 27(Winter): 15–44.

Bryant, Douglas H. 2002. "Unorthodox and Paradox: Revisiting the Ratification of the Fourteenth Amendment." *Alabama Law Review* 53: 555–581.

Bryant, Irving. 1965. *The Bill of Rights: Its Origin and Meaning.* Indianapolis, IN: Bobbs-Merrill.

Bryce, James. 1906. *The American Commonwealth.* 3d ed. 2 vols. New York: Macmillan.

———. 1905. "Flexible and Rigid Constitutions." In *Constitutions.* Germany: Scientia Verlag Aalen. Reprint of New York and London edition, 1980.

Buchanan, James M. 2005. "Three Amendments: Responsibility, Generality, and Natural Liberty." *Cato Unbound,* December 5, http://www .cato-unbound.org/2005/12/05/james -m-buchanan/three-amendments.

Budziszewski, J. 2002. "Judicial Restraints." *World* 17 (June 8): 16–18.

Bumiller, Elisabeth. 2002. "Bush to Undergo Colon Procedure: President Will Transfer Power to Cheney before Sedation." *New York Times,* 29 June, A1 and A11.

Burke, Yvonne B. 1976. "Validity of Attempts to Rescind Ratification of the Equal Rights Amendment." *University of Los Angeles Law Review* 8: 1–22.

Burgess, Susan R. 1992. *Contest for Constitutional Authority: The Abortion and War Powers Debates.* Lawrence: University Press of Kansas.

Burnham, Walter D. 1995. "Realignment Lives: The 1994 Earthquake and Its Implications." In *The Clinton Presidency: First Appraisals,* ed. Colin Campbell and Bert Rockman. Chatham, NJ: Chatham House.

———. 1970. *Critical Elections and the Mainsprings of American Politics.* New York: W. W. Norton.

Burns, James MacGregor. 1963. *The Deadlock of Democracy: Four-Party Politics in America.* Englewood Cliffs, NJ: Prentice-Hall, Inc.

Butler, David, and Bruce Cain. 1992. *Congressional Redistricting: Comparative and Theoretical Perspectives.* New York: Macmillan.

Butts, R. Freeman. 1978. *Public Education in the United States: From Revolution to Reform.* New York: Holt, Rinehart, and Winston.

Butzner, Jane, comp. 1941. *Constitutional Chaff— Rejected Suggestions of the Constitutional Convention of 1787 with Explanatory Argument.* New York: Columbia University Press.

Bybee, Jay S. 1997. "Ulysses at the Mast: Democracy, Federalism, and the Sirens' Song of the Seventeenth Amendment." *Northwestern University Law Review* 91 (Winter): 500–569.

Cahn, Edmond. 1954. "An American Contribution." In *Supreme Court and Supreme Law.* Bloomington: Indiana University Press.

Calhoun, John C. 1953. *A Disquisition on Government and Selections from the Discourse.* Edited by C. Gordon Post. Indianapolis, IN: Bobbs-Merrill. [Originally published as part of *The Works of John C. Calhoun.* Edited by Richard K. Crallé. New York: D. Appleton and Company, 1851–1856.] Reprint, New York: Russell and Russell, 1968.

———. 1851–1856. *The Works of John C. Calhoun,* ed. Richard K. Crallé. Reprint, New York: Russell and Russell, 1968.

Calmes, Jackie. 1996. "In Symbolical Gesture, House Is to Vote Today on Amendment Making It Harder to Boost Taxes." *Wall Street Journal* 127 (April 15): A20.

Caplan, Russell L. 1988. *Constitutional Brinkmanship: Amending the Constitution by National Convention.* New York: Oxford University Press.

———. 1983. "The History and Meaning of the Ninth Amendment." *Virginia Law Review* 69 (March): 223–268.

Carleton, David. 2002. *Student's Guide to Landmark Congressional Laws on Education.* Westport, CT: Greenwood Press.

Carroll, John. 1982. "Constitutional Law: Constitutional Amendment. Rescission of Ratification. Extension of Ratification Period. *State of Idaho v. Freeman.*" *Akron Law Review* 14 (Summer): 151–161.

Carson, Gerald. 1973. "The Income Tax and How It Grew." *American Heritage* 25 (December): 5–9, 79–88.

Carter. Dan T. 1964. *Scottsboro: A Tragedy of the American South.* New York: Oxford University Press.

Carter, Stephen L. 1994. *The Confirmation Mess: Cleaning Up the Federal Appointments Process.* New York: Basic Books.

Casey, Samuel B. 1995. "Religious Freedom Makes Good Neighbors." *Christian Legal Society Quarterly* 16 (Summer): 3.

Cassell, Paul G. 1999. "Barbarians at the Gates? A Reply to the Critics of the Victims' Rights Amendment." *Utah Law Review* 1999: 479–537.

Cassell, Paul G., and Steven J. Twist. 1996. "A Bill of Rights for Crime Victims." 127 *Wall Street Journal* (24 April): A15.

Ceaser, James W. 1988. "The Reagan Presidency and American Public Opinion." In *The Reagan Legacy: Promise and Performance,* ed. Charles O. Jones. Chatham, NJ: Chatham House.

———. 1986. "In Defense of Separation of Powers." In *Separation of Powers—Does It Still Work?* Ed. Robert A. Goldwin and Art Kaufman. Washington, DC: American Enterprise Institute.

Ceaser, James W., and Andrew W. Busch. 2001. *The Perfect Tie: The True Story of the 2000 Presidential Election.* Lanham, MD: Rowman & Littlefield.

"A Celebration of Women's Right to Vote." 1995. *New York Times,* 27 August, 9.

Chang, Stanley. 2007. "Updating the Electoral College: The National Popular Vote Legislation." *Harvard Journal on Legislation* 44 (Winter): 205–229.

Chapin, Bradley. 1964. *The American Law of Treason: Revolutionary and Early National Origins.* Seattle: University of Washington Press.

Chemerinsky, Erwin. 2000. "Citizens for the Constitution." *Insights on Law & Society* 1 (Fall): 14–15.

Chen, Paul. 2006. "The Constitutional Politics of Roads and Canals: Inter-branch Dialogue Over Internation Improvements, 1800–1828. *Whittier Law Review* 28 (Winter): 625–662.

Chernow, Ron. 2004. *Alexander Hamilton.* New York: Penguin.

"Children Adopted Abroad Win Automatic Citizenship." 2001. *Migration World Magazine* 19 (March): 12.

Chin, Gabriel J., and Angali Abraham. 2008. "Beyond the Supermajority: Post-Adoption Ratification of the Equality Amendments." *Arizona Law Review* 50 (Spring): 25–47.

Chittenden, Lucius E. 1864. *A Report of the Debates and Proceedings in the Secret Sessions of the Conference Convention for Proposing Amendments to the Constitution of the United States.* New York: D. Appleton & Company. Reprint, New York: Da Capo Press, 1971.

Christensen, Terry. 1995. *Local Politics: Governing at the Grassroots.* Belmont, CA: Wadsworth.

Christman, Henry M., ed. 1985. *Kingfish to America: Share Our Wealth: Selected Senatorial Papers of Huey P. Long.* New York: Shocken Books.

Church, Joseph. 1982. *America the Possible: Why and How the Constitution Should Be Rewritten.* New York: Macmillan.

Citizens for the Constitution. 1999. *Great and Extraordinary Occasions.* New York: Century Foundation, Inc.

Clapp, Rodney. 1990. *The Reconstructionists.* Downers Grove, IL: Intervarsity Press.

Clark, James C. 1985. *Faded Glory: Presidents out of Power.* New York: Praeger.

Clark, Walter. 1913. Address by Chief Justice Walter Clark Before the Federation of Women's Clubs, New Bern, N.C. 8 May 1913: Electronic Edition. http://doesouth.une.edu/nc/clark13/clark13.html.

Clark, Walter. 1906. "Some Defects of the Constitution of the United States." In *The Papers of Walter Clark.* Vol. 2, 1902–1924, ed. Aubrey L. Brooks and Hugh T. Lefler. Reprint, Chapel Hill, NC: University of North Carolina Press, 1950.

Claude, Inis L., Jr. 1971. *Swords into Plowshares: The Problems and Progress of International Organization.* 4th ed. New York: Random House.

Clem, Alan L. 1989. *Congress: Powers, Processes, and Politics.* Pacific Grove, CA: Brooks/Cole.

Clinton, Robert L. 1989. Marbury v. Madison *and Judicial Review.* Lawrence: University Press of Kansas.

Clotfetter, Charles T., and Phillip Cook. 1989. *Selling Hope: State Lotteries in America.* Cambridge, MA: Harvard University Press.

Clymer, Adam. 1996. "Senator Still Plans to Push Amendment on Tax Increase." *New York Times* 145 (April 17): A12.

Cobb, Frank. 1924. "A Twentieth Amendment." In *Cobb of "The World": A Leader in Liberalism,* ed. John L. Heaton. New York: E. P. Dutton.

Cochrane, Thad. 1994. "Constitutional Amendment Restoring the Right to the Free Exercise of Religion." *Congressional Record,* U.S. Senate, 14 June, 103rd Cong., 2d sess., 1994, Vol. 140, pt. 9.

Cogan, Neil H. ed. 1997. *The Complete Bill of Rights: The Drafts, Debates, Sources, and Origins.* New York: Oxford University Press.

Cohen, Charles E. 2006. "Eminent Domain After Kelo v. City of New London: An Argument for Banning Economic Development Takings." *Harvard Journal of Law and Public Policy* 29 (Spring): 491–565.

Cohen, Patricia. 2002. "9/11 Law Means More Snooping? Or Maybe Less?" *New York Times,* 7 September, B9.

Coit, Margaret L. 1961. *John C. Calhoun: American Portrait.* Boston: Houghton Mifflin.

Colantuono, Michael G. 1987. "The Revision of American State Constitutions: Legislative Power, Popular Sovereignty, and Constitutional Change." *California Law Review* 75 (July): 1473–1512.

Cole, Wayne S. 1962. *Senator Gerald P. Nye and American Foreign Relations.* Minneapolis: University of Minnesota Press.

Coleman, Charles. 1938. *The Constitution up to Date.* Bulletin no. 10. Cambridge, MA: National Council for Social Studies.

Coleman, Peter J. 1992. "Bankruptcy and Insolvency Legislation." In *The Oxford Companion to the Supreme Court of the United States,* ed. Kermit L. Hall. New York: Oxford University Press.

———. 1974. *Debtors and Creditors in America: Insolvency, Imprisonment for Debt, and Bankruptcy, 1607–1900.* Madison: State Historical Society of Wisconsin.

Committee on Federal Legislation of the Bar Association of the City of New York. n.d. *The Law of Presidential Impeachment.* New York: Harrow Books.

Committee on Federal State Relations. 1963. "Amending the Constitution to Strengthen the States in the Federal System." *State Government* 10 (Winter): 10–15.

The Committee to Frame a World Constitution. 1948. *Preliminary Draft of a World Constitution.* Chicago: University of Chicago Press.

"Composition and Jurisdiction of the Supreme Court—Proposed Constitutional Amendment." 1953. In *Congressional Record.* U.S. Senate, 16 February, 1106–1108.

"Conference of the States: An Action Plan to Restore Balance in the Federal System." 1995. Concept paper adopted by the Council of State Governments, the National Governors' Association, and the National Conference of State Legislatures. 1 February.

"Congressional Bomb Shelter Revealed." 1992. *Facts on File* 52: 681.

Congressional Quarterly. 2000. *American Political Leaders, 1789–2000.* Washington, DC: Congressional Quarterly.

———. 1991. *Guide to Congress.* 4th ed. Washington, DC: Congressional Quarterly.

Conklin, Curt E. 1996. "The Case of the Phantom Thirteenth Amendment: A Historical and Bibliographic Nightmare." *Law Library Journal* 88 (Winter): 121–127.

Conlan, Timothy J., James D. Riggle, and Donna E. Schwartz. 1995. "Deregulating Federalism? The Politics of Mandate Reform in the 104th Congress." *Publius: The Journal of Federalism* 25 (Summer): 23–40.

Conley, Patrick T., and John P. Kaminski, eds. 1992. *The Bill of Rights and the States: The Colonial and Revolutionary Origins of American Liberties.* Madison, WI: Madison House.

"The Conservation Bill of Rights." *Congressional Record,* 90th Cong., 2d sess., 13 June 1968, Vol. 114, pt. 13: 17116–17117.

"Constitution for a United Republic of America, Followed by an Index." 1970. *Center Magazine* 3 (September/October): 24–49.

"Constitution Party 2000 National Platform." http://www.constitutionpar ty.com/ustp–99p1. html. Accessed 29 May 2002.

"The Constitutional Amendment Process." http://www.archives.gov/federal_register/constitution/amendment_process.html. Accessed 11/26/02.

Constitutional Rights Foundation. "America Responds to Terrorism." http://www.crfusa/terror/America. Accessed 18 May 2002.

Contemporary Authors Online. 2001. The Gale Group.

"Continuity of Congress." http://www.aeipolitical-corner.org/continuity.htm. Accessed 20 May 2002.

Cooke, Edward F. 1984. *A Detailed Analysis of the Constitution.* 5th ed. Savage, MO: Littlefield Adams Quality Paperbacks.

Cooley, Thomas M. 1893. "The Power to Amend the Federal Constitution." *Michigan Law Journal* 2 (April): 109–120.

Cooper, Phillip, and Howard Ball. 1996. *The United States Supreme Court from the Inside Out.* Upper Saddle River, NJ: Prentice Hall.

Cornwell, Elmer E., Jr. 1981. "The American Constitutional Tradition: Its Impact and Development." In *The Constitutional Convention as an Amending Device,* ed. Kermit L. Hall, Harold M. Hyman, and Leon V. Sigal. Washington, DC: American Historical Association.

Cornwell, Elmer E., Jr., Jay S. Goodman, and Wayne R. Swanson. 1975. *State Constitutional Conventions: The Politics of the Revision Process in Seven States.* New York: Praeger.

Correspondents of *New York Times.* 2001. *36 Days: The Complete Chronicle of the 2000 Presidential Election Crisis.* New York: Henry Holt.

Cortner, Richard C. 1993. *The Iron Horse and the Constitution: The Railroads and the Transformation of the Fourteenth Amendment.* Westport, CT: Greenwood Press.

Corwin, Edward S. 1981. "The Constitution as Instrument and as Symbol." In *Corwin on the Constitution,* vol. 1, ed. Richard Loss. Ithaca, NY: Cornell University Press.

———. 1955. *The "Higher Law" Background of American Constitutional Law.* Ithaca, NY: Cornell University Press.

Cottrol, Robert J., ed. 1993. *Gun Control and the Constitution: Sources and Explorations of the Second Amendment.* 3 vols. New York: Garland.

"Covenant, Polity, and Constitutionalism." 1980. Special issue of *Publius: The Journal of Federalism* (Fall).

Craig, Barbara H. 1988. *Chadha: The Story of an Epic Constitutional Struggle.* New York: Oxford University Press.

Craig, Barbara H., and David M. O'Brien. 1993. *Abortion and American Politics.* Chatham, NJ: Chatham House.

Cram, Ralph. 1937. *The End of Democracy.* Boston: Marshall Jones Company.

———. 1935. *Convictions and Controversies.* Reprint, Freeport, NY: Books for Libraries Press, 1970.

Cramer, Clayton E. 1994. *For the Defense of Themselves and the State: The Original Intent and Judicial Interpretation of the Right to Keep and Bear Arms.* Westport, CT: Praeger.

Critchlow, Donald T. 2008. *Phyllis Schlafly and Grassroots Conservatism.* Princeton, NJ: Princeton University Press.

Critchlow, Donald T. and Cynthia L. Stacheki. 2008. "The Equal Rights Amendment Reconsidered: Politics, Policy, and Social Mobilization in a Democracy." *Journal of Policy History* 20: 157–176.

Crockett, David A. 2003. "Dodging the Bullet: Election Mechanics and the Problem of the Twenty-third Amendment." *PS: Political Sciene and Politics* 36 (July): 423–426.

Croly, Herbert. 1914. *Progressive Democracy.* New York: Macmillan. Reprint, New Brunswick, NJ: Transaction Publishers, 1998.

———. 1909. *The Promise of American Life.* New York: Macmillan Company. Reprint, Indianapolis: Bobbs-Merrill, 1965.

Cronin, Thomas E. 1989. *Direct Democracy: The Politics of Initiative, Referendum, and Recall.* Cambridge, MA: Harvard University Press.

Cronin, Thomas E., and Jeffrey J. Weill. 1985. "An Item Veto for the President?" *Congress & the Presidency* 12 (Autumn): 127–151.

Crook, Sara Brandes, and John R. Hibbing. 1997. "A Not-So-Distant Mirror: The 17th Amendment and Congressional Change." *American Political Science Review* 91 (December): 845–853.

Cullinan, Gerald. 1968. *The Post Office Department.* New York: Praeger.

Cummings, Richard. 1980. *Proposition Fourteen: A Secessionist Remedy.* Sagaponack, NY: The Permanent Press.

Cunningham, Noble E. 1987. *The Pursuit of Reason: The Life of Thomas Jefferson.* Baton Rouge: Louisiana State University Press.

Curriden, Mark, and Leroy Phillips Jr. 1999. *Contempt of Court: The Turn-of-the-Century Lynching That Launched 100 Years of Federalism.* New York: Faber and Faber, Inc.

Currie, David P. 1985. *The Constitution in the Supreme Court: The First One Hundred Years, 1789–1888.* Chicago: University of Chicago Press.

Curry, James A., Richard B. Riley, and Richard M. Battistoni. 1989. *Constitutional Government: The American Experience.* St. Paul, MN: West.

Curtis, Michael Kent. 2003. "John A. Bingham and the Story of American Liberty: The Lost Cause Meets the "Lost Clause."" *Akron Law Review* 36:617–69.

Curtis, Michael K. 1986. *No State Shall Abridge: The Fourteenth Amendment and the Bill of Rights.* Durham, NC: Duke University Press.

Curtis, Michael K., ed. 1993. *The Constitution and the Flag.* Vol. 2 of *The Flag Burning Cases.* New York: Garland.

Cushman, Barry. 2002. "Mr. Dooley and Mr. Gallop: Public Opinion and Constitutional Change in the 1930s." *Buffalo Law Review* 50 (Winter): 7–101.

Cutler, Lloyd N. 1986. "To Form a Government." in *Separation of Powers—Does It Still Work?* ed. Robert Al Goldwin and Art Kaufman. Washington, DC: American Enterprise Institute for Public Policy Research.

Dahl, Robert. 2001. *How Democratic Is the American Constitution?* New Haven, CT: Yale University Press.

Dalzell, Stewart, and Eric J. Beste. 1994. "Is the Twenty-seventh Amendment 200 Years Too Late?" *George Washington Law Review* 62 (April): 501–545.

D'Amato, A. D. 1995. "Conflict of Laws Rules and the Interstate Recognition of SameSex Marriages." *University of Illinois Law Review* 1995: 911–943.

Danforth, John C. 1994. *Resurrection: The Confirmation of Clarence Thomas.* New York: Viking.

Daniels, Roger. 1968. *The Politics of Prejudice.* New York: Antheneum.

DaSilva, Virgilio Afonso. 2007. "A Fossilized Constitution?" *Ratio Juris* 17 (December): 454–473.

Davidson, Elizabeth H. 1939. *Child Labor Legislation in the Southern Textile States.* Chapel Hill: University of North Carolina Press.

Davidson, James D. 1992. "Yes, to Save Congress from Itself." *The World & I* 7 (August): 110, 112–115.

Davidson, Jim, with Eric Klien, Norm Doering, and Lee Crocker. 1994. *The Atlantis Papers.* Houston, TX: Interglobal Paratronics, Inc.

Davidson, Michael. 2002. "Notes on Proposed Constitutional Amendments on Temporary Appointments of Members of the House." 20 January. www.aeipoliticalcorner.org/continuity.htm. Accessed 16 May 2002.

Davidson, Roger H., and Walter J. Oleszek. 1994. *Congress and Its Members.* 4th ed. Washington, DC: Congressional Quarterly.

Davis, Richard. 1985. *Proposed Amendments to the Constitution of the United States of America Introduced in Congress from the 91st Congress, 1st Session, through the 98th Congress, 2d Session, January 1969–December 1984.* Washington, DC: Congressional Research Service Report no. 85–36 GOV.

Davis, Sue. 2008. *The Political Thought of Elizabeth Cady Stanton.* New York: New York University Press.

Davis, William C. 1994. *"A Government of Our Own": The Making of the Confederacy.* New York: Free Press.

Deale, Frank E. L. 2000. "The Unhappy History of Economic Rights in the United States and Prospects for Their Creation and Renewal." *Howard Law Journal* 43 (Spring): 281–342.

DeConde, Alexander. 1971. *A History of American Foreign Policy.* 2d ed. New York: Charles Scribner's Sons.

DeHart, Paul R. 2007. *Uncovering the Constitution's Moral Design.* Columbia: University of Missouri Press.

Dellinger, Walter. 1983. "The Legitimacy of Constitutional Change: Rethinking the Amending Process." *Harvard Law Review* 97 (December): 380–432.

———. 1979. "The Recurring Question of the 'Limited' Constitutional Convention." *Yale Law Journal* 88: 1623–1640.

Denning, Brannon P. 2001. "Reforming the New Confirmation Process: Replacing 'Despise and

Resent' with 'Advice and Consent'" *Administrative Law Review* 53 (Winter): 1–44.

———. 1998. "Gun Shy: The Second Amendment as an 'Underenforced Constitutional Norm.'" *Harvard Journal of Law & Public Policy* 21 (Summer): 719–791.

Denning, Brannon P., and Brooks R. Smith. 1999. "Uneasy Riders: The Case for a Truth-in-Legislation Amendment." *Utah Law Review* (1999): 957–1025.

Denning, Brannon P., and John R. Vile. 2002. "The Relevance of Constitutional Amendments: A Response to David Strauss." *Tulane Law Review* 77 (November): 247–282.

———. 2000. "Necromancing the Equal Rights Amendment." *Constitutional Commentary* 17 (Winter): 593–602.

Dennison, George M. 1976. *The Dorr War: Republicanism on Trial, 1831–1861*. Lexington: University Press of Kentucky.

DeRosa, Marshall L. 1996. *The Ninth Amendment and the Politics of Creative Jurisprudence: Disparaging the Fundamental Right of Popular Control*. New Brunswick, NJ: Transaction Publishers.

———. 1991. *The Confederate Constitution of 1861: An Inquiry into American Constitutionalism*. Columbia: University of Missouri Press.

Dershowitz, Alan M. 2001. *Supreme Injustice: How the High Court Hijacked Election 2000*. New York: Oxford University Press.

Diamond, Martin. 1976. "The Revolution of Sober Expectations." In *America's Continuing Revolution*. Garden City, NY: Anchor Press.

Dierenfield, Bruce J. 2007. *The Battle Over School Prayer: How Engel v. Vitale Changed America*. Lawrence: University Press of Kansas.

Diller, Daniel C. 1989. "Chief of State." In *Guide to the Presidency*, ed. Michael Nelson. Washington, DC: Congressional Quarterly.

Dillon, Conley. 1977. "American Constitutional Review: Are We Preparing for the 21st Century?" *World Affairs* 140 (Summer): 5–24.

———. 1974. "Recommendation for the Establishment of a Permanent Commission of Constitutional Review." *Bureaucrat* 3 (July): 211–224.

Dillon, Merton L. 1974. *The Abolitionists: The Growth of a Dissenting Minority*. De Kalb: Northern Illinois University Press.

Dionne, E. J., and William Kristol, eds. 2001. *Bush v. Gore: The Court Cases and the Commentary*. Washington, DC: The Brookings Institution.

Dirksen, Everett M. 1968. "The Supreme Court and the People." *Michigan Law Review* 66 (March): 837–874.

DiTullo, James E., and John B. Schochet. 2004. "Saving This Honorable Court: A Proposal to Replace Life Tenure on the Supreme Court with Staggered, Nonrenewable Eighteen-year Terms." *Virginia Law Review* 90 (June):1093–1149.

Dodd, Walter F. 1921. "Amending the Federal Constitution." *Yale Law Journal* 30 (February): 321–354.

———. 1910. *The Revision and Amendment of State Constitutions*. Baltimore: Johns Hopkins University Press.

Doherty, Brian. 2008. *Gun Control on Trial: Inside the Supreme Court Battle Over the Second Amendment*. Washington, DC: Cato Institute.

Dolbeare, Kenneth M., and Janette K. Hubbell. 1996. *USA 2012: After the Middle-Class Revolution*. Chatham, NJ: Chatham House Publishers.

Donald, David H. 1995. *Lincoln*. New York: Simon & Schuster.

Dorsen, Norman. 2000. "Flag Desecration in Courts, Congress, and Country." *Thomas M. Cooley Law Review* 17 (Michaelmas Term): 417–442.

Douglass, Frederick. 1845. *Narrative of the Life of Frederick Douglass: An American Slave*. Boston: Anti-Slavery Office. Reprint, New York: Signet Books, 1968.

Dow, David R. 1990. "When Words Mean What We Believe They Say: The Case of Article V." *Iowa Law Review* 76 (October): 1–66.

Dreisbach, Daniel L. 1996. "In Search of a Christian Commonwealth: An Examination of Selected Nineteenth-Century Commentaries on References to God and the Christian Religion in the United States Constitution." *Baylor Law Review* 48: 928–1000.

Dry, Murray. 1991. "Flag Burning and the Constitution." In *The Supreme Court Review, 1990*, ed. Gerhard Casper et al. Chicago: University of Chicago Press.

Dubois, Ellen Carol. 1991. "Frances Willard." *The Reader's Companion to American History*. P. 1151. Accessed through http://www.galenet.com.

———. 1978. *Feminism and Suffrage: The Emergence of an Independent Women's Movement in America, 1848–1869*. Ithaca, NY: Cornell University Press.

Du Bois, W. E. Burghardt. 1928–1936. "Frederick Douglass." *Dictionary of American Biography*. American Council of Learned Societies. Accessed through http://www.galenet.com.

Duker, William F. 1977. "The President's Power to Pardon: A Constitutional History." *William and Mary Law Review* 18 (Spring): 475–538.

Duggin, Sarah Helene, and Mary Beth Collins. 2005. "'Natural Born' in the USA: The Striking Unfairness and Dangerous Ambiguity of the Constitution's Presidential Qualifications Clause and Why We Need to Fix It." *Boston University Law Review* 85 (February): 53–154.

Dumond, Dwight L. 1973. *The Secession Movement, 1860–1861*. New York: Octagon Books.

Dunne, Gerald T. 1977. *Hugo Black and the Judicial Revolution*. New York: Simon & Schuster.

Durst, Jack. 2000. "Constitution of the Republic." http://synx_jd.tripod.com. Accessed 18 May 2002.

Earle, W. H. 1987. "The Phantom Amendment and the Duchess of Baltimore." *American History Illustrated* 22 (November): 32–39.

Eastland, Terry. 1996. *Ending Affirmative Action: The Case for Colorblind Justice.* New York: Basic Books.

Eastland, Terry, and William J. Bennett. 1979. *Counting by Race.* New York: Basic Books.

Edel, Wilbur. 1981. *A Constitutional Convention: Threat or Challenge?* New York: Praeger.

Edgar, William. 2001. "The Passing of R. J. Rushdonny." *First Things: A Monthly Journal of Religion and Public Life* (August): 24.

Edwards, George C. III. 2004. *Why the Electoral College Is Bad for America.* New Haven: Yale University Press.

Ehrlich, Walter. 1965. *They Have No Rights: Dred Scott's Struggle for Freedom.* Westport, CT: Greenwood Press.

Eidelberg, Paul. 1968. *The Philosophy of the American Constitution: A Reinterpretation of the Intentions of the Founding Fathers.* New York: Free Press.

Eiselen, Malcolm R. 1941. "Can We Amend the Constitution?" *South Atlantic Quarterly* 40 (October): 333–341.

———. 1937. "Dare We Call a Federal Convention?" *North American Review* 244 (Autumn): 27–28.

Eisenach, Eldon J. 1994. *The Lost Promise of Progressivism.* Lawrence: University Press of Kansas.

Ekirch, Arthur A., Jr. 1974. *Progressivism in America: A Study of the Era from Theodore Roosevelt to Woodrow Wilson.* New York: New Viewpoints.

Elliott, Ward. 1974. *The Rise of Guardian Democracy.* Cambridge, MA: Harvard University Press.

Elliott, William Y. 1935. *The Need for Constitutional Reform: A Program for National Security.* New York: Whittlesey House.

Ellis, Frederick, with Carl Frederick. 2000. *The Oakland Statement: A Political Adventure Novel.* Miami, FL: Synergy International of the Americas.

Ellis, L. Ethan. 1961. *Frank B. Kellogg and American Foreign Relations, 1925–1929.* New Brunswick, NJ: Rutgers University Press.

Ellis, Richard E. 2007. *Aggressive Nationalism: McCulloch v. Maryland and the Foundation of Federal Authority in the Young Republic.* New York: Oxford University Press.

Elster, Joh. 2000. *Ulysses Unbound.* Cambridge: Cambridge University Press.

Ely, James W. 1992. *The Guardian of Every Other Right: A Constitutional History of Property Rights.* New York: Oxford University Press.

Ely, John Hart. 1993. *War and Responsibility: Constitutional Lessons of Vietnam and Its Aftermath.* Princeton, NJ: Princeton University Press.

———. 1980. *Democracy and Distrust.* Cambridge, MA: Harvard University Press.

Engdahl, David E. 1994. "The Spending Power." *Duke Law Journal* 44 (October): 1–109.

The English Language Amendment. 1985. Hearings before the Subcommittee on the Constitution of the Committee on the Judiciary, U.S. Senate. Washington, DC: U.S. Government Printing Office.

English Language Constitutional Amendments. 1989. Hearings before the Subcommittee on the Judiciary, House of Representatives. Washington, DC: U.S. Government Printing Office.

Epstein, Barbara L. 1981. *The Politics of Domesticity: Women, Evangelism, and Temperance in Nineteenth-Century America.* Middletown, CT: Wesleyan University Press.

Epstein, Richard A. 2006. *How Progressives Rewrote the Constitution.* Washington, DC: Cato Institute.

Epstein, Lee, and Joseph F. Kobylka. 1992. *The Supreme Court and Legal Change: Abortion and the Death Penalty.* Chapel Hill, NC: University of North Carolina Press.

Erdman, Sol, and Lawrence Susskind. 1995. *Reinventing Congress for the 21st Century: Toward a Politics of Accountability, Participation and Consensus.* New York: Frontier Press.

Ernst, Morris L. 1973. *The Great Reversals: Tales of the Supreme Court.* New York: Weybright and Talley.

Ervin, Sam J., Jr. 1984. *Preserving the Constitution: The Autobiography of Sam J. Ervin Jr.* Charlottesville, VA: Michie.

———. 1968. "Proposed Legislation to Implement the Convention Method of Amending the Constitution." *Michigan Law Review* 66 (March): 875–902.

Eskridge, William N., Jr. 2008. "No Easy Constitutional Solution for Big Government." *Northwestern University Law Review* 102 (Winter): 457–460.

———. 1991. "Overriding Supreme Court Statutory Interpretations Decisions." *Yale Law Journal* 101 (November): 331–455.

Eskridge, William N., Jr., and Sanford Levinson. 1998. *Constitutional Stupidities, Constitutional Tragedies.* New York: New York University Press.

Eskridge, William N., Jr., and John Ferejohn. 2001. "Super-statutes." *Duke Law Journal* 50 (March): 1215–76.

Estaville, Lawrence E. 1990. "The Louisiana French Language in the Nineteenth Century." *Southeastern Geographer* 30 (November): 107–120.

Euchner, Charles C., and John A. Maltese. 1989. "The Electoral Process." In *Guide to the Presidency,* ed. Michael Nelson. Washington, DC: Congressional Quarterly.

Fairman, Charles. 1949. "Does the Fourteenth Amendment Incorporate the Bill of Rights? The Original Understanding." *Stanford Law Review* 2 (December): 5–139.

Fallon, Richard H., Jr. 2001. *Implementing the Constitution.* Cambridge, MA: Harvard University Press.

Farber, Daniel A. 2007. *Retained By the People: The "Silent" Ninth Amendment and the Constitutional Rights Americans Don't Know They Have.* New York: Basic Books.

Farnsworth, Ward. 2005. "The Regulation of Turnover on the Supreme Court." *University of Illinois Law Review* 2005: 407–453.

Farnsworth, Ward. 2000. "Women under Reconstruction: The Congressional Understanding." *Northwestern University Law Review* 94 (Summer): 1229–1295.

Farrand, Max, ed. 1966. *The Records of the Federal Convention.* 4 vols. New Haven, CT: Yale University Press.

Farris, Michael P. 1999. "Only a Constitutional Amendment Can Guarantee Religious Freedom for All." *Cardozo Law Review* 21 (December): 689–706.

Feerick, John D. 1992. *The Twenty-fifth Amendment: Its Complete History and Applications.* New York: Fordham University Press.

———. 1965. *From Failing Hands: The Story of Presidential Succession.* New York: Fordham University Press.

Fehrenbacher, Don E. 1978. *The Dred Scott Case: Its Significance for American Law and Politics.* New York: Oxford University Press.

Fernandez, Ferdinand F. 1966. "The Constitutionality of the Fourteenth Amendment." *Southern California Law Review* 39: 378–407.

Ferrell, Claudine L. 1986. *Nightmare and Dream: AntiLynching in Congress 1917–1922.* New York: Garland.

Ferreres-Comella, Victor. 2000. "A Defense of Constitutional Rigidity." In *Analysis and Right,* ed. Paul Comanducci and Riccardo Guastini. Turin, Italy: G. Giappichelli Publisher.

Fineman, Howard. 2002. "One Nation, Under . . . Who?" *Newsweek* 140 (July 8): 20–25.

Finer, Herman. 1960. *The Presidency, Crisis and Regeneration: An Essay in Possibilities.* Chicago: University of Chicago Press.

Fink, Richard H., and Jack C. High, eds. 1987. *A Nation in Debt: Economists Debate the Federal Budget Deficit.* Frederick, MD: University Publications of America.

Finkelman, Paul. 2000. "'A Well Regulated Militia': The Second Amendment in Historical Perspective. *Chicago-Kent Law Review* 76: 195–236.

———. 1992. "Slavery." In *The Oxford Companion to the Supreme Court of the United States,* ed. Kermit L. Hall. New York: Oxford University Press.

———. 1991. "James Madison and the Bill of Rights: A Reluctant Paternity." In *The Supreme Court Review, 1990.* Chicago: University of Chicago Press.

———. 1981. *An Imperfect Union: Slavery, Federalism and Comity.* Chapel Hill: University of North Carolina Press.

Finletter, Thomas K. 1945. *Can Representative Government Do the Job?* New York: Reynal and Hitchcock.

Fisch, William B. 2006. "Constitutional Referendum in the United States of America." *The American Journal of Comparative Law* 54(Fall):485–504.

Fiscus, Ron. 1992. *The Constitutional Logic of Affirmative Action.* Durham, NC: Duke University Press.

Fisher, Louis. 1993. "The Legislative Veto: Invalidated, It Survives." *Law and Contemporary Problems* 56 (Autumn): 273–292.

———. 1991. *Constitutional Conflicts between Congress and the President.* 3d ed. Lawrence: University Press of Kansas.

Fisher, Sidney G. 1862. *A Philadelphia Perspective: The Diary of Sidney George Fisher Covering the Years 1834–1871.* Reprint, Philadelphia: Historical Society of Pennsylvania, 1967.

———. 1862. *The Trial of the Constitution.* Reprint, New York: Da Capo Press, 1972.

Fitzpatrick, John C. 1931–1944. *The Writings of George Washington.* 39 vols. Washington, DC: U.S. Government Printing Office.

Flack, Horace E. 1908. *The Adoption of the Fourteenth Amendment.* Baltimore: Johns Hopkins. Reprint, Gloucester, MA: Peter Smith, 1965.

Flaherty, Martin S. 2002. "The Legacy of Chief Justice John Marshall: John Marshall, McCulloch v. Maryland, and 'We the People': Revisions in Need of Revising." *William and Mary Law Review* 43 (March): 1339–1397.

Fleming, James M. 2009. "Toward a More Democratic Congress?" *Boston University Law Review* 89 (April): 629–40.

Flexnor, Eleanor. 1974. *Century of Struggle: The Woman's Rights Movement in the United States.* New York: Atheneum.

Fogleson, Robert M., and Richard E. Rubenstein. 1969. *Mass Violence in America: Invasion at Harper's Ferry.* New York: Arno Press.

Foley, Michael. 1989. *The Silence of Constitutions: Gaps, "Abeyances" and Political Temperament in the Maintenance of Government.* London: Routledge.

Folton, Richard T. 1996. "Horror Stories." *Liberty* (March/April): 6–8.

Foner, Eric. 1970. *Free Soil, Free Labor, Free Men: The Ideology of the Republican Party before the Civil War.* New York: Oxford University Press.

Foner, Eric, and John A. Garraty, eds. 1991. *The Reader's Companion to American History.* Boston: Houghton Mifflin.

Ford, Paul L., ed. 1898. *The Federalist.* New York: Henry Holt. [Originally published as series of newspaper articles from 1787–1788.]

"Forum: Historians and Guns." 2002. *William and Mary Quarterly* 59, 3d Series (January): 203–268.

Fowler, Robert B. 1986. *Carrie Catt: Feminist Politician.* Boston: Northeastern University Press.

Fraley, Colette. 1995. "House Opponents Savor Gains; Senate Outlook Is Unclear." *Congressional Quarterly Weekly Report* 53 (29 July): 2276–2277.

"Francis Elizabeth Caroline Willard." 1928–1936. *Dictionary of American Biography* Base Set. American Council of Learned Societies. Accessed through http://www.galenet.com.

Frank, Jerome. 1969. *Courts on Trial: Myth and Reality in American Justice.* New York: Atheneum.

Frankfurter, Felix. 1974. *The Commerce Clause under Marshall, Taney and Waite.* Chicago: Quadrangle Books.

Freedman, Russell. 1994. *Lewis Hine and the Crusade against Child Labor.* New York: Clarion Books.

Freedman, Samuel S., and Pamela J. Naughton. 1978. *ERA: May a State Change Its Vote?* Detroit, MI: Wayne State University Press.

Freedoms Foundation. 1985. "Bill of Responsibilities." Valley Forge: Freedom Foundation.

Frenzel, Bill. 1992. "Term Limits and the Immortal Congress." *Brookings Review* 10 (Spring): 18–22.

Freyer, Tony. 1990. *Hugo L. Black and the Dilemma of American Liberalism.* Glenville, IL: Scott Foresman.

Friedman, Barry. 1992. "When Rights Encounter Realitiy: Enforcing Federal Remedies." *Southern California Law Review* 65 (January): 7354–7780.

Friedman, Barry, and Scott B. Smith. 1998. "The Sedimentary Constitution." *University of Pennsylvania Law Review* 147 (November): 1–90.

Friendly, Henry J. 1968. "The Fifth Amendment Tomorrow: The Case for Constitutional Change." *University of Cincinnati Law Review* 37 (Fall): 671–726.

Frierson, William. 1920. "Amending the Constitution of the United States: A Reply to Mr. Marbury." *Harvard Law Review* 33 (March): 659–666.

Fritz, Christian G. 2004. "Fallacies of American Constitutionalism." *Rutgers Law Journal* 35 (Summer): 1327–1369.

Fry, Amelia R. 1986. "Alice Paul and the ERA." In *Rights of Passage: The Past and Future of the ERA,* ed. Joan Hoff-Wilson. Bloomington: Indiana University Press.

Fuess, Calude Moore. 1928–1936. "William Lloyd Garrison." *Dictionary of American Biography,* Base Set. American Council of Learned Societies. Accessed through http://www.galenet.com.

Funston, Richard Y. 1977. *Constitution Counterrevolution? The Warren Court and the Burger Court: Judicial Policy Making in Modern America.* New York: Schenkman.

Gabriel, Mary. 1998. *Notorious Victoria: The Life of Victoria Woodhull,* Uncensored. Chapel Hill, NC: Algonquin Books.

Gallagher, Maggie. 2002. "Live Your Life, but Marriage Is for Men and Women." *The Tennessean,* 30 May, 9A.

Gammie, Beth. 1989. "State ERA's: Problems and Possibilities." *University of Illinois Law Review* 1989: 1123–1159.

Gangala, Thomas. 2007. *From the Primaries to the Polls: How to Repair America's Broken Presidential Nomination Process.* Westport, CT: Praeger.

Garcia, Alfredo. 1992. *The Sixth Amendment in Modern American Jurisprudence: A Critical Perspective.* New York: Greenwood Press.

Gardiner, William. 1973. *A Proposed Constitution for the United States of America.* Summerfield, FL: William Gardiner.

Garrett, Stephen A. 1972. "Foreign Policy and the American Constitution: The Bricker Amendment in Contemporary Perspective." *International Studies Quarterly* 16 (June): 187–220.

Garrow, David J. 2000. "Mental Decrepitude on the U.S. Supreme Court: The Historical Case for a 28th Amendment." *University of Chicago Law Review* 67: 995–1087.

———. 1994. *Liberty and Sexuality: The Right to Privacy and the Making of* Roe v. Wade. New York: Macmillan.

Gatell, Frank O. 1969. "John McLean." In *The Justices of the United States Supreme Court, 1789–1969: Their Lives and Major Opinions.* Vol. 1, ed. Leon Friedman and Fred L. Israel. New York: R. R. Bowker.

Gavzer, Bernard. 1995. "Life behind Bars." *Parade Magazine* 13 August, 4–7.

Geiger, Virginia, and Jeanne H. Stevenson. 1989. *The Living Constitution, 1787, 1987, 2187.* Lanham, MD: University Press of America.

George, Henry. 1938. *Progress and Poverty: An Inquiry into the Cause of Industrial Depressions and of Increase of Want with Increase of Wealth, the Remedy.* 50th anniversary ed. New York: Robert Schalkenback Foundation.

George, Robert P. 2001. "The 28th Amendment: It Is Time to Protect Marriage, and Democracy, in America." *National Review* 53 (July 23): 32–34.

Gerber, Scott D. 1995. *To Secure These Rights: The Declaration of Independence and Constitutional Interpretation.* New York: New York University Press.

Gerhardt, Michael J. 2008. "Non-Judicial Precedent." *Vanderbilt Law Review* 61 (April): 713–784.

———. 2002. "The Rhetoric of Judicial Critique: From Judicial Restraint to the Virtual Bill of Rights." *William and Mary Bill of Rights Journal* 10 (April): 585–645.

Gerken, Heather K. 2007. "The Hydraulics of Constitutional Reform: A Skeptical Response to Our Undemocratic Constitution." *Drake Law Review* 55 (Summer): 925–943.

Germond, Jack W., and Jules Witcover. 1999. "After the Trial, Revisions Are in Order." *National Journal* 31 (January 30): 296.

Gettlinger, Stephen. 1994. "New Filibuster Tactics Imperil Next Senate." *Congressional Quarterly* 52 (5 November): 3198.

Gerring, John and Strom C. Thacker. 2008. *A Centripetal Theory of Democratic Goverance.* New York: Cambridge University Press.

Gildor, Dan L. 2005. "Preserving the Priceless: A Constitutional Amendment to Empower Congress to Preserve, Protect, and Promote the Environment." *Ecology Law Quarterly* 32: 821–61.

Gillespie, Ed, and Bob Schellhas, eds. 1994. *Contract with America: The Bold Plan by Rep. Newt Gingrich, Rep. Dick Armey, and the House Republicans to Change the Nation.* New York: Random House.

Gillespie, Michael L., and Michael Lienesch, eds. 1989. *Ratifying the Constitution.* Lawrence: University Press of Kansas.

Gillman, Howard. 2001. *The Votes That Counted: How the Court Decided the 2000 Presidential Election.* Chicago: University of Chicago Press.

———. 1997. "The Collapse of Constitutional Originalism and the Rise of the Notion of the 'Living Constitution' in the Course of American State-Building." *Studies in American Political Development* 11 (Fall): 191–247.

———. 1993. *The Constitution Besieged: The Rise and Demise of Lochner Era Police Powers Jurisprudence.* Durham, NC: Duke University Press.

Gillmor, Paul, and Fred Eames. 1994. "Reconstruction of Federalism: A Constitutional Amendment to Prohibit Unfunded Mandates." *Harvard Journal on Legislation* 31 (Summer): 395–413.

Gilmore, Al-Tony. 1973. "Jack Jackson and White Women: The National Impact." *Journal of Negro History* 58 (January):18–38.

Ginsburg, Ruth B. 1989–1990. "On Amending the Constitution: A Plea for Patience." *University of Arkansas at Little Rock Law Journal* 12: 677–694.

———. 1969. "Ratification of the Equal Rights Amendment: A Question of Time." *Texas Law Review* 57: 919–945.

Glasson, William H., and David Kinley. 1918. *Federal Military Pensions in the United States.* New York: Oxford University Press.

Glendon, Mary Ann. 1992. "Rights in Twentieth-Century Constitutions." *University of Chicago Law Review* 59 (Winter): 519–538.

———. 1991. *Rights Talk: The Impoverishment of Political Discourse.* New York: Free Press.

———. 1987. *Abortion and Divorce in Western Law.* Cambridge, MA: Harvard University Press.

Glick, Henry R. 1988. *Courts, Politics, and Justice.* 2d ed. New York: McGraw-Hill.

Godkin, E. L. 1864. "The Constitution and Its Defects." *North American Review* 99 (July): 117–143.

Goldsmith, Barbara. 1998. *Other Powers: The Age of Suffrage, Spiritualism, and the Scandalous Victoria Woodhull.* New York: Alfred A. Knopf.

Goldstein, Leslie F. 1991. *In Defense of the Text: Democracy and Constitutional Theory.* Savage, MD: Rowman and Littlefield.

———. 1987. "The ERA and the U.S. Supreme Court." In *Research in Law and Policy Studies,* ed. Stuart S. Nagel. Greenwich, CT: JAI.

Goldstein, Robert J. 2000. *Flag Burning and Free Speech.* Lawrence: University Press of Kansas.

———. 1996. *The American Flag Desecration Controversy: A Collection of Documents from the Civil War to 1990.* Kent, OH: Kent State University Press.

———. 1995. *Burning the Flag: The Great 1989–1990 American Flag Desecration Controversy.* Kent, OH: Kent State University Press.

———. 1994. *Saving "Old Glory": The History of the American Flag Desecration Controversy.* Boulder, CO: Westview.

———. 1990. "The Great 1989–1990 Flag Flap: A Historical, Political, and Legal Analysis." *University of Miami Law Review* 45 (September): 19–106.

Gonzalez, Carlos E. 2005. "Representational Structures Through Which We the People Ratify Constitutions: The Troubling Original Understanding of the Constitution's Ratification Clauses." *University of California Davis Law Review* 38 (June): 1373–1504.

Goodnow, Frank J. 1911. *Social Reform and the Constitution.* New York: The Macmillan Co. Reprint, New York: Burt Franklin, 1970.

Goodstein, Laurie. 1995. "Religious Freedom Amendment Passed." *Washington Post,* 9 June, A12.

Gordon, Charles. 1982. "The Power of Congress to Terminate United States Citizenship." *Connecticut Law Review* 4 (Spring): 611–632.

———. 1968. "Who Can Be President of the United States: The Unresolved Enigma." *Maryland Law Review* 28 (Winter): 1–32.

Gordon, Sarah Barringer. 2002. *The Mormon Question: Polygamy and Constitutional Conflict in Nineteenth-Century America.* Chapel Hill: University of North Carolina Press.

Gould, Lewis L., ed. 1974. *The Progressive Era.* Syracuse, NY: Syracuse University Press.

Graber, Mark. 2006. *Dred Scott and the Problem of Constitutional Evil.* New York: Cambridge University Press.

———. 1995. "Unnecessary and Unintelligible." *Constitutional Commentary* 12 (Summer): 167–170.

Grad, Frank P. and Robert F. Williams. 2006. *Drafting State Constitutions, Revisions, and Amendments.* vol. 2 of *State Constitutions for the Twenty-first Century.* Albany: State University of New York Press.

Graetz, Michael J. 1997. *The Decline (and Fall?) of the Income Tax.* New York: W.W. Norton & Company.

Graham, Tim. 2002. "Prenuptial Disagreement." *World* 17 (June 8): 14–18.

Gravel, Mike. 1995. "Philadelphia II: National Initiatives." *Campaigns and Elections* 16 (December): 25.

Greenfield, Kent. 1993. "Original Penumbras: Constitutional Interpretation in the First Year of Congress." *Connecticut Law Review* 26 (Fall): 79–144.

Gregg, Gary L. II, ed. 2001. *Securing Democracy: Why We Have an Electoral College.* Wilmington, DE: ISI Books.

Green, Steven K. 1999. "Justice David Josiah Brewer and the 'Christian Nation' Maxim." *Albany Law Review* 63: 427–476.

———. 1992. "The Blaine Amendment Reconsidered." *American Journal of Legal History* 36 (January): 38–69.

Greenawalt, Kent. 1998a. "Introduction: Should the Religion Clauses of the Constitution Be Amended?" *Loyola of Los Angeles Law Review* 32 (November): 9–25.

———. 1998b. "Symposium: Reflections of *City of Boerne v. Flores:* Why Now Is Not the Time for Constitutional Amendment: The Limited Reach of *City of Boerne v. Flores.*" *William and Mary Law Review* 39 (February): 689–698.

Greenhouse, Linda. 1996. "Justices Curb Federal Power to Subject States to Lawsuits." *New York Times,* 28 March, A1, A12.

Gregg, Gary L., II, ed. 2001. *Securing Democracy: Why We Have an Electoral College.* Wilmington, DE: ISI Books.

Grey, Thomas C. 1975. "Do We Have an Unwritten Constitution?" *Stanford Law Review* 27 (February): 703–718.

Griffin, Stephen M. 1996. *American Constitutionalism: From Theory to Practice.* Princeton, NJ: Princeton University Press.

Griffith, Elisabeth. 1984. *In Her Own Right: The Life of Elizabeth Cady Stanton.* New York: Oxford University Press.

Grimes, Alan P. 1978. *Democracy and the Amendments to the Constitution.* Lexington, MA: Lexington Books.

Gringer, David. 2008. "Why the National Popular Vote Plan Is the Wrong Way to Abolish the Electoral College." *Columbia Law Review* 108 (January):182–230.

Grinnell, F. W. 1925. "Finality of State's Ratification of a Constitutional Amendment." *American Bar Association Journal* 11 (March): 192–193.

Grinnell, Frank W. 1959. "Petitioning Congress for a Convention: Cannot a State Change Its Mind?" *American Bar Association Journal* 45: 1164–1165.

Grodzins, Morton. 1966. *The American System: A New View of the Government in the United States.* Chicago: Rand McNally.

Grossman, Joel B., and David A. Yalof. 2000. "The Day After: Do We Need a 'Twenty-Eighth' Amendment?" *Constitutional Commentary* 17 (Spring): 7–17.

Grunder, Garel A., and William E. Livezey. 1973. *The Philippines and the United States.* Westport, CT: Greenwood Press.

Guelzo, Allen C. 2005. *Lincoln's Emancipation Proclamation: The End of Slavery in America.* New York: Simon and Schuster.

Gulliuzza, Frank, III. 2000. *Over the Wall: Protecting Religious Expression in the Public Square.* Albany, NY: State University of New York Press.

Gunderson, Robert Gray. 1961. *Old Gentleman's Convention: The Washington Peace Conference of 1861.* Madison: University of Wisconsin Press.

Guy-Urid, E. Charles. 2003. "Racial Identity, Electoral Structures, and the First Amendment Right of Association." *California Law Review* 91 (October):1209–1280.

Hahn, Jeanne. 1987. "Neo-Hamiltonianism: A Democratic Critique." In *The Case against the Constitution from AntiFederalists to the Present,* ed. John F. Manley and Kenneth M. Dolbeare. New York: M. E. Sharpe.

Halbrook, Stephen P. 2008. *The Founders' Second Amendment: Origins of the Right to Bear Arms.* Chicago: Ivan R. Dee.

———. 1994. *That Every Man Be Armed: The Evolution of a Constitutional Right.* Oakland, CA: Independent Institute.

Hall, Kermit L. 1989. *The Magic Mirror: Law in American History.* New York: Oxford University Press.

Hall, Kermit L., ed. 2005. *The Oxford Companion to the Supreme Court of the United States.* 2nd ed. New York: Oxford University Press.

———, ed. 1991. *By and for the People: Constitutional Rights in American History.* Arlington Heights, IL: Harlan Davidson.

Halper, Louise A. 1990. "Christopher G. Tiedeman, 'Laissez-Faire Constitutionalism' and the Dilemma of Small-Scale Property in the Gilded Age." *Ohio State Law Journal* 51: 1349–1384.

Halpern, Stephen C., and Charles M. Lamb, eds. 1982. *Supreme Court Activism and Restraint.* Lexington, MA: Lexington Books.

Hamburger, Philip A. 2002. *Separation of Church and State.* Cambridge, MA: Harvard University Press.

———. 1993. "Natural Rights, Natural Law, and American Constitutionalism." *Yale Law Journal* 102 (January): 907–960.

Hamilton, Alexander, James Madison, and John Jay. 1787–1788. *The Federalist Papers.* Reprint, New York: New American Library, 1961.

Hamilton, Hugh L. 1938. *A Second Constitution for the United States of America.* Richmond, VA: Garrett and Massie.

Hamilton, Robert W. 1987. *The Law of Corporations.* St. Paul, MN: West.

Hamm, Richard F. 1995. *Shaping the 18th Amendment: Temperance Reform, Legal Culture and the Polity, 1880–1920.* Chapel Hill: University of North Carolina Press.

Hammond, Rayne L. 2000. "Trial and Tribulation: The Story of United States v. Anthony." *Buffalo Law Review* 48 (2000): 981–1045.

Handy, Robert T. 1971. *A Christian America: Protestant Hopes and Historical Realities.* New York: Oxford University Press.

Hanlon, Michael C. 2000. "Note: The Need for a General Time Limit on Ratification of Proposed Constitutional Amendments." *Journal of Law & Politics* 16 (Summer): 663–698.

Hansen, Richard H. 1962. "Barriers to a National Primary Law." *Law and Contemporary Problems* 27 (Spring): 178–87.

Hardaway, Robert M. 1994. *The Electoral College and the Constitution: The Case for Preserving Federalism*. Westport, CT: Praeger.

Hardin, Charles M. 1989. *Constitutional Reform in America: Essays on the Separation of Powers*. Ames: Iowa State University Press.

———. 1974. *Presidential Power and Accountability: Toward a New Constitution*. Chicago: University of Chicago Press.

Hare, Lloyd C. 1970. *The Greatest American Woman: Lucretia Mott*. New York: Negro Universities Press.

Harrigan, John J. 1994. *Politics and Policy in States and Communities*. 5th ed. New York: Harper-Collins College Publishers.

Harriger, Katy J. 2000. Independent Justice: The Federal Special Prosecutor in American Politics. 2nd ed. Lawrence: University Press of Kansas.

Harris, Daryl B. 1992. *Proposed Amendments to the U.S. Constitution: 99th–101st Congresses (1985–1990)*. Washington, DC: Congressional Research Service, Library of Congress.

Harris, William F., II. 1993. *The Interpretable Constitution*. Baltimore: Johns Hopkins University Press.

Harrison, John. 2001. "The Lawfulness of the Reconstruction Amendments." *University of Chicago Law Review* 68 (Spring): 375–462.

Hart, Vivien. 1994. *Bound by Our Constitution: Women, Workers, and the Minimum Wage*. Princeton, NJ: Princeton University Press.

Hartnett, Edward. 1998. "A 'Uniform and Entire' Constitution: Or, What if Madison Had Won?" *Constitutional Commentary* 15 (Summer): 251–297.

Hatch, Orrin. 1991. "Constitutional Convention Implementation Act." *Congressional Record*, U.S. Senate, 15 January, S559–S565.

———. 1979. "Should the Capital Vote in Congress? A Critical Analysis of the Proposed D.C. Representation Amendment." *Fordham Urban Law Journal* 7: 479–539.

Hawes, Robert F., Jr. 2006. *One Nation, Indivisible? A Study of Secession and the Constitution*. n.p.: Fultus Books.

Haynes, George H. 1960. *The Senate of the United States, Its History and Practice*. New York: Russell and Russell.

Hazlitt, Henry. 1987. "A Proposal for Two Constitutional Amendments." In *A Nation in Debt: Economists Debate the Federal Budget Deficit*, ed. Richard H. Fink and Jack H. High. Frederick, MD: University Publications of America.

———. 1974. *A New Constitution Now*. New Rochelle, NY: Arlington House.

———. 1942. *A New Constitution Now*. New York: Whittlesey House.

———. 1931. "Our Obsolete Constitution." *Nation* 132 (4 February): 124–125.

Heater, Derek. 2004. *A Brief History of Citizenship*. New York: New York University Press.

Hehmeyer, Alexander. 1943. *Time for Change: A Proposal for a Second Constitutional Convention*. New York: Farrar and Rinehart.

Held, Allison L., Sheryl L. Herndon, and Danielle M. Stager. 1997. "The Equal Rights Amendment: Why the ERA Remains Legally Viable and Properly before the States." *William and Mary Journal of Women and Law* 3: 113.

Heller, Francis H. 1982. "Limiting a Constitutional Convention: The State Precedents." *Cardozo Law Review* 3: 563–579.

Heller, Scott. 1995. "The Right to Bear Arms." *Chronicle of Higher Education* 41 (21 July): A8, A12.

Henderson, Yandell. 1913. "The Progressive Movement and Constitutional Reform." *Yale Review* n.s. 3: 78–90. Henkin, Louis. 1972. *Foreign Affairs and the Constitution*. Mineola, NY: Foundation Press.

Henneberg, Molly. 2002. "Marriage Amendment Preserves MaleFemale Union." 16 May. http://www.foxnews.com. Accessed 16 May 2002.

Hensler, Louis W. III. 2003. "The Recurring Constitution Convention: Therapy for a Democratic Constitutional Republic Paralyzed by Hypocrisy." *Texas Review of Law and Politics* 7 (Spring): 263–312.

Herlighy, Sarah P. 2006. "Amending the Natural Born Citizen Requirement: Globalization as the Impetus and the Obstacle." *Chicago-Kent Law Review* 81: 275–300.

Hillhouse, [James]. 1808a. *Amendments to the Constitution of the United States Submitted for Consideration by Mr. Hillhouse, April 12, 1808*. Printed by Order of the Senate, 7 pp.

———. 1808b. *Propositions for Amending the Constitution of the United States Submitted by Mr. Hillhouse to the Senate on the Twelfth Day of April, 1808, with his Explanatory Remarks*. U.S. Senate.

Hitchcock, Ripley. 1903. *The Louisiana Purchase, and the Exploration, Early History and Building of the West*. Boston: Ginn & Company.

Ho, James C. 2000. "Unnatural-Born Citizens and Acting Presidents." *Constitutional Commentary* 17: 575–585.

Hoban, Thomas M., and Richard O. Brooks. 1987. *Green Justice: The Environment and the Courts*. Boulder, CO: Westview Press.

Hobson, Charles F. 1979. "The Negative on State Laws: James Madison, the Constitution, and the Crisis of Republican Government." *William and Mary Quarterly* 3rd ser. 36 (April): 214–235.

Hoebeke, C. H. 1995. *The Road to Mass Democracy: Original Intent and the Seventeenth Amendment*. New Brunswick, NJ: Transaction

Hoffman, Joseph L., and William J. Stuntz. 1994. "Habeas after the Revolution." In *Supreme Court Review*. Chicago: University of Chicago Press.

Hoffman, Ronald, and Peter J. Albert, eds. 1997. *The Bill of Rights: Government Proscribed*. Charlottesville: University Press of Virginia.

Hoff-Wilson, Joan, ed. 1986. *Rights of Passage: The Past and Future of ERA*. Bloomington: Indiana University Press.

Holden, Matthew, Jr. 1973a. *The Politics of the Black Nation*. New York: Chandler.

———. 1973b. *The White Man's Burden*. New York: Chandler.

Holmes, Stephen. 1995. *Passions and Constraint: On the Theory of Liberal Democracy*. Chicago: University of Chicago Press.

Holt, J.C. 1992. *Magna Carta*. New York: Cambridge University Press.

Hook, Janet, and Donna Cassata. 1995. "Low-Key Revolt May Spur Thurmond to Give Colleagues Freer Hand." *Congressional Quarterly Weekly Report* 53 (11 February): 466.

Hopkins, Caspar T. 1885. "Thoughts toward Revising the Federal Constitution." *Overland Monthly* n.s. 6 (October): 388–398.

Horn, Dottie. 1990. "Another Star for the Stripes?" *Endeavors* 8 (Fall): 4–6.

Horwill, Herbert W. 1925. *The Usages of the American Constitution*. Reprint, Port Washington, NY: Kennikat Press, 1969.

Hosanky, David. 1995. "Mandate Bill Is More Moderate Than Proposed in 'Contract.'" *Congressional Quarterly Weekly Report* 53 (7 January): 40.

"House Resolution 14." *Congressional Record* 89th Cong., 1st sess., 1965, Vol. 111, pt. 12: 15770.

Hsieh, Christine J. 1998. "Note: American Born Legal Permanent Residents? A Constitutional Amendment Proposal." *Georgetown Immigration Law Journal* 12 (Spring): 511–529.

Huckabee, David C. September 30, 19097. "Ratification of Amendments to the U.S. Constitution." Congressional Research Service: Library of Congress.

Hudson, David L, Jr. 2002. "Top Court Docket: Copyright to Cross Burning." *Chicago Daily Law Bulletin,* 16 September, 1.

Hudson, David L., Jr, and John R. Vile. 2011. *Encyclopedia of the Fourth Amendment*. Washington, DC: CQ Press.

Hunter, James D. 1994. *Before the Shooting Begins: Searching for Democracy in America's Culture War*. New York: Free Press.

Hurst, James W. 1971. *The Law of Treason in the United States: Collected Essays*. Westport, CT: Greenwood Press.

Imari, Brother (Richard B. Henry). 1968. War in America: The Malcolm X Doctrine. Detroit, MI: Malcolm X Doctrine. *Information Please Almanac: Atlas and Yearbook*. 1993. 43d ed. Boston: Houghton Mifflin.

Irons, Peter. 1989. *Justice Delayed: The Record of the Japanese Internment Cases*. Middletown, CT: Wesleyan University Press.

———. 1983. *Justice at War*. New York: Oxford University Press.

Irons, Peter, and Stephanie Guitton, eds. 1993. *May It Please the Court*. New York: New Press.

Isaacson, Eric A. 1990. "The Flag-Burning Issue: A Legal Analysis and Comment." *Loyola of Los Angeles Law Review* 23 (January): 535–600.

Ishikawa, Brendon T. 2000. "The Stealth Amendment: The Impending Ratification and Repeal of a Federal Budget Amendment." *Tulsa Law Journal* 33 (Winter): 353–381.

———. 1997. "Everything You Always Wanted to Know about How Amendments Are Made, but Were Afraid to Ask." *Hastings Constitutional Law Quarterly* 24 (Winter): 545–597.

———. 1996a. "Amending the Constitution: Just Not Every November." *Cleveland State Law Review* 44: 303–343.

———. 1996b. "Toward a More Perfect Union: The Role of Amending Formulae in the United States, Canadian, and German Constitutional Experiences." *Journal of International Law & Policy* 2 (Spring): 267–294.

Jackson, Donald W. 1992. *Even the Children of Strangers: Equality under the U.S. Constitution*. Lawrence: University Press of Kansas.

Jackson, Jesse L., Jr., with Frank E. Watkins. 2001. *A More Perfect Union: Advancing New American Rights*. New York: Welcome Rain Publishers.

Jackson, Robert H. 1941. *The Struggle for Judicial Supremacy*. New York: Vintage Books.

Jacob, Clyde E. 1972. *The Eleventh Amendment and Sovereign Immunity*. Westport, CT: Greenwood Press.

Jacob, Herbert. 1995. *Law and Politics in the United States*. 2d ed. New York: HarperCollins College Publishers.

Jacoby, Steward O. 1984. *The Religious Amendment Movement: God, People and Nation in the Gilded Age*. 2 vols. PhD dissertation, University of Michigan.

Jaffa, Harry V. 1994. *Original Intent and the Framers of the Constitution: A Disputed Question*. Washington, DC: Regnery Gateway.

James, Joseph B. 1984. *The Ratification of the Fourteenth Amendment*. Macon, GA: Mercer University Press.

———. 1956. *The Framing of the Fourteenth Amendment*. Urbana: University of Illinois Press.

Jameson, John A. 1887. *A Treatise on Constitutional Conventions: Their History, Powers, and Modes of Proceeding*. 4th ed. Chicago: Callaghan and Company.

Jaschik, Scott, and Douglas Lederman. 1996. "Appeals Court Bars Racial Preference in College Admissions." *Chronicle of Higher Education* 43 (29 March): A26–A27.

Jefferson, Thomas. 1964. *Notes on the State of Virginia*. New York: Harper and Row. [Originally published as part of Vol. VIII of *The Writings of Thomas Jefferson,* ed. by H. A. Washington. New York: H. W. Darby, 1861.]

————. 1905. *The Works of Thomas Jefferson,* ed. Paul Leicester Ford. 12 vols. New York: G. P. Putnam's Sons, Knickerbocker Press.

————. 1902. *The Jefferson Bible: The Life and Morals of Jesus of Nazareth.* St. Louis, MO: N. D. Thompson. Reprint, Introduction by F. Forrester Church. Boston: Beacon Press, 1989.

————. 1791. "Opinion of the Constitutionality of a National Bank." In *Documents of American Constitutional and Legal History,* ed. Melvin I. Urofsky. New York: Alfred A. Knopf, 1989.

Jeffries, Judson L. 1998. "Black Panther Party." In *The Encyclopedia of Civil Rights in America.* Ed. David Bradley and Shelley Fisher Fishkin. Armond, NY: M. E. Sharpe, Inc.

Jeffs, Daniel B. 2000. *America's Crisis: The Direct Democracy and Direct Education Solution.* Amherst Junction, WI: Hard Shell Word Factory.

Jennings, Thelma. 1998. "Nashville Convention." In *The Tennessee Encyclopedia of History and Culture,* ed. Carroll Van West. Nashville, TN: Rutledge Hill Press.

————. 1980. *The Nashville Convention: Southern Movement for Unity, 1848–1851.* Memphis, TN: Memphis State University Press.

Jenkins, David. 2003. "From Unwritten to Written: Transformation in the British Common-law Constitution." *Vanderbilt Journal of Transnational Law* 36 (May): 863–960.

Jensen, Erik M. 2001. "The Taxing Power, the Sixteenth Amendment, and the Meaning of 'Incomes,'" *Arizona State Law Journal* 33 (Winter): 1057–1158.

Jensen, Merrill. 1966. *The Articles of Confederation.* Madison: University of Wisconsin Press.

Johannsen, Robert W., ed. 1965. *The LincolnDouglas Debates of 1858.* New York: Oxford University Press.

Johnsen, Julia E., ed. 1948. *Federal World Government.* Vol. 19, no. 5 of the Reference Shelf. New York: H. W. Wilson.

————. 1947. *United Nations or World Government.* Vol. 20, no. 5 of the Reference Shelf. New York: H. W. Wilson.

Johnson, Calvin H. 2005. "The Dubious Enumerated Power Doctrine." *Constitutional Commentary* 22 (Spring): 25–95.

————. 2003–2004. "Homage to CLIO: The Historical Continuity From the Articles of Confederation into the Constitution." *Constitutional Commentary* 20 (Winter): 463–513.

Johnson, John W. 2005. *Griswold v. Connecticut: Birth Control and the Constitutional Right of Privacy.* Lawrence: University Press of Kansas.

Johnstone, Frederic B. 1912. "An Eighteenth-Century Constitution." *Illinois Law Review* 7 (December): 265–290.

Jonas, Gilbert. 2007. *Freedom's Sword: The NAACP and the Struggle Against Racism, 1909–1969.* New York: Routledge.

Kalfus, Mason. 1999. "Why Time Limits on the Ratification of Constitutional Amendments Violate Article V." *University of Chicago Law Review* 66 (Spring): 437–467.

Kammen, Michael. 1987. *A Machine That Would Go of Itself: The Constitution in American Culture.* New York: Alfred A. Knopf.

Kanowitz, Leo, and Marilyn Klinger. 1978. "Can a State Rescind Its Equal Rights Amendment Ratification: Who Decides and How?" *Hastings Law Journal* 28 (March): 969–1009.

Kaplan, Morton A. 1991. "Freedom of Speech: Its Constitutional Scope and Function." *This World & I* 7 (July): 531–541.

Kares, Lauren. 1995. "Note: The Unlucky Thirteenth: A Constitutional Amendment in Search of a Doctrine." *Cornell Law Review* 80 (January): 372–412.

Katz, Elai. 1996. "On Amending Constitutions: The Legality and Legitimacy of Constitutional Entrenchment." *Columbia Journal of Law and Social Problems* 29 (Winter): 251–292.

Kaufman, Burton I. 1969. *Washington's Farewell Address: The View from the 20th Century.* Chicago: Quadrangle Books.

Kauper, Paul G. 1968. "The Alternate Amending Process: Some Observations." *Michigan Law Review* 66 (March): 903–920.

Kay, Julie. 2002. "War of, for Words: South Florida Lawyers on ABA Task Force Lead Fight for Right of Enemy Combatants to Counsel." *Broward Daily Business Review* 43 (21 October): A10.

Kay, Richard S. 1987. "The Illegality of the Constitution." *Constitutional Commentary* 4 (Winter): 57–80.

Kelbley, Charles A. 2004. "Are There Limits to Constitutional Change? Rawls on Comprehensive Doctrines, Unconstitutional Amendments, and the Basis of Equality." *Fordham Law Review* 72: 1487–1536.

Keller, Morton. 1987. "Failed Amendments to the Constitution." *The World & I* 9 (September): 87–97.

Kelly, Frank K. 1981. *Court of Reason: Robert Hutchins and the Fund for the Republic.* New York: Free Press.

Kennedy, Devin C. 1991. "We Need a Fresh Start; Repeal the Seventh Amendment." *Detroit College of Law Review* (Winter): 1289–1301.

Kens, Paul. 1990. *Judicial Power and Reform Politics: The Anatomy of* Lochner v. New York. Lawrence: University Press of Kansas.

Kenyon, Cecelia, ed. 1985. *The Antifederalists.* Boston: Northeastern University Press.

Keogh, Stephen. 1987. "Formal and Informal Constitutional Lawmaking in the United States in the Winter of 1860–1861." *Journal of Legal History* 8 (December): 275–299.

Kerber, Linda K. 1998. *No Constitutional Right to Be Ladies: Women and the Obligations of Citizenship.* New York: Hill and Wang.

Kerr, K. Austin. 1985. *Organized for Prohibition: A New History of the Anti-Saloon League.* New Haven, CT: Yale University Press.

Kershen, Drew L. 1992. "Agriculture." In *The Oxford Companion to the Supreme Court of the United States,* ed. Kermit L. Hall. New York: Oxford University Press.

Kesler, Charles R. 1990. "Bad Housekeeping: The Case against Congressional Term Limits." *Policy Review* 53 (Summer): 20–25.

Keynes, Edward, with Randall K. Miller. 1989. *The Court vs. Congress: Prayer, Busing, and Abortion.* Durham, NC: Duke University Press.

Keyssar, Alexander. 2000. *The Right to Vote: The Constitutional History of Democracy in the United States.* New York: Basic Books.

Killenback, Mark R., ed. 2002. *The Tenth Amendment and State Sovereignty: Constitutional History and Contemporary Issues.* Lanham, MD: Rowman & Littlefield.

Kincaid, John. 2000. "Constitutional Proposals from the States." *Insights on Law & Society* 1 (Fall): 15.

———. 1989. "A Proposal to Strengthen Federalism." *The Journal of State Government* 62 (January/February): 36–45.

Kirstein, Herbert C. 1994. *U.S. Constitution for 21st Century and Beyond.* Alexandria, VA: Realistic IDEALIST Enterprise.

———. 1992. *Ideology of Freedom and Democracy.* Alexandria, VA: Realistic IDEALIST Enterprise.

Kirwan, Albert D. 1962. *John J. Crittenden: The Struggle for the Union.* n.p.: University of Kentucky Press.

Klein, Alana. 2008. "Judging as Judging: New Governance Approaches for the Enforcement of Constitutional Social and Economic Rights." *Columbia Human Rights Law Review* 39 (Spring): 351–422.

Klinkhammer, Marie C. 1965. "The Blaine Amendment of 1875." *Catholic Historical Review* 21: 15–49.

Kluger, Richard. 1975. *Simple Justice: The History of* Brown v. Board of Education *and Black America's Struggle for Equality.* 2 vols. New York: Alfred A. Knopf.

Knappman, Edward W., ed. 1994. *Great American Trials.* Detroit, MI: Visible Ink Press.

Knipprath, Joerg W. 1987. "To See the Trees, but Not the Forest in Constitution Making: A Commentary on Professor Miller's Proposed Constitution." *Southwestern University Law Review* 17: 239–256.

Knowles, Robert. 2003. "The Balance of Forces and the Empire of Liberty: States' Rights and the Louisiana Purchase." *Iowa Law Review* 88 (January): 343–419.

Kobach, Kris W. 1999. "May 'We the People' Speak? The Forgotten Role of Constituent Instructions in Amending the Constitution." *University of California Davis Law Review* 33 (Fall): 1–94.

Kraditor, Aileen S. 1981. *The Idea of the Woman's Suffrage Movement, 1890–1920.* New York: W. W. Norton.

Kramer, Daniel C. 2001. "The Constitution and the Right to Leisure." *The Good Society* 10: 64–67.

Kramnick, Isaac, and R. Laurence Moore. 1996. *The Godless Constitution: The Case against Religious Correctness.* New York: W. W. Norton.

Kravitz, Walter. 1993. *American Congressional Dictionary.* Washington, DC: Congressional Quarterly.

Kromkowski, Charles A. 2002. *Recreating the American Republic: Rules of Apportionment, Constitutional Change, and American Political Development, 1700–1870.* New York: Cambridge University Press.

Krusch, Barry. 1992. *The 21st Century Constitution: A New America for a New Millennium.* New York: Stanhope Press.

Ku, Raymond. 1995. "Consensus of the Governed: The Legitimacy of Constitutional Change." *Fordham Law Review* 64 (November): 535–586.

Kuic, Vukan. 1983. "John C. Calhoun's Theory of the 'Concurrent Majority.'" *American Bar Association* 69: 482–486.

Kurland, Philip B., and Ralph Lerner, eds. 1987. *The Founders' Constitution.* 5 vols. Chicago: University of Chicago Press.

Kuroda, Tadahisa. 1994. *The Origins of the Twelfth Amendment: The Electoral College in the Early Republic, 1878–1804.* Westport, CT: Greenwood Press.

Kyl, John. 1996. "Why Victims Need a Bill of Rights." *Washington Times* (22 April): A21.

Kyvic, David D. 2008. *The Age of Impeachment: American Constitutional Culture Since 1960.* Lawrence: University Press of Kansas.

———. 2000. *Unintended Consequences of Constitutional Amendments.* Athens: University of Georgia Press.

———. 1996a. *Explicit and Authentic Acts: Amending the Constitution, 1776–1995.* Lawrence: University Press of Kansas.

———. 1996b. "Appealing Supreme Court Decisions: Constitutional Amendments as Checks on Judicial Review." *Journal of Supreme Court History* 2: 105–119.

———. 1995. "Reforming or Resisting Modern Government? The Balanced Budget Amendment to the U.S. Constitution." *Akron Law Review* 28 (Fall/Winter): 97–124.

———. 1989. "The Road Not Taken: FDR, the Supreme Court and Constitutional Amendment." *Political Science Quarterly* 104 (Fall): 463–481.

———. 1988. "Can the Constitution Be Amended? The Battle over the Income Tax, 1895–1913." *Prologue* 20 (Fall): 181–200.

———. 1979. *Repealing National Prohibition.* Chicago: University of Chicago Press.

Kyvig, David E., ed. 1985. *Alcohol and Order: Perspectives on National Prohibition.* Westport, CT: Greenwood Press.

Labbe, Donald M., and Jonathan Lurie. 2005. *The Slaughterhouse Cases: Regulation, Reconstruction, and the Fourteenth Amendment.* Lawrence: University Press of Kansas.

Labunski, Richard. 2006. *James Madison and the Struggle for the Bill of Rights.* New York: Oxford University Press.

_____. 2000. *The Second Constitutional Convention: How the American People Can Take Back Their Government.* Versailles, KY: Marley and Beck Press.

____. 2007. "The Second Convention Movement, 1787–1789," *Constitutional Commentary* 24 (Fall): 567–600.

Laham, Nicholas. 1993. *Why the United States Lacks a National Health Insurance Program.* Westport, CT: Greenwood Press.

Landry, Thomas K. 1993. "Constitutional Invention: A Patent Perspective." *Rutgers Law Journal* 25 (Autumn): 67–104.

Lane, Charles. 2002. "High Court Denies Texas Death Appeal: Court Declines to Intervene in 'Sleeping Lawyer Case,'" *The Washington Post,* 3 June, at washingtonpost.com.

Lane, Eric, and Michael Orekes. 2007. *The Genius of America: How the Constitution Saved Our Country—And Why It Can Again.* New York: Bloomsbury.

Langum, David J. 1994. *Crossing Over the Line: Legislating Morality and the Mann Act.* Chicago: University of Chicago Press.

Larson, Edward J. 2008. *A Magnificent Catastrophe: The Tumultuous Election of 1800, America's First Presidential Campaign.* New York: Free Press.

_____. 1993. "The 'Blaine Amendment' in State Constitutions." In *The School-Choice Controversy: What Is Constitutional?* Ed. James W. Skillen. Grand Rapids, MI: Baker Books.

Larson, Gustave O. 1971. *The "Americanization" of Utah for Statehood.* San Marino, CA: Huntington Library.

Lasch, Christopher. 1995. "Progress." In *A Companion to American Thought,* eds. Richard Wightman Fox and James T. Kloppenberg. Malden, MA: Blackwell Publishers.

Lash, Kurt T. 2009. *The Lost History of the Ninth Amendment.* New York: Oxford University Press.

_____. 2001. "The Constitutional Convention of 1937: The Original Meaning of the New Jurisprudential Deal." *Fordham Law Review* 70 (November): 459–525.

_____. 1994. "Rejecting Conventional Wisdom: Federalist Ambivalence in the Framing and Implementation of Article V." *American Journal of Legal History* 38 (April): 197–231.

Latham, Darren R. 2005. "The Historical Amendability of the American Constitution: Speculations on an Empirical Problematic." *American University Law Review* 55 (October): 145–264.

Laubach, John H. 1969. *School Prayers: Congress, the Courts and the Public.* Washington, DC: Public Affairs Press.

Lawrence, William B. 1880. "The Monarchical Principle in Our Constitution." *North American Review* 288 (November): 385–409.

Lawson, Gary, and Guy Seidman. 2001. "When Did the Constitution Become Law?" *Notre Dame Law Review* 77 (November): 1–37.

Lawson, Steven F. 1976. *Black Ballots: Voting Rights in the South, 1944–1969.* New York: Columbia University Press.

Lawton, Kim A. 1996. "'The Right to Parent': Should It Be Fundamental?" *Christianity Today* 40 (29 April): 57.

Lazare, Daniel. 2001. *The Velvet Coup: The Constitution, the Supreme Court, and the Decline of American Democracy.* New York: Verso.

———.1996. *The Frozen Republic: How the Constitution Is Paralyzing Democracy.* New York: Harcourt Brace & Company.

Leach, Robert S. "House Rule XXI and an Argument against a Constitutional Requirement for Majority Rule in Congress." *UCLA Law Review* 44 (April): 1253–1288.

Lee, Calvin B. T. 1967. *One Man One Vote: WMCA and the Struggle for Equal Representation.* New York: Charles Scribner's Sons.

Lee, Charles Robert, Jr. 1963. *The Confederate Constitutions.* Chapel Hill, NC: University of North Carolina Press.

Lee, R. Alton. 1961. "The Corwin Amendment in the Secession Crisis." *Ohio Historical Quarterly* 70 (January): 1–26.

Lee, Robert W. 1999. "Battling for the Constitution." *The New American* 15 (26 April), at http://www.thenewamerican.com/tna/1999/04/vol5no09_constitution.htm. Accessed 24 April 2002.

Leedham, Charles. 1964. *Our Changing Constitution: The Story behind the Amendments.* New York: Dodd, Mead & Company.

Legislative Reference Service of the Library of Congress. 1936–1996. *Digest of Public General Bills and Resolutions.* Washington, DC: Library of Congress.

Leinwand, Gerald. 1994. *Do We Need a New Constitution?* New York: Franklin Watts.

Leish, Kenneth W., ed. 1968. *The American Heritage Pictorial History of the Presidents of the United States.* 2 vols. n.p.: American Heritage.

Leuchtenburg, William E. 1995. *The Supreme Court Reborn: The Constitutional Revolution in the Age of Roosevelt.* New York: Oxford University Press.

Levinson, Sanford. 2006. *Our Undemocratic Constitution: Where the Constitution Goes Wrong (and How the People Can Correct It).* New York: Oxford University Press.

———.1996a. "Constitutional Imperfection, Judicial Misinterpretation, and the Politics of Constitutional Amendment: Thoughts Generated by Some Current

Proposals to Amend the Constitution." *Brigham Young University Law Review* (1996): 611–626.

———. 1996b. "The Political Implications of Amending Clauses," *Constitutional Commentary* 13 (Spring): 107–123.

———. 1995. "Presidential Elections and Constitutional Stupidities." *Constitutional Commentary* 12 (Summer): 183–186.

———. 1994. "Authorizing Constitutional Text: On the Purported Twenty-seventh Amendment." *Constitutional Commentary* 11 (Winter): 101–113.

———. 1992. "Contempt of Court: The Most Important 'Contemporary Challenge to Judging.'" *Washington and Lee Law Review* 49 (Spring): 339–343.

———. 1990a. "On the Notion of Amendment: Reflections on David Daube's 'Jehovah the Good.'" *S'vara: A Journal of Philosophy and Judaism* 1 (Winter): 25–31.

———. 1990b. "'Veneration' and Constitutional Change: James Madison Confronts the Possibility of Constitutional Amendment." *Texas Tech Law Review* 21: 2443–2461.

———. 1989. "The Embarrassing Second Amendment." *Yale Law Journal* 99 (December): 637–660.

Levinson, Sanford, ed. 1995. *Responding to Imperfection: The Theory and Practice of Constitutional Amendment.* Princeton, NJ: Princeton University Press.

Levy, Leonard W. 1995. *Seasoned Judgments: The American Constitution, Rights, and History.* New Brunswick, NJ: Transaction Publishers.

———. 1988. *Original Intent and the Framers' Constitution.* New York: Macmillan.

———. 1986. *The Establishment Clause and the First Amendment.* New York: Macmillan.

———. 1968. *Origins of the Fifth Amendment: The Right against Self-Incrimination.* New York: Oxford University Press.

Lewis, Anthony. 1991. *Make No Law: The Sullivan Case and the First Amendment.* New York: Random House.

———. 1974. *Gideon's Trumpet.* New York: Vintage Books.

Lieber, Benjamen, and Patrick Brown. 1995. "On Supermajorities and the Constitution." *Georgetown Law Journal* 83(July):2347–84.

Lieber, Francis. 1888. *Manual of Political Ethics, Designed Chiefly for the Use of Colleges and Students at Law.* 2d ed. Philadelphia: Lippincott.

———. 1881. *Reminiscences, Addresses, and Essays.* Ed. Daniel G. Bilman. 2 vols. Philadelphia: J. B. Lippincott.

———. 1865. *Amendments of the Constitution Submitted to the Consideration of the American People.* New York: Loyal Publication Society.

Lieberman, Jethro K. 1992. *The Evolving Constitution: How the Supreme Court Has Ruled on Issues from Abortion to Zoning.* New York: Random House.

Lind, Michael. 1995. *The Next American Nation: The New Nationalism and the Fourth American Revolution.* New York: The Free Press.

Lind, Michael. 1966. "Pat Answers." *New Republic* 214 (February 19): 13–14.

Linder, Douglas. 1981. "What in the Constitution Cannot Be Amended?" *Arizona Law Review* 23: 717–731.

Link, Arthur S. 1963. *Woodrow Wilson: A Brief Biography.* Cleveland, OH: World.

Link, Arthur S., and Richard L. McCormick. 1983. *Progressivism.* Arlington Heights, IL: Harlan Davidson.

Little, Laura E. 1991. "An Excursion into the Uncharted Waters of the Seventeenth Amendment." *Temple Law Review* 674 (Fall): 629–658.

Lively, Donald E. 1992. *The Constitution and Race.* New York: Praeger.

Livingston, Steven G. 2002. *Student's Guide to Landmark Congressional Legislation on Social Security and Welfare.* Westport, CT: Greenwood Press.

Livingston, William S. 1956. *Federalism and Constitutional Change.* Oxford, UK: Clarendon Press.

Lockwood, Henry C. 1884. *The Abolition of the Presidency.* New York: R. Worthington. Reprint, Farmingdale, NY: Darbor Social Science Publications, 1978.

Lofgren, Charles A. 1987. *The Plessy Case: A Legal-Historical Interpretation.* New York: Oxford University Press.

———. 1975. "*Missouri v. Holland* in Historical Perspective." In *The Supreme Court Review.* Chicago: University of Chicago Press.

Long, Huey P. 1935. *My First Days in the White House.* Harrisburg, PA: Telegraph Press.

Longley, Lawrence D., and Alan G. Braun. 1972. *The Politics of Electoral College Reform.* New Haven, CT: Yale University Press.

Lowell, A. Lawrence. 1886. "Ministerial Responsibility and the Constitution." *Atlantic Monthly* 57:180–193.

Lugosi, Charles I. 2005. "Respecting Human Life in 21st-century America: A Moral Perspective to Extend Civil Rights to the Unborn from Creation Until Death." *Issues in Law & Media* 20 (Spring): 211–258.

Lunardini, Christine A. 1986. *From Equal Suffrage to Equal Rights: Alice Paul and the National Woman's Party, 1910–1928.* New York: New York University Press.

Lutz, Donald S. 1994. "Toward a Theory of Constitutional Amendment." *American Political Science Review* 88 (June): 355–370.

———. 1992. *A Preface to American Political Theory.* Lawrence: University Press of Kansas.

———. 1988. *The Origins of American Constitutionalism.* Baton Rouge, LA: Louisiana State University Press.

Lyman, Edward L. 1986. *Political Deliverance: The Mormon Quest for Utah Statehood.* Urbana: University of Illinois Press.

Lynch, Michael J. 2001. "The Other Amendments: Constitutional Amendments That Failed." *Law Library Journal* 92 (Spring): 303–310.

Macdonald, Dwight. 1968. "The Constitution of the United States Needs to Be Fixed." *Esquire* 70 (October): 143–146, 238, 240, 243–244, 246, 252.

MacDonald, William. 1922. *A New Constitution for a New America.* New York: B. W. Heubsch.

———. 1921. "A New American Constitution." *Proceedings of the American Antiquarian Society* 2 (October): 439–447.

Macedo, Stephen. 2009. "Our Imperfect Democratic Constitution: The Critics Examined." *Boston University Law Review* (April): 609–28.

Machen, Arthur W., Jr. 1910. "Is the Fifteenth Amendment Void?" *Harvard Law Review* 23 (January): 169–193.

MacPherson, Peter. 1995. "Contested Winners Seated; Challengers in Pursuit." *Congressional Quarterly Weekly Report* 53 (7 January): 28.

Madry, Alan R. 1994. "Private Accountability and the Fourteenth Amendment, State Action, Federalism and Congress." *Missouri Law Review* 59 (Summer): 499–568.

Madueno, Emily L. 2007. "The Fifth Amendment's Taking Clause: Public Use and Private Use; Unfortunately, There Is No Difference." *Loyola of Los Angeles Law Review* 40 (Winter): 809–52.

Maier, Pauline. 1997. *American Scripture: Making the Declaration of Independence.* New York: Alfred A. Knopf.

Main, Jackson T. 1961. *The Antifederalists: Critics of the Constitution, 1781–1788.* Chicago: Quadrangle Books.

Malone, Dumas, ed. 1961. *Dictionary of American Biography.* 10 vols. New York: Charles Scribner's Sons.

Maltz, Earl M. 2002. "The Fourteenth Amendment and Native American Citizenship." *Constitutional Commentary* 17 (Winter): 555–573.

———. 1995. "The Impact of the Constitutional Revolution of 1937 on the Dormant Commerce Clause—A Case Study in the Decline of State Autonomy." *Harvard Journal of Law & Public Policy* 19 (Fall): 121–145.

———. 1990. *Civil Rights, the Constitution, and Congress, 1863–1869.* Lawrence: University Press of Kansas.

"The Man Who Would Not Quit." 1992. *People* 37 (April 1): 72.

Manfredi, Christopher and Michael Lusztig. 1998. "Why Do Formal Amendments Fail? An Institutional Design Analaysis." *World Politics* 50: 377–400.

Mangone, Gerald J. 1951. *The Idea and Practice of World Government.* New York: Columbia University Press.

Mann, Thomas E. 1992. "The Wrong Medicine." *Brookings Review* 10 (Spring): 23–25.

Mansbridge, Jane J. 1986. *Why We Lost the ERA.* Chicago: University of Chicago Press.

Marberry, M. M. 1967. *Vicky: A Biography of Victoria C. Woodhull.* New York: Funk and Wagnalls.

Marbury, William L. 1920. "The Nineteenth Amendment and After." *Virginia Law Review* 7 (October): 1–29.

———. 1919. "The Limitations upon the Amending Power." *Harvard Law Review* 33 (December): 223–235.

Marduke, P. G. 1970. *The CASCOT System for Social Control of Technology.* Silver Spring, MD: Citizens' Association for Social Control of Technology.

Marshall, Patrick. 2001. "Religion in Schools." *CQ Researcher.* 12 January. http://library.cqpress.com/cqres/lpext.dll/cqpres/print/ print20010112?.

Marshall, Price. 1998. "'A Careless Written Letter'—Situating Amendments to the Federal Constitution." *Arkansas Law Review* 51: 95–115.

Martin, Jil L. 2000. "United States v. Morrison: Federalism Against the Will of the States." *Loyola University of Chicago Law Review* 32 (Fall): 243–333.

Marx, Michael. 1999. *Justus—A Utopia: Formation of a Tax Free Constitutional Democracy.* Flat Rocik, IL: Marx & Marx.

Masei, David. 1995. "Flag Resolution's Future Murky in More Divided Senate." *Congressional Quarterly Weekly Report* 53 (22 July): 2195.

Mason, Alpheus T. 1964. *The States' Rights Debate: Antifederalism and the Constitution.* Englewood Cliffs, NJ: Prentice-Hall.

Mason, Alpheus T., and Gordon E. Baker. 1985. *Free Government in the Making: Readings in American Political Thought.* 4th ed. New York: Oxford University Press.

Mason, Alpheus T., and Donald G. Stephenson Jr. 2007. *American Constitutional Law: Introductory Essays and Selected Cases.* 15th ed. Upper Saddle River: Pearson/Prentice-Hall.

Mason, John Lyman, and Michael Nelson. 2001. *Governing Gambling.* New York: The Century Foundation Press.

Massaro, John. 1990. *Supremely Political: The Role of Ideology and Presidential Management in Unsuccessful Supreme Court Nominations.* Albany, NY: State University of New York Press.

Massey, Calvin R. 1995. *Silent Rights: The Ninth Amendment and the Constitution's Unenumerated Rights.* Philadelphia: Temple University Press.

Masters, Brooke A. 2001. "Va. Minute of Silence Survives Test in High Court: 4th Circuit Ruling Allowed to Stand Without Comment." *Washington Post,* 30 October, B01.

Mathews, John M. 1908. *Legislative and Judicial History of the Fifteenth Amendment.* Reprint, New York: Da Capo Press, 1971.

Mathis, Doyle. 1967. "*Chisholm v. Georgia:* Background and Settlement." *Journal of American History* 54: 19–29.

Matthews, Richard K. 1995. *If Men Were Angels: James Madison and the Heartless Empire of Reason.* Lawrence: University Press of Kansas.

Mauro, Tony. 2001. "The Age of Justice." *American Lawyer* 23 (March): 67.

May, Christopher N. 1989. *In the Name of War.* Cambridge, MA.: Harvard University Press.

May, James. 1992. "Antitrust." In *The Oxford Companion to the Supreme Court of the United States,* ed. Kermit L. Hall. New York: Oxford University Press.

May, Janice C. 1987. "Constitutional Amendment and Revision Revisited." *Publius: The Journal of Federalism* 17 (Winter): 153–179.

Mayer, Carl J. 1990. "Personalizing the Impersonal: Corporations and the Bill of Rights." *Hastings Law Journal* 41 (March): 577–667.

Mayer, David N. 1994. *The Constitutional Thought of Thomas Jefferson.* Charlottesville: University Press of Virginia.

———. 1990. "The Jurisprudence of Christopher G. Tiedeman: A Study in the Failure of Laissez-Faire Constitutionalism." *Missouri Law Review* 55 (Winter): 93–161.

Mayer, Henry. 2008. *All on Fire: William Lloyd Garrison and the Abolition of Slavery.* New York: W.W. Norton.

Mayers, Lewis. 1959. *Shall We Amend the Fifth Amendment?* New York: Harper and Brothers.

Mayhew, David R. 1991. *Divided We Govern: Party Control, Lawmaking, and Investigations, 1946–1990.* New Haven, CT: Yale University Press.

Mays, David John. 1984. *Edmund Pendleton, 1721–1803: A Biography.* 2 vols. Richmond: Virginia State Library. Reprint of Harvard University Edition of 1952.

Mazzone, Jason. 2005. "Unamendments." *Iowa Law Review* 90 (May):1747–1855.

McBain, Howard Lee. 1927. *The Living Constitution: a Consideration of the Realities and Legends of Our Fundamental Law.* New York: Macmillian.

McBride, James. 1991. "'Is Nothing Sacred?' Flag Desecration, the Constitution and the Establishment of Religion." *St. John's Law Review* 65: 297–324.

McClurg, Andrew J., David B. Kopel, and Brannon P. Denning, eds. 2002. *Gun Control & Gun Rights: A Reader & Guide.* New York: New York University Press.

McConnell, Michael W. 1995. "Originalism and the Desegregation Decisions." *Virginia Law Review* 81 (May): 947–1140.

McCullough, David. 1992. *Truman.* New York: Simon and Schuster.

McDonald, Forrest. 1992. "Pardon Power." In *The Oxford Companion to the Supreme Court of the United States,* ed. Kermit L. Hall. New York: Oxford University Press.

———. 1982. *A Constitutional History of the United States.* New York: Franklin Watts.

———. 1979. *Alexander Hamilton: A Biography.* New York: Norton.

McFeely, William S. 1991. *Frederick Douglass.* New York: W. W. Norton.

McGinnis, John O., and Michael B. Rappaport. 2002. "Our Supermajoritarian Constitution." *Texas Law Review* 80 (March): 703–805.

———. 1999. "Supermajority Rules as a Constitutional Solution." *William and Mary Law Review* 40 (February): 365–470.

———. 1995. "The Constitutionality of Legislative Supermajority Requirements: A Defense." *Yale Law Journal* 105 (November): 483–511.

McGrath, Patrick J. 2000. *The Way to Responsible Government: The Constitutional Re-Structuring America Needs.* San Jose: Writer's Showcase.

McHenry, Robert, ed. 1980. *Liberty's Women.* Springfield, MA: G. and C. Merriam.

McIntyre, Robert S. 1992. "No, It Would Wreck the Economy." *The World & I* 7 (August): 111, 116–117, 119.

McKee, Henry S. 1933. *Degenerate Democracy.* New York: Thomas Y. Crowell. Meador, Lewis H.

———. 1898. "The Council of Censors." *Pennsylvania Magazine of History and Biography* 22: 265–300.

McLaughlin, Michael. 2008. "Direct Democracy and the Electoral College: Can a Popular Initiative Change How a State Appoints its Electors?" *Fordham Law Review* 76 (May): 2943–3000.

Melendez, Edgardo. 1988. *Puerto Rico's Statehood Movement.* New York: Greenwood Press.

Meltsner, Michael. 1974. *Cruel and Unusual: The Supreme Court and Capital Punishment.* New York: William Morrow.

Merriam, Charles E. 1931. *The Written Constitution and the Unwritten Attitude.* New York: Richard R. Smith.

Mertens, John. 1997. *The Second Constitution for the United States of America.* Cottonwood, CA: Gazelle Books.

Meyer, Alfred W. 1951. "The Blaine Amendment and the Bill of Rights." *Harvard Law Review* 64: 939–945.

Meyer, Karl E. 1968. "So Does the Bill of Rights." *Esquire* 70 (October): 147–148.

Meyers, Marvin, ed. 1973. *The Mind of the Founder: Sources of the Political Thought of James Madison.* Indianapolis, IN: Bobbs-Merrill.

Meyerson, Michael I. 2008. *Liberty's Blueprint: How Madison and Hamilton Wrote the Federalist Papers, Defined the Constitution, and Made Democracy Safe for the World.* New York: Basic Books.

Mickelman, Frank I. 2006. "What Do Constitutions Do That Statutes Don't (Legally Speaking)?" in Bauman, Richard W. and Tsvi Kahana, *The Least Examined Branch: The Role of Legislatures in the Constitutional State.* New York: Cambridge University Press.

Miller, Arthur S. 1987. *The Secret Constitution and the Need for Constitutional Change.* Westport, CT: Greenwood Press.

———. 1984. "The Annual John Randolph Tucker Lecture: Taking Needs Seriously: Observations on the Necessity for Constitutional Change." *Washington and Lee Law Review* 41 (Fall): 1243–1306.

———. 1982. *Toward Increased Judicial Activism: The Political Role of the Supreme Court.* Westport, CT: Greenwood Press.

Miller, Jeremy. 1987. "It's Time for a New Constitution." *Southwestern University Law Review* 17: 207–237.

Miller, John C. 2001. "Immigrants for President: Why the Foreign-born Should Be Allowed to Compete for the Big Job." *National Review* 53 (6 August): 22–24.

Miller, Robert S., and Donald O. Dewey. 1991. "The Congressional Salary Amendment: 200 Years Later." *Glendale Law Review* 10: 92–109.

Miller, William L. 1992. *The Business of May Next: James Madison and the Founding.* Charlottesville: University Press of Virginia.

Monaghan, Henry P. 1996. "We the People[s], Original Understanding, and Constitutional Amendment." *Columbia Law Review* 96 (January): 121–177.

Monsma, Stephen V. 1993. *Positive Neutrality: Letting Religious Freedom Ring.* Westport, CT: Greenwood Press.

Moore, Charles Forrest. 1925. *The Challenge of Life.* New York: William Edwin Rudge.

Moore, John. 1995. "Pleading the 10th." *National Journal* 28 (29 July): 1940–1944.

Moore, Trevor W. 1970. "A Rumbling in Babylon: Panthers Host a Parley." *Christian Century* 87 (28 October): 1296–1300.

Moore, W. S., and Rudolph G. Penner, eds. 1980. *The Constitution and the Budget: Are Constitutional Limits on Tax, Spending and Budget Powers Desirable at the Federal Level?* Washington, DC: American Enterprise Institute for Public Policy Research.

Morehead, Joe. 1985. "Private Bills and Private Laws: A Guide to the Legislative Process." *Serials Librarian* 9 (Spring): 115–125.

Morgan, Robert J. 1988. *James Madison on the Constitution and the Bill of Rights.* New York: Greenwood Press.

Morgan, Thomas J. 1963. "Seventeen States Vote to Destroy Democracy as We Know It." *Look* 27 (3 December): 76–88.

Morin, Isobel V. 1998. *Our Changing Constitution: How and Why We Have Amended It.* Brookfield, CT: Millbook Press.

Morris, Henry O. 1897. *Waiting for the Signal, a Novel.* Chicago: Schulte.

Morris, Thomas D. 1974. *Free Men All: The Personal Liberty Laws of the North, 1780–1861.* Baltimore: Johns Hopkins University Press.

Morrison, Charles C. 1972. *The Outlawry of War: A Constructive Policy for World Peace.* New York: Garland Publishing.

Morrison, Stanley. 1949. "Does the Fourteenth Amendment Incorporate the Bill of Rights? The Judicial Interpretation." *Stanford Law Review* 2 (December): 140–173.

Morton, Robert K. 1933. *God in the Constitution.* Nashville, TN: Cokesbury Press.

Murdock, Joyce and Deb Price. 2001. *Courting Justice: Gay Men and Lesbians v. the Supreme Court.* New York: Basic Books.

Murphy, Bruce A. 1988. *Fortas: The Rise and Ruin of a Supreme Court Justice.* New York: William Morrow.

Murphy, Cornelius F., Jr. 1988. "Constitutional Revision." In *Philosophical Dimensions of the Constitution,* ed. Diana T. Meyers and Kenneth Kipnis. Boulder, CO: Westview Press.

Murphy, Walter F. 2007. *Constitutional Democracy: Creating and Maintaining a Just Political Order.* Baltimore: Johns Hopkins University Press.

Murphy, Walter F. 1995. "Merlin's Memory: The Past and Future Imperfect of the Once and Future Polity." In *Responding to Imperfection,* ed. Sanford Levinson. Princeton, NJ: Princeton University Press.

———. 1992a. "Consent and Constitutional Change." In *Human Rights and Constitutional Law: Essays in Honour of Brian Walsh,* ed. James O'Reilly. Dublin, Ireland: Found Hall Press.

———. 1992b. "Staggering Toward the New Jerusalem of Constitutional Theory: A Response to Ralph F. Graebler." *American Journal of Jurisprudence* 37: 337–357.

———. 1990. "The Right to Privacy and Legitimate Constitutional Change." In Constitutional Bases of Political and Social Change in the United States, ed. Shlomo Slonin. New York: Praeger.

———. 1987. "*Slaughterhouse, Civil Rights,* and Limits on Constitutional Change." *American Journal of Jurisprudence* 23: 1–22.

———. 1980. "An Ordering of Constitutional Values." *Southern California Law Review* 53: 703–760.

———. 1978. "The Art of Constitutional Interpretation: A Preliminary Showing." In *Essays on the Constitution of the United States,* ed. M. Harmon. Port Washington, NY: Kennikat Press.

———. 1962. *Congress and the Court.* Chicago: University of Chicago Press.

Murphy, Walter F., James E. Fleming, and Sotirios Barber. 1995. *American Constitutional Interpretation,* 2d ed. Westbury, NY: Foundation Press.

Musmanno, M. A. 1929. *Proposed Amendments to the Constitution.* Washington, DC: U.S. Government Printing Office.

Myles, John. 1989. *Old Age in the Welfare State: The Political Economy of Public Pensions.* Lawrence: University Press of Kansas.

Nader, Ralph, and Carl J. Mayer. 1988. "Corporations Are Not Persons." *New York Times* (9 April), sect. 1, p. 31.

Nagel, Stuart S. 1965. "Court-Curbing Proposals in American History." *Vanderbilt Law Review* 18: 925–944.

Nagle, John Copeland. 1997. "Essay: A Twentieth Amendment Parable." *New York University Law Review* 72 (May): 470–494.

Natelson, Robert G. 2002. "A Republic, Not a Democracy? Initiative, Referendum, and the Constitution's Guarantee Clause." *Texas Law Review* 80 (March): 807–857.

Naylor, Thomas H., and William H. Willimon. 1997. *Downsizing the U.S.A.* Grand Rapids, MI: William B. Eerdmans.

Nelson, Michael, ed. 2008. *Guide to the Presidency.* 4th ed., 2 vols. Washington, DC: Congressional Quarterly.

———. 1987. "Constitutional Qualifications for President." *Presidential Studies Quarterly* 17 (Spring): 383–399.

Nelson, William E. 1988. *The Fourteenth Amendment: From Political Principle to Judicial Doctrine.* Cambridge, MA: Harvard University Press.

Newbold, Robert C. 1955. *The Albany Congress and Plan of Union of 1954.* New York: Vantage Press.

Newman, Roger K. 1994. *Hugo Black: A Biography.* New York: Pantheon Books.

Newmyer, R. Kent. 1968. *The Supreme Court Under Marshall and Taney.* New York: Thomas Y. Crowell.

"New Proposal for Constitutionalizing Victims' Rights Introduced in Congress." 2002. *U.S. Law Week* 70 (30 April): 2679.

Nisbet, Robert. 1980. *The Idea of Progress.* New York: Basic Books.

Niven, John. 1988. *John C. Calhoun and the Price of Union: A Biography.* Baton Rouge: Louisiana State University Press.

Nordeen, Ross. "Home Page." http://www.amatec on.com. Accessed 5/7/02.

Norham, George W. 1988. "A Constitutional Door Is Opened for Amendment." *Texas Bar Journal* 51 (September): 804–806.

"North Carolina Ratifies the 24th Amendment." 1989. *We the People: A Newsletter of the Commission on the Bicentennial of the United States Constitution* 5 (July): 10.

Oates, Stephen B. 1970. *To Purge This Land with Blood: A Biography of John Brown.* New York: Harper and Row.

O'Brien, Aaron J. 1996. "States' Repeal: A Proposed Constitutional Amendment to Reinvigorate Federalism." *Cleveland State Law Review* 44: 547–76.

O'Brien, David M. 2005a. *Civil Rights and Civil Liberties.* Vol. 2 of *Constitutional Law and Politics.* 6th ed. New York: W. W. Norton.

———. 2005b. *Struggles for Power and Governmental Accountability.* 6th ed., Vol. 1 of *Constitutional Law and Politics.* New York: W. W. Norton.

O'Brien, F. William. 1965. "The States and 'No Establishment': Proposed Amendments to the Constitution since 1798." *Washburn Law Journal* 4: 183–210.

———. 1963. "The Blaine Amendment, 1875–1876." *University of Detroit Law Journal* 41 (December): 137–205.

O'Connell, Frank J., Jr. 2001. "Estate Tax Repeal: What Now?" *The Tax Adviser* 32 (September): 588.

O'Connor, Karen. 1996. *No Neutral Ground? Abortion Politics in an Age of Absolutes.* Boulder, CO: Westview.

O'Conor, Charles. 1881. "Democracy." In *Johnson's New Universal Cyclopaedia: A Treasury of Scientific and Popular Treasure of Useful Knowledge.* Vol. 1, Part 2. New York: A. J. Johnson.

———. 1877. Address by Charles O'Conor Delivered before the New York Historical Society at the Academy of Music. 8 May. New York: Anson D. F. Randolph.

Ogden, Frederic D. 1958. *The Poll Tax in the South.* Tuscaloosa: University of Alabama Press.

O'Neil, Patrick M. 1995. "The Declaration as Un-Constitution: The Bizarre Jurisprudential Philosophy of Professor Harry V. Jaffa." *Akron Law Review* 28 (Fall/Winter): 237–252.

Onuf, Peter. 1984. "Territories and Statehood." In *Encyclopedia of American Political History: Studies of Principal Movements and Ideas,* ed. Jack P. Greene. Vol. 3. New York: Charles Scribner's Sons.

Orentlicher, David. 2002. "Conflict of Interest and the Constitution." *Washington and Lee Law Review* 59 (Summer): 713–766.

Orfield, Lester B. 1942. *The Amending of the Federal Constitution.* Ann Arbor: University of Michigan Press.

Ornstein, Norman J. 2002. "Preparing for the Unthinkable: Bush's 'Shadow Government' Plan Is a Start—But Only a Start." *Wall Street Journal,* 11 March, A18.

———. 1994. "Congress Inside Out." *Roll Call* 39 (10 March): 5–6.

Ornstein, Norman J., and Amy L. Schenhenberg. 1995. "The 1995 Congress: The First Hundred Days and Beyond." *Political Science Quarterly* 110 (Summer): 183–206.

Orth, John V. 1992. "Eleventh Amendment." In *The Oxford Companion to the Supreme Court of the United States,* ed. Kermit L. Hall. New York: Oxford University Press.

———. 1987. *The Judicial Power of the United States: The Eleventh Amendment in American History.* New York: Oxford University Press.

O'Toole, Lawrence J., Jr., ed. 1985. *American Intergovernmental Relations: Foundations, Perspectives, and Issues.* Washington, DC: Congressional Quarterly.

Pace, James O. 1986. *Amendment to the Constitution: Averting the Decline and Fall of America.* Los Angeles: Johnson, Pace, Simmons and Fennell.

Padover, Saul K. 1962. *To Secure These Blessings.* New York: Washington Square Press/Ridge Press.

Palm, Kirby. n.d. "The U.S. Constitution: Formal Additions." http://www.nettally.com/palmk/ConstitutionSections.html.

Palmer, Kris E. 2000. *Constitutional Amendments: 1789 to the Present.* Detroit, MI: Gale Group.

Paludan, Phillip S. 1994. *The Presidency of Abraham Lincoln.* Lawrence: University Press of Kansas.

"Panthers Plan New Convention." 1971. In *Facts on File Yearbook, 1970.* Vol. 30. New York: Facts on File.

Paschal, Richard A. 1991. "The Continuing Colloquy: Congress and the Finality of the Supreme Court." *Journal of Law and Politics* 8 (Fall): 143–226.

Paternoster, Raymond and Robert Brane, and Sarah Baron. 2007. *The Death Penalty: America's Experience with Capital Punishment.* New York: Oxford University Press

Patrick, John J. 1994. *The Young Oxford Companion to the Supreme Court of the United States.* New York: Oxford University Press.

Patterson, Bennett B. 1955. *The Forgotten Ninth Amendment.* Indianapolis, IN: Bobbs-Merrill.

Paulsen, Michael S. 1995. "The Case for a Constitutional Convention." *Wall Street Journal,* 3 May, A15.

———. 1994. "Is Lloyd Bentsen Unconstitutional?" *Stanford Law Review* 46 (April): 907–918.

———. 1993. "A General Theory of Article V: The Constitutional Issues of the Twenty-seventh Amendment." *Yale Law Journal* 103: 677–789.

Peabody, Bruce G. 2007. "Reversing Time's Arrow: Law's Reordering of Chronology, Causality, and History." *Akron Law Review* 40: 587–621.

Peabody, Bruce G., and Scott E. Gant. 1999. "The Twice and Future President: Constitutional Interstices and the Twenty-second Amendment." *Minnesota Law Review* 83 (February): 565–635.

Pear, Robert. 1994. "State Officials Worry That a Federal Budget Will Be Balanced on Their Books." *New York Times,* 11 December, 34.

Pearson, Hugh. 1994. *The Shadow of the Panther: Huey Newton and the Price of Black Power in America.* Reading, MA: AddisonWesley.

Pease, William H., and June H. Pease, eds. 1965. *The Antislavery Argument.* Indianapolis, IN: Bobbs-Merrill.

Peck, Robert S. 1992. *The Bill of Rights and the Politics of Interpretation.* St. Paul, MN: West.

Pei, Mario. 1967–1968. "The Case for a Constitutional Convention." *Modern Age* 12 (Winter): 8–13.

Peirce, Neal R. 1968. *The People's President: The Electoral College in American History and the Direct-Vote Alternative.* New York: Simon and Schuster.

Peltason, Jack W. 1994. *Corwin and Peltason's Understanding the Constitution.* 13th ed. Fort Worth, TX: Harcourt Brace College Publishers.

Pendergast, Tom, Sara Pendergast, and John Sousanis, with Elizabeth Shaw Grunow, ed., 2001. *Constitutional Amendments: From Freedom of Speech to Flag Burning.* 3 vols. Detroit, MI: U.X.L. imprint of Gale Group.

Pendleton, Edmund. 2004. "The Danger Not Over." In *Liberty and Order: The First American Party Struggle,* ed. Lance Banning. Indianapolis: Liberty Fund.

Penn, William. 2002. *The Political Writings of William Penn,* intro by Andrew R. Murphy. Indianapolis: Liberty Fund.

Penney, Annette C. 1968. *The Golden Voice of the Senate.* Washington, DC: American Enterprise Institute for Public Policy Research.

Penniman, Clara. 1980. *State Income Taxation.* Baltimore: Johns Hopkins University Press.

Perry, Barbara A. 2007. *The Michigan Affirmative Action Cases.* Lawrence: University Press of Kansas.

Perry, Michael J. 1999. *We the People: The Fourteenth Amendment and the Supreme Court.* Oxford, UK: Oxford University Press.

Peters, Ronald M., Jr. 1990. "Repeal the Seventeenth!" *Extensions* 2 (Spring): 16–17.

Peters, William. 1987. *A More Perfect Union: The Making of the United States Constitution.* New York: Crown.

Peterson, Charles S. 1977. *Utah: A Bicentennial History.* New York: W. W. Norton.

"Philippines, Republic of the." 1994. *Microsoft Encarta Multimedia Encyclopedia.*

Piburn, John L. 1932. *A Constitution and a Code.* San Diego, CA: Bowman Printing Company.

Pious, Richard M. 1978. "Introduction." In *The Abolition of the Presidency.* Farmingdale, NY: Darbor Social Science Publications.

Pitts, Michael J. 2003. "Section 5 of the Voting Rights Act: A Once and Future Remedy?" *Denver University Law Review* 81:225–88.

Pizzigati, Sam. 1994. "Salary Caps for Everyone!" *New York Times,* 28 August, 15.

———. 1992. *The Maximum Wage: A Common-Sense Prescription for Revitalizing America—By Taxing the Very Rich.* New York: Appex Press.

Planell, Raymond M. 1974. "The Equal Rights Amendment: Will States Be Allowed to Change Their Minds?" *Notre Dame Lawyer* 49 (February): 657–670.

Political Economy and Constitutional Reform. 1982. Hearings before the Joint Economic Committee of the Congress of the United States. 97th Cong., 2nd Sess.

Political staff of *The Washington Post.* 2001. *Deadlock: The Inside Story of America's Closest Election.* New York: Public Affairs.

Pollard, Vincent Kelly, and Bruce E. Tonn. 1998. "Revisiting the 'Court of Generations' Amendment." *Futures* 30: 345–352.

Pollack, Malla. 2001. "What Is Congress Supposed to Promote? Define 'Progress' In Article I, Section

8, Clause 8 of the United States Constitution, or Introducing the Progress Clause." *Nebraska Law Review* 80: 754–813

Porter, Kirk H., and Donald B. Johnson. 1966. *National Party Platforms, 1840–1964.* Urbana : University of Illinois Press.

Posner, Richard A. 1999. *An Affair of State: The Investigation, Impeachment, and Trial of President Clinton.* Cambridge, MA: Harvard University Press.

Powe, Lucas A., Jr. 1991. *The Fourth Estate and the Constitution: Freedom of Press in America.* Berkeley: University of California Press.

Presser, Stephen B. 2000. "Constitutional Amendments: Dangerous Threat or Democracy in Action?" *Texas Review of Law and Politics* 5 (Fall): 209–225.

Preston, Robert L. 1972. *The Plot to Replace the Constitution.* Salt Lake City: Hawkes Publications.

Prinz, Timothy S. 1992. "Term Limitation: A Perilous Panacea." *The World & I* 7 (January): 143–153.

Proceedings of the National Convention to Secure the Religious Amendment of the Constitution of the United States Held in Pittsburgh, February 4, 5, 1874, with an Account of the Origin and Progress of the Movement. 1874. Philadelphia: Christian Statesman Association.

"Proper Government." http://www.ebtx.com. Accessed 5/17/02.

Proposals for a Constitutional Convention to Require a Balanced Federal Budget. 1979. Washington, DC: American Enterprise Institute for Public Policy Research.

Proposed Amendments to the Constitution of the United States of America Introduced in Congress from the 69th Congress, 2d Session through the 87th Congress, 2d Session, December 6, 1926, to January 3, 1963. 1963. Washington, DC: U.S. Government Printing Office.

Proposed Amendments to the Constitution of the United States of America Introduced in Congress from the 88th Congress, 1st Session through the 90th Congress, 2d Session, January 9, 1963, to January 3, 1969. 1969. Washington, DC: U.S. Government Printing Office.

Proposed Amendments to the Constitution of the United States, Introduced in Congress from the 69th Congress, 2d Session through the 84th Congress, 2d Session, December 6, 1926, to January 3, 1957. 1957. Washington, DC: U.S. Government Printing Office.

"Proposed Legislation on the Convention Method of Amending the United States Constitution." 1972. *Harvard Law Review* 85: 1612–1648.

Pullen, William R. 1948. *Applications of State Legislatures to Congress for the Call of a National Constitutional Convention, 1788–1867.* Master's thesis, University of North Carolina at Chapel Hill.

Quirk, William J. 2008. *Courts and Congress: America's Unwritten Constitution.* New Brunswick, NJ: Transaction Publishers.

Radin, Max. 1930. "The Intermittent Sovereign." *Yale Law Journal* 30: 514–531.

Rakove, Jack N., ed. 1990. *Interpreting the Constitution: The Debate over Original Intent.* Boston: Northeastern University Press.

Ranney, Austin. 1978. "The United States of America." In *Referendums: A Comparative Study of Practice and Theory,* ed. David Butler and Austin Ranney. Washington, DC: American Enterprise Institute for Public Policy Research.

Raskin, Jamin B. 2001. "A Right to Vote." *The American Prospect* 12 (27 August): 10–12.

Rasmussen, Jorgen S., and Joel C. Moses. 1995. *Major European Governments.* 9th ed. Belmont, CA: Wadsworth.

RavenHansen, Peter. 1975. "Congressional Representation for the District of Columbia: A Constitutional Analysis." *Harvard Journal of Legislation* 12: 167–192.

Rawley, James A. 1981. *The Transatlantic Slave Trade: A History.* New York: W. W. Norton.

Reagan, Ronald, et al. 1990. *Restoring the Presidency: Reconsidering the Twenty-second Amendment.* Washington, DC: National Legal Center for Public Interest.

Records of the Council of Censors. 1783–1784. Journal vols. 1–3. Division of Archives and Manuscripts, Pennsylvania Historical and Museum Commission.

Redinger, Paul. 1996. "The Faltering Revolution." *ABA Journal* 82 (February): 56–59.

Reed, Ralph. 1995. *Contract with the American Family: A Bold Plan by Christian Coalition to Strengthen the Family and Restore CommonSense Values.* Nashville, TN: Moorings.

Rees, Grover, III. 1986. "The Amendment Process and Limited Constitutional Conventions." *Benchmark* 2: 67–108.

Rehnquist, William H. 1976. "The Notion of the Living Constitution." *Texas Law Review* 54: 693–706.

Reid, John P. 1993. *Constitutional History of the American Revolution. The Authority of Law.* Madison: University of Wisconsin Press.

Reidinger, Paul. 1996. "The Faltering Revolution." *ABA Journal* 82 (February): 56–59.

Renehan, Edward J., Jr. 1995. *The Secret Six: The True Tale of the Men Who Conspired with John Brown.* New York: Crown.

"The Report of the National Symposium on Presidential Selection." 2001. The Center for Governmental Studies at the University of Virginia. http://www.goodpolitics.org/reform/repor t/ electoral.htm. Accessed 11/29/02.

Report on the Condition of Women and Children as Wage Earners. 1910–1913. U.S. Department of Labor. 19 vols. Washington, DC: U.S. Government Printing Office.

Report to the Attorney General. 1987. *The Question of Statehood for the District of Columbia.* 3 April. Washington, DC: U.S. Government Printing Office.

"Rethinking the Electoral College Debate: The Framers, Federalism, and One Person, One Vote." 2001. *Harvard Law Review* 114 (June): 2526–2549.

"Retroactive Tax Increases: No Problem, Say Justices." 1994. *Congressional Quarterly Weekly Report* 52 (18 June): 1588.

Reynolds, Edward. 1985. *Stand the Storm: A History of the Atlantic Slave Trade.* London: Allison and Busby.

Reynolds, Eustace. 1915. *A New Constitution: A Suggested Form of Modified Government.* New York: Nation Press.

Rhodehamel, John. 1998. *The Great Experiment: George Washington and the American Republic.* New Haven, CT: Yale University Press.

Richards, Nelson. 2006. "The Bricker Amendment and Congress's Failure to Check the Inflation of the Executive's Foreign Affairs Powers, 1951–1954. *California Law Review* 94 (January):175–213.

Rice, Isaac. 1884. "Work for a Constitutional Convention." *Century Magazine* 28 (August): 534–540.

Rich, Bennett M. 1960. *Major Problems in State Constitutional Revision,* ed. W. Brooke Groves. Chicago: Public Administration Service.

Richards, David A. J. 1993. *Conscience and the Constitution: History, Theory, and Law of the Reconstruction Amendments.* Princeton, NJ: Princeton University Press.

Richardson, James E., ed. 1908. *A Compilation of the Messages and Papers of the Presidents, 1789–1908.* 11 vols. n.p.: Bureau of National Literature and Art.

Richardson, Sula. 1991. *Congressional Terms of Office and Tenure: Historical Background and Contemporary Issues.* Washington, DC: Congressional Research Service, Library of Congress.

———. 1989. *Congressional Tenure: A Review of Efforts to Limit House and Senate Service.* Washington, DC: Congressional Research Service, Library of Congress.

Richie, Robert. 1995. "Democracy and Majority Preference Voting." *Rainbow* 3, no. 30 (27 July).

Riker, William H. 1954. "Sidney George Fisher and the Separation of Powers during the Civil War." *Journal of the History of Ideas* 15 (June): 397–412.

"Rising Clamor for Black Separatism." 1970. *U.S. News and World Report* 69 (21 September): 82.

Robinson, Donald. 1989. *Government for the Third American Century.* Boulder, CO: Westview Press.

———. 1987. "Adjustments Are Needed in the System of Checks and Balances." *Polity* 19: 660–666.

———. 1985. *Reforming American Government: The Bicentennial Papers of the Committee on the Constitutional System.* Boulder, CO: Westview Press.

Robinson, Lloyd. 1996. *The Stolen Election, Hayes versus Tilden—1876.* New York: Forge.

Robinson, Roger W., and Herschel B. Burt., ed. by Robert Edwards. 1996. *The Willard House and Clock Museum and the Willard Family Clockmakers.* Columbia, PA: National Association of Watch and Clock Collectors, Inc.

Rodick, Burleigh C. 1953. *American Constitutional Custom: A Forgotten Factor in the Founding.* New York: Philosophical Library.

Roemer, Arthur C. 1983. "Classification of Property." In *The Property Tax and Local Finance,* ed. C. Lowell Harris. New York: Proceedings of the Academy of Political Science.

Rogers, James Kenneth. 2007. "The Other Way to Amendment the Constitution: The Article V Constitutional Convention Amendment Process." *Harvard Journal of Law and Public Policy* 30 (Summer):1005–22.

Rohde, David W. 1994. "The Fall Elections: Realignment or Dealignment." *Chronicle of Higher Education* 41 (14 December): B1–B2.

Roman, Jose D. 2002. "Trying to Fit an Oval Shaped Island into a Square Constitution: Arguments for Puerto Rican Statehood." *Fordham Urban Law Journal* 29 (April): 1681–1713.

Romana, John. 2005. "State Militias in the United States: Changed Responsibilities for a New Era." *The Air Force Law Review* 56: 233–47.

Rose, Judith H. "An American Bill of Responsibilities." http://charltonrose.com/misc/billresp.

Rosen, Jeffrey. 1996. "Just a Quirk." *New Republic* 214 (March 18): 16–17.

———. 1991. "Was the Flag Burning Amendment Unconstitutional?" *Yale Law Review* 100: 1073–1092.

Rosenberg, Gerald N. 1991. *The Hollow Hope: Can Courts Bring about Social Change?* Chicago: University of Chicago Press.

Rosenbloom, David H. 1971. *Federal Service and the Constitution: The Development of the Public Employment Relationship.* Ithaca, NY: Cornell University Press.

Ross, Russell M., and Fred Schwengel. 1982. "An Item Veto for the President?" *Presidential Studies Quarterly* 12 (Winter): 66–79.

Ross, William G. 2005. "When Did the 'Switch in Time' Actually Occur?: Re-discovering the Supreme Court's 'Forgotten' Decisions of 1936–1937." *Arizona State Law Journal* 37 (Winter):1153–1220.

———. 2000. "The Contemporary Significance of *Meyer* and *Pierce* for Parental Rights Issues Involving Education." *Akron Law Review* 34: 177–207.

———. 1990. "The Hazards of Proposals to Limit the Tenure of Federal Judges and to Permit Judicial Removal without Impediment." *Villanova Law Review* 35 (November): 1063–1138.

Rossiter, Clinton. 1987. *1787: The Grand Convention.* New York: W. W. Norton.

———. 1964. *Alexander Hamilton and the Constitution.* New York: Harcourt, Brace and World.

Rossum, Ralph A. 2001. *Federalism, the Supreme Court, and the Seventeenth Amendment: The Irony of Constitutional Democracy.* Lanham, MD: Lexington Books.

Rossum, Ralph A., and G. Alan Tarr. 1999. *American Constitutional Law: The Structure of Government.* 5th ed. New York: St. Martin's Press.

Rothwax, Harold J. 1996. *Guilty: The Collapse of Criminal Justice.* New York: Random House.

Rousseau, JeanJacques. 1762. *On the Social Contract with Geneva Manuscript and Political Economy.* Reprint, ed. Roger D. Masters. New York: St. Martin's Press, 1978.

Rubenfeld, Jed. 2001. "The New Unwritten Constitution." *Duke Law Journal* 51 (October): 289–305.

Rubin, Alissa J. 1995. "Democrats Hope Tax-Raising Rule Will Come Back to Haunt GOP." *Congressional Quarterly Weekly Report* 53 (15 July): 2045–2046.

Rubin, Irene S. 1990. *The Politics of Public Budgeting: Getting and Spending, Borrowing and Balancing.* Chatham, NJ: Chatham House.

Ruhl, J. B. 1999. "The Metrics of Constitutional Amendments: Why Proposed Environmental Quality Amendments Don't Measure Up." *Notre Dame Law Review* 74 (January): 245–281.

Rushdoony, Rousas J. 1973. *The Institutes of Biblical Law.* Phillipsburg, NJ: Presbyterian and Reformed Publishing Co.

Rutland, Robert A. 1987. *James Madison: The Founding Father.* New York: Macmillan.

Sabato, Larry J. 2007. *A More Perfect Constitution: 23 Proposals to Revitalize Our Constitution and Make America a Fairer Country.* New York: Walker and Company.

Sabourin, Jennifer L. 1999. "Note: Parental Rights Amendments: Will a Statutory Right to Parent Force Children to 'Shed Their Constitutional Rights' at the Schoolhouse Door?" *Wayne State University Law Review* 44 (Winter): 1899–1926.

Sager, Lawrence Gene. 1978. "Fair Measure: The Legal Status of Underenforced Constitutional Norms." *Harvard Law Review* 92: 1212–1264.

Salins, Peter D., ed. 1987. *Housing America's Poor.* Chapel Hill: University of North Carolina Press.

Samaha, Adam M. 2008. "Dead Hand Arguments and Constitutional Interpretation." *Columbia Law Review* 108 (April): 606–680.

Sargentich, Thomas O. 1993. "The Limits of the Parliamentary Critique of the Separation of Powers." *William and Mary Law Review* 34 (Spring): 679–739.

Sartori, Giovanni. 1994. *Comparative Constitutional Engineering: An Inquiry into Structures, Incentives and Outcomes.* New York: New York University Press.

Savage, James D. 1988. *Balanced Budgets and American Politics.* Ithaca, NY: Cornell University Press.

"Sawing a Justice in Half." 1939. *Yale Law Journal* 48: 1455–1458.

Schaffner, Joan. 2005. "The Federal Marriage Amendment: To Protect the Sanctity of Marriage or Destroy Constitutional Democracy?" *American University Law Review* 54 (August): 1487–1526.

Schaller, Thomas F. 1998. "Democracy at Rest: Strategic Ratification of the Twenty-First Amendment." *Publius: The Journal of Federalism* 28 (Spring): 81–97.

Schapsmeier, Edward L., and Frederick H. Schapsmeier. 1985. *Dirksen of Illinois: Senatorial Statesman.* Urbana: University of Illinois Press.

Scharpf, Fritz W. 1966. "Judicial Review and the Political Question: A Functional Analysis." *Yale Law Journal* 75 (March): 517–597.

Schechter, Stephen L. 2000. "Amending the Constitution: Current Proposals." *Insights on Law & Society* 1 (Fall): 11–13.

Scheef, Robert W. 2001. "'Public Citizens' and the Constitution: Bridging the Gap between Popular Sovereignty and Original Intent." *Fordham Law Review* 69 (April): 2201–2251.

Scheiber, Harry N. 1992. "Police Power." In *The Oxford Companion to the Supreme Court of the United States,* ed. Kermit L. Hall. New York: Oxford University Press.

Scheuerman, William E. 2002. "Constitutionalism in an Age of Speed." *Constitutional Commentary* 19 (Summer): 353–390.

Schlesinger, Arthur M., Jr. 1974. "On the Presidential Succession." *Political Science Quarterly* 89 (Fall): 475–505.

Schlickeisen, Rodger. 1994. "Protecting Biodiversity for Future Generations: An Argument for a Constitutional Amendment." *Tulane Environmental Law Journal* 8 (Winter): 181–221.

Schmidt, David D. 1989. *Citizen Law Makers: The Ballot Initiative Revolution.* Philadelphia: Temple University Press.

Schmidt, Peter. 2002. "Next Stop, Supreme Court? Appeals Court Upholds Affirmative Action at University of Michigan Law School." *Chronicle of Higher Education* 48 (24 May): A24–26.

Schneier, Edward V., and Bertram Gross. 1993. *Legislative Strategy.* New York: St. Martin's Press.

Schotten, Peter, and Dennis Stevens. 1996. *Religion, Politics, and the Law: Commentaries and Controversies.* Belmont, CA: Wadsworth.

Schouler, James. 1908. "A New Federal Constitution." In *Ideals of the Republic,* ed. James Schouler. Boston: Little, Brown.

Schrader, George D. 1970. "Constitutional History of the Income Tax." *Georgia State Bar Journal* 7 (August): 39–55.

Schrag, Philip G. 1985. *Behind the Scenes: The Politics of a Constitutional Convention.* Washington, DC: Georgetown University Press.

Schwartzberg, Melissa. 2008. "Ratification Rules and the New (and Old) Constitutional Convention."

Papers presented at the 2008 Annual Meeting of the American Political Science Association in Boston.

———. 2007. *Democracy and Legal Change.* New York: Cambridge University Press.

———. 2004. "Athenian Democracy and Legal Change." *American Political Science Review* 98 (May): 311–325.

Schubert, Glendon. 1954. "Politics and the Constitution: The Bricker Amendment during 1953." *Journal of Politics* 16 (May): 257–298.

Schuck, Peter H., and Rogers M. Smith. 1985. *Citizenship without Consent: Illegal Aliens in the American Polity.* New Haven, CT: Yale University Press.

Schultz, David. 2006. "Economic Development and Eminent Domain After Kelo: Property Rights and 'Public Use' Under State Constitutions." *Albany Law Environmental Outlook Journal* 11: 41–88.

Schwartz, Victoria. 2005. "The Victims' Rights Amendment." *Harvard Journal on Legislation* 42 (Summer): 525–555.

Scott, Rodney D. 1999. *The Great Debate: The Need for Constitutional Reform.* Chicago: Rampant Lion Press.

Schwartz, Bernard. 1992. *The Great Rights of Mankind: A History of the American Bill of Rights.* Madison, WI: Madison House.

———. 1988. *Super Chief: Earl Warren and His Supreme Court—A Judicial Biography.* New York: New York University Press.

———. 1986. *Swann's Way: The School Busing Case and the Supreme Court.* New York: Oxford University Press.

Schwartz, Bernard, ed. 1980. *The Roots of the Bill of Rights.* 5 vols. New York: Chelsea House.

Scigliano, Robert. 1994. "The Two Executives: The President and the Supreme Court." In *The American Experiment: Essays on the Theory and Practice of Liberty,* ed. Peter A. Lawler and Robert M. Schoefar. Lanham, MD: Rowman and Littlefield.

Scott, Rodney. 1999. *The Great Debate: The Need for Constitutional Reform.* Chicago: Rampant Lion Press.

"Second Amendment Symposium." 1995. *Tennessee Law Review* 62 (Spring): 443–821.

Seelye, Katharine Q. 1995. "Congress Members off Hook on Reelection, but Not Issue." *New York Times,* 23 May, A1, A11.

Seitz, Don C. 1929. *Famous American Duels: With Some Account of the Causes That Led up to Them and the Men Engaged.* Reprint, Freeport, NY: Books for Libraries Press, 1966.

Senese, Donald J. 1989. *George Mason and the Legacy of Constitutional Liberty: An Examination of the Influence of George Mason on the American Bill of Rights.* Fairfax County, VA: Fairfax County Historical Commission.

"Separation of Church and Stats: An Examination of State Constitutional Limits on Government Funding for Religious Institutions." 2003. *The First Amendment Law Review* 2 (Winter).

Setty, Sudha. 2008. "The President's Question Time: Power, Information, and the Executive Credibility Gap." *Cornell Journal of Law and Public Policy* 17 (Spring):247–294.

Shalom, Stephen R. 1981. *The United States and the Philippines: A Study of Neocolonialism.* Philadelphia: Institute for the Study of Human Issues.

ShandTucci, Douglass. 1995. *Ralph Adams Cram: Life and Architecture.* Vol. 1. Amherst, MA: University of Massachusetts Press.

———. 1975. *Ralph Adams Cram: American Medievalist.* Boston: Boston Public Library.

Shannon, David A. 1967. *The Socialist Party of America: A History.* Chicago: Quadrangle Books.

Shermer, Matt. 1969. *"The Sense of the People" or the Next Development in American Democracy.* New York: American Referendum Association.

Sidak, J. Gregory. 1995. "The LineItem Veto Amendment." *Cornell Law Review* 80 (July): 1498–1505.

———. 1989. "The Recommendation Clause." *Georgetown Law Journal* 77 (August): 2070–2135.

Siegal, Reva B. 2006. "Constitutional Culture, Social Movement Conflict and Constitutional Change: The Case of the de facto ERA; 2005–2006 Brennan Center Symposium Lecture." *California Law Review* 94 (October): 1323–1419.

Siegel, Reva B. 2002. "She the People: The Nineteenth Amendment, Sex Equality, Federalism, and the Family." *Harvard Law Review* 115 (February): 947–1046.

———. 2001. "Gender and the Constitution From a Social Movement Perspective." *University of Pennsylvania Law Review* 150 (November): 297–351.

Sigler, Jay A. 1969. *Double Jeopardy: The Development of a Legal and Social Policy.* Ithaca, NY: Cornell University Press.

Sigmund, Paul E. 1971. *Natural Law in Political Thought.* Cambridge, MA: Winthrop Publishers.

Silva, Edward J. 1970. "State Cohorts and Amendment Clusters in the Process of Federal Constitutional Amendments in the United States, 1869–1931." *Law and Society Review* 4 (February): 445–466.

Silversmith, Jol A. 1999. "The 'Missing Thirteenth Amendment': Constitutional Nonsense and Titles of Nobility." *Southern California Interdisciplinary Law Journal* 8 (Spring): 577–611.

Sisk, Gregory C. 2002. "Suspending the Pardon Power during the Twilight of a Presidential Term." *Missouri Law Review* 67 (Winter): 13–27.

Skillen, James W., ed. 1993. *The School Choice Controversy: What Is Constitutional?* Grand Rapids, MI: Baker Books.

Smith, Goldwin. 1906. "Chief Justice Clark on the Defects of the American Constitution." *North American Review* 183 (1 November): 845–851.

———. 1898. "Is the Constitution Outworn?" *North American Review* 166 (March): 257–267.

Smith, Jean Edward. 1996. *John Marshall: Definer of a Nation.* New York: Henry Holt and Company.

Smith, Page. 1995. *Democracy on Trial: The Japanese American Evacuation and Relocation in World War II.* New York: Simon and Schuster.

Smith, Rodney K. 1987. *Public Prayer and the Constitution: A Case Study in Constitutional Interpretation.* Wilmington, DE: Scholarly Resources.

Smith, Steven. 1989. "Taking It to the Floor." In *Congress Reconsidered,* ed. Lawrence C. Dodd and Bruce I. Oppenheimer. Washington, DC: Congressional Quarterly.

Smith, Terry. 1996. "Rediscovering the Sovereignty of the People: the Case for Senate Districts." *North Carolina Law Review* 75(November):1–74.

Solberg, Winton, ed. 1958. *The Federal Convention and the Formation of the Union.* Indianapolis, IN: Bobbs-Merrill.

Soller, Christopher J. 1995. "Newtonian Government: Is the Contract with America Unconstitutional?" *Duquesne Law Review* 33 (Summer): 959–984.

Solomon, Stephen D. 2007. *Ellery's Protest: How One Young Man Defied Tradition & Sparked a Battle Over School Prayer.* Ann Arbor: University of Michigan Press.

Somin, Ilya. 2003. "Voter Knowledge and Constitutional Change: Assessing the New Deal Experience." *William and Mary Law Review* 45 (December): 595–674.

Somin, Ilya, and Neal Devins. 2007. "Can We Make the Constitution More Democratic? *Drake Law Review* 55 (Summer): 971–1000.

Sorauf, Frank J. 1988. *Money in American Elections.* Glenview, IL: Scott, Foresman.

Spence, Karl. 2006. *Yo! Liberals! You Call This Progress? Crime, Race, Sex, Faith, Law and the Culture War.* Converse, TX: Fielding Press.

Spitzer, Robert J. 1995. *The Politics of Gun Control.* Chatham, NJ: Chatham House Publishers.

———. 1988. *The Presidential Veto: Touchstone of the American Presidency.* Albany, NY: State University of New York Press.

Spotts, JoAnne D. 1994. "The Twenty-seventh Amendment: A Late Bloomer or a Dead Horse?" *Georgia State University Law Review* 10 (January): 337–365.

Stanwood, Edward. 1903. *American Tariff Controversies in the Nineteenth Century.* 2 vols. Reprint, New York: Russell and Russell, 1967.

Stathis, Stephen. 1990. "The Twenty-second Amendment: A Practical Remedy or Partisan Maneuver?" *Constitutional Commentary* 7 (Winter): 61–88.

Steamer, Robert J. 1992. "Commerce Power." In *The Oxford Companion to the Supreme Court of the United States,* ed. Kermit L. Hall. New York: Oxford University Press.

Stein, Edward. 2004. "Past and Present Proposed Amendments to the United States Constitution Regarding Marriage." *Washington University Law Quarterly* 82 (Fall): 611–85.

Stern, Madeline B., ed. 1974. *The Victoria Woodhull Reader.* Weston, MA: M & S Press.

Sterling, Dorothy. 1999. *Lucretia Mott.* New York: The Feminist Press at CUNY.

Stevens, Doris. 1995. *Jailed for Freedom: American Women Win the Vote.* Troutdale, OR: New Sage.

Stickney, Albert. 1879. *A True Republic.* New York: Harper and Brothers.

Stone, Geoffrey R., Richard A. Epstein, and Cass R. Sunstein, eds. 1992. *The Bill of Rights in the Modern State.* Chicago: University of Chicago Press.

Stoner, James R., Jr. 1995. "Amending the School Prayer Amendment." *First Things* 51 (May): 16–18.

Storing, Herbert, ed. 1981. *The Complete Anti-Federalist.* 7 vols. Chicago: University of Chicago Press.

———, ed. 1970. *What Country Have I? Political Writings by Black Americans.* New York: St. Martin's Press.

Story, Joseph. 1987. *Commentaries on the Constitution of the United States.* Durham, NC: Carolina Academic Press.

———. 1833. *Commentaries on the Constitution of the United States.* Boston: Hilliard, Gray. Reprint, New York: Da Capo Press, 1970.

Stowe, Steven M. 1987. *Intimacy and Power in the Old South: Ritual in the Lives of the Planters.* Baltimore: Johns Hopkins University Press.

Strauss, David A. 2001. "Commentary: The Irrelevance of Constitutional Amendments." *Harvard Law Review* 114 (March): 1457–1505.

Strickland, Ruth A. 1993. "The Twenty-seventh Amendment and Constitutional Change by Stealth." *P.S. Political Science and Politics* 26 (December): 716–722.

———. 1989. *The Ratification Process of U.S. Constitutional Amendments: Each State Having One Vote as a Form of Malapportionment.* PhD dissertation, University of South Carolina.

Strittmatter, Bill. n.d. "A Christian Constitution and Civil Law for the Kingdom of Heaven on Earth." Lakemore, OH: 28 pp.

Struble, Robert, Jr. "Redeeming U.S. Democracy." http://temnet.com/~rusd. Accessed 11 July 1997. No longer available on the Internet.

Sturm, Albert L., and Janice May. 1982. "State Constitutions and Constitutional Revision: 1980–81 and the Past 50 Years." In *The Book of the States: 1982–1983.* Lexington, KY: Council of State Governments.

Suber, Peter. 1990. *The Paradox of SelfAmendment: A Study of Logic, Law, Omnipotence, and Change.* New York: Peter Lang.

———. 1987. "Population Changes and Constitutional Amendments: Federalism versus Democracy." *Journal of Law Reform* 20 (Winter): 409–490.

Sullivan, J. W. 1893. *Direct Legislation by the Citizenship*. New York: Nationalist Publishing Company.

Sullivan, Kathleen M. 1995. "Constitutional Constancy: Why Congress Should Cure Itself of Amendment Fever." *Record of the Bar of the City of New York* 50 (November): 724–735.

Sundquist, James L. 1986. *Constitutional Reform and Effective Government*. Washington, DC: Brookings Institution.

Suthon, Walter J., Jr. 1953. "The Dubious Origin of the Fourteenth Amendment." *Tulane Law Review* 28: 22–44. Swanson, Wayne R. 1990. *The Christ Child Goes to Court*. Philadelphia: Temple University Press.

Swindler, William. 1963. "The Current Challenge to Federalism: The Confederating Proposals." *Georgetown Law Review* 52 (Fall): 1–41.

"Symposium: A Religious Equality Amendment?" 1996. *Brigham Young University Law Review* 1996: 561–688.

"Symposium on the Reuss Resolution: A Vote of No Confidence in the President." 1975. *George Washington Law Review* 43 (January): 328–500.

Taft, Henry. 1930. "Amendment of the Federal Constitution: Is the Power Conferred by Article V Limited by the Tenth Amendment?" *Virginia Law Review* 16 (May): 647–658.

Tananbaum, Duane. 1988. *The Bricker Amendment Controversy: A Test of Eisenhower's Political Leadership*. Ithaca, NY: Cornell University Press.

Tansill, Charles C. 1926. *Proposed Amendments of the Constitution of the United States Introduced in Congress from December 4, 1889, to July 2, 1926*. Washington, DC: U.S. Government Printing Office.

Tarr, G. Alan. 1994. *Judicial Process and Judicial Policymaking*. St. Paul, MN: West.

Tarr, G. Alan and Robert F. Williams, eds. 2006a. *The Politics of State Constitutional Reform*. Vol. 1 of *State Constitutions for the Twenty-first Century*. Albany: State University of New York Press.

———. 2006b. *The Agenda of State Constitutional Reform*. Vol. 3 of *State Constitutions for the Twenty-first Century*. Albany: State University of New York Press.

Tatalovich, Raymond. 1995. *Nativism Reborn? The Official English Language Movement and the American States*. Lexington: University Press of Kentucky.

Taylor, A. Elizabeth. 1957. *The Woman Suffrage Movement in Tennessee*. New York: Bookman Associates.

Taylor, Andrew. 1997. "Senate Again One Vote Short: GOP Says House Will Act." *Congressional Quarterly* 55 (8 March): 577–578.

———. 1996a. "Congress Hands Presidency a Budgetary Scalpel." *Congressional Quarterly Weekly Report* 54 (30 March): 864–867.

———. 1996b. "Republicans Break Logjam on LineItem Veto Bill." *Congressional Quarterly Weekly Report* 54 (16 March): 687.

Taylor, Arthur H. 2006. "Fear of an Article V Convention." *Brigham Young University Journal of Public Law*. 20: 497–438.

Taylor, George R., ed. 1993. *The Great Tariff Debate, 1820–1830*. Boston: D. C. Heath.

Taylor, Joe Gray. 1976. *Louisiana: A Bicentennial History*. New York: W. W. Norton.

Taylor, Stuart, Jr. 2000. "Victims' Rights: Leave the Constitution Alone." *National Journal* 32 (22 April): 1254.

TenBroek, Jacobus. 1951. *The Antislavery Origins of the Fourteenth Amendment*. Berkeley: University of California Press.

"Text of Amendment." 1995. *Congressional Quarterly Weekly Report* 53 (4 March): 673.

Thierer, Adam D. 1999. "The Bliley 'States' Initiative': Empowering States and Protecting Federalism." 2 March. No. 576. The Heritage Foundation Executive Memorandum.

"33 States Ask Congress for Constitutional Convention." 1969. *Congressional Quarterly Weekly Report* 27 (1 August): 1372–1373.

Thomas, Chantal. 2000. "Constitutional Change and International Government." *Hastings Law Journal* 52 (November): 1–46.

Thomas, Tracy A. 2005. "Elizabeth Cady Stanton on the Federal Marriage Amendment: A Letter to the President." *Constitutional Commentary* 22 (Spring): 137–159.

Thorpe, Francis N. 1909. *The Federal and State Constitutions, Colonial Charters and Other Organic Laws of the States, Territories, and Colonies Now or Heretofore Forming the United States of America*. 7 vols. Washington, DC: U.S. Government Printing Office.

Tiedeman, Christopher G. 1890. *The Unwritten Constitution of the United States*. New York: G. P. Putnam's Sons.

Tillman, Seth Barrett. 2005. "A Textualist Defense of Article I, Section 7, Clause 3: Why Hollingsworth v. Virginia Was Rightly Decided, and Why INS v. Chadha Was Wrongly Reasoned." *Texas Law Review* 83 (April): 1265–1372.

Timberlake, James H. 1970. Prohibition and the Progressive Movement, 1900–1920. New York: Atheneum.

Tocqueville, Alexis de. 1835, 1840. *Democracy in America*. 2 vols. Reprint, ed. J. P. Mayer. Garden City, NY: Anchor Books, 1969.

Toffler, Alvin, and Heidi Toffler. 1995. *Creating a New Civilization: The Politics of the Third Wave*. Atlanta: Turner Publishing.

Tolchin, Mark. 1990. "Fifteen States Rally behind Calls for Amendment to Gain More Powers." *New York Times*, 26 June, A12, col. 3–6.

Tomlins, Christopher L. 1985. *The State and the Unions: Labor Relations, Law, and the Organized Labor Movement in America, 1880–1960*. Cambridge, UK: Cambridge University Press.

Toner, Robin. 1995. "Flag Burning Amendment Fails in Senate, but Margin Narrows." *New York Times*, 13 December, 1.

Tonn, Bruce E. 1996. "A Design for Future-Oriented Government." *Futures* 28 (June): 413–431.

———. 1991. "The Court of Generations: A Proposed Amendment to the U.S. Constitution." *Futures* 21: 482–498.

Toole, James F., Robert J. Joynt, and Arthur S. Link, eds. 2001. *Presidential Disability: Papers, Discussions, and Recommendations on the Twenty-Fifth Amendment and Issues of Inability and Disability among Presidents.* Rochester, NY: University of Rochester,

Torke, James W. 1994. "Assessing the Ackerman and Amar Theses: Notes on Extratextual Constitutional Change." *Widener Journal of Public Law* 4: 229–271.

Trattner, Walter I. 1970. *Crusade for the Children: A History of the National Child Labor Committee and Child Labor Reform in America.* Chicago: Quadrangle Books.

Traynor, Roger J. 1927. *The Amending System of the United States Constitution, a Historical and Legal Analysis.* PhD dissertation, University of California.

Tribe, Laurence H. 1990. *Abortion: The Clash of Absolutes.* New York: W. W. Norton.

———. 1983. "A *Constitution* We Are Amending: In Defense of a Restrained Judicial Role." *Harvard Law Review* 97 (December): 433–445.

Tribe, Laurence H., and Michael C. Dorf. 1991. *On Reading the Constitution.* Cambridge, MA: Harvard University Press.

Tsesis, Alexander. 2004. *The Thirteenth Amendment and American Freedom: A Legal History.* New York: New York University Press.

Tugwell, Rexford. 1974. *The Emerging Constitution.* New York: Harper and Row.

Tuller, Walter K. 1911. "A Convention to Amend the Constitution—Why Needed—How It May Be Obtained." *North American Review* 193: 369–387.

Turner, John J., Jr. 1973. "The Twelfth Amendment and the First American Party System." *Historian* 35: 221–237.

Tushnet, Mark. 2005. "Democracy Versus Judicial Review." *Dissent* 52 (Spring): 59–63.

———. 1990. "The Flag-Burning Episode: An Essay on the Constitution." *University of Colorado Law Review* 61: 39–53.

Twelve Southerners. 1930. *I'll Take My Stand: The South and the Agrarian Tradition.* Introduction by Louis D. Rubin Jr. Reprint, Baton Rouge: Louisiana State University Press, 1977.

Twentieth Century Fund Task Force on the Vice Presidency. 1988. *A Heartbeat Away.* New York: Printing Press Publications.

"The Twenty-fifth Amendment: Preparing for Presidential Disability." 1995. *Wake Forest Law Review* 30 (Fall): 427–648.

Unger, Sanford J. 1972. *The Paper and the Papers.* New York: E. P. Dutton.

Upham, Thomas C. 1941. *Total Democracy: A New Constitution for the United States. A Democratic Ideal for the World.* New York: Carlyle House.

Uradnik, Kathleen. 2002. *Student's Guide to Landmark Congressional Laws on Youth.* Westport, CT: Greenwood Press.

Ure, James Christian. 2007. "You Scratch My Back and I'll Scratch Yours: Why the Federal Marriage Amendment Should Also Repeal the Seventh Amendment." *South Texas Law Review* 49 (Fall): 277–305.

Urofsky, Melvin I. 1988. *A March of Liberty: A Constitutional History of the United States.* New York: Alfred A. Knopf.

U.S. Senate Committee on the Judiciary, *Proposing an Amendment to the Constitution of the United States Relative to Taxes on Incomes, Inheritance, and Gifts: Hearings on S.J. Res. 23,* 83rd Cong., 2d sess., 1954.

U.S. Senate Committee on the Judiciary, *Proposing an Amendment to the Constitution of the United States Relative to Taxes on Incomes, Inheritance, and Gifts: Hearings on S.J. Res. 23,* 84th Cong., 2d sess., 1956.

U.S. Senate Committee on the Judiciary, Subcommittee on Constitutional Amendments, *Lowering the Voting Age to 18,* 90th Cong., 2d sess., 14, 15, 16 May 1968.

U.S. Senate Committee on the Judiciary, Subcommittee on Constitutional Amendments, *Lowering the Voting Age to 18,* 91st Cong., 2d sess., 16, 17 February, 9, 10 March 1970.

U.S. Senate Committee on the Judiciary, Subcommittee on the Constitution, *Affirmative Action and Equal Protection: Hearings on S.J. 41,* 97th Cong., 1st sess., 11 May, 18 June, and 16 July 1981.

U.S. Senate Committee on the Judiciary, Subcommittee on the Constitution, *Amendments to the Constitution: A Brief Legislative History.* 1985. Washington, DC: U.S. Government Printing Office.

Utley, Robert L., Jr., and Patricia B. Gray. 1989. *Principles of the Constitutional Order: The Ratification Debates.* Lanham, MD: University Press of America.

Van Alstine, Michael P. 2002. "The Costs of Legal Change." *UCLA Law Review* 49 (February): 789–870.

Van Alstyne, William. 1993. "What Do You Think About the Twenty-seventh Amendment?" *Constitutional Commentary* 10 (Winter): 9–18.

———. 1979. "The Limited Constitutional Convention—The Recurring Answer." *Duke Law Journal* 1979 (September): 985–1001.

———. 1978. "Does Article V Restrict the States to Calling Unlimited Conventions Only?—A Letter to a Colleague." *Duke Law Journal* 1978 (January): 1295–1306.

Van Burkleo, Sandra F. 1990. "No Rights but Human Rights." *Constitution* 2 (Spring/Summer): 4–19.

Van Deusen, Glyndon. 1937. *The Life of Henry Clay.* Boston: Little, Brown.

Van Doren, Carl. 1948. *The Great Rehearsal: The Story of the Making and Ratifying of the Constitution of the United States.* New York: Viking Press.

Van Riper, Paul P. 1958. *History of the United States Civil Service.* Evanston, IL: Row, Peterson.

Van Sickle, Bruce M., and Lynn M. Boughey. 1990. "Lawful and Peaceful Revolution: Article V and Congress' Present Duty to Call a Convention for Proposing Amendments." *Hamline Law Review* 14 (Fall): 1–115.

Vandercoy, David E. 1994. "The History of the Second Amendment." *Valparaiso University Law Review* 28 (Spring): 1007–1039.

Vanguard, Virginia. 1995. *The Populis: A Draft Constitution for a New Political Age.* Brentsville, VA: The Wingspread Enterprise.

Vergara, Vanessa B. M. 2000. "Comment: Abusive MailOrder Bride Marriage and the Thirteenth Amendment." *Northwestern University Law Review* 94 (Summer): 1547–1599.

Vermeule, Adrian. 2006. "Constitutional Amendments and the Constitutional Common Law." In *The Least Examined Branch: The Role of Legislatures in the Constitutional State,* ed. Richard W. Bauman and Tsvi Kahana. New York: Cambridge University Press.

———. 2001. "The Facts about Unwritten Constitutionalism: A Response to Professor Rubenfeld." *Duke Law Journal* 51 (October): 473–476.

Vidal, Gore. 1997. "Time for a People's Convention." *The Nation* 254 (27 January): 73.

Vierra, Norman. 1981. "The Equal Rights Amendment: Rescission, Extension and Justiciability." *Southern Illinois Law Journal* 1981: 1–29.

Vile, John R. 2010. *A Companion to the United States Constitution and Its Amendments.* 5th ed. Westport, CT: Praeger.

———. 2005. *The Constitutional Convention of 1787: A Comprehensive Encyclopedia of America's Founding.* 2 vols. Santa Barbara, CA: ABC-CLIO.

———. 2003a. *Great American Judges: An Encyclopedia.* 2 vols. Santa Barbara: ABC-CLIO.

———. 2002. *Presidential Winners and Losers: Words of Victory and Concession.* Washington, DC: Congressional Quarterly.

———. 2001. *Great American Lawyers: An Encyclopedia.* 2 vols. Santa Barbara: ABC-CLIO.

———. 2000. "Up Close: Three Recent Amendments." *Insights on Law & Society* 1 (Fall): 8–11.

———. 1998a. "Francis Lieber and the Constitutional Amending Process." *The Review of Politics* 60 (Summer): 524–543.

———. 1998b. *The United States Constitution: Questions and Answers.* Westport, CT: Greenwood Press.

———. 1996–1997. "Truism, Tautology or Vital Principle? The Tenth Amendment Since *United States v. Darby.*" *Cumberland Law Review* 27: 446–532.

———. 1995. "The Case against Implicit Limits on the Constitutional Amending Process." In *Responding to Imperfection,* ed. Sanford Levinson. Princeton, NJ: Princeton University Press.

———. 1994a. *Constitutional Change in the United States: A Comparative Study of the Role of Constitutional Amendments, Judicial Interpretations, and Legislative and Executive Actions.* Westport, CT: Praeger.

———. 1994b. "The Selection and Tenure of Chief Justices." *Judicature* 78 (September-October): 96–100.

———. 1993a. *Contemporary Questions Surrounding the Constitutional Amending Process.* Westport, CT: Praeger.

———. 1993b. *The Theory and Practice of Constitutional Change in America: A Collection of Original Source Materials.* New York: Peter Lang.

———. 1993c. "Three Kinds of Constitutional Founding and Change: The Convention Model and Its Alternatives." *Political Research Quarterly* 46: 881–895.

———. 1992. *The Constitutional Amending Process in American Political Thought.* New York: Praeger.

———. 1991a. "Just Say No to 'Stealth' Amendment." *National Law Journal* 14 (22 June): 15–16.

———. 1991b. "Proposals to Amend the Bill of Rights: Are Fundamental Rights in Jeopardy?" *Judicature* 75 (August/September): 62–67.

———. 1991c. *Rewriting the United States Constitution: An Examination of Proposals from Reconstruction to the Present.* New York: Praeger.

———. 1990–1991. "Legally Amending the United States Constitution: The Exclusivity of Article V's Mechanisms." *Cumberland Law Review* 21: 271–307.

———. 1990. "Permitting States to Rescind Ratifications of Pending Amendments to the U.S. Constitution." *Publius: The Journal of Federalism* 20 (Spring): 109–122.

———. 1989. "How a Constitutional Amendment Protecting the Flag Might Widen Protection of Symbolic Expression." *Louisiana Bar Journal* 37 (October): 169–172.

———. 1985. "Limitations on the Constitutional Amending Process." *Constitutional Commentary* 2 (Summer): 373–388.

———. 1980. "The Supreme Court and the Amending Process." *Georgia Political Science Association Journal* 8 (Fall): 33–66.

Vile, John R., and Mario PerezReilly. 1991. "The U.S. Constitution and Judicial Qualifications: A Curious Omission." *Judicature* 74 (December-January): 198–202.

Vile, John R., David L. Hudson, Jr, and David Schultz. 2008. *The Encyclopedia of the First Amendment.* 2 vols. Washington, DC: CQ Press.

Vile, John R., and William Pederson, and Frank Williams. 2008. *James Madison: Philosopher, Founder, and Statesman.* Athens: Ohio University Press.

Vile, John R., ed. 2002. *Proposed Amendments to the U.S. Constitution, 1787–2001.* 3 Vols. Union, NJ: Law Book Exchange.

Virginia Commission on Constitutional Government. 1967. *The Reconstruction Amendments Debates.* Richmond, VA: Virginia Commission on Constitutional Government.

Volcansek, Mary L. 1993. *Judicial Impeachment: None Called for Justice.* Urbana: University of Illinois Press.

Voorhis, Jerry. 1947. *Confessions of a Congressman.* Reprint, Westport, CT: Greenwood Press, 1970.

Vorenberg, Michael. 2001. *Final Freedom: The Civil War, the Abolition of Slavery, and the Thirteenth Amendment.* Cambridge, UK: Cambridge University Press.

———. 2000. "Bringing the Constitution Back In: Amendment, Innovation, and Popular Democracy during the Civil War Era." Paper presented at the "Democracy in America" Conference, M.I.T., Cambridge, Massachusetts, September 21–23.

Vose, Clement E. 1979. "When District of Columbia Representation Collides with the Constitutional Amendment Institution." *Publius: The Journal of Federalism* 9 (Winter): 105–125.

———. 1972. Constitutional Change: Amendment Politics and Supreme Court Litigation since 1900. Lexington, MA: D. C. Heath.

Wade, Edwin. 1995. *Constitution 2000: A Federalist Proposal for the Next Century.* Chicago: Let's Talk Sense.

Walker, David M. 1980. *The Oxford Companion to Law.* Oxford, UK: Clarenden Press.

Wallace, William Kay. 1932. *Our Obsolete Constitution.* New York: John Day.

Walcoff, Jonathan L. 1985. "The Unconstitutionality of Voter Initiative Applications for Federal Constitutional Conventions." *Colorado Law Review* 85: 1525–1545.

Walsh, Edward. 2002. "U.S. Argues for Wider Gun Rights: Supreme Court Filing Reverses Past Policy," *Washington Post,* 8 May, A01.

Wardle, Lynnd. 2007. "Lessons from the Bill of Rights About Constitutional Protection for Marriage." *Loyola University Chicago Law Review* 38 (Winter): 279–322.

———. 2006. "Federal Constitutional Protection for Marriage: Why and How." *Brigham Young University Journal of Public Law* 20:439–85.

Watkins, William. 2004. *Reclaiming the American Revolution: The Kentucky and Virginia Resolutions and Their Legacy.* New York: Palgrave Macmillan.

Watson, Gregory. 2000. "I Have a Better Way." *Insights on Law & Society* 1 (Fall): 16.

Watson, Richard A. 1985. *Promise and Performance of American Democracy.* 5th ed. New York: John Wiley & Sons.

Weber, Paul. 1989. "Madison's Opposition to a Second Convention." *Polity* 20 (Spring): 498–517.

Weber, Paul J., and Barbara A. Perry. 1989. *Unfounded Fears: Myths and Realities of a Constitutional Convention.* New York: Praeger.

Wedgwood, William B. 1861. *The Reconstruction of the Government of the United States of America: A Democratic Empire Advocated and an Imperial Constitution Proposed.* New York: John H. Tingley.

Weeks, Kent M. 1971. *Adam Clayton Powell and the Supreme Court.* New York: Dunellen.

Weiser, Philip J. 1993. "Ackerman's Proposal for Popular Constitutional Lawmaking: Can It Realize His Aspirations for Dualist Democracy?" *New York University Law Review* 68 (October): 907–959.

Welch, Susan, et al. 1993. *Understanding American Government.* 2d ed. Minneapolis–St. Paul, MN: West.

Wenner, Lettie M. 1982. *The Environmental Decade in Court.* Bloomington: Indiana University Press.

Westin, Alan. 1990. *The Anatomy of a Constitutional Law Case:* Youngstown Sheet & Tube Co. v. Sawyer; *the Steel Seizure Decision.* New York: Columbia University Press.

Westover, Casey L. 2003. "The Twenty-eighth Amendment: Why the Constitution Should Be Amended to Grant Congress the Power to Legislate in Furtherance of the General Welfare." *John Marshall Law Review* 36 (Winter): 327–369.

Wheeler, Marjorie S. 1993. *New Women of the New South: The Leaders of the Woman Suffrage Movement in the Southern States.* New York: Oxford University Press.

Wheeler, Marjorie S., ed. 1995a. *One Woman, One Vote: Rediscovering the Woman Suffrage Movement.* Troutdale, OR: New Sage.

———. 1995b. *Votes for Women! The Woman Suffrage Movement in Tennessee, the South, and the Nation.* Knoxville: University of Tennessee Press.

Whitaker, L. Paige. 1992. *The Constitutionality of States Limiting Congressional Terms.* Washington, DC: Congressional Research Service, Library of Congress.

White, G. Edward. 2000. *The Constitution and the New Deal.* Cambridge, MA: Harvard University Press.

———. 1991. *The Marshall Court and Cultural Change 1815–1835.* New York: Oxford University Press.

White, James J. 1991. "One Hundred Years of Uniform State Laws: *Ex Proprio Vigore.*" *Michigan Law Review* 89 (August): 2096–2133.

White, Welsh S. 1991. *The Death Penalty in the Nineties: An Examination of the Modern System of Capital Punishment.* Ann Arbor: University of Michigan Press.

Whitehead, John W. 2002. "Forfeiting 'Enduring Freedom' for 'Homeland Security': A Constitutional Analysis of the USA Patriot Act and the Justice Department's Anti-Terrorism Initiatives." *American University Law Review* 51 (August): 1081–1133.

Whitman, Alden, ed. 1985. *American Reformers.* New York: H. W. Wilson.

Whitten Nathaniel. *The Do-It-Yourself Constitutional Amendment Kit.* n.p.: Vitally Important Books, 2008.

Whittington, Keith E. 1999. *Constitutional Construction: Divided Powers and Constitutional Meaning.* Cambridge, MA: Harvard University Press.

Wiecek, William. 1992. "Subversion." In *The Oxford Companion to the Supreme Court of the United*

States, ed. Kermit L. Hall. New York: Oxford University Press.

———. 1977. *The Sources of Antislavery Constitutionalism in America, 1760–1848.* Ithaca, NY: Cornell University Press.

———. 1972. *The Guarantee Clause of the U.S. Constitution.* Ithaca, NY: Cornell University Press.

Wiggins, Charles. 1973. "A Constitutional Amendment Concerning Information Proceedings and Grand Jury Indictments." *Congressional Record.* 93rd Cong. 1st sess., 1973, Vol. 119, pt. 25: 32911–32912.

Wilcox, Clyde. 1995. *The Latest American Revolution? The 1994 Elections and Their Implications for Governance.* New York: St. Martin's Press.

Wilkinson, J. Harvie, III. 1979. *From Brown to Bakke: The Supreme Court and School Integration: 1954–1978.* New York: Oxford University Press.

Will, George W. 2001. "Congress Just Isn't Big Enough." *Washington Post* 14 January.

Willard, John Ware. 1968. *Simon Willard and His Clocks.* New York: Dover Publications, Inc. Unabridged and corrected version of 1911, *A History of Simon Willard, Invention and Clockmaker.*

Willard, Simon, Jr., 1815. *The Columbian Union, Containing General and Particular Explanations of Government, and the Columbian Constitution, Being an Amendment to the Constitution of the United States: Providing a Yearly Revenue to Government of About Forty Millions of Dollars, and the Inevitable Union of the People by a Rule of Voting, and Exemption from Unnecessary Taxation, Consequently Their Permanent and Perpetual Freedom.* Albany, NY: printed for the author.

Williams, T. Harry. 1970. *Huey Long.* New York: Alfred A. Knopf.

Willis, Clyde E. 2002. *Student's Guide to Landmark Congressional Laws on the First Amendment.* Westport, CT: Greenwood Press.

Willis, Paul G., and George L. Willis. 1952. "The Politics of the Twenty-second Amendment." *Western Political Quarterly* 5 (September): 469–482.

Wills, Garry. 1981. *Explaining America: The Federalist.* Garden City, NY: Doubleday.

———. 1978. *Inventing America: Jefferson's Declaration of Independence.* New York: Doubleday.

Wilson, James G. 1992. "American Constitutional Conventions: The Judicially Unenforceable Rules That Combine with Judicial Doctrine and Public Opinion to Regulate Political Behavior." *Buffalo Law Review* 40 (Fall): 645–738.

Wilson, Justin T. 2007. "Preservationism, or The Elephant in the Room: How Opponents of Same-Sex Marriage Deceive Us into Establishing Religion." *Duke Journal of Gender Law & Policy* 14 (January): 561–679.

Wilson, (Thomas) Woodrow. 1908. *Constitutional Government in the United States.* Reprint, New York: Columbia University Press, 1961.

———. 1885. *Congressional Government: A Study in American Politics.* Boston: Houghton Mifflin.

———. 1882. "Government by Debate: Being a Short View of Our National Government as It Is and as It Might Be." In *The Papers of Woodrow Wilson,* Vol. 2, ed. Arthur S. Link. Reprint, Princeton, NJ: Princeton University Press, 1967.

———. 1879. *Cabinet Government in the United States.* In *The Papers of Woodrow Wilson,* Vol. 1, ed. Arthur S. Link. Reprint, Princeton, NJ: Princeton University Press, 1966.

Wirenius, John F. 1994. "The Road to *Brandenburg:* A Look at the Evolving Understanding of the First Amendment." *Drake Law Review* 43: 1–49.

Wolfe, Christopher. 1991. *Judicial Activism: Bulwark of Freedom or Precarious Security?* Pacific Grove, CA: Brooks/Cole.

Wood, Charles. 1999. "Losing Control of America's Future: The Census, Birthright Citizenship, and Illegal Aliens." *Harvard Journal of Law and Public Policy* 22 (Spring): 465–522.

Wood, Gordon S. 1969. *The Creation of the American Republic, 1776–1787.* New York: W. W. Norton.

Wood, Stephen B. 1968. *Constitutional Politics in the Progressive Era: Child Labor and the Law.* Chicago: University of Chicago Press.

Woodward, Augustus B. 1825. *The Presidency of the United States.* New York: J. & J. Harper.

Wright, Benjamin F. 1938. *The Contract Clause of the Constitution.* Cambridge, MA: Harvard University Press.

Wright, R. George. 1991. "Could a Constitutional Amendment Be Unconstitutional?" *Loyola University of Chicago Law Review* 22: 741–764.

Wunder, John R. 1994. *"Retained by the People": A History of American Indians and the Bill of Rights.* New York: Oxford University Press.

WyattBrown, Bertram. 1948. *Southern Honor: Ethics and Behavior in the Old South.* New York: Oxford University Press.

Yandle, Bruce. 1995. *Land Rights: The 1990s' Property Tax Rebellion.* Lanham, MD: Rowman & Littlefield.

Yarbrough, Tinsley E. 1988. *Mr. Justice Black and His Critics.* Durham, NC: Duke University Press.

Young, Donald. 1974. *American Roulette: The History and Dilemma of the Vice Presidency.* New York: Viking Press.

Zuckerman, Edward. 1984. *The Day after World War III.* New York: Viking Press.

Zywicki, Todd J. 1997. "Beyond the Shell and Husk of History: The History of the Seventeenth Amendment and Its Implications for Current Reform Proposals." *Cleveland State Law Review* 45:165–234.

———. 1994. "Senators and Special Interests: A Public Choice Analysis of the Seventeenth Amendment." *Oregon Law Review* 73 (Winter): 1007–1055.

❖ LIST OF CASES ❖

❖ ABOUT THE AUTHOR ❖

Dr. John R. Vile is professor of political science and dean of the University Honors College at Middle Tennessee State University. He has written and edited more than 25 books including *Great American Lawyers: An Encyclopedia*, 2 vols., (2001); *A Companion to the United States Constitution and Its Amendments*, 5th ed., (2010); *Presidential Winners and Losers: Words of Victory and Concession* (2002); *Proposed Amendments to the U.S. Constitution, 1787–2002*, 3 vols., (2002); *Great American Judges: An Encyclopedia*, 2 vols., (2003); *The Constitutional Convention of 1787: A Comprehensive Encyclopedia of America's Founding*, 2 vols., (2005); the *Encyclopedia of the First Amendment*, 2 vols. (with David L. Hudson Jr. and David Schultz), as well as earlier editions of the *Encyclopedia of Constitutional Amendments, Proposed Amendments, and Amending Issues.* The first edition of this work, published in 1996, received a starred review in *The Library Journal*, and was selected by the *Journal*'s editors as one of the best reference books of 1996. The Reference and User's Association of the American Library Association listed it as one of the 30 best reference books of 1996. The *Law Library Journal* listed the first edition as one of the best legal reference books of the year, and the Society of School Librarians International selected it as an honor book in 7–12 Social Studies. This revised third edition builds on the edifice of the two editions, with not only new entries but also updates and revisions of almost every entry in the book.